D1542824

THE LAW AND
THE COLLEGE STUDENT

JUSTICE IN EVOLUTION

By

WILLIAM G. MILLINGTON

Department of Higher and Postsecondary Education
University of Southern California

87216

ST. PAUL, MINN.
WEST PUBLISHING CO.
1979

CI   FEB. 1 3 1980

COPYRIGHT © 1979 By WEST PUBLISHING CO.

All rights reserved

Printed in the United States of America

Library of Congress Cataloging in Publication Data

Millington, William G

    The law and the college student.

    Bibliography: p.

    Includes index.

    1.   College students—Legal status, laws, etc.—United States. 2. Universities and colleges—Law and legislation—United States. I. Title.

KF4243.M54   344'.73'079   79–14211

ISBN 0–8299–2047–1

Millington—Just. In Evolution

For

Earl V. Pullias

Professor Emeritus, Higher and Postsecondary Education
School of Education, University of Southern California

I have never heard him state his own case; he is utterly
honorable

There is nothing of the 'superior person' about him; he
simply, patiently and unflinchingly wants to know, to
hear the essence of things, and from the center of his
own crystal

He is meditative, but intimates praise his conversation
and students memorize his words

He is kind, as wise men are, and has an unfailing habit
of extending to each person a feeling that he or she has
much worth

The temptation to lie down is very great, but his human-
ness re-charges us.

*

ACKNOWLEDGMENTS

Every year, if not every day, we have to wager our salvation upon a prophecy based upon imperfect knowledge.

The law . . . . In order to know what it is, we must know what it has been, and what it tends to become.

Oliver Wendell Holmes, Jr.

ACKNOWLEDGMENTS

The important role of the American college and university in American society, a concern but not the major focus of the book, raises an intriguing set of questions for which the present status of student rights on campus can provide only partial answers. Clearly, moreover, an analysis of the full scope and all the ramifications of federal and state case-law, statutes and regulations in the student province alone would transcend available space; yet, almost every column of fine print in such law may in untold ways affect the structure, mission and performance of higher educational institutions in the United States. I have, therefore, tried to create a volume to which any American might turn for an understanding of the special province the law has staked out for students and of its effects on the relationships of colleges and universities with their clientele.

Any person who writes a book, however, is indebted to others for encouragement, ideas and materials. In fact, perhaps the most bizarre kind of pretense is that of originality and such intellectually fraudulent terrain I attempt to avoid by first extending my thanks to West Publishing Company's Law School Department staff for their advice and cooperation in preparing the manuscript, and to Dean Stephen J. Knezevich, USC School of Education, whose encouragement bespeaks his fierce devotion to scholarly endeavor.

I am also deeply indebted to Lawrence Raful, Assistant Dean, USC School of Law, who critiqued the manuscript in draft, pro-

ACKNOWLEDGMENTS

vided valuable comments and kept the writer abreast of related developments in the law.

Others who should be acknowledged include Professors Les Wilbur, Clive Grafton, Bill Maxwell, and Penny Richardson, my colleagues in the Department of Higher and Postsecondary Education, USC School of Education, whose friendly assistance to scholarly inquiry inspired and encouraged the writer; and Charles Kane, President of Riverside City College, with whom I had frequent discussions of many ideas contained herein; Professors Don Mills, Al Gilpin and Jim Epperson, and Dean John Geyer, all of Long Beach City College, and Mary Berry Brennen, teacher in the Long Beach Unified School District, who, in one version or another, read the manuscript and offered key assistance as to form and style; Vance Nolan, Jeannine Andrews and Gary Blount, graduate students in Education at USC, who spent countless hours in the USC School of Law Library confirming legal citations and briefing law cases that are digested and discussed in the book.

Chris Maas, Lori Nishimura, Flo Acohido, and Marge Herrera responded with the utmost courtesy and promptness in typing and preparing the manuscript for the press.

And finally—to Jere Millington for tranquility and a debt of gratitude to my children and their husbands, David and Melinda Hughes, Don and Kim Carlson, David and Jerilyn Bourdon (and grandson, Brandon), Bill Millington, Lili Millington, and Brett Rodgers, for just being, and to my old friend, Professor Myron Pelsinger, El Camino College, without whose advice and criticism I would have finished the book two years earlier.

INTRODUCTION

When I arise in the morning I am torn by the twin desires to reform the world and enjoy the world. This makes it hard to plan the day.

E. B. White

Some Legal Quicksand in the Old Sandbox

Preparation of this book actually began during the campus turbulence of the middle and late 1960s. From 1964 to 1967, as Dean of Student Affairs at a large multi-campus public college in California, this writer became acutely aware that the judiciary had substituted a constitutional standard in the relationship between the tax-supported college and the student for yesteryear's standards of *"in loco parentis,"* "privilege" and "contract." That is to say, the college's control and discipline of students could no longer be rationalized on the ground that the administration and faculty stood in place of the parent or that attendance at a college was merely a privilege or that the student by enrolling at a college had bound himself contractually to the rules and procedures previously established or to be established by college officials.[1]

The fact was that the traditional disciplinary stance of higher education and the increasingly politicized student of the 1960s were on a collision course. The collision which occurred is now, it seems, largely prologue, but higher education is still attempting to determine where it ought to have been when that collision occurred.

Student activism produced a needed awareness that something was wrong within our institutions of higher education. It also brought about an increased visibility of these educational institutions—particularly because of their inability to handle conflict resolution effectively. Under the conditions of *ad hoc* extemporization, at best, and arrogant institutional abuses of disciplinary authority, at worst, the judiciary ultimately rejected its

---

[1] See *Dixon v. Alabama State Board of Education* (1961) in Chapter 2.

traditional policy of nonintervention and extended constitutional rights to students.

Today, student activism has largely peaked out, but in its wake the academic world has been left in a state of anxiety, with a battle-scarred sensitivity to the force and power of public opinion, and among academic executives especially, with an almost insatiable need for public approval. The scars are much deeper than one might imagine. Thus higher education's attention is now primarily focused externally on its credibility gap with the larger society which is demanding such pragmatic responses as accountability, more concentrated technical training, cost efficiency, and an overall sharp reduction in the gap between academic life and "real" life.

Internally, expending enormous energy on such external pressures and having become weary of a decade of student problems, institutional policy (probably unconsciously) has been in part to lead the public from its dangerous hostility by lulling and maneuvering students not so much into a state of tranquility as into a condition of apathy and inertia. A serious reduction in academic standards, for one instance, has been an uncomfortably frequent technique of reducing student conflict potential, and in such short-range expedients there is a strong suggestion that American colleges and universities have been drifting in a direction that will serve neither educational nor public interest well. Even among students there seems to be a growing undercurrent of distrust and contempt for the academic system. Thus with such dysfunctional response, we may find ourselves witnessing not only continuing governmental and judicial intervention with an increasing reduction in the traditional autonomy of educational institutions, but also a continuation of the sinking prestige of the college degree and the end of America's love affair with higher education.

The point is that no wise decisions can be made about structure or control or power that do not derive from a prior examination of what will happen to the people who teach and the people who learn and the process of teaching and learning both within and outside the classroom. Institutional structures and policies which grew out of the experiences of the last couple of decades—in particular the last tumultuous years of campus activism—must be reshaped to respond well to the coming years. The quality of education can best be measured by its capacity to assist students in achieving moral and intellectual maturity. This does not suggest a stoic acceptance of the way things are, but the development of critical responsibility.

Unfortunately, it appears that it was precisely this principle that was among the casualties of the sixties. Martin Kaplan put it this way:

> No sooner had the 1970–71 academic year begun than a startlingly different montage began to take shape. Accompanied by snippy captions like 'The New Mood on Campus' and 'The Return of Romance,' the first image of the emergent seventies to capture the public imagination was the quivering face of Ali McGraw. Bare-assed streakers, four years later, were an obvious extension of the same cultural infantilism, as were the switch from dope to booze, the astrology boom, and the nostalgia industry. Instead of the student striker in blue jeans and head band, the seventies montage gave us the taxi driver with a PhD and the cutthroat premed. In the sixties we were radicals; in the seventies we tended our own gardens, baked organic bread, and learned we were OK from paperbacks. In the sixties we were enraged by government lying; in the seventies we yawned at deceit, bitched about gas lines, and knew everyone was out for his own good.[2]

Thus, the 1970's began with new problems along with the intensification of old ones, and they, too, have been affecting the purposes, goals, and functions of our educational institutions. The exponential growth of knowledge continues at an accelerating pace, and the increasing emphasis on technology is demanding more concentrated specialization. It goes without saying that higher education is facing many dilemmas. Under such conditions, for instance, how can these institutions circumscribe an area of knowledge from such a vast and expanding pattern and claim that that is what "every educated person ought to know"? Even with the renewed discussion of fundamentals one finds few orderly patterns and instead a remarkable degree of confusion. To be sure, the flurry of words in the liberal arts debate is permitting (perhaps insuring) a new style of carelessness in what had once been considered essentials of definition. Meanwhile,

---

[2] Martin Kaplan, "The Idealogies of Tough Times," *Change* VIII (August, 1976), p. 25.

national literacy rates are plummeting unbelievably as we place the feet of a new generation on the shifting sands of educational relativism.

At the same time higher education is everywhere being challenged. As the relative value of higher education in the world of unemployment seems to be declining, the costs are inexorably rising; and the cost increase appears to be an aspect of a labor-intensive industry that has not—and may never—discover significant economies of scale. The best colleges and universities are not immune to this trend either, and public disenchantment is growing. Public criticism reaches its polar limit in the concept of education as consisting of Mark Hopkins at one end of a log and the student at the other end. But Mark Hopkinses do not come cheap. Professors and their mates must eat too. Thus, as they say on the streets, when the paddy wagon comes, it takes the good girls along with the bad; in tough times, the bell tolls even for the Ivy League institutions, albeit, perhaps not so dolefully.

Scholastic Aptitude Test scores have dropped from 478 (verbal) and 502 (math) in 1962–63 to 434 (verbal) and 472 (math) in 1975–76. Students are less ready to sit at anyone's feet, and both they and the public are increasingly less respectful of and responsive to educators' prescriptions for higher education. There are many open questions: Who should be admitted and why? Who teaches what to whom, when, where, and why? And then come the jurisdictional questions: Who decides, who must be consulted, and who can approve or disapprove?

But as soon as one raises the issue of purposes and values within higher education, the importance of the student as a person becomes central. There is general agreement, for example, that an important mission of colleges and universities is to produce good citizens capable of functioning in the democratic process. Yet, simultaneously, the advancement of such an aim requires the translation of democratic concepts into realities reflected in the behavior of the institutions toward their students. However, while some college authorities do not openly proclaim their disillusionment with the principles of democracy and justice, they confess it by their conduct. Action talks. It speaks more plainly than words. It can shout the truth where words lie. Obviously, what people do is ultimately more important and revealing than what they say. If this book does nothing more than to plant this idea, it will have served a useful purpose.

If the managers of our society are largely produced by its colleges and universities, then these institutions should get down to the business of turning out the best. Included somewhere in the achievement of this vision is the recognition that students no longer leave their constitutional rights at the college door and that a historically derived rule of law is safer, for all its failings, than the rule of men. It could be hoped that these would be such deeply held convictions that they would realize themselves in institutional behavior.

If one needs convincing beyond the moral and educational levels then one should consider the 1975 Supreme Court decision, *Wood v. Strickland,*[3] in which it was ruled that educators are individually liable for damages if they abridge the "unquestioned constitutional rights" of students. The decision states specifically that ignorance of these rights is no excuse for their violation. Therefore, it is now legally imperative that public college personnel understand and practice such constitutional principles. The constitutional theory of democracy is no longer an abstract issue to be discussed only in the classroom. The Supreme Court has introduced a new legal as well as educational element into the educator's work day.

The challenge to American higher education is important and real. Fueled by court decisions in the last two decades, students are being encouraged to sue their colleges and universities if any institutional decision impedes their march toward graduation day; and the courts are mandating a vast network of due process and equal protection requirements for all such decisions that are appealed to them. Thus, administrators, professors and trustees are finding that they must be aware of, and responsive to, the decisional law of the courts. At the same time, however, the seemingly complex logic of the courts presents a formidable obstacle to an evaluation of the status of the law which, of course, must precede any meaningful implementation of it.

The purpose of this book, therefore, is to enhance this understanding by recognition of the fact that there are certain basic principles of law upon which the courts are disposed to rely, faced with given general situations. Moreover, if an educator under-

---

[3] 420 U.S. 308 (1975).

stands the logic behind a court's decision, it not only makes the adjustment more rational, but it also alleviates much of the emotional anxiety and inertia which typically accompany lack of information. The point is that our legal system is a major force for justice and productive change—to be used rather than ignored or opposed. And finally, the reader should discover that behind the apparent mystery, confusion and disorganization of the judicial interpretation of such legal terms as due process, there is order; and that this understanding will set him to re-examine his professional activities and even make him a better educator.

The Meaning of Law

The law seems to be a bundle of contradictions. Americans are fond of saying that we have "a government of laws and not of men"; nevertheless, most laws are made by men to rule other men. Moreover, judges piously announce that "ignorance of the law is no excuse," but in addition to managing to live in a very complicated society, is a person supposed to know all the laws governing his complicated existence? For instance, it would probably be optimistic to say that fifty percent of the professional educators in this country know that it is a violation of the Family Education and Privacy Act of 1974 to post official grades or class standings together with names of students or that Title IX of the Education Amendments of 1972 prohibits most institutions from having separate men's honorary societies.

Dr. Samuel Johnson said, "Law is the last result of human wisdom acting from human experience for the benefit of the public." But wouldn't the ordinary woman or man go broke if she or he should become embroiled in the legal process? As a matter of fact, most laymen look upon the law as something to avoid, at least when they find themselves on its receiving end. It is prohibition and the threat of prosecution. It is lawyer's fees, delay and court costs. It is complex and mysterious; it's the fine print in the contract, and the name of the game seems to be the words and phrases that only a lawyer or a judge can read or write. To some, in fact, the power of the law seems to be at the end of a policeman's nightstick, and its majesty a judge in a black robe.

Professional students of the law have described it in quite different ways. Thus law has been identified as the consequence of God's will, of nature, of the judges, of "doing what comes naturally," of what is good and right for people to do to one another, of the "decencies of civilized conduct," of commands from political superiors that are binding on inferiors, of the "logical outcome of past experience" or of the social and economic system. Some of us might even recall the Lord Chancellor in Gilbert and Sullivan's *Iolanthe* singing:

> The law is the true embodiment
> Of everything that's excellent.
> It has no kind of fault or flaw,
> And I, my Lords, embody the Law.

However, Mr. Bumble in *Oliver Twist* described it somewhat differently when he complained, "The law is a ass, a idiot."

But what, precisely, is law? It is not an easy concept to define, and as you have observed, attempts to do so frequently reveal the human tendency to give mere subjective definitions. Hence, to avoid any further obfuscation, "law" in this book is defined as the formal means of social control that involves the use of rules for human behavior that are interpreted, and are enforceable, by the courts and the quasi-judicial agencies of the political community. This is also consistent with Pound's definition of law as "the systematic and orderly application of force by the appointed agents" of politically organized society.[4] Thus sanction (enforceability) contributes the legal characteristic to a rule, for if it is not enforceable, a rule of human behavior has no juristic significance.

Law as a Part of Culture

The structure of the law *is* civilization. As a part of society's system of social control, law is an essential aspect of the social organization of the political community. It is a part of the culture—the habits, attitudes, ideas, objects, possessions and values that are transmitted from one generation to another. Specifically, law is an aspect of the institutionalized part of culture; that is, the agreements that are conceived as desirable upon which social institutions are organized. These agreements then become

---

[4] Roscoe Pound, *Social Control through Law* (New Haven: Yale University Press, 1942), p. 25.

expectations which are stated as explicit rules that are obligatory. According to Llewellyn,

> All you have to do is to borrow a concept from sociology: *Institution*, and to make explicit that you include therein the relevant going practices and the relevant specialists and the relevant physical equipment and the manner of organization of the whole; and Pound's picture of law—the *institution* of law—becomes forwith a something which any social scientist can look at, understand, make friends with, learn from, and comfortably contribute to. The central aspect of an institution is organized activity, activity organized around the cleaning up of some job.[5]

In this sense institutions are defined as distinctive patterns that are centered around major human needs and accompanied by particular modes of social interaction.

Federal and State Law

Although many question the desirability of the national government's increasing role in the governance of higher education, few dispute its legality today. Yet, the United States Constitution by virtue of its silence on the topic would appear to leave to the states the exclusive responsibility for the education of their citizens. In fact the Tenth Amendment claims that "The powers not delegated to the United States by the Constitution, nor prohibited by it to the States, are reserved to the States respectively, or to the people."

The extent of the national government's mandate over higher education, however, has never been fully ascertained. As previously noted, the Constitution did not endow the federal government with direct and specific authority related to the administration of education. In accordance, the first Justice Harlan, in *Cumming v. Board of Education* (1899), observed that education

> . . . is a matter belonging to the respective states, and any interference on the part of Federal authority with the management of such schools cannot be justified except in

---

5 Karl N. Llewellyn, "Law and the Social Sciences—Especially Sociolo- gy," *American Sociological Review*, 14 (August, 1949), p. 453.

the case of a clear and unmistakable disregard of rights secured by the supreme law of the land.[6]

Our dualistic form of government necessarily creates two governments in every state—the state and federal governments. Each state possesses all the attributes of sovereignty and each is endowed with all governmental powers except those conferred exclusively upon the United States, denied to the states, or reserved to the people. Thus, the exclusion of education from federally delegated powers would seem to preclude interference with the routine administration of colleges and universities by the national government.

On the other hand, Congress is endowed with sufficient jurisdiction to enable that legislative body to exercise rather broad functions, except as it may be restrained by constitutional provisions. In fact the selection of areas subject to statutory regulation is greatly expanded because of its constitutionally delegated power to tax and provide for the general welfare. However, during the formative period of our national existence, many endorsed the argument that since the national government was endowed exclusively with express or delegated powers, the authority to levy and expend tax revenue in the interest of the general welfare was necessarily restricted to those purposes enumerated in the Federal Constitution. Thus in conformity with this version, allocation of national funds in support of education would not be permissible since education was not an express power delegated to Congress.

A contrary view supported the contention that the constitutional mandate to tax and provide for the general welfare was comprehensive and not restricted to the purposes specifically enumerated in the Constitution. In this respect, two of the most famous of all judicial comments on the Constitution presage what would eventually transpire:

> In considering this question, then, we must never forget, that it is a *constitution* we are expounding.

And later in the same opinion:

> Let the end be legitimate, let it be within the scope of the constitution, and all means which are appropriate, which are plainly adapted to that end, but consist with the letter and spirit of the constitution are constitutional.

---

[6] 175 U.S. 528, 545 (1899).

INTRODUCTION

Both of these comments came from the pen of John Marshall in
McCulloch v. Maryland (1819).

Of course today this latter interpretation prevails since the
United States Supreme Court adopted the broader construction
of the Constitution in 1936 holding that Congress was authorized
to tax and expend revenues for any purpose that promotes the
general welfare.[7] Thus this decision removed any uncertainty
shrouding Congressional authority to expend money in support
of public education. Additionally, when this interpretation is
coupled with Article VI of the Constitution (which renders the
Constitution and all laws passed under it as the supreme law of
the land), the recipe becomes powerfully tempting for the national government to increase its involvement in determining the
direction of education throughout the nation.

Thus the reasons for the growing involvement of the national
government in the affairs of higher education are not hard to
find. Simply put, the legal power is there. Furthermore, in-
centives for such involvement have grown daily; that is, higher
education has moved front and center on the stage of American
life and, not surprisingly, has therefore found itself the object of
nearly everyone's attention. As Martin Trow commented, "Postsecondary education has been perceived as having become too
important . . . and too costly to be left to professors and
educators alone."[8]

Of course from the inception of our nation, higher education
has been a necessary aspect of American life, and the national
government has, from its earliest beginnings, been involved. For
instance, President George Washington advocated a federal university in his inaugural address. Moreover, the Northwest Ordinance of 1787 implicitly provided endowments for institutions
of higher education, and the Morrill Acts of 1862 and 1890 clearly show that the federal government's interest and involvement
in the financing and shaping of higher education has not been
merely a recent phenomenon. Nevertheless, it was not until the
post-World War II years that the federal government moved into
education in a big way. It is interesting to note, by way of example, that the United States Office of Education boasted on the

---

[7] *United States v. Butler*, 297 U.S.
1 (1936).

[8] Quoted in B. Israel, *Can Higher
Education Recapture Public Support?*
(New York: International Council for
Educational Development, 1974), p.
35.

XVI

occasion of its 100th birthday in 1967 that Congress had passed more major pieces of legislation for education in the previous three years than in the preceding ninety-seven years combined.[9]

A glance at selected figures provides some of the explanation for this new focus. As Halstead pointed out,

> The 1960's decade is likely to have recorded higher education's greatest growth. Enrollment increased from 3.8 to 8.6 million students, annual expenditures rose from 7.7 to 27.1 billion dollars, and the instructional staff grew from 292,000 to 592,000. In this ten-year span higher education expenditures tripled and enrollments more than doubled while the college-age population expanded by only fifty percent.[10]

Specific Kinds of Law

Our law can be found in four kinds of documents. The most fundamental is the United States Constitution and its amendments and the constitutions of the states. The other three are the statutes enacted by the legislative branch, the orders and regulations issued by the executive branch, and the court decisions rendered by the federal government and by fifty state governments. To know the law on a question, therefore, one must look to the constitutions, statutory law, administrative law, and court case (or common) law in one's jurisdiction.

Constitutional Law

The United States Constitution appears to be a simple document. It definitely is a short document; therefore, since the Constitution contains only 7,500 words or so and can be read in half an hour, it is frequently assumed that any person can learn constitutional law after a little study. But its wording is highly generalized and thus reading the document itself gives few clues to the actual application of the principles embodied therein. In fact constitutional law is full of phrases like an "ordered concept of liberty," "reasonableness," "fair play," "the clear and present danger rule," and "selective absorption" that are not to be found in the written words of the Constitution. Furthermore, the ap-

---

[9] M. L. Zoglin, *Power and Politics in the Community College* (Palm Springs, California: ETC Publications, 1976), p. 13.

[10] K. K. Halstead, *Statewide Planning* (Washington, D. C.: U. S. Government Printing Office, 1974), p. 1.

plication of any principles in question—for instance, freedom of speech, press, and assembly—is often dependent upon a balancing of extrinsic interests rather than a mere interpretation of the intrinsic document itself. As Mr. Justice Holmes declared, "a word is not a crystal, transparent and unchanged, it is the skin of a living thought and may vary greatly in color and content according to the circumstances and the time in which it is used." [11]

Actually, then, constitutional law consists of case-law statements about the interpretation of the Constitution that have been given Supreme Court sanction. Hence its meaning can be changed, and it frequently is modified in this way—that is, through a case-by-case analysis, interpretation and application of its phrases and words as issues arise through the eyes of each new generation. And so the Constitution remains, in our extremely complex age, flexible and as useful and alive as when it was written. "We are under a Constitution," Charles Evans Hughes claimed in 1907, "but the Constitution is what the judges say it is," and the Supreme Court says various things about it depending upon the era.

It is no mere coincidence, therefore, that constitutional law is constantly in a state of flux. Try as it may, the Court has found it impossible to maintain a high degree of historical consistency. As Carl Brent Swisher commented, "Throughout its entire history . . . the Supreme Court has been in search of the Constitution as the judges sitting were able to see and define the Constitution, and throughout its entire history the Court has been seeking to determine the character and dimensions of its own role in the government." [12] Consequently, one of the major paradoxes of American constitutional law is that about the only thing that is historically constant is constant continual change.

Both the search and change are perpetual because not only do times change, but the Constitution itself is elusive. After all, the document seems to be only words, but then it must be something in addition because words alone are never enough, and they are seldom if ever precise and certain. Of course there are the

---

[11] *Towne v. Eisner*, 245 U.S. 418, 425 (1918).

[12] Carl Brent Swisher, *The Supreme Court in Modern Role* (N. Y.: New York University Press, 1958), p. 6.

"strict constructionists" who think otherwise, but they are a growing minority. If you viewed the Watergate hearings, for instance, you could not have avoided the penetrating logic and eloquence of Senator Sam J. Ervin, Jr., a preeminent advocate of the position that the words of the Constitution never change. He put it this way:

> We are told that the words of the Constitution automatically change their meaning from time to time without any change in phraseology being authorized by Congress and the states in the manner prescribed by Article V, and that a majority of the Supreme Court justices possess the omnipotent power to declare when these automatic changes occur, and their scope and effect. This notion is the stuff of which a judicial oligarchy is made. . . . Everyone will concede that the Constitution is written in words. If these words have no fixed meaning, they make the Constitution conform to Mark Twain's description of the dictionary. He said the dictionary has a wonderful vocabulary, but no plot.[13]

Senator Ervin's position, however, is supported by neither the history of the Court nor the rulings of those who have sat on it. Indeed, one needs only to review a small part of the Court's history to dislodge such a belief. The great precedent for "judicial review" in the case of *Marbury v. Madison* (1803), in which the Supreme Court declared invalid a part of the Federal Judiciary Act of 1789, is perhaps the best historical example. Even though Marshall's argument for judicial review might appear reasonable, there was no explicit statement in the Constitution establishing the power of the federal courts to strike down acts of Congress or state legislatures which the courts might find inconsistent with the Constitution. Yet this power has become one of the most salient characteristics of the American system of government, and the power to interpret the Constitution has strengthened the political position of American judges even more than their power to construe statutes. That is, since no federal or state law can be contrary to the Constitution, any decision interpreting the Constitution is in effect a top-level political decision. As David Trumen put it, "Interpretation of the Constitution through judicial review imposes upon the judiciary, particularly the Supreme Court, a task of statemanship no less po-

---

13 Quoted in Robert Sherrill, *Why* Harcourt Brace Jovanovich, Inc., *They Call It Politics* (New York: 1974), p. 163.

litical than that assumed at Philadelphia in 1787." [14] However, the first Justice Harlan placed a somewhat different twist on this power when he told a group of law students: "I want to say to you young gentlemen that if we don't like an act of Congress, we don't have much trouble to find grounds for declaring it unconstitutional." [15]

Less obviously, but not necessarily less significantly, at least two other judicial-review factors should be considered in the execution of court decisions. For example, one of the hoariest and most significant propositions concerning the function of judicial review involves "legitimacy." That is to say, according to some authorities on constitutional law, the mere power of judicial review, especially as brandished by the Supreme Court, confers a stamp of legitimacy throughout American society.[16] In other words, the bald possibility that *any* law can be declared unconstitutional affords an "air" of legality to *all* acts of American government.[17]

It is also frequently urged that constitutional checks on political power, enforced vigorously by judicial institutions, provide the best defense of individual liberties. In fact, as early as 1835, Alexis de Tocqueville proclaimed that the American judiciary, with its power of judicial review, was "one of the most powerful barriers which has ever been devised" to prevent mass tyranny.[18] Similarly, implicit in much of our contemporary legal writing is the thesis that courts are the major protectors of freedom. Charles Black, for instance, stated this position forthrightly:

> The judicial power is one of the accredited means by which
> our nation seeks its goals, including the prime goal . . .
> of self-limitation. Intellectual freedom, freedom from irra-
> tional discrimination, immunity from unfair administration

---

14 David Trumen, *The Governmental Process: Political Interests and Public Opinion* (New York: Alfred A. Knopf, 1951), p. 48.

15 Quoted in E. S. Corwin, *Constitutional Revolution* (Claremont Associated Colleges, 1941), p. 38.

16 See, e. g., Charles Black, *The People and the Court* (New York: Macmillan, 1960), pp. 34 *et seq.*

17 Black believes this "air" possesses a "sweetness" that is the envy of people everywhere and to which Frenchmen are peculiarly unaccustomed. Id., p. 35.

18 Alexis de Tocqueville, *Democracy in America*, trans. Phillips Bradley (New York: Vintage Books, 1954, I, pp. 102–09.

of the law—these (and others similar) are the constitutional interests which the Court can protect on ample doctrinal grounds. They often cannot win protection in rough-and-tumble politics. The Supreme Court is more and more finding its highest institutional role is the guarding of such interests.[19]

The Constitution, for instance, guarantees that neither the federal nor the state governments can deny a person life, liberty, or property without due process of law, but it is the judiciary that supplies definition and determination as to just what due process is. For example, the right of freedom of speech and press is generally considered a "preferred status" guarantee of the Constitution, but does this protect one who writes or speaks obscenely? In fact, what is obscenity anyhow? You guessed it; the courts will tell you and that is precisely what Justice Oliver Wendell Holmes meant when he said, "The prophecies of what the courts will do in fact, and nothing more pretentious are what I mean by the law." This is not to say that the courts do not need authority in the Constitution for what they decide. But this authority is broad indeed so it depends on a doctrine of judicial restraint—which has not always been characteristic of the Supreme Court and subordinate federal courts—to limit judges in demanding what they think is right as well as what they believe to be within the Constitution.

State tax-supported institutions of higher education, such as public colleges and universities, are entities of state government, and today are subject to judicial scrutiny under the obligations of the Fourteenth Amendment: "No State . . . shall . . . deprive any person of life, liberty, or property, without due process of the laws; nor deny to any person within its jurisdiction the equal protection of the laws." Consequently, "state action" is the basis (and therefore becomes the prerequisite) upon which unreasonable, arbitrary, or unequally applied regulations and actions of public college and university officials have been declared unconstitutional.

Equal protection deals with the unreasonable classification and treatment of individuals and groups and will be dealt with thoroughly in Part IV of the book. Therefore, since Chapter I deals

---

[19] Charles Black, *Perspectives on Constitutional Law* (Englewood Cliffs, New Jersey: Prentice-Hall, 1963), p. 5.

with due process, let's briefly examine this rather vague and general concept. Here neither Congress (Section 5 of the Fourteenth Amendment allows for Congressional implementation) nor the courts have attempted to set up a definitive formula. Rather, Congress has essentially avoided the task, and the courts have followed the suggestion of Justice Miller in *Davidson v. New Orleans* that the meaning of due process should be determined by the "gradual process of judicial inclusion and exclusion, as the cases presented for decision shall require." [20]

In effect, we may distinguish between two kinds of due process of law, *substantive* and *procedural*. They are not as clearly or cleanly separable as we might wish, or as some members of the legal profession at times claim, but it is possible—and indeed vital—to understand the basic distinction. At the risk of oversimplifying, *substantive* due process refers to the content or subject matter of legislation or administrative regulations, whereas *procedural* due process refers to the manner in which the mandates of the legislative and/or administrative process are carried out by public officials.

For our purposes, then, whenever a governmental body such as a public college acts so as to injure an individual, the Constitution requires that the act be consonant with due process of law. Next, once it is determined that due process applies, the question remains what process is due. As will be explained more thoroughly later in the book, a multitude of factors enter at this point, but to simplify, two kinds of possible inquiry are involved in this situation—again, substantive and procedural. Thus, substantive due process requires that a law or regulation a person is accused of violating must be consonant with the fundamental rights and liberties of American democratic concepts, and at this point one generally looks to the First Amendment which spells out the basic rights of the people against unreasonable governmental interference.

"Congress shall make no law," declares the First Amendment, "respecting an establishment of religion, or prohibiting the free exercise thereof; or abridging the freedom of speech, or of the press, or the right of the people peaceably to assemble, and to petition the Government for a redress of grievances." Hence

---

[20] 96 U.S. 97 (1878).

right here in bold and imposing terms are the substantive or fundamental supports of a free society—freedom of conscience and freedom of expression. However, at this point it should be emphasized that although due-process-of-law-clauses are found in both the federal and most state constitutions, the Federal Bill of Rights is not automatically applicable or transferable to the states, since it was originally conceived—and long judicially regarded [21]—as a restriction against the national government only. But then in 1925, in *Gitlow v. New York,* the Supreme Court announced: "For present purposes we may and do assume that freedom of speech and of press . . . are . . . liberties protected by the due process clause of the Fourteenth Amendment from impairment by the states." [22] Subsequently the Supreme Court gradually began to "incorporate" or "nationalize" these rights until today it has brought within the protection of the Fourteenth Amendment almost every applicable provision of the Bill of Rights. Therefore, even though you will find First Amendment questions at the heart of many student-public college conflicts, technically they are decided on the grounds of a substantive interpretation of the Fourteenth Amendment due process clause.

Obviously, there must be limits to the kinds of laws regulating life, liberty, and property that a legislative body may enact. Generally speaking, however, most state laws, as well as rules and regulations promulgated by state-supported educational institutions, will be upheld as legitimate exercises of governmental power if there is a "rational basis" to justify the law or regulation. Moreover, constitutional rights are not absolute. This principle was well stated by the Fourth Circuit Court of Appeals in *Baines v. City of Danville, Virginia*:

> First Amendment rights of free speech and assembly incorporated into the Fourteenth Amendment are not a license to trample on rights of others and First Amendment rights must be exercised responsibly and without depriving others of their rights.[23]

However, laws and regulations which have the effect of infringing upon First Amendment guarantees as applied to the states

---

[21] See *Barron v. Baltimore,* 7 Peters 243 (1833); *The Slaughterhouse Cases,* 16 Wallace 36 (1873); and *Palko v. Connecticut,* 302 U.S. 319 (1937).

[22] 268 U.S. 652 (1925).

[23] 337 F.2d 579 (1964).

by the Fourteenth Amendment (substantive due process) will be held to restrictive standards. Van Alstyne states it this way:

> A university rule which threatens a student with dismissal for any activity he is constitutionally entitled to pursue as a citizen carries the burden of establishing precisely how that activity would specifically interfere with the legitimate business of the university.[24]

The Fourth (protection against unreasonable government searches), Fifth (guaranteed protections in trials), Sixth (rights of an accused person in criminal cases), and Eighth (prohibition of excessive bail, fines, and punishment) Amendments as noted are also essentially applicable to the several states of the Union but are generally considered procedural issues of the Fourteenth Amendment due process clause. More specifically, procedural due process typically implies regular allegations, an opportunity to answer the allegations, and a hearing according to some settled course of judicial proceedings. "Its quintessence is the philosophic notion that the end does not justify the means . . . In the due process sense it connotes that no one should be harmed by an *ex parte* [one-sided] accusation of having violated a valid rule or regulation." [25]

Statutory Law

In many instances, a judicial decision is based on statutory law. This is law formulated and enacted by a legislative body (Congress, state legislature, or local legislative body) and is enforceable in the courts as long as the legislative assembly possesses the Constitutional authority to enact it. Legislative bodies, however, have little choice but to state rules in general terms since it is nearly, if not always, impossible to anticipate all the questions that will arise over their meaning. Therefore, although the initial interpretation is nearly always made by some administrator, the final interpretation generally rests with the judges.

Administrative Law

A relatively new kind of law that has become increasingly prominent in the decisions of judges is administrative law. More

---

[24] William Van Alstyne, "Student Academic Freedom and the Rule-Making Power of Public Universities: Some Constitutional Considerations," *Law in Transition Quarterly,* I (Winter, 1965).

[25] *Slochower v. Board of Higher Education,* 350 U.S. 551 (1956).

specifically, as the complexity of social life has increased, legislative bodies have found it necessary to establish more and more administrative agencies and to delegate rule-making authority to them. However, just as statute law must be enacted within the constitutional authority granted to legislative bodies, administrative law must lie within the authority and intent granted in statute law. Administrative law, therefore, is supplementary to statutory and constitutional law; but in today's gigantic modern government, administrative law has grown more voluminous than statute law. Frequently, in fact, statutes are little more than delegations of authority to administrative officers to write rules and regulations in their areas of expertise, but judges are often called on to determine whether the administrators have acted properly and within their authority.

Common Law

When there is no valid statute or regulation to help reach a decision, the courts must apply common law. That is, the courts must follow precedent wherein each decision has a basis in some past decision. Therefore, common law rests on judicial precedent, "the fruit of reason ripened by experience," but contrary to popular misconception, common law is not "unwritten law"; it is very much written, for it has been recorded for hundreds of years in court reports. Moreover, common law continues to be developed by court decisions according to the rule of *stare decisis,* which means "let the decision stand," a principle of Anglo-American jurisprudence that a precedent once established in the decision of a case should be followed in other similar cases unless it is found to be in conflict with established principles of justice. Obviously, *stare decisis* offers the advantage of certainty and stability in common law disputes, and even where this kind of law has been superseded by statute or regulation, the statutory or administrative law is normally interpreted according to the common-law tradition. In effect, then, common law is law made by judges—either through their interpreting statutes or regulations or through their adapting legal traditions or precedents to new situations.

Other Classifications of Law

Law may also be classified as criminal, civil, or equity. *Criminal law,* which is almost entirely statutory, is concerned with offenses against the public—that is, crimes. *Civil law,* much of which is common law, governs the relations among individuals and defines their legal rights. The United States courts, for example, hear a great many civil suits involving federal statutes, regulatory and precedent law on such matters as copyrights, patents, labor-management relations, civil rights and, of course, student-college relations.

Still another kind of law that is also found in both the federal and state courts is called *equity*. Like the common law, equity has its roots in history, but in common law, the remedies for private wrongs usually take the form of monetary compensations for damages suffered. The remedies in equity, however, take the form of court orders to prevent the wrong from occurring. The writ of *injunction* or *mandamus* is illustrative of the use of equity rather than other forms of the law, and procedure is quite different in equity than in ordinary trials. In equity cases there are no juries, and violations of court decrees are punished as contempt of court. The injunction, a cease and desist order from a court, is used most frequently in equity disputes in which there is little likelihood that the parties who contemplate the objectionable actions would be able to compensate the injured parties fully. On the other hand, the writ of mandamus provides a means by which a private citizen may petition a court to require a government official to perform a legally established duty.

As we look back on this brief explanation of American jurisprudence, it should be clear that its *corpus* (body) comprises some distinct types of law, which differ somewhat in subject matter and in source, but whatever its classification, the principal purpose of it all is to control relations among people. In fact the very core of law is the relationship between rights and duties, and that is why so many of the subject titles in the law have to do with reciprocal relations: husband and wife, parent and child, guardian and ward, student and school, landlord and tenant, vendor and purchaser, and so forth.

Finally, it should be recalled that law does not consist of absolute or immutable rules, for it is a product of changing human relations. In effect, law is what the government enforces at a particular time in a particular place, and thus the effectiveness of the law depends on its suitability to the facts of contemporary society.

INTRODUCTION

Finding the Law

The Sources of Law

H. L. Mencken once observed that Americans seem to think that any problem whatever can be easily solved by the old-fashioned method of passing a law—either for or against something. At least the nation's legislatures seem to support this view; by one estimate, legislative bodies ranging from city councils to Congress pass something like 150,000 new laws every year,[26] and the number of administrative regulations is inestimable. Now if the thought of 150,000 new laws a year and the bombardment of fresh administrative regulations, not to mention their accumulation over the years, boggles your mind, be patient. There is, fortunately, some order to this apparent chaos.

First, however, a word of caution. You cannot effectively study the American system of law if at this stage of the investigation you permit your spectacles to be fogged by the notion that the law can be understood by specific reference to constitutional provisions, legislation, or administrative regulations alone. Both the federal and state constitutions are notoriously ambiguous documents, and statutes and regulations, though generally more explicit, are typically far from being models of clarity. Hence most laws seem to breed lawsuits; in fact every case-law rule which is formulated by a court comes into existence because somebody has conceived that he was aggrieved by the action of somebody else, and so instituted a lawsuit of some sort. This is the interpretative and dispute-setting function of the courts. With the occasional exception of the federal or state supreme courts, the rule articulated by a court to resolve some instant litigation must also be a generalized rule applicable to all other parties in similar situations.

The Concept of Law as a Unity

The American system of common law, moreover, is not simply a narrow set of rules which have been applied by the courts to specific areas such as contracts, property, torts, criminal justice or education. It is, rather, *all* of the law, and thus for all prac-

---

[26] "Too Much Law," *Newsweek* (January 10, 1977), p. 43. Little wonder that Chief Justice Burger has been asking Congress to produce a "judicial impact statement" as it considers every new law, outlining its probable effect on the courts.

tical purposes the law is a unity; there is, really, no such thing as higher education law *per se*. We shall therefore be looking for "principles of law," from whatever areas of the law they derive, not just at the rules which the courts have said are applicable to specific factual situations involving the student-college relationship.

For instance, to lawyers and judges it is axiomatic that fundamental constitutional rights, like the constitutional guarantee of freedom of expression, exist in relation to the circumstances of their exercise. Hence, it is inappropriate to say that students in high school have *less* rights than adults in society. Rather, students in school have the same First Amendment rights as adults, but those rights may be curtailed upon the proper showing of a governmental interest in preserving the proper operation of the school. Correspondingly, it is also inappropriate to say that college students have *more* First Amendment rights than high school students. Both groups have the same right to express their views in school. On the other hand, the high school environment would probably present different circumstances than the college environment. Thus a showing which might be sufficient to restrict student expression in high school, might not be adequate where more mature individuals of college age are concerned.

While this distinction may seem a niggling detail, it is nevertheless crucial to an understanding of the broad sweep of the law. With this perspective one can then draw conclusions from any area of the law which has relevance for the student-college relationship. By adopting this view, a student demonstration or protest on a university campus becomes a test of free expression and as such is subject to the protections and limitations of a wide-range of First Amendment rulings. For example, the particular circumstances of the protest might cause a court to apply the *Schenck v. U. S.* [27] "clear and present danger" test, the *Milk Wagon Drivers' Union v. Meadow Moore Company* [28] "utterance in a context of violence" test, the *Miller v. California* [29] standards for the determination of obscenity, all of which represent First Amendment case law developed outside the higher education environment. The university protest becomes then not a unique,

---

[27] 249 U.S. 47 (1919).   [29] 413 U.S. 15 (1973).
[28] 312 U.S. 287 (1941).

free-expression phenomenon of the moment or place, but the legitimate heir of a half century of legal development in the United States.

One court has noted that "the relevant legal principles apply generally both to high schools and universities."[30] What distinguishes high school from college cases is the same thing that distinguishes one First Amendment case from another: the particular facts and circumstances presented and whether the government has advanced adequate reasons for restricting the exercise of that right. That is, when weighing the "reasonableness" of a governmental action restricting the free exercise of expression, the courts will assess the total environment in which the free exercise was curtailed—the danger involved, the personality of the speaker, the composition of the audience, the content of the speech, the nature of the forum, and so on. Thus, it is not surprising to find that a high school case such as *Tinker*[31] is frequently cited by courts ruling on college cases, or to find courts relying on college cases to reach a decision involving high school students, or even to find a court applying a case like the *New York Times Co. v. Sullivan*[32] "actual malice" test to a student publication case involving a libel issue.

Case Law

Many lawsuits are clear cases. They call for the application of pre-existing rules—that is, precedent law (*stare decisis*). In difficult cases, however, in which the rules themselves are at issue, the traditional resolution process requires that each party to the dispute must demonstrate that his claimed rule of law rests on at least one possible reading of existing rules which are accepted as such (e. g., see *Dixon* and the contending parties' use of conflicting case law regarding the constitutional status of students in public institutions of higher education, chapter 1). The decision-making process in these difficult cases provides the best example of judicial comparison and differentiation of precedent. Nevertheless, the rule output of the courts, even in the more difficult cases, generally involves incremental, rather than radical, change.

---

[30] *Scoville v. Board of Education of Joliet*, 425 F.2d 10, 13 (1970).

[31] *Tinker v. Des Moines Independent Community School District*, 393 U.S. 503 (1969).

[32] 376 U.S. 254 (1963).

INTRODUCTION

A sharp exception, however, must be made of the Supreme Court of the United States in the 1950s and 1960s (but tapering off to a more conservative role in the 1970s). During that period, the Court more than ever before, became the nation's moral entrepreneur in Constitutional litigation and in the process changed the central thrust of entire institutions. Of course, the Supreme Court's authority of judicial review of legislation or actions by any governmental body in the nation in effect gives it the power to change radically the essence of existing institutions.

Thus, needless to say, the level at which decisions are made in the country's courts is important. Decisions made at the United States Supreme Court level, for instance, are binding on all lower federal and state courts. Therefore, the Supreme Court's reasoning must be adhered to in all lower court decisions. In other circumstances, a court is bound to follow only the rulings of higher courts of record within whose jurisdiction the court is located.

In a sense, *all* court decisions, even those not legally binding on a particular court, may prove to be persuasive authority leading to a judicial determination. In America, as every lawyer knows, great weight is placed on the authority of precedent; each argues accordingly, knowing the benefits of fitting one's case into previously-adjudicated categories. As you will see, this approach is clearly evident in judicial cases dealing with student rights.

A number of publishers and governmental agencies now report every case decided in a federal court or in appellate jurisdictions of the state courts. What follows is a list of the major publications to which an individual interested in identifying cases similar to pending litigation is referred; obviously, these reports are highly significant in terms of arriving at an opinion as to how some future court will rule on the same or similar subject matter and factual situations.

First, attention should be paid to three sources—the first two of which are legal encyclopedias—*American Jurisprudence,* Second Series (Am.Jur.2d), and *Corpus Juris Secundum* (C. J. S.). Generally similar, each is alphabetically arranged by topic and subtopics, providing a comprehensive coverage of American law. In effect, the topic and subtopics categorize and summarize rules of law and provide supporting case law and other legal references.

INTRODUCTION

A researcher who has found an opinion is now ready to assess its importance. Perhaps the single best authority for a thorough reading of a case in point is contained in Karl Llewellyn's book *The Bramble Bush.** He puts it this way:

" . . . The first thing to do with an opinion, then, is read it. The next thing is to get clear the actual decision, the judgment rendered. Who won, the plaintiff or defendant? And watch your step here. You are after in first instance the plaintiff and defendant *below,* in the trial court. In order to follow through what happened you must therefore first know the outcome *below;* else you do not see what was appealed from, nor by whom. You now follow through in order to see exactly what *further* judgment has been rendered on appeal. The stage is then cleared of form—although of course you do not yet know all that these forms mean, that they imply. You can turn now to what you want peculiarly to know. Given the actual judgments below and above as your indispensable framework—what has the case decided, and what can you derive from it as to what will be decided later?

"You will be looking, in the opinion, or in the preliminary matter plus the opinion, for the following: a statement of the facts the court assumes; a statement of the precise way the question has come before the court—which includes what the plaintiff wanted below, and what the defendant did about it, the judgment below, and what the trial court did that is complained of; then the outcome on appeal, the judgment; and finally the reasons this court gives for doing what it did. This does not look so bad. But it is much worse than it looks.

"For all our cases are decided, all our opinions are written, all our predictions, all our arguments are made, on certain four assumptions. They are the first presuppositions of our study. They must be rutted into you till you can juggle with them standing on your head and in your sleep.

"(1) *The court must decide the dispute that is before it.* It cannot refuse because the job is hard, or dubious, or dangerous.

---

* Copyright © 1960 by K. N. Llewellyn and reprinted here by special permission of Soia M. Llewellyn and Oceana Publications, New York, and as cited in Arval A. Morris, *The Constitution and American Education.* West Publishing Co.

INTRODUCTION

"(2) *The court can decide only the particular dispute which is before it.* When it speaks to that question it speaks ex cathedra, with authority, with finality, with an almost magic power. When it speaks to the question before it, it announces *law,* and if what it announces is new, it legislates, it *makes* the law. But when it speaks to any other question at all, it says mere words, which no man needs to follow. Are such words worthless? They are not. We know them as judicial *dicta*; when they are wholly off the point at issue we call them *obiter dicta*—words dropped along the road, wayside remarks. Yet even wayside remarks shed light on the remarker. They may be very useful in the future to him, or to us. But he will not feel bound to them, as to his ex cathedra utterance. They came not hallowed by a Delphic frenzy. He may be slow to change them; but not so slow as in the other case.

"(3) *The court can decide the particular dispute only according to a general rule which covers a whole class of like disputes.* Our legal theory does not admit of single decisions standing on their own. If judges are free, are indeed forced, to decide new cases for which there is no rule, they must at least make a new rule as they decide. So far, good. But how wide, or how narrow, is the general rule in this particular case? That is a troublesome matter. The practice of our case-law, however, is I think fairly stated thus: it pays to be suspicious of general rules which look too wide; it pays to go slow in feeling *certain* that a wide rule has been laid down at all, or that, if seemingly laid down, it will be followed. For there is a fourth accepted canon:

"(4) *Everything, everything, everything, big or small, a judge may say in an opinion, is to be read with primary reference to the particular dispute, the particular question before him.* You are not to think that the words mean what they might if they stood alone. You are to have your eye on the case in hand, and to learn how to interpret all that has been said *merely* as a reason for deciding *that* case *that* way. . . .

"What now of preparation for your case class? Your cases are assigned. Before they can be used they have to be digested. Experience shows that it is well to brief them. Briefing is valuable if only for the impending discussion. Briefing is well nigh essential when it comes to the review. . . .

INTRODUCTION

" . . . Briefing is also the saddest trap that ever awaited a law student, if he does not watch his step. For the practice under pressure of time, as eyes grow tired in the evening, or the movies lure, is to brief cases, *one by one,* and therefore blindly. Now if I have made one point in this discussion it should be this: that a case read by itself is meaningless, is nil, is blank, is blah . . . Briefing, I say again, is a problem of putting down what in the one case bears upon the problem stated by the other cases. Each brief should be in terms of *what this case adds to what I already know about* this subject . . . What does the case *add, what difference does it make,* to what I already know? This is the keynote of the brief. . . .

"What, now, should a brief contain? (1) First, as a finder: the title and its page in the casebook. (2) Second, to orient it in the law, the state and date. From now on, the order becomes largely immaterial. I give you one possible and useful order. (3) What, precisely, did the plaintiff want? What did he ask for? This is one most vital and one almost regularly overlooked feature of a brief. This is the first start in coming to the *question.* (4) Contrariwise, what did the defendant want and how did the case come to an issue? (5) What did the trial court do; that is, what was the judgment below? (6) Finally, what action of the trial court is complained of? When you have these things in your brief, and only then, are you prepared to look for either relevant facts or relevant rules of law. When you have found these things, and only then, have you your cross-lines laid to spot *the question* in the case. (7) I find it useful to put down next the outcome of appeal. You see why that is useful. It at once makes clear whether the language of the court in a given passage was or was not necessary to the decision. (8) Then come the facts of the case as assumed by the court. I warn you, I warn you strongly, against cutting the facts down too far. If you cherish any hope of insight into *what difference the rules make* to people, you will have to keep an eye out to some of the more striking details of the facts, as the court gives them. I know you will lose patience with them. But observe this, my friends. *You will be impatient with the facts to the precise extent to which you need them.* If you do not need them, if you already have some knowledge of the background of the case, the facts will not be boring; they will interest you. If they pester and upset you, that is a sign that you know so little about what the case means in life that these facts need desperate study.

"Which facts, then, are significant? I recur again to my proposition. One case will not tell you. Only the group of cases will give you any start at solving that. The more cases you read, therefore, before you brief any, the better off you are, provided only that you brief them each one in the light of all.

"And finally, remember this: it is where the facts (as illumined, as *selected,* as *classified* in the light of other cases) *cross* with the issue given by the procedural set-up, that the narrow-issue question of the case is found. *And only there.*

"(9) After the facts, the ratio decidendi, phrased preferably substantially along the lines taken by the court. (10) If you do not like the language of the court, in the light of the other cases, here is the place to note down how you think it should have phrased the rule.

"Beyond this, notes are a matter of discretion. (11) I have always found it useful to indicate something of the line of argument the court indulged in, for reasons which I hope to make appear. (12) A beginning law student, moreover, finds in the cases many remarks as to the law, which although they have no bearing on the subject he is studying, are highly interesting and informative. It was my practice when a student to note those down, but to note them by themselves, where they helped memory but did not get in the way of review.

"So much for the brief.   .   .   ."

SUMMARY OF CONTENTS

SUMMARY OF CONTENTS

TABLE OF CONTENTS

TABLE OF CONTENTS

TABLE OF CONTENTS

TABLE OF CONTENTS

TABLE OF CONTENTS

TABLE OF CONTENTS

THE LAW AND THE COLLEGE STUDENT
JUSTICE IN EVOLUTION

Part I

HIGHER EDUCATION AND THE LAW: NEW DEMANDS AND EXPECTATIONS

Chapter 1

DIXON GOES TO COURT

No State . . . shall . . . deprive any person of life, liberty, or property, without due process of law; nor deny to any person within its jurisdiction the equal protection of the laws.

> (Fourteenth Amendment, U.S. Constitution)

College authorities stand *in loco parentis* concerning the physical and moral welfare and mental training of the pupils, and we are unable to see why, to that end, they may not make any rule or regulation for the government or betterment of their pupils than a parent could for the same purpose.

> (Kentucky Court of Appeals' ruling in *Gott v. Berea*, 156 Ky. 376, 161 S.W. 204 (1913))

It is shocking that the officials of a state educational institution, which can function properly only if our freedoms are preserved, should not understand the elementary principles of fair play. It is equally shocking that a court supports them in denying to a student the protection given to a pickpocket.

> (Professor Warren Seavey's illuminating criticism of the generally accepted legal relation-

ship between students and colleges in 1957, *Harvard Law Review, LXX*)

The courts have consistently upheld the validity of regulations that have the effect of reserving to the college the right to dismiss students at any time for any reason without divulging the reason other than its being for the general good of the institution. The prevailing law does not require the presentation of formal charges or a hearing prior to expulsion by (college) authorities.

(The District Court's ruling in *Dixon v. Alabama State Bd. of Educ.* 1960).

The question presented by the pleadings and evidence, and decisive of this appeal, is whether due process requires notice and some opportunity for hearing before students at a tax-supported college are expelled for misconduct. We answer that question in the affirmative . . . Whenever a governmental body acts so as to injure an individual, the Constitution requires the act to be consonant with due process of law.

(The Fifth Circuit Court of Appeals overruling the above lower court upon appeal in 1961).

What happened? Well, for one thing the presiding judge in the *Dixon* appeal had read Warren Seavey's article; at least he quoted from it in his decision, but perhaps Tom Sawyer and Huck Finn can explain the change better so read on—

When Tom Sawyer and Huck Finn had determined to rescue Jim by digging under the cabin where he was confined, it seemed to the uninformed lay mind of Huck Finn that some old picks the boys had found were the proper implements to use. But Tom knew better. From reading he knew what was the right course in such cases, and he called for case-knives. "It doesn't make no difference," said Tom, "how foolish it is, it's the *right* way and it's the regular way. And there ain't no other way that I ever head of, and I've read all the books that gives any information about these things. They always dig out with a case-knife." So in deference to the books and to the proprieties the boys set to work with case-knives. But after they had dug till nearly midnight and they were tired and their hands were blistered and they had made little progress, a light came to Tom's legal mind. He dropped his knife, and turning to

Huck, said firmly, "Gimmie a case-knife." Let Huck tell the rest:

"He had his own by him, but I handed him mine. He flung it down and says, '*Gimmie a case-knife.*'

"I didn't know just what to do—but then I thought. I scratched around amongst the old tools and got a pickax and give it to him, and he took it and went to work and never said a word.

"He was always just that particular. Full of principle."

Tom Sawyer had made over again one of the earliest discoveries of the law. When legislation or tradition prescribed case-knives for tasks for which pickaxes were better adapted, it seemed better to our forefathers, after a little vain effort with case-knives, to adhere to principle—but use the pickax. They granted that law ought not to change. Changes in law were full of danger. But on the other hand, it was highly inconvenient to use case-knives. And so the law has always managed to get a pickax in its hand, though it steadfastly demanded a case-knife and to wield it in the virtuous belief that it was using the approved instrument.

(From Roscoe Pound's *The Spirit of the Common Law*, 1921)

THE EVOLUTION OF LAW ON CAMPUS

One authority on educational jurisprudence established that between 1789 and 1896 there were 3,096 court cases that significantly affected the organization, administration, and programs of our schools and colleges. By contrast, in the latter half of the sixties there were more than 3,500 such cases—nearly five hundred more than in the formative period of over one hundred years![1] It would appear, then, that during the sixties there was established a growing trend in the field of educational jurisprudence and, in fact, the above numbers could very well underestimate the magnitude of the legal problems and potential pitfalls which now confront the postsecondary education community.

Thus to tell a college trustee, administrator or faculty member today that legal activism has found a home on campus would

1. John C. Hogan, *The Schools, the Courts and the Public Interest*   (Lexington: D. C. Heath and Co., 1974), p. 7.

be stating the obvious; for good or ill, Americans have come to rely on the courts to solve educational problems to an unprecedented degree. Educational reformers, for instance, who found legislatures, boards and administration slow to act have suddenly discovered that major changes can often be wrought far more quickly and effectively by the judiciary. At the same time, students, parents and faculty, awakened to rights only recently defined, are finding more occasions to tell their troubles to a judge. The mounting influence of the law and judges on modern colleges and universities, therefore, constitutes one of the great revolutions in the history of American higher education. It is not without reason that the National Association of College and University Attorneys moved from nonexistence in 1961 to one of the fastest growing higher education associations in the United States today.[2]

Such an awesome preoccupation with the law, of course, is not relegated to the field of education alone, nor in areas outside of education is it a recent phenomenon. Alexis de Tocqueville spied the legalistic proclivity of Americans during his visit here in the early 1830s and wrote about it in his two-volume classic *Democracy in America,* published in 1835 and 1840. But perhaps he captured this propensity somewhat more succinctly in 1848 when he wrote, "If I were asked where I place the American aristocracy, I should reply without hesitation . . . that it occupies the judicial bench and bar . . . scarcely any political question arises in the United States that is not resolved, sooner or later, into a judicial question." [3]

To grasp the prescience of Tocqueville's statement, especially his "sooner or later" claim, one needs only to consider a very brief list of recent legal issues involving just the college-student relationship: In a student-suspension proceeding, is a private university acting under color of state law and thus Fourteenth Amendment requirements if it is chartered by the state, enjoys tax-exempt status and receives federal grants? Does a student have the constitutional right to wear long hair while attending a public college? Must there be meticulous specificity in state college regulations relating to student conduct? Do students have the constitutional right to march or demonstrate at

2. *Legal Issues for Postsecondary Education,* ed. Dennis H. Blumer (American Association of Community and Junior Colleges, 1975), I, p. 1.

3. *Democracy in America,* ed. Phillips Bradley (Knopf, 1944), I, pp. 278–80.

will on a state college campus? Must a public college accord students the due process requirement of notice and hearing before dismissing them for academic failure? Is a college legally liable for breach of contract if a student proves that he has experienced incompetent instruction? May a state university professional school give special consideration to minority students in its admission procedure?

Today most people assume that these are matters for a court to decide—and this is precisely the point. For until the sixties, these issues hardly ever required the attention of a court. Yet, almost unavoidably, unfortunate things are always happening to students, but there was a time when victims were advised, "Don't make a Federal case out of it." Since the early sixties, however, more and more students have been inclined to do just that. For many years, as an example, administrators and faculty members sometimes punished student misconduct by suspension or expulsion. Often the student's side of the story was not heard, but that's the way things were. Then someone got the reasonable enough idea that if students were dismissed from a public college without adequate notice and a fair hearing, they were being deprived of due process of the law. The due process claim by students, however, had been attempted before, but it was at variance with the "case-knife" concept of legal precedent. Nevertheless, when a lawsuit making this claim reached the United States Fifth Circuit Court of Appeals in 1961, the Court "managed to get a pickax in its hands" and the Supreme Court subsequently refused to review the case.[4] That was the crack in the dam. The legal relationship between the public institution of higher education and the student had changed, but in countless colleges and universities the decision was either not known or simply ignored.

Then, thanks in good part to the decade of Berkeley, institutions of higher education found themselves rudely yanked into the central legal system. Increasingly their decisions were made for them off-campus—by the courts, legislatures and executive agencies. Ivory tower images faded, external vetoes multiplied, and thus today it seems that even the simplest internal action should be handled in a way designed more to stand up to external review than to solve an urgent problem.

4. Dixon v. Alabama State Bd. of Educ., 294 F.2d 150 (5th Cir. 1961), cert. denied 286 U.S. 930 (1961).

Protest on Campus

As we look back on this scenario, we might recall that protests on campus inevitably led to institutional disciplinary reaction which in turn focused attention on the administrative procedures used in dealing with student discipline. But most colleges were caught unprepared for the changes which ensued in the institutional-student relationship. By analogy with the game theory, the game was changing, but the game plan remained much the same. Higher education had become increasingly necessary as society's push and emphasis on technology made life more complex. Many more students enrolled in the college with the idea of using higher education as an avenue to a better life. An increasing birth rate added another factor, and eventually most colleges found themselves almost unavoidably transforming into large, bureaucratized, impersonal institutions.

Thus educators were caught in the operational trap of playing the catch-up game. It became more and more apparent that "the dean" was no longer humanly capable of handling conflict resolution and student misconduct cases with the traditional private conference technique; it was obvious that out of frustration he tended to react arbitrarily. Too many problems and public demands for appropriate institutional control were building up pressures for flagrant abuse of authority, and the familial aspect of student discipline began to disappear.

Such embarrassing new accounts triggered additional squabbles between the administrators of the institutions under attack and their protesting students, and a number of these colleges quickly became repressive enclaves. The primary question soon became the whole moral tone of the college environment. Perhaps some educators observed these events and swallowed hard; others might have gagged, from Berkeley to Harvard. And in regards to the much needed campus morality, the reader may find his mind drifting back *Through the Looking Glass* to Tweedledee, speaking contrarily wise: "If it was so, it might be; and if it were so, it would be; but as it isn't, it ain't."

Since these friction points more and more failed to yield to academic lube jobs, sooner or later it was inevitable that the judiciary would reconsider its traditional hands-off policy regarding the student-college relationship. This principle had excluded the college student from the penumbra of protections under academic freedom but, in addition, had essentially excluded the public college from most of the Fourteenth Amendment due process obligations in its relationship with the student.

The Occasion for Judicial Intervention

In fact there was very little time lag between the changed conditions in higher education and judicial intervention. At first gradually, and then with mounting student dissent, the courts, at an ever accelerating pace, came to regard students as something more than second-class citizens. Apparently all that was needed to begin this process was a judicial recognition that higher education was no longer a privilege but an "important benefit," should combine with some flagrant abuse of college disciplinary authority. The first part of this equation had already arrived front and center by the late fifties, and the latter part of the combination presented itself at Alabama State College in 1960. The circumstances provided an ideal setting for a test case. First, the case involved minority students; second, it involved the ultimate sanction power of higher education-expulsion; third, the expulsion was based upon a vague and nonspecific conduct rule; and fourth, the procedure (or lack of procedure) upon which such severe punishment was meted out provided the students with neither notification nor hearing.

The subsequent 1961 appellate decision, Dixon v. Alabama State Bd. of Educ., therefore, found conditions "ripe" for changing the legal relationship between the public institution of higher education and the student. Then in a series of cases following *Dixon*, there again appeared a revealing common denominator: institutional abuse of authority. In fact in each of the cases where the "*Dixon* Doctrine" was later expanded and refined, generally the same element was clearly present.

It is apparent that both the public and the courts felt that academic self-regulation was not working properly, particularly in the area of student discipline and conflict resolution; what ensued amounts to a serious reduction in the traditional autonomy of public colleges and universities. How much further is this encroachment likely to go? The law in this area is still in a state of becoming, thus perhaps the qualities of a prophet rather than those of a researcher are needed for such an answer. Yet the past can be instructive, and lest the colleges eventually choose to surrender their disciplinary functions to the exclusive jurisdiction of the courts, that past deserves careful examination.

PRE–DIXON OBSERVATIONS

The Good Old Days

In the past, it seems that campus disciplinary mechanisms functioned with a maximum of flexibility and informality. The dean of students, for instance, did not typically separate his function of providing advice, guidance and assistance, on the one hand, from his function of dispensing punishment, on the other. The dean usually looked on student punishment as only a continuation of the guidance and counseling function much in the same way that Clausewitz saw war as a continuation of diplomacy. Thus, under such circumstances, the dean might have advised a particular student that his campus conduct was sufficiently immature to require him to withdraw from the college for a year to grow up. When the occasional appeal was heard by the college president or the governing board, a general informality continued to be the rule rather than the exception.

There were obvious advantages to such informal disciplinary procedures. Decision-making processes tended to be individualized and personal. Colleges were typically small, and there existed little need for more formalized, impersonal social controls. Indeed, the persuasiveness of the dean seemed to be heightened by the non-criminal tone of the student misconduct interview.

In this approach the relationship between the college and the student was considered to be familial, a concept which led to nonspecific rules and informal procedures. The general feeling was that strict legalities created a "wrong tone" on campus. Furthermore, before 1961 the courts supported this rationale with the development of some descriptive legal analogies, such as in loco parentis, "contract" and "privilege," and consequently refused to enter the student disciplinary arena unless the student had been subjected to arbitrary or capricious punishment. The courts thought such a position was required not only by the traditional principle of academic self-regulation but also by the sub-category of academic self-regulation, academic freedom.

In the United States, academic freedom generally referred to the freedom of the professor to express diverse opinions in teaching and writing. The Germans, however, had made a distinction in academic freedom including the freedom of the student to arrange his own academic life; American college students of course began demanding such a distinction, very dramatically, during the turbulent decade of the sixties.

Autonomy and Judicial Restraint

Thus for many years, American colleges and universities enjoyed almost total autonomy in such matters as admissions, graduation requirements, determining the curriculum, grading, and disciplining students. They merited this autonomy because those who operated the institutions were considered the experts in higher education, and, as the rationale went, who was to judge expertise but the experts themselves? Accordingly, the courts were expressly unwilling to substitute their judgment for that of the educators and therefore gave almost unlimited support to the unilateral use of disciplinary authority in the educational setting. Moreover, the rather loose way in which the courts interpreted the student-college relationship added legal presumptions of reasonableness to all rules and regulations instituted by lawfully constituted college boards. And when state statutes were passed which embodied this philosophy, these laws were buttressed by the judicial precedents which were stacked on top of them.

Legal Relationships

Some of the courts which dealt with litigation in this area did not even attempt to define the relationship between the student and the college, but contented themselves with describing the extent of power allotted the college in matters of discipline. However, most courts specifically pointed out the existence of a contract or alluded to the existence of some predetermined understanding. Furthermore, it seems that recognition of the controlling contractual relationship pretty well negated any reason for the differentiation between the private and public institution of higher education. Therefore, when the student-college relationship was looked at in this way, there was no application of due process requirements in the "state-action" sense and thus the principles of justice in civil life did not apply.

An old decision cited as authority in many cases that involved both public and private institutions was Goldstein v. New York Univ. (1902). There the Court pointed out:

> The relation existing between the university and the student is contractual. . . . obviously and of necessity, there is implied in such contract a term or condition that the student will not be (involved in) such misconduct as would be subversive of the discipline of the college or school, or as would show him to be morally unfit to be continued as a member thereof.[6]

6. 76 App.Div. 80, 78 N.Y.S. 739, 740 (1902).

What terms could the college or university establish in its contract with students?   In referring to educational institutions, the Illinois Supreme Court said:

> Its charter gives to the trustees and faculty the power "to adopt and enforce such rules as may be deemed expedient for the government of the institution," a power which they would have possessed without such express grant, because [it was] incident to the very object of their incorporation, and indispensable to the successful management of the college.[7]

Another explanation frequently advanced to emphasize the institution's advantage in the contractual relationship was that college matriculation was a privilege rather than a right.   Consequently, since enrollment was intended solely at the pleasure of the college, the college had the right to dismiss students at any time for any reason without divulging its reason other than its being for the general benefit of the institution.   Quite frankly, then, attempts to curb certain kinds of student behavior were sometimes masked by an assertion that the college or university had a privilege to be arbitrary.   A classic example of this brand of support for university regulations was relied upon in Anthony v. Syracuse Univ. (1928):

> Attendance at the University is a privilege and not a right.   In order to safeguard its scholarship and its moral atmosphere, the University reserves the right to request withdrawal of any student whose presence is deemed detrimental.   Specific charges may or may not accompany a request for withdrawal.   (Statement in Syracuse University Catalog) [8]

Therefore, Syracuse University, labeled a private entity, was not required to prefer charges or hold a hearing before dismissing a co-ed for the ludicrous reason of failing to be a "typical Syracuse girl," whatever that meant.   Yet despite the impenetrable vagueness of the reason given for the school's action, it was not discussed by the Court; in fact the dismissal was upheld on the grounds that Miss Anthony was absolutely bound by the registration agreement.   Concerning the application of the regulation, the Court observed that:

> The regulation   .   .   .   does not reserve to the defendant an absolute right to dismiss the plaintiff for any cause what-

7. People ex rel. Pratt v. Wheaton College, 40 Ill. 186, 187 (1866).

8. 224 App.Div. 487, 489, 231 N.Y.S. 435, 438 (1928).

ever. Its right to dismiss is limited, for the regulation must be read as a whole. The University may only dismiss a student for reasons falling within two classes, one, in connection with safeguarding the University's ideal of scholarship, and the other in connection with safeguarding the University's moral atmosphere. *When dismissing a student, no reason for dismissing need be given.* The University must, however, have a reason . . . Of course the University authorities have wide discretion in determining what situation does and what does not fall within the classes mentioned and the courts would be slow in disturbing any decision of the University authorities in this respect.[9]

In this case, therefore, expulsion was not only a severe deprivation, but it also was an arbitrary one. Moreover, while the courts were still indulging in the presumption that schools acted reasonably, that blind-folded lady holding those scales would have insisted that reasonableness was more a question of fact.

The Contract and Privilege Approach to Fair Proceedings

In reviewing the main body of case-law prior to 1961 courts were reluctant to interfere in the campus disciplinary arena and frequently alluded to the right of the college or university, whether private or public, to dismiss students summarily without hearing and on any grounds the institution deemed sufficient. Generally the only question on an appeal to the courts was whether the institution acted without malice and in accordance with its own rules. In brief, it seems that the language used in a Maryland court in 1924 fairly well sums up the almost unchallenged authority of college officials to discipline students with little if any possibility of judicial interference:

The maintenance of discipline, the upkeep of the necessary tone and standards of behavior in a body of students in a college is, of course, a task committed to its faculty and officers; not to the courts. It is a task which demands special experience, and is often one of much delicacy . . . and the officers must, of necessity, be left untrammeled in handling the problems which arise as their judgment and discretion may dictate, looking to the ends to be accomplished. Only in extraordinary situations can a court of law ever

9. Id., at 440 (emphasis added). If "no reason for dismissing must be given", it is difficult to conceive of any method short of mind reading by which Miss Anthony could have convinced the University authorities that she should remain in school.

be called upon to step in between students and the officers in charge of them.[10]

At this point in time, therefore, the courts seemed to be content to satisfy themselves that there was a reason for dismissing a student and were not concerned with the manner in which colleges and universities determined the sufficiency of the reason. To somewhat the same effect, moreover, was State of Mont. ex rel. Ingersoll v. Clapp (1928),[11] which though it involved a state university drew no distinction between public and private institutions. The plaintiff student, a married female, had been accused of serving intoxicating liquors in her home, and, after a brief interview with the Dean's Council, she was dismissed from the university. Hill v. McCauley (1887),[12] apparently the only authority her counsel could find requiring a formal notice and hearing in this setting, was expressly rejected by the *Ingersoll* Court as "a wholly unworkable and impractical solution" and concluded the issue with the view that the opportunity of the expelled student to present her side of the question to the Dean's Council constituted for all purposes a sufficient hearing. Nevertheless, the court at least mentioned the reasonableness of having some type of hearing before expelling a student. But while resting on the easy use of legal analogies, the court failed to supply meaningful content to this reasonableness rule.

Fourteen years after the *Ingersoll* case, the first mention of due process was encountered in State of Tenn. ex rel. Sherman v. Hyman (1942).[13] Here the *Sherman* Court somewhat solidified the requirements of disciplinary proceedings within a state university by paying more heed to the question of what it *would* consider to be a fair method of disposition, as distinguished from the *Ingersoll* Court's extensive treatment of what procedures it *would not* consider necessary.

The *Sherman* case involved an action by a student seeking reinstatement following his expulsion on a charge of stealing examinations (plaintiff had denied the charge). Here it was paradoxically stated that all authorities agreed that a student could not be dismissed without notice and a fair hearing, but that the due process clause of the Constitution had no application to such proceedings. Well, it was clear enough that due process

10. Woods v. Simpson, 146 Md. 547, 551, 126 A. 882, 883 (1924).

11. 263 P. 433 (1928), cert. denied 277 U.S. 591 (1928).

12. 3 Pa. County Ct. 77 (1887).

13. 171 S.W.2d 822 (Tenn.1942), cert. denied 319 U.S. 748 (1943).

was not a limitation on college disciplinary authority, but it was less clear that the total weight of case precedent supported notice and hearing requirements in such proceedings. As a matter of fact, the notice and hearing requirement issue was a mixed bag at this time; some courts required this and others did not. Actually some courts provided that notice and hearing were necessary only when a state law or the rules of an institution's governing board required such. Thus here the situation was that no hearing needed to be held but if one was held, or required by either state or board policy, then the hearing had to conform to some judicial notion of fairness. Conversely, some other courts placed a generalized, minimal standard of notice and hearing on college disciplinary authority.

The first instance of a student plaintiff specifically pleading constitutional protection, however, occurred in People ex rel. Bluett v. Board of Trustees of the Univ. of Illinois (1956).[14] The expelled student alleged that the action taken against her was arbitrary and unconstitutional, but there was no reported claim specifically indicating a denial of due process. The Illinois Court used the Ingersoll v. Clapp and Anthony v. Syracuse cases as controlling and decided that the plaintiff was not entitled to a full-dress hearing. Again the issue involved was the adequacy and sufficiency of the hearing, not whether one should be held.

Still, it is difficult to determine in a positive way what the court considered an "adequate" and "sufficient" hearing to be. But it is not difficult to detect elements of unfairness in what the court accepted as adequate and sufficient. For example, apparently all that the court required in proceedings resulting in the expulsion of a student was that the institution's authorities should have heard "some evidence" and acted in "good faith." Some evidence and good faith? A bit vague but quite clearly the court allowed the real issue to be dodged. Of course there would not need to be much justification to establish an educational institution's right to dismiss for cheating any more than there would need be for a medical doctor's refusal to continue his professional relationship with a patient who failed to follow his prescribed treatment. But the right to dismiss was never the issue in the university's proceedings—it was wholly as to the existence of the alleged offense. Moreover, the student was

---

14. 10 Ill.App.2d 207, 134 N.E.2d 635 (1956). This case aroused the wrath of Professor Warren A. Seavey which found expression in some blistering comments on the topic in Seavey "Dismissal of Students: Due Process," 70 *Harvard Law Review* (1957).

never told what evidence there was against her nor the identity of her accusers. She was merely informed that she had been accused of cheating and then subsequently allowed to present her side of the issue. Therefore, not only was the burden of disproving the alleged offense placed on the student rather than on the institution to prove otherwise (to be kind, a somewhat unusual idea of justice), but additionally, when she sought relief from the courts, she was left with the impossible task of proving that the university officials had acted arbitrarily or capriciously without having the information from which evidence to support her claim could be found.[15] A real life "Catch–22," a metaphor that would soon help shape the moral vision of the sixties.

In his analysis of the *Bluett* case, Professor Seavey pointed out that had the University of Illinois been a private institution, it might have been somewhat easier to support the action of the University authorities; that is, the plaintiff's claim then would not have been based upon what should have been a public right to more formalized notification and hearing protection. Whatever, Seavey was quite adamantly opposed to the prevailing contract rationale in either public or private colleges because the results tended to be unfair, even contractually illegal:

> . . . since the courts depart from the usual rule of contracts which requires one terminating a contract for breach to justify his action. Here again the dismissed student bears the burden of showing that the school has acted arbitrarily, although he lacks information as to the source of the charges against him, or even as to their nature.[16]

Seavey, moreover, believed that the contract analogy used to explain the student-college relationship was even less fair as applied to the private college since it had " . . . been held that a private institution may dismiss a student not guilty of an 'overt act' and that 'it is not incumbent on the institution to prefer charges and prove them at trial.' " [17]

Some twelve years after the *Bluett* Court's rather abbreviated consideration of the fair hearing issue within a public university, the United States Second Circuit Court of Appeals was presented with a similar problem, but in this case the student who had been dismissed from Brooklyn College (also a public institution),

15. Seavey, op. cit.

16. Id.

17. Id. Seavey quoting in part from John B. Stetson Univ. v. Hunt, 88 Fla. 510, 514, 102 So. 637, 641 (1924).

raised the problem in the federal rather than state courts and among other assertions, specifically claimed that he had been deprived of due process as guaranteed under the Fourteenth Amendment.   Nevertheless, the judge writing the opinion of the court in this case, Steier v. New York State Educ. Comm'r (1959), denied due process jurisdiction over disciplinary problems within a state college or university by observing that:

> Education is a field of life reserved to the individual states. *The only restriction the Federal Government imposes is that in their educational program no state may discriminate against an individual because of race, color or creed.*   (Italics added for emphasis) [18]

Apparently the Second Circuit Court was feeling the impact of the Supreme Court's Brown v. Board of Educ. decision (347 U.S. 483, 1954).   But regardless of mounting racial unrest and the Supreme Court's accentuated interest in the civil rights movement, it seems curious that the judge delivering the Court of Appeals ruling would indicate that he could find the Fourteenth Amendment equal protection clause applicable in the student-college relationship and not the adjacent due process protection. Perhaps he had never encountered the intransigency of being just a little pregnant.   However, the other two judges on the panel held that there was both due process and equal protection jurisdiction, and thus, as precedent, the *Steier* case stands as the first existence of federal jurisdiction to review state college and university expulsions.

That conclusion in fact was inherent in the Supreme Court ruling enunciated in West Virginia State Bd. of Educ. v. Barnette and in subsequent cases for which the West Virginia case was used as a precedent.   However, the courts mean what they say when they warn again and again that each problem must be considered on a case-by-case basis.   But the essence was there as early as 1943:

> The Fourteenth Amendment as now applied to the State, protects the citizen against the State itself and all of its creatures—Boards of Education not excepted.   These have, of course, important, delicate, and highly discretionary functions, but none that they may not perform within the limits of the Bill of Rights.   That they are educating the young for citizenship is reason for scrupulous protection of constitution-

18.   271 F.2d 13, 15 (2d Cir. 1959), cert. denied 361 U.S. 966 (1960).

al freedoms of the individual if we are not to discount important principles of our government as mere platitudes.[19]

The above would appear to have broadened the constitutional
community to include students within the protection of the due
process clause of the Fourteenth Amendment in a variety of
ways. But this was narrowly interpreted by later court decisions, and thus a broader view of constitutional due process protection for students in public institutions of higher education was
slow in evolving.

As a matter of record, then, until 1961 courts were essentially
operating under the assumption that constitutional guarantees
were inapplicable to student-college conflicts. Rather, the courts
usually looked to contract law to rationalize their decisions in
suits involving such conflicts. That is, if the student registered,
he became a member of that academic community for limited,
quasi-contractual purposes, and the provisions of the student-college contract were considered to be embodied in college bulletins,
the catalog, materials signed during the registration process, et
cetera. Provided the student accepted and fulfilled such obligations contained therein, the college agreed to confer the appropriate degree, certificate of course completion, or transcript.

Included somewhere in the catalog or registration forms of
most institutions, however, was a statement to the effect that the
college reserved the right to require withdrawal of any student
without having to state a reason for its action. Moreover, the
courts generally focused on this purported right, upheld it, and
gave it broad construction in cases involving both public and
private institutions of higher education. Of course prior to 1961
the courts were judging the adequacy or inadequacy of such hearings that were held, but nonetheless it seems apparent that they
were measuring these proceedings against a somewhat minimal
concept of substantial justice. In fact, the usual qualification
that dismissal must not be arbitrary, in bad faith, or in abuse of
discretion remained largely undefined. Thus although acknowl-
edging their jurisdiction, courts still seemed unwilling to create
that set of standards necessary to establish substantial "fair play"
in the disciplining of students on campus and that reluctance, of
course, was reflected in the rarity in which student suits prevailed.

19. West Virginia State Bd. of Educ.
v. Barnette, 319 U.S. 624, 637
(1943).

Arriving at Fair Proceeding Through Due Process

With the advent of the civil rights movement, however, changes occurred. Students were dismissed from public colleges because they participated in civil rights activities which eventually the federal courts would decide were legitimate constitutional activities. Still, relying on the case law prevailing in 1960, a federal district court concluded in Dixon v. Alabama State Bd. of Educ. that students had no procedural or substantive due process rights as long as a public college acted without malice in expelling them. The United States Fifth Circuit Court of Appeals, however, reversed the lower court, holding that state colleges— like all other governmental bodies—were constitutionally required to provide procedural due process when inflicting expulsion deprivations.[20]

Heretofore, judicial analysis concerning the adequacy of a student disciplinary hearing had not evolved to a point where the analysis demanded that before the sufficiency of a hearing be judged, the due process right to have such a hearing be firmly fixed. However, the *Dixon* appellate decision sliced through the subtleties involved in the determination of procedural niceties by determining decisively that the due process clause controlled and that a hearing must be held.

Indeed, the game was changing.

Thus, the disciplining of a student used to be a simple matter within the nearly autonomous discretion of a dean or faculty disciplinary committee. However, during the sixties a rather abrupt decline in judicial support occurred for the arbitrary use of authority to suppress the constitutional rights of students enrolled in public institutions of higher education. And today, the deference once shown to the expertise of college authorities has declined to the point that the courts now recognize a duty to intervene where the Fourteenth Amendment and other rights of students are infringed.

THE *DIXON* CASES

Dixon and the Federal District Court

Since 1961, the courts have been exhibiting increasing interest in the constitutional "rights" of expelled or suspended students. The preliminary *Dixon* case, to wit, Dixon v. Alabama State Bd. of Educ. (1960), involved the summary dismissal of students who

---

20.   186 F.Supp. 945 (D.C.Ala.1960),
rev'd 294 F.2d 150 (5th Cir. 1961).

participated in an off-campus lunch counter "sit in" and other civil rights activities which allegedly disrupted campus life. The students were not given any notice or hearing and were advised of their dismissals via letter. The issue was whether Fourteenth Amendment "due process" required notice and some opportunity for hearing before students at a tax-supported college could be separated from the institution for misconduct.[21]

Relying on the case law prevailing in 1960, the United States District Court for the Middle District of Alabama concluded the following in this first *Dixon* case:

> The courts have consistently upheld the validity of regulations that have the effect of reserving to the college the right to dismiss students at any time for any reason without divulging the reason other than its being for the general good of the institution. The prevailing law does not require the presentation of formal charges or a hearing prior to expulsion by the school authorities.[22]

Furthermore, the Federal District Court pointed out that the regulations of the College provided for expulsion for ". . . conduct prejudicial to the school and for conduct unbecoming a student or future teacher in schools in Alabama, [or] . . . for insubordination." [23]

On appeal, the Fifth Circuit Court of Appeals was appalled by the lower court's preoccupation with the functioning of the college and its insensitivity to the rights of the expelled student, " '. . . our sense of justice should be outraged by the denial to students of the normal safeguards . . . . given to a pickpocket.' " [24] The Court of Appeals consequently reversed and remanded the finding of the lower court.[25]

The reversal of the first *Dixon* case by the Fifth Circuit Court of Appeals, and the subsequent approval of the Court of Appeals' decision by almost every court handling a major student "due process" case,[26] as well as the refusal of the Supreme Court to

21. Dixon v. Alabama State Bd. of Educ., 186 F.Supp. 945 (D.C.Ala. 1960).

22. Id., at 951.

23. Id., at 951.

24. Dixon v. Alabama State Bd. of Educ., 294 F.2d 150, 158 (5th Cir. 1961) quoting Professor Warren Seavey.

25. Id., at 159.

26. Thomas C. Fischer, *Due Process in the Student-Institutional Relationship* (Washington, D.C.: American Association of State Colleges and Universities, 1970), p. 34.

review that decision,[27] has pretty well eclipsed any value the District Court's logic or reasoning might have had.

Still, the first *Dixon* case is instructive, because it indicates how narrow the decisions in these difficult cases can be. Both the District Court and the Court of Appeals cited many of the same precedents. The District Court simply found itself interpreting the precedents conservatively at a time when individual rights were being expanded. The first *Dixon* case remains valuable, therefore, because it reflects the generally accepted state of the law and the point of view of the courts prior to the landmark *Dixon* appellate decision. The first *Dixon* case is also a well written exposition of the conservative point of view of student-institutional relationships in disciplinary cases. Now this is all history, for the second *Dixon* case, and later cases, wrought a new legal concept of student rights.

Dixon and the Federal Court of Appeals

The second *Dixon* case, the appeal of the prior case decision, is, as previously mentioned, the granddaddy of the recent strain of student "due process" decisions. This case is considered a "landmark" decision not because it marked the first occasion in which students successfully challenged institutional authority; rather, the reason is that the decision gave students a constitutional "right" to *notice* and a *hearing* before they could be dismissed from a public institution of higher education, and also that the Court spelled out with some particularity the procedural due process safeguards to which students were entitled when facing serious institutional penalties. But by far the most important was the fact that *Dixon* was the first case in which constitutional rights were expressly extended to students in public colleges and universities.

In essence, the second *Dixon* case required the following procedural safeguards: (1) *Notice*, containing a statement of the specific charges and grounds which, if proven, would justify expulsion under the regulations of the college; and (2) a *hearing* that must amount to more than an informal interview with an administrative authority, and which must preserve at least the "rudiments of an adversary proceeding": (a) an opportunity for the student to present his own defense against the charges and to produce either oral testimony or written affidavits of witnesses

27. Dixon v. Alabama State Bd. of
Educ., 294 F.2d 150 (5th Cir. 1961),
cert. denied 368 U.S. 930 (1961).

in his behalf; and (b) if cross-examination of witnesses is not allowed, the student "should be given the names of the witnesses against him and an oral or written report on the facts to which each witness testifies." [28]

The second *Dixon* case obviously did not answer all the questions concerning the character of the hearing which is constitutionally required in order to discipline a student at a tax-supported institution of higher education. Nor did the opinion state any constitutional guidelines concerning such substantive issues as expression, association and assembly. Nevertheless, Knight v. State Bd. of Educ. (1961),[29] which closely followed *Dixon*, gave some indication of the eventual influence that case would have. The *Knight* case involved a state college's suspension of students without a hearing pursuant to a regulation of the Tennessee State Board of Education requiring dismissal of any student arrested and convicted on charges "involving personal misconduct." The District Court cited *Dixon* as controlling and found the regulation reasonable, but declared its application unreasonable. That is, the Court ruled that an off-campus arrest and conviction without a hearing by the college to determine whether in fact the students actually had been involved in "personal misconduct" constituted an inadequate application of procedural due process protection. The Court then concluded with the statement that "the rudiments of fair play and the requirements of due process rested in the plaintiffs' right to be forewarned or advised of the charges to be made against them and to be afforded an opportunity to present their side of the case . . ."

In summary, these significant points in both *Dixon* and *Knight* should be noted: (1) The precedent setting significance of *Dixon* was not the requirement of notice and hearing, but the express notion that student expulsion was controlled by the Fourteenth Amendment. With just a few exceptions, prior authorities had not even mentioned Fourteenth Amendment guarantees; in fact, even if the Court had omitted Fourteenth Amendment application, by establishing the "rudiments of an adversary proceeding" requirement, it would still have been at variance with the trend of the precedents. (2) Both *Dixon* and *Knight* involved black students who were dismissed from college because of off-campus civil rights activities. The Warren Court had already expressed considerable sensitivity about racial discrimination, and since

28. Dixon v. Alabama State Bd. of   29. 200 F.Supp. 174 (D.C.Tenn.1961).
Educ., 294 F.2d at 158–159.

the Supreme Court has no judicial peer, it was inevitable, sooner or later, that other courts would react similarly. Moreover, as one reads the gross lack of specific evidence considered by the Alabama State Board of Education upon which it based its decision to expel the students (see pp. 22–31 for the complete *Dixon* decision), one can hardly avoid the suspicion that what might really have been the heart of the issue was an effort by a politically rather than an educationally oriented board to utilize the disciplinary discretion of a college to impress its will on the civil rights problems prevalent in the area at the time. In other words, it appears that the expulsions were an arbitrary act motivated by a spirit of retaliation. Faced with this possibility, one can probably assume that the *Dixon* Court was quite ready to be impressed with the lack of "fundamental fairness." (3) Confining itself to the issue at point, the *Dixon* Court ruled due process applicable to expulsion of students, but the *Knight* issue was specifically concerned with student suspensions. Therefore, although *Knight* made reference to the belief that suspension was tantamount to expulsion, it nevertheless raised the question of whether all disciplinary actions, however minimal, might now be open to due process review by the courts. (4) Both *Dixon* and *Knight* fumbled around with "privilege" and "right" alternatives as to public college attendance, but neither of them reached the position that it was a constitutional right. (5) It is interesting to note that by disposing of the appeal on purely procedural grounds, the *Dixon* Court avoided the difficult substantive question of whether students may be expelled from a tax-supported college for participating in sit-ins or similar demonstrations with the objective of achieving civil rights recognized under the U. S. Constitution. (6) And finally, rather than ignoring the quasi-contractual nature of the student-college relationship, why didn't the Fifth Circuit seize upon this well-established analogy as the device to specify its ". . . rudimentary elements of fair play [to be] followed in a case of misconduct . . ."? By simply drawing on basic principles of contract law, the Court could have riddled the notion that the college, one party to the educational contract, could constitute itself as the *ex parte* authority to determine whether or not to sever the student-school relationship. Moreover, this kind of approach not only would have been more in harmony with precedent, but, at the same time, the ruling then would have denominated an expanded "fair play" framework for the private as well as the public disciplinary arena. However, even though one might understandably wonder if the difference between public and private colleges is sufficiently significant to justify different kinds of dismissal procedures, Judge Rives was most explicit in confining his holding to "public" institutions. In fact, Judge Rives probably solidified the power imbalance existing between a student and his private institution by dispensing with the lower court's application of the Anthony v. Syracuse principle on the ground that it involved a *private* university and thus merely followed ". . . the well-settled rule that the relations between a student and a private university are a matter of contract."

Of course an analysis of significant points could go much further, but still it would be difficult to substitute that for a reading of the case—so read on.   .   .   .

DIXON v. ALABAMA STATE BOARD OF EDUCATION

United States Court of Appeals, Fifth Circuit, 1961.
294 F.2d 150, cert. denied 286 U.S. 930 (1961).

RIVES, Circuit Judge.

The question presented by the pleadings and evidence, and decisive of this appeal, is whether due process requires notice and some opportunity for hearing before students at a tax-supported college are expelled for misconduct. We answer that question in the affirmative.

The misconduct for which the students were expelled has never been definitely specified. Defendant Trenholm, the President of the College, testified that he did not know why the plaintiffs and three additional students were expelled and twenty other students were placed on probation. The notice of expulsion which Dr. Trenholm mailed to each of the plaintiffs assigned no specific ground for expulsion, but referred in general terms to "this problem of Alabama State College."

.   .   .

As shown by the findings of the district court,   .   .   .   the only demonstration which the evidence showed that *all* of the expelled students took part in was that in the lunch grill located in the basement of the Montgomery County Courthouse. The other demonstrations were found to be attended "by several if not all of the plaintiffs." We have carefully read and studied the record, and agree with the district court that the evidence does not affirmatively show that *all* of the plaintiffs were present at any but the one demonstration.

Only one member of the State Board of Education assigned the demonstration attended by all of the plaintiffs as the sole basis for his vote to expel them.   Mr. Harry Ayers testified:

"Q.   Mr. Ayers, did you vote to expel these negro students because they went to the Court House and asked to be served at the white lunch counter?   A.   No, I voted because they violated a law of Alabama.

"Q.   What law of Alabama had they violated?   A.   That separating of the races in public places of that kind.

"Q.   And the fact that they went up there and requested service, by violating the Alabama law, then you voted to have them expelled?   A.   Yes.

"Q.   And that is your reason why you voted?   A.   That is the reason."

The most elaborate grounds for expulsion were assigned in the testimony of Governor Patterson:

"Q.   There is an allegation in the complaint, Governor, that—I believe it is paragraph six, the defendants' action of expulsion was taken without regard to any valid rule or regulation concerning student conduct and merely retaliated against, punished, and sought to intimidate plaintiffs for having lawfully sought service in a publicly owned lunch room with service; is that statement true or false?

"A.   Well, that is not true; the action taken by the State Board of Education was—was taken to prevent—to prevent incidents happening by students at the College that would bring—bring discredit upon—upon the School and be prejudicial to the School, and the State—as I said before, the State Board of Education took—considered at the time it expelled these students several incidents, one at the Court House at the lunch room demonstration, the one the next day at the trial of this student, the marching on the steps of the State Capitol, and also this rally held at the church, where— where it was reported that—that statements were made against the administration of the School.   In addition to that, the—the feeling going around in the community here due to—due to the reports of these incidents of the students, by the students, and due to reports of incidents occurring involving violence in other States, which happened prior to these things starting here in Alabama, all of these things were discussed by the State Board of Education prior to the taking of the action that they did on March 2 and as I was present and acting as Chairman, as a member of the Board, I voted to expel these students and to put these others on probation because I felt that that was what was in the best interest of the College. And the—I felt that the action should be—should be prompt and immediate, because if something—something had not been done, in my opinion, it would have resulted in violence and disorder, and that we wanted to prevent, and we felt that we had a duty to the—to the— to the parents of the students and to the State to require that the students behave themselves while they are attending a State College, and that is (sic) the reasons why we took the action that we did. That is all."

Superintendent of Education Stewart testified that he voted for expulsion because the students had broken rules and regulations pertaining to all of the State institutions, and, when required to be more specific, testified:

"The Court: What rule had been broken is the question, that justified the expulsion insofar as he is concerned?

"A. I think demonstrations without the consent of the president of an institution."

The testimony of other members of the Board assigned somewhat varying and differing grounds and reasons for their votes to expel the plaintiffs.

The district court found the general nature of the proceedings before the State Board of Education, the action of the Board, and the official notice of expulsion given to the students as follows:

"Investigations into this conduct were made by Dr. Trenholm, as president of the Alabama State College, the Director of Public Safety for the State of Alabama under directions of the Governor, and by the investigative staff of the Attorney General for the State of Alabama.

"On or about March 2, 1960, the State Board of Education met and received reports from the Governor of the State of Alabama, which reports embodied the investigations that had been made and which reports identified these six plaintiffs, together with several others, as the 'ring leaders' for the group of students that had been participating in the above-recited activities. During this meeting, Dr. Trenholm, in his capacity as president of the college reported to the assembled members of the State Board of Education that the action of these students in demonstrating on the college campus and in certain downtown areas was having a disruptive influence on the work of the other students at the college and upon the orderly operation of the college in general. Dr. Trenholm further reported to the Board that, in his opinion, he as president of the college could not control future disruptions and demonstrations. There were twenty-nine of the Negro students identified as the core of the organization that was responsible for these demonstrations. This group of twenty-nine included these six plaintiffs. After hearing these reports and recommendations and upon the recommendation of the Governor as chairman of the Board, the Board voted unanimously, expelling nine students, including these six plaintiffs, and placing twenty students on probation. This action was taken by Dr. Trenholm as president of the college, acting pursuant to the instructions of the State Board of Education. Each of these plaintiffs, together with the other students expelled, was officially notified of his expulsion on March 4th or 5th, 1960. No formal charges were placed against these students and no hearing was granted any of them prior to their expulsion."

The evidence clearly shows that the question for decision does not concern the sufficiency of the notice or the adequacy of the hearing, but is whether the students had a right to any notice or hearing whatever before being expelled. The district court wrote at some length on that question, as appears from its opinion. Dixon v. Alabama State Board of Education, supra, 186 F.Supp. at pages 950–952. After careful study and consideration, we find ourselves unable to agree with the conclusion of the district court that no notice or opportunity for any kind of hearing was required before these students were expelled.

It is true, as the district court said, that ". . . there is no statute or rule that requires formal charges and/or a hearing . . .," but the evidence is without dispute that the usual practice at Alabama State College had been to give a hearing and opportunity to offer defenses before expelling a student. Defendant Trenholm, the College President, testified:

"Q. The essence of the question was, will you relate to the Court the usual steps that are taken when a student's conduct has developed to the point where it is necessary for the administration to punish him for that conduct?

"A. We normally would have conference with the student and notify him that he was being asked to withdraw, and we would indicate why he was being asked to withdraw. That would be applicable to academic reasons, academic deficiency, as well as to any conduct difficulty.

"Q. And at this hearing ordinarily that you would set, then the student would have a right to offer whatever defense he may have to the charges that have been brought against him?

"A. Yes."

Whenever a governmental body acts so as to injure an individual, the Constitution requires that the act be consonant with due process of law. The minimum procedural requirements necessary to satisfy due process depend upon the circumstances and the interests of the parties involved. As stated by Mr. Justice Frankfurter concurring in Joint Anti-Fascist Refugee Committee v. McGrath, 1951, 341 U.S. 123, 163:

"Whether the *ex parte* procedure to which the petitioners were subjected duly observed 'the rudiments of fair play', . . . cannot . . . be tested by mere generalities or sentiments abstractly appealing. The precise nature of the interest that has been adversely affected, the manner in which this was done, the reasons for doing it, the available alternatives to the procedure that was followed, the protection implicit in the office of the functionary whose conduct is challenged, the balance of hurt complained of and good accomplished—these are some of the considerations that must enter into the judicial judgment."

Just last month, a closely divided Supreme Court held in a case where the governmental power was almost absolute and the private interest was slight that no hearing was required. Cafeteria and Restaurant Workers Union v. McElroy et al., 1961, 367 U.S. 886. In that case, a short-order cook working for a privately operated cafeteria on the premises of the Naval Gun Factory in the City of Washington was excluded from the Gun Factory as a security risk. So, too, the due process clause does not require that an alien never admitted to this Country be granted a hearing before being *excluded*. United States ex rel. Knauff v. Shaughnessy, 1950, 338 U.S. 537, 542, 543. In such case the executive power as implemented by Congress to *exclude* aliens is absolute and not subject to the review of any court, unless expressly authorized by Congress. On the other hand, once an alien has been admitted to lawful residence in the United States and remains physically present here it has been held that, "although Congress may prescribe conditions for his expulsion and deportation, not even Congress may expel him without allowing him a fair opportunity to be heard." Kwong Hai Chew v. Colding, 1953, 344 U.S. 590, 597, 598.

It is not enough to say, as did the district court in the present case, "The right to attend a public college or university is not in and of itself a constitutional right." 186 F.Supp. at page 950. That argument was emphatically answered by the Supreme Court in the Cafeteria and Restaurant Workers Union case, supra, [367 U.S. 893.] when it said that the question of whether ". . . summarily denying Rachel Brawner access to the site of her former employment violated the requirements of the Due Process Clause of the Fifth Amendment . . . cannot be answered by easy assertion that, because she had no constitutional right to be there in the first place, she was not deprived of liberty or property by the Superintendent's action. 'One may not have a constitutional right to go to Bagdad, but the Government may not prohibit one from going there unless by means consonant with due process of law.' " As in that case, so here, it is necessary to consider "the nature both of the private interest which has been impaired and the governmental power which has been exercised."

The appellees urge upon us that under a provision of the Board of Education's regulations the appellants waived any right to notice and a hearing before being expelled for misconduct.

> "Attendance at any college is on the basis of a mutual decision of the student's parents and of the college. Attendance at a particular college is voluntary and is different from attendance at a public school where the pupil may be required to attend a particular school which is located in the neighborhood or district in which the pupil's family may live. Just as a student may choose to withdraw from a particular college at any time for any personally-determined reason, the college may also at any time decline to continue to accept responsibility for the supervision and service to any student with whom the relationship becomes unpleasant and difficult."

We do not read this provision to clearly indicate an intent on the part of the student to waive notice and a hearing before expulsion. If, however, we should so assume, it nonetheless remains true that the State cannot condition the granting of even a privilege upon the renunciation of the constitutional right to procedural due process. See Slochower v. Board of Education, 1956,

350 U.S. 551, 555; Wieman v. Updegraff, 1952, 344 U.S. 183, 191, 192; United Public Workers of America (C.I.O.) v. Mitchell, 1947, 330 U.S. 75, 100; Shelton v. Tucker, 1960, 364 U.S. 479. Only private associations have the right to obtain a waiver of notice and hearing before depriving a member of a valuable right. And even here, the right to notice and a hearing is so fundamental to the conduct of our society that the waiver must be clear and explicit. Medical and Surgical Society of Montgomery County v. Weatherly, 75 Ala. 248, 256–259. In the absence of such an explicit waiver, Alabama has required that even private associations must provide notice and a hearing before expulsion. In Medical and Surgical Society of Montgomery County v. Weatherly, supra, it was held that a physician could not be expelled from a medical society without notice and a hearing. In Local Union No. 57, etc. v. Boyd, 1944, 245 Ala. 227, 16 So.2d 705, 711, a local union was ordered to reinstate one of its members expelled after a hearing of which he had insufficient notice.

The precise nature of the private interest involved in this case is the right to remain at a public institution of higher learning in which the plaintiffs were students in good standing. It requires no argument to demonstrate that education is vital and, indeed, basic to civilized society. Without sufficient education the plaintiffs would not be able to earn an adequate livelihood, to enjoy life to the fullest, or to fulfill as completely as possible the duties and responsibilities of good citizens.

There was no offer to prove that other colleges are open to the plaintiffs. If so, the plaintiffs would nonetheless be injured by the interruption of their course of studies in mid-term. It is most unlikely that a public college would accept a student expelled from another public college of the same state. Indeed, expulsion may well prejudice the student in completing his education at any other institution. Surely no one can question that the right to remain at the college in which the plaintiffs were students in good standing is an interest of extremely great value.

Turning then to the nature of the governmental power to expel the plaintiffs, it must be conceded, as was held by the district court, that that power is not unlimited and cannot be arbitrarily exercised. Admittedly, there must be some reasonable and constitutional ground for expulsion or the courts would have a duty to require reinstatement. The possibility of arbitrary action is not excluded by the existence of reasonable regulations. There may be arbitrary application of the rule to the facts of a particular case. Indeed, that result is well nigh inevitable when the

Board hears only one side of the issue. In the disciplining of college students there are no considerations of immediate danger to the public, or of peril to the national security, which should prevent the Board from exercising at least the fundamental principles of fairness by giving the accused students notice of the charges and an opportunity to be heard in their own defense. Indeed, the example set by the Board in failing so to do, if not corrected by the courts, can well break the spirits of the expelled students and of others familiar with the injustice, and do inestimable harm to their education.

The district court, however, felt that it was governed by precedent, and stated that, "the courts have consistently upheld the validity of regulations that have the effect of reserving to the college the right to dismiss students at any time for any reason without divulging its reason other than its being for the general benefit of the institution." [186 F.Supp. 951.] With deference, we must hold that the district court has simply misinterpreted the precedents.

The language above quoted from the district court is based upon language found in 14 C.J.S. Colleges and Universities § 26, p. 1360, which, in turn, is paraphrased from Anthony v. Syracuse University, 224 App.Div. 487, 231 N.Y.S. 435, reversing 130 Misc. 2d 249, 223 N.Y.S. 796, 797. (14 C.J.S. Colleges and Universities § 26, pp. 1360, 1363 note 70.) This case, however, concerns a private university and follows the well-settled rule that the relations between a student and a private university are a matter of contract. The Anthony case held that the plaintiffs had specifically waived their rights to notice and hearing. See also Barker v. Bryn Mawr, 1923, 278 Pa. 121, 122 A. 220. The precedents for public colleges are collected in a recent annotation cited by the district court. 58 A.L.R.2d 903–920. We have read all of the cases cited to the point, and we agree with what the annotator himself says: "The cases involving suspension or expulsion of a student from a public college or university all involve the question whether the hearing given to the student was adequate. In every instance the sufficiency of the hearing was upheld." 58 A.L.R.2d at page 909. None held that no hearing whatsoever was required. Two cases not found in the annotation have held that some form of hearing is required. In Commonwealth ex rel. Hill v. McCauley, 1886, 3 Pa.Co.Ct.R. 77, the court went so far as to say that an informal presentation of the charges was insufficient and that a state-supported college must grant a student a full hearing on the charges before expulsion for misconduct. In Gleason v. University of Minnesota, 1908, 104 Minn. 359, 116 N.W. 650, on reviewing the overruling of the state's demurrer to a petition for mandamus for reinstatement, the court held that the plaintiff stated a prima facie case upon showing that he had been expelled without a hearing for alleged insufficiency in work and acts of insubordination against the faculty.

The appellees rely also upon Lucy v. Adams, D.C.N.D.Ala.1957, 134 F.Supp. 235, where Autherine Lucy was expelled from the University of Alabama without notice or hearing. That case, however, is not in point. Autherine Lucy did not raise the issue of an absence of notice or hearing.

It was not a case denying any hearing whatsoever but one passing upon the adequacy of the hearing, which provoked from Professor Warren A. Seavey of Harvard the eloquent comment:

> "At this time when many are worried about dismissal from public service, when only because of the overriding need to protect the public safety is the identity of informers kept secret, when we proudly contrast the full hearings before our courts with those in the benighted countries which have no due process protection, when many of our courts are so careful in the protection of those charged with crimes that they will not permit the use of evidence illegally obtained, our sense of justice should be outraged by denial to students of the normal safeguards. It is shocking that the officials of a state educational institution, which can function properly only if our freedoms are preserved, should not understand the elementary principles of fair play. It is equally shocking to find that a court supports them in denying to a student the protection given to a pickpocket."

Dismissal of Students: "Due Process," Warren A. Seavey, 70 Harvard Law Review 1406, 1407. We are confident that precedent as well as a most fundamental constitutional principle support our holding that due process requires notice and some opportunity for hearing before a student at a tax-supported college is expelled for misconduct.

For the guidance of the parties in the event of further proceedings, we state our views on the nature of the notice and hearing required by due process prior to expulsion from a state college or university. They should, we think, comply with the following standards. The notice should contain a statement of the specific charges and grounds which, if proven, would justify expulsion under the regulations of the Board of Education. The nature of the hearing should vary depending upon the circumstances of the particular case. The case before us requires something more than an informal interview with an administrative authority of the college. By its nature, a charge of misconduct, as opposed to a failure to meet the scholastic standards of the college, depends upon a collection of the facts concerning the charged misconduct, easily colored by the point of view of the witnesses. In such circumstances, a hearing which gives the Board or the administrative authorities of the college an opportunity to hear both sides in considerable detail is best suited to protect the rights of all involved. This is not to imply that a full-dress judicial hearing, with the right to cross-examine witnesses, is required. Such a hearing, with the attending publicity and disturbance of college activities, might be detrimental to the college's educational atmosphere and impractical to carry out. Nevertheless, the rudiments of an adversary proceeding may be preserved without encroaching upon the interests of the college. In the instant case, the student should be given the names of the witnesses against him and an oral or written report on the facts to which each witness testifies. He should also be given the opportunity to present to the Board, or at least to an administrative official of the college, his own defense against the charges and to produce either oral testimony or written affidavits of witnesses in his behalf. If the hearing is not before the Board directly, the results and findings of the hearing should be presented in a report open to the student's inspection. If these rudimentary elements of fair play are followed in a case of misconduct of this particular type, we feel that the requirements of due process of law will have been fulfilled.

The judgment of the district court is reversed and the cause is remanded for further proceedings consistent with this opinion.

Reversed and remanded.

Chapter 2

HIGHER EDUCATION UNDER JUDICIAL SCRUTINY

The French writer Charles Peguy said that everything begins in mysticism and ends in politics. In America the aphorism needs rewording: everything begins in mysticism and ends in the federal courtrooms.

> (Joseph Featherstone, *What Schools Can Do,* 1976)

During the halcyon days of the fifties and early sixties, many people invested higher education with some sort of magic—perhaps as a symbol of their own hunger for a moment of purpose and perfection. Nevertheless, there seemed to be ample evidence to support such approbation. American higher education had emerged from World War II as the world leader in research and scholarship. By the mid-fifties our universities were producing more Nobel laureates than any other nation and were beginning to occupy a position of world-wide primacy similar to that held by the late nineteenth century German universities. Higher education's response to the educational expectations of returning veterans and a burgeoning population appeared to be equally successful. Moreover, with society's growing emphasis and push on knowledge and technology, many were led to believe that higher education had become the pivotal institution for the achievement of national goals.

Thus the "revolution of rising expectations" came to the campus, and colleges and universities gradually began to falter. New demands with expectations of immediate gratification began to push higher education into an ecological cul-de-sac. Fissures began to appear in its success record. Solutions for mounting societal problems were not forthcoming from the academic community, and when the "Great Refusal" of youth to go along with the system hit the campus, there was a strong suggestion in the air that higher education itself might have been more than just peripherally implicated in the problems of society.[1] By the mid-sixties, in fact, the growing perception of higher education was a little like the hero of Clifford Odet's early play, *Waiting for*

1. Lewis B. Mayhew, "American Higher Education Now and in the Future" *The Annals*, ed. Marving Bressler (Philadelphia: The American Academy of Political and Social Science, 1972), pp. 46–47.

32

Lefty: "the stage is set for the hero, everyone measures his life and aspirations by him, but he never shows up because he has fallen victim to the forces of greed and reaction." [2]

NEW WINE IN OLD BOTTLES

A great deal was new on the campus in the sixties, and only vaguely understood, even by those who were most directly involved. The astonishing growth of colleges and universities, the massive knowledge explosion, the growing involvement of higher education with government and societal problems, the rising influence of the counterculture which was tough on traditional values, student activism and protest, increasing judicial intervention in college and university processes—all of these and more constituted new elements which took higher education into uncharted areas. As a consequence, it appeared that no one in academe was behaving according to traditional pattern. Apparently many thought that such behavior was equivalent to men biting dogs. In other words, it was the first time in American history that the campus was really news.

Particularly for students, it appears that the sixties brought first apathy, then anomie, then alienation—flaring into the 1964 Berkeley demonstrations and subsequently spreading throughout campuses with the seeming capriciousness of a plague striking innocent and guilty alike. And then almost as suddenly, social disorders on campuses seemed to flare out—largely culminating in the protest aftermath of the 1970 invasions of Cambodia. The Cambodian protest along with the resulting student deaths at Kent State and Jackson State symbolized the massive outpouring of anti-war sentiment during the most turbulent week in American college and university history.

Traditionally, students had been accorded few if any rights in their relationship with colleges and universities. However, as early as 1961 the judiciary began to change its long-term policy of nonintervention in this area and gradually extended constitutional protections to students. Yet, as the courts removed many of the former *in loco parentis* strictures, colleges and universities reacted in ways so artful and ambiguous as to make little difference. Left-wing student groups continued to be driven off campus, and unpopular visiting speakers as well. Student newspapers

2. Metaphor adapted from Max Lerner's, *America as a Civilization: Life and Thought in the United* *States Today* (New York: Simon and Schuster, 1957).

were still censored, and many students were dismissed from the institutions without the protections of the newly imposed judicial standards of due process.

But this system ultimately depended upon student compliance. When during the growing controversies in the mid-sixties they refused to cooperate, it fell apart, and the judiciary began to move into this arena in a big way. The courts were especially concerned about the erosion of due process of law—that combination of rules and safeguards built up over the centuries to make sure that every person is treated fairly. One should remember that due process was designed not only for desperate characters and criminals; it was designed for everyone which now began to include (even) students. Nor was due process merely for the benefit of the individual. As Justice Robert Jackson said, "It is the best insurance for the Government itself against those blunders which leave lasting stains on a system of justice . . ." Needless to say, American higher education was soon experiencing the reputation of those "lasting stains" (and still is).

In looking back at these "due process" decisions during the sixties, one might believe that judicial interest in student rights began with the *Dixon* decision. However, as we shall see, the long-term "hands-off" attitude of the courts in this area began to decline some years earlier.

THE CHANGING ROLE OF THE FEDERAL COURTS IN EDUCATION

Throughout most of our country's history with but few notable exceptions,[3] the federal courts had little to do with cases affecting education (public or private), and consequently a body of

3. Among some of those notable exceptions were Meyer v. Nebraska, 262 U.S. 390 (1923), a Nebraska statute forbidding the teaching of any subject in any language but English in the schools held unconstitutional; Pierce v. Society of the Sisters of the Holy Names of Jesus and Mary, 268 U.S. 510 (1925), constitutional for states to require parents to send their children to public schools when parents wished to educate their children in religious schools; Hamilton v. Regents of the Univ. of Cal., 293 U.S. 245 (1934), freedom of religion held to be protected by 14th Amendment, although Court held that Hamilton's religious liberty was not violated by University requirement that he take ROTC; West Virginia State Bd. of Educ. v. Barnette, 319 U.S. 624 (1943), reversed the Minersville School Dist. v. Gobitis, 310 U.S. 586 (1940) ruling by holding that school flag-salute requirement violated religious liberty of Jehovah's Witnesses; and other cases involving religious issues such as Everson v. Board of Educ., 330 U.S. 1 (1947) and People of State of Illinois ex rel. McCollum v. Board of Educ., 333 U.S. 203 (1948).

case law developed at the state level which permitted, if not actually sanctioned, educational policies and practices which frequently fell far short of meeting federal constitutional standards and requirements.[4] The "due process" panoply of protections, for instance, was generally withheld from students on the basis of a long-standing judicial doctrine that took the position that society extended a "privilege" to a student when it provided him with a tax-supported education. Therefore, if attendance at a public school or college was so classified, the state could deprive a student of that privilege without meeting a constitutional issue.

However, a significant shift in the attitude of the federal courts began with the 1954 Brown v. Board of Educ. case,[5] which overturned the "separate but equal" doctrine in connection with state-required, racially-segregated facilities in public education. Yet it seems today that the landmark *Brown* decision was the subject of this change only as a corpse is to a murder mystery. The real shift in judicial policy resulted from the reaction of social forces to that decision; and what eventually came out of that milieu was a new judicial focus wherein hardly a thread of the educational fabric would be immune from "judicial scrutiny."

With the *Brown* decision, of course, there is no discounting the fact that the Supreme Court had spoken and the law had been determined. Nonetheless, the judicial decision-making process includes application as well as formulation and promulgation of policy. For one thing, those whose behaviors are affected by any new policy unavoidably participate in the decision-making; that is, by either conforming to or disregarding the policy they help determine whether it is or is not in fact an effective policy. Therefore, in order for the new *Brown* policy to have a general effect in our political system, the behavior of many individuals had to be affected; but the overall response to desegregation, especially in the South, was avoidance, evasion and delay. More than that, the *Brown* ruling inspired one of the strongest backlashes the country has ever experienced.

However, the Supreme Court had recognized that desegregation would be a bitter constitutional pill for many whites in the South. Consequently, instead of the customary mandate that would take effect immediately, the Court adopted the unusual practice of restoring the case to its docket for further argument on the question of appropriate implementation and invited the legal officers of interested states to appear and propose plans for the integra-

4. See Chapter 1, pp. 8–17.   5.   347 U.S. 483 (1954).

tion of public schools. Then, on May 31, 1955, the Court directed federal district courts to "take such proceedings and enter such orders and decrees . . . as are necessary and proper to admit to public schools on a racially nondiscriminatory basis *with all deliberate speed* the parties to these cases." [6]

But the forces that had opposed integration before the *Brown* decision pounced on the Court's failure to order immediate desegregation as the justification for an endless variety of evasive and delaying tactics. Not surprisingly, the response to this resistance was a stepped-up judicial activism, the target of which was public education and the message was that it should mend its ways.[7] And as the visibility of the country's system of public education was heightened, other questions outside the equal protection clause began to arise.[8]

The Civil Rights Movement and Higher Education

Black leaders had observed rather early in the Civil Rights Movement that planned nonviolent activism got some results. On the other hand, so long as blacks confined themselves to verbally proclaiming their aspiration for equality, concrete concessions by the white majority were few and far between. But when blacks demonstrated, picketed, paraded, boycotted, engaged in sit-ins, lie-ins, wade-ins, or whatever, and risked fire hoses, cattle prods, tear gas, police dogs, billy clubs, and jail sentences, at least more began to happen. Whites who sympathized with the blacks over their abuse, businessmen who feared

---

6. 349 U.S. 294, 300 (1954) (emphasis added).

7. See, e. g., Cooper v. Aaron, 358 U.S. 5 (1958), the Little Rock decision where the Court stated: "The constitutional rights of children not to be discriminated against in school admission on grounds of race or color . . . can neither be nullified openly and directly by state legislators or state executives or judicial officers, nor nullified indirectly by them through evasive schemes for segregation whether attempted 'ingeniously or ingenuously.' " Watson v. Memphis, 373 U.S. 526 (1963), the Court pointedly stated: "Given the extended time that has elapsed, it is far from clear that the mandates of the several *Brown* decisions . . . would

today be fully satisfied by types of plans or programs for desegregation of public educational facilities which eight years ago might have been deemed sufficient. *Brown* never contemplated that the concept of 'deliberate speed' would countenance indefinite delay in elimination of racial barriers in schools."

8. See, e. g., Engle v. Vitale, 370 U.S. 421 (1962), a prescribed prayer in the New York public schools held in violation of the First Amendment's proscription against the establishment of a religion; Abington School Dist. v. Schempp, 374 U.S. 203 (1963), prohibiting the reading of Bible passages or saying of prayers as religious exercises in public schools.

direct economic sanctions, citizens who wanted a peaceful community, and politicians who wanted to solve problems (and get reelected) were stimulated to act. But as "things got better," as is true with almost all social revolutions, discontent became more intense.

The immediate origin of nonviolent activism was on December 1, 1955, when Rosa Parks, a black Montgomery seamstress, was riding the city bus home after a hard day's work. In Alabama at that time, blacks were supposed to sit in a special section in back of the bus, and that's what Parks was doing. However, as the bus became more crowded and the "white" section became filled, the bus driver ordered Parks and three other blacks to give up their seats to whites just getting on the bus. Parks' refusal and her immediate arrest drew national attention to the situation prevailing in Alabama, and when the black community subsequently engaged in a boycott of the city buses to protest segregation on them, the boycott worked. And from the Montgomery incident the civil rights movement produced its first charismatic leader—the Reverend Martin Luther King, who, through his Southern Christian Leadership Conference and his belief in nonviolent resistance, provided a new dimension in black-white relations in America.

By the early sixties, apathy among blacks and a lack of organization and concerted effort were no longer major obstacles in their struggle for equality. In effect, blacks were no longer sleeping on their constitutional rights; they had become increasingly unwilling to forfeit their civil rights by default. Organizations such as the NAACP, the Urban League, CORE, SNCC, and of course (the Reverend Dr.) King's SCLC were providing leadership, funds, and education to support and sponsor passive resistance, sit-ins, freedom rides, boycotts, live-ins, picketing and mass demonstrations in almost every city in the nation.

Many black youths were fired with a burning passion to give themselves unreservedly for a larger cause—the winning of political, economic and social parity. The crusade gave intensified meaning, purpose and moral dignity to their lives as well as vitality to their cause which soon was to become one of the central facts of black life on and off college campuses. The civil rights struggle was now in full bloom, and picketing, sit-ins, boycotts and freedom rides all captured the imagination of many blacks and whites alike. In fact an increasing number of black students went to restaurants, lunch counters, parks, swimming pools, and other public places, demanding admission and equal service. Although their motivation was apparently to get what they were entitled to without going to court, the students often wound up in court despite their intentions. That is, when they were arrested, they became defendants, whether they liked it or not. Moreover, these off-campus activities frequently resulted in their dismissal from college, and therefore they were faced with the necessity of filing lawsuits for reinstatement.

Actually a great number of individuals and groups decided to press for constitutional protections within a short time after Earl Warren was appointed Chief Justice in 1953. Such diverse groups as racial and religious minorities, classroom teachers, welfare recipients and booksellers felt they were under attack by government, especially by state and local governments, and asked the Supreme Court for protection; and of course this gave the Court the responsibility to examine the applicability of the Fourteenth Amendment. It was faced with the old question: does the amendment say what it seems to say, and, if so, can it be modified just a little to prohibit certain kinds of conduct that someone in authority opposes?

One way that had been used to limit the Fourteenth Amendment was to say that particular groups of people were not covered—for example, public school and college students, teachers, prisoners, draftees or military service personnel. Still other limitations were attempted by saying that a "compelling state interest" such as education must win over "freedom," or that certain places were not part of what Justice Holmes considered the free marketplace of ideas—that is, the marketplace did not extend to the prison, the draftboard, the classroom or the college campus. Furthermore, some constitutional authorities argued that citizens brought to *state* courts for violation of *state* laws or regulations were not entitled to invoke the Bill of Rights protections that might be appropriate against the federal government.

The above list of possible limitations placed upon constitutional protections is merely illustrative, not exhaustive. Whatever, the number of cases involving such issues increased markedly during the Warren era. In fact the Warren Court, sitting for sixteen years (1953–1969), agreed to hear more Fourteenth Amendment cases than all previous Supreme Courts put together. This was undoubtedly due, in part, to the fact that the Court demonstrated an accentuated interest in the protection of civil liberties and ruled in favor of the parties claiming constitutional protections in many cases. Thus many groups and individuals decided that the time had come to insist upon their rights, and though the Warren Court refused to handle even one student-college disciplinary appeal, its message in terms of expanded civil liberties in other areas was not overlooked by the lower courts when they reviewed student-college conflicts.

The Bill of Rights and the Fourteenth Amendment on the Public Campus

While operating under the assumption that constitutional guarantees were inapplicable to student-college conflicts, the courts were reluctant to review the disciplining of students for alleged violations of college regulations unless it could be shown that the college acted maliciously, in bad faith, arbitrarily, or unreasonably. For a student to prevail, he had to prove the college wrong. Frequently such judicial restraint was proclaimed as necessary to preserve the freedom of the academic community. Yet, even though such freedom was regarded primarily as a means for furthering the scholarly pursuits of that community, paradoxically institutional autonomy often allowed the repression of that freedom. However, with the *Dixon* appellate decision, the focus shifted toward the constitutional protection of student rights, and the burden of justification shifted more to the college authorities.

State-Supported Higher Education as a "Public Benefit"

Public education may not be a right, in the strictest sense, but neither is it to be regarded as a matter of incidental importance. Thus, while no state legislature requires any of the 3,000 odd institutions of higher education to compel students to attend —and in truth a fair percentage of students pay handsomely for the opportunity to do so—the evidence of government (and in particular, judicial) interest is unmistakable. In fact, higher education is considered so centrally important in this society that entrance to a public institution or dismissal from it can be subject to court review.[9] Hence, in Dickey v. Alabama State

9. See, e. g., Frasier v. Board of Trustees of Univ. of North Carolina, 134 F.Supp. 589 (D.C.N.C. 1955); affirmed 350 U.S. 979 (1956); the district court applied the *Brown* decision to public higher education by ruling that the university policy of denying admission to blacks was unconstitutional; in Goss v. Lopez, 419 U.S. 565, 576 (1975), the Supreme Court treated education in a public secondary school as a public benefit and sustained a due process challenge; the *General Order* . . . 45 F.R.D. 133, 141 (1968) declares: "The federal constitution protects the equality of opportunity of all qualified persons to attend public colleges and universities. Whether this

Bd. of Educ. (1967), the district court treated education at a state university as a public benefit and upheld a First Amendment complaint; [10] in Knight v. State Bd. of Educ. (1961), the interest in pursuing a higher education was described by the court as "an interest of almost incalculable value"; [11] and, as you will recall, in Dixon v. Alabama State Bd. of Educ. (1961), the Fifth Circuit held that higher "education is vital and, indeed, basic to civilized society and . . . an interest of extremely great value." [12]   But perhaps more significant, *Dixon* held that whether or not attendance at a public college was a privilege, a right, or something in between was irrelevant to the existence of an unconstitutional condition:

> "One may not have a constitutional right to go to Bagdad, but the Government may not prohibit one from going there unless by means consonant with due process of law." [13]

The Doctrine of Unconstitutional Conditions

Thus, needless to say, persons today do not lose their constitutional rights by enrolling as students in a state-supported college or university. This proposition has been termed "the doctrine of unconstitutional conditions," since it prohibits the conditioning of the enjoyment of a government-connected interest upon a rule requiring that one abstain from the exercise of some right protected by the Constitution. Even though this principle was almost totally inapplicable to the student-public education setting until 1961, the underlying rationale was explained by the Supreme Court more than a half century ago:

> It would be a palpable incongruity to strike down an act of state legislation which, by words of express divestment, seeks to strip the citizen of rights guaranteed by the federal Constitution, but to uphold an act by which the same result is accomplished under the guise of a surrender of a right in exchange for a valuable privilege which the state threatens otherwise to withhold . . .. If the state may compel the surrender of one constitutional right as a condi-

protected opportunity be called a qualified 'right' or 'privilege' is unimportant."

10. 273 F.Supp. 613, 618 (D.C.Ala. 1967).

11. 200 F.Supp. 174, 178 (D.C.Tenn. 1961).

12. 294 F.2d 150, 157, cert. denied 368 U.S. 930 (1961).

13. Id., at 156 quoting from Cafeteria and Restaurant Workers Union v. McElroy (citation omitted).

tion of its favor, it may, in like manner, compel a surrender of all. It is inconceivable that guarantees embedded in the Constitution of the United States may thus be manipulated out of existence.[14]

Therefore, the unconstitutional condition doctrine prohibits government from imposing a choice between enjoyment of an important public benefit or privilege and assertion of fundamental constitutional rights. Such a choice necessarily produces coercion against exercise of that right, whether it is enjoyment of religious freedom,[15] exercise of free speech,[16] or another basic constitutional right.[17]

Nonetheless, that a student's constitutional rights place the same limitations on his private college has not yet been established by modern judicial holdings. Rather, at private colleges and universities, the contractual relationship between students and the institution prevails unless rare or unusual circumstances exist, such as would constitute "state action." The state action concept, however, is difficult to define; in fact, the elusiveness

---

14. Frost & Frost Trucking Co. v. Railroad Comm. of Cal., 271 U.S. 583, 593 (1926).

15. See, e. g., Sherbert v. Verner, 374 U.S. 398 (1963). The Supreme Court held that the state may not condition receipt of unemployment compensation benefits on subordination of sabbatarian (Saturday worship) convictions. Id. at 406. An eligibility rule for welfare required acceptance of any available employment, Id., at 400–01, including jobs involving Saturday work, and Mrs. Sherbert's religion forbade labor on that day. Id. at 399. Consequently the state had "forced her to choose between following the precepts of her religion and forfeiting benefits, on the one hand, and abandoning one of the precepts of her religion in order to accept work, on the other hand." Id. at 404. The Court thus ruled this to be an unconstitutional choice since "the disqualification for benefits imposed a burden on the free exercise of appellant's religion." Id. at 403.

16. See, e. g., Speiser v. Randall, 357 U.S. 513, 581 (1958) (choice between tax exemption and loyalty oath causes "deterrence of speech"); American Communications Ass'n, C. I. O. v. Douds, 339 U.S. 382, 402 (1950) ("Under some circumstances, indirect 'discouragements' undoubtedly have the same coercive effect upon the exercise of First Amendment rights as imprisonment, fines, injunctions or taxes.")

17. See, e. g., United States v. Jackson, 390 U.S. 570, 581 (1968) (making death penalty possible in jury trial but not in nonjury trial inevitably acts "to discourage assertion of the Fifth Amendment right not to plead guilty and to deter exercise of the Sixth Amendment right to demand a jury trial."); Spevack v. Klein, 385 U.S. 511, 516 (1967) ("The threat of disbarment and the loss of professional standing, professional reputation, and of livelihood are powerful forms of compulsion to make a lawyer relinquish the privilege" against self-incrimination.)

of this concept was recorded by the Supreme Court in Burton
v. Wilmington Parking Auth. (1961):

> . . . to fashion and apply a precise formula for recogni-
> tion of state responsibility under the Equal Protection Clause
> is an "impossible task" which this court has never attempt-
> ed . . . . Only by sifting facts and weighing circum-
> stances can the nonobvious involvement of the State in priv-
> ate conduct be attributed its true significance . . . [18]

Still, though difficult to predict what precisely establishes the
state-action nexus, the significance of the concept lies in the fact
that it plays a major role in the determination of a court's involvement in cases concerning private colleges and universities.
Thus, regardless of personal feelings about "due process" and
"equal protection," it must be acknowledged that there are times
when the officials of private institutions must adjust their conduct to these standards or, failing to do so, suffer reversal in the
courts.

The solution to this problem necessitates an excursion into the
legal realm of private higher education which, in the process,
can shed some light on the problem of defining and understanding the authority and responsibility of the institution vis-a-vis
its students.

HIGHER EDUCATION—THE PUBLIC/PRIVATE DISTINCTION

The Contract Approach—Private Institutions

Though for many years the basic yardstick used to measure
the legal relationship between students and private as well as
public institutions was that of contract, since 1961 the utility
of that concept's application to the student-public college relationship has been reduced and somewhat overshadowed by the
new constitutionally protected rights of public college students.
Of course the contractual theory is still dusted off occasionally
and used by certain courts in the public college context (especially in cases involving admissions and academic requirements),[19]
but most commonly when private institutions are involved. In

---

18. 365 U.S. 715, 722 (1961).

19. See, e. g., Eden v. Board of Trustees of State Univ., 49 A.D.2d 277,
374 N.Y.S.2d 686 (1975); Healy v.
Larsson, 67 Misc.2d 374, 323 N.Y.
S.2d 625 (1971); Mahavongsanan v.

Hall, 529 F.2d 448 (5th Cir. 1976);
Tanner v. Board of Trustees of
Univ. of Illinois, 48 Ill.App.3d 680,
6 Ill.Dec. 679, 363 N.E.2d 208
(1977); Basch v. George Washington Univ., 370 A.2d 1364 (D.C.App.
1977).

fact, it appears essentially settled that the basic relationship between the private college and its students is one of contract.[20]

When the contract relationship is viewed in juxtaposition with the tremendous power that certain "private" entities have over vital segments of social life, however, it poses some frustrating problems for courts and the public alike. One result has been that many commentators have urged that private organizations as such be subject to the same constitutional restrictions as public entities. Nevertheless, the judicial break with the past in the *Dixon* case did not break so clearly for private colleges and universities. The distinction between "constitutionally" permissible conduct for private and public institutions is evident when one considers the case of Carr v. St. John's Univ.,[21] in which the plaintiffs, who were in their senior year at the private Roman Catholic institution, had been dismissed from the institution as a result of their marriage in a civil ceremony.

According to Canon Law of the Catholic Church, a civil marriage by members of the Catholic faith is not only invalid, but also the act of each person who participates in such a ceremony, whether as a party to the marriage or as a witness, is considered a serious sin. Furthermore, St. John's Catalog stated that "In conformity with the ideals of Christian education and conduct, the University reserves the right to dismiss a student at any time on whatever grounds the University judges advisable." Using this right, the University dismissed the students; yet, a lower New York court ordered the students reinstated on the grounds that the regulation stipulating the standard of "Christian ideals" was so ambiguous and uncertain that even though the contract relationship was controlling, the students could not understand the obligation which they had implicitly agreed to obey.

The New York Appellate Division, however, reversed the lower court's decision and sustained the dismissal. Also citing the special relationship (implied contract) which exists between a student admitted to a private university and that university, the Court went on to say that "To the Catholic students and authorities at the University, 'Christian education and conduct' meant and means 'Catholic education and conduct.' "[22] The Court, therefore, ruled that the regulation was not ambiguous and that

20. See, e. g., Zumbrun v. University of Southern Cal., 25 Cal.App.3d 1, 101 Cal.Rptr. 499 (1972) and cases cited therein.

21. 34 Misc.2d 319, 231 N.Y.S.2d 403 (1962).

22. Id., at 414.

students could and should be held to the knowledge that a civil ceremony would be antithetical to the requirements of "Catholic education and conduct." But perhaps the most revealing statement regarding the judiciary's position of restraint in the area of a student's relationship to the private institution of higher education was the following:

> With respect to rules and regulations for breach of which students of a private university may be expelled, courts will not consider whether they are wise or expedient but whether they are a reasonable exercise of power and discretion of college authorities.[23]

In Jones v. Vassar College [24] a similar position of judicial restraint was used in upholding the right of a private institution to govern itself in any manner it chose so long as there was an absence of clearly unreasonable action. Again, the issue was of a contractual nature. For years Vassar had been a college strictly for women, but in the trend toward coeducation in the late sixties, the college finally yielded to the new direction. With male students on the campus, the issue of visiting hours for men in women's dormitories presented itself, and the students elected unrestricted hours. The President of Vassar College did not exercise his power of veto over the student enacted legislation, thereby giving approval to the change in the rules and regulations. However, the mother of one of the female students claimed that the college had a duty to her and other parents to maintain the old dormitory rules and that allowing the students to make this drastic change amounted to a breach of contract. The court disagreed:

> The judiciary must exercise restraint in questioning the wisdom of specific rules or the manner of their application, since such matters are ordinarily in the prerogative of school administrators rather than the courts.

> There has been no showing by plaintiffs that there was an abuse of discretion by defendants in . . . adopting the new . . . regulations and this court will not interfere with defendants' discretion. Private colleges and universities are governed on the principle of academic self-regulation, free from judicial restraints . . . [25]

23. Id.

24. 59 Misc.2d 296, 299 N.Y.S.2d 283 (1969).

25. Id., at 287–288.

In general, therefore, the basic relationship between the private institution and its students is one of contract.   Under this condition, and in the absence of state action, private colleges and universities generally reserve the right to admit only students of their choosing and to require withdrawal of any student at any time for any reason regarded sufficient to them.   In general, the only limit to this theory is that the private institution must state these specifications in its catalog or in its rules and regulations and make them available to all students.   If the institution does this, then such provisions become part of the contract between the institution and the student.

The critical determination in this area, of course, is that constitutional mandates are uniquely applied to state, not private, conduct.

State Action

The distinction between public and private institutions, in the legal sense at least, is that public educational institutions, like all other governmental entities of a state, are bound by the guarantees of the Fourteenth Amendment, and in the education setting, especially by the equal protection of the laws and the due process of the law clauses.   On the other hand, private persons, groups, associations, corporations, and of course private educational institutions, do not appear to be limited by these constitutional restrictions.   Yet, for reasons that will be advanced later, the courts on occasion have treated the conduct of a private entity as though it were public when certain vital rights have been adversely affected by that conduct.

Actually, the legal distinction between public and private higher education goes back to Dartmouth College v. Woodward,[26] decided in 1819.   In that case, the United States Supreme Court rejected the argument that Dartmouth was a state institution because it was incorporated by the state and involved in a vital state interest—education.[27]   More recently, however, with the

26.   17 U.S. (4 Wheaton) 518 (1819); Dartmouth College had been the beneficiary of "great value" granted by the states of Vermont and New Hampshire, Id. at p. 538. However, this did not interfere with Chief Justice Marshall in concluding that Dartmouth's trustees and professors were not "public officers, invested with any portion of political power, partaking in any degree in the administration of civ-il government, and performing duties which flow from sovereign authority." Id. at 634.

27.   Art. I, Section 10 of the U. S. Constitution forbids State legislatures "to pass any law impairing the obligation of contracts," and in 1769, Dartmouth College was chartered by the English Crown which the Court considered a contract.

advent of the modern university, the question of "state action" has been raised since many private institutions of higher education derive a large portion of their support from federal and state funds.

One of the most forthright statements denying the *Dartmouth College* case distinction between public and private institutions appeared in a 1962 case involving Tulane University (Guillory v. Tulane Univ.). Here a federal district court in Louisiana stated:

> At the outset, one may question whether any school or college can ever be so private as to escape the reach of the Fourteenth Amendment—No one any longer doubts that education is a matter affected with the greatest public interest. And this is true whether it is offered by a public or private institution—Clearly, the administrators of a private college are performing a public function .   .   . often in the place of the state. Does it not follow that they stand in the state's shoes? [28]

The Federal District Court ruled that Tulane did and thus that a racially discriminatory admission policy could not stand. However, the finding of the District Court was reversed on rehearing, with the subsequent court holding that state action in the affairs of the Tulane Board of Trustees was not so significant that it could be said that the actions of the Board were the actions of the State of Louisiana.[29]

This reversal at a subsequent sitting clearly demonstrates the elusive nature of the "state action" concept. One thing does clearly appear, though, and that is that it is most difficult to establish a condition of "state action" in the behavior of private college or university officials.

This difficulty is reflected in the case of Grossner v. Trustees of Columbia Univ. There, a federal district court ruled that "receipt of money from the state is not, without a good deal more, enough to make the recipient an agency or instrumentality of the Government." [30] The *Grossner* case also discussed the contention that the process of educating persons constituted state action. This argument for the public function of education was dismissed as lacking any basis:

> Plaintiffs are correct in a trivial way when they say education is "impressed with a public interest." Many things are.

28. Guillory v. Tulane Univ., 203 F. Supp. 855, 858–859 (D.C.La.1962), reversed on rehearing 212 F.Supp. 674 (D.C.La.1962).

29. 212 F.Supp. 674 (D.C.La.1962).

30. 287 F.Supp. 535, 547–548 (D.C.N. Y.1968).

And it may even be that action in some context or other by such a University as Columbia would be subject to limitations like those confining the State. But nothing supports the thesis that university "education" as such is "state action." [31]

For these reasons a suit for an injunction to prevent disciplinary action against student leaders involved in the 1968 spring riots and building seizures was disallowed.

Again, a like effect was reached in Browns v. Mitchell,[32] the University of Denver sit-in case. Here, the Tenth Circuit Court of Appeals held that institution to be private, in spite of significant tax exemptions on property the University used for both educational and commercial purposes. Therefore, the procedural guarantees of the Fourteenth Amendment were not applicable to the student disciplinary proceedings.

As already noted, there is not yet a universal test to determine if "state action" exists in private conduct; rather, each case must be weighed on its own facts and circumstances. Thus, even though the 1962 *Guillory* reversal found that Tulane University was not sufficiently involved in state action to render its racially discriminatory admissions policy violative of constitutional equal protection. The Fifth Circuit Court of Appeals found otherwise in the 1965 Hammond v. Univ. of Tampa case.[33] In this case, the Court found that the University of Tampa, a private institution, had a sufficiently "public" nexus to inhibit racial discrimination in admissions, largely because a surplus city building had been made available to the University founders and city land had been leased to the institution.

At this point at least one feature of the state action concept clears up; that is, racial discrimination is considered so offensive by the courts that a *lesser* degree of state involvement is necessary in determining what constitutes "state action" than in other contexts. Therefore, where the action complained of is racially motivated, the receipt of government funds by a private institution, for instance, could be considered by the courts as sufficient "state action" to trigger constitutional guarantees for those dealing with the recipient. In fact, there is a long list of cases supporting the conclusion that state action findings are normally

31. Id., at 549.

32. 409 F.2d 593 (10th Cir. 1969).

33. 344 F.2d 951 (5th Cir. 1965).

reached *only* in those cases where the recipient is engaged in invidious discrimination on the basis of race.[34]

An instance not involving discrimination, but where a court found the "state action" concept applicable to a private university can be found in Ryan v. Hofstra Univ. (1971).[35] In this case, a freshman student who had been dismissed from Hofstra for allegedly throwing a rock through a bookstore window on campus sued for reinstatement claiming that his rights to due process had been denied. The University, however, claimed that it was a private institution and was not obliged therefore to afford due process. Hence, the validity of the student's claim that the University's disciplinary action had violated his due process rights hinged on a determination of "state action"; that is, was Hofstra so entwined with the State of New York that the "state action" concept would apply to the University's disciplinary action?

The New York Supreme Court held that it did. After a careful and detailed examination of the relationship of Hofstra University with the State of New York, the Court wrote:

> Plainly, Hofstra exists as largely a governmental manifestation. The public appearance of the Dormitory Authority is marked by signs. The Dormitory Authority built, owns, and leases to it the individual bulk of its plant, including the area where the charged vandalism took place. Over one-half of its land stems from federal donation. State scholarship and incentive funds attach to the majority of its students. It has millions of dollars in government grants and subsidies, not to mention real estate tax exemption which makes its maintenance on its present basis practicable.

34. See, e. g., Powe v. Miles, 407 F.2d 73 (2d Cir. 1968), ". . . we recognize that discrimination may stand somewhat differently, because of [its] peculiar offensiveness . . . ." Id. at 82; Grafton v. Brooklyn Law School, 478 F.2d 1137 (2d Cir. 1973), cert. denied 423 U.S. 995 (1973), "It could well be that such grants by the state . . would afford a ground for constitutional complaint if the charges here were an admission policy discriminating against racial . . . groups." Id. at p. 1142; Greenya v. George Washington Univ., 512 F.2d 556 (D.C.Cir. 1975), Court held that state action requires less government involvement if issue is racial discrimination, Id. at 560; Spark v. Catholic Univ., 510 F.2d 1277 (D.C.Cir. 1975), state action normally found only when private institution involved in discriminatory act, Id. at 1282; Williams v. Howard Univ., 528 F.2d 658 (D.C. Cir. 1976), cert. denied, 429 U.S. 850, "We assume that the allegation of substantial federal funding would be enough to demonstrate governmental action as to appellant's claim of racial discrimination." Id. at 660.

35. 67 Misc.2d 651, 324 N.Y.S.2d 964 (1971) supplemented 68 Misc.2d 890, 328 N.Y.S.2d 339 (1972).

Hofstra is franchised by the State, controlled in its degree requirements by the State, and subject to the State's visitation.[36]

It is important to recognize that this decision was rendered by a state court. Moreover, while an action to be declared unconstitutional under the "due process" or "equal protection" clauses of the Fourteenth Amendment requires that it be a "state action," the New York Constitution merely requires that "no person" be denied his rights and "makes no provision in terms that 'state action' be the negating force." [37]   The Court pointed out, however, that *some* state action is prerequisite in New York since the constitutional provisions are coordinate commands.[38]

It should be noted, also, that the New York Court provided two fundamental points that must be weighed in the determination of state action. First, "The characterization of state action for constitutional purposes rests in part on the particular purposes for which it is sought." [39]   The Court found here that if the purposes for which state action is sought are the protection of due process and equal protection rights, then the effort to find state action will be given high priority. Second, the Court indicated that state action is difficult to define and to determine what constitutes state action compounds the problem. Therefore, the determination and application of that most elusive concept must derive from a careful analysis of the facts and circumstances of each case.

This latter piece of reasoning, however, is rather nebulous; in fact, it can make the layman rather humble. Relax! On closer inspection at least one thing becomes clear—there is a certain lack of clarity and a distinct paucity of concrete facts in the Court's reasoning. For one thing, what exactly constitutes *some* state action? Next, what conditions in brute reality indicate its existence? And then, what precisely is a "high priority" effort? To paraphrase Gertrude Stein's last, last words, "What are the questions?" (and to expect some exactitude in the asking of them.) To be frank, the same questions could be asked of the other cases that have been discussed.

In the area of possible "due process" constraints placed on private institutions, it should be noted that the courts have almost overwhelmingly failed to find state action on such bases as

36.   Id., at 982.

37.   Id., at 977.

38.   Id., at 977.

39.   Id., at 982.

receipt of government funds,[40] tax exempt status,[41] state charter-
ing or accreditation of academic programs,[42] or the public function of private education.[43] Besides *Ryan*, the only approach
that the courts have determined which may lead to state action
in this area is that of state contracts wherein the private institution acts as a representative of the state. This position was taken
in Powe v. Miles,[44] where the court held that the contractual arrangement between Alfred University and the State of New
York's College of Ceramics at Alfred University constituted state
action but only so far as the College of Ceramics was concerned.
Thus, it is generally impossible to establish sufficient government involvement in the area of due process unless it is shown
that the government exercises some form of control over the
challenged actions of the private institutions.

Perhaps one day the courts will go even further in extending
the application of the present meaning of state action. Language
indicating such a possibility was used by Chief Justice Warren
and Justices Black and Douglas in a dissenting opinion during
the summer of 1956: ". . . the courts may not be implicated
in . . . a discriminatory scheme," wrote the dissenters, but
"[o]nce the courts put their imprimatur on such a contract, government, speaking through the judicial branch, acts . . .
And it is governmental action that the Constitutions control."[45]
This represented an extremely broad reading of the restrictive
covenant case of Shelley v. Kraemer [46] where the Supreme Court
declared only that the state could not enforce private discrimina-
tions. According to the Warren-Black-Douglas view, however,
any slight participation by any state instrumentality in a discriminatory scheme—no matter how limited that participation
—was unconstitutional state action.

Though the Supreme Court never quite arrived at the Warren-
Black-Douglas position, the Court nevertheless increasingly found

40. Grossner v. Trustees of Columbia Univ., supra; Browns v. Mitchell, supra; Blackburn v. Fisk Univ., 443 F.2d 121 (6th Cir. 1971); Williams v. Howard Univ., 174 U.S. App.D.C. 85, 528 F.2d 658 (1976), cert. denied, 429 U.S. 850 (1977).

41. Case examples same as above.

42. Grafton v. Brooklyn Law School, 478 F.2d 1137 (2d Cir. 1973), cert. denied 423 U.S. 995 (1973); Krohn v. Harvard Law School, 552 F.2d 21 (1st Cir. 1977).

43. Counts v. Voorhees College, 312 F.Supp. 598 (D.C.S.C.1970).

44. 294 F.Supp. 1269 (D.C.N.Y.1968) modified 407 F.2d 73.

45. Black v. Cutter Laboratories, 351 U.S. 292, 302 (1956).

46. 334 U.S. 1 (1948).

ways to declare invalid the racial discrimination practiced by private institutions.

Since the Fourteenth Amendment has thus far been interpreted not to restrict purely private action, it would seem likely that state or local governments would sometimes attempt to do indirectly (through private bodies) that which they could not do directly. Of course, this has been done; however, the courts have held that "governmental action" includes not only any action taken directly by state or local governments, but also action taken indirectly by delegating public functions to private organizations; or by controlling, affirming, or to some significant extent becoming involved in private action.

Then, too, the Fourteenth Amendment contains an enabling clause which gives Congress the power to enforce that amendment by "appropriate legislation." Such legislation is evident in the Civil Rights Acts of 1870, 1871, 1957 and 1964, and Title IX of the Higher Education Amendments of 1972 (the latter prohibiting sex discrimination). However, since the Fourteenth Amendment forbids only state action, the question arises whether Congress is limited to laws preventing the state from discriminating, or whether the enabling clause also confers power on Congress to outlaw even private acts of discrimination. The United States Supreme Court in United States v. Price (1966)[47] answered the latter part of the question in the affirmative; that is, the enabling clause gives Congress the power to regulate and punish discrimination by private individuals collaborating with state officials; and in United States v. Guest (1966)[48] it was deter-

---

47. United States v. Price, 383 U.S. 787 (1966), in which the Supreme Court upheld the conviction of Ku Klux Klan members, including county and city police officers as well as a number of private citizens. Unable to get an indictment from the state courts for the murder of three young civil rights workers, Michael Schwerner and Goodman (both white) and James Chaney (black), federal officials took the case to a federal court where the accused were charged with (and later convicted of) violating the 1870 Civil Rights Act provision making it a crime to "conspire to injure, oppress, threaten or intimidate any citizen in the free exercise . . . of any right or privilege secured to him by the Con-

stitution." (The federal charges carried a maximum penalty of ten years in prison and/or a $5,000 fine. A murder conviction could carry a death penalty under Mississippi law.)

48. United States v. Guest, 383 U.S. 745 (1966), in which the Supreme Court handed down its decision on the same day it decided the United States v. Price case and used the same 1870 statute. Here the Court upheld a federal court conviction of six white men for conspiring to deprive black citizens of the exercise of rights. In this instance, two of the defendants had been tried for murder in a Georgia State Court and acquitted.

mined that even purely private acts of discrimination, under certain conditions, can be regulated.

Following somewhat the same principles as applied in *Price* and *Guest* and after reviewing other pertinent case law, the Supreme Court held in the 1976 Runyon v. McCrary case [49] that a federal statute which provided that:

> All persons within the jurisdiction of the United States shall have the same right in every State and Territory to make and enforce contracts, to sue, be parties, give evidence, and to the full and equal benefit of all laws and proceedings for the security of persons and property as is enjoyed by white citizens, and shall be subject to like punishment, pains, penalties, taxes, licenses, and exactions of every kind, and to no other.[50]

prohibited racial discrimination in the making and enforcement of private contracts and, more specifically, made it illegal for private schools to be involved in racially-discriminatory admissions.

It is this type of action that limits the life expectancy of political trickery, and it is likely that if *Guillory* were to be argued today a different result would follow. As noted earlier (p. 48 fn. 34, supra); federal funding will most likely constitute sufficient state action in the private sector where the action complained of is racially motivated discrimination.

CONCLUDING OBSERVATIONS

Beginning in 1961, the federal courts have been deciding that the disciplinary actions of officials in publicly supported colleges and universities must adhere to the due process standards of the Fourteenth Amendment. One may note that the cases setting the legal precedent involved the interests of black students who had been punished for participating in off-campus, civil rights demonstrations by administrators of black colleges under pressure from Southern whites. Clearly, the judicial concern for student rights was inspired by a judicial concern for civil rights and not by purely academic considerations. Moreover, it appears that higher education, in acquiring new social significance, lost a substantial measure of its old autonomy. In fact the result of this chain of consequences was a greater loss of internal authority for public colleges and universities than any may have anticipated

49. 427 U.S. 160 (1976).   **50.** 42 U.S.C.A. § 1981.

or approved. But here one may be permitted the conclusion that, on balance, justice gained.

In terms of providing an understanding of the Fourteenth Amendment's applicability to the student/public institution context, an exemplary judicial statement is presented nearly *in toto* at the end of this chapter.

As previously indicated, courts will only interfere with the actions of private institutions when certain factors such as "state action" are present. The crucial determination in this area is that constitutional commands, especially due process, equal protection, and First Amendment guarantees—as applied to the states through the Fourteenth Amendment—and most mandates of federal statutes prohibiting the deprivement of civil rights, are singularly applied to state, not private conduct. Thus, without some determination of state action, a private institution is not required to extend to its students the array of federal rights afforded those attending a public institution. Accordingly, the chapter will conclude with two cases involving the state action concept.

GENERAL ORDER ON JUDICIAL STANDARDS OF PROCEDURE AND SUBSTANCE IN REVIEW OF STUDENT DISCIPLINE IN TAX SUPPORTED INSTITUTIONS OF HIGHER EDUCATION

United States District Court for the Western District of Missouri,
En Banc, 1968.
45 F.R.D. 133.

RELATIONS OF COURTS AND EDUCATION

Achieving the ideal of justice is the highest goal of humanity. Justice is not the concern solely of the courts. Education is equally concerned with the achievement of ideal justice. The administration of justice by the courts in the United States represents the people's best efforts to achieve the ideal of justice in the field of civil and criminal law. It is generally accepted that the courts are necessary to this administration of justice and for the protection of individual liberties. Nevertheless, the contributions of the modern courts in achieving the ideals of justice are primarily the products of higher education. The modern courts are, and will continue to be, greatly indebted to higher education for their personnel, their innovations, their processes, their political support, and their future in the political and social order. Higher education is the primary source of study and support of improvement in the courts. For this reason, among others, the courts should exercise caution when importuned to intervene in the important processes and functions of education. A court should never intervene in the processes of education without understanding the nature of education.

Before undertaking to intervene in the educational processes, and to impose judicial restraints and mandates on the educational community, the courts should acquire a general knowledge of the lawful missions and the continually changing processes, functions, and problems of education. Judicial action without such knowledge would endanger the public interest and be likely to lead to gross injustice.

Education is the living and growing source of our progressive civilization, of our open repository of increasing knowledge, culture and our salutary democratic traditions. As such, education deserves the highest respect and the fullest protection of the courts in the performance of its lawful missions.

There have been, and no doubt in the future there will be, instances of erroneous and unwise misuse of power by those invested with powers of management and teaching in the academic community, as in the case of all human fallible institutions. When such misuse of power is threatened or occurs, our political and social order has made available a wide variety of lawful, non-violent, political, economic, and social means to prevent or end the misuse of power. These same lawful, non-violent, political, economic and social means are available to correct an unwise but lawful choice of educational policy or action by those charged with the powers of management and teaching in the academic community. Only where erroneous and unwise actions in the field of education deprive students of federally protected rights or privileges does a federal court have power to intervene in the educational process.

LAWFUL MISSIONS OF TAX SUPPORTED
HIGHER EDUCATION

The lawful missions of tax supported public education in the United States are constantly growing and changing. For the purposes of this analysis, it is sufficient to note some of the widely recognized traditional missions of tax supported higher education in this country.   Included in these lawful missions of education are the following:

(1) To maintain, support, critically examine, and to improve the existing social and political system;

(2) To train students and faculty for leadership and superior service in public service, science, agriculture, commerce and industry;

(3) To develop students to well rounded maturity, physically, socially, emotionally, spiritually, intellectually and vocationally;

(4) To develop, refine and teach ethical and cultural values;

(5) To provide fullest possible realization of democracy in every phase of living;

(6) To teach principles of patriotism, civil obligation and respect for the law;

(7) To each the practice of excellence in thought, behavior and performance;

(8) To develop, cultivate, and stimulate the use of imagination;

(9) To stimulate reasoning and critical faculties of students and to encourage their use in improvement of the existing political and social order;

(10) To develop and teach lawful methods of change and improvement in the existing political and social order;

(11) To provide by study and research for increase of knowledge;

(12) To provide by study and research for development and improvement of technology, production and distribution for increased national production of goods and services desirable for national civilian consumption, for export, for exploration, and for national military purposes;

(13) To teach methods of experiment in meeting the problems of a changing environment;

(14) To promote directly and explicitly international understanding and cooperation;

(15) To provide the knowledge, personnel, and policy for planning and managing the destiny of our society with a maximum of individual freedom; and

(16) To transfer the wealth of knowledge and tradition from one generation to another.

The tax supported educational institution is an agency of the national and state governments. . . .

The nihilist and the anarchist, determined to destroy the existing political and social order, who direct their primary attacks on the educational institutions, understand fully the missions of education in the United States.

Federal law recognizes the powers of the tax supported institutions to accomplish these missions and has frequently furnished economic assistance for these purposes.

The genius of American education, employing the manifold ideas and works of the great Jefferson, Mann, Dewey and many other living authorities, has made the United States the most powerful nation in history. In so doing, it has in a relatively few years expanded the area of knowledge at a revolutionary rate.

With education the primary force, the means to provide the necessities of life and many luxuries to all our national population, and to many other peoples, has been created. This great progress has been accomplished by the provision to the educational community of general support, accompanied by diminishing interference in educational processes by political agencies outside the academic community.

If it is true, as it well may be, that man is in a race between education and catastrophe, it is imperative that educational institutions not be limited in the performance of their lawful missions by unwarranted judicial interference.

OBLIGATIONS OF A STUDENT

Attendance at a tax supported educational institution of higher learning is not compulsory. The federal constitution protects the equality of opportunity of all qualified persons to attend. Whether this protected opportunity be called a qualified "right" or "privilege" is unimportant. It is optional and voluntary.

The voluntary attendance of a student in such institutions is a voluntary entrance into the academic community. By such voluntary entrance, the student voluntarily assumes obligations of performance and behavior reasonably imposed by the institution of choice relevant to its lawful missions, processes, and functions. These obligations are generally much higher than those imposed on all citizens by the civil and criminal law. So long as there is no invidious discrimination, no deprival of due process, no abridgement of a right protected in the circumstances, and no capricious, clearly unreasonable or unlawful action employed, the institution may discipline students to secure compliance with these higher obligations as a teaching method or to sever the student from the academic community.

No student may, without liability to lawful discipline, intentionally act to impair or prevent the accomplishment of any lawful mission, process, or function of an educational institution.

THE NATURE OF STUDENT DISCIPLINE COMPARED TO CRIMINAL LAW

The discipline of students in the educational community is, in all but the case of irrevocable expulsion, a part of the teaching process. In the case of irrevocable expulsion for misconduct, the process is not punitive or deterrent in the criminal law sense, but the process is rather the determination that the student is unqualified to continue as a member of the educational community. Even then, the disciplinary process is not equivalent to the criminal law processes of federal and state criminal law. For, while the expelled student may suffer damaging effects, sometimes irreparable, to his educational, social, and economic future, he or she may not be imprisoned, fined, disenfranchised, or subjected to probationary supervision. The attempted analogy of student discipline to criminal proceedings against adults and juveniles is not sound.

In the lesser disciplinary procedures, including but not limited to guidance counseling, reprimand, suspension of social or academic privileges, probation, restriction to campus and dismissal with leave to apply for readmission, the lawful aim of discipline may be teaching in performance of a lawful mission of the institution. The nature and procedures of the disciplinary process in such cases should not be required to conform to federal processes of criminal law, which are far from perfect, and designed for circumstances and ends unrelated to the academic community. By judicial mandate to impose upon the academic community in student discipline the intricate, time consuming, sophisticated procedures, rules and safeguards of criminal law would frustrate the teaching process and render the institutional control impotent.

A federal court should not intervene to reverse or enjoin disciplinary actions relevant to a lawful mission of an educational institution unless there appears one of the following:

    (1) a deprival of due process, that is, of fundamental concepts of fair play;

(2) invidious discrimination, for example, on account of race or religion;

(3) denial of federal rights, constitutional or statutory, protected in the academic community; or

(4) clearly unreasonable, arbitrary or capricious action.

PROVISIONAL PROCEDURAL AND JURISDICTIONAL STANDARDS

In the absence of exceptional circumstances these standards are applicable.

Jurisdiction

1. Under Sections 1343(3), Title 28, and 1983, Title 42, U.S.C.A., and also in appropriate cases under Sections 2201, 1331(a) or 1332(a), Title 28, U.S.C.A., the United States District Courts have jurisdiction to entertain and determine actions by students who claim unreasonably discriminatory, arbitrary or capricious actions lacking in due process and depriving a student of admission to or continued attendance at tax supported institutions of higher education.

Nature of Action

2. The action may be

(a) Under Section 1983, an action at law for damages triable by a jury;

(b) Under Section 1983, a suit in equity; or

(c) Under Section 1983 and Section 2201, a declaratory judgment action, which may be legal or equitable in nature depending on the issues therein.

Question of Exhaustion of Remedies

3. In an action at law or equity under Section 1983, Title 42, U.S.C.A., the doctrine of exhaustion of state judicial remedies is not applicable. The fact that there is an existing state judicial remedy for the alleged wrong is no ground for stay or dismissal.

Ordinarily until the currently available, adequate and effective institutional processes have been exhausted, the disciplinary action is not final and the controversy is not ripe for determination.

Right to Jury Trial

4.   In an action at law under Section 1983, the issues are triable by jury and equitable defenses are not available.

Trial of Equitable Actions

5.   In an equitable action by a court without a jury under Section 1983, equitable doctrines and defenses are applicable.

(a)   There must be an inadequate remedy at law.

(b)   The plaintiff must be in a position to secure equitable relief under equitable doctrines, for example, must come with "clean hands."

Question of Mootness

6.   In an action at law or equity under Section 1983, Title 42, U.S.C.A., to review severe student disciplinary action, the doctrine of mootness is not applicable when the action is timely filed.

PROVISIONAL SUBSTANTIVE STANDARDS IN STUDENT DISCIPLINE CASES UNDER SECTION 1983, TITLE 42

1.   Equal opportunity for admission and attendance by qualified persons at tax supported state educational institutions of higher learning is protected by the equal privileges and immunities, equal protection of laws, and due process clauses of the Fourteenth Amendment to the United States Constitution.   It is unimportant whether this protected opportunity is defined as a right or a privilege.   The protection of the opportunity is the important thing.

2.   In an action under Section 1983, issues to be determined will be limited to determination whether, under color of any statute, ordinance, regulation, custom or usage of a state ("state action"), a student has been deprived of any rights, privileges, or immunities secured by the Constitution and laws of the United States.

3.   State constitutional, statutory, and institutional delegation and distribution of disciplinary powers are not ordinarily matters of federal concern.   Any such contentions based solely on claims of unlawful distribution and violation of state law in the exercise of state disciplinary powers should be submitted to the state courts.   Such contentions do not ordinarily involve a substantial

federal question of which the district court has jurisdiction under Section 1983. This rule does not apply, however, to actions based on diversity jurisdiction under Sections 1331, 1332 or 2201, Title 28, U.S.C.A.

4. Disciplinary action by any institution, institutional agency, or officer will ordinarily be deemed under color of a statute, ordinance, regulation, custom or usage of a state ("state action") within the meaning of Section 1983, Title 42, U.S.C.A.

5. In the field of discipline, scholastic and behavioral, an institution may establish any standards reasonably relevant to the lawful missions, processes, and functions of the institution. It is not a lawful mission, process, or function of an institution to prohibit the exercise of a right guaranteed by the Constitution or a law of the United States to a member of the academic community in the circumstances. Therefore, such prohibitions are not reasonably relevant to any lawful mission, process or function of an institution.

6. Standards so established may apply to student behavior on and off the campus when relevant to any lawful mission, process, or function of the institution. By such standards of student conduct the institution may prohibit any action or omission which impairs, interferes with, or obstructs the missions, processes and functions of the institution.

Standards so established may require scholastic attainments higher than the average of the population and may require superior ethical and moral behavior. In establishing standards of behavior, the institution is not limited to the standards or the forms of criminal laws.

7. An institution may establish appropriate standards of conduct (scholastic and behavioral) in any form and manner reasonably calculated to give adequate notice of the scholastic attainments and behavior expected of the student.

The notice of the scholastic and behavioral standards to the students may be written or oral, or partly written and partly oral, but preferably written. The standards may be positive or negative in form.

Different standards, scholastic and behavioral, may be established for different divisions, schools, colleges, and classes of an institution if the differences are reasonably relevant to the missions, processes, and functions of the particular divisions, schools, colleges, and classes concerned.

8. When a challenged standard of student conduct limits or forbids the exercise of a right guaranteed by the Constitution or a law of the United States to persons generally, the institution must demonstrate that the standard is recognized as relevant to a lawful mission of the institution, and is recognized as reasonable by some reputable authority or school of thought in the field of higher education.   This may be determined by expert opinion or by judicial notice in proper circumstances.   It is not necessary that all authorities and schools of thought agree that the standard is reasonable.

9. Outstanding educational authorities in the field of higher education believe, on the basis of experience, that detailed codes of prohibited student conduct are provocative and should not be employed in higher education.

For this reason, general affirmative statements of what is expected of a student may in some areas be preferable in higher education.   Such affirmative standards may be employed, and discipline of students based thereon.

10. The legal doctrine that a prohibitory statute is void if it is overly broad or unconstitutionally vague does not, in the absence of exceptional circumstances, apply to standards of student conduct.   The validity of the form of standards of student conduct, relevant to the lawful missions of higher education, ordinarily should be determined by recognized educational standards.

11. In severe cases of student discipline for alleged misconduct, such as final expulsion, indefinite or long-term suspension, dismissal with deferred leave to reapply, the institution is obligated to give to the student minimal procedural requirements of due process of law.[51]   The requirements of due process do not demand an inflexible procedure for all such cases.   "But 'due process' unlike some legal rules, is not a technical conception with a fixed content unrelated to time, place and circumstances."   Three minimal requirements apply in cases of severe discipline, growing out of fundamental conceptions of fairness implicit in procedural due process.   First, the student should be given adequate notice in writing of the specific ground or grounds and the nature of the evidence on which the disciplinary proceedings are based.   Second, the student should be given an opportunity for a hearing in which the disciplinary authority provides

51. More recently, however, the U. S. Supreme Court has ruled that before a student can be suspended for even one day, he must first be accorded some kind of notice and hearing. Goss v. Lopez, 419 U.S. 565 (1975).

a fair opportunity for hearing of the student's position, explanations and evidence. The third requirement is that no disciplinary action be taken on grounds which are not supported by any substantial evidence. Within limits of due process, institutions must be free to devise various types of disciplinary procedures relevant to their lawful missions, consistent with their varying processes and functions, and which do not impose unreasonable strain on their resources and personnel.

There is no general requirement that procedural due process in student disciplinary cases provide for legal representation, a public hearing, confrontation and cross-examination of witnesses, warnings about privileges, self-incrimination, application of principles of former or double jeopardy, compulsory production of witnesses, or any of the remaining features of federal criminal jurisprudence. Rare and exceptional circumstances, however, may require provision of one or more of these features in a particular case to guarantee the fundamental concepts of fair play.

It is encouraging to note the current unusual efforts of the institutions and the interested organizations which are devising and recommending procedures and policies in student discipline which are based on standards, in many respects far higher than the requirements of due process. See for example the Joint Statement on Rights and Freedoms of Students, 54 A.A.U.P. Bulletin No. 2, Summer 1968, 258, a report of a joint committee of representatives of the U. S. National Students Association, Association of American Colleges, American Association of University Professors, National Association of Student Personnel Administrators, National Association of Women's Deans and Counselors, American Association of Higher Education, Jesuit Education Association, American College Personnel Association, Executive Committee, College and University Department, National Catholic Education Association, Commission on Student Personnel, American Association of Junior Colleges; and the University of Missouri, Provisional Rules of Procedure In Student Disciplinary Matters.

Many of these recommendations and procedures represent wise provisions of policy and procedure far above the minimum requirements of federal law, calculated to ensure the confidence of all concerned with student discipline.

The excellent briefs and arguments, including those of amici curiae, have been of great assistance in the preparation of this memorandum.

GREENE v. HOWARD UNIVERSITY

United States District Court, District of Columbia, 1967.
271 F.Supp. 609.

HOLTZOFF, District Judge.

.   .   .

The defendant in [this case] is Howard University, an institution of higher learning located in Washington, D. C. The plaintiffs   .   .   .   are students, whose status was terminated by the University as of the close of the academic year ending June 30, 1967.   .   .   .

In view of the disposition of the issues about to be made by this Court, it would be superfluous to review in detail the incidents that led to the action taken by the University against the plaintiffs. Suffice it to say that it arose out of a series of disorders that took place on the campus of Howard University. In one instance, the head of the Selective Service System of the United States had been invited to make a speech at the University. A group of students created such a disturbance as made it impossible for him to address the audience. At another time the University authorities were about to conduct a hearing on charges of misconduct against a student. A group composed of some students and of some members of the faculty created such a commotion and uproar as to render its impracticable for the hearing to proceed. Threatening utterances were heard on the campus. Several fires took place. The University authorities concluded, after a careful and thorough investigation, that the student plaintiffs   .   .   .   actively participated in creating these chaotic conditions and disorder. Accordingly, in an effort to bar a continuation and repetition of such disruptive incidents, the University in June 1967, sent a formal letter to each of the student plaintiffs, notifying him that he would not be permitted to return to the institution for the next academic year.   .   .   .

.   .   .   [The student plaintiffs'] complaint is predicated on the contention that they were not accorded their alleged Constitutional right to receive notices of charges and a hearing, but were dismissed from the University by *ex parte* decisions. The relief that they seek is to require the University to vacate its action and to give them notices of charges and a hearing.

This contention is based on a misconception of the scope of the Bill of Rights. The procedural safeguards and the privileges accorded by the Constitution of the United States are confined solely to judicial and quasi-judicial proceedings, either in the courts or before administrative agencies. They are directed solely against Governmental action. They do not extend to any other relation in life, such as that of parent and child, teacher and pupil, or employer and employee. These relations are of a private character. While some of them, such as that of employer and employee, may be circumscribed by contract or by statute, they are not controlled by the Constitution. For example, until the enactment of the Civil Service laws, the Federal Government had the right to discharge any of its employees at will. In fact, it may do so even now in respect to those persons who are exempt from the various limitations of the Civil Service statutes. To take another example, arbitrary discharge of employees of private concerns may be limited by statute or by agreements between the employers and labor unions, but Constitutional restrictions are not applicable.

Counsel for the plaintiffs rely principally on the decision of the Court of Appeals for the Fifth Circuit in Dixon v. Alabama State Board of Education, 294 F.2d 150, which held a vote of 2 to 1, that a State College had no authority to expel a student without first giving him notice and some opportunity for a hearing. The Court referred to the State college as "a governmental body". Counsel for the student plaintiffs in the case at bar argued that there are sufficient contacts and a strong enough connection between Howard University and the Federal Government to render the principle of the *Dixon* case applicable. Decisions of Courts of Appeals of other circuits must be regarded with respect and may be persuasive, but they are not necessarily controlling. For the reasons about to be stated, it is not necessary, however, to determine whether the principle evolved by the *Dixon* case, should constitute the law in the District of Columbia.

Unlike the college involved in the *Dixon* case, Howard University is not a governmental body. It is a private corporation created by an Act of Congress. True, a large percentage of its expenses are paid by annual appropriations made by Congress. As a condition of receiving such money, the Secretary of Health, Education and Welfare is given authority to visit and inspect Howard University and to control and supervise the expenditures of those funds which have been appropriated by Congress, 20 U.S.C.A. § 122. In addition, the President and Directors of Howard University are required to file an annual report with the Secretary. No Government officer, however, is a member of the

Board of Trustees of the Institution, nor is any control over the institution vested in the Federal Government.

The status of Howard University is not open for determination by this Court, for it has already been held by the Court of Appeals for this Circuit that the University is a private corporation and is not a public institution, Maiatico Const. Co. v. United States, 65 App.D.C. 62, 79 F.2d 418. Speaking for a unanimous bench, Groner, J., in that case wrote as follows:

> Howard University is a private corporation. It was incorporated under an act passed March 2, 1867 (14 Stat. 438), and its charter gives it all the rights and powers usually vested in private corporations, including the right to purchase and sell real estate, and the right to contract and to sue and to be sued.

Judge Groner then referred to the fact that in 1928, a statute was enacted enabling Congress to make annual appropriations for the support of the University. Judge Groner continued:

> This amendment of the charter of the university goes no farther than its terms. If it successfully legalizes the appropriation out of the Treasury of money of the government in aid of a private institution, it does not, nor does it purport to, change the fundamental character of the institution or make it any the less private; for Congress has passed no law giving the Secretary of the Interior or any other officer of the government control of the university, and we think it is obvious it could not do so without the consent and approval of the corporate authorities of that institution. Hence, in the view we take, the generosity of the government is not enough in itself to change a private into a public institution.

The *Maiatico* case was cited with approval and its doctrine reaffirmed and applied in Irwin v. United States, 74 App.D.C. 296, 122 F.2d 73. It is clear, therefore, that the principle which counsel for the plaintiffs seek to invoke namely, that a Government college or university may not expel its students without notice of charges and an opportunity to be heard, is not applicable to Howard University, for it is not a public institution nor does it partake of any governmental character.

It would be a dangerous doctrine to permit the Government to interpose any degree of control over an institution of higher learning, merely because it extends financial assistance to it. There are numerous colleges in this country, whose establishment was made financially possible by grants of land by the Federal Government. It is inconceivable that for this reason every "land grant college", as such institutions are generally denominated, should to some degree be subject to the control of the Federal Government, or that the Federal courts should be empowered to interfere with the administration of discipline, or the appointment of members of the faculty in such schools. In recent years, numerous universities, colleges and technical schools have received Governmental aid of various kinds by being granted funds to carry on scientific research projects. Surely it should not be held that any institution by entering into a contract with the United States for the conduct of some project of this sort and receiving funds for that purpose, has placed its head in a noose and subjected itself to some degree of control by the Federal Government. Such a result would be intolerable, for it would tend to hinder and control the progress of higher learning and scientific research. Higher education can flourish only in an atmosphere of freedom, untrammelled by Governmental influence in any degree. The courts may not interject themselves into the midst of matters of school discipline. Such discipline cannot be administered successfully in the same manner as governs the trial of a criminal case or a hearing before an administrative agency.

Students entering Howard University are formally advised by the University authorities that attendance at the institution is not a right but a privilege. In that important respect, among many others, Howard University differs from some State colleges. It is further indicated that this privilege may be withdrawn by the authorities if in their own judgment a student, who has been accepted for admission, does not conform to standards of conduct that the University exacts from its student body. Nowhere is it stated directly or by implication that a student would be accorded a hearing before his connection with the University could be terminated.

The University catalog, which is available to all prospective students and to members of the student body, as well as to the general public, enunciates the relation between the University and its students as follows:

Attendance at Howard University is a privilege. In order to protect its standards of scholarship and character, the University reserves the right, and the student concedes to the University the right, to deny admission to and require the withdrawal of any student at any time for any reason deem-

ed sufficient to the University. Admission to and enrollment in the University include obligations in regard to conduct, both inside and outside the classroom, and students
are expected to conduct themselves in such a manner as to be
a credit both to themselves and to the University. They are
amenable to the laws governing the community as well as to
the rules and orders of the University and University officials, and are expected to conform to the standards of conduct approved by the University.

In this important respect, among many others, Howard University differs from some State institutions to which all qualified
residents of the State are entitled to be admitted. As indicated
in its catalog, this is not the case at Howard University, which
partakes of the character of a private institution. If there is any
contractual relation between the University and its students, the
foregoing provisions are part of the contract.

The conclusion necessarily follows that the student plaintiffs
had no constitutional, statutory, or contractual right to a notice
of charges and a hearing before they could be expelled or their
connection with the University could be otherwise severed. It
was entirely within the discretion of the University authorities
to grant or withhold a hearing. Consequently, the student plaintiffs are not entitled to any relief requiring the University to reinstate them until they have received a notice of charges and a
hearing.

.   .   .

BROWN v. VILLANOVA UNIVERSITY

United States District Court, E.D.Penn.1974.
378 F.Supp. 342.

J. NEWCOMER, District Judge.

Findings of Fact

1.   Plaintiffs are twelve former and present students of defendant Villanova University.

2.   Defendants are Villanova University, a private, parochial
institution of higher education located in Villanova, Pennsylvania; its President, the Rev. Edward J. McCarthy; Dr. James F.
Duffy, Vice-President charge of student affairs; and other officers of Villanova University.

3.   In early 1974, a group of students, including some of the plaintiffs, formed an organization to seek more protection for the rights of students and a greater voice for students in school affairs.   The immediate catalyst for the formation of this organization, called the "Ad Hoc Committee", was the disciplinary action taken against certain students in January, 1974.   The members of the Ad Hoc Committee complained that these students had been expelled or suspended without due process.

4.   On April 6, 1974, there was a school event known as "Candidates Day", during which prospective candidates for admission to the school visited campus.

5.   On that date, there are many visitors on campus, and many parties in various parts of campus, including students' residence halls.

6.   In order to allow the candidates and their families inside the dormitories where they might live, Villanova's regular parietal (visitation) rules were suspended so that individuals of one sex could be in the residence, washroom, and hallway areas of the opposite sex until 9:00 p. m.

7.   Under Villanova's parietal rules, students are allowed to remain in the lounge areas of the residence halls of the opposite sex until 3:00 a. m. on weekends.

8.   On April 6, several students, including some of the plaintiffs, distributed throughout campus fliers inviting students to attend a rally in Sheehan Hall, a residence for women students at the University.

9.   Approximately fifteen minutes before the special visitation hours were to elapse, numerous male students came to Sheehan Hall, entered the washroom and hallway areas, and began to distribute beer from kegs.

10.   Alarmed by this influx of male visitors, the resident counselors of Sheehan Hall asked for the help of male counselors. The Assistant Dean of Men, Anthony Martin, soon appeared on the scene and ordered the males to leave.

11.   By this time—approximately 9:30 p. m.—there were over a hundred males in all areas of Sheehan Hall.   When Mr. Martin and his cohorts were not able to convince the men to leave Sheehan Hall the police were called in.

12.   When the police arrived, they were met by a group of students at the door who locked arms to resist their entry, but as the police approached this human barrier it voluntarily disband-

ed. Various members of the police entered the building but the police eventually left without making any arrests.

13. This melee-party-rally lasted into the night, and it was only much later that the University's disciplinary officers were able to disband it.

14. The plaintiffs were present at this event. Plaintiff Richard E. Brown, the President of the Student Body, and a student of high academic standing testified that he arrived at Sheehan Hall at approximately 10:00 p. m. and attempted to assist Dean Martin in clearing the building. Brown stated that he did lock arms as the result of peer pressure, but ended his resistance as soon as police approached. Plaintiff Brown testified that he was thanked by a police lieutenant for his assistance in clearing the building. As a result of the disturbance at Sheehan Hall 56 students—allegedly those who could be identified from photographs by Dean Martin and his assistants—were charged with insubordination and participation in an unauthorized mass demonstration. Ten minute hearings were set for these students, but upon protest of counsel during the first such hearing a new hearing process was established. This revised process provided for a factual determination by a panel to be composed of the Dean of the Villanova Law School, the Dean of the Faculty of Arts and Sciences, and the Dean of Men. Students were given the right to be represented by counsel, the right to cross-examine, and the right to present evidence at these hearings. They were fully notified of the subject matter of these hearings. The panel's factual findings were then transmitted to Dr. James Duffy, Vice-President in Charge of Student Affairs, who then assessed the penalties. Of the fifty-six students originally charged, 31 were punished. Of a total of seven students who were expelled, six are plaintiffs here. The remaining plaintiffs received sentences ranging from suspension from 12 months to suspension for 15 months.

15. Several of the named plaintiffs, including plaintiffs Brown and Pakuris were members of the Ad Hoc Committee, and this fact was known to the officials of Villanova. Dr. Duffy testified that his decision as to punishments was based totally on the findings of the hearing panel. But upon cross-examination it was revealed that he himself was involved in making certain decisions for the administration on the night of April 6, and that he had discussed the events of the night of April 6 with other Villanova officials. Dr. Duffy also testified that past records of the students played a role in determining what punishment they received.

16.   The attitude of the President of the University, Rev. Mc-Carthy, was hostile to the presence and activities of the Ad Hoc Committee.   Rev. McCarthy testified at the hearing that he held the Ad Hoc Committee's speech and organizational activities responsible for an environment in which acts of violence and desecration could exist.   Father McCarthy did not attempt to hide this attitude from his subordinates or the students.

17.   Those students who were expelled have experienced extreme difficulty in attempting to gain admission to other universities.   The expulsion of plaintiff Brown came too late to allow him to gain admission to a university for the semester beginning this August or September.

18.   Plaintiffs who were suspended are experiencing and will experience a delay and disruption of their education and careers.

19.   The expulsion and suspension of the plaintiffs will result in a blot upon their records which will inhibit them from pursuing their university-level education, graduate education, and careers.

CONCLUSIONS OF LAW

1.   This Court does not have jurisdiction by reason of 42 U.S.C.A. § 1983.   The action of the officials at Villanova University was not state action within the meaning of that section.

2.   Jurisdiction over this action cannot be based on the diversity jurisdiction statute, 28 U.S.C.A. § 1332, since complete diversity is lacking.

3.   Jurisdiction of this court over the action is properly based on 42 U.S.C.A. § 1985, in that there is a substantial probability that plaintiffs will show at trial that there was a conspiracy among some of the defendants to deny plaintiffs rights which are guaranteed them under the constitution, and that such a conspiracy was based upon an invidiously discriminatory animus in that they were punished severely because they had exercised in the past and continued to exercise their first amendment rights through membership on the Ad Hoc Committee.

4.   Plaintiffs will suffer irreparable injury unless the imposition of their penalties is enjoined.

Part II

PROCEDURAL GUARANTEES

Chapter 3

SOME PROCEDURAL PRELIMINARIES

The case before us requires something more than an informal interview with an administrative authority of the college.

(Judge Rives in *Dixon*, 1961)

The Party Over There

A Man in a Hurry, whose watch was at his lawyer's asked a Grave Person the time of day.

"I heard you ask that Party Over There the same question," said the Grave Person. "What answer did he give you?"

"He said it was about three o'clock," replied the Man in a Hurry; "but he did not look at his watch, and as the sun is nearly down I think it is later."

"The fact that the sun is nearly down," the Grave Person said, "is immaterial, but the fact that he did not consult his timepiece and make answer after due deliberation and consideration is fatal. The answer given," continued the Grave Person, consulting his own timepiece, "is of no effect, invalid, and void."

"What, then," said the Man in a Hurry, eagerly, "is the time of day?" "The question is remanded to the Party Over There for a new answer," replied the Grave Person, returning his watch to his pocket and moving away with great dignity.

He was a Judge of an Appellate Court.

(Ambrose Bierce)

After the 1961 Dixon v. Alabama State Bd. of Educ. appellate ruling, campus decisions involving student discipline in public colleges and universities still had to follow a rather undefined set of standards under the rubric of due process, and chapters 1 and 2 indicate that since that time the judiciary has manifested a searching interest in this procedure. In fact, the accumulation of case law in the procedural area is now almost staggering, at least in part because such a focus allows courts to dispose of cases on issues where the judiciary considers it has most competence. Moreover, as to the courts' propensity to reverse on procedural rather than substantive grounds, the above fable by Ambrose Bierce might seem in point to the confused student personnel administrator.

In a general sense and at the risk of oversimplifying, procedural due process is a combination of procedures that, if followed in the spirit of fair play, is more likely to result in truth and justice being achieved than if the procedures were not followed. Sounds something like the truth-seeking process of the higher learning, doesn't it? Then was higher education hoisted by its own petard with *Dixon*? Well, whatever, during the sixties a growing number of the thousands of students who felt "folded, stapled and mutilated" after their encounters with institutional bureaucracies gradually turned to the courts to get some kind of relief. Too frequently, they had no place else to go.

As the consequences of such action were recorded in case law and court practice, public colleges and universities were increasingly in need of constitutionally acceptable guidelines to respond fairly and legally to student misconduct, but, perhaps more important, these guidelines were essential for educational and moral purposes as well. Metaphorically, Justice Brandeis made this latter point very clear, but from a different time and from a somewhat different perspective:

> Our government is the potent, omnipresent teacher. For good or ill, it teaches the whole people by its example . . If the government becomes a law breaker, it breeds contempt for the law . . . To declare that in the administration of . . . laws the end justifies the means—to declare that the government may commit crimes in order to secure the conviction of a private criminal—would bring terrible retribution.[1]

Thus a variation of the same problem that Justice Brandeis was addressing was that if students found that college officials

---

1. Olmstead v. United States, 277 U.
S. 438, 485 (1928).

made arbitrary use of their authority, they could come to expect that people in authority should not be trusted, or even worse, that the irresponsible use of power, although not desirable, was to be expected and tolerated.

THE JUDICIAL MAZE

Since preventive law is just as desirable as preventive medicine, it should be useful in this section of the book to spell out the specifics of procedural due process as the courts are likely to define them in the context of college student discipline. Nevertheless, one may search the case reports in vain for some meaningful verbal encapsulation of procedural due process, for even in criminal proceedings the Supreme Court " . . . has always declined to give a comprehensive definition of it, and has preferred that its full meaning should be gradually ascertained by the process of inclusion and exclusion in the course of the decision of cases as they arise." [2] Furthermore, " . . . it [procedural due process] contains the garnered wisdom of the past in assuring fundamental justice [and] . . . is also a living principle not confined to the past." [3] As a "living principle" due process "cannot be imprisoned within the treacherous limits of any formula . . . [It] is not a yardstick. It is a process." [4] The case findings dealing with due process, then, are at best but indications of general principles "compounded of history, reason, the past course of decisions, and stout confidence in the strength of the democratic faith which we profess." [5]

Following this case-by-case process, the United States Supreme Court in a series of state criminal case appeals during the sixties dealt with many details of Fourteenth Amendment procedural due process requirements.[6] Thus, if one had carefully read each of those cases and put their findings together, he would have possessed a rather up-to-date guideline for criminal proce-

2. Twining v. New Jersey, 211 U.S. 78, 100 (1908).

3. Joint Anti-Fascist Refugee Committee v. McGrath, 341 U.S. 123, 174 (1951).

4. Id., at 162–163.

5. Id., at 163.

6. See, e. g., Washington v. Texas, 388 U.S. 14 (1967) (compulsory proc-

ess); Klopfer v. North Carolina, 386 U.S. 213 (1967) (speedy trial); Parker v. Gladden, 385 U.S. 363 (1966) (impartial jury); Sheppard v. Maxwell, 384 U.S. 333 (1966) (prejudicial publicity); Griffin v. California, 380 U.S. 609 (1965) (prohibition against prosecution comment on privilege); Pointer v. Texas, 380 U.S. 400 (1965) (confrontation); Gideon v. Wainwright, 372 U.S. 335 (1963) (right to counsel).

dural jurisprudence. However, student disciplinary proceedings have been held to be civil and not criminal proceedings and therefore do not necessarily require all of the judicial safeguards and rights accorded to criminal proceedings.

The Balancing of Interests

Today, court decisions involving student discipline employ the judicial test of "fair play" as the rough equivalent of procedural due process. As Mr. Justice Frankfurter wrote in Joint Anti-Fascist Refugee Committee v. McGrath: [7]

> The heart of the matter is that democracy implies respect for the elementary rights of men, however suspect or unworthy; a democratic government must therefore practice fairness . . . [8]

Essentially what the Court deemed "fair" follows:

> [F]airness . . . cannot be tested by mere generalities or sentiments abstractly applied. The precise nature of the interest that has been adversely affected, the manner in which it was done, the reasons for doing it, the available alternatives to the procedure that was followed, the protection implicit in the office of the functionary whose conduct is challenged, the balance of hurt complained of and good accomplished—these are some of the considerations that must enter into judicial judgment.[9]

One key to the diversity of court opinions in student discipline cases, then, is the courts' changing evaluation of "the precise nature of the interest that has been adversely affected" and, as a consequence, the direction of "the balance of hurt complained of and good accomplished." Formerly the courts concentrated on the "good accomplished" by the college in the pursuit of its "lawful mission" and were not very concerned if any interest of a student was "adversely affected." However, such judicial predilection is now history, and the courts since *Dixon* are relying more on "the interest that has been adversely affected" and are therefore requiring the "rudiments of an adversary proceeding" in public college disciplinary hearings.

In the area of substantive due process, moreover, the United States Supreme Court has established a "balancing test" which is to guide public education authorities when seeking to regulate

7. 341 U.S. 163 (1951).

8. Id., at 170.

9. Id., at 163.

student behavior in constitutionally protected interests.[10]   The interests which are in conflict are the rights of students to be protected in constitutionally assured areas of behavior as opposed to the necessity of the state to maintain an effective system of public education.   Therefore, student conduct rules regulating constitutional freedoms must be judged by balancing the interest to be secured by the regulations against the amount of freedom that is lost or impaired.   When the student meets the burden of showing that the state is intruding into an area of constitutionally protected activity, the burden of proof shifts to the state to show some compelling reason for establishing rules and regulations in this area.   The most frequently cited justification for attempted regulation here, of course, has been that of "disruption" but there have been a number of dissimilar court rulings as to the boundaries of its application.

Different Jurisdictions—Sometimes Different Rulings

Still another barrier to a more precise definition of due process in student disciplinary proceedings is the fact that different courts may view a question differently in their respective jurisdictions.   Although courts generally abide by the doctrine of *stare decisis*, there is the possibility that each of the state courts will view a question differently and set forth even conflicting opinions at times.   In fact at least one prominent jurist believed that judges should, on occasion, ignore the origins and precedents of law because, "outworn concepts which no longer fit the facts must be vacated.   The judge should fit his decision to the facts; if he cannot find the precedents he must create new precedents." [11]

Even though access may be had directly to the United States District Courts when there is an alleged United States Constitutional violation, there still remains the fact that what definitions these courts may give to due process apply only to the jurisdiction of that court.   The Court of Appeals, to which cases are appealed from the United States District Courts, may issue further definitions and they are then applicable to all of the United States District Courts within that circuit.   Only the United States Supreme Court's definitions are applicable to the entire United States, and to date that court has ruled on only one case (Goss v. Lopez, 419 U.S. 565 (1975)) regarding student disciplinary

---

10. Tinker v. Des Moines Independent Community School Dist., 393 U.S. 503 (1969).

11. William O. Douglas, "Stare Decisis", *Columbia Law Review*, XLIX (1949) p. 735.

proceedings and that ruling involved secondary rather than post-secondary students.

Waiting for the Supreme Court to Rule

The Supreme Court may refuse to hear a case being appealed from the Court of Appeals and frequently does. When this is done, it has the effect of upholding the lower court's ruling and, in turn, tends to produce court compliance throughout the entire United States. An example of this was the case of Dixon v. Alabama State Bd. of Educ. when the United States Supreme Court denied *certiorari*.

Then, too, one should understand that dissenting opinions often become the law of the land some years later after the inevitable changes in the membership of the Court, shifts in the political winds, or the arrival of new concepts and practices in social organization and purpose. Thus in decisions by a divided Court, particularly if the vote is close, we find an "early warning system" that the minority opinion might well be adopted by the Court in subsequent cases. This, of course, indicates flexibility and a degree of progressiveness, but it also runs contrary to the advantages of stability and predictability and thus can make the Court appear erratic and unstable.

Finally, we must face the fact that frequently a Supreme Court decision comes many months or even years after the legal questions have been passed upon in lower federal or state courts. Thus the problem of "judicial lag" can create at least two additional problems for those attempting to use case law as a guideline. First, many lower court judges facing similar issues that are at the same time being reviewed by the high tribunal purposely postpone a decision until after the Supreme Court has pronounced its judgment. Second, when the Supreme Court finally breaks the log-jam, conditions are all too frequently favorable for hasty and sometimes "over-interpreted" conceptions of the Court's ruling principles, especially by laymen but also by lawyers, and even on occasion by judges in high echelons.

SOURCES OF INSTITUTIONAL AUTHORITY

In setting up the adjudicatory system for student discipline in the public institution, the fundamental rights of the student may not be unreasonably denied or limited. The student does not, nor can he be required to, sacrifice his constitutional rights as a condition of entering or continuing at the college. Many students, however, are accustomed to finding rights where no constitutionally protected rights exist and are used to thinking of rights in absolute terms.

An Ordered Educational Environment

Actually, no person possesses absolute rights. Each person's right to "absolute" freedom, for instance, is curtailed to the extent that that freedom is given to any other person. Thus in addition to the time-worn standard of shouting "fire" in a crowded theater, courts have added other restrictions such as: "gross disrespect and contempt for officials of an educational institution" (Schwartz v. Schuker, 298 F.Supp. 238 (D.C.N.Y.1969)); "behavior which materially and substantially disrupt[s] the work and discipline of the school" (Tinker v. Des Moines Independent Community School Dist., 393 U.S. 503 (1969)); "utterances in a context of violence [used as an] . . . instrument of force" (Siegel v. Regents of Univ. of Cal., 308 F.Supp. 832 (D.C.Cal. 1970)) or "abrasive and contemptuous behavior" (Lipkis v. Caveney, 19 Cal.App.3d 383, 96 Cal.Rptr. 779 (1971)). In brief then, the essential issue to be resolved is whether the limitations the college places on its students' rights are reasonable.

This concept of reasonableness, however, lies in a rather narrow territory between students' constitutionally protected rights on one hand, and the college's interest in the peaceful pursuit of its legitimate mission on the other. The problem, therefore, is how to balance individual rights against collective needs such as the compelling interest of the state to educate, remembering that individual freedom and social order are necessary to each other.

The Legal and Inherent Power to Discipline

The governing boards of public colleges and universities are creatures of the state and have authority to make regulations to the education of students and their conduct. This authority is nearly always specifically provided by state law. For example, the *California Education Code* gives the following disciplinary powers to its public community colleges:

> The governing board of any [community college] district shall prescribe rules not inconsistent with law . . . for the government of the schools under its jurisdiction. (Section 1052)

> Any governing board may enforce the provisions of Section 1052 by suspending, or if necessary, expelling a pupil

. . . . who refuses or neglects to obey any rules prescribed pursuant to that section. (Section 10604)

The governing board of any [community college] district shall suspend or expel students for misconduct when other means of correction fail to bring about proper conduct. (Section 10605)

Most of the cases resolving conflicts between students and college authorities, however, open with a general rule, variously stated, that the college has the authority, the power, and the duty to make regulations as to the conduct of students and to enforce its rules. In Goldberg v. Regents of the Univ. of Cal., the court put it this way:

. . . the university disciplinary action . . . was a proper exercise of its inherent general powers to maintain order on the campus and to exclude therefore those who are detrimental to its well being.[12]

The court also took notice of the unique place and nature of the academic community, saying:

Historically the academic community has been unique in having its own standards, rewards and punishments. Its members have been allowed to go about their business of teaching and learning largely free of outside interference. To compel such a community to recognize and enforce precisely the same standards and penalties that prevail in the broader social community would serve neither the special needs and interest of the educational institutions, nor the ultimate advantages that society derives therefrom. Thus, in an academic community, greater freedoms and greater restrictions may prevail than in society at large, and the subtle fixing of these limits should, in large measure, be left to the educational institution.[13]

So, of necessity, college officials have been given considerable discretion in formulating and enforcing rules and regulations to prescribe and control student conduct within the institution. Yet whatever control college authorities attempt to exercise in this area should have a legitimate governmental purpose since they could well find themselves required to come forward with a substantial showing of a necessary relationship of any regulation to a compelling state interest. Otherwise, it would seem safe to assume that the courts will continue to reflect a respect for the

12. 248 Cal.App.2d 867, 881, 57 Cal. Rptr. 463, 473 (1967).   13. Id., at 472.

unique problems of higher education and the clientele with which it deals while insisting upon an observance of current constitutional protections in the educational setting.

Legal Relationships

The body of law governing student-college relationships is still in a state of evolution. The essential conflict underlying each case, however—the duty of the college to educate in face of the equally important need to protect the free flow of activity and thought remains constant. It is in the resolution of the conflict that the focus shifts constantly. Nevertheless, if the college or university is an institution based on controversy and dedicated to the rigorous exchange of ideas and clash of concepts in search of truth and understanding, then surely it has no claim to an institutional need for autocratic power.

Not too many years ago judges were reluctant to interfere in most aspects of educational decision making. During that time, as previously noted, judges generally accepted "expert" testimony of educators as reasonable and nonarbitrary. However, the docility of the courts has changed markedly in recent years, and, consequently, courts have become an integral part of the educational decision-making process. The result has been a dramatic change in the student-college relationship and the way in which public institutions of higher education may operate within the area of student discipline.

As mentioned in Chapter 1, in the past courts make little distinction between the public and private institution in respect to the student-college relationship. Many courts developed legal analogies such as *in loco parentis*, "privilege" and "contract" to describe this relationship; however the courts have progressively retreated from the concept that the college (or its administration) should act as parents for its students or that college attendance is a privilege. In fact the proposition that summary discipline by a public college is justified because it is dealing with "legal infants" or that a student can or must waive his rights has been repudiated in numerous court decisions.[14]

Again, as noted in Chapter 2, the contract analogy is still used as a method of settling conflicts between students and their private colleges, and occasionally it is even applied in the public

14.   See, e. g. *Goldberg*, 57 Cal.Rptr. at 470; ". . . state universities . . . no longer stand in loco parentis in relation to their students." Zanders v. Louisiana State Bd. of Educ., 281 F.Supp. 747 (D.C.La.1968); Buttny v. Smiley, 281 F.Supp. 280 (D.C.Colo.1968).

college context. In the Andersen v. Regents of the Univ. of Cal. case,[15] for instance, a California court of appeals ruled that a contract existed between a student and his public university:

> [B]y the act of matriculation, together with payment of required fees, a contract between the student and the institution is created containing two implied conditions: (1) that the student will not be arbitrarily expelled, and (2) that the student will submit himself to reasonable rules and regulations for the breach of which, in a proper case he may be expelled . . . [16]

Nonetheless, the state cannot condition even a contractual obligation upon the renunciation of constitutional rights.

In terms of the student-public college relationship in the area of constitutional issues, therefore, the better approach recognizes that student

> . . . attendance at publicly financed institutions of higher education should be regarded as a benefit analogous to that of public employment. The test is whether conditions annexed to the benefit reasonably tend to further the purposes sought by conferment of that benefit and whether the utility of imposing the conditions manifestly outweighs any resulting impairment of constitutional rights.[17]

Thus the public college or university is viewed as a semi-independent agency of the state and the students as employees or appointees of the agency. It indicates that the public institution of higher education, like an agency, has a purpose of its own and that students, like agency members, have important obligations to help achieve the institution's mission. Likewise, the institution's commitment to the student is a firm one because, like an agency, it must remain true to its purposes.

For example, in order to foster a campus environment conducive to educational purposes, the public institution of higher education has the right to establish and enforce *reasonable* regulations designed to maintain discipline over students. The key constitutional test would be whether such institutional regulations and actions are so necessary in carrying out a college's educational purpose that they *reasonably* outweigh any resulting impairment of constitutional rights.

---

15. 22 Cal.App.3d 763, 99 Cal.Rptr. 531 (1972).

16. Id., at 535.

17. *Goldberg*, 57 Cal.Rptr. at 470.

The Student Conduct Code—Reasonable Rules Reasonably Applied

Whether it is literally true that "the history of liberty has largely been the history of procedural safeguards" [18] a proper respect for the fairness of public college student rules is not irrelevant in determining appropriate rights of college students. In ordinary legal terminology, this latter area is generally considered "substantive," but in the process of its clarification college officials will necessarily have to give careful consideration to the formulation of rules.

Since entrance into a public postsecondary institution is completely voluntary, it is inherent that, upon admission to the institution, the student has an obligation to adhere to the standards established by the college as long as there is no conflict with his legal or constitutional rights. A 1968 Fifth Circuit Court of Appeals' ruling makes this point clear:

> It is equally well settled, we think, that by seeking admission to and obtaining the benefits of attending a college or university the student agrees that he will abide by and obey the rules and regulations promulgated for the orderly operation of the institution and for the effectuation of its purposes. . . . [19]

In point of fact, many states require that their public colleges and universities provide for the adoption and availability of "specific" rules and regulations governing student behavior along with appropriate penalties. However, even though the law might stipulate that rules be "specific", it is probably impossible to cover every conceivable situation in a set of rules pertaining to students. Regardless of this fact, due process would seem to require that there should not be undue "vagueness" or "overbreadth" in the rules governing students. For instance, in Soglin v. Kauffman the Federal District Court declared:

> A standard of "misconduct", without more, may not serve as the sole foundation for the imposition of the sanction of expulsion, or the sanction of suspension for any significant time, throughout the entire range of student life in the university.[20]

18.   McNabb v. United States, 318 U.S. 347 (1943).

19.   Wright v. Texas Southern Univ., 392 F.2d 728, 729 (5th Cir. 1968).

20.   295 F.Supp. 978, 991 (D.C.Wis. 1968).

In upholding the lower court's decision upon appeal, the United States Court of Appeals, Seventh Circuit, pointed out that

> . . . expulsion and prolonged suspension may not be imposed simply on the basis of allegations of "misconduct" without reference to any preexisting rule which supplies an adequate guide.[21]

Moreover, many courts have been concerned with the sweeping dragnet potential in such boilerplate proscriptions as "misconduct", "behavior unbecoming a college student," "social conduct which reflects discredit upon the university," or "immoral or disreputable conduct." What do these statements mean? That is the critical question, and of course therein lies the legal friction point. The rub is that such regulations are so uncertain that reasonable people could disagree as to their interpretation and do not provide whether such behavior as, say, card playing, smoking, gluttony, holding hands on campus, failing to tip one's hat to a woman professor or whatever might be susceptible to punishment by the college.

In a student disciplinary case, then, must the rule alleged to have been broken be a written rule that has been made known to the student? It would seem so, but in Richards v. Thurston,[22] the Court predicated its decision upon an important assumption. This was that the regulation itself need not always be in writing in the form of a code or even promulgated in advance since school authorities could not always anticipate student conduct *or* the circumstances that might arise.

However, the importance of the written rule was emphasized in a case dating back more than a hundred years in Murphy v. Board of Directors of the Independent Dist. of Marengo.[23] It involved a student who was expelled for writing an article that allegedly held up to ridicule the members of the school board and tended to impair the influence and control of the board over the school. In the absence of any regulation prohibiting such acts, the Court concluded that the efforts of the school authorities constituted an *ex post facto* attempt to impose penalties, and said:

> When proper regulations for the government of the school are made and brought to the knowledge of the pupils, they may well be held to the penalties for their violation; but for the board to visit the severest penalty within their power

21. 418 F.2d 163, 168 (7th Cir. 1969). 23. 30 Iowa 429 (1870).

22. 424 F.2d 1281 (1st Cir. 1970).

upon a pupil . . . not prohibited either expressly or
by implication, even by a general regulation, is at variance
with both the letter and spirit of our laws.[24]

Whether or not the regulations are written and promulgated
in advance, it appears that the first minimum requirement of due
process should be that students have a reasonable opportunity to
know what types of conduct are prohibited. Therefore, in order
to be fair and to avoid possible judicial intervention it would
seem more appropriate to have written rules with a becoming
specificity and clarity. It is not to say that a spectacular degree
of preciseness, narrowness, and specificity in rulemaking should
be imposed upon the college; rather, the rules should be clear
enough for a reasonable person to understand them. Otherwise
the application of vague or overly broad rules would have an un-
savory *ex post facto* flavor. In fact, a fairly large pattern of
court decisions in this area imposes more than a moderate degree
of precision and narrowness and specificity on rulemaking; [25]
nevertheless, a majority of the courts have given a broad scope to
colleges and universities in the formulation of student conduct
standards.

Merely because a college board establishes a written student
conduct standard, therefore, does not necessarily mean that constitutional requirements have been met. The standard itself, for
instance, may be challengeable unless it is sufficiently explicit to
inform those who are subject to it what conduct on their part will
render them liable to its penalties. Obviously, it is difficult, if
not nearly impossible, to get a sharply defined idea of what the
constitutional requirements might be for rulemaking. In the
attempt, however, one would do well by first recognizing that
the very essence of due process is "tailoring" in that appropriate
protections vary depending upon the circumstances of a particular case. Thus, three court rulings, Lowery v. Adams (344 F.
Supp. 446 (D.C.Ky.1972)), Goldberg v. Regents of the Univ. of
Cal. (248 Cal.App.2d 867, 57 Cal.Rptr. 463 (1967)), and Esteban
v. Central Missouri State College (415 F.2d 1077 (8th Cir. 1969)),

---

24. Id., at 432.

25. See, e. g., Soglin v. Kaufman, 295
F.Supp. at 991; ". . . constitutional doctrines of vagueness and
overbreadth are . . . to be applied by the university in disciplining its students." Dickson v. Sitterson, 280 F.Supp. 486, 499 (D.C.N.C.

1968); "Precision of regulation
must be the touchstone in an area
so closely touching our most precious freedoms." Synder v. Board
of Trustees of Univ. of Illinois, 286
F.Supp. 927, 934 (D.C.Ill.1968); "A
[regulation] which fails to provide
an ascertainable standard of conduct . . . is void."

because of the special circumstances of the first two cases and the contrast of the third case, *Esteban*, with *Soglin*, will help clarify some important principles concerning constitutionally allowable breadth and vagueness.

In the *Lowery* case, students who had been involved in protest activity at Murphy State University in Kentucky were suspended for violating student conduct regulation which prohibited

> . . . any disruptive or disorderly conduct which inter-feres with the rights and opportunities of those who attend the University for the purpose of which the University ex-ists—the right to utilize and enjoy facilities provided to ob-tain an education.[26]

Based upon the following rationale, the court ruled that the regu-lation was neither impermissible vague nor overbroad:

> [The regulation] . . . . is not such that a person of common intelligence is in doubt both as to its meaning and its application. While the language used could be more pre-cise, it is the opinion of this Court that it is sufficient to con-vey a definite warning as to the proscribed conduct when measured by common understanding and practices.[27]

Thus, although the language of the regulation could have been more precise, the common-sense test applied by the court was that the plaintiff students had at least average intelligence, could read, and possessed sufficient powers of comprehension so that a reasonable person would find it difficult to accept the student claim that they were unable to understand the warning implied in the regulation.

The student conduct regulation involved in the *Goldberg* case, however, was considerably more nebulous and would, in most cir-cumstances, appear as unable to pass constitutional muster. Here the conduct standard upon which several students were either suspended or dismissed failed to contain even the most gen-eral description of the kinds of conduct which might be pro-scribed:

> It is taken for granted that each student . . . will ad-here to *acceptable standards of personal conduct*; and that all students . . . will act and observe among them-selves *proper standards of conduct and good taste* . . .
> This presumption in favor of the students . . . con-tinues until . . . by misconduct, it is reversed, in

26. *Lowery*, 344 F.Supp. at 446–447.   **27.** Id., at 456.

which case the University authorities will take such action as the particular occurrence judged in the light of the attendant circumstances may seem to require.

The University authorities take it for granted that a student enters the University with an earnest purpose and will so conduct himself. *Unbecoming behavior* . . . will result in curtailment or withdrawal of the privileges or other action of the University authorities that they deem warranted by the student's conduct.[28]

When the students complained that the disciplinary committee's sanction was based upon an unconstitutionally vague and overbroad regulation, the California Appeals Court gave it short shrift and upheld the regulation as constitutionally valid. The basic facts of the students' misbehavior, however, were never in dispute. That is, Goldberg had participated in rallies on the Berkeley campus and in the course thereof had "repeatedly used the work 'fuck' in its various declensions." At another rally on the steps of the Student Union Building, he used the terms, "fuck," "bastard," "asshole," and "pissed off." Another student, Klein, used the word "fuck" at two rallies on campus, and Bills had manned a table with a container labeled "Fuck Fund" along with a large sign that read: "Support the Fuck Defense Fund. Raise money for the bail and legal defense of John Thomson. Combat hypocrisy. Sponsored by Student Committee for a Good Fuck." The other student, Zvegintzov, had participated in a rally "by leading a yell or cheer consisting of first spelling and then shouting the word 'fuck.' "

Quite obviously the Court recognized that a student could be on notice of impropriety from the circumstances of a case without the necessity of an explicit regulation. In effect, then, the *Goldberg* Court expressed an important judicial principle, that is, public postsecondary institutions may most certainly discipline a student pursuant to such a vague regulation when the student's conduct is so gross as to render a more explicit prohibition superfluous.

Most courts, in fact, have held that colleges and universities are not obligated to have specific rules and regulations to the extent necessary in criminal statutes. The *Soglin* appellate decision departs from this position and presents itself as the most severe test of required specificity in student conduct rules. The

---

28. *Goldberg*, 57 Cal.Rptr. at 466
(emphasis added).

classic case on the other side of the spectrum, however, is the Esteban v. Central Missouri State College decision, which, by contrast, represents the greatest allowable breadth and generality in the formulation of rules and regulations and standards of student conduct. It is interesting to note that both of these decisions occurred in 1969, and that each case was decided by a United States Court of Appeals.

A number of legal issues were decided in the *Esteban* case by Judge Harry Blackmun (appointed to the U. S. Supreme Court as an Associate Justice shortly thereafter), but the one of most interest in light of Soglin v. Kauffman was this:

> . . . *we see little basically or constitutionally wrong with flexibility and reasonable breadth rather than meticulous specificity* in college regulations relating to [student] conduct. Certainly these regulations are not to be compared with the criminal statute. They are codes of general conduct which those qualified and experienced in the field have characterized not as punishment but as part of the educational process itself and as *preferably to be expressed in general rather than in specific terms* . . .
>
> Let there be no misunderstanding as to our precise holding. We do not hold that any college regulation, however loosely framed, is necessarily valid. We do not hold that a school has the authority to require a student to discard any constitutional right. . . . We do hold that a college has the inherent power to promulgate rules and regulations; that it has power appropriately to protect itself and its property; that it may expect that its students adhere to generally accepted standards of conduct; that, as to these, *flexibility and elbow room are to be preferred over specificity*; . . . that school standards are not to be measured by the standards which prevail for the criminal law and criminal procedure; and that the courts should interfere only where there is a clear case of constitutional infringement.[29]

When considerable heterogeneity of opinion develops among lower federal courts or in state supreme or appellate courts regarding such a constitutional issue, and especially if there are distinct conflicts among the judgments of the eleven Circuits of the United States Courts of Appeals, the Supreme Court sometimes consents to review an appealed case which it deems typical,

29. Esteban v. Central Missouri State College, 415 F.2d 1077, 1088– 1089 (8th Cir. 1968) (emphasis added).

so that its decision will add something to the harmony and predictability of the law throughout the nation. To date the high tribunal has not so acted on rulemaking standards for students' conduct.[30]

Nevertheless, it would seem unfair, if not constitutionally impermissible, for a college to punish a student for violating a policy he had no reason to believe existed. Of course "prior restraint" regulations touching First Amendment freedoms are generally subjected to a more rigid standard by the courts. That is, any student conduct regulation that allows those who administer it so much discretion that the administrators could discriminate against those whose views they disapprove, comes to the courts "with a 'heavy presumption' against its constitutional validity." But more of this later in Part III of the book .   .   .

The College Adjudicatory System—Student Discipline

Governing boards often adopt extensive written policies concerning rules for suspension and expulsion of students, but regarding hearing procedure, comparable information is generally unavailable. The result is that college officials are often confused about what procedures to use, and students are unsure of their rights before the hearing board. Consequently, the student case is often not presented as effectively as it might have been, and the possibility of procedural error and subsequent judicial intervention is heightened.

Whatever the courts might or might not do, it is nevertheless expedient for the college to develop its own internal adjudicatory system. Its system should be aimed at dealing promptly with internal disciplinary problems, but it should guarantee at the same time due process to the accused student. This system can be called into use whenever it is necessary to review an alleged violation of the student conduct code.

Some college official must process cases initially. Generally, it is the Dean of Students or Dean of Student Affairs. This official's office receives and investigates complaints; determines their seriousness; interviews alleged offenders; seeks cooperation, accommodation, informal solution; and imposes minimal sanctions, for instance, warnings, if appropriate. Even in the more serious cases, many times the student admits guilt at the point of the initial interview and waives a hearing. Therefore,

---

30. See, e. g., *Esteban*, supra, cert. denied 398 U.S. 965 (1970).

the type of due process provided by a more formalized adjudicatory hearing is generally necessary only in the relatively few cases where there is a dispute concerning the guilt of the accused party or the appropriateness of his punishment.

In establishing the adjudicatory system of the college, the governing board must be aware that it is required to prescribe rules not inconsistent with law for the governance of the institution. Under this provision a governing board may adopt disciplinary procedures to be followed in cases involving suspension or expulsion of students. If such procedures are adopted, the governing board cannot suspend or expel a student without complying with its own procedural regulations. Thus the failure of a governing board to accord a student procedural protections in accordance with its own published regulations would be considered a denial of due process, even though those same procedures might not be required by either state statute or constitutional law.[31]

In the event that there are no disciplinary procedures established by the governing board to be followed in cases involving suspension or expulsion of students, or if such procedures are established but the appropriate officials either do not perform their duties or in performing their duties act in an arbitrary or unreasonable manner, the student could, by writ of *mandamus,* seek judicial aid in requesting that a complete hearing be given to the matter involved.

JUDICIAL RESTRAINT

It is not just anyone who can sue for relief in a court. The courts, in fact are rightfully concerned about the possibility of getting bogged down in the dismal swamp of attempting to be all things to all people. Therefore a person must have "standing to sue"—that is, must have "sustained or is immediately in danger of sustaining a direct injury. It is not sufficient that he has merely a general interest common to all members of the public." This self-imposed limitation is also in line with Article III of the Constitution which limits the jurisdiction of all federal courts to "cases and controversies." The Supreme Court has construed this to require a real and substantial dispute affecting the legal rights and obligations of parties having adverse interests which permit specific relief through a conclusive judicial de-

31. Vitarelli v. Seaton, 359 U.S. 535 (1969) supports the view that once the institution provides greater procedural protections than the Constitution requires, those greater protections must be complied with by the institution.

cree.[32]   Moreover, the federal courts will not render advisory opinions [33] (state courts may be so empowered but few are), and, furthermore, an actual controversy must exist at all stages of review, not merely when the complaint is filed.   The Supreme Court has called such cases "moot" and thus "does not sit to decide arguments after events have put them to rest." [34]

The Rule of Parsimony

The logic involving the very nature of the adversary system and the incredible demands that are placed on the judiciary require that judges decide only what is necessary to dispose of a specific case before them.   Of course judges often find the temptation irresistable to take up some point not argued in a case, or not a part of the conclusion necessary to support a judgment, but this is called *obiter dicta* and not binding as precedent.   Nevertheless, the Supreme Court has clearly expressed the judicial reluctance to go beyond a case at hand, especially when constitutional issues are involved, in Ashwander v. Tennessee Valley Auth.   Here Justice Brandeis wrote:

1. The court will not pass upon the constitutionality of legislation in a friendly, non-adversary proceeding .   .

2. The Court will not "anticipate a question of constitutional law in advance of the necessity of deciding it." .   .   .

3. The Court will not "formulate a rule of constitutional law broader than is required by the precise facts to which it is to be applied."   .   .   .

4. The Court will not pass upon a constitutional question although properly presented by the record, if there is also present some other ground upon which the case may be disposed of.   .   .   .

5. The Court will not pass upon the validity of a statute upon complaint of one who fails to show that he is injured by its operation   .   .   ..

6. The Court will not pass upon the constitutionality of a statute at the instance of one who has availed himself of its benefits   .   .   ..

32.   Aetna Life Ins. Co. v. Haworth, 300 U.S. 227 (1937).

33.   Muskrat v. United States, 219 U.S. 346 (1911)—holding invalid a statute which purported to confer appellate jurisdiction on the Court to render advisory opinions as to the validity of Acts of Congress.

34.   Doremus v. Bd. of Educ., 342 U.S. 429 (1952).

7. "When the validity of an act of the Congress is drawn
    in question, and even if a serious doubt of constitution-
    ality is raised, it is a cardinal principle that this Court
    will first ascertain whether a construction of the statute
    is fairly possible by which the question may be avoid-
    ed."   .   .   .[35]

Special Areas

The courts are also reluctant to impose their judgment in
areas beyond their competence unless justice clearly requires intervention. Exercising restraint at this point, the bench typically limits its intervention to righting the wrong and not to policing
the expertise of the professionals in the field. Moreover, as Alvin Goldman writes, "Some institutions by their very nature require a high degree of autocratic control—a religious group, a
fraternal order, a political action group." If a member disagrees
with its internal operations, he is free to resign and join some
other organization. Thus, after joining and agreeing to abide
by the group's internal discipline, a "member has little cause
to expect judicial aid if the group treats him arbitrarily. And,
in fact courts seldom interfere with the internal activities of
such organizations." [36]

Some associations, however, seem to have a "strangle-hold"
on their members "through their control of an occupation or
property that can ill be spared. In such a situation, there is
operative a [judicial] policy in favor of relief against wrongful
treatment." [37] As we have seen, however, judicial relief was indeed rare in the student-college relationship until the sixties. At
this point, the right of federal courts to intervene in the student-
public college relationship was established through the analogy
of education as property and the liberty to take advantage of
such.

Still, it is interesting to note that until the last few years most
decisions affecting colleges and universities were made by state
and lower federal courts. Remarkably, for nearly forty years,
the United States Supreme Court did not review and decide a
single case involving the student-college internal relationship.
That is, earlier, in 1934, the nation's top Court had ruled that

35. 297 U.S. 288, 346–348 (1936).

36. Alvin L. Goldman, "The Uni-
     versity and the Liberty of Its Stu-
     dents—a Fiduciary Theory," *Ken-*

tucky Law Journal, 54 (1966), pp.
655–657.

37. Id., at 656.

the University of California could constitutionally require all male students to participate in ROTC.[38] It was not until mid-1972 that the Supreme Court again ruled on a student-college relationship issue; in this case the Court held that Central Connecticut State College had violated Fourteenth Amendment rights of a student group when the institution refused recognition of a chapter of Students for a Democratic Society.[39]

Scholastic Affairs

As previously noted, many judges assigned as the cause of their unwillingness to provide relief for a student's complaint against a college disciplinary action, the fear of treading into the academic swamp. In matters of deportment, extracurricular activities and student expression and association, this position is now untenable, but in matters of scholastic achievement and teaching effectiveness, this generally makes sense. There is a valid objection to judicial interference because discretion here is a question of scholarly expertise known best to the faculty and administration. Professor Charles Alan Wright provides an insightful reason for the distinction between discipline cases and those involving academic matters:

> [C]ourts are expert in applying the first amendment and the due process clause, but the persons on campus are the experts in deciding the academic value of a piece of work . . . I perceive no basis on which a student can claim a constitutional right to a D rather than an F, so long as the grade given him was the good faith academic judgment of his instructor.[40]

An important and often quoted decision which embodies this approach is Connelly v. University of Vermont.[41] In this case, a third year medical student missed nearly a month of classes in the spring of 1964 because of illness. Although he was given the opportunity to make up the missed work the following summer, the student failed to earn a satisfactory grade on the make-up work and was hence dismissed. The student alleged that the summer professor arbitrarily decided to fail him regardless of how well he performed, but a petition by the student to repeat

---

38. Hamilton v. Regents of the Univ. of Cal., 293 U.S. 245 (1934).

39. Healy v. James, 408 U.S. 169 (1972).

40. Charles Alan Wright, "The Constitution on the Campus" *Vanderbilt Law Review*, XXII (1969), p. 1070.

41. 244 F.Supp. 156 (D.C.Vt.1965).

his third year was denied. He then brought court action to require reinstatement; however, after citing several prior cases involving student-school controversies, the *Connelly* Court explicitly concluded that academic conflicts warranted different judicial treatment from those involving disciplinary disputes:

> The effect of these decisions is to give the school authorities absolute discretion in determining whether a student has been delinquent in his studies and to place the burden on the student of showing that his dismissal was motivated by arbitrariness, capriciousness or bad faith. The reason for this rule is that in matters of scholarship, the school authorities are uniquely qualified by training and experience to judge the qualifications of a student, and efficiency of instruction depends in no small degree upon the school faculty's freedom from interference from other noneducational tribunals. It is only when the school authorities abuse this discretion that a court may interfere with their decision to dismiss a student.[42]

The Federal District Court in Keys v. Sawyer, while observing some practical disadvantages to judicial intervention, came to a similar conclusion:

> The federal judiciary should not adjudicate the soundness of a professor's grading system, nor make a factual determination of the fairness of the individual grades. Such an inquiry would necessarily entail the complete substitution of a court evaluation of a complainant's level of achievement in the subject under review, and the standard by which such achievement should be measured, for that of the professor. It would be difficult to prove by reason, logic or common sense that the federal judiciary is either competent, or more competent, to make such an assessment.[43]

Failure to attain an acceptable standard in academic studies, therefore, is a very different matter from misconduct. That is, if a public college dismisses a student for disciplinary reasons, the student is constitutionally entitled to some sort of institutional review of the dismissal decision and to a subsequent judicial review if he can show unfairness in the procedures used in reaching the decision. However, if the same student were dismissed for academic reasons, the public college would not be required to provide any kind of review of the academic judgment which led to the dismissal decision. Nonetheless, the courts' reluctance here

---

42. Id., at 160.

43. 353 F.Supp. 936, 940 (D.C.Tex. 1973).

does not completely rule out the possibility of judicial relief; but if relief is to occur, it imposes on the academically aggrieved student an extremely heavy burden of proving that his dismissal had been arbitrary, capricious, or in bad faith.

When the basis for dismissal is a student's failure to maintain satisfactory academic standing, therefore, it seems that no hearing is necessary, and mere notice of dismissal is sufficient. In other words, dismissal for poor scholarship does not appear to involve disputed facts that have to be adjudicated. In essence, this rationale was used by the Supreme Court in Board of Curators of the Univ. of Missouri v. Horowitz (1978):

> Academic evaluations of a student, in contrast to disciplinary determinations, bear little resemblance to the judicial and administrative fact finding proceedings to which we have traditionally attached a full hearing requirement. . . .
> The decision to dismiss respondent . . . rested on the academic judgment of school officials that she did not have the necessary clinical ability to perform adequately as a medical doctor . . .[44]

Hence, the Court declined to ignore the judgment of educators, refused to formalize the academic dismissal process by requiring a hearing, and declined to view the academic dismissal process as adversarial. (See the *Horowitz* case reported at end of chapter).

Thus the courts have repeatedly declared that they do not have the expertise and experience to judge the academic qualifications of a student and that interference by noneducational tribunals only diminishes the efficiency of instruction. The *Education Code* of California, for instance, recognizes this rationale by giving the community college teacher complete authority to grade students:

> When grades are given for any course of instruction taught in the public [community colleges] the grade given to each [student] shall be the grade determined by the teacher of the course, and the determination of the [student's] grade by the teacher, in the absence of mistake, fraud, bad faith, or incompetency, shall be final. (Section 10753)

Case law indicates, however, that if a student plagiarizes or cheats on an examination and is dismissed from a public institution for such misconduct, the proceedings resulting in the student's dismissal must be conducted in accordance with the re-

44. 430 U.S. 964 (1978).

quirements of due process of law.[45] Cheating, then, is considered more a behavioral problem than an academic one.

Drawing the line between behavioral and academic matters, therefore, can be tricky. Another illustration of just how elusive that border can be is found in Woody v. Burns.[46] The issue here was whether procedural protections are due before a student can be dismissed from a state university for failing to take a required course. It would seem that such action would be within a university's academic purview, but the court thought otherwise. After equating the student's failure to take the required course with misconduct, the court stated that "the principles of fair play require that before a student may be denied the right to continue his studies at a state-supported university due to misconduct he shall be advised of all the charges against him and be given a chance to refute same." [47]

Similarly, a public community college in Pennsylvania admitted a male student to its nursing program but later informed him that he must withdraw because he (1) failed to submit a medical examination, (2) failed to submit a transcript of courses taken at another nursing school, and (3) did not attend classes regularly after admission. The student filed suit in a federal district court claiming that reasonable explanations could have been made in rebuttal to all three charges but that he had not been given the opportunity for a due process hearing.

While the court observed that had the student been denied admission because of failure to meet admission requirements there would have been no basis for a hearing of the type required in suspension or expulsion cases, it noted that the student had been admitted and was interrupted from pursuing a course of study by the college's action. Under these circumstances, the court stated:

> Scholastic standards are not involved, but rather disputed facts concerning whether plaintiff [the student] did or did not comply with certain school regulations. These issues adapt themselves readily to determination by a fair and impartial "due process" hearing.[48]

45. See e. g., Anderson v. Regents of the Univ. of Cal., 22 Cal.App. 763, 99 Cal.Rptr. 531 (1972); McDonald v. Board of Trustees of the Univ. of Ill., 375 F.Supp. 95 (D.C.Ill. 1974); aff'd 503 F.2d 105 (1975); Roberts v. Knowlton, 377 F.Supp. 1381 (D.C.N.Y.1974); and Hill v. Trustees of Indiana Univ., 537 F.2d 248 (7th Cir. 1976).

46. 188 So.2d 56 (1966).

47. Id., at 58.

48. Brookins v. Bonnell, 362 F.Supp. 379, 383 (D.C.Pa.1973).

The *Woody* and *Brookins* decisions tend to exceed opinions of other courts in related matters; nonetheless, to date these seem to be the only precedents for handling this precise issue. Thus, while the fog factor rises, the significance to the conceptual line between disciplinary and academic matters lies in the fact that it can play a major part in the determination of a court's involvement in certain student dismissal cases.

The readmission of students formerly dismissed because of poor scholastic achievement, however, falls within the purview of the public college's academic expertise. In Wright v. Texas Southern Univ., for example, former students were denied readmission to the university on the basis that they were still scholastically ineligible. The Fifth Circuit Court of Appeals ruled that if the institution's scholastic requirements for readmission were uniformly applied, notice and hearing were not necessary.[49]

Admission of Guilt

It has been said that the maintenance of procedural due process for student offenders is substantially unnecessary because very few students deny the misconduct with which they are charged or take exception to the discipline imposed. Additionally, most students don't have the money, the inclination, nor the know-how to institute judicial action. Regardless of these claims, the college for obvious reasons should be wary of becoming complacent over simplistic solutions.

If an accused student facing a disciplinary sanction, however, admits his guilt and waives a hearing, as many students are inclined to do, and signs a written statement to that effect, the courts will not accept the case if the student later changes his mind unless the student can produce substantial evidence that he was forced or "tricked" into such an acknowledgment of guilt.

Exhaustion of Administrative Remedies

It is a long-settled rule of law that no one is entitled to judicial relief for a supposed or threatened injury until the prescribed administrative remedy has been exhausted.[50] As applied to student disciplinary proceedings in public colleges, a student must first appeal his case to the proper administrative authority. This may be the governing board of the college, the president, a hearing committee, or an administrative officer designated by the gov-

49. 392 F.2d 728, 729 (5th Cir. 1968).   50. Myers v. Bethlehem Shipbuilding
                                                 Corp., 303 U.S. 41 (1938).

erning board or president. There may be direct appeal to the courts, however, in the case of no administrative appeal available, or where irreparable damage might occur, or when the constitutional rights of a student have been violated by public officials such as board members or administrators in state-operated colleges.

In respect to the latter exception, that is, the exception to the general principle of exhaustion of institutional processes when the constitutional rights of a student have been abridged by a public institution, the United States District Court for the Western District of Missouri, *en banc,* had this to say:

> In an action at law or equity under § 1983, Title 42, U.S. C.A., the doctrine of exhaustion of state judicial remedies is not applicable. The fact that there is an existing state judicial remedy for the alleged wrong is no ground for stay or dismissal.[51]

The Civil Rights Act of 1871 (42 U.S.C.A. § 1983)

The Civil Rights Act of 1871, known as the Ku Klux Klan Act and found at Title 42 United States Code § 1983 and 28 U.S.C.A. § 1343(3), reads as follows:

> Every person who, under color of any statute, ordinance, regulation, custom, or usage, of any State or Territory, subjects, or causes to be subjected, any citizen of the United States or other persons within the jurisdiction thereof to the deprivation of any rights, privileges, or immunities secured by the Constitution and laws, shall be liable in an action of law, suit in equity, or other proper proceedings for redress.

Title 23 U.S.C.A. § 1343 grants to the federal courts, rather than the state courts, jurisdiction to hear causes of action which arise under § 1983, and state officers, agents, and representatives are, according to the U. S. Supreme Court, "persons" under this provision.[52]

After the Civil War the Reconstruction Congress passed a series of civil rights laws—the Civil Rights Acts of 1866, 1870, 1871 and 1875—designed to protect the constitutional and legal rights of the newly freed slaves. Yet, despite the specific purpose of these acts, they were cast in broad and general language and thus § 1983 provides a cause of action for every person (black or white) who is deprived of a constitutional or legal right by state

---

51. *General Order* . . ., 45 F. R.D. 133 at 143–44 (1968).

52. See Monroe v. Pape, 365 U.S. 167 (1961).

officials. Nevertheless, § 1983 was seldom used until the 1960's. In 1961, for instance, 296 cases based on § 1983 were filed in federal courts, but in 1973, 6,133 such cases were filed there which represented an increase of 1,972 percent.[53]

Justice Douglas, in delivering a Supreme Court majority opinion in 1961, looked back at the adoption of the Civil Rights Act of 1871. The Reconstruction law, he said, had several purposes: first, to override state laws calling openly for racial discrimination; second, to provide a remedy where state law was inadequate and third, "to provide a federal remedy where the state remedy, though adequate in theory, was not available in practice."[54]

Therefore, said the Court, state and federal laws can provide alternate routes to recovery for the same wrongful conduct; however, the injured party need not first ask for and be refused the state remedy before trying for the federal remedy. Furthermore, state officials must be sued in their individual capacities since it was determined that government entities were not "persons" for purpose of § 1983.[55]

Whether the plaintiff can recover money damages, however, depends not only on whether his constitutional rights have been violated by the state official he sues, but also on the scope of *immunity* accorded to the state official being sued. And in the context of § 1983 actions, the precise scope of official immunity has been a much contested issue. In fact, the doctrine of sovereign immunity renders a state immune from tort [56] when acting in a governmental capacity unless consent is expressly granted by statutory provisions permitting suit. Therefore, tort liability cannot be maintained against a state-supported institution of higher education in the absence of specific legislation allowing such. That is to say, since state colleges and universities are instrumentalities of the state, immunity is extended to them as governmental agencies. Thus if a suit is brought against a state, the courts will dismiss the suit on the basis of the Eleventh Amendment unless, again, the state has expressly waived its immunity from the particular kind of suit involved. (It should be noted here that at least six states—Arizona, California, Illinois,

---

53. Deborah Crandall, *The Personal Liability of Community College Officials* (Los Angeles: Eric Clearinghouse for Junior Colleges, UCLA, 1977), fn. 22.

54. Monroe v. Pape, 365 U.S. at 174.

55. Id., at 191–192.

56. In brief, a tort is a civil suit not involving a contract.

Indiana, New Jersey, and Wisconsin—have specifically waived the immunity of their state offices.)

The Eleventh Amendment provides that: "The judicial power of the United States shall not be construed to extend to any suit in law or equity, commenced or prosecuted against one State by citizens of another state, or by citizens or subjects of any foreign state." Yet even though this does not expressly bar suits in federal courts against a state by citizens of the state sued, it has been so interpreted. As a result, no state may be sued in a federal court without its consent by any private individual, and with this interpretation, in effect, ". . . judicially enacting the 11½ Amendment." [57]

Additionally, the courts have developed a "doctrine of official immunity" designed to shield public officials from any torts they might commit while performing their public duties. Although this doctrine originally barred all suits against public officials as long as any action on which liability was based was taken in the course and scope of the official's public duties, gradually various federal courts began to take varying stances on this protection. Some did not apply this standard at all. The Court of Appeals for the Third Circuit allowed absolute immunity to all public officials who performed discretionary acts [58] while the standard used by the Fifth Circuit was that of absolute immunity as long as the official was acting within the scope of his employment when he took the action involved.[59] But in direct contrast was the standard employed by the Eighth Circuit which allowed no immunity for any public official sued under Section 1983.[60]

Finally, in 1975 the United States Supreme Court brought some legal harmony to all of this, at least as far as public school officials are concerned, in its Wood v. Stricklin [61] decision.

The issue in this case began when some high school girls in Mena, Arkansas, were suspended from school for pouring a relatively small amount of beer into a relatively large amount of soda pop to be used as punch at a school function. The school regulation that the girls were found guilty of violating stated that possession by any student (or the serving of any) "intoxicating" bev-

57.   Hans v. Louisiana, 134 U.S. 1 (1890).

58.   Fidtler v. Rundle, 497 F.2d 794 (3rd Cir. 1974).

59.   Norton v. McShane, 332 F.2d 855 (5th Cir. 1964).

60.   Board of Trustees of Ark. A and M College v. Davis, 396 F.2d 730 (8th Cir. 1968).

61.   420 U.S. 308 (1975).

erages at the school function would be regarded as grounds for
suspension. The District Court and the Court of Appeals disagreed over whether the punch was really "intoxicating." Actually the school officials meant to ban "alcoholic" beverages from
the campus, but the Supreme Court, refusing to play a nitpicking
semantics' game, found nothing wrong with either the wording or
the regulation. It was when the school board exercised its judicial function—to judge whether its rule had been violated—that
it ran into trouble.

The problem was that the board voted to suspend the girls for
the remainder of the semester—a period of approximately three
months—but neither the girls nor their parents were in attendance
at the session. The board met a couple of weeks afterwards, and
at this meeting the girls, their parents and their legal counsel attended. At this point the girls asked the board to reduce the punishment, but the board voted not to rescind its earlier decision
and therein lay the heart of matter. The Supreme Court's majority (5–4) ruled that the board members should have known
that what they were doing was wrong. That is, it is a well-
settled standard of procedural due process that a quasi-judicial
body should not go into a hearing having already made up its
mind. And in terms of official immunity under 42 U.S.C.A.
§ 1983, the Court had this to say:

> The disagreement between the Court of Appeals and the Dis-
> trict Court over the immunity standard in this case has been
> put in terms of an "objective" versus a "subjective" test of
> good faith. As we see it, the appropriate standard neces-
> sarily contains elements of both. *The official must himself
> be acting sincerely and with belief that he is doing right, but
> an act violating a student's constitutional rights can be no
> more justified by ignorance or disregard of settled, indis-
> putable law on the part of one entrusted with supervision
> of student's daily lives than by the presence of actual malice.*
> To be entitled to a special exemption from the categorical
> remedial language of § 1983 in a case, in which his action
> violated a student's constitutional rights, a school board
> member, who has voluntarily undertaken the task of super-
> vising the operation of the school and the activities of the
> students, must be held to a standard of conduct based not
> only on permissible intention, but also *on knowledge of the
> basic, unquestioned constitutional rights of his charges.*
> Such a standard neither imposes an unfair burden upon a
> person assuming a responsible public office requiring a high

degree of intelligence and judgement for the proper fulfillment of its duties, not an unwarranted burden in light of
the value which civil rights have in our legal system. Any
lesser standard would deny much of the promise of § 1983.
Therefore, in the specific context of school discipline, we hold
that a school board member is not immune from liability for
damages under § 1983 *if he knew or reasonably should have
known that the action he took within his sphere of official
responsibility would violate the constitutional rights of the
students affected,* or if he took the action with the malicious
intention to cause a deprivation of constitutional rights or
other injury to the student. That is not to say that school
board members are "charged with predicting the future
course of constitutional law." A compensatory award will
be appropriate only if the school board member has acted
with an impermissible motivation or with such *disregard of
the student's clearly established constitutional rights that
his action cannot reasonably be characterized as being in
good faith.*[62]

Thus, after *Wood,* official immunity means that public college
officials are protected against personal liability under § 1983
only when they have no "constructive knowledge"[63] that they
are violating the constitutional rights of another person. Therefore, it is clear that trustees and administrators of public colleges and universities can suffer personal liability for any action which denies a student, faculty member, or any other person
the rights and liberties guaranteed by the Constitution.

It is important to note, however, that the *Wood* decision does
not charge public school officials with "predicting the future
course of constitutional law." Thus if the particular right involved was not undisputed at the time the official action was
taken, there can be no liability under § 1983, even if that right
became undisputed before the trial took place. The fact of the
matter is that constitutional law is constantly changing and evolving so that it is sometimes impossible even for constitutional
scholars to identify areas of "settled, indisputable law" or "unquestioned constitutional rights." Moreover, the Supreme Court
in the *Wood* decision relied upon its own recently established
standard of "good faith" announced in Scheuer v. Rhodes (1974)[64]

---

62. Id., at 321–323 (emphasis added).

63. "Constructive Knowledge" is a
legal concept charging a person
with knowledge he did not have on
the theory that he should have had
it.

64. 416 U.S. 232 (1974).

as the appropriate standard to be applied to public school officials. The *Scheuer* case involved the suit brought against the Governor of Ohio and the President of Kent State University by the parents of the three students killed by national guardsmen in the Kent State incident. Here the Supreme Court ruled that state executive officers were immune from § 1983 suits, if, in the light of the discretion and responsibilities of their offices, and under all of the circumstances as they appeared at the time, the officers had acted reasonably and in good faith.

Yet there has been criticism of the *Wood* decision. In fact the decision itself was far from unanimous; of the nine Supreme Court Justices, four thought it was wrong. The dissenting opinion of Justice Powell, joined by Chief Justice Burger and Justices Blackmun and Rehnquist, claimed that the majority opinion imposed a higher standard of personal responsibility upon public school officials than that previously required of any other public officials:

> The holding of the Court . . . would impose personal liability on a school official who acted sincerely and in the utmost good faith, but who was found—after the fact—to have acted in "ignorance . . . of settled, indisputable law." Or, as the Court also puts it, the school official must be held to a standard of conduct based not only on good faith "but also on knowledge of the basic, unquestioned constitutional rights of his charges." Moreover, ignorance of the law is explicitly equated with "actual malice." This harsh standard, requiring knowledge of what is characterized as "settled, indisputable law," leaves little substance to the doctrine of qualified immunity. The Court's decision appears to rest on an unwarranted assumption as to what lay school officials know or can know about the law and constitutional rights. These officials will now act at the peril of some judge or jury subsequently finding that a good-faith belief as to the applicable law was mistaken and hence actionable.

The Court states the standard of required knowledge in two cryptic phrases: "settled, indisputable law" and "unquestioned constitutional rights." Presumably these are intended to mean the same thing, although the meaning of neither phrase is likely to be self-evident to constitutional law scholars—much less the average school board members.[65]

65. *Wood*, 420 U.S. at 327–329.

Despite such criticism, the *Wood* standard will probably prove to be beneficial for public education officials. In fact, precisely because there are so few areas of "settled, indisputed law" and so few "unquestioned constitutional rights," it would seem that this standard will shield school officials from liability more often than it will impose it.

Tailoring the Procedure

In determining the requirements of procedural due process for students in public colleges, a number of applicable principles should be borne in mind, particularly since student procedural rights in misconduct cases vary and are not the same as required for persons in criminal proceedings. As said in Esteban v. Central Missouri State College:

> By judicial mandate to impose upon the academic community in student discipline the intricate, time consuming, sophisticated procedures, rules, and safeguards of criminal law would frustrate the teaching process and render the institutional control impotent.[66]

Therefore, procedures for dismissing college students are not completely analogous to criminal proceedings, and it appears that they could not be so without at the same time being both impractical and detrimental to the control and function of a college.

In Perlman v. Shasta Joint Junior College Dist. Bd. of Trustees, the Court stated:

> . . . that except for expulsion proceeding (expulsion means that the student may never again attend the college) the rule appears to be that each disciplinary hearing is *sui generis* of its own kind, and if under all the circumstances the student was given a fair hearing and opportunity to meet any charges brought against him, the courts will not interfere.[67]

Therefore, the concept of procedural due process is not a frozen thing. It does not refer to a single, fixed style of procedure. The general observation of the *Perlman* Court is that the quality of the procedure must be directly proportioned to the gravity of the harm which may befall the student whose guilt is ascertained pursuant to that procedure. Put more directly, the degree of procedural due process is a function of the seriousness of the offense and the complexity of the issues to be determined. As a result

66. 290 F.Supp. 622, 629 (D.C.Mo. 1968).   67. 9 Cal.App.3d 873, 880, 88 Cal. Rptr. 563, 568 (1970).

of the application of this principle, there is a judicially allowable scaling down from higher procedural safeguards required in student expulsion cases to lower requirements in proceedings involving lighter sanctions.

Intuitively, one can conclude that it would be absurd to afford a student accused of making noise in the library the procedural guarantees required in expulsion cases. Again, as Fisher points out, procedural safeguards should be "tailored" to fit the seriousness of the alleged misconduct and the severity of the sanctions available under the circumstances.[68]

> A scaling down of the procedure . . . . to fit the lower procedure requirements of less aggravated offenses (and lighter sanctions) is what is meant by due process.[69]

In French v. Bashful, the Court indicated

> We are also of the opinion . . . that disciplinary proceedings which do not involve expulsion or suspension, but which only deal with lesser penalties such as the loss of social privileges, do not have to be protected by the same procedural safeguards which are necessary in expulsion or suspension proceedings.[70]

In deciding cases on the basis of the "tailoring" concept, the Supreme Court finally had to answer some difficult questions: Are *all* students charged with misconduct entitled to some kind of procedural protections? Could these governmental units provide fewer procedural protections to students receiving short-term suspensions, say ten days, than those meted out long-term suspensions of one semester or more? At what point does a student have a right to due process? Does due process require notice and a hearing only when a major disciplinary matter is involved? Compounding the problem here was not only the status of somewhat mixed lower court rulings, but also the position of the United States District Court for the Western District of Missouri sitting *en banc*, which, taken as a whole is probably the most significant and comprehensive statement made by any court regarding the relationship between the courts and student disciplinary matters in public education. In regards to the "tailoring" guidelines, the District Court's statement was that only "In severe cases of student discipline for alleged misconduct, such as

68. Thomas C. Fischer, *Due Process in the Student-Institutional Relationship* (Washington, D.C.: AAS CU, 1970), p. 12.

69. Id.

70. 303 F.Supp. 1333 (D.C.La.1969).

final expulsion, indefinite or long-term suspension, dismissal with deferred leave to reapply, is the institution . . . obligated to give to the student minimal procedural requirements of due process of law.[71]

Most educators tend to dislike students charged with misconduct. Most of us are inclined to think that a student accused of some dereliction must be guilty. In fact most of us probably look upon procedural protections, especially in short-term suspensions, as a pain in the middle backside. But in its 1975 Goss v. Lopez decision, the Supreme Court didn't think so:

> The prospect of imposing elaborate hearing requirements in every suspension case is viewed with great concern, and many school authorities may well prefer the untrammeled power to act unilaterally, unhampered by rules about notice and hearing. But it would be a strange disciplinary system in an educational institution if no communication was sought by the disciplinarian with the student in an effort to inform him of his dereliction and to let him tell his side of the story . . . .

> Students facing temporary suspension have interests qualifying for protection of the Due Process Clause, and *due process requires, in connection with a suspension of 10 days or less,* that the student be given oral or written notice of the charges against him, and if he denies them, an explanation of the evidence the authorities have and an opportunity to present his side of the story.[72]

The Court then went on to rule that in short-term suspensions (probably one or two days) that

> *There need be no delay between the time "notice" is given and the time of the hearing.* In the great majority of cases the disciplinarian may informally discuss the alleged misconduct with the student minutes after it has occurred. We hold only that, in being given an opportunity to explain his version of the facts at the discussion, the student first be told what he is accused of doing and what the basis of the accusation is.[73]

In brief, then, for suspension of only a few days, the college may convene an informal conference at which the student meets

---

71. *General Order* . . . ., 45 F.
R.D. 133, 147 (1968).

72. 419 U.S. 565, 580–81 (1975) (emphasis added).

73. Id., at 582 (emphasis added).

with a college official to discuss the reasons for the suspension, but most importantly, the student must be allowed to present his side of the issue. And at an even lower level of required protection, student conduct cases involving sanctions less severe such as verbal reprimand and loss of some social privilege, would in almost all circumstances be regarded by the courts as an extension of the college's teaching-guidance function and the injury *de minimus* (insufficient); the outcome, accordingly, would be judicially non-reviewable. With the above exceptions, the courts will hold that the student is entitled to procedural protections of a more formal nature, especially in any college disciplinary proceeding involving expulsion and suspension for such a period of time that the student's educational career is substantially affected.

Interim Suspension

At this point it is important to note that there may be emergency circumstances where it appears advisable to suspend a student temporarily before a hearing can be held. There is authority for such action required by reason of the physical or emotional safety of the student, or the safety or well being of other students, faculty, other college personnel, or college property.[74] A preliminary hearing must be held, however, if reasonably possible. In the words of the *Stricklin* Court, "An interim suspension may not be imposed without a prior preliminary hearing, unless it can be shown that it is impossible or unreasonably difficult to accord it prior to an interim suspension.[75] And if an interim suspension is warranted without a prior preliminary hearing, the college must simultaneously or within a few days provide the student with notice and shortly thereafter a hearing where he can perhaps show that he was wrongly accused or that suspension was not justified.[76]

The fleshing out of due process takes time, but eventually the Supreme Court was confronted with this issue in Goss v. Lopez (1975) and offered the following clarification:

> We agree . . . however, that there are recurring situations in which prior notice and hearing cannot be insisted upon. Students whose presence poses a continuing danger to persons or property or an ongoing threat of disrupting the

---

74. See, e. g., Marzette v. McPhee, 294 F.Supp. 562 (D.C.Wis.1968); Stricklin v. Regents of Univ. Wis., 297 F.Supp. 416 (D.C.Wis.1969); Gardenhire v. Chalmers, 326 F. Supp. 1200 (D.C.Kan.1971); Goss v. Lopez, 419 U.S. 565 (1975).

75. *Stricklin*, 297 F.Supp. at 420.

76. *Gardenhire*, 326 F.Supp. at 1205.

academic process may be immediately removed from school. In such cases, the necessary notice and . . . hearing should follow as soon as practicable . . . [77].

CONCLUDING OBSERVATIONS

The landmark case of Dixon v. Alabama State Bd. of Educ. (1961) marks the historic turning-point toward closer judicial attention to the constitutional rights of public college students. No rigid procedural steps were required by the court, but broad guidelines were established requiring notice and a hearing, and since *Dixon*, those guidelines have been added to and refined by other courts.

Thus far the courts have generally *not* required procedural protections for disciplinary action involving academic matters. Yet, as we have observed, on occasion there seems to be no clear distinction between judicially mandated due process requirements for "disciplinary" and "academic" dismissals. There is an old but wise maxim that "nothing is settled until it is settled right." In the United States legal system, more often than not, the ultimate responsibility of such resolution lies with the Supreme Court. Accordingly, as a means of ascertaining the current status of due process in academic affairs, the basic text of the Supreme Court's *Horowitz* decision follows.

BOARD OF CURATORS OF THE UNIVERSITY OF MISSOURI v. HOROWITZ

Supreme Court of the United States, 1978.
430 U.S. 964.

Mr. Justice REHNQUIST delivered the opinion of the Court.

Respondent, a student at the University of Missouri-Kansas City Medical School, was dismissed by petitioner officials of the School during her final year of study for failure to meet academic standards. Respondent sued petitioners under 42 U.S.C.A. § 1983 in the United States District Court for the Western District of Missouri alleging, amongst other constitutional violations, that petitioners had not accorded her procedural due process prior to her dismissal. The District Court, after conducting a full trial, concluded that respondent had been afforded all of the rights guaranteed her by the Fourteenth Amendment to the United States Constitution and dismissed her complaint. The Court of

---

77. 419 U.S. at 582–83.

Appeals for the Eighth Circuit reversed, 538 F.2d 1317 (1976), and a petition for rehearing en banc was denied by a divided Court. 542 F.2d 1335. We granted certiorari, 430 U.S. 964, to consider what procedures must be accorded to a student at a state educational institution whose dismissal may constitute a deprivation of "liberty" or "property" within the meaning of the Fourteenth Amendment. We reverse the judgment of the Court of Appeals.

I

Respondent was admitted with advanced standing to the Medical School in the fall of 1971. During the final years of a student's education at the School, the student is required to pursue in "rotational units" academic and clinical studies pertaining to various medical disciplines such as Obstetrics-Gynecology, Pediatrics, and Surgery. Each student's academic performance at the School is evaluated on a periodic basis by the Council on Evaluation, a body composed of both faculty and students, which can recommend various actions including probation and dismissal. The recommendations of the Council are reviewed by the Coordinating Committee, a body composed solely of faculty members, and must ultimately be approved by the Dean. Students are not typically allowed to appear before either the Council or the Coordinating Committee on the occasion of their review of the student's academic performance.

In the spring of respondent's first year of study, several faculty members expressed dissatisfaction with her clinical performance during a pediatrics rotation. The faculty members noted that respondent's "performance was below that of her peers in all clinical patient-oriented settings," that she was erratic in her attendance at clinical sessions, and that she lacked a critical concern for personal hygiene. Upon the recommendation of the Council on Evaluation, respondent was advanced to her second and final year on a probationary basis.

Faculty dissatisfaction with respondent's clinical performance continued during the following year. For example, respondent's docent, or faculty adviser, rated her clinical skills as "unsatisfactory." In the middle of the year, the Council again reviewed respondent's academic progress and concluded that respondent should not be considered for graduation in June of that year; furthermore, the Council recommended that, absent "radical improvement," respondent be dropped from the School.

Respondent was permitted to take a set of oral and practical examinations as an "appeal" of the decision not to permit her to graduate. Pursuant to this "appeal," respondent spent a substantial portion of time with seven practicing physicians in the area who enjoyed a good reputation among their peers. The physicians were asked to recommend whether respondent should be allowed to graduate on schedule and, if not, whether she should be dropped immediately or allowed to remain on probation. Only two of the doctors recommended that respondent be graduated on schedule. Of the other five, two recommended that she be immediately dropped from the school. The remaining three recommended that she not be allowed to graduate in May and be continued on probation pending further reports on her clinical progress. Upon receipt of these recommendations, the Council on Evaluation reaffirmed its prior position.

The Council met again in mid-May to consider whether respondent should be allowed to remain in school beyond June of that year. Noting that the report on respondent's recent surgery rotation rated her performance as "low-satisfactory," the Council unanimously recommended that "barring receipt of any reports that Miss Horowitz has improved radically, [she] not be allowed to re-enroll in the . . . School of Medicine." The Council delayed making its recommendation official until receiving reports on other rotations; when a report on respondent's emergency rotation also turned out to be negative, the Council unanimously reaffirmed its recommendation that respondent be dropped from the School. The Coordinating Committee and the Dean approved the recommendation and notified respondent, who appealed the decision in writing to the University's Provost for Health Sciences. The Provost sustained the School's actions after reviewing the record compiled during the earlier proceedings.

II

A

To be entitled to the procedural protections of the Fourteenth Amendment, respondent must in a case such as this demonstrate that her dismissal from the School deprived her of either a "liberty" or a "property" interest. Respondent has never alleged that she was deprived of a property interest. Because property interests are creatures of state law . . . respondent would have been required to show at trial that her seat at the Medical School was a "property" interest recognized by Missouri state law. Instead, respondent argued that her dismissal deprived her of "liberty" by substantially impairing her opportunities to continue her medical education or to return to employment in a medically related field.

The Court of Appeals agreed, citing this Court's opinion in Board of Regents v. Roth, 408 U.S. 564 (1972). In that case, we held that the State had not deprived a teacher of any liberty or property interest in dismissing the teacher from a nontenured position, but noted that

> ".   .   . there is no suggestion that the State, in declining to re-employ the respondent, imposed on him a stigma or other disability that foreclosed his freedom to take advantage of other employment opportunities. The State, for example, did not invoke any regulations to bar the respondent from all other public employment in state universities."

We have recently had an opportunity to elaborate upon the circumstances under which an employment termination might infringe a protected liberty interest. In Bishop v. Wood, 426 U.S. 341, we upheld the dismissal of a policeman without a hearing; we rejected the theory that the mere fact of dismissal, absent some publication of the reasons for the action, could amount to a stigma infringing one's liberty:

> "In Board of Regents v. Roth, 408 U.S. 564, we recognized that the nonretention of an untenured college teacher might make him somewhat less attractive to other employers, but nevertheless concluded that it would stretch the concept too far 'to suggest that a person is deprived of "liberty" when he simply is not rehired in one position but remains as free as before to seek another.' This same conclusion applies to the discharge of a public employee whose position is terminable at the will of the employer when there is no public disclosure of the reasons for the discharge.
>
> "In this case the asserted reasons for the City Manager's decision were communicated orally to the petitioner in private and also were stated in writing in answer to interrogatories after this litigation commenced. Since the former communication was not made public, it cannot properly form the basis for a claim that petitioner's interest in his 'good name, honor, or integrity' was thereby impaired."

The opinion of the Court of Appeals, decided only two weeks after we issued our opinion in *Bishop,* does not discuss whether a state university infringes a liberty interest when it dismisses a student without publicizing allegations harmful to the student's reputation. Three judges of the Court of Appeals for the Eighth Circuit dissented from the denial of rehearing en banc on the ground that "the reasons for Horowitz's dismissal were not released to the public but were communicated to her directly by school officials." Citing *Bishop,* the judges concluded that "[a]bsent such public disclosure, there is no deprivation of a liberty." Petitioners urge us to adopt the view of these judges and hold that respondent has not been deprived of a liberty interest.

B

We need not decide, however, whether respondent's dismissal deprived her of a liberty interest in pursuing a medical career. Nor need we decide whether respondent's dismissal infringed any other interest constitutionally protected against deprivation without procedural due process. Assuming the existence of a liberty or property interest, respondent has been awarded at least as much due process as the Fourteenth Amendment requires. The School fully informed respondent of the faculty's dissatisfaction with her clinical progress and the danger that this posed to timely graduation and continued enrollment. The ultimate decision to dismiss respondent was careful and deliberate. These procedures were sufficient under the Due Process Clause of the Fourteenth Amendment. We agree with the District Court that respondent

"was afforded full procedural due process by the [school]. In fact, the Court is of the opinion, and so finds, that the school went beyond [constitutionally required] procedural due process by affording [respondent] the opportunity to be examined by seven independent physicians in order to be absolutely certain that their grading of the [respondent] in her medical skills was correct."

In Goss v. Lopez, 419 U.S. 565 (1975), we held that due process requires, in connection with the suspension of a student from public school for disciplinary reasons, "that the student be given oral or written notice of the charges against him and, if he denies them, an explanation of the evidence the authorities have and an opportunity to present his side of the story." The Court of Appeals apparently read *Goss* as requiring some type of formal hearing at which respondent could defend her academic ability and performance. All that *Goss* required was an "informal give-and-take" between the student and the administrative body dismissing him that would, at least, give the student "the opportunity to characterize his conduct and put it in what he deems the proper context." But we have frequently emphasized that "[t]he very nature of due process negates any concept of inflexible procedures universally applicable to every imaginable situation." Cafeteria Workers v. McElroy, 367 U.S. 886, 895 (1961). The need for flexibility is well illustrated by the significant difference between the failure of a student to meet academic standards and the violation by a student of valid rules of conduct. This difference calls for far less stringent procedural requirements in the case of an academic dismissal.

Since the issue first arose 50 years ago, state and lower federal courts have recognized that there are distinct differences between decisions to suspend or dismiss a student for disciplinary purposes and similar actions taken for academic reasons which may call for hearings in connection with the former but not the latter. Thus, in Barnard v. Inhabitants of Shelburne, 216 Mass. 19, 102 N.E. 1095 (1913), the Supreme Judicial Court of Massachusetts rejected an argument, based on several earlier decisions requiring a hearing in disciplinary contexts, that school officials must also grant a hearing before excluding a student on academic grounds. According to the court, disciplinary cases have

> "no application. . . . Misconduct is a very different matter from failure to attain a standard of excellence in studies. A determination as to the fact involves investigation of a quite different kind. A public hearing may be regarded as helpful to the ascertainment of misconduct and useless or harmful in finding out the truth as to scholarship."

A similar conclusion has been reached by the other state courts to consider the issue. See, e. g., Mustell v. Rose, 282 Ala. 358, 367, 211 So.2d 489, 498 (1968), cert. denied, 393 U.S. 936 (1968); cf. Foley v. Benedict, 122 Tex. 193, 55 S.W.2d 805 (1932). Indeed, until the instant decision by the Court of Appeals for the Eighth Circuit, the Courts of Appeals were also unanimous in concluding that dismissals for academic (as opposed to disciplinary) cause do not necessitate a hearing before the school's decisionmaking body. See Mahavongsanan v. Hall, 529 F.2d 448 (CA5 1976); Gaspar v. Bruton, 513 F.2d 843 (CA10 1975). These prior decisions of state and federal courts, over a period of 60 years, unanimously holding that formal hearings before decisionmaking bodies need not be held in the case of academic dismissals, cannot be rejected lightly . . .

Reason, furthermore, clearly supports the perception of these decisions. A school is an academic institution, not a courtroom or administrative hearing room. In *Goss,* this Court felt that suspensions of students for disciplinary reasons have a sufficient resemblance to traditional judicial and administrative factfinding to call for a "hearing" before the relevant school authority. While recognizing that school authorities must be afforded the necessary tools to maintain discipline, the Court concluded that

> "it would be a strange disciplinary system in an educational institution if no communication was sought by the disciplinarian with the student in an effort to inform him of his dereliction and to let him tell his side of the story in order to make sure that an injustice is not done. . . .
>
> [R]equiring effective notice and informal hearing permitting the student to give his version of the events will provide a meaningful hedge against erroneous action. At least the disciplinarian will be alerted to the existence of disputes about facts and arguments about cause and effect." 419 U.S. 565, 580, 583–584.

Even in the context of a school disciplinary proceeding, however, the Court stopped short of requiring a *formal* hearing since "further formalizing the suspension process and escalating its formality and adversary nature may not only make it too costly as a regular disciplinary tool but also destroy its effectiveness as a part of the teaching process."

Academic evaluations of a student, in contrast to disciplinary determinations, bear little resemblance to the judicial and administrative fact-finding proceedings to which we have traditionally attached a full hearing requirement. In *Goss,* the school's decision to suspend the students rested on factual conclusions that the individual students had participated in demonstrations that had disrupted classes, attacked a police officer, or caused physical damage to school property. The requirement of a hearing, where the student could present his side of the factual issue, could under such circumstances "provide a meaningful hedge against erroneous action." The decision to dismiss respondent, by comparison, rested on the academic judgment of school officials that she did not have the necessary clinical ability to perform adequately as a medical doctor and was making insufficient progress toward that goal. Such a judgment is by its nature more subjective and evaluative than the typical factual questions presented in the average disciplinary decision. Like the decision of an individual professor as to the proper grade for a student in his course, the determination whether to dismiss a student for academic reasons requires an expert evaluation of cumulative information and is not readily adapted to the procedural tools of judicial or administrative decisionmaking.

Under such circumstances, we decline to ignore the historic judgment of educators and thereby formalize the academic dismissal process by requiring a hearing. The educational process is not by nature adversarial; instead it centers around a continuing relationship between faculty and students, "one in which the teacher must occupy many roles—educator, adviser, friend, and at times, parent-substitute." Goss v. Lopez, 419 U.S. 565, 594 (1975) (Powell, J., dissenting). This is especially true as one advances through the varying regimes of the educational system, and the instruction becomes both more individualized and more specialized. In Goss, this Court concluded that the value of some form of hearing in a disciplinary context outweighs any resulting harm to the academic environment. Influencing this conclusion was clearly the belief that disciplinary proceedings, in which the teacher must decide whether to punish a student for disruptive or insubordinate behavior, may automatically bring an adversarial flavor to the normal student-teacher relationship. The same conclusion does not follow in the academic context. We decline to further enlarge the judicial presence in the academic community and thereby risk deterioration of many beneficial aspects of the faculty-student relationship. We recognize, as did the Massachusetts Supreme Judicial Court over 60 years ago, that a hearing may be "useless or even harmful in finding out the truth as to scholarship." Barnard v. Inhabitants of Shelburne, supra.

"Judicial interposition in the operation of the public school system of the Nation raises problems requiring care and restraint. . . . By and large, public education in our Nation is committed to the control of state and local authorities." Epperson v. Arkansas, 393 U.S. 97, 104 (1968). We see no reason to intrude on that historic control in this case.

III

In reversing the District Court on procedural due process grounds, the Court of Appeals expressly failed to "reach the substantive due process ground advanced by Horowitz." 538 F.2d 1317, 1321 n. 5. Respondent urges that we remand the cause to the Court of Appeals for consideration of this additional claim. In this regard, a number of lower courts have implied in dictum that academic dismissals from state institutions can be enjoined if "shown to be clearly arbitrary or capricious." Mahavongsanan

v. Hall, supra, 529 F.2d, at 449. See Gaspar v. Bruton, supra, 513 F.2d, at 850, and citations therein. Even assuming that the courts can review under such a standard an academic decision of a public educational institution, we agree with the District Court that no showing of arbitrariness or capriciousness has been made in this case. Courts are particularly ill-equipped to evaluate academic performance. The factors discussed in Part II with respect to procedural due process speak *a fortiori* here and warn against any such judicial intrusion into academic decisionmaking.

The judgment of the Court of Appeals is therefore reversed.

Chapter 4

THE SPECIFICS OF PROCEDURAL DUE PROCESS

It is not without significance that most of the provisions of the Bill of Rights are procedural. It is procedure that spells much of the difference between rule by law and rule by whim or caprice. Steadfast adherence to strict procedural safe-guards is our main assurance that there will be equal justice under the law.

(Justice Douglas concurring in Joint Anti-Fascist Refugee Committee v. McGrath, 341 U.S. 123, 179 (1951)).

GENERAL CONSIDERATIONS

Fleshing Out the Dixon Precedent

Once *Dixon* established the precedent that students dismissed from public colleges and universities for disciplinary reasons must first be given at least the rudiments of due process protection, subsequent cases somewhat filled out the *"Dixon* Doctrine" by specifying what processes would be required to meet procedural standards and what kind of substantive regulations could be enacted by the schools. Though some courts have gone further than others, the general guidelines which have emerged from these cases are that the student should receive adequate notice, be advised of the specific charges against him, and be given the opportunity of a fair hearing at which he can present his side of the case. Constitutional requirements for college regulations indicate that these rules must be neither overly broad in limiting student freedom nor overly vague in prescribing student conduct.

While it is nearly impossible, however, to predict unerringly what any given court will decide in any given fact situation, it is still possible to trace the trends of recent decisions and to anticipate the "due process" or "rudiments of an adversary proceeding" requirements that will likely be imposed on public college administrators disciplining students for misconduct. But these findings, of course, are only general guidelines and must be carefully circumscribed by an awareness of the continually evolving character of "due process" itself and the particular facts of each instant case.

A Comparison with Criminal Jurisprudence

This writer's examination, nevertheless, indicates that the "rudiments of an adversary proceeding" in *criminal jurisprudence* is almost universally regarded as requiring (1) adequate notice; (2) a fair tribunal and impartial hearing; (3) representation by legal counsel; (4) confrontation and cross-examination of witnesses; (5) a decision based upon adequate evidence; (6) privilege against compulsory self-incrimination; and (7) a right of appeal from the original determination.[1]

In the following "adversary proceeding" analysis, then, an attempt is made to ascertain which of the basic criminal law standards might be applied to the administrative law regarding the public college student disciplinary context.

"THE RUDIMENTS OF AN ADVERSARY PROCEEDING"

The Right to an Adequate Notice

Although the courts have not been of one mind regarding the precise "notification" procedure which constitutionally must be followed before an expulsion or suspension may be imposed upon a student, an increasing number have recognized the 1961 *Dixon* ruling:

> For the guidance of the parties in the event of further proceedings, we state our views on the nature of the notice . . . required by due process . . . The notice should contain a statement of the specific charges and grounds . . . the student should be given the names of the witnesses against him and an oral or written report on the facts to which each witness testifies.[2]

These *Dixon* guidelines have been subsequently cited by almost every major student due process case decision. Nevertheless, adequate notice is an issue for case by case determination in view of the circumstances, and, as a result of somewhat different circumstances, later cases have gone some distance in refining, clarifying, and extending these criteria.

At this point it is once again important to note the application of the "tailoring" concept in terms of a graduated scale of constitutional notification requirements. Whereas the *Dixon* requirements involved expulsion cases, the Federal District Court

---

1. See, e. g., Osmond K. Fraenkel, *The Supreme Court and Civil Liberties* (Dobbs Ferry: N.Y.: Occana Pub., Inc. (1963).

2. Dixon v. Alabama State Bd. of Educ., 294 F.2d 150, 158–59 (5th Cir. 1961), cert. denied 368 U.S. 930 (1961).

for the Western District of Missouri, *en banc* (all judges sitting), extended these same requirements to sanctions involving "indefinite or long-term suspension," [3] and the *Perlman* Court held that the student is entitled to reasonable notice in "any college disciplinary proceeding."[4] The following highly informal notice was ruled adequate in the *Perlman* case since the student only received a three day suspension:

> . . . where the dean discussed with the student his refusal to comply with the dean's instructions and told the student to report to the president's office an hour later for a disciplinary interview, it would be absurd to require the dean to write a formal notice to the student to appear and to set forth what the student already knew was his claimed offense.[5]

However, the Court, in turn, issued an interesting caveat:

> . . . the differing rules of fair play encompassed by the concept of due process vary according to specific factual concepts and different types of proceedings. It could very well be that where charges of infractions of college rules are more than one or require the presence of witnesses a more formal notice . . . would be required than was the situation here . . . [6]

Adequate notice is a variation of the previously presented problem of rule promulgation, but constitutionally required notification requirements are considerably greater. Obviously, a hearing would be useless if a student had no idea of what accusations he was supposed to be defending himself against. That is, if a college dean, for instance, sent a letter to a student charging him with "violating college rules," and "serious misconduct," without specifically defining what those charges meant the student would have insufficient opportunity prior to the hearing to examine the charges, prepare a defense and gather evidence and witnesses. That, according to the "fair play" concept of due process, would constitute inadequate notice.

The "fair play" principle here is that before a student can be punished, he has the right to know the specific acts he is charged

---

3. *General Order on Standards of Judicial Procedure* . . ., 45 F.R.D. 133, 147 (1968).

4. Perlman v. Shasta Joint Junior College Dist. Bd. of Trustees, 9 Cal.App.3d 873, 879, 88 Cal.Rptr.

563, 567 (1970); see also Goss v. Lopez, 419 U.S. 565 (1975).

5. Id., at 881.

6. Id., at 880.

with committing. Accordingly, there is authority since the *Dixon* decision that a notice of charges which is not sufficiently specific invalidates a disciplinary proceeding. In fact, a number of courts have ruled that in college/student disciplinary cases involving severe sanctions, the charges must be both specific and clear enough to allow accused students a reasonable opportunity to prepare a defense.[7] But probably the best description of this requirement was provided in a secondary school context. Here a Federal District Court in Washington, D. C. required, among other things, that the notice state specific, clear and full reasons for the proposed action, including the specifications of the alleged act upon which the disciplinary action is to be based and the reference to regulation subsection under which such action is proposed.[8]

The courts also have delved into the question of how much time must be afforded between the receipt of the charges by the student and the date of hearing. In the *Jones* [9] case it was two days, and in the *Esteban* [10] case ten days. In general, depending upon both the complexity and seriousness (tailoring) of the case, the courts are requiring notice sufficiently prior to the hearing to provide the accused student adequate time for preparation.

An interesting aspect of notice occurred in Wright v. Texas Southern Univ. where the Court ruled that a student could not frustrate the constitutionally required notice process by failure to keep the institution informed of change of address and by subsequent failure to actually receive the notice. This decision stated that "nothing more is required of college officials than that their best efforts be employed to give written notice." [11]

---

7. See, e. g. Scott v. Alabama State Bd. of Educ., 300 F.Supp. 163 (D.C.Ala.1969); Scoggin v. Lincoln Univ., 291 F.Supp. 161 (D.C.Mo. 1968).

8. Mills v. Board of Educ. of the Dist. of Columbia, 348 F.Supp. 866, 880 (D.C.D.C.1972). See also Gonzales v. McEuen, 435 F.Supp. 460, 465 (D.C.Cal.1977) where the court held that in expulsion cases a student must also be notified of his basic rights before the hearing body: "It is not 'fair' if the student does not know, and is not told, that he has certain rights which he may exercise at the proceedings."

9. Jones v. State Bd. of Educ., 279 F.Supp. 191 (D.C.Tenn.1968).

10. Esteban v. Central Missouri State College, 290 F.Supp. 630 (D.C. Mo.1968).

11. 392 F.2d 728, 731 (5th Cir. 1968).

In brief, constitutionally required "notice" can be defined as
. . . reasonably calculated, under all the circumstances,
to apprise interested parties of the pendency of the action
and afford them an opportunity to present their objection.[12]

More specifically, Thomas C. Fisher of the Georgetown University Law Center has indicated that procedural due process requirements of notice require that the accused student receive

(1) . . . adequate (5–10 days) (prior) *written* notice
of the charges against him, the section of the code upon
which the charges are based, and the sanctions which may
be applied if the charges are proven; (2) . . . written
notice of the date, time, and place of the hearing (this should
accompany the charges); (3) . . . the names of the
witnesses who will appear against him and the substance of
their testimony.[13]

The Right to a Fair Tribunal and Impartial Hearing

The *Dixon* Court said, in substance, that the student should
have reasonable notice and a fair hearing and that the nature of
the hearing could vary, depending upon the circumstances of the
case. The Court then proceeded to outline those fundamentals:

By its nature, a charge of misconduct . . . depends
upon a collection of the facts concerning the charged misconduct easily colored by the point of view of the witnesses.
In such circumstances, a hearing which gives the Board, or
the administrative authorities of the college an opportunity
to hear both sides in considerable detail is best suited to
protect the rights of all involved. This is not to imply that
a full-dress judicial hearing, with the right to cross-examine
witnesses, is required. Such a hearing, with the attending
publicity and disturbance of college activities might be detrimental to the college's educational atmosphere and impractical to carry out. Nevertheless, the rudiments of an adversary proceeding may be preserved without encroaching upon
the interest of the college.[14]

The *Dixon* decision made no mention of requirements regarding the composition of the hearing tribunal. In regard to the

12. Mullane v. Central Hanover
Bank and Trust Company, 339 U.S.
306, 314 (1950).

13. Thomas C. Fischer, *Due Process
in the Student-Institutional Rela-*tionship (Washington, D. C.: AASCU, 1970), p. 12.

14. *Dixon,* 294 F.2d at 158–159.

question of trial by one's peers, the writer has found no court decision requiring, in that sense, the Sixth Amendment notion of trial by jury; nor does there appear to be constitutional authority requiring plural or mixed (student, faculty, administrator) hearing tribunals.

It is not altogether clear from *Dixon* whether or not the student is entitled to have the hearing open to the public (it was implied that whether the decision was to be open or closed should be left to the discretion of the institution),[15] but the writer knows of no case in which it has been held that the student is so entitled. The *Zanders'* case ruled as follows:

> The fact that the public was not allowed to attend the hearing before the State Board in no way tends to establish bias or unfairness in those proceedings.[16]

However, the *Moore* Court recommended that hearings should be public and open to the press, but it stated that this was not necessary insofar as compliance with a student's procedural rights was concerned.[17]

It has occurred that a member of the hearing body was also a testifying witness with respect to the events involving the student, but this has been held not to disqualify him as a "judge" or to invalidate the hearing if it is otherwise fair.[18] On the other hand, in Wasson v. Trowbridge, the Court of Appeals ruled that "an impartial trier of fact" is fundamental to a "fair hearing."[19] It should be noted, however, that this case involved the federal government, not a state government, in the operation of a federal college (United States Merchant Marine Academy), not a state college. The decision, therefore, rested on the due process clause of the Fifth Amendment (federal) not the Fourteenth (state).[20]

While it might be desirable to have an adjudicatory body which is not also the investigator and prosecutor, such conditions have not been required by the courts, even in the most serious student

---

15. Id.

16. Zanders v. Louisiana State Bd. of Educ., 281 F.Supp. 747, 768 (D.C. La.1968).

17. Moore v. Student Affairs Committee of Troy State Univ., 284 F. Supp. 725, 731 (D.C.Ala.1968).

18. Zanders, 281 F.Supp. at 769; Jones v. State Bd. of Educ., 279 F.Supp. 191 (D.C.Tenn.1968); see also, Blanton v. State Univ. of New York, 489 F.2d 377 (2d Cir. 1973), and Brown v. Knowlton, 370 F. Supp. 1119 (D.C.N.Y.1974).

19. 382 F.2d 807, 813 (2d Cir. 1967).

20. Id., at 807.

expulsion cases. Illustrative of this point is the Wright v. Texas Southern Univ. case, in which a student was expelled for misconduct. After a disciplinary conference with a dean, the student had a hearing with the university president. In a *mandamus* hearing before the Federal District Court, the student claimed that he had been denied a fair hearing since both the dean and the president each acted in dual capacities—that of prosecutor and judge. The Court ruled that since the student had been given a "fair" opportunity to explain his conduct, he had been given a fair hearing and that no violation of due process was involved.[21]

In a similar but somewhat different context, a student at the University of Connecticut was suspended for having disrupted a class. A hearing was conducted by the Associate Dean of Students since the Student Conduct Committee had disbanded at the end of the academic year. The student claimed that his procedural due process protection had been violated because the sole judge in the disciplinary hearing was an administrator in the Office of Men's Affairs, the office which formally initiated the suspension proceedings. However, the United States Court of Appeals, Second Circuit, ruled as follows:

> It may well be that having an administrator as the sole judge in student disciplinary proceedings is undesirable. In fact, the University's regulations recognize that a tribunal of students and faculty is preferable. Nevertheless, the mere fact that the decision maker in a disciplinary hearing is also an administrative officer of the University does not in itself violate the dictates of due process.[22]

Similarly, the Perlman[23] Court ruled, "Due process does not forbid the combination of judging and prosecuting in administrative proceedings."[24] However, the Court further ruled that an adjudicatory body should not discuss a scheduled case before the hearing nor should this body permit ex-parte (one-sided) com-

---

21. 392 F.2d 728, 731 (5th Cir. 1968).

22. Winnick v. Manning, 460 F.2d 545, 548–549 (2d Cir. 1972).

23. The *Perlman* case involved an appeal of two disciplinary proceedings: in the first proceeding Perl-man was suspended and this was upheld by the Court; in the second proceeding Perlman was expelled and the Court reversed this sanction for lack of "due process."

24. *Perlman*, 9 Cal.App.3d at 875, 88 Cal.Rptr. 563.

munication to take place between themselves and defendants or prosecutors.[25]

Preceding Perlman's expulsion hearing before the Shasta Joint Junior College District Board of Trustees, members of the College Board decided to expel the student through numerous telephone discussions with one another. After these discussions one member of the Board requested a resolution from the Anderson Chamber of Commerce in support of the pending action.[26] With this evidence, the Court set aside Perlman's expulsion and provided the following rationale:

> The inference drawn by the court from . . . the testimony summarized above, is that the board in fact made its decision prior to the hearing and, hence, was not an impartial board . . . if the record of such proceedings show bias and prejudice upon the part of the administrative body, its decision will not be upheld by the courts.[27]

What is constitutionally necessary for a fair hearing process is only the *opportunity* to be heard. This implies that the student has been sufficiently advised of the charges against him, and their possible consequences, and has been given the opportunity to refute those charges in a hearing. Whether he actually *takes* the opportunity for a hearing is not important to the courts.[28]

25. Id., at 883. See also Gonzales v. McEuen, 435 F.Supp. 460 (D.C.Cal. 1977); high school board of trustees hearing which resulted in expulsion of eleven students held to be in violation of students' due process rights to a hearing before an impartial body on the following grounds: (1) having attorneys act as prosecutors at the Board hearing contemporaneously with role as legal advisors to the supposedly impartial tribunal created what the court termed an "unacceptable risk of bias;" and (2) superintendent sat with Board during its expulsion proceedings and later spent at least 45 minutes with the Board while it was deliberating on whether to expel students. School attorneys argued that the superintendent did not participate in the Board's deliberations and in fact did no more than "serve cookies and coffee." The court found this argument irrelevant: "Whether he did or did not participate, his presence to some extent might operate as an inhibiting restraint upon the freedom of action and expression of the Board." Id., at 465.

26. Id., at 882–883.

27. Id., at 883; see also Goss v. Lopez, 419 U.S. 565, 580 (1975) quoting Justice Frankfurter in Joint Anti-Fascist Refugee Committee v. McGrath, 341 U.S. 123, 170–172 (1951). " 'Fairness can rarely be obtained by secret, one-sided determination of facts decisive of rights . . . Secrecy is not congenial to truth-seeking and self-righteousness gives too slender an assurance of rightness.' "

28. *Wright*, 392 F.2d at 731.

This approach to non-appearance prevents the student from blocking the progress of the disciplinary process simply by not appearing.   This principle is akin to the legal concept of "confession of judgment."   Fischer indicates, however, that under the circumstances of non-appearance, the student does not necessarily admit guilt, nor does he waive due process protections, but the student does imply by such absence that he will accept the judgment of the tribunal.   Consequently, Fischer contends that the tribunal is obligated to afford the same due process as if the defendant were present.   Under these circumstances the student neither attends the hearing nor presents a defense.[29]

The Right to Representation by Counsel

The *Dixon* decision did not deal with the counsel issue directly.   However, it did establish the procedural framework of "the rudiments of an adversary proceeding" into which the student's right to counsel could be logically incorporated.[30]   In fact, the 1967 *Esteban* decision appeared to be developing this possibility.

> . . .   plaintiffs shall be permitted to have counsel present with them at the (college disciplinary) hearing to advise (not represent) them   . . .   plaintiffs shall be permitted to hear the evidence presented against them, and plaintiffs (not their attorney) may question at the hearing any witness who gives evidence against them   . . . [31]

This protection was a considerable extension of the standards laid down in either the *Dixon* (1961) or the Due v. Florida A. and M. Univ. (1963) cases.   In fact, the court in the latter case completely refused to flesh out the *Dixon* possibility of "right to counsel."

> A fair reading of the *Dixon* case shows that it is not necessary to due process requirements that a full scale judicial trial be conducted by a university disciplinary committee with qualified attorneys either present or formally waived as in a felonious charge under the criminal law.[32]

Since the *Esteban* extension came later (1967), had it been allowed to stand unchanged, it would have required reasonably strict legal standards (at least in the Federal District Court in

29. *Fischer*, op. cit., p. 25.

30. *Dixon*, 294 F.2d at 159.

31. Esteban v. Central Missouri State College, 277 F.Supp. 649, 651–52 (D.C.Mo.1967).

32. 233 F.Supp. 403, 407 (D.C.Fla. 1963).

the Western District of Missouri) including legal counsel for students involved in disciplinary hearings in public colleges, and would have been, it seems, the furthest extension of students' rights in disciplinary hearings to date. As the following cases will make clear, however, this decision did not remain unchanged.

Illustrative of this change in the *Esteban* "right to counsel" (in an advisory but not representative capacity) requirement are the following cases presented in chronological order:

Barker v. Hardway (1968)

> *Dixon* significantly failed to include . . . counsel as a required safeguard in its enumeration of recommended minimum requirements . . . *Madera* and *Zanders,* although envisioning possible situations where the right might be required, avoided a definitive ruling on the point . . . I share that reluctance.[33]

Perlman v. Shasta Joint Junior College Dist. Bd. of Trustees (1970) considered procedural fairness in the "suspension" aspect of the case:

> The student did not assert that the notice of the hearing was too short, that he wanted the hearing continued or that he wanted a lawyer. As said in Madera v. Bd. of Educ. of City of New York (1967) . . . "The right to representation by counsel is not an essential ingredient to a fair hearing in all types of proceedings." [34]

Andersen v. Regents of Univ. of Calif. (1972)

> Plaintiff cites no authority, and we have found none, holding that in a disciplinary proceeding a college is required to supply counsel for the student.[35]

Therefore, at this time, it can be concluded that the right to counsel is generally not extended to student disciplinary proceedings, and accordingly, neither is the college obliged to provide counsel for the indigent student.[36] However, one might understandably wonder about the *Madera* decision, supra, upon which the *Perlman* case partially rested: " . . . counsel is not an

---

33. Barker v. Hardway, 283 F.Supp. 236, 237 (D.C.W.Va.1968).

34. *Perlman,* 9 Cal.App.3d at 879, 88 Cal.Rptr. 563.

35. Andersen v. Regents of Univ. of Calif., 22 Cal.App.3d 763, 765, 99 Cal.Rptr. 531 (1972).

36. Id.; see also French v. Bashful, 303 F.Supp. 1333, 1338 (D.C.La. 1969), where the court stipulates that ". . . we are limiting this holding to *retained* legal counsel as opposed to *appointed* counsel."

essential ingredient . . . in all types of proceedings." In what type of student disciplinary proceeding then would it be an essential ingredient?

Professor Charles Wright takes the position that the right to counsel should be recognized in "major disciplinary proceedings" in colleges and universities.[37] Professor Arthur Sherry perhaps goes a bit further with this protection in his claim that at a university disciplinary proceeding the student's "right to counsel, should the matter appear to him to be of sufficient gravity to make legal assistance desirable, should receive ungrudging recognition . . . "[38] Even in Wasson v. Trowbridge, where the Second Circuit Court held that the student did not have the right to counsel in expulsion hearings, the Court qualified its holding by saying:

> The requirement of counsel as an ingredient of fairness is a function of all of the other aspects of the hearing. Where the proceeding is non-criminal in nature, where the hearing is investigative and not adversarial and the government does not proceed through counsel, where the individual concerned is mature and educated, where his knowledge of the events . . . should enable him to develop the facts adequately through available sources, and where the other aspects of the hearing taken as a whole are fair, due process does not require representation by counsel.[39]

In French v. Bashful, for an example of the *Wasson* qualification, a Federal District Court ruled that a college student is entitled to counsel if the administration proceeds through counsel at the hearing; the requirement was declared a "balancing" aspect of fairplay.[40] This idea, of course, was first established in criminal law but now has become required in such administrative proceedings as student disciplinary hearings. Moreover, the underlying logic of the adversary system is that the best way for the hearing tribunal to discover the truth is for each side to strive as hard as it can to present its point of view. Then if we view the hearing as a neutral arena, in which two parties fight

---

37. Charles Alan Wright, "The Constitution on the Campus," *Vanderbilt Law Review*, XXII (1969), p. 1075.

38. Arthur Sherry, "Governance of the University: Rules, Rights, and Responsibilities," *California Law Review*, LIV (1966), p. 37.

39. 382 F.2d 807, 812 (2d Cir. 1967).

40. 303 F.Supp. 1333, 1338 (D.C.La. 1969); see also Madera v. Board of Educ. of City of New York, 267 F.Supp. 356 (D.C.N.Y.1967), rev'd 386 F.2d 778 (2d Cir. 1967).

out their differences before an impartial tribunal, it would seem only reasonable that the test of fair play would require, among other things, at least minimal safeguards in terms of some kind of equality of representation between the contestants.

Furthermore, the *French* Court indicated that the need for higher "education is so vital in our present day society that the procedure under which one may lose this right should be heavily stocked with procedural safeguards." [41]   But the balancing safeguard of "counsel versus counsel" was not precisely the point in this case.   More specifically, the University allowed the prosecution of the students before the disciplinary committee to be conducted by a senior law student who was rather well-versed in legal proceedings and shortly thereafter became a member of the bar.

Thus the *French* ruling provides another dimension to the balancing concept of legal assistance; that is, where an institution proceeds through a law student, even though not a certified attorney, and the institution refuses to permit participation by the student's retained counsel, due process will be violated.   But does this formulation of "appropriate protection" go far enough?   What if, for merely one example, an institution conducts its prosecution through a brilliant, enormously articulate professor of logic and debate?   If the student then is not allowed representation at the hearing by retained counsel, or at least by someone of comparable verbal ability, among other things it fills one's mind with the imagery of verbal surgery.

Whatever, it follows logically that the general prohibition against being represented, or advised, by legal counsel is applied only to the actual conduct of the hearing itself.   It does not restrict in any way the student's "right" to legal counsel and legal representation *outside* the hearing room.

It should also be pointed out that in many of the court cases involving student disciplinary proceedings the students had been given the right to counsel.   Of course, no court has or will bar such a practice if the college administration allows such at the hearing, and the principle should also be recalled that if college regulations stipulate the right to legal assistance, then due process would require that the opportunity be provided the student. The courts hold that the procedures may and indeed should be flexible, that it is impossible to be absolute, and that each set of circumstances must be weighed separately in determining what

41.   Id., at 1337.

meets due process and what will not hinder the implementation of the lawful aims and objectives of the institution.

As the Court said in the *General Order on Judicial Standards of Procedure and Substance in Review of Student Discipline in Tax Supported Institutions of Higher Education* (1968):

> Within limits of due process, institutions must be free to devise various types of disciplinary procedures relevant to their lawful missions, consistent with their varying processes and functions, . . . resources and personnel.[42]

However, does the following provide an opening for a possible evolving trend?

> There is no general requirement that procedural due process in student disciplinary cases provide for legal representation . . . Rare and exceptional circumstances, however, may require provision [for counsel] in a particular case to guarantee the fundamental concepts of fair play.[43] [See *Gabrilowitz* at pp. 150–59 for an example of the "rare and exceptional circumstances" application.]

The Right to Confrontation and Cross-Examination of Witnesses

After examining the Sixth Amendment's guarantee of confrontation and cross-examination of witnesses, Justice Black, writing for the majority in Pointer v. Texas, noted:

> There are few subjects, perhaps, upon which this Court and other courts have been more nearly unanimous than in their expressions of belief that the right of confrontation and cross-examination is an essential and fundamental requirement for the kind of fair trial which is this country's constitutional goal.[44]

Since expulsion or long-term suspension can be a harsher penalty than certain criminal sanctions, it would seem logical to require these rights in college disciplinary hearings. The courts, however, have been extremely reluctant to require cross-examination in such hearings, unless in cases of substantial penalties which turn upon questions of witness credibility, "cross examination of witnesses might be essential to a fair hearing." [45]

---

42. *General Order*, 45 F.R.D. at 147.

43. Id., at 148.

44. 380 U.S. 400, 405 (1965).

45. Blanton v. State Univ. of New York, 489 F.2d 377, 385 (2d Cir. 1973).

There are several reasons for this refusal. First, college disciplinary proceedings are not considered a part of criminal jurisprudence. Second, college boards, unlike courts, do not have the subpoena power; that is, college authorities cannot compel witnesses to attend disciplinary hearings. Another result of the lack of the subpoena power is that witnesses who voluntarily testify do not have absolute immunity from libel laws, as they would if they were legally compelled to speak.[46] Moreover, at least one court feels that it may be harmful to make students confront those whom they have accused of misconduct:

> . . . honorable students do not like to be known as snoopers and informers against their fellows . . . they should not be subjected to a cross-examination . . . to their displeasure if not their public humiliation.[47]

For these among other reasons, the most adversary-oriented courts have generally required the colleges to give the accused student only the names of adverse witnesses and a summary of what they have said.[48] In other words, witnesses are seldom constitutionally required to be present at any time during the disciplinary hearing.

Despite these considerations, there could be times when a witness's testimony is so damaging and the potential harm to the student so great that the college could be required either to present the witness for cross-examination at the hearing or forego his testimony. The Blanton v. State Univ. of New York warning of "witness credibility," or the "rare and exceptional circumstances" concept of the courts or the great value of cross-examination in arriving at the truth could force this choice. Wigmore has illustrated the importance of cross-examination as follows:

> . . . the belief that no safeguard for testing the value of human statements is comparable to that furnished by cross-examination, and the conviction that no statement . . . should be used in testimony until it has been probed and

---

46. William Van Alstyne, "Procedural Due Process and State University Students," *UCLA Law Review*, X (1963), p. 371.

47. State ex rel. Sherman v. Hyman, 180 Tenn. 99, 110, 247 S.W. 984 (1942).

48. See, e. g., *Dixon*, 294 F.2d at 159; *Barker*, 283 F.Supp. at 236; *General Order*, 148; Brown v. Knowlton, 370 F.Supp. 1119 (D.C.N.Y. 1974); and *Winnick*, 460 F.2d at 549, in which the U.S. Court of Appeals, 2nd Circuit, pointed out that "the right to cross-examine witnesses generally has not been considered an essential requirement of due process in school disciplinary proceedings."

sublimated by that test, has found increasing strength in lengthening experience.[49]

Even though *Dixon* did not require cross-examination of witnesses, it indicated the difficulty and importance of fact-finding and truth discovery in the student disciplinary proceeding:

> . . . [the proof of misconduct] depends upon a collection of the facts concerning the charged misconduct, easily colored by the point of view of the witnesses . . . [And if cross-examination of witnesses is not allowed, there is still the requirement that adequate notification must include] names of the witnesses against him and an oral or written report on the facts to which each witness testifies . . . [and at the hearing] to produce either oral testimony or written affidavits of witnesses in his behalf.[50]

The Right to a Decision Based Upon Adequate Evidence

Since student disciplinary proceedings are non-criminal in nature, the standard of evidence used to establish misconduct does not seem to have to meet the more severe constitutional test of "beyond a reasonable doubt" or "preponderance of evidence" or any other test common to legal adjudication. In fact, *Dixon* avoids the issue of establishing a constitutionally required fact-finding standard necessary to support a hearing committee's decision. There is subsequent authority, however, indicating that there must be "substantial evidence" to support the findings.[51] For example, the *General Order* stipulates "that no disciplinary action be taken on grounds which are not supported by any substantial evidence." [52] According to Fischer, "substantial evidence" is the test of sufficiency; that is, "the evidence is just enough to be more convincing as to its truth when weighed against the evidence in opposition thereto." [53]

There is, regarding the above, a somewhat different dimension to the constitutional requirement of establishing "substantial evidence." It involves mass disruptive behavior. In the mass situation, where the means of identifying the participants and

49. John Henry Wigmore, *Evidence in Trials at Common Law*, V (Boston: Little Brown and Company, 1940), p. 29.

50. *Dixon*, 294 F.2d at 159.

51. See e. g., *General Order*, 45 F.R.D. at 148; *Esteban*, 277 F.Supp. at 650–651; *Zanders*, 281 F.Supp. at 769; *Jones*, 297 F.Supp. at 191; McDonald v. Board of Trustees of Univ. of Ill., 375 F.Supp. 95 (D.C. Ill.1974).

52. *General Order*, 45 F.R.D. at 148.

53. *Fisher*, op. cit., p. 12.

getting evidence against them is frequently lacking, it seems that even the most conscientious tribunal might try to make do with a kind of second-rate form of evidence. Such a situation was reviewed by a federal court in San Francisco.[54]

The case involved many hundreds of San Francisco State College students allegedly involved in the disruption at the college. As there were not enough witnesses, not enough photographs, not enough firsthand evidence to make the case, the hearing committee at the college relied in each case upon the police record of arrest as sufficient to establish disruptive conduct in violation of the college rule, in the absence of any evidence to the contrary offered by the student. A number of students were put on probation and some were suspended. Some of these students proceeded to the federal district court where their reinstatement was ordered on constitutional grounds. The basis for the order is very straightforward:

> . . . The mere recordation by a police officer that he placed Mr. X. under arrest at a given time and place does not by itself show, even by substantial evidence, that X was violating the disruptive conduct rule of the university. It is consistent with the known information, for instance, that he was a spectator at the time, or a passerby at the scene, or was there trying to render aid to someone else. The evidence by itself is not enough.[55]

The above case, it appears, involved an important kind of constitutional *caveat*—given the procedural integrity of the hearing board, ultimately all hearing decisions, perhaps even those involving sanctions as light as a one-day suspension, must be backed by some form of written record containing at least "substantial evidence" considered as a whole, that the material elements of the campus rule have in fact been violated. That is a rather stringent test to meet in view of possible mass civil disobedience on campus, but it seems, as a result of this case, to be an emerging constitutional demand.

But in some circumstances it seems that even "substantial evidence" could be constitutionally insufficient upon which to base a severe disciplinary sanction. In the Smyth and Smith v. Lubbers (1975) case, for instance, the court concluded

> that at least *where an adult student is charged by a college with committing an act which is a crime* (even though the

54.   Wong v. Hayakawa, 464 F.2d   55.   Id., at 1283.
1282 (9th Cir. 1972).

college did not bring criminal charges for the student's possession of marijuana), *the Due Process Clause requires that some articulated and coherent standard of proof be formally adopted and applied* at the college hearing which determines the student's guilt or innocence of the charge. If such a standard is not adopted and applied, then the college hearing board is totally free to exercise its prejudices or to convict for the purpose of vindicating "order and discipline" rather than on the evidence presented. All the rest of the procedural guarantees become or threaten to become meaningless as even a well-intentioned hearing board is adrift in uncertainty over the measure of persuasion to be applied . . .

The *substantial evidence* formula standing alone as a standard of proof . . .   need only present a certain quantum of evidence . . .   that a party was guilty as charged . . .   Assuming this definition embodies an intelligible standard of proof for a trier of fact, *that standard is too low. The application of any standard lower than a "preponderance of evidence"* would have the effect of requiring the accused to prove his innocence. Under the circumstances of this case, at least, it would be fundamentally unfair to shift the burden of proof to the accused . . .

However, given the nature of the charges and the serious consequences [suspension for a period of two years for Smyth and one term for Smith], the court believes the *higher standard* of *"clear and convincing evidence"* may be required. The "clear and convincing standard" is well below the criminal standard . . .   [and] would be consistent with the general proposition that "school regulations are not to be measured by the standards which prevail . . .   for criminal procedures" . . . [56]

The courts have noted again and again that the procedures due depend upon the nature of the "interests affected and the circumstances of the deprivation." [57] Thus, the "rare and exceptional circumstances" test can and most certainly will be applied, but with the exception of the *Smyth* case, the courts so far have relied on the "substantial evidence" test.[58]

---

56. 398 F.Supp. 777, 797–799 (D.C. Mich.1975). (emphasis added)

57. Marin v. Univ. of Puerto Rico, 377 F.Supp. 613, 623 (D.C.Puerto Rico 1974).

58. See, e. g. Jones v. State Bd. of Educ., 407 F.2d 834 (6th Cir. 1969); *Esteban*, 415 F.2d 1077 (8th Cir. 1969); Keene v. Rodgers, 316 F. Supp. 217 (D.C.Me.1970); and Speake v. Grantham, 317 F.Supp.

Attendant to the judicial requirement that disciplinary action only be taken if supported by the minimal standard of "substantial evidence," however, is the constitutional question of rules of evidence to be followed within the disciplinary hearing. It appears that this aspect of the procedure is even less precise than the former. According to Goldberg v. Regents of Univ. of California, rules of evidence which apply to criminal proceedings, such as heresay, are not applicable.[59]   Therefore, and again with the exception of *Smyth,* it appears that as a general rule college hearing tribunals are left relatively free to determine their own rules of evidence according to the circumstances of each individual case.

The Privilege Against Unreasonable Search and Seizure

The right of the people to be secure in their persons, houses, papers and effects against unreasonable searches and seizures, shall not be violated, and no Warrants shall issue, but upon probable cause, supported by Oath or affirmation, and particularly describing the place to be searched, and the persons or things to be seized.[60]

As noted in the preceding section on evidence, certain types of evidence are inadmissible in criminal proceedings.   "Hearsay" was used as an example, but undoubtedly an even more important procedural protection for the accused is the judicial position that evidence obtained through "unreasonable search and seizure" cannot be used in a federal [61] (Fourth Amendment) or state [62] (Fourteenth Amendment due process) court against persons from whom it was seized.   The argument is that if a person's private effects can be unconstitutionally seized and yet be used as admissible evidence, the Fourth Amendment protection is of no value.   From this standpoint, if any court allows such evidence to be used in the trial, it will have committed a prejudicial error, and thus stands to have its decision reversed in any subsequent appeal to a higher court (exclusionary rule).

1253 (S.D.Miss.1970), aff'd 440 F.2d 1351 (5th Cir. 1971); in fact at 1283 the District Court specifically ruled that a higher standard of "beyond a reasonable doubt" was constitutionally unnecessary.

59. Goldberg v. Regents of Univ. of Calif., 248 Cal.App.2d 867, 884, 57 Cal.Rptr. 463, 475 (1967).

60. U. S. Constitution, Amend. IV.

61. Weeks v. United States, 232 U.S. 383 (1914).

62. Mapp v. Ohio, 367 U.S. 643 (1961).

In order to conduct a lawful search, for instance, a police officer has three basic alternatives: (1) He must obtain a warrant from a judge specifying the person and place to be searched and the material to be seized, or (2) he must get the consent of the individual whose person or place will be searched, or (3) he must be able to prove to a court that he had "probable cause" to believe that a crime was committed and the person to be searched committed it.

What is written above of course is applicable to criminal jurisprudence. Nevertheless, it still has some utility for the college disciplinary context, for it is not altogether uncommon for college officials to search students' private effects in such places as dormitory rooms, automobiles and gymnasium lockers for evidence upon which to base a disciplinary action. Furthermore, evidence obtained as a result of "unreasonable search and seizure" and submitted and used in determining a student misconduct decision could, in some cases, provide grounds for judicial review. A careful analysis of three federal court decisions, Moore v. Student Affairs Committee of Troy State Univ. (1968), Smyth and Smith v. Lubbers (1975), and Piazzola and Marinshaw v. Watkins (1971), provide some interesting information pertinent to such a possibility.

In the *Moore* case the plaintiff's name was on a list of students suspected of possession of marijuana. Late one morning, the list was presented by police officers to the dean of men at the university for permission to search the students' dormitory rooms. The list had been drawn up on the basis of information from reputedly reliable sources. In the early afternoon of the same day, the police received further information that some of the students named were packing to leave the campus for a break, and fearing that their quarry might escape, the police and the dean searched the plaintiff's room *without* a warrant and *without* his consent. The search turned up a quantity of marijauna, and as a result, the plaintiff was indefinitely suspended. He sought reinstatement primarily because his Fourth Amendment (more technically his Fourteenth Amendment) freedom from "unreasonable search and seizure" had been invaded and, therefore, the marijuana should not have been permitted as evidence in the university disciplinary hearing.

The university quoted a leaflet on residence hall policies which stated that the university reserved the right to enter rooms for inspection purposes and that if the administration deemed it necessary students' rooms might be searched.[63] The Court declared:

> A student naturally has the right to be free of unreasonable searches and seizures, and a tax-supported public college may not compel a "waiver" of that right as a condition precedent to admission . . .
>
> The student is subject only to reasonable rules and regulations, but his rights must yield to the extent that they would interfere with the institution's fundamental duty to operate the school as an educational institution. A reasonable right of inspection is necessary to the institution's performance of that duty even though it may infringe on the outer boundaries of a dormitory student's Fourth Amendment rights . . . The regulation of the Troy State University issue here is thus facially reasonable . . .
>
> The regulation was reasonably applied in this case. The constitutional boundary line between the right of a dormitory student to privacy must be based on a *reasonable belief* on the part of the college authorities that a student is using a dormitory room for a purpose which is illegal or which would otherwise seriously interfere with campus discipline—upon this submission, it is clear that such a belief existed in this case . . .
>
> This standard of *"reasonable cause to believe"* to justify a search by college administrators—even where the sole purpose is to seek evidence of suspected violations of law—is *lower* than the constitutionally protected criminal law standard of *"probable cause."* This is true because of the special necessities of the student-college relationship and because college disciplinary proceedings are not criminal proceedings in the constitutional sense. It is clearly settled that due process in college disciplinary proceedings does not require . . . hearings subject to rules of evidence and all constitutional criminal guarantees.[64]

The Court pointed out, in other words, that the college would merely have to establish "reasonable cause to believe" before a student's private effects could be searched and seized and subsequently used as evidence for a misconduct decision. Not much of a test. In point of fact, no other evidence was offered by the

---

63. Moore v. Student Affairs Committee of Troy State Univ., 284 F. Supp. 725, 731–33 (D.C.Ala.1968).

64. Id., at 729–730 (emphasis added).

University in justification of the search other than that the dean and the police officers "had information," that they believed that information, and that, implied by the testimony, there were more unnamed informers whose information or credibility as informers was never discussed. Thus the *Moore* test was merely something more than suspicion.

But whatever the test, tests do not decide cases—judges do. And judges are constantly searching and seeking and explaining. Tests are judges' starting points, not their conclusions; each case requires them to weigh a variety of factors. For instance, what were the events leading to the charge? Did the student have a "reasonable expectation of privacy?" How complex were the issues at hand? Where was the burden of proof located, with the institution or the student? How severe was the disciplinary sanction? Under all of the circumstances of the particular case, taken as a whole, was there "fair play?" These and scores of other considerations are involved. In short, no test has been devised that will weigh all the factors.

The implications of the above qualification are somewhat more subtle and considerably more significant than one might think. As Justice Powell has written, "Searches and seizures are an opaque area of the law; flagrant Fourth Amendment abuses will rarely escape detection but there is a vast twilight zone with respect to which our own 'decisions . . . are hardly noted for their predictability.' " [65] Thus one should be wary of over-interpreting any court-announced standard and in terms of the present issue, the *Moore* criterion of "reasonable cause to believe," the Smyth and Smith v. Lubbers' decision provides an excellent case in point.

On January 30, 1974, Charles Smyth and Greg Smith, both students at Grand Valley State College in Allendale, Michigan, were living in Kistler Hall on the College campus. Each had signed a "Residence Hall Contract" which provided that they would agree to abide by the terms and conditions of residence in college dormitories as stated in the current housing handbook. Of importance was Section 2(c) of the "Room Entry Procedures" in the handbook which provided that "If College officials have reasonable cause to believe that students are continuing to violate federal, state, or local laws or college regulations, the room is subject to search by college authorities."

65. Concurring in Schneckloth v. Bustamonte, 412 U.S. 218 (1973) and quoting Justice Harlan in Ker v. California, 374 U.S. 23 (1963).

On the above date, the rooms of Smyth and Smith were entered and searched under the authority of the Room Entry Procedures, Rule 2(c). The students were not present during the searches, no consent was given for the searches, the searches were conducted by college officials without warrants, and evidence (marijuana) was seized in both rooms. Based upon the evidence seized, the students were charged with disorderly conduct and possession of narcotic drugs in violation of Michigan law and/or College regulations. After a hearing by the All College Judiciary, both students were found guilty of possession of marijuana and Smyth was suspended from the College for a period of two years and Smith for one term.

Subsequently, the students brought civil rights action (42 U.S. C.A. § 1983) against the college officials, including Arend Lubbers, President of Grand Valley State College, seeking declaration that the search of their rooms was unconstitutional and seeking injunctive relief with respect to the college disciplinary proceedings.

Judge Fox of the United States District Court, Western District, Michigan, first took issue with the regulation upon which the students' suspension was based:

> The College contends it is an institution having "special characteristics" which justify the regulation and search in question . . . The College advances a general proposition that regulations which are essential to the maintenance of order and discipline on school property are constitutionally reasonable even though such regulations infringe on outer limits of constitutional rights, citing . . . *Moore*, supra, 284 F.Supp. at 730. The College argues that the search regulation is essential to the maintenance of order and discipline on the campus, and that the search conducted pursuant to that regulation was accordingly reasonable within the meaning of the Fourth Amendment. The theory is that the special characteristics of the College defeat or seriously qualify whatever expectation of privacy the student might have in other contexts or vis-a-vis other social institutions.

> The court rejects the theory that College officials acting pursuant to regulations may infringe on the outer limits of an adult's constitutional rights . . . *Moore,* upon which the College relies, [was] decided before *Tinker,* which rejected the proposition that students "shed their constitutional rights . . . at the schoolhouse gate." 393 U.S. at 506,

1969 . . . "In our system, state-operated schools may not be enclaves of totalitarianism. School officials do not possess absolute authority over their students." *Tinker,* supra . . . at 511 . . .

The College is unjustifiably claiming extraordinary powers. The College drug regulations track federal and state laws, yet the College contends that its interests are so important that it may use means of enforcement—warrantless police searches on less than probable cause—which are not available to either the federal or state governments. Indeed, the College is claiming that its drug regulations are more important than the domestic security of the United States, which will not justify such action as the College took here . . . Since nearly all college students in Michigan are adults, the College cannot have such a high interest in maintaining strict discipline as elementary and secondary schools. The College is also unlike military or quasi-military organizations, where the need for discipline is more acute than in civilian society . . .

The court concludes that under the circumstances presented here, the defendants were constitutionally required to get a search warrant from a neutral and detached magistrate before searching . . . and the failure of the defendants to secure such a warrant renders the search and seizure unreasonable and constitutionally invalid. The failure of the College regulation to require a warrant in the absence of exigent circumstances renders the regulation constitutionally invalid.[66]

Subsequently, the Court ruled that the "exclusionary rule" applied to the evidence seized in the search:

If there were no exclusionary rule in this case, the College authorities would have no incentive to respect the privacy of its students . . . Where, as here, the authorities who violated the Constitution were not demonstrably guilty of bad faith, the exclusionary rule remains the only possible deterrent, the only effective way to positively encourage respect for the constitutional guarantee . . .

The court concludes that the evidence seized in the illegal search . . . could not be used . . . in the College disciplinary proceedings. Accordingly, the College must re-

66. Smyth and Smith v. Lubbers, 398 F.Supp. at 789–793.

try (the case), without the evidence, or dismiss the charges.[67]

Thus the *Smyth and Smith* (1975) ruling on Fourth Amendment rights was quite different from that of the *Moore* (1968) decision.   As you will recall, the principles laid down in the *Moore* case indicated that whereas a student cannot be required to waive his/her Fourth Amendment rights, colleges may have catalog stipulations reserving the right to enter and inspect student rooms.   It was pointed out that colleges may do this for purposes of safety or if college authorities have a "reasonable cause to believe" that the room is being used for illegal purposes or for activity that would otherwise seriously interfere with campus discipline.   Furthermore, the "reasonable cause to believe" test was a standard much lower than that of "probable cause" and one that was justified on the special necessities in the student-college relationship.   And any evidence secured during such an inspection was ruled constitutionally admissible as evidence against a student in college disciplinary proceedings.

But why did the *Smyth and Smith* Court expressly refuse to follow the *Moore* precedent?   The two cases certainly had elements of factual similarity; nevertheless, the answer seems simply to be that times had changed.   With that said, let us turn back to the *Smyth and Smith* opinion and attempt a brief analysis of the change factor inherent in the reasoning of that opinion.

First, the District Court in Michigan indicated that *Moore* (1968), upon which the court relied, was ".   .   .   decided before *Tinker* (1969), which rejected the proposition that students 'shed their constitutional rights   .   .   .   at the schoolhouse gate.' "   Apparently, the Supreme Court's *Tinker* decision was especially noteworthy because it was the first student disciplinary case decided by the high tribunal in the sixties, and it seemed to mark a reinforcement of the judicial trend to surround the college-student relationship with restraints embodied in the concepts of due process of law.   Second, the Court indicated that both Smyth and Smith were adults (Amendment Twenty Six was ratified on June 30, 1971), and their rooms were deemed their place of "residence by the State of Michigan for voting purposes."   In fact, the constitutional amendment allowing citizens who were eighteen years of age or older the right to vote made, for all intent and purposes, the vast majority of undergraduate students legal adults.   Third, the Court alluded to the fact that the possession

67.   Id., at 794–795.

of marijuana in 1968 was considered a much more serious offense than in the mid-1970's. Accordingly, the Court claimed that the suspensions meted out to Smyth and Smith were far harsher than they would have received "... from either a state court for conviction on or after April 9, 1974, or a federal court for a first-time offense of simple possession of marijuana." In fact, "... the policy of the United States and the State of Michigan is that ... simple possession of marijuana ... is best treated by leaving the offender in society without serious social disability other than close supervision." The Court went on to say, however, that the matter was still quasi-criminal in that the Michigan Controlled Substances Act required that seized marijuana be forfeited to the state. Thus, at the very least, the seized marijuana could "be the basis of state or federal grand jury questions ... ."

The decision in this case runs counter to most other search and seizure cases involving public college residence halls. But one thing both *Moore* and *Smyth and Smith* seem to make clear is how uncertain and perhaps unreliable the courts might be in the determination of due process protections. Generally, however, evidence discovered as a result of a search based upon "reasonable cause to believe" may be used against the student in a campus hearing. Nonetheless, the legal status of Fourth Amendment rights on campus are still evolving so that, if at all possible, college officials should procure a warrant from a disinterested magistrate prior to any search of a student's room or personal belongings.

In any event, a very different set of guidelines from that of *Moore* controls when one seeks to use such evidence in a criminal proceeding or when the public college permits law enforcement personnel to enter a student's room to secure evidence for criminal prosecution. For instance, Judge Frank Johnson of the Federal District Court in Alabama, the judge who decided the 1968 *Moore* case, was presented the Piazzola and Marinshaw v. Watkins [68] case in 1970. This case was an appeal from a state court by students from the same university as involved in the *Moore* case, Troy State University. However, the situation was somewhat different in Piazzola and Marinshaw v. Watkins. Here the University again delegated to local police its right to search dormitory rooms without a warrant; however, in this case, after

<hr/>

68. 316 F.Supp. 624 (D.C.Ala.1970).
See also People v. Cohen, 57 Misc.
2d 366, 292 N.Y.S.2d 706 (1968).

discovery of marijuana, the students were charged and convicted in the state criminal courts.

Recognizing that the University had the right to search and seizure—for a restricted purpose—the Court went on to say that this ". . . does not mean that the college may exercise the right by admitting a third party." In other words, evidence secured by searching a student's room may only be used for institutional purposes, not in criminal proceedings. In order to be admissible in a criminal court, the evidence secured from a dormitory room must be acquired in full compliance with the requirements of the Fourth Amendment.

In concluding its decision, the court held that

> Since there was no warrant, no probable cause for searching without a warrant, and no waiver or consent, the search of petitioners' dormitory rooms by State law enforcement officers, including narcotic agents and Troy city police officers, on February 28, 1968, was in violation of the petitioners' rights as guaranteed by the Fourth Amendment to the Constitution . . . It follows that the convictions of the petitioners, having been based solely upon the fruits of such search, are likewise illegal and cannot stand. Accordingly, it is the

> Order, judgment and decree of this Court that the conviction of Frank Piazzola on April 25, 1968, and the conviction of Terrance Marinshaw on April 26, 1968, both in the Circuit Court of Pike County, Alabama, which convictions form the basis for the incarceration of each, be and each of said convictions is hereby set aside. It is further

> Ordered that Frank Piazzola and Terrance Marinshaw be released immediately by the State authorities now holding them in custody pursuant to said convictions.[69]

The Privilege Against Compulsory Self-Incrimination

The provision against self-incrimination in the First Amendment is designed to strengthen the fundamental principle of Anglo-American justice that no man has any obligation to prove he is innocent; rather, the burden is on the government to prove him guilty. This privilege has two aspects: (1) it can be invoked by an individual in order to prevent his being compelled to give incriminating testimony in a present investigation or prosecution; or (2) it can be invoked in a proceeding by any party or

69. Id., at 628–629.

witness in order to keep from giving evidence which might pertain to or lead to a subsequent criminal prosecution.[70]

Thus far, however, no student disciplinary proceeding has been regarded as sufficiently criminal in character that a student could justly claim the privilege against self-incrimination.[71]   There is, however, the crossover problem—the very practical problem—of the student who has been involved or alleged to have been involved in the commission of misconduct on campus that is also a crime against the state, city, or federal government.   In such a case does the college need to suspend its disciplinary proceeding on the basis that the information thus required of the student might be used to his inconvenience in the outside government proceeding?

In several such cases, students sought unsuccessfully to enjoin the college from proceeding with its disciplinary hearing until the criminal action had been adjudicated.   In support of their injunction applications, the students asserted that unless the college disciplinary proceeding were stayed, they had to testify in their own defense or risk suspension or expulsion by remaining silent; if they testified at the college hearing, they claimed their testimony would be used against them in the subsequent trial of the criminal action.[72]

Several grounds for denying the students' motions for stays of college disciplinary hearings were given by the courts.   In Goldberg v. Regents of the Univ. of Cal., the earliest of the cases, the court noted that university rules and community criminal statutes do not serve the same ends and recognized the university's interest in the swift conclusion of disciplinary proceedings.[73]

The Federal Court for the Southern District of New York was presented with the same issue in Grossner v. The Trustees of Columbia Univ.   Judge Frankel, who heard the application, commented in his opinion that the simultaneous pendency of an administrative proceeding and a criminal action involving the same event does not require that the administrative proceeding be stayed.   For an analogy, the court noted that a motor vehicle

70. See, e. g., Murphy v. Waterfront Comm., 378 U.S. 52 (1964).

71. See, e. g., Goldberg v. Regents of Univ. of Cal., 248 Cal.App.2d 867, 884, 57 Cal.Rptr. 463, 476 (1967).

72. See, e. g., *Goldberg*, 248 Cal.App. 2d 867, 57 Cal.Rptr. 463 (1967);

Grossner v. Trustees of Columbia Univ. in City of New York, 287 F. Supp. 535 (D.C.N.Y.1968); Furutani v. Ewigleben, 297 F.Supp. 1163 (D.C. Cal.1969).

73. *Goldberg*, 57 Cal.Rptr. at 476.

commissioner authorized to suspend a driver's license for speeding need not wait the outcome of a negligent homicide prosecution before considering administrative action.[74]

In Furutani v. Ewigleben a federal court in California while denying the students' application to enjoin San Mateo College's disciplinary proceeding, pointed out that if the plaintiff students were obliged to testify in the college proceeding to avoid expulsion, their testimony could be excluded in the subsequent criminal trial based upon the decision of the United States Supreme Court in Garrity v. New Jersey.[75]

Garrity, however, has been somewhat altered by later Supreme Court decisions and should not be relied upon as ruling law in this area, especially when college students are involved. Thus it now seems that testimony in a college hearing that precedes a court appearance can be used against the student at the subsequent trial. Therefore, at this date there is no judicial ruling providing students with either self-incrimination or double jeopardy protections in campus disciplinary proceedings pending completion of state or federal criminal trials.

Of course students cannot be disciplined by college authorities on the basis of an off-campus arrest alone. One of the most fundamental concepts of American justice is that a person be deemed to be innocent until proven guilty. Therefore, since an arrest is only an accusation and not a conviction, disciplinary action based solely on an arrest would be illegal. However, a college may hold a disciplinary hearing to try to prove that the student actually committed the offense for which he was arrested. If the evidence then proves that the student committed the offense, he can be disciplined by the college even before his court trial.

Today, however, many colleges are deciding on their own that a student's off-campus activities are no concern of theirs unless that behavior relates to the general order and welfare of the institution. The commission of serious criminal acts, including narcotics offenses, are probably the most relevant examples of this exception, and the courts have held these to be justifiable causes for college disciplinary action even though such activities take place off campus. Yet even if the student has been convicted of a criminal offense by a state or federal court, the student is entitled to notice and hearing before the college can mete out its own penalty.

74. *Grossner,* 287 F.Supp. at 537.   75. *Furutani,* 297 F.Supp. at 1169.

This is precisely where the University of Texas System ran into trouble since the Regents of that system promulgated a rule which called for an *automatic* two-year suspension of any student "placed on probation for or finally convicted of the illegal use, possession and/or sale of a drug or narcotic." Students afflicted by this rule initiated court action claiming that the regulation violated the double jeopardy clause of the Fifth Amendment as well as the due process and equal protection clause of the Fourteenth Amendment.

The United States District Court ruled that the regulation did not violate the double jeopardy clause of the Fifth Amendment since the sanction imposed was civil and not criminal. However, the Court ruled that the regulation did violate due process in that students were not provided an opportunity to show that they posed "no substantial threat of influencing other students to use, possess or sell drugs or narcotics." Moreover, the Court stated that equal protection was violated in that only students charged under this rule would be denied an opportunity for a hearing.[76]

The Right of Appeal from the Original Determination

Although right of appeal is not constitutionally guaranteed through "due process," [77] it is so much a part of the American tradition that most authorities recommend that a system of appeal be made available, under certain circumstances, within the college's procedural structure. In most of the leading court cases, however, the suggestion that there should be a system of appeal within the college is notable by its absence. The few courts that do refer to this aspect of appealability do so only marginally. These court comments are as follows:

Dixon v. Alabama State Board of Education (1961)

If the hearing is not before the Board directly, the results and findings should be presented in a report open to the student's inspection.[78]

This case indicated that a written report of "the results and findings" should be made if the hearing is not before the ultimate authority of the institution. The primary purpose of recordation is to provide a basis for review, and since the Court indicated that a record should be made only if the hearing took place be-

---

76. Paine v. Bd. of Regents of Univ.
of Texas System, 355 F.Supp. 199
(W.D.Tex.1972).

77. National Union of Marine Cooks
and Stewards v. Arnold. 348 U.S.
37 (1954).

78. *Dixon*, 294 F.2d at 159.

neath the Board, it could be inferred that the Court was considering the possibility of appeal and the necessary condition of recordation attached thereto.

Esteban v. Central Missouri State College (1967)

The parties acknowledge that only the President has the authority to expel a student from the college, and it is therefore necessary that all evidence be before him in some appropriate manner, as the transcript of an authorized hearing or before him directly . . .[79]

Again, it appears that the *Barker* Court was considering the need of a record for appeal purposes.

Barker v. Hardway (1968)

. . . the determinative factor . . . was whether the proceeding was investigative or adjudicative . . . Applying this criterion to the facts of the instant case . . . it unmistakably appears from the evidence and the [student] handbook that its Faculty Committee on Student Affairs only function was to gather facts and make recommendations to the president and faculty who could accept or reject them as they might choose. The adjudicative authority at the college rested at all times with the president and faculty and was never delegated to the Committee, as indeed it could not lawfully have been under state law.[80]

In a sense, the courts were referring to a quasi-appeal procedure, i. e., since the hearing committee's function was only "to gather facts and make recommendations" then its results had to be reviewed by the lawful "adjudicative" authority of the college for final determination. In fact, the two prior cases referred roughly to the same review condition.

The policy the above mentioned courts worked out involving a distinction between the "investigative" and "adjudicative" functions of the college hearing procedure appears constitutionally applicable to most public colleges. For example, in California the *Education Code* gives the "adjudicative" authority for student suspensions of ten days or less to the president of the college.[81] Under this provision, of course, he may delegate the "investigative" responsibility to a hearing committee, but by law his "adjudicative" authority is non-delegable. Therefore, unless the college president hears the case in its first instance, there is not

79. *Esteban*, 277 F.Supp. at 651.

80. *Barker*, 283 F.Supp. at 238.

81. State of California, *Education Code*, § 10605.5.

only a lawful requirement of review but a constitutional "due process" mandate as well.[82]

Many colleges, in fact, permit an appeal after the campus hearing. The appeal usually goes to the president and then to the governing board of the institution, and under such circumstances the letter advising the student of the campus hearing committee's sanction should provide information about how to appeal. Furthermore, since there also exists the possibility of the student appealing the college decision to the courts, it is important to have a written decision that discusses the testimony and states the reason for imposing the disciplinary action. Otherwise, the persons or judge reviewing the case cannot determine whether or not there was a legal basis for the disciplinary sanction. Therefore, a written memorandum with only the conclusion of "guilty of misconduct as charged" will be insufficient to permit adequate review.

The courts in terms of the appeal process from the college disciplinary decision to the judiciary have laid down some additional and fundamental guidelines. For example:

A federal court should not intervene to reverse or enjoin disciplinary actions relevant to a lawful mission of an educational institution unless there appears one of the following:

(1) A deprival of due process, that is, fundamental concepts of fair play;

(2) Invidious discrimination, for example, on account of race or religion;

(3) Denial of federal rights, constitutional or statutorily protected in the academic community; or

(4) Clearly unreasonable, arbitrary or capricious action.[83]

CONCLUDING OBSERVATIONS

Allowing for reasonable rules, the courts' insistence upon suitable warning of the circumstances in which disciplinary action may be imposed is a procedural limit upon rule application; and the doctrine of reasonable application of reasonable rules seems to call for other procedural limitations in which needs of both college and student are to be considered. An administrator

---

82. Vitarelli v. Seaton, 359 U.S. 535 (1975). (due process requires that a government agency accord an employee procedural protections in ac-

cordance with its own lawful regulations).

83. *General Order*, 45 F.R.D. at 143.

might be impelled to suggest that the college's interest is in utilizing the most expedient route to disciplinary action. Thus, in the administration of a system, there exists the problem caused by a tendency to confuse that which makes administrative jobs easier with that which furthers the goals of the institution. However, both college and students share an interest in an inquiry which is fair, can be seen to be fair, and can be relied upon to find facts accurately. The procedures to be required for any given form of disciplinary action will, of course, depend upon a multitude of factors. That is, the more complex, serious, and disputed an issue, the more procedure will become important, and the more formal will the proceedings of any campus tribunal become.[84]

In some instances, the actual guilt of the student is so evident that his only means of avoiding the consequences is to challenge the procedure. If, under such circumstances, the campus disciplinary procedure becomes abbreviated and therefore appears to be devoid of fairness, challenges to such procedure may receive much sympathy on the campus, particularly when the college community views the disciplinary process as an extension of the college's parental function, or when the offense is rationalized in a context of moral righteousness or on emotional or political grounds. It would seem that the maxim "not only must justice be done, it must be made to appear to be done" becomes very applicable at this point.[85]

There seems to be no formula which can be strictly applied in each instance to determine the proper procedure for student misconduct adjudication. Since most cases involve minor violations, it appears that such cases can be handled rather informally. That does not mean to say that an adequate notice and a fair disciplinary decision can be eliminated.

Acting in a disciplinary role, the college administrator can many times find himself in an uncertain area between what is to be considered a serious offense and what is to be considered a minor violation. If, for instance, a student is suspended for one day, does the imposition of such a penalty require a formalized procedure? One might advise caution at this point. Judges are

---

84. See, e. g., Speiser v. Randall, 357 U.S. 513, 520–521 (1958); it has always been recognized that "the more important the rights at stake the more important must be the procedural safeguards surrounding those rights."

85. As Mr. Justice Frankfurter declared in another connection: "Justice must satisfy the appearance of justice." Offut v. United States, 348 U.S. 11, 14 (1954).

talking about "rare and exceptional circumstances;" courts examine each case carefully—just as the colleges must "tailor" the procedure in each instance to the seriousness and complexity of the case at issue. In this approach, if a college records one-day suspensions on students' permanent records, a fairly formalized procedure ought to be followed, along with a mechanical recordation of the hearing. The possibility of subsequent judicial review might be remote at that time because the injury to the student would probably be considered insufficient. However, at a later time the student might be denied employment or admission to a professional school on the basis of the disciplinary recordation on his permanent record. At this point, the injury becomes sufficient, and the possibility of court intervention increases.

In the development and refinement of student disciplinary hearing procedures, colleges must face at least another problem. The Scranton Commission reported that

> . . . the disciplinary tribunal may be unwilling to impose meaningful sanctions, and if it does it may risk losing broad support within the community. Moreover, because campus tribunals usually are lacking the sanctions as well as the respect that protect a court of law from disruption, the proceedings themselves can become the focus of mass disturbance. In sum, disciplinary hearings for those involved in disruptions are apt to become political circuses rather than procedures for determining culpability and for imposing appropriate sanctions.[86]

This problem could be especially evident when college officials feel in order that "justice must appear to be done" that students and faculty as well as administrators should be represented on the hearing tribunal. Perhaps such a problem could be partially circumvented by making these tribunals ad hoc, and continuity, experience, and special skills could still be assured for the hearing committee by the appointment of a permanent chairperson. It should be recognized that students and faculty usually do not share the feelings of institutional responsibility which typically characterize administrators. Therefore, it might be advantageous in certain cases to have only administrators on the hearing committee. Such a decision, of course, will have to be decided after considering all the circumstances and possibilities surrounding each case.

86. William W. Scranton, *Campus Unrest: The Report of the President's Commission on Campus Unrest* (Washington, D.C.: U.S. Government Printing Office, 1970), p. 129.

Testing the Limits

In the early seventies, student dissent largely "peaked out." Perhaps this problem was resolved, or at least considerably mitigated, because superior conflict resolution techniques were adopted by colleges and universities and "fair play" disciplinary procedures were judicially imposed upon higher education. However, student disciplinary problems still exist in varying degrees on numerous campuses throughout the nation. The recurring theme or thread common to all such activity may be summed up in three words, namely, "testing the limits." Our society sets the limits by the development of laws and general policy in accordance with such documents as the Constitution of the United States and the constitutions of the fifty states. Therefore, the question of legally acceptable student disciplinary procedures confronting both student and college personnel concerns the identification of the limits in light of current federal and state court rulings.

The Flexible Nature of Due Process

In the court decisions analyzed so far, judges were found to be interpreting the appropriateness of student disciplinary procedure with concepts difficult for laymen to define. Those frequently recurring concepts included "fair play," "reasonableness," "rudiments of an adversary proceeding," "substantial evidence," "reasonable cause to believe," "rare and exceptional circumstances," et cetera. It seems almost that the judges were setting up a reasonable person in abstract and asking him, given the facts and circumstances in a particular case, whether the procedure used could insure justice. It should be emphasized once again that colleges will have to use much the same method in deciding what kind of a procedure will be used for a particular case.

The recurrence in court decisions of phrases like "fair play" is added evidence that "due process" as recorded in this chapter is to travel only around the next bend of what promises to be a considerably longer journey. What the new Supreme Court appointees and the "Burger Court" might or might not do are, of course, problematical. However, it seems to be an historical fact that when more conservative judges appear on the bench, they at least tend to abide by the legal precedents already established.

Public and Private Institutions—Due Process Limitations

Clearly, students at publicly controlled colleges and universities have gained significant protections in the area of institutional control of student conduct. Yet post-*Dixon* case law has been limited by two significant factors. First and most obvious is that these protections are only applicable under the Fourteenth Amendment when a "state" denies due process. Although the argument has been made in several cases that the amount of state and federal aid received by private colleges, as well as various other entanglements in which they have become involved, is a sufficient nexus to constitute "state action," almost every judicial decision on this point has taken the position that such aid and entanglements are not sufficient. In fact the few "maverick" decisions in this regard have not won any significant judicial following.[87] However, despite this somewhat bleak legal position for students at private colleges, many such institutions have "voluntarily" set up disciplinary review boards that comply with the constitutional standards described in this chapter. Moreover, private colleges must conform to such procedures once established.[88]

Indeed, the *Joint Statement on Rights and Freedoms of Students* (see Appendix B), unlike the Fourteenth Amendment, makes no distinction between public and private institutions, and the reason appears self-evident: as a matter of sound educational philosophy it is difficult to rationalize a distinction in terms of fundamentally fair standards.

The second limitation of *Dixon* and its progeny is that these protections have been almost universally limited to student discipline and held inapplicable to student complaints about academic dismissals or unfair grades. As you will recall from Chapter 3, in *Horowitz* the Supreme Court concluded that for academic evaluations, a hearing is not required by the due process clause of the Fourteenth Amendment. However, the Court was badly divided in its reasoning, and Justice Marshall sharply pointed out that Horowitz was dismissed largely because of her conduct, as were the students in Goss v. Lopez. Moreover, under consideration were none of the inflammatory issues that civil rights lawyers might use in future academic appeals—e. g., changes in grading procedures and published requirements, undocumented clinical evaluations, a student's refusal to submit to a professor's personal request (sex, for example) or anything else

87. As you will recall from Chapter 2, however, where "invidious discrimination" is involved in private college affairs, the courts tend to find sufficient "state action."

88. See, e. g., Kwiatkowski v. Ithaca College, 82 Misc.2d 43, 368 N.Y.S. 2d 973 (1975).

that could be construed as being prejudicial, arbitrary, malicious or capricious on the part of professors or administrators. (See Part V).

As noted earlier, the *Dixon* doctrine was essentially established because of racial discrimination and the flagrant abuse of a state college's disciplinary authority. Subsequently, the technical formalism that was fleshed out of *Dixon* occurred largely because of similar reasons. Therefore, it might seem reasonable to conclude that if the black students in *Dixon* had been dismissed because of poor grades assigned unfairly by professors who disapproved of the students' civil rights activities, the Fifth Circuit would have required procedural protections for academic dismissals. Then, too, if under the same circumstances the institution had been private, "state action" would most assuredly have been found.

The fact of the matter is that due process is an evolving concept. For example, a competent attorney reading precedents in 1960 could say that procedural protections were not required for student conduct dismissals from public institutions. The same attorney reading precedents today could still say that procedural protections are not required for academic dismissals, but he might not be reading trends. Thus, the conclusion toward which these considerations ultimately lead is that the present involvement of the judiciary in the student-institutional relationship may merely be the tip of an iceberg.

GABRILOWITZ v. NEWMAN

United States Court of Appeals, First Circuit, 1978.
582 F.2d 100.

BOWNES, Circuit Judge.

This is an appeal by defendants-appellants, officials of the University of Rhode Island, pursuant to 28 U.S.C.A. § 1292(a) from an order of the United States District Court for the District of Rhode Island granting a preliminary injunction restraining appellants from conducting a disciplinary hearing against plaintiff-appellee, Steven A. Gabrilowitz, unless he is allowed to be represented by an attorney of his choice.

At the outset, we note that the issue before us is somewhat different than that presented by the terms of the injunction. We interpret the injunction to mean, as counsel did in their briefs, that appellee's attorney, if allowed to represent him at the hearing, would do so in the traditional sense, i. e., he would conduct direct and cross-examination. At oral argument, counsel for appellee stated in response to a question from the bench that it was not necessary for the lawyer to participate in direct or cross-examination; all that appellee wanted was that a lawyer be at his side during the hearing for consultation and advice. It is in this context, therefore, that we address ourselves to the case.

On November 11, 1977, the South Kingstown, Rhode Island, Police Department charged appellee, a senior at the University of Rhode Island (U.R.I.), with assault with intent to commit rape on another student on October 18, 1977. While appellee was at the police station being charged, a U.R.I. employee delivered a letter to him notifying him that he had been suspended from the school and barred from entering the campus. On November 16, 1977, U.R.I. sent appellee another letter informing him that the campus police had charged him with violating the U.R.I. *Community Standards of Behavior.* Gabrilowitz was directed to defend against the specific allegations of assault with intent to rape and an additional allegation of a later assault on the same student before the University Board on Student Conduct (U.B. S.C.). The letter outlined the procedures of the hearing and informed appellee of the existence of rules defining his rights at the hearing. One of the rules prohibits the existence or presence of legal counsel at the hearing. Appellee, thereupon, petitioned the district court for an injunction pursuant to 42 U.S.C.A. § 1983.

The procedural guidelines for a disciplinary hearing are set forth in Section 23 of Part 2 of RamPages, a student's guide to the University. While the student is not "permitted to employ professional legal counsel or other persons from outside the University community to present the case before the hearing board," he "shall have the right to request the assistance of an advisor of his/her choice from the community." Section 23.6.

"The technical rules of evidence applicable to civil and criminal trials are not applicable and the board shall rule on the admissibility of evidence." Section 23.8.

"During the hearing, the accused student and/or his/her advisor shall have the right to cross-examine all witnesses and to view and question all evidence presented to the judicial board. .   .   . " Section 23.9.

"Decisions shall be based only upon evidence and testimony introduced at the hearing." Section 23.10.

"In cases in which a student denies an allegation, the burden of proof shall rest upon the person bringing the charge." Section 23.11.

"All decisions made by a judicial board shall be by a majority vote. . . ." Section 23.12.

There is a right of appeal: "Such appeals shall be based only on specific evidence, presenting [sic] in writing, of fraud, denial of rights, procedural error, or on the claim of new evidence not previously available which would have materially affected the decision of the board." Section 23.22.

After a two-day hearing, the district court found irreparable harm and, while noting that the weight of authority supported the position of appellant, decided that, under the circumstances of this case, there was a due process violation.

[1] We note preliminarily that this action is not barred by the doctrine of Younger v. Harris, 401 U.S. 37 (1971). *Younger* applies to some civil and administrative proceedings, Geiger v. Jenkins, 401 U.S. 985 (1971), but is not a bar to a challenge to a state proceeding claimed to be constitutionally defective. Withrow v. Larkin, 421 U.S. 35, 44 n. 8 (1975); Gibson v. Berryhill, 411 U.S. 564 (1973). *Younger* presupposed the existence of a competent state forum. The U.R.I. *Community Standards of Behavior* prohibit legal counsel under all circumstances. There is no opportunity here to present the federal claim in a state judicial proceeding. *Cf.* Juidice v. Vail, 430 U.S. 327, 337 n. 15 (1977).

The issuance of a preliminary injunction lies within the sound discretion of the trial court and will not be reversed absent a clear abuse of that discretion, Grimard v. Carlston, 567 F.2d 1171 (1st Cir. 1978), or a clear error of law, Automatic Radio Mfg. Co. v. Ford Motor Company, 390 F.2d 113, 115 (1st Cir.), cert. denied, 391 U.S. 914 (1968). The power of a federal court to stay a civil proceeding because of a nexus between that proceeding and a pending criminal case is well established. United States v. Kordel, 397 U.S. 1, 12 n. 25, n. 27 (1970); Arthurs v. Stern, 560 F.2d 477, 479 (1st Cir. 1977); Silver v. McCamey, 95 U.S.App. D.C. 318, 221 F.2d 873 (1955).

Appellants' position is that the district court committed errors of law of such magnitude in issuing the injunction as to amount to an abuse of discretion. In addition to claiming that the order requiring the appointment of counsel in a student disciplinary hearing is contrary to authority, appellants also claim that it was

error for the district court to take into consideration the effect
that the disciplinary proceeding might have on the pending criminal action.

We deal first with the alleged error of considering the implications of the criminal case. We reject at the outset appellants' assertion that criminal and civil proceedings arising out of the same
facts are unrelated and must be treated as separate entities. Judicial deference to academic autonomy is not a before-the-fact
policy. Rather, it emerges from a balancing of the interests of
the parties. *See e. g.*, Downing v. LeBritton, 550 F.2d 689 (1st
Cir. 1977); Wasson v. Trowbridge, 382 F.2d 807 (2d Cir. 1967).

Were the appellee to testify in the disciplinary proceeding, his
statement could be used as evidence in the criminal case either
to impeach or as an admission if he did not choose to testify. Appellee contends that he is, therefore, impaled on the horns of a
legal dilemma: if he mounts a full defense at the disciplinary
hearing without the assistance of counsel and testifies on his own
behalf, he might jeopardize his defense in the criminal case; if
he fails to fully defend himself or chooses not to testify at all,
he risks loss of the college degree he is within weeks of receiving
and his reputation will be seriously blemished. Appellants respond that appellee risks nothing by mounting a full defense at
the hearing because his words would be compelled testimony
precluded from admission at the criminal case under the doctrine of Garrity v. New Jersey, 385 U.S. 493 (1967). *See also*
Lefkowitz v. Cunningham, 431 U.S. 801 (1977). It is our opinion
that neither *Garrity* nor *Lefkowitz* apply to the facts of this
case.

In Garrity v. New Jersey, supra, 385 U.S. 493, police officers
were questioned in the course of a state investigation of ticket
fixing.

> Before being questioned, each appellant was warned (1)
> that anything he said might be used against him in any state
> criminal proceeding; (2) that he had the privilege to refuse
> to answer if the disclosure would tend to incriminate him;
> but (3) that if he refused to answer he would be subject to
> removal from office. *Id.* at 494.

In setting aside the convictions that resulted from testifying at
the investigation, the Court focused on the fact that "[t]he
choice imposed on petitioners was one between self-incrimination
or job forfeiture." *Id.* at 496. The Court found: "Where the

choice is 'between the rock and the whirlpool,' duress is inherent in deciding to 'waive' one or the other." *Id.* at 498.[89]

Duress was also the key factor in Lefkowitz v. Cunningham, supra, 431 U.S. 801. At issue was the constitutionality of a New York statute providing that, if an officer of a political party was subpoenaed by a grand jury to testify about the conduct of his office and refused to testify or waive immunity against criminal prosecution, his term of office would be terminated and he would be disqualified from holding any party or public office for five years. In holding the statute unconstitutional, the Court said: "These cases settle that government cannot penalize assertion of the constitutional privilege against compelled self-incrimination by imposing sanctions to compel testimony which has not been immunized." *Id.* at 806.

The case at bar does not involve compelled testimony. The U.R.I. standards governing a disciplinary hearing neither require nor prohibit the drawing of an adverse inference from the silence of the accused. The procedures outlined in Section 23.10 state simply: "Decisions shall be based only upon evidence and testimony introduced at the hearing." The letter of suspension enclosed a list of procedures to be followed during the hearing which included the right "[t]o remain silent and not testify against himself/herself." The outline of procedures also stated: "Student[s] should remember that if they remain silent, the Board is compelled to hear the case and render a decision based on the evidence presented." Exhibit No. 4 at I(c)(5). There is no indication that the hearing board will consider the silence of an accused as either pointing to or being conclusive evidence of guilt. Appellee's testimony would be, therefore, entirely voluntary and subsequently admissible at the criminal case. Although the possibility of expulsion may make participation a wise choice, the hearing procedures do not place appellee "be-

---

89. Appellants misconstrue the reliance of the Vermont Supreme Court on *Garrity* in Nzuve v. Castleton State College, 133 Vt. 225, 232, 335 A.2d 321, 326 (1975), a case involving a factual situation nearly identical to the one at hand. The court in *Nzuve* concurred with the line of reasoning advanced in Furutani v. Ewigleben, 297 F.Supp. 1163 (N.D.Cal.1969), that any statement made under compulsion by students subject to disciplinary proceedings would not be admissible at a subsequent criminal proceeding. However, the court also found no compulsion to exist in *Nzuve*, and ruled that any statement made by the student would be voluntary and subsequently admissible at the criminal proceeding. We also note that the student in *Nzuve* was entitled to counsel at the disciplinary proceeding. *Nzuve*, supra, 133 Vt. at 232, 335 A.2d at 326.

tween the rock and the whirlpool." Garrity v. New Jersey, supra, 385 U.S. at 498. He can, if he wishes, stay out of the stream and watch the proceedings from dry land. But, if he does so, he forfeits any opportunity to control the direction of the current. Appellee must decide whether or not to testify at the hearing with the knowledge that, if he does, his statements may be used against him in the criminal case.

A factor which further complicates the choice is an awareness of his own inability to evaluate the effect his statements may have in the criminal case. Although the choice facing him is difficult, that does not make it unconstitutional. In McGautha v. California, 402 U.S. 183 (1971), a case involving a convicted murderer faced with the Hobson's choice of testifying in the hope of a lenient sentence and risking self-incrimination or remaining silent and facing a harsh sentence, the Court said: "The criminal process, like the rest of the legal system, is replete with situations requiring the 'making of difficult judgments' as to which course to follow." *Id.* at 213. This court followed *McGautha* when considering the case of a convicted felon found in violation of a deferred sentence agreement. Flint v. Mullen, 499 F.2d 100 (1st Cir. 1974). In rejecting the contention that defendant was unconstitutionally forced to choose between testifying at the sentencing hearing and risking self-incrimination at a criminal trial arising out of the same facts, we noted the applicability of the principle applied in *McGautha:*

> A defendant at a criminal trial for a substantive offense may wish to speak in his own defense but refrain, fearing a subsequent conspiracy prosecution. The choice is a strategic one, within a setting which requires many strategic choices.
>
> We would view the choice as less strategic were an adverse finding to be based on the fact of defendant's silence, rather than independent evidence, as here.

Flint v. Mullen, supra, 499 F.2d at 103.

The issue is not whether it is unconstitutional to force appellee to decide whether or not to testify in the disciplinary proceeding. The issue is whether he is unconstitutionally deprived of due process of law because he is forced to make that choice, or other choices, without the benefit of a lawyer in the face of a pending criminal case arising from the same facts that triggered the disciplinary proceeding.

We recognize, as did the district court, that most courts have declined to grant students the right to counsel in disciplinary proceedings. But, with the exception of Nzuve v. Castleton State College, 133 Vt. 225, 232, 335 A.2d 321, 326 (1975), and Furutani v. Ewigleben, 297 F.Supp. 1163 (N.D.Cal.1969), these cases did not involve the specter of a pending criminal case hovering over the hearing. *See e. g.,* Wasson v. Trowbridge, supra, 382 F.2d 807; Garshman v. Pennsylvania State University, 395 F.Supp. 912; Haynes v. Dallas County Junior College District, 386 F. Supp. 208 (N.D.Tex.1974); Barker v. Hardway, 283 F.Supp. 228 (S.D.W.Va.), cert. denied, 394 U.S. 905 (1969); Due v. Florida A. & M. University, 233 F.Supp. 396 (N.D.Fla.1963).

There are cases, however, holding that due process mandates the right to counsel at student expulsion proceedings. Mills v. Board of Education of District of Columbia, 348 F.Supp. 866, 881 (D.D.C.1972); Givens v. Poe, 346 F.Supp. 202, 209 (W.D. N.C.1972); Esteban v. Central Missouri State College, 277 F. Supp. 649, 651 (W.D.Mo.1967).

Because of the lack of compelling precedent, we apply the traditional due process balancing test as delineated by the Supreme Court in Mathews v. Eldridge, 424 U.S. 319, 334–335 (1976):

> More precisely, our prior decisions indicate that identification of the specific dictates of due process generally requires consideration of three distinct factors: First, the private interest that will be affected by the official action; second, the risk of an erroneous deprivation of such interest through the procedures used, and the probable value, if any, of additional or substitute procedural safeguards; and finally, the Government's interest, including the function involved and the fiscal and administrative burdens that the additional or substitute procedural requirement would entail.

See also Board of Curators of University of Missouri v. Horowitz, 435 U.S. 78, 99–100 (1978); Goldberg v. Kelly, 397 U.S. 254, 263–271 (1970).

The private interest and risk of erroneous deprivation that will be affected by the refusal of the hearing board to allow appellee the assistance of counsel depend upon the choice made at the hearing. If appellee chooses not to risk self-incrimination, he risks loss of his college degree. If he chooses to protect his degree, he risks self-incrimination and possible imprisonment of up to twenty years. All that appellee asks is that he be allowed the advice of counsel when he throws his college degree into the balance against a possible loss of liberty. Appellee has not asked that the hearing be postponed until after the criminal case has been tried; he is willing to participate in the hearing provided he is accompanied by counsel to advise and guide him. The role of his attorney could be analogized to that of counsel representing a client at a congressional investigative hearing. We echo the comments of the district judge:

> Further, the charge of assault with intent to rape is decidedly a matter of legal construction. Indeed, the definition of assault by itself, known and applied by legal professionals, is markedly different from the concept of laymen of what actions constitute an assault. The consequences of this plaintiff's participation in what otherwise might be strictly a University affair, reaches well beyond the University walls in terms of potential effect upon this plaintiff.

In Flint v. Mullen, supra, 499 F.2d 100, we found the convicted felon not to be presented with an unconstitutional choice because, *inter alia*, "[p]etitioner, however, was provided with counsel, and both petitioner and his counsel had full opportunity to cross-examine every adverse witness and could have called their own." Id. at 103. More recently, we reversed the enjoining of disciplinary proceedings against a physician until criminal charges arising out of the same actions were completed, finding: "The disciplinary proceeding was not brought solely to obtain evidence for the criminal prosecution; the doctor was aware during the hearing of the pending criminal actions; *the doctor had counsel;* . . . ." (emphasis added). Arthurs v. Stern, supra, 560 F.2d at 479 n. 5. *See also* United States v. Kordel, supra, 397 U.S. at 12 n. 25, n. 27.

Appellee's need for an attorney at the hearing seems obvious. With the exception of the denial of counsel, the disciplinary proceedings are, in many respects, similar to that of a criminal trial. Only a lawyer is competent to cope with the demands of an adversary proceeding held against the backdrop of a pending criminal case involving the same set of facts. The risk involved in participation at the hearing is substantial with counsel present; without counsel, it is enormous. The presence of counsel will, of course, not remove all risks. It will, however, enable appellee to make an intelligent, informed choice between the risks presented.

Academic institutions have a significant interest in the promulgation of procedures for the resolution of student disciplinary problems. Healy v. James, 408 U.S. 169, 184 (1972); Wasson

v. Trowbridge, supra, 382 F.2d 807; Dixon v. Alabama State Board of Education, 294 F.2d 150 (5th Cir.), cert. denied, 368 U.S. 930 (1961); Morales v. Grigel, 422 F.Supp. 988, 997 (D.N.H. 1976); Furutani v. Ewigleben, supra, 297 F.Supp. 1163. The limited role of counsel that we are considering, however, would not be very intrusive. Counsel would be present only to safeguard appellee's rights at the criminal proceeding, not to affect the outcome of the disciplinary hearing. Counsel's principal functions would be to advise appellee whether he should answer questions and what he should not say so as to safeguard appellee from self-incrimination; and to observe the proceeding first-hand so as to be better prepared to deal with attempts to introduce evidence from the hearing at a later criminal proceeding. To fulfill these functions, counsel need speak to no one but appellee. Counsel should, however, be available to consult with appellee at all stages of the hearing, especially while appellee is being questioned. Appellee, or his chosen U.R.I. counsel, will conduct the defense. The board will be conscious of the presence of an outsider, but this will emphasize the potential as well as present gravity of the charge. The presence of counsel will not place any financial or administrative burden on the University. It will set a precedent only for a truly unusual situation. *See* Garshman v. Pennsylvania State University, 395 F.Supp. 912 (M.D.Pa.1975). The most serious effect on the hearing of having counsel present that we can anticipate is that it will probably take longer to complete.

We hold that, because of the pending criminal case, the denial to appellee of the right to have a lawyer of his own choice consult with and advise him during the disciplinary hearing without participating further in such proceeding would deprive appellee of due process of law.

The order of the district court as modified is affirmed.

LEVIN H. CAMPBELL, Circuit Judge (dissenting).

As the court points out, the pendency of serious criminal charges against him could complicate appellee's defense at the University's disciplinary hearing, perhaps making the presence of counsel more valuable to him than in the ordinary disciplinary proceeding. Confronted with a similar situation involving prison disciplinary proceedings against convicts facing possible criminal charges arising out of the same incident, this court once held that the potential for self-incrimination required the presence of counsel to assist those convicts. Palmigiano v. Baxter, 487 F.2d 1280 (1st Cir. 1973), vacated and remanded, 418 U.S. 908 (1974), reaffirmed, 510 F.2d 534 (1st Cir. 1974). The Supreme Court disagreed, ruling

> "[n]either *Miranda* [*v. Arizona,* 384 U.S. 436 (1966)], nor *Mathis* [*v. United States,* 391 U.S. 1 (1968)], has any substantial bearing on the question whether counsel must be provided at '[p]rison disciplinary hearings [which] are not part of a criminal prosecution.' Wolff v. McDonnell, 418 U.S. 539 (1974). The Court has never held, and we decline to do so now, that the requirements of those cases must be met to render pretrial statements admissible in other than criminal cases."

Baxter v. Palmigiano, 425 U.S. 308, 315 (1976). After *Palmigiano,* I think we must accept that the pendency of criminal charges is irrelevant to the question of whether the due process clause allows a person to insist upon having counsel present at a separate civil proceeding involving similar facts. Although the Supreme Court's decision in *Palmigiano* drew upon its earlier ruling in Wolff v. McDonnell, another prisoner case, I do not see how its rationale can be meaningfully limited to prison disciplinary proceedings only. All the key factors present here were present there. Because I believe that *Palmigiano* applies here, and also because like my brothers I am not prepared to rule that due process requires the presence of retained counsel at all or most student disciplinary proceedings, I am unable to join the opinion of the court.

Not only does the court's decision run counter to the most directly applicable Supreme Court precedent, but I fear that it opens the door to a claim of right to counsel in almost all student disciplinary proceedings. Although the court stresses this case "will set a precedent only for a truly unusual situation," *ante* at 106, I do not see how the right recognized here can be so easily confined. Most conduct of a serious enough nature to merit disciplinary action will involve at least colorable misdemeanors, if not felonies, and a student very well might contend that the fact that criminal charges may be brought, even if they are not pending, requires the presence of counsel at his hearing. Furthermore, I believe most of the benefits of the passive assistance of counsel, the only right involved in the court's decision, can be realized through consultations between the student and his counsel before the proceeding begins or perhaps by periodic consultations outside the room while the hearing is in progress. For these reasons, I respectfully dissent.

Part III

SUBSTANTIVE GUARANTEES

Chapter 5

TINKER GOES TO COURT: CONSTITUTIONAL RIGHTS INSIDE THE SCHOOLHOUSE GATE

Congress shall make no law respecting an establishment of religion, or prohibiting the free exercise thereof; or abridging the freedom of speech, or of the press; or of the right of the people peaceably to assemble, and to petition the government for a redress of grievances.

(First Amendment, U. S. Constitution)

Thus, it seems reasonable that—

In our system, state-operated schools may not be enclaves of totalitarianism. School officials do not possess absolute authority over their students. Students in school as well as out of school are "persons" under our Constitution. They are possessed of fundamental rights which the state must respect, just as they themselves must respect their obligations to the State . . . It can hardly be argued that either students or teachers shed then their constitutional rights . . . at the schoolhouse gate.

(Justice Fortas in *Tinker*, 1969)

But there have been times—

Dear Gentlemen: We note your threat to take what you call "direct action" unless your demands are immediately met. We feel that it is only sporting to let you know that our governing body includes three experts in chemical warfare, two ex-commandos skilled with dynamite and torturing prisoners, four qualified marksmen in both small arms and rifles, two ex-artillerymen, one holder of the Victoria Cross, four Karate experts and a chaplain. The governing body has authorized me to tell you that we look forward with confidence to what you call a "confrontation," and, I may say, even with anticipation.

> (A letter from the Warden and Fellows of Wadham College, Oxford in reply to a set of non-negotiable demands by students—widely publicized in U.S. newspapers during the late sixties which seemingly captured the feelings of many Americans concerned with troubled campuses.)

> And long ago in France, even the peasants were becoming unruly—

And then there was a nasty spirit abroad in the village; the people were getting impudent, slacker about paying their feudal dues, and sulking about the performance of Manorial Corvees. In some districts peasants have begun "to stare proudly and insolently" at their lord, and are putting their hands in their pockets instead of saluting him. . . . A noble has been executed for squeezing his peasants a little too hard; it is becoming quite common for peasants to go to law with their seigneur. Things have come to a pretty pass in France.

> (W. H. Lewis in his study of life in France during the reign of Louis XIV, entitled *The Splendid Century*)

THE PROTEST SETTING

And in the 1960s, so too did things come to a pretty pass in American higher education. There was a nasty spirit abroad on the college campus; students were becoming impudent and slacker about paying their academic dues; "sulking and unwilling simply to attend classes and take notes, they [were] protesting, striking, sitting in, demanding a voice in the governance of their colleges, staring proudly and insolently at college presidents and professors alike." [1] And, yes, it too was becoming quite common for students to go to law with their masters. Indeed, things had certainly come to a pretty pass in the American college and university.

1. Edward J. Bloustein, "The New Student and His Role in American Colleges," in Metzger, Kadish, DeBardeleben and Bloustein, *Dimensions of Academic Freedom,* (Urbana: University of Illinois Press, 1969), pp. 92–93.

Just as significant, if not more so, is the fact that the highly publicized student unrest of the sixties, widespread and often violent, thrust the academic community into a posture of self-justification. On the one hand, institutional insecurity bred a remarkable public relations' effort—as if it could never be admitted that things were going badly. On the other, guilt feelings among some members of the academic community motivated loud cries of *mea culpa* along with quick promises of a new age of institutional reform. For some period of time, in fact, it seemed that higher education was taking on the characteristics of an advanced schizophrenic as a defense against the threats of the new realities. It was a time (and in many ways still is—but for some other reasons) when educators might have recalled with poignant empathy the plight of Socrates and with good reason figure that he might have been but the first among an increasing number of professors to drink themselves to death.

Actually, a great variety of voices were speaking protest on campus. Not all were saying the same thing, and not all of those who did agree were doing so for the same reasons. To be sure, many of the troubles on campus during the sixties had their origins off campus, but it would still seem myopic to attribute campus troubles solely to external causes. Of course the civil rights movement first and later the Vietnam War provided student activists with bountiful moral anger and energy. But then the indubitable fact is that some of the same moral inconsistencies and even some new ones (not withstanding Watergate) have little troubled the present generation; or at least they have not expressed much open and hostile frustration with the gap between America as it is and as it could be. Furthermore, if racial injustice and war provided the *sine qua non* for the moral outrage expressed by students in the sixties, it appears strange that racism and the Korean War in the fifties, together with McCarthyism and the loyalty oath issues, did not flatten the academic landscape with student protest.

While it is risky to attribute a list of specific reasons for radical student activism, it nevertheless came with a force that hindsight makes appear inevitable. Even on the threshold of 1964, virtually no one predicted it. The vision of hindsight, of course, is well known, but in using it to advantage one can see a plethora of discrete causal issues which impacted American colleges and universities—to which they responded and with which they interacted—but typically each issue was closely intermingled with others, and all were part of and suffused by the extraordinary social ferment and activism of those years. Moreover, even though societal issues are intimately related to the purposes of the higher learning, the growing problems within the larger context of the contemporary world also coincided with some festering internal problems on campus. Thus, as student awareness and sensitivity over outside societal issues increased, these concerns became catalytic and set in motion the assimilation of internal institutional tensions.

Thus, the interactive friction of external and internal problems, it seems, produced the spark to flame tactics of student protest which soon led to the virtual annulment of a whole set of attitudes and principles within the academic community. Along side and exacerbated by the problems engendered from outside, the internal issues were legion: bureaucratic depersonalization and authoritarian notions of discipline; constitutional rights of expression, fair rules and procedural requirements of notice and process before disciplinary action; the relevancy of curriculum and the effectiveness of instructional delivery systems; the fairness of admission policies and the efficacy of academic standards; the relationship of higher education with the military-industrial complex; the governance of colleges and universities and the participatory requirements of democracy; the condition of minorities on campus and so forth.

These issues certainly deserved contemplation and resolution. In fact, all of them, including the outside societal issues, needed the exposure that objectivity, disinterest and academic freedom could provide. Such a process, of course, implied not only the efficacy of the "robust and free exchange of ideas," but also that the process be performed within the framework of polite controversy. However, it appears that it was precisely these principles that were among the first casualties in the student revolution.

In this sense one is compelled to ask: Was higher education's process ideal of truth-seeking a mere shibboleth, an eminent fiction of the past? Or was it that students refused to play by the rules?

With this line of questioning we are driven to seek answers, and find them by discovering a necessary relation between the institutional behavior of colleges and universities during the sixties and student reasons and techniques for protest at that time. Educators and students, as with most people, many times, of course, say one thing but do something else, so the widespread and highly-publicized confrontation on campuses probably did more to point out the contrast between the academic community's outer image and its inner qualities than anything else in its history. Moreover, student protest forced colleges and universities to "look in the mirror," and for better or worse and, undoubtedly, some of both, the result was change. Pressure almost unavoidably means change. To react is in some part to transform. And all forms of pressure, from simple rhetoric to mass rebellion, share in this subtle or not so subtle process of alteration. In any case, it may be a truism to say that institutions acquire their philosophical underpinnings less in the course of their origins than after they are in place and come under attack. As seemingly resistent to change as educational institutions might appear, they are not exempt from this process as the events of the turbulent sixties so aptly demonstrate.

Thus one of the more important stories to be told about college and university issues during the sixties lies in the growth and development of a new political force—student activism. With its intensity, its focus on both academic and social problems, and its widespread base, the primary relevance of that movement today is that it challenged the way in which colleges and universities were run, and in so doing it sharpened awareness of some deep-seated flaws in American higher education—at least as seen from many students' point of view. Some of those perceived flaws such as bureaucratic depersonalization, restrictions on information access, *in loco parentis* kinds of student conduct surveillance, and assembly-line techniques in the teaching-learning function most certainly needed exposure. In a manner of speaking, campus disorders applied public light and political heat to an academe, which for generations had dispatched its products to an acquiescent public.

The Cumulative Chain Reaction
Even though the decade of the sixties began with almost totally apathetic students, it ended with students who had become increasingly active and militant. The result, of course, had many campuses considerably immobilized, disrupted and confused. There had been incidents of student protest in earlier decades, but for the most part such incidents involved only a few students protesting isolated issues in localized settings. In 1960, students protested at the House Un-American Activities Committee hearings in San Francisco, and in 1960 and 1961 the Freedom Riders and black college students employed collective agitation (basic-

ally sit-ins) in the South. The years 1961 and 1962 witnessed nonviolent student protests over President Kennedy's Cuban policy, and the same impulse to protest took many students south to join the Student Nonviolent Coordinating Committee (SNCC) in 1963.[2]

When one looks at the situation historically, therefore, one can see that injustice was not new, nor was hypocrisy. Neither was student unrest; nor an establishment bent on maintaining order by force. What seems almost entirely new was the way a growing number of young people were learning to look at life and to perceive at once its glaring inconsistencies. Along with this, college students were beginning to recognize the power and impact of an organized, unified minority. The foremost example of this new situation was the Civil Rights Movement, and, largely from this experience, college students began to organize unified protests, not only against assumed injustices in society in general, but also against injustices they felt existed on their own campuses.

Thus one might say that just as the 1954 Supreme Court decision, Brown v. Board of Educ., was the legal turning point in racial relations, the sit-ins were the psychological turning point in both race relations and in student political involvement throughout the country.[3] However, the earliest and most dramatic area of on-campus student protest took place on the Berkeley Campus during the 1964 Free Speech Movement. At this point not only the location of protest changed from off-campus to on-campus, but the technique of protest changed as well—from nonviolent to violent forms.

Following the Berkeley crisis, which now seems to have been the Bastille of higher education as well as the prototype of things to come, hundreds of colleges and university campuses in all regions of the country experienced organized student protest. For the most part these incidents involved students at four-year institutions of higher education, but inevitably such widespread protest activity had an impact on students at two-year community colleges, high schools, junior high schools, and even some elementary schools.

2. Paul Jacobs and Saul Landau, *The New Radicals: A Report with Documents* (New York: Vintage Books, 1966), pp. 3–4.

3. Jack Newfield, *A Prophetic Minority* (New York: The New American Library, 1966), p. 38.

The entire affair was magnified by immediate and simultaneous news coverage which kept everyone informed of the latest student eruptions. Protests were then imitated by many who shared the general rationale of dissent and disillusionment with the college or university at hand—most convenient, unprotected, open targets. The point should be made, however, that confrontation and violence made the headlines while the peaceful pursuit of other educational activities went relatively unnoticed. Thus, it was easy for the public to visualize most campuses as being in flames; too many people lost perspective by believing that student revolt had become a way of life on most campuses, and, accordingly, public disenchantment with higher education soon became greater than the actual cause would justify.

Yet, as the technique of protest achieved public attention and often recognizable results for the students, the technique itself became contagious. The increased attention, especially from the major news media and many of the nation's leading dignitaries, was a heady discovery which encouraged many to try even harder to attract more attention. Regardless of motivations, however, these protestors could not be written off as a bearded, long-haired, exhibitionist minority. In fact, some of the top students—neat and cleanshaven—were sometimes in the front lines of protest demonstrations. Then, too, even though the student protest movement in general remained "peripheral to the philosophies and lives of the vast number of American students," [4] many in this majority appeared to be interested in and sympathetic toward the concerns of the protesting minority.

Obviously, the condition of campus disorders and the resulting external scrutiny and repudiation pulled our colleges and universities several ways, making for an extraordinarily complex experience and an unprecedented degree of confusion. Solution seemed to pose many vexing problems. Indeed, the woods were soon full of task forces but there were few generals. The system was tampered with, some improvements were effected, but overall the initial response was largely an unsophisticated and/or insensitive search for efficiency—to bring students under control.

The impulse for this solution, apparently, was not appropriately anchored to a most revealing inquiry into the fundamental purpose and mode of higher education and, of course, how students should relate to them. President Levi of the University of Chi-

4. Lewis S. Feuer, *The Conflict of Generations/The Character and Significance of Student Move-* ments (New York: Basic Books, 1969), p. 481.

cago struck to the core of this relationship when he declared that American colleges and universities are not neutral. They exist to propagate a special point of view: "the worthwhileness of the intellectual pursuit of truth." Put quite simply, we should foster academic freedom in this pursuit in order to avoid error and discover truth; so far, we have found no other way to achieve this objective.

So, too, with dissent. The higher learning should not encourage dissent for sentimental reasons; dissent should be encouraged because we have learned that we cannot effectively perform our purposes without it. A college or university that silences dissent, whether by force, intimidation, the withholding or rigging of information or a foggy intellectual climate, invites failure and eventually disaster for the society it serves. An institution of higher learning that discourages criticism and originality is left with passive acquiescence of error and minds that are unimaginative and dull. And with stunted minds, as with stunted people and institutions, few great things can be accomplished.

With students the protective cloak of academic freedom had hardly ever been apparent, and in the sixties, of course, the mode and purpose of the higher learning seemed too fragile to withstand the combination of student activism and public scrutiny. Thus when students began to lay claim to academic freedom by going to court, institutional response was often merely that of creating among students an illusion of certain rights while withholding the substance of them where possible.

Briefly, the emphasis was supposed to be on teaching students how to think rather than what to think; ideally it sought to open minds, not close them. But students were becoming more and more capable of spotting a fast "snow" job. They knew, for instance, that we had not found final truth in physics or biology. Then how were they supposed to know that we had found final truth in politics?

But had we? Speaker bans and censorship of student newspapers, for instance, said as much. The thrust was almost everywhere the same: To equate student dissent with lawlessness and nonconformity with insult and disloyalty. It was as if to argue that unacknowledged problems disappear. It seems that discontent was not to be considered an honest expression of genuine grievances but of willfulness, or perversity, or perhaps of the crime of being young, and that if it could only be stifled, harmony would be restored to our distracted campuses and society. It must have been obvious to most students that the principle of truth-seeking was not to be applied to them or, perhaps worse, that it was more a shibboleth than a dynamic application and practice.

What was needed in higher education was a re-affirmation of the intimate tie between critical dissent and democracy, for the absence of one always signals the demise of the other, and all too often neither is appreciated until both disappear. More basically, technical information alone has never been enough to produce the thoughtful and self-critical society we need, any more than technology has been enough to produce humanistic progress. As Walt Whitman wrote in *Democratic Vistas*:

> Know you not, dear, earnest reader, that the people of our land may all read and write, and may all possess the right to vote—and yet the main things may be entirely lacking?

Colleges and universities, therefore, needed to abandon the comforts of *in loco parentis* and to examine critically, as many students were, the distinction between those privileges that could be withheld and those which were the national birthright of students. Early on, it should have been apparent that we could no longer afford the cynicism engendered by the wide discontinuities between the social science classroom, for instance, and the real world of the student's total educational experience. During the sixties, however, public confidence in higher education began to decline rather rapidly, and soon the academic community was able to count on few dependable allies. The dominant public response to student activism revealed the limits that continued to define conceptions of student rights.

The Erosion of Authority and Purpose

In retrospect, the decade of the sixties seems like a "bad trip." The war in Vietnam and racial injustices on one hand and the shortcomings of higher education on the other stirred one student protest after another. In fact many college and university administrators those days were nearly driven to despair by the disruptions and disorders that frequently threatened both the tranquility of their campuses and the traditional organization of collegiate authority.

The student movement's frequent arrogance, self-righteousness, unrestrained emotionalism and impatience, its strident, action-oriented anti-intellectualism and its proclivity for adventurism and physical destruction, and its frequent hypocrisy, intimi-

dation and locker-room scatology—were, to say the least, serious
threats to the disciplined freedoms and functions of higher education. Repeatedly, in fact, there were breakdowns in the area
of old-fashioned, courteous, civil communication. Professor L. G.
Heller of the City College of New York describes one such example which, on the eve of the *Tinker* decision, took place at his
institution:

> "Go fuck yourself, you cock-sucking, mother-fucking bas-
> tard," snarled the leader of the revolutionists when Dr. Buell
> Gallagher, the Christian minister serving as president of the
> college, moved as though to say something. The clergyman
> sank back into his cair, and the obscene verbal abuse mount-
> ed in intensity. Possibly six or seven hundred faculty mem-
> bers—many, scholars of international reputation—sat in
> stunned silence. Forty or fifty armed militants crowded the
> steps across the podium, brandishing makeshift weapons—
> jagged metal bars, clubs, knives, and spears—while the
> vituperation continued. Behind them, towered an enorm-
> ous, world-famous mural depicting Alma Mater presenting a
> diploma to a new graduate, who stood clad in cap and gown,
> as the Muses, and also a solemn assemblage of scholars,
> scientists, and various other learned men from the past and
> present watched. This was Great Hall, pressed into service
> in recent years for registration, but ofttimes the scene of
> solemn academic ceremony or scholarly activity. From the
> very same podium senators, governors, mayors, Nobel laure-
> ates, Pulitzer Prize winners, philosophers, physicists—dis-
> tinguished men of every type—had spoken. Now a very be-
> ligerent "student" stood there—mouthing obscenities.[5]

Yale University's Professor Kenneth Keniston, an articulate observer of the student protest scene, explained the consequences
of such tactics at the 1971 Notre Dame Commencement: the
"movement and new culture, dedicated above all to peace, justice,
democracy and equality was moving toward the systematic violation of these various principles." [6]

In terms of causing durable change, moreover, the general
mode of student activism had an overall dysfunctional element—
that is, mere confrontation was not the answer to either campus

5. L. G. Heller, *The Death of the
    American University* (New Rochelle,
    New York: Arlington House, 1973),
    p. 100. Reprinted by permission.

6. Quoted in *The New York Times*,
    June 14, 1971, p. 44.

or societal ills, especially when done hatefully. Gandhi explained this best in his wise counsel that the confronter should aim at
future community with the confronted. But student radicals too
frequently harried administrators into extreme positions, and
gradually the middle ground was blasted away. The accepted and
logical strategem of much of the radical ideology was to wear
down the other side, emotionally and physically. Thus, behavior
on both sides generally became self-defeating in that its alienat-
ing circumstances proved too strong for a later reconciliation of
differences upon which to build viable agreements.

The sheer recklessness of much activism of student radicals also
reflected a rather disconcerting lack of commitment to their college or university. To explicate, Joseph Schwab aptly pointed
out:

> . . . their "involvement" with the institution [of higher
> education] is inadequate: that is, their felt sense of its life
> expectancy does not exceed the four years of their tenure;
> their sense of the threat of having to undergo the conse-
> quences of a bad decision is pale and dilute by virtue of their
> merely peripheral membership in the community and remote
> connection with those among the faculties whose member-
> ship is intimate and durable.[7]

Yet, in returning to the harried administrator, one might have
reasonably wondered whether the spirit of Munich had really retreated into the past. Many times, too frequently in fact, institutional policy became one with public opinion and thus there were
some flagrant abuses of students' constitutional rights. Then,
when the courts seriously began to intervene in this scenario, and
all the horror stories of due process violations and court put-
downs were discussed and digested, many professors and administrators rushed to embrace the student activist in an orgy of guilt
and often condescension. Speaker heckling, the occupation of
buildings and offices, classroom disruption, the pelting of unpopular speakers or college administrators with rotten vegetables
and other such forms of behavior were often overlooked or gin-
gerly side-stepped. And was such feckless tolerance not as
brutalizing as rigid tolerance? In a condition of anarchy, of
course, neither freedom nor dignity could prosper.

Also, campus disorders all too frequently evoked reforms more
to appease students than to implement powerfully-felt education-

---

7. Joseph J. Schwab, *College Curriculum and Student Protest* (University of Chicago Press, 1969), pp.
8–9.

al principles. Consider, for instance, the following phenomena: grade inflation, the elimination of foreign language requirements from the curricula, the steady dilution even of mild distribution requirements in the general education curriculum, and the regularity with which course achievement standards were lowered—simply less reading, writing and study. Even though one may have approved or disapproved of one or another of these developments, not one of them appears to have been the product of fundamental educational principles. As Charles Frankel rightfully claimed, "they were decisions made of short-range expediency, made not out of conviction but dispiritedness, confusion, demoralization, and absence of confidence and an indisposition to exercise authority and to lead." [8]

College and university leaders seemed to be torn between the need to take a stand and a strategic desire to shift with the winds. Retrospectively, one must recall that the new sound and fury surrounding the decision-making processes, signified something. The student thrust toward greater involvement in processes formerly dominated by college authorities, for instance, many times resulted in fears about status and power, particularly among administrators who correctly perceived their traditional prerogatives eroding. Moreover, administrators not only had to contend with fears of losing power, they also had to face continuing pressures from trustees, alumni and the general public to behave in traditional patterns. This condition, of course, led to a serious dilemma.

If administrators clung to the modes of behavior that coincided with public stereotypes, they ran the risk of further antagonizing students, thus provoking more confrontations which generally culminated in public censure and lack of confidence. On the other hand administrators who tended to relate creatively to the new forces at work within their institutions were likely to be labeled as "fuzzy-headed" liberals and severely castigated, especially if incidents arose over issues traditionally unrelated to the internal affairs of these institutions and consequently beyond the control of the administrators. Demonstrations against the war in Vietnam or national policy were illustrations of this dilemma. Caught between the two, many administrators found themselves whip-sawed. If they sought to gain public confidence by prevent-

8.   Charles Frankel, "Reflections on a   Worn-Out   Model," *Daedalus*, Fall, 1974, p. 25.

ing student demonstrations, they alienated students and, in the process, escalated the violence of the confrontation. But then if they supported the causes espoused by the demonstrators, they became the targets of outraged citizens who felt such issues were clearly beyond the scope of student concern.

Perhaps more dangerous than either of the above extremes were attempts to occupy some kind of middle ground. Most attempts to compromise only served in fact, to alienate both public and internal constituencies. More than that, the compromising of the higher learning's vital doctrines of disinterested inquiry and academic excellence that occurred meant giving in to some strong anti-intellectual motivations among both students and the general public. As for suspending classes in order to allow students to participate in demonstrations, for instance, President Kingman Brewster of Yale later commented, "One thing they didn't accomplish, really, was getting down to the serious business of improving the world. People accept the therapeutic bash as a substitute for hard work."

Coupled with the alienation from authority and regimentation that characterized the changing values among students, neither crisis management, nor abuse of institutional authority, nor even compromise worked. After each uprising the students seemed more alienated than ever, the faculty and administration humiliated and dismayed. A number of presidents resigned. Middle Americans and their political representatives turned against higher education as such. Thus, something like an interactive and self-defeating cycle was set in motion supported in considerable depth by guilt and by rationalized theories of failure which appeared to be confirmed. Under such conditions, we had the recipe for professional cynicism and skepticism—a perception that almost anything one might do was fundamentally meaningless. The more pronounced the condition became, the more that healthy coping mechanisms became damaged and the more that the deteriorating climate became inviting for a veritable inundation of external interference. Excessive self-rejection, therefore, came perilously close to producing a condition in which we knew who we were not, but not who we were which, in turn, eventually flirted with the equivalency of being nothing.

Meanwhile, these forces did much to obfuscate the nature and purpose of the higher learning. Even though we frequently claimed that we could not afford to be indifferent or neutral in this regard, evidence seems to indicate otherwise. Moreover, the crucial issue of the higher learning and the principles upon which it rested, or should have rested, was big enough and broad enough to be for without supposing that one could personally do all that much about it or that individual gestures one might make would, in turn, make any difference. Beyond that, when some did do something about it, there was the problem of the sheer size and perhaps even capriciousness of the whole concept so that it often seemed to be a catchall so loose and ill-defined that when placed in the pressure cooker of student activism and public scrutiny it was peculiarly susceptible to posturing, pointlessness, and fecklessness.

PRE-TINKER OBSERVATIONS

Confusion, or at least uncertainty, about the objectives of the higher learning was matched by disappointment in the apparent inability of higher education to bring its clientele under control. As you will recall, the budget of student discontent with their colleges and universities was in part a balance brought forward from the fifties and early sixties. In fact, it is a good idea to get a running start here with the reminder that as early as 1957, and well before disruption on campuses became common, the question had arisen among some whether students were being pushed around without due regard to their civil liberties.[9] Yet, it was in the widespread confrontations with academic authorities in the next decade that the courts were provided repeated opportunities to test and delimit the area of student rights. Of course most colleges and universities had rules to keep disorder in hand, but violations of those rules led to suspensions and even expulsions. To gain redress for these disciplinary measures (many of such were constitutionally questionable at best), students often turned to the courts.

The demonstrations of the early sixties alone, nonetheless, would never have been enough to label the sixties the "turbulent decade." The protests that did occur at that time had two main targets: first, civil rights, especially for blacks; and second, the banning of nuclear weapons and disarmament. Student protest tactics during this period were generally off-campus and non-violent, and thus such activities did little to excite and alarm the population as a whole. In fact, according to the *President's Commission on Student Unrest*, "When the decade began, the Ameri-

9. See, e. g., Warren Seavy, "Dismissals of Students," *Harvard Law Review*, Vol. 70, June, 1975, p. 1406.

can public was impressed with the courage, idealism, and restraint of student civil rights workers."[10]

Actually, it took the Vietnam conflict in the latter part of the sixties to jolt the student movement into massive protest. The turn from the civil rights issues to Vietnam was explained in part by Lewis Feuer: "It was not that the problems of civil rights had suddenly ceased to exist; rather the issue no longer offered as good an emotional opportunity for conducting a generational struggle." [11] However, the manner in which the Supreme Court would treat this protest was not completely clear, since the Court did not make any decisions directly on the subject until 1969, in Tinker v. Des Moines Independent Community School Dist.[12] Nevertheless, a brief analysis of some specific lower court decisions suggests that there was a developing pattern.

The First and the Fourteenth Amendments to the Constitution proved to be critical here. Again, as you will recall, on the procedural side of due process it was decided in the 1961 *Dixon* decision that students were entitled to notice and hearing before a public institution could impose severe disciplinary penalties. But you should also note that the right to procedural due process is only half the student's battle in obtaining fair treatment. Notice and a hearing only guarantee the student time to prepare an adequate defense and at the hearing to show that he did not violate a college rule. Hearings will not determine whether the rule was a fair one in the first place. If, for instance, a college had a rule against holding hands on campus, the right to notice and hearing would not protect students if they were, in fact, holding hands. Therefore, the due process constraints of the Fourteenth Amendment inhibit unfair rules as well as unfair procedures; or, in other words, on the substantive side of due process students are protected from arbitrary or unreasonable regulations of the public college or university.

The Nature of Freedom of Expression and its Role in a Democratic Society

The first task—i. e., before analyzing the early legal responses to student demonstrations—will be to consider at least a part of the historical formulation of First Amendment freedoms of speech and assembly. Needless to say, perhaps, this consideration is important because, with mounting student protest, courts were in-

10. Published by the Government Printing Office, 1969.

11. Feuer, op. cit.

12. 393 U.S. 503 (1969).

creasingly called upon to draw the lines between First Amendment guarantees and the necessarily associated rights of others; and, since there was virtually no First Amendment case law in sync with the constitutional mandate of *Dixon,* these courts generally relied on case law related to, but existing outside of, the educational context.

At this point it is possible only to state certain broad generalizations, but certainly, the criterion most frequently used by these early student protest decisions to distinguish between protected and unprotected expression was the "clear and present danger" test; i. e., whether the danger to public welfare outweighs the interest in freedom of expression. The test was first announced in 1919 by Justice Holmes in Schenck v. United States [13] as follows:

> . . . the character of every act depends upon the circumstances in which it is done. . . . The most stringent protection of free speech would not protect a man in *falsely shouting fire in a theatre* and causing a panic. . . . The question in every case is whether the words used are used in such circumstances and are of such a nature as to create a clear and present danger that they will bring about the substantive evils that Congress has the right to prevent. It is a question of proximity and degree.[14]

Later, in Whitney v. California (1927),[15] the Supreme Court modified the test somewhat by indicating that *imminency of danger* is an essential requirement to the validity of any curb on free expression. Here, the Court stated:

> . . . no danger flowing from speech can be deemed clear and present unless the incidence of the evil is so *imminent* that it may befall before there is opportunity for full discussion.[16]

Actually, by the 1960s, the Supreme Court had adopted the view that there should be "more exacting judicial scrutiny" of the First Amendment freedoms. The Court, however, had not

13. 249 U.S. 47 (1919).

14. Id., at 52 (emphasis added). The "falsely shouting fire in a theatre" phrase is one of the most frequently repeated interpretations of constitutional law one will encounter inside or outside the courtroom; nonetheless, in 1978, apparently Steve Martin extended its meaning:

"Can you shout 'MOVIE' in a crowded firehouse? To date, the Supreme Court hasn't rendered a decision on that one, but some of my firemen friends are waiting in tense anticipation.)

15. 274 U.S. 357 (1927), p. 373.

16. Id., at 377 (emphasis added).

stopped here, but moved on to the principle that these freedoms were so vitally essential, and of more fundamental importance than the other provisions of the Constitution, that they occupied a preferred place in our scheme of constitutional values.   In this sense, the Court required a weighing or balancing of any competing interests which, in effect, meant that any regulation of First Amendment freedoms had to be judged by the interests to be secured by the regulation against the amount of freedom that was lost or impaired.[17]   In fact, even though there is a presumption in favor of the constitutionality of most laws and regulations, by this time the Court was holding that any law or regulation that on its face limited First Amendment freedoms, the presumption was *against* rather than in favor of its validity.

Laws or regulations trespassing on First Amendment freedoms, therefore, were now facing the so-called "reverse presumption of constitutionality" test.   The Supreme Court had clearly pointed out this condition in United States v. C.I.O. (1948): [18]

> Thus, the burden is always on the party seeking to uphold the statute to establish constitutionally sufficient grounds for the restraint   .   .   .   i. e., a sufficient government interest to justify the impairment of the rights involved.[19]

Thus, in Terminiello v. Chicago (1949),[20] the Court, by a 5–4 decision, reversed Terminiello's conviction and $100 fine under a broadly-worded Chicago ordinance which permitted the punishment for breach of the peace by speech that "stirs the public to anger, invites disputes, brings about a condition of unrest, or creates a disturbance."   The controversy resulted from a highly inflamatory address by Terminiello, a defrocked Catholic priest, in which he denounced Eleanor Roosevelt as "Queen of the World's Communists," professed knowledge of a Jewish conspiracy to sterilize the entire German population through syphillis inoculations, referred to Jews as "filthy scum," and linked Democrats, Jews and Communists together in remarks filled with race hatred.   The speech took place in an auditorium in Chicago before a crowd of about 800 persons.   Meanwhile, outside the auditorium, a protesting crowd of over 1,000 milled about, yelling and throwing stones at the windows.   A cordon of policemen as-

17.   See, e. g., Joint Anti-Fascist Refugee Committee v. McGrath, 341 U. S. 123 (1951).

18.   335 U.S. 106 (1948).

19.   Id., at 107.

20.   337 U.S. 1 (1949).

signed to the meeting was unable to prevent several outbreaks of violence, including the smashing of doors and windows.

The Supreme Court never reached the question whether the speech itself might be punishable, because it found that the Chicago ordinance as interpreted by the lower court permitted the punishment of speech that was protected by the Constitution:

> [A] function of free speech under our system of government is to invite dispute. It may indeed best serve its high purpose when it induces a condition of unrest, creates dissatisfaction with conditions as they are, or even stirs people to anger. Speech is often provocative and challenging. It may strike at prejudices and preconceptions and have profound unsettling effects as it presses for acceptance of an idea. . . . The ordinance as construed by the trial court seriously invaded this province. It permitted conviction of petitioner if his speech stirred people to anger, invited public dispute, or brought about a condition of unrest. A conviction resting on any of those grounds may not stand. . . . [In addition, the Court concluded], freedom of speech, though not absolute . . . is nevertheless protected against censorship or punishment, unless shown likely to produce a clear and present danger of a serious substantive evil that rises far above public convenience, annoyance, or unrest.[21]

It might appear that the Supreme Court in its *Terminiello* decision rejected the "fighting words" theory of Chaplinski v. New Hampshire (1942); [22] however, as already mentioned, the *Terminiello* holding never reached the question of whether the speech itself might be punishable. Instead, the Court struck at the Chicago ordinance, holding it "void on its face"—interestingly, an issue that was raised by *neither* of the parties to the litigation.

21. Id. at 4–5.

22. In Chaplinsky v. New Hampshire, 315 U.S. 568 (1942), a Jehovah's Witness called a police officer a "God damned racketeer" and "a damned Fascist," in violation of a state statute whose purpose, the state court held, was to forbid words "such as have a direct tendency to cause acts of violence by the persons to whom, individually, the remark is addressed." The Supreme Court agreed: "There are certain well-defined and limited classes of speech, the prevention and punishment of which have never been thought to raise any constitutional problem. These include the lewd and obscene, the profane, the libelous, and the insulting or 'fighting' words—those which by their very utterance inflict injury or tend to incite an immediate breach of the peace. . . the appellations 'damned racketeer' and 'damned Fascist' are epithets likely to provoke the average person to retaliation, and thereby cause a breach of the peace."

The fact of the matter is that one of the oldest and best-established rights of any organized community is the right to protect itself from a breach of the peace. Such a breach is a "substantive evil which the state can prevent" through the exercise of its police power; therefore, a speech or assembly which presents a "clear and present danger" of causing a breach of the peace is punishable, even though the "substantive evil which the state can prevent" might not actually occur. Thus the courts, in reviewing cases which allege a violation of freedom of speech or assembly on this ground, must determine (1) that the statute really defines a breach of the peace, and (2) that a clear and present danger of such a breach actually existed.

A case in which the making of a speech was punished as a breach of the peace, and such action later upheld by the Supreme Court, can be found in Feiner v. New York (1951).[23]   In this case, the Supreme Court, dividing six to three denied the free speech claim of Irving Feiner, a young sidewalk orator, who had used derogatory language about public officials and certain pressure groups to a crowd of some 80 people clustered around him in a predominantly black residential area of Syracuse, New York. Feiner was arrested by two policemen at the scene on a charge of disorderly conduct and incitement to riot,[24] after one man had threatened to haul him from his platform. The Supreme Court's majority of six held that the New York statute, which provided for the preservation of order and protection of the general welfare, and the officers' action in light of their perception that a clear danger of disorder was threatened, did not violate the constitutional guarantees of freedom of expression. The three dissenting judges, however, argued that the record showed merely an unsympathetic audience; that there was no danger of a riot; and that if the police had been really interested in preserving order, they would have arrested those who were threatening to break up the gathering.

The *Feiner* case has never been overruled, but later the Supreme Court tended to emphasize the need for governments to act under more precisely-drawn statutes. For example, in Edwards v. South Carolina (1963) [25] the Supreme Court reversed

---

23. 340 U.S. 315 (1951).

24. Feiner, for example, had called President Truman "a bum," Mayor O'Dwyer "a bum," the American Legion "a Nazi Gestapo," Syracuse's Mayor Costello a "champagne-sipping bum," and exhorted the blacks to "rise up in arms and fight for their right." (However, not very inciteful when compared with *Terminiello*.)

25. 372 U.S. 229 (1963), a case that was off-campus and did not directly involve an educational institution.

the convictions of 187 black high school and college students who had been arrested for holding a mass meeting in front of the South Carolina State House to protest denial of their civil rights. The police protected the students from a crowd of about 300 onlookers for approximately forty-five minutes and then gave the students fifteen minutes in which to disperse. When the students refused to do so, they were arrested for breach of the peace. The Supreme Court ruled that "The Fourteenth Amendment does not permit a State to make criminal the peaceful expression of unpopular views." Moreover, the Court stressed that the convictions of the students had not been based upon a violation of a precise and narrowly-drawn statute limiting or prescribing specific conduct, such as interfering with traffic.

Thus, at this point, the status of the law was that persons could assemble at public facilities for protest purposes so long as they did not interfere with programs or attempt to appropriate those facilities for their own use.[26] On the other hand, if the manner of expression was incompatible with the normal activity of a particular place at a particular time, prohibition or punishment was constitutionally permissible. It was clear, therefore, that under the guise of exercising freedom of speech and peaceful assembly, people were *not* free to incite riots, to block traffic, to take over a public building (or a college), to seize and hold the office of a mayor (or a university president), to hold demonstrations or parades, or to make speeches in the public streets during heavy traffic hours. In sum, the government could make reasonable regulations over time, place, and manner in order to preserve order in the midst of possible chaos.

In brief, there was more, much more, case law upon which courts relied when called on to decide protest cases prior to *Tinker*. Nevertheless, the general principle of constitutional law that was at the bottom of the aforementioned Supreme Court logic was that the right to express one's opinion is so indispensable to the democratic process that any restriction on such is justified only by the existence of a "clear and present danger." In fact, the high priority in which the Supreme Court held First Amendment freedoms can be recognized in the action of the Court, beginning with the *Gitlow*[27] case back in 1925, in assimilating these liber-

---

26. See, e. g., Brown v. Louisiana, 383 U.S. 131 (1965), where the Supreme Court ruled that five blacks could not be punished for merely remaining quietly in a public library for ten to fifteen minutes in order to protest racial discrimination.

27. Gitlow v. New York, 268 U.S. 652 (1925); in this case Benjamin Gitlow had challenged a state stat-

ties, and not others for some time, into the concept of liberty in the due process clause of the Fourteenth Amendment.

Withal, we can now proceed somewhat more prepared to those selected student protest cases which illustrate where the First Amendment lines were drawn.   It was here, perhaps more than in any other area involving civil liberties at that time, that the difficulties of ascertaining the line between freedom and the abuse of freedom became painfully apparent.   As we shall see, the all-American, born on the fourth of July cry "it's a free country and I can say what I please" was as appealing and touching as it was complicated and misleading (The problem, as always, occurred in the movement from generalities to specifics.   "All declare for liberty," wrote one justice "and proceed to disagree among themselves as to its true meaning.").

Permissible Limitations on Expression

Goldberg v. Regents of the Univ. of Cal. (1967)

The first significant court decision on college demonstrations begins appropriately enough in Berkeley, California.   As previously noted, the University of California campus in that city sustained the nation's first large-scale student disruptions in the fall of 1964 and spring of 1965.   The particular brand of protest that became the subject of judicial review involved several types of issues simultaneously, but what was especially significant was that the protest in 1965 contained the use of signs and speaker amplification equipment which placed the participants under the standard of "captive audience" rather than the less restrictive "voluntary audience" category.   Further, the language used by the students (e. g., signs labeled "Fuck Fund" and yells consisting of spelling out and shouting the word "fuck"—see Chapter 3, pp. 84–85) was considered to be obscene by the University administration.

In this case a California Court of Appeals made a distinction between what is and what is not protected by the mantle of "free speech and assembly."   It ruled that these freedoms do not mean

ute as violating his freedom of speech and thereby denying him due process. The Supreme Court took jurisdiction under the due process clause declaring that: "For present purposes we may and do assume that freedom of speech and of the press—which are protected by the First Amendment from abridgment by Congress—are among the fundamental personal rights and 'liberties' protected by the due process clause of the Fourteenth Amendment from impairment by the states."

"[c]onduct involving rowdiness, rioting, destruction of property, reckless display of impropriety or any unjustifiable disturbance of public order on or off [the] . . . campus" for such, said the court, ". . . is indefensible, however sincere to some cause or ideal." [28] Moreover, the court seemed inclined to elaborate this principle further:

> An individual cannot escape from social constraint merely by asserting that he is engaged in political talk or action. . .
> Thus, reasonable restrictions on the freedoms of speech and assembly are recognized in relation to public agencies that have a valid interest in maintaining good order and proper decorum.[29]

Buttney v. Smiley (1968)

On October 25, 1967, a number of students at the University of Colorado, a public institution, demonstrated against the recruiting activity of the Central Intelligence Agency on campus. The primary tactic of the demonstrators was that of joining hands and arms in order to block entrance to the campus Placement Bureau where the CIA was recruiting. The obvious result was that students who had interviews scheduled, as well as others, were deprived of the right of access to the building. When asked by University officials to cease this activity, the students refused. Subsequently, after notice, hearing and appeal, the students were suspended either indefinitely or for shorter terms.

After their dismissal, the students entered suit for reinstatement in the Federal District Court of Colorado, claiming (*inter alia*) that the suspensions were incompatible with the "free-speech" guarantee of the First Amendment. In considering the constitutional validity of this claim, the court relied heavily on *Goldberg* and, in fact, quoted part of that decision as follows:

> "Broadly stated, the function of the University is to impart learning and to advance the boundaries of knowledge. This carries with it the administrative responsibility to control and regulate that conduct and behavior of the students which tend to impede, obstruct or threaten the achievements of its educational goals."[30]

---

28. *Goldberg*, 248 Cal.App.2d 867, 57 Cal.Rptr. 463, 473 (1967).

29. Ibid., at 471

30. Buttney, 281 F.Supp. 280, 284 (D.C.Colo.1968), quoting Goldberg v. Regents of the Univ. of Cal., 248 Cal.App.2d 867, 57 Cal.Rptr. 463 at 472 (1967).

Moreover, the *Buttney* court made a distinction between conduct (the physical blocking of entrance to the building) and speech (what the students said):

> Plaintiffs contended that the action of the University officials had a "chilling" effect on the First Amendment right of freedom of speech. What they said on the occasion in question is not the basis for the disciplinary proceedings; it is what they did. We hold that the First Amendment guarantee of freedom of speech, as it is related to plaintiffs' activities here, does not give them the right to prevent lawful access to campus facilities. We have been unable to find any case that holds that active, aggressive physical action may properly be characterized by the courts as free speech.[31]

Grossner v. Trustees of Columbia Univ. (1968)

Actually, the magnitude of student upheavals on campus from 1965–69 brought an unprecedented number of cases dealing with the control of student behavior to the courts. Given the basic constitutional right of freedom of expression and assembly, the central question was more often whether the freedom had been abused by students and the sanctions justified on the ground of a "compelling state interest." The courts steadily insisted on the "principle that debate on public issues should be uninhibited, robust, and wide open. . . ."[32] At the same time, the courts warned against the gross error of believing that every kind of conduct must be treated simply as protected expression. As was noted in *Grossner:*

> Without such inescapably necessary limits, the First Amendment would be a self-destroying license for "peaceful expression" by the seizure of streets, buildings, and offices by mobs, large or small, driven by motives (and toward objectives) that different viewers might deem "good or bad."[33]

The *Grossner* case resulted from one of the most notorious instances of student rioting that occurred in 1968. Between January 1 and June 15, 1968, the National Student Association counted 221 major demonstrations at 101 colleges and universities. But Columbia, by far the most spectacular, could easily have

---

31. Id., at 286. See also Zanders v. Louisiana State Bd. of Educ., 281 F.Supp. 747 (D.C.La.1968) where the dismissal of students at Grambling College for blocking entrances to the Administration Building was upheld by the court.

32. Grossner v. Trustees of Columbia Univ., 287 F.Supp. 535, 544 (D.C. N.Y.1968) quoting with approval New York Times Co. v. Sullivan, 376 U.S. 254 (1964).

33. Id., at 544.

stood for all the rest. Several elements combined to inflame emotions there. One was a vigorous and hot-blooded SDS chapter. Another was that the University, an important landlord in Harlem, was building a lavish gymnasium partly on land taken from an adjoining recreation space for nearby Harlem blacks. Though blacks in the neighboring ghetto were to have use of part of the new facility, militant black leaders remained dissatisfied. "This community is being raped" was how the chairman of the Harlem CORE put it. At this point, SDS merged its effort to have Columbia divorce itself from the Institute of Defense Analysis (a university consortium for military research) with black resentment against Columbia's real estate operations. After addressing their grievances through normal channels with no acceptable results, on April 23 a mixed band of SDS and Students' Afro-American Society members marched on Low Memorial Library. Repulsed by guards, they went to the gymnasium site shouting "Gym Crow Must Go," and tore down a section of fencing. They then occupied Hamilton Hall, the administrative center of the undergraduate college. The following day, black militants seceded from the allied force. They retained Hamilton Hall while the whites occupied Low Library where they ransacked President Grayson Kirk's files, drank his sherry, and smoked his cigars.

In the next few days other buildings were occupied and converted into "revolutionary communes." Attempts by the administration to negotiate failed, but by this time it was too late— if such had not been the case from the very outset. Meanwhile, a "majority coalition" was formed against the seven hundred or so insurgents. The coalition, largely dominated by athletes, surrounded Low Library and successfully cut off relief supplies from reaching rebel hands. One veteran observer of Columbia football defeats commented: "It's probably the first time Columbia has ever held a line." Then, President Kirk, under enormous pressure to act, suddenly discarded his hitherto deliberately patient conduct and called in the police. The buildings were taken by storm, and the rebellion was quickly suppressed. In the process something like seven hundred students were arrested and 150 injured. Overall, "things had certainly come to a pretty pass."

A student sympathy strike followed the new quietude, which made it nearly impossible to carry on classes, and thus the University closed early that semester. Construction of the new gymnasium stopped. Physical damage to University buildings required expensive repair. A history instructor's notes and manuscripts had been burned in the melee. Seventy-three students were eventually suspended, and President Kirk resigned soon afterward. But, perhaps not surprisingly, SDS claimed a great victory, and its newest star, Mark Rudd, became a television personality. Yet, from the perspective of 20/20 hindsight, SDS did for dissent what the Hindenburg did for air travel: it gave a worthy enterprise a bad name.

In any event, four students who were dismissed for their part in these disturbances sought relief in the United States District Court for the Southern District of New York. They appealed to the Court on constitutional grounds and alleged that Columbia, although a private university, was involved in "state action." The alleged state action consisted of the fact that over 40 percent of the university budget for the preceding two years had been derived from public funds, a considerable portion of which went for military-related research; thus it was in the very nature of its functioning so impregnated with a governmental character as to become subject to the constitutional limitations upon state action.

The Court did not accept this postulation, deciding that neither the fact that Columbia received some government funds nor the fact that education is generally a state function was sufficient to subject a private university to constitutional limitations in the discipline of its students. Therefore, the Court held that much more was necessary than the receipt of public money to prove state action. The point was made that it was not the source of funds but whether there was an interdependence between Columbia University and the government that was the deciding factor. As the Court found no such connection, it became unnecessary to examine whether due process had been exercised in suspending the plaintiffs.

The plaintiffs were in a better position, however, in showing that the state, by exercising its governing power through the intervention of the New York City Police, had been closely involved in the action that resulted in the curtailment of their First Amendment protections. Yet the Court merely alluded to such a nexus, rather obliquely, as it quickly went to the heart of the matter and made clear that the constitutional safeguards which protect dissenters are also available as a bulwark against anarchy and violence:

> Plaintiffs maintain, consistent with the American tradition of democratic and legal confrontation, that the non-

violent occupation of five buildings of Columbia University
for less than one week in the circumstances of this case is
fully protected by the First Amendment guarantees of the
right to petition government for the redress of grievances,
. . . to assemble and to speak. Plaintiffs maintain that
the nonviolent occupation of the buildings was absolutely
necessary to breathe life into the First Amendment principle
that government institutions should reflect the will of the
people and that this interest must prevail under any balancing test against the inconvenience to defendant Columbia
University in having five of its buildings occupied by students for approximately one week.

Embellishing such untenable propositions, plaintiffs (or,
more fairly, the sixteen attorneys who sign their brief) proceed to argue that the rhetoric and the tactics of the American Revolution are the guides by which judges are to construe the First Amendment. The "rule of law," they explain,
must not be overrated: "Had Americans agreed that the rule
of law, however despotic, must always prevail, had the
Americans felt that dropping the tea in the harbor was going
too far, had the Americans not focused on fundamental principles, this country might still be a colony today." The message, insofar as it is intelligible, possibly means that a tea
party today, if nothing else could achieve repeal of a hated
tax, would be protected by the First Amendment. Or possibly it means something else. Whatever it is meant to
mean, and whatever virtues somebody might think such
ideas might have in other forms, arguments like this are at
best useless (at worst deeply pernicious) nonsense in courts
of law. . . .

It is surely nonsense . . . to argue that a court of
law should subordinate the "rule of law" in favor of
more "fundamental principles" of revolutionary action designed forcibly to oust government, courts and all. But this
self-contradictory sort of theory . . . is ultimately at
the heart of plaintiffs' case. And so it is not surprising that
plaintiffs' efforts to implement the theory have led them to
champion a series of propositions of unsound constitutional
law.[34]

----

34. Id., at 545.

Impermissible Limitations on Expression

The Free Speech Movement which transpired at the University of California at Berkeley during 1964 and which thereafter ignited a flurry of similar activities on its own campus, as well as on campuses throughout the nation, however, did not in actuality serve as one of the better testing grounds for the constitutional rights of expression and assembly. As seen above, the FSM was the procreator of many campus disruptions where one party, in exercising the liberty to voice a particular view, abridged other freedoms on the part of a second party. In his 1970 treatise on the American student revolt, Nathan Glazer noted:

> "The Free speech Movement," which stands at the beginning of the student rebellion in this country, seems now to almost mock its subsequent course. In recent years, the issue has been how to *defend* the speech. . . .[35]

Actually, it is difficult to remember a period in our history in which due process had achieved more victories in the courts and suffered more setbacks in the arena of politics and public opinion. There was widespread harassment of the young, directed superficially at little more than hair-style, dress or manners— but directed in fact to their opinions, or perhaps to their youthfulness. And throughout the country, government officials were busy compiling dossiers on almost all citizens, young and old, noisy enough to come to their attention.

Government itself, as well as many colleges and universities, was engaged increasingly in violating what President Dwight David Eisenhower chose as the motto for the Columbia University bicentenary in 1954: "Man's right to knowledge and the free use thereof." Meanwhile, the growing influence of the military and its intervention in areas long supposed to be exclusively civilian gravely threatened the principle of the superiority of the civil to the military power. Military considerations were advanced to justify the revival of the shabby practices of the McCarthy era—for instance, security clearances for all civilians working in all establishments that had contracts with the Defense Department—a category that included laboratories, educational institutions and research organizations. What the standards were that could be expected to dictate security clearance was suggested by Vice President Spiro Agnew's 1969 proposal to "separate the [protest leaders] from our society—with no more

---

35. *Remembering the Answers*, (New York: Basic Books, 1970), p. 275.

regret than we should feel over discarding rotten apples from a barrel." That, of course, was precisely the philosophy that animated the Nazi. Eventually, secrecy embraced the significant facts of the Vietnam War. For example, it was reported that Attorney General John Mitchell hoped to keep the Cambodian invasion secret from Congress and the people until it was a *fait accompli*. So, too, the CIA, in theory merely an information-gathering agency, covered its far-flung operations in over 60 countries with a cloak of secrecy so thick that even Congress could not penetrate it.

Of course there is much more to this list, but the importance of it all is to point out the broad attack on freedoms that took place during this period. The motivation behind all of this, probably unconscious, was to silence criticism of government and of the war and thus to encourage an attitude that Americans have thought odious ever since the days of George III. Unfortunately, higher education was not immune to this repressive condition. In fact, institutions of higher education, thrown on the defensive by student activism, found themselves even more vulnerable because more of them were publicly-controlled than in the past. Up to the 1950s, more than 50 percent of the students enrolled in colleges and universities were in private institutions. By the end of the 1960s, however, 76 percent were enrolled in public institutions. And publicly-controlled colleges and universities, "by their very nature, had less autonomy and flexibility and tended to be more strictly accountable to voters, taxpayers, state officials, and federal bureaucracies." [36]

Then, too, because higher education was prepared neither in doctrine nor in management for the great growth of student enrollments during the post-World War II period, rather suddenly it was faced with enormous needs for funds which neither the institutions nor society and neither fiscal policy nor tax structures were adequately prepared. The consequences are not difficult to uncover, but among the more significant was the almost overwhelming need for institutions of higher education to reach out for new resources. Of course tuition rates steadily increased; yet the percentage of the total cost this source was capable of supporting steadily decreased. Thus the task of selling the utilitarian advantages of higher education to the public, especially as they might relate to or be transformed into perceived national goals,

36. John S. Brubacher and Willis Rudy, *Higher Education in Transi-* *tion* (New York: Harper and Row, Publishers, 1976), p. 389.

became an increasingly essential element in every budget consideration—even in private colleges and universities.

One might have rightfully applauded the generous public response to the financial needs of higher education, but there was another side to that "coin." That is, the growing dependence of colleges and universities on both public approbation and funds made these institutions increasingly vulnerable to a vigorous application of Barry Commoner's fourth law: "There's no such thing as a free lunch." True, the need for public financial assistance was urgent and real, but to surrender virginity for money has rarely been a graceful exercise. In these events, a presentiment appeared for what was becoming and would become of higher education—a growing loss of college and university autonomy along with an increasing erosion of principle and integrity.

Someone else put it more bluntly:

> There was a young lady from Kent
> Who said that she knew what it meant
> When men took her to dine
> Gave her cocktails and wine
> She knew what it meant—but she went.[37]

The Kent projection was just another way of suggesting that higher education was increasingly becoming an agent rather than a principal—an agent whose facilities were available and whose activities were determined more and more by the requirements of the state. As James Perkins (at that time President of Cornell) observed, "In this image, the university would become an institution always for hire, and increasingly for hire for the short-run rather than for the long-run needs of society." [38]

In the past it had been fashionable to think of higher education as "apolitical," as somehow set apart from other social institutions. But as higher education in America grew to great prominence as a result of the expertise and service it supplied to the World War II effort and to the prestige-motivated rush to the moon after Sputnik, that myth fast disappeared. Simultaneously, as society—through the federal, state and local governments—supplied more and more funds for higher education, it became increasingly interested in what was happening in academia. Then, with general disruption and the proliferation of nonconformist

37. Quoted in James A. Perkins, 38. Id.
    The University in Transition
    (Princeton University Press, 1967),
    p. 26.

lifestyles on campus, the bloom was off the rose. Societal interest escalated into a disenchanted obsession, and the operations
of higher education came under closer and more critical scrutiny.

Other societal trends also reinforced the move towards government control. Internally, society was being compelled to face
drastic adjustments to novel conditions, major modifications of
its economic, political and social structure. Increasingly this
meant the general ascension throughout American society of public policy control over previously semi-autonomous institutions.
Externally, we faced a fundamental alteration in our relations
with the rest of the world. The pace was urgent. Yet, as our
society grew older and more institutionalized, its rigidities seemed
to increase. Pressing against these inflexibilities of status quo,
the insistent forces of change tended to arouse in the body politic
anxiety, fear, hostility and bewilderment. Ofttimes these irrational responses were deliberately stimulated.

Probably the most far-reaching development in post-World War
II America, however, was the change in the nature of the political process, especially the impact of mass public opinion. Because of increased literacy and education, the growth of widespread, rapid communication and the influence of mass media,
public opinion became broader, more uniform, less independent.
Because political issues were more complex, more dependent on
specific information not available to the general public, and more
remote, public opinion became more apathetic, less well informed,
less focused on precise issues, and less confident. Hence, public
opinion became more susceptible to manipulation.

Significantly, all of these conditions raised obvious problems
for a system of free expression, particularly in areas where government possessed a monopoly or quasi-monopoly, and particularly in light of the consistent tendency to overestimate the need
for restriction upon freedom of expression. Such a condition
arose in the field of higher education. Here the possibilities of
nongovernmental communication offsetting the government influence was frequently reduced by governmental fiat. In fact
higher education itself had no precise guidelines to determine
proper and improper constraints. Thus there was a great need
for the countervailing judicial power to protect nonconforming
individuals and small minority groups, both in their relations with
the legislature and executive and in their voluntary participation
in government-controlled institutions.

Dickson v. Sitterson (1968)

"The unexamined life is not worth living," Socrates said, and implied in that statement is the further thought that the unexamined society is not worth living in. Thus, in theory at least, the "community of scholars" should thrive on the "robust and free exchange of ideas;" after all, this process provides the means by which man can overcome the precarious and contingent forces in his environment. And the role of open inquiry and the productive tension of conflict (but within an *ad valorum*, not *ad hominum*, framework) in such a philosophy is clear. But despite the fundamental importance of this philosophy in academe, not to mention in a democracy, some people always believe that speech should be free for only those who agree with them.

Thus, as we leave the level of abstractions and move to the level of specifics with Dickson v. Sitterson,[39] we can see, early on, an example of the discouragingly low level of support for free speech among the public, especially through its mirror images—the executive and legislative branches of government. The issue in this case arose in the winter of 1966 when Frank Wilkinson, Executive Director of the National Committee to Abolish the House Un-American Activities Committee and Herber Aptheker, Director of the American Institute for Marxist Studies, were denied permission to speak on the University of North Carolina campus. Both men had been invited to speak by student representatives from several recognized campus organizations, among whom were Paul Dickson, student body president, George Nicholson, Chairman of the Carolina Forum, and James Medford, President of the campus Young Men's Christian Association.[40] Nevertheless, both men were denied permission to speak on campus pursuant to a 1963 statute, "commonly referred to as the 'Speaker Ban' law."

The statute provided in essence that the Board of Trustees of each state college or university publish regulations governing the use of campus facilities for speaking purposes according to the following guidelines:

§ 116–119. No college or university, which receives any State funds in support thereof, shall permit any person to

39. 280 F.Supp. 486 (D.C.N.C.1968), aff'd 415 F.2d 228 (5th Cir. 1969).

40. Id., at 487. Others were Robert Powell, Executive Director, Carolina Forum; John Greenbacker, President, Dialectic and Philanthropic Literary Society; Eric Van Loon, Chairman, Carolina Political Union; Ernest McCrary, Editor, *Daily Tar Heel*; Gary Waller, Member of Steering Committee, SDS; Stuart Matthews, Member of Steering Committee, SDS.

use the facilities of such college or university for speaking purposes, who:

(A) Is a known member of the Communist Party;

(B) Is known to advocate the overthrow of the Constitution of the United States or the State of North Carolina;

(C) Has pleaded the Fifth Amendment of the Constitution of the United States in refusing to answer any question, with respect to Communist or subversive connections, or activities, before any duly constituted legislative committee, any judicial tribunal, or any executive or administrative board of the United States or any state.[41]

Thereafter, the Executive Committee of the University of North Carolina Board of Trustees, on July 8, 1963, adopted its own regulations and policy statement in full compliance with the law.[42] Then, on February 28, 1966, after Wilkinson and Aptheker had been asked to speak on campus by the student representatives, the Board met and adopted the following procedures and regulations regarding the appearance of visiting speakers:

1. The officers of a recognized student club or society desiring to use University facilities for a visiting speaker shall consult with the club's faculty adviser concerning the proposed speaker.

2. The head of a student organization shall submit to the Chancellor a request for reservation of a meeting place along with the following information:

(a) Name of the sponsoring organization and the proposed speaker's topic.

(b) Biographical information about the proposed speaker.

(c) Request for a date and place of meeting.

3. Upon receipt of the above information, the Chancellor shall refer the proposed invitation to a joint student-faculty standing committee on visiting speakers for advice. He may consult such others as he deems advisable.

4. The Chancellor shall then determine whether or not the invitation is approved.[43]

41. Id., at 488.

42. Id., at 488-89.

43. Id., at 492-93.

The trend of events was all too evident. Aptheker had been a member of the Communist Party since 1939, and Wilkinson had served a term in federal prison for unlawfully refusing to answer questions with respect to Communist or subversive connections.[44] Clearly, both fell within the classifications set forth in the state statute and the rules and regulations established pursuant to that statute. Interestingly, two members of the Communist Party had delivered speeches at the University of North Carolina campus after passage of the "Speaker Ban" statute and the February 28, 1966, adoption of procedures and regulations. However, these two speakers had appeared upon the invitation of the faculty, and "Chancellor Sitterson did not consider the invitations by faculty groups to be subject to the statute."[45]

With this double standard, one might appropriately recall the words Mr. Dooley (mouthpiece for the great American humorist, Peter Finnely Dunne) put in the mouth of a college president greeting a freshman: "Now my friend," he inquired, "in what subject would you like your thinking done for you by our learned professors? "

The court in the *Dickson* case did not feel called upon to deal with any of the other free speech issues (e. g., political censorship and "clear and present danger" test) which appeared clearly involved in the controversy. Instead, the court focused its attention on the statute and regulations and declared them unconstitutional solely on the grounds of vagueness. More specifically, the court indicated that statutes and regulations governing the access of outside speakers to the public campus must contain clear, narrow, precise and objective standards because the "standards of permissible statutory vagueness are particularly strict when First Amendment rights are involved." [46]

The chief points presented in the court's application of the vagueness doctrine to rules governing external speakers follow:

It is firmly established that a statute "which either forbids or requires the doing of an act in terms so vague that men of common intelligence must necessarily guess at its meaning and differ as to its application . . . " violates the due process clause of the Fourteenth Amendment because of vagueness. Connally v. General Constr. Co., 269 U.S. 385 (1926) . . .

44. Id., at 496.   46. Id., at 498.

45. Id., at 497.

The first provision of the statute under attack covers a "known member of the Communist Party." "Known" to whom, and to what degree of certainty? "Known" according to what standard? A "member" in what sense? Does it include membership in a Communist "front" organization? Is it a matter of general reputation or rumor, or the personal knowledge of the Chancellor? The statutes and regulations provide no clues to any of these questions. Without such answers, neither those who must obey nor those who must enforce the statutes and regulations can determine the extent of their obligation.

The next provision of the statute requires regulations covering visiting speakers who are "known to advocate the overthrow of the Constitution of the United States or the State of North Carolina." Does it mean with force and arms or is the advocacy of ideas sufficient? Must the advocacy be public or private? Is the advocacy of peaceful change included? It is sufficient to say that reasonable men might differ on the answers to these questions.

The third section of the statute covers speakers who have "pleaded the Fifth Amendment of the Constitution of the United States." Presumably, this means the "self-incrimination" class, although this is a matter of conjecture. What is meant by "subversive connections?" Here again, since reasonable men might differ, the statute is unconstitutionally vague. Moreover, the imposition of any sanction by reason of the invocation of the Fifth Amendment is constitutionally impermissible. Spevack v. Klein, 385 U.S. 511 (1967).

The statement of policy and the procedures and regulations adopted by the Board of Trustees suffer from the same infirmities. In order to withstand constitutional attack, they must impose a purely ministerial duty upon the person charged with approving or disapproving an invitation to a speaker falling within the statutory classifications, or contain standards sufficiently detailed to define the bounds of discretion. Neither criteria has been met with respect to the procedures and regulations in question.

Loyalty oaths have recently been declared unconstitutional because of vagueness in the cases of Baggett v. Bullitt, 377 U.S. 360 (1964) and Elfbrandt v. Russell, 384 U.S. 11 (1966). In Whitehill v. Elkins, 389 U.S. 54 (1967), the Supreme Court, in another teacher oath case, again emphasized the need for "precision and clarity" in the "sensitive and important First Amendment area."

Similarly, in Keyishian v. Board of Regents, 385 U.S. 589 (1967), the Supreme Court in striking down certain New York statutes and administrative regulations dealing with the employment or retention of State employees because of vagueness, stated:

> "There can be no doubt of the legitimacy of New York's interest in protecting its education system from subversion. But 'even though the governmental purpose be legitimate and substantial, that purpose cannot be pursued by means that broadly stifle fundamental personal liberties when the end can be more narrowly achieved.'" Shelton v. Tucker, 364 U.S. 479.

We emphasize once again that "[p]recision of regulation must be the touchstone in an area so closely touching our most precious freedoms," N.A.A.C.P. v. Button, 371 U.S. 415 (1963); "[f]or standards of permissible statutory vagueness are strict in the area of free expression. . . . Because First Amendment freedoms need breathing space to survive, government may regulate in the area only with narrow specificity." Id., at 432–433. New York's complicated and intricate scheme plainly violates that standard. When one must guess what conduct or utterance may lose him his position, one necessarily will "steer far wider of the unlawful zone . . . ." Speiser v. Randall, 357 U.S. 513. For "[t]he threat of sanctions may deter . . . almost as potently as the actual application of sanctions." N.A.A.C.P. v. Button, supra [371 U.S.] at 433. The danger of that chilling effect upon the exercise of vital First Amendment rights must be guarded against by sensitive tools which clearly inform teachers what is being proscribed. See Stromberg v. [People of State of] Cal., 283 U.S. 359; Cramp v. Board of Public Instruction, 368 U.S. 278; Baggett v. Bullitt, supra.

The regulatory maze created by New York is wholly lacking in "terms susceptible of objective measurement." Cramp v. Board of Public Instruction, supra, at 286. It has the quality of "extraordinary ambiguity" found to be fatal to the oaths considered in *Cramp* and Baggett v. Bullitt. "[M]en of common intelligence must necessarily guess at its meaning and differ as to its application . . . ." Baggett v. Bullitt, supra [377 U.S.] at 367. Vagueness of wording is aggravated by prolixity and profusion of statutes, regulations, and administrative machinery, and by manifold cross-references to interrelated enactments and rules.

When the statutes and regulations in question are applied to the unbroken line of Supreme Court decisions respecting the necessity for clear, narrow and objective standards controlling the licensing of First Amendment rights, the conclusion is inescapable that they run afoul of constitutional principles.[47]

Snyder v. Board of Trustees of Univ. of Ill. (1968)

It is obvious that the *Dickson* case, closely reasoned as it was, left unanswered a good many important questions regarding the permissible scope of government power to limit expression on public campuses. However, whereas the *Dickson* decision was based solely on the grounds of vagueness, the court in *Snyder*, though also citing the vagueness principle, employed some additional means in its determination that a state statute unconstitutionally abridged students' freedom of speech and peaceful assembly.

The *Snyder* case arose from the persistent refusal of University of Illinois officials to approve a student organization's invitation to one Louis Diskin to speak on campus. The sole reason given by University officials was that Mr. Diskin was a professed member of the Communist Party of the United States, and therefore to allow him the use of University facilities would violate the provisions of an Illinois statute, commonly known as the "Clabaugh Act." Somewhat similar to the North Carolina "Speaker Ban" statute, the "Clabaugh Act" provided the following:

> No trustees, official, instructor, or other employee of the University of Illinois shall extend to any subversive, seditious, and un-American organization, or to its representatives the use of any facilities of the University for the purpose of carrying on, advertising or publicizing the activities of such organization.[48]

The Federal District Court found the Act to be unconstitutional on these grounds:

> "[A]ny system of prior restraints [on First Amendment rights] comes to this Court bearing a heavy burden against its constitutionality . . . Bantam Books, Inc. v. Sullivan, 372 U.S. 58, 70 (1963).[49]

> "A statute which fails to provide an ascertainable standard of conduct and which because of its vagueness inhibits the exercise of constitutionally protected freedoms of speech and assembly is void. Baggett v. Bullitt, 377 U.S. 360 (1964)".
> . . . . The North Carolina Court [referring to *Dickson*]

47. Id., at 498–99.   **49.** Id., at 934.

48. 286 F.Supp. 927, 930 (D.C.Ill. 1968).

found the quoted language impermissibly vague, and struck down the statute. Quite obviously, the language of the Clabaugh Act is even more vague . . .[50]

"A statute purporting to regulate expression may not be so broad in its sweep as to hazard the loss or impairment of First Amendment freedoms . . . . Dombrowski v. Pfister, 380 U.S. 479 (1965)."[51]

Disregarding for present purposes the special cases of obscenity and libel, it is accurate to state that speech may be suppressed only when it presents a "clear and present danger" that substantive evil will result.[52]

The Clabaugh Act in part proscribes the "advertising" and "publicizing" of activities of "subversive, seditious, and un-American" organizations. Except in the most extraordinary factual setting where there would be a clear danger of immediate violent audience reaction at the mere mention of the activities of an organization, it would seem that the "advertising" and "publicizing" of the political viewpoints in the market place of ideas is close to the very heart of what the First Amendment was intended to protect. Yet the Clabaugh Act prohibits the described speech in all contexts, without regard to the likelihood that the audience will immediately and violently react to the words of the speaker, either by committing acts of violent overthrow of the government; by turning violently against the speaker; or by committing other illegal acts after incitement by the speaker.[53]

Hammond v. South Carolina State College (1967)

Even before *Dickson*, on another southern campus students thought that a college regulation denying them the opportunity to "celebrate, parade, or demonstrate on the campus without the approval of the Office of the President" had a "chilling" effect on First Amendment freedoms. In this case, Hammond v. South Carolina State College,[54] the court agreed. Many of the students in attendance at the College had assembled on the campus to express their disapproval of certain college practices. Subsequently, several of these students were suspended for violating the rule prohibiting student demonstrations without prior approval from the administration.

50. Id.

51. Id.

52. Id., at 933.

53. Id., at 935.

54. 272 F.Supp. 947 (D.C.S.C.1967).

The court held the college regulation constitutionally void on the following grounds. First, the regulation constituted a prior restraint on the students' First Amendment rights to expression and assembly, and "there exists a heavy constitutional presumption in favor of such rights." [55] Second:

> These rights of the First Amendment, including the right to peaceably assemble, are not to be restricted except upon the showing of a clear and present danger, or riot, disorder, or immediate threat to public safety, peace, or order. [56]

Recognizing the students' rights to assemble at "the site of government for peaceful expression of grievances constituted exercise of First Amendment rights in their pristine form," [57] the Court found the student suspensions unconstitutional.

THE TINKER CASE

Thus the First Amendment principles suggested by the lower courts were in part a product of student protest litigation in which the courts struggled with their own libertarian impulses. At the same time, the courts battled head on with an instinctive notion that *some* First Amendment regulation was both permissible and desirable, especially within the context of campus protest. As would be expected, these courts relied heavily upon First Amendment interpretations of the Supreme Court, but, as already noted, those holdings were essentially in areas not connected to the students' claim for the protective cloak of constitutionally guaranteed rights of free expression.

Of course, some twenty-six years prior to *Tinker,* the Supreme Court had announced the First Amendment's hostility to state-coerced belief. That principle was stated in the famous words of Justice Jackson in the 1943 West Virginia State Bd. of Educ. v. Barnette case:

> If there is any fixed star in our constitutional constellation, it is that no official, high or petty, can prescribe what shall be orthodox in politics, nationalism, religion or other matters of opinion or force citizens to confess by word or act their faith therein. If there are any circumstances which permit an exception, they do not now occur to us. [58]

55. Id., at 947.

56. Id., at 949.

57. Id., at 951.

58. 319 U.S. 624, 642 (1943). In this case the Court held invalid a state statute imposing a compulsory requirement that school children recite the pledge of allegiance to the

Thus the *Barnette* decision had put an end to compulsory participation in school flag ceremonies. Later the Court struck down the compulsory hearing of classroom prayers and Bible readings because such activities violated freedom of speech and the establishment and free exercise of religion clauses.[59]

In 1968 the Court also invalidated an Arkansas statute prohibiting the teaching of evolution as violative of the establishment clause.[60] But undoubtedly most revealing to the lower courts in the pre-*Tinker* period—i. e., in terms of the Supreme Court's potential position in regards to free expression rights of students—must have been a series of Court decisions providing for the protection of faculty rights to free speech and association.[61] Apparently, these decisions had been based in part on the interest of students in uncensored instruction.

Nevertheless, Tinker v. Des Moines Independent Community School Dist. (1969) [62] was the first Supreme Court decision to establish that public high school students have a positive, though limited, constitutional right to express themselves both on the campus and in the classroom. More specifically, the *Tinker* Court thought that the First Amendment protects a learning process in state schools which is open, vigorous, disputatious, disturbing—an educational environment in which error is combatted with reason, not fiat. The Court stressed that school authorities

flag. However, one should not apply this holding as a general rule in support of free expression for students; more appropriately, the holding was one of freedom of religion. Nevertheless, Jackson's statement indicates that freedom of expression for students did not spring full-grown in *Tinker*.

59. Engel v. Vitale, 370 U.S. 421 (1962) (prayers); and Abington School Dist. v. Schempp, 374 U.S. 203 (1963) (Bible reading). Again, however, both cases should be read as freedom of religion rather than freedom of expression cases.

60. Epperson v. Arkansas, 393 U.S. 97 (1968).

61. See, e. g., Sweezy v. New Hampshire, 354 U.S. 234 (1957), in which the Court invalidated the dismissal of a professor for refusing to answer questions about possible sub-

versive ideas in his teaching. Chief Justice Warren commented: "Teachers and students must always remain free to inquire, to study and to evaluate, to gain new maturity and understanding; otherwise our civilization will stagnate and die" (Id. at 250); Keyishian v. Board of Regents, 385 U.S. 589 (1967), in which the Court invalidated a loyalty oath required of all state teachers. Justice Brennan in delivering the majority opinion stated: "The classroom is peculiarly the 'marketplace of ideas.' The Nation's future depends upon leaders trained through wide exposure to that robust exchange of ideas which discovers truth 'out of a multitude of tongues, [rather] than through any kind of authoritative selection.'" (Id. at 603; revealingly quoted at length in *Tinker*, 393 U.S. 503, 511 (1969).

62. 393 U.S. 503 (1969).

may never merely suppress "feelings with which they do not wish to contend," [63] nor may they treat students as "closed-circuit recipients" [64] of the dominant opinions of the community. In short, the Court established a principle of educational philosophy based on the First Amendment.

But what are the implications of *Tinker* for public college and university students? Certainly, since its promulgation *Tinker* has been the most frequently used case reference in student/public postsecondary conflicts over the boundaries of free expression. In this regard you should recall that First Amendment rights are contextually dependent, and their exercise must be judged protected or not with reference to the context. For example, by virtue of *Tinker* school authorities may prohibit student expression when that expression is disruptive or invades the rights of others, or, when the authorities are reasonably led to forecast such disruption. Presumably, high school students are more easily disrupted than college students of more mature age, and thus subsequent courts have, on a number of occasions, allowed greater restrictions on high school students' free expression.

The emerging doctrine for higher education after *Tinker* may be uncertain in its own way, but Mr. Justice Sutherland summarized well the necessarily contextual character of regulations prohibiting offensive behavior. "A nuisance," he said, "may be merely a right thing in the wrong place—like a pig in the parlor instead of the barnyard." [65] Hence, in any judicial determination of constitutionally permissible or impermissible limitations of expression on campus, the major factors distinguishing parlors from barnyards will undoubtedly be the nature of the forum and composition of the audience.

Despite the continuing need for ad hoc resolution of conflicting forces, there was after *Tinker* at least hope that the lines of battle would be more aptly drawn.

Thus, since "[i]t can hardly be argued that . . . students . . . shed their constitutional rights to freedom of speech or expression at the school house gate," [66] the full exercise of these rights—e. g., wearing black armbands—cannot be precluded absolutely by school authorities unless currently existing facts reasonably lead school officials to forecast that the exercise of such

63. Id., at 511, quoting Burnside v. Byars, 363 F.2d 744, 749 (5th Cir. 1966).

64. Id.

65. Village of Euclid v. Ambler Realty Co., 272 U.S. 365, 388 (1926).

66. *Tinker*, 393 U.S. at 508.

First Amendment rights in the particular educational context [67] will "materially and substantially interfere with the requirements of appropriate discipline in the operation of the school," [68] or collide with the constitutionally protected rights of others.

As you read the *Tinker* case (which follows), pay particular attention to its "forecast" rule; it does not authorize prior restraint or a system of censorship, but rather, it authorizes the curtailment of First Amendment rights only on the basis of existing facts and not on the basis of some "undifferentiated fear or apprehension of disturbance" or "a mere desire to avoid the discomfort and unpleasantness that always accompany an unpopular viewpoint." [69] However, the forecast rule implies that an institution's curtailment of these rights may prevail if it can demonstrate that the exercise of such rights, in the context of a particular setting, has, for instance, continually led to disruptive action on the part of other students.

At this point you should note that the Court reflects briefly on the hazards of exercising the constitutionally protected right to express unpopular ideas, but does not comment on the possibility that that right could be vetoed by the disruptive reaction of others to it. The danger here is that a person could be restrained from performing a constitutionally protected act merely because hostile individuals or groups might cause a disturbance. Of course "hostile audience" reaction was not in actuality at issue in the present case since there was no disorder. If that had been the case, according to the Court's "least means" [70] requirement, the appropriate response of the school officials would have been to discipline the students who tried to stop the exercise of free expression. Thus the school officials' responsibility would have been to protect freedom of expression, rather than to require the

---

67. The Court "pointed out that a school is not like a hospital or a jail enclosure"; and distinguished the case at bar from Adderley v. Florida, 385 U.S. 39 (1966), and Cox v. Louisiana, 379 U.S. 536 (1965), in which civil rights advocates who had demonstrated at a jail and at a courthouse were denied full First Amendment protection because they had chosen to demonstrate on public property which the state could lawfully dedicate to nonexpressive purposes. Id., at 512 fn. 6.

68. Id., at 509 and again quoting *Burnside* at 749.

69. Id., at 510.

70. See, e. g. Shelton v. Tucker, 364 U.S. 479 (1960), where the Court held that if a law or regulation impinges on the First Amendment, "even though the governmental purpose be legitimate and substantial, that purpose cannot be achieved by means that broadly stifle fundamental personal liberties when that end can be more narrowly achieved."

Tinker children to remove their armbands. In fact, in 1970 the United States Court of Appeals, Seventh Circuit, held that school officials could not curtail the exercise of First Amendment rights when they are exercised in front of a hostile audience that reacts unfavorably to their exercise "unless school officials have [first] actively tried and failed to silence those persons actually engaged in disruptive conduct." [71]

Attention should also be placed on the *Tinker* holding that the wearing of black armbands is "closely akin to 'pure speech.'" [72] The question presented by *Tinker* was not, therefore, whether the wearing of armbands was within the context of speech—admittedly it was. It is interesting to note, however, that the Court stated that the "problem posed by the present case does not relate to regulation of the length of skirts or the type of clothing, [or] to hair style . . . " [73] Thus it appears that the Court was reluctant to wander into the "hair thicket" or the hippie *cum* military surplus mode of dress and, in fact, undoubtedly considered such symbolism as a less crucial form of expression than political protest. Obviously, the Court considered the students' black armband message as political and hence their conduct as deserving of protection against the unwarranted interference of public officials.

It is also interesting to note that in *Tinker* the Court constructed its opinion with great care, but, in so doing, relied heavily upon two apparently contradictory precedents. Of course one of the essential keys to evaluating judicial logic is to recognize its reliance on prior decisions. Precedents, under some circumstances, may be binding on a court; in some other situations, prior decisions may be only persuasive. Nonetheless, to the Supreme Court—which has no peer—only its own decisions can be binding; yet, it can, and frequently does, permit itself to be instructed by the holdings of other courts.

71. Crews v. Clones, 432 F.2d 1259, 1265 (7th Cir. 1970); see also Richards v. Thurston, 304 F.Supp. 449, 454, aff'd 424 F.2d 1281 (D.C.Mass. 1970).

72. 393 U.S. at 505. See also Stromberg v. California, 283 U.S. 359 (1931), forbidding display of red flag symbolizing anarchism held to violate freedom of speech. In West Virginia State Bd. of Educ. v Barnette, 319 U.S. 624 (1943), the Court commented at length on the communicative force of saluting the United States flag:

"There is no doubt that . . . the flag salute is a form of utterance. Symbolism is a primitive but effective way of communicating ideas. The use of an emblem or flag to symbolize some system, idea, institution, or personality is a short cut from mind to mind" (at 632).

73. Id., at 507–08.

In *Tinker,* the Court looked to two decisions of the Fifth Circuit Court of Appeals for guidance. In Blackwell v. Issaquena City Bd. of Educ. (1966),[74] the Court of Appeals upheld a regulation which forbade the wearing of freedom buttons in school. These buttons were inscribed "SNCC" or "Freedom Now," and were worn by students in support of the civil rights movement.

The same court, the Fifth Circuit, on the same day, struck down as unconstitutional another such regulation in a different school, in Burnside v. Byars.[75] However, *Burnside* and *Blackwell* were nearly identical in every respect; in legal parlance, they were, to all immediate appearances, "on all fours." Yet, one significant factual difference between the two cases provided the Supreme Court with its rationale for following *Burnside* and thereby for ruling that the Des Moines armband prohibition was unconstitutional.

In *Burnside,* the Court of Appeals refused to allow the button prohibition to stand because there had been no showing in the trial court that exercise of the right would "materially and substantially interfere with the requirements of appropriate discipline in the operation of the school." [76] On the other hand, in *Blackwell*, where the prohibition stood, the school successfully showed that the restriction of expression was justified because of disruptive and disorderly behavior growing out of the proscribed conduct; that is, the students wearing buttons behaved discourteously toward school officials, attempted to pin buttons on other students, left their classes without permission, and engaged in loud and distracting conversations in halls and corridors.

The stature of *Tinker* has grown rapidly since the decision was handed down in February, 1969, until it has come to be perhaps the leading First Amendment case in school law today. Read the case carefully and when you finish the reading, think about the late Justice Black's vigorous dissent. Has *Tinker* actually worked to place our public schools under "the whims and caprices of their loudest-mouthed but maybe not their brightest, students" ? [77] There are two directions to that question: one for the secondary setting and the other for higher education.

A number of appealing arguments can be marshalled to support Justice Black's position, all premised on the special environment of the secondary school and the "compelling state interest"

74. 363 F.2d 749 (5th Cir. 1966).   **76.** Id., at 749.

75. 363 F.2d 744 (5th Cir. 1966).   **77.** *Tinker,* 393 U.S. at 525.

to educate within that environment. For instance, it is well settled that reasonable time, place, and manner regulations of expressive activity are permitted when necessary to further significant governmental interests. Here again, the crucial question in determining whether regulation of expressive activity is reasonable is whether the manner of expression is basically incompatible with the normal activity of a particular place at a particular time.

In this regard, *Tinker's* holding that secondary school authorities must tolerate "intellectual disruption" (as contrasted with "actual (physical) disruption," which is not permissible) seems to ignore such relevant factors as the intellectual maturity of the particular audience and the normal activities and purposes of the secondary school. Moreover, one should examine carefully the implications of *Tinker* in light of the "captive nature" of the high school audience.

Argu̇ably, the *Tinker* holding would have been more appropriate for the higher education setting, and since that is our purpose here, two cases follow which, in that sense, should set and hold the *Tinker* principles for the reader.

TINKER v. DES MOINES INDEPENDENT COMMUNITY SCHOOL DIST.

Supreme Court of the United States, 1969.
393 U.S. 503.

Mr. Justice FORTAS delivered the opinion of the Court.

Petitioner John F. Tinker, 15 years old, and petitioner Christopher Eckhardt, 16 years old, attended high schools in Des Moines, Iowa. Petitioner Mary Beth Tinker, John's sister, was a 13-year-old student in junior high school.

In December 1965, a group of adults and students in Des Moines held a meeting at the Eckhardt home. The group determined to publicize their objections to the hostilities in Vietnam and their support for a truce by wearing black armbands during the holiday season and by fasting on December 16 and New Year's Eve. Petitioners and their parents had previously engaged in similar activities, and they decided to participate in the program.

The principals of the Des Moines schools became aware of the plan to wear armbands. On December 14, 1965, they met and adopted a policy that any student wearing an armband to school would be asked to remove it, and if he refused he would be suspended until he returned without the armband. Petitioners were aware of the regulation that the school authorities adopted.

On December 16, Mary Beth and Christopher wore black armbands to their schools. John Tinker wore his armband the next day. They were all sent home and suspended from school until they would come back without their armbands. They did not return to school until after the planned period for wearing armbands had expired—that is, until after New Year's Day.

This complaint was filed in the United States District Court by petitioners, through their fathers .   . . It prayed for an injunction restraining the respondent school officials and the respondent members of the board of directors of the school district from disciplining the petitioners, and it sought nominal damages.

The District Court dismissed the complaint. It upheld the constitutionality of the school authorities' action on the ground that it was reasonable in order to prevent disturbance of school discipline. The court referred to but expressly declined to follow the Fifth Circuit's holding in a similar case that the wearing of symbols like the armbands cannot be prohibited unless it "materially and substantially interfere[s] with the requirements of appropriate discipline in the operation of the school." Burnside v. Byars, 363 F.2d 744, 749 (1966). [But compare, Blackwell v. Issaquena County Bd. of Educ., 363 F.2d 749 (5th Cir. 1966).]

On appeal, the Court of Appeals for the Eighth Circuit considered the case *en banc*. The court was equally divided, and the District Court's decision was accordingly affirmed, without opinion. We granted certiorari.

The District Court recognized that the wearing of an armband for the purpose of expressing certain views is the type of symbolic act that is within the Free Speech Clause of the First Amendment. See West Virginia State Board of Education v. Barnette. As we shall discuss, the wearing of armbands in the circumstances of this case was entirely divorced from actually or potentially disruptive conduct by those participating in it. It was closely akin to "pure speech" which, we have repeatedly held, is entitled to comprehensive protection under the First Amendment.

First Amendment rights, applied in light of the special characteristics of the school environment, are available to teachers and students. It can hardly be argued that either students or teachers shed their constitutional rights to freedom of speech or expression at the schoolhouse gate. This has been the unmis-

takable holding of this Court for almost 50 years. In Meyer v.
Nebraska, this Court, . . . held that the Due Process
Clause of the Fourteenth Amendment prevents States from for-
bidding the teaching of a foreign language to young students.
Statutes to this effect, the Court held, unconstitutionally interfere
with the liberty of teacher, student, and parent. . . .

. . . On the other hand, the Court has repeatedly emphasized the need for affirming the comprehensive authority of the
States and of school officials, consistent with fundamental constitutional safeguards, to prescribe and control conduct in the
schools. See Epperson v. Arkansas, supra, 393 U.S. at 104; Meyer
v. Nebraska, supra, 262 U.S. at 402. Our problem lies in the
area where students in the exercise of First Amendment rights
collide with the rules of the school authorities.

The problem posed by the present case does not relate to regulation of the length of skirts or the type of clothing, to hair style,
or deportment.   It does not concern aggressive, disruptive action or even group demonstrations. Our problem involves direct,
primary First Amendment rights akin to "pure speech."

The school officials banned and sought to punish petitioners for
a silent, passive expression of opinion, unaccompanied by any
disorder or disturbance on the part of petitioners. There is here
no evidence whatever of petitioners' interference, actual or nas-
cent, with the schools' work or of collision with the rights of
other students to be secure and to be let alone. Accordingly, this
case does not concern speech or action that intrudes upon the
work of the schools or the rights of other students.

Only a few of the 18,000 students in the school system wore
the black armbands. Only five students were suspended for wearing them. There is no indication that the work of the schools
or any class was disrupted. Outside the classrooms, a few students made hostile remarks to the children wearing armbands,
but there were no threats or acts of violence on school premises.

The District Court concluded that the action of the school authorities was reasonable because it was based upon their fear of
a disturbance from the wearing of the armbands. But, in our
system, undifferentiated fear or apprehension of disturbance is
not enough to overcome the right to freedom of expression. Any
departure from absolute regimentation may cause trouble. Any
variation from the majority's opinion may inspire fear. Any
word spoken, in class, in the lunchroom, or on the campus, that
deviates from the views of another person may start an argument

or cause a disturbance. But our Constitution says we must take this risk, and our history says that it is this sort of hazardous freedom—this kind of openness—that is the basis of our national strength and of the independence and vigor of Americans who grow up and live in this relatively permissive, often disputatious, society.

In order for the State in the person of school officials to justify prohibition of a particular expression of opinion, it must be able to show that its action was caused by something more than a mere desire to avoid the discomfort and unpleasantness that always accompany an unpopular viewpoint. Certainly where there is no finding and no showing that engaging in the forbidden conduct would "materially and substantially interfere with the requirements of appropriate discipline in the operation of the school," the prohibition cannot be sustained.

In the present case, the District Court made no such finding, and our independent examination of the record fails to yield evidence that the school authorities had reason to anticipate that the wearing of the armbands would substantially interfere with the work of the school or impinge upon the rights of other students. Even an official memorandum prepared after the suspension that listed the reasons for the ban on wearing the armbands made no reference to the anticipation of such disruption.

On the contrary, the action of the school authorities appears to have been based upon an urgent wish to avoid the controversy which might result from the expression, even by the silent symbol of armbands, of opposition to this Nation's part in the conflagration in Vietnam. It is revealing, in this respect, that the meeting at which the school principals decided to issue the contested regulation was called in response to a student's statement to the journalism teacher in one of the schools that he wanted to write an article on Vietnam and have it published in the school paper. (The student was dissuaded.)

It is also relevant that the school authorities did not purport to prohibit the wearing of all symbols of political or controversial significance. The record shows that students in some of the schools wore buttons relating to national political campaigns, and some even wore the Iron Cross, traditionally a symbol of Nazism. The order prohibiting the wearing of armbands did not extend to these. Instead, a particular symbol—black armbands worn to exhibit opposition to this Nation's involvement in Vietnam—was singled out for prohibition. Clearly, the prohibition of expression of one particular opinion, at least without evidence that it is necessary to avoid material and substantial interference with schoolwork or discipline, is not constitutionally permissible.

In our system, state-operated schools may not be enclaves of totalitarianism. School officials do not possess absolute authority over their students. Students in school as well as out of school are "persons" under our Constitution. They are possessed of fundamental rights which the State must respect, just as they themselves must respect their obligations to the State. In our system, students may not be regarded as closed-circuit recipients of only that which the State chooses to communicate. They may not be confined to the expression of those sentiments that are officially approved. In the absence of a specific showing of constitutionally valid reasons to regulate their speech, students are entitled to freedom of expression of their views. As Judge Gewin, speaking for the Fifth Circuit, said, school officials cannot suppress "expressions of feelings with which they do not wish to contend." Burnside v. Byars, supra, 363 F.2d at 749.

In Meyer v. Nebraska, supra, Mr. Justice McReynolds expressed this Nation's repudiation of the principle that a State might so conduct its schools as to "foster a homogeneous people." He said:

"In order to submerge the individual and develop ideal citizens, Sparta assembled the males at seven into barracks and intrusted their subsequent education and training to official guardians. Although such measures have been deliberately approved by men of great genius, their ideas touching the relation between individual and State were wholly different from those upon which our institutions rest; and it hardly will be affirmed that any Legislature could impose such restrictions upon the people of a state without doing violence to both letter and spirit of the Constitution."

This principle has been repeated by this Court on numerous occasions during the intervening years. In Keyishian v. Board of Regents, Justice Brennan, speaking for the Court, said:

" 'The vigilant protection of constitutional freedoms is nowhere more vital than in the community of American schools.' Shelton v. Tucker. The classroom is peculiarly the 'marketplace of ideas.' The Nation's future depends upon leaders trained through wide exposure to that robust exchange of ideas which discovers truth 'out of a multitude of tongues, [rather] than through any kind of authoritative selection.' "

The principle of these cases is not confined to the supervised and ordained discussion which takes place in the classroom. The principal use to which the schools are dedicated is to accommodate students during prescribed hours for the purpose of certain types of activities. Among those activities is personal intercommunication among the students. This is not only an inevitable part of the process of attending school; it is also an important part of the educational process. A student's rights, therefore, do not embrace merely the classroom hours. When he is in the cafeteria, or on the playing field, or on the campus during the authorized hours, he may express his opinions, even on controversial subjects like the conflict in Vietnam, if he does so without "materially and substantially interfer[ing] with the requirements of appropriate discipline in the operation of the school" and without colliding with the rights of others.

But conduct by the student, in class or out of it, which for any reason—whether it stems from time, place, or type of behavior— materially disrupts classwork or involves substantial disorder or invasion of the rights of others is, of course, not immunized by the constitutional guarantee of freedom of speech.

Under our Constitution, free speech is not a right that is given only to be so circumscribed that it exists in principle but not in fact. Freedom of expression would not truly exist if the right could be exercised only in an area that a benevolent government has provided as a safe haven for crackpots. The Constitution says that Congress (and the States) may not abridge the right to free speech. This provision means what it says. We properly read it to permit reasonable regulation of speech-connected activities in carefully restricted circumstances. But we do not confine the permissible exercise of First Amendment rights to a telephone booth or the four corners of a pamphlet, or to supervised and ordained discussion in a school classroom.

If a regulation were adopted by school officials forbidding discussion of the Vietnam conflict, or the expression by any student of opposition to it anywhere on school property except as part of a prescribed classroom exercise, it would be obvious that the regulation would violate the constitutional rights of students, at least if it could not be justified by a showing that the students' activities would materially and substantially disrupt the work and discipline of the school. . . . In the circumstances of the present case, the prohibition of the silent, passive "witness of the armbands," as one of the children called it, is no less offensive to the constitution's guarantees.

As we have discussed, the record does not demonstrate any facts which might reasonably have led school authorities to forecast substantial disruption of or material interference with school activities, and no disturbances or disorders on the school premises in fact occurred. These petitioners merely went about their ordained rounds in school. Their deviation consisted only in wearing on their sleeve a band of black cloth, not more than two inches wide. They wore it to exhibit their disapproval of the Vietnam hostilities and their advocacy of a truce, to make their views known, and, by their example, to influence others to adopt them. They neither interrupted school activities nor sought to intrude in the school affairs or the lives of others. They caused discussion outside of the classrooms, but no interference with work and no disorder. In the circumstances, our Constitution does not permit officials of the State to deny their form of expression.

. . .

Reversed and remanded.

Mr. Justice STEWART, concurring.

Although I agree with much of what is said in the Court's opinion, and with its judgment in this case, I cannot share the Court's uncritical assumption that, school discipline aside, the First Amendment rights of children are co-extensive with those of adults. Indeed, I had thought the Court decided otherwise just last Term in Ginsberg v. New York, 390 U.S. 629 . . . . I continue to hold the view I expressed in that case: "[A] State may permissibly determine that, at least in some precisely delineated areas, a child—like someone in a captive audience—is not possessed of that full capacity for individual choice which is the presupposition of First Amendment guarantees." Id., at 649–650.

Mr. Justice WHITE, concurring.

While I join the Court's opinion, I deem it appropriate to note, first, that the Court continues to recognize a distinction between communicating by words and communicating by acts or conduct which sufficiently impinges on some valid state interest; and, second, that I do not subscribe to everything the Court of Appeals said about free speech in its opinion in Burnside v. Byars, a case relied upon by the Court in the matter now before us.

Mr. Justice BLACK, dissenting.

The Court's holding in this case ushers in what I deem to be an entirely new era in which the power to control pupils by the

elected "officials of state supported public schools . . . " in
the United States is in ultimate effect transferred to the Supreme
Court. The Court brought this particular case here on a petition for certiorari urging that the First and Fourteenth Amendments protect the right of school pupils to express their political
views all the way "from kindergarten through high school."
Here the constitutional right to "political expression" asserted
was a right to wear black armbands during school hours and at
classes in order to demonstrate to the other students that the
petitioners were mourning because of the death of United States
soldiers in Vietnam and to protest that war which they were
against. Ordered to refrain from wearing the armbands in school
by the elected school officials and the teachers vested with state
authority to do so, apparently only seven out of the school system's 18,000 pupils deliberately refused to obey the order. One
defying pupil was Paul Tinker, 8 years old, who was in the second grade; another, Hope Tinker, was 11 years old and in the
fifth grade; a third member of the Tinker family was 13, in the
eighth grade; and a fourth member of the same family was
John Tinker, 15 years old, an 11th grade high school pupil. Their
father, a Methodist minister without a church, is paid a salary
by the American Friends Service Committee. Another student
who defied the school order and insisted on wearing an armband
in school was Christopher Eckhardt, an 11th grade pupil and a
petitioner in this case. His mother is an official in the Women's
International League for Peace and Freedom.

    .   .   .

Assuming that the Court is correct in holding that the conduct
of wearing armbands for the purpose of conveying political ideas
is protected by the First Amendment, the crucial remaining questions are whether students and teachers may use the schools at
their whim as a platform for the exercise of free speech—"symbolic" or "pure"—and whether the courts will allocate to themselves the function of deciding how the pupils' school day will be
spent. While I have always believed that under the First and
Fourteenth Amendments neither the State nor the Federal Government has any authority to regulate or censor the content of
speech, I have never believed that any person has a right to give
speeches or engage in demonstrations where he pleases and when
he pleases. This Court has already rejected such a notion.   .   .

While the record does not show that any of these armband
students shouted, used profane language, or were violent in any
manner, detailed testimony by some of them shows their arm-

bands caused comments, warnings by other students, the poking of fun at them, and a warning by an older football player that other, nonprotesting students had better let them alone. There is also evidence that a teacher of mathematics had his lesson period practically "wrecked" chiefly by disputes with Mary Beth Tinker, who wore her armband for her "demonstration." Even a casual reading of the record shows that this armband did divert students' minds from their regular lessons, and that talk, comments, etc., made John Tinker "self-conscious" in attending school with his armband.   .   .   . And I repeat that if the time has come when pupils of state-supported schools, kindergartens, grammar schools, or high schools, can defy and flout orders of school officials to keep their minds on their own schoolwork, it is the beginning of a new revolutionary era of permissiveness in this country fostered by the judiciary. The next logical step, it appears to me, would be to hold unconstitutional laws that bar pupils under 21 or 18 from voting, or from being elected members of the boards of education.

.   .   .

In my view, teachers in state-controlled public schools are hired to teach there. Although Mr. Justice McReynolds may have intimated to the contrary in Meyer v. Nebraska, supra, certainly a teacher is not paid to go into school and teach subjects the State does not hire him to teach as a part of its selected curriculum. Nor are public school students sent to the schools at public expense to broadcast political or any other views to educate and inform the public. The original idea of schools, which I do not believe is yet abandoned as worthless or out of date, was that children had not yet reached the point of experience and wisdom which enabled them to teach all of their elders. It may be that the Nation has outworn the old-fashioned slogan that "children are to be seen not heard," but one may, I hope, be permitted to harbor the thought that taxpayers send children to school on the premise that at their age they need to learn, not teach.

.   .   .

Change has been said to be truly the law of life but sometimes the old and the tried and true are worth holding. The schools of this Nation have undoubtedly contributed to giving us tranquility and to making us a more law-abiding people. Uncontrolled and uncontrollable liberty is an enemy to domestic peace. We cannot close our eyes to the fact that some of the country's greatest problems are crimes committed by the youth, too many of school age. School discipline, like parental discipline, is an integral and important part of training our children to be good citizens—to be better citizens. Here a very small number of students have crisply and summarily refused to obey a school order designed to give pupils who want to learn the opportunity to do so. One does not need to be a prophet or the son of a prophet to know that after the Court's holding today some students in Iowa schools and indeed in all schools will be ready, able, and willing to defy their teachers on practically all orders. This is the more unfortunate for the schools since groups of students all over the land are already running loose, conducting break-ins, sit-ins, lie-ins, and smash-ins. Many of these student groups, as is all too familiar to all who read the newspapers and watch the television news programs, have already engaged in rioting, property seizures, and destruction. They have picketed schools to force students not to cross their picket lines and have too often violently attacked earnest but frightened students who wanted an education that the pickets did not want them to get. Students engaged in such activities are apparently confident that they know far more about how to operate public school systems than do their parents, teachers, and elected school officials. It is no answer to say that the particular students here have not yet reached such high points in their demands to attend classes in order to exercise their political pressures. Turned loose with lawsuits for damages and injunctions against their teachers as they are here, it is nothing but wishful thinking to imagine that young, immature students will not soon believe it is their right to control the schools rather than the right of the States that collect the taxes to hire the teachers for the benefit of the pupils. This case, therefore, wholly without constitutional reasons in my judgment, subjects all the public schools in the country to the whims and caprices of their loudest-mouthed, but maybe not their brightest, students. I, for one, am not fully persuaded that school pupils are wise enough, even with this Court's expert help from Washington, to run the 23,390 public school systems in our 50 States. . . . I dissent.

Mr. Justice HARLAN, dissenting.

. . . I would, in cases like this, cast upon those complaining the burden of showing that a particular school measure was motivated by other than legitimate school concerns—for example, a desire to prohibit the expression of an unpopular point of view, while permitting expression of the dominant opinion.

Finding nothing in this record which impugns the good faith of respondents in promulgating the armband regulation, I would affirm the judgment below.

BROOKS v. AUBURN UNIV.

United States District Court, Middle Dist., Ala., 1969.
296 F.Supp. 188, aff'd 412 F.2d 1171.

JOHNSON, Chief Judge.

In this class action plaintiffs seek to have this Court issue a preliminary injunction restraining defendants from interfering with a scheduled speaking appearance at Auburn University of the Reverend William Sloan Coffin. Plaintiffs also seek a declaratory judgment of the unconstitutionality of certain regulations, rules, and guidelines concerning inviting speakers to the Auburn University campus. . . .

Plaintiffs in this action are students and faculty members of Auburn University, and the Human Rights Forum, an officially chartered Auburn University student organization. Defendants are Auburn University, a state-operated institution of higher learning located at Auburn, Alabama, Dr. Harry M. Philpott, individually and as President of Auburn University, and Frank P. Samford, Sr., Chairman of the Board of Trustees of Auburn University.

The events immediately triggering this action commenced November 13, 1968, when the Chairman of the Human Rights Forum, David Jeffers, made a written request to the Public Affairs Seminar Board requesting $650 to pay the Reverend William Sloan Coffin to speak at the University on February 7, 1969. The Public Affairs Seminar Board was chartered by Auburn University for the purpose of "allocating funds to departments or groups for the presentation of seminars, conferences, individual lecturers, or other activities which encourage the worthwhile discussion of public affairs." The Public Affairs Seminar Board met on November 20 and approved unanimously the Human Rights Forum's request. . . .

On November 22 President Philpott told the Chairman of the Public Affairs Seminar Board that the Reverend Mr. Coffin would not be allowed to come to the Auburn University campus because he might advocate breaking the law and because he was a convicted felon. . . . President Philpott then laid down what the plaintiffs have termed "the oral Philpott rules" relative to inviting outside speakers. These rules consist of three provisions:

> Student organizations could not invite (a) a speaker that could reasonably be expected to advocate breaking a law, (b) a speaker who had been previously convicted of a felony, and (c) a speaker of the type as the Reverend Mr. Coffin because it would be tantamount to Auburn University's sanctioning what the Reverend Mr. Coffin advocated.

On December 4 the Public Affairs Seminar Board met with President Philpott at his request. At this time President Philpott stated he was using his power as President to veto the expenditure of the money and was banning the appearance of the Reverend Mr. Coffin at Auburn University, and he again stated the "oral Philpott rules" upon which he based this action. At this meeting President Philpott handed out "Guidelines for Issuing Invitations to Outside Speakers." He stated these were for study and discussion only and were not being handed out as "rules." These guidelines are attached as Exhibit "A." The most relevant guideline for present purposes is guideline 2 which provides:

> "Invitations to speak at Auburn University should not be extended to persons who by prior expression might reasonably be expected to advocate:
>
> a.   Disregard for the laws of our society or the breaking of these laws.
>
> b.   The violent overthrow of our government."

Several other background facts are worthy of note. The Reverend William Sloan Coffin is the active Chaplain of Yale University and has been an outspoken leader of the opposition to American involvement in the Vietnam war. In connection with these activities, the Reverend Mr. Coffin has been arrested and has been convicted by a United States District Court in Massachusetts for conspiracy to counsel and aid and abet young men in resisting the draft. That conviction is currently on appeal. The Reverend Mr. Coffin has frequently lectured on college campuses in the last twelve months.

Prior to the invitation to the Reverend Mr. Coffin, Auburn University had no written or orally announced policy or guidelines for inviting speakers to the campus. In the last several years speakers have been invited, some at University expense, to speak to student and faculty groups on campus. Among others, these speakers included Whitney Young, George C. Wallace, Admiral John Crommelin, and Lurleen B. Wallace.

President Philpott has made it clear that the fact that the funds of the Public Affairs Seminar Board were to be used to pay the Reverend Mr. Coffin was a significant consideration but was not critical to his decision. It also seems clear that the ban is not based upon the probability of violence, riots, or other disorders accompanying the proposed speech. It is also clear from Dr. Philpott's testimony that the scheduled appearance of the Reverend Mr. Coffin would not unduly interfere with the discipline or the orderly operation of Auburn University. In short, the basic reasons Dr. Philpott advances in support of his decision to ban the Reverend Mr. Coffin's appearance and payment therefor at Auburn University are based upon a "philosophical concept" and his decision in the matter constitutes a "philosophical decision."

.　.　.

There can no longer be much doubt that constitutional freedoms must be respected in the relationships between students and faculty and their university.　.　.　.

.　.　. Auburn University is, of course, a state agency, and in terms of freedom of expression what is true of elementary and secondary education must be true *a fortiori* of colleges and universities. Indeed, it could be argued that an open forum is even more important on a campus than among the public generally. Chief Justice Warren seemed to be suggesting just that in Sweezy v. New Hampshire, 354 U.S. 234, 250, when he stated:

"The essentiality of freedom in the community of American universities is almost self-evident.　.　.　. Teachers and students must always remain free to inquire, to study and to evaluate, to gain new maturity and understanding; otherwise our civilization will stagnate and die."

It is these considerations which have repeatedly led courts to strike down restrictions on First Amendment rights in this context.

Given that students and faculty are not second class citizens, one can turn to the many cases and scholarly articles from which emerge the nature and scope of their First Amendment rights.

The broad issue of whether Auburn might close its campus altogether to outside speakers is not raised in this case. Rather, we have a situation similar to that facing a New York court in which the observation was made:

"The over-riding issue as to use of school facilities for nonacademic purposes is not raised. Thus, while there may be no duty to open the doors of the school houses for uses other than academic—and I have some doubt even as to this proposition—once they are opened they must be opened under conditions consistent with constitutional principle." Buckley v. Meng, supra, 230 N.Y.S.2d at 933.

. . .

Among other things, plaintiffs contend that Auburn's rules are vague and overbroad. Certainly they are that. In barring anyone who "advocates" breaking of the laws, the regulations run afoul of the almost constitutional ambiguity of "advocate." . . .

. . .

In barring all speakers convicted of a felony, the regulations run afoul of the ambiguity of "convicted." In most instances lawyers would use "convicted" to refer to a final conviction after all appeals had been exhausted. The meaning must be unclear, however, since here President Philpott has applied it to a speaker whose conviction is still on appeal. . . . As stated earlier, the Reverend Mr. Coffin has been "convicted" of a felony in a United States District Court in Massachusetts. This conviction is presently on appeal, and although there is no testimony on this particular point it is common knowledge that the matter will be, if necessary, litigated through the courts, including the Supreme Court of the United States. This Court is of the opinion that the present status of the criminal prosecution against the Reverend Mr. Coffin cannot be used as a justification for the regulations in question. . . .

. . .

The vice in these regulations, however, is really far more basic than their just being vague and overbroad. *These regulations of Dr. Philpott are not regulations of conduct at all.* That would presuppose that they dealt with activities which the state had a legitimate interest in restricting. No such interest has been suggested here. Rather, we have here direct regulation of speech, regulations which on their face restrict the nature and source— both the medium and the message—to which these student and faculty plaintiffs may be exposed. In plain words these regulations must fall because they constitute blatant political censorship. . . .

. . . The State of Alabama cannot, through its President of Auburn University, regulate the content of the ideas students may hear. To do so is illegal and thus unconstitutional censorship in its rawest form. In reaching this conclusion upon the facts in this case, this Court makes no new law and advances no novel constitutional concepts to support its decision. The cases on similar questions are practically unanimous in holding and declaring that such action as attempted by President Philpott in this case is unconstitutional censorship in violation of the First Amendment. . . .

. . .

There is no doubt that the powers and responsibilities of a university president are awesome and extensive. Those powers include wide discretion in dealing with allocating funds, with educational policy, with the requirements of campus order and discipline, and with the time, place, and manner of extracurricular lectures. This Court will not ordinarily sit to review the wisdom with which that discretion is exercised.

It is the duty of this Court, however, to review the exercise of governmental power where there is a tenable claim that it has been exercised in a manner inconsistent with the Constitution of the United States. The point which defendants have forgotten, as persons in authority are wont to forget, is that the First and Fourteenth Amendments are *limitations on governmental power*. They were intended to have and do have the force of law. If Acts of Congress, state statutes, or administrative actions conflict with these limitations, they must yield; the Constitution is the supreme law of the land.

Thus, while it can be said that President Philpott has the ultimate power to determine whether a speaker is invited to the campus, the First Amendment right to hear of the students and faculty of Auburn University means that this determination may not be made for the wrong reasons or for no reason at all.

. . .

If the banning of the right to hear this speaker be seen as independent of the stated reasons, as indicated by the testimony to the effect that Dr. Philpott had not seen fit to apply these reasons to those who fit within the loose criteria as well as the Reverend Mr. Coffin, it must fall because it becomes the act of an unbridled censor. The arbitrary acts of a censor cannot be tolerated; not because arbitrary power will be abused in every case but because of its inherent potential for discrimination against unorthodox views. . . .

The prohibition on arbitrary or discriminatory action also relates to President Philpott's power to control the use of University facilities and funds where that control affects the right to listen. In this case it is clear that the University authorities allocated $10,000 from student fees to be used to pay speakers invited to campus by student organizations. . . .

. . . Having allocated the money, however, and having paid other speakers with no questions asked, Auburn may not in this instance, for no constitutionally acceptable reason, withhold the funds for the Reverend Mr. Coffin as a censorship device.

Nor may Auburn withhold available facilities. While Auburn may establish neutral priorities and require adequate coordination, this Court is clear to the conclusion that it cannot altogether close its available facilities to outside speakers. But here there is no claim that space would not be available, and it is clear that facilities have always been available to speakers invited by student groups. Suitable space must be provided the Reverend Mr. Coffin too.

In the oft quoted words of Judge Learned Hand:

> "It [the First Amendment] presupposes that right conclusions are more likely to be gathered out of a multitude of tongues, than through any kind of authoritative selection. To many this is, and always will be, folly; but we have staked upon it our all." United States v. Associated Press, 52 F.Supp. 362, 372 (S.D.N.Y.1943).

This Court is aware of the many forces which tend to foster the fear that the First Amendment is "folly." The paranoia of living under a nuclear balance of terror, the divisiveness of an unpopular war, the racial tensions existing throughout the country, the economic and social deterioration of our inner cities, and the insecurity of unprecedented technological change are but a few of the forces which continue to threaten our constitutional form of government. If our First Amendment's freedom to speak and freedom to listen are unduly infringed, our plan of self-government is seriously weakened.

. . . Conflicting points of view on sensitive current topics must be—where people want to hear them—afforded a forum. The denial of the right to hear these conflicting views—even though those in authority believe them to be unwise or un-American—violates the very ideas of our government. As Alexander Meikeljohn wrote:

> "When men govern themselves, it is they—and no one else—who must pass judgment upon unwisdom and unfairness and danger. And that means that unwise ideas must

have a hearing as well as wise ones, unfair as well as fair, dangerous as well as safe, un-American as well as American. . . . "

The denial of that right to hear:

" . . . is that mutilation of the thinking process of the community against which the First Amendment to the Constitution is directed." . . .

. . .

SMITH v. UNIVERSITY OF TENNESSEE

United States District Court, Eastern Dist. of Tenn., 1969,
300 F.Supp. 777.

ROBERT L. TAYLOR, Chief Judge.

Plaintiffs seek to enjoin officials of the University of Tennessee from enforcing rules which prohibit students from inviting as speakers for university sponsored programs persons who do not meet certain standards. Jurisdiction is based on Title 28 U.S. C.A. Sections 1331, 1343, 2201 and 2202, and Title 42 U.S.C.A. Sections 1981 and 1983.

Plaintiffs are primarily students and faculty of the defendant university who sue individually and on behalf of all those similarly situated under Rule 23 of the Federal Rules of Civil Procedure.

. . .

Throughout the period of the operative facts in this suit and until the present the University has had in force guidelines for student invitations to speakers. Those guidelines appear in the student handbook as follows:

A. *Choice of Speaker*

An invitation to a speaker who is to be sponsored by a student organization must be approved by the appropriate officers and faculty-alumni advisers to that organization and registered with and approved by the Dean of Students as meeting the following criteria:

(1) The speaker's competence and topic shall be relevant to the approved constitutional purpose of the organization;

(2) There is no reason to believe that the speaker intends to present a personal defense against alleged misconduct or crime which is being adjudicated in the courts;

(3) There is no reason to believe that he might speak in a libelous, scurrilous or defamatory manner or in violation of public laws which prohibit incitement to riot and conspiracy to overthrow the government by force.

. . .

C. *Appeal or Referral*

In addition to the criteria in (A) above, the University Faculty Committee must consider the general question of whether the invitation and its timing are in the best interests of the University.

Issues is one of two officially sanctioned lecture series at the University of Tennessee. Unlike Man and his Environment, the other lecture series, Issues is presently composed solely of student members. Both Issues and Man and his Environment are financed through the Student Activities and Services Fee which is assessed quarterly upon all full-time university students to defray the cost of a long list of student activities and services. . . .

As one of the speakers for its fall quarter program Issues had selected Dick Gregory, the Negro civil rights activist who at the time of the invitation was a candidate for President of the United States. After the invitation was initially approved by the administrative officials as required by the handbook rules, the contract for Mr. Gregory's appearance was duly forwarded by Issues to defendant Gordon for execution by the appropriate financial officers of the University.

On or about September 10, 1968, officers of Issues were informed by Chancellor Weaver . . . that Mr. Gregory would not be permitted to appear on the University campus as a student invited speaker. Two days later, Chancellor Weaver issued a statement entitled "Freedom of Speech on the Campus" in which he said that the administration fully supported unhindered freedom of speech by faculty, students and speakers invited by the academic departments. He expressed the view that student speaker invitation programs constituted in effect a separate university of questionable educational benefit, and which created problems in maintaining the freedom of speech of the faculty.

The Issues program issued an invitation to Dr. Timothy Leary to speak on February 27, 1969 as a part of Winter Quarter Issues schedule. Leary is known primarily as an advocate of the use of the hallucinogenic drug LSD. On February 4, Chancellor Weaver announced that the University administration had refused finally to issue a contract for the appearance on campus of Dr. Leary.

During its October meeting the Board of Trustees adopted a resolution which directed the chancellors of the individual campuses of the university to develop speaker policies which must be submitted to and approved by the Trustees before becoming effective. At its February meeting, the Board set up a committee to recommend a new speakers policy for the consideration of the Board at its June gathering.

The Issues program has scheduled an appearance by Leary for May 6, 1969; but the Acting Vice Chancellor for Student Affairs has declined to approve the invitation. Plaintiffs allege present and future injury in the nature of a violation of their First and Fourteenth Amendment rights because of the refusal of the defendants to allow Gregory and Leary to speak. They contend that the policy as announced in the student handbook is unconstitutionally broad and vague. Temporary and permanent injunctive relief are sought and in addition a declaratory judgment that the current policy of the University is unconstitutional.

. . .

Although the invited speaker is not a plaintiff in this suit, the legal interests of the students who sought to invite Dr. Leary and who would have made up the audience are sufficient to present a substantial legal controversy with the persons whose actions barred the appearance. Snyder v. Board of Trustees of University of Illinois, D. C., 286 F.Supp. 927.

. . .

This case involves the balancing of rights of students and teachers proteced by the First and Fourteenth Amendments of the Federal Constitution and of the officials of the University of Tennessee to control and regulate public speaking on University property. If possible, the rights of the parties should be reconciled so as to avoid the destruction of the rights of either.

The First Amendment provides in pertinent part:

> "Congress shall make no law . . . abridging the freedom of speech, . . . or the right of the people peaceably to assemble, and to petition the Government for a redress of grievances."

The right of freedom of speech is applicable to States under the Due Process Clause of the Fourteenth Amendment. Gitlow v. New York, 268 U.S. 652; De Jonge v. Oregon, 299 U.S. 353.

The First Amendment protection of free speech extends to listeners. On April 7, 1969, the Supreme Court wrote on the case of Stanley v. Georgia, 394 U.S. 557, as follows:

"It is now well established that the Constitution protects the right to receive information and ideas. 'This freedom [of speech and press] . . . necessarily protects the right to receive . . .' (Citing cases) This right to receive information and ideas, regardless of their social worth, see Winters v. New York, 333 U.S. 507, 510 (1948), is fundamental to our free society. . . ." 394 U.S. 557.

Further, it has long been recognized that in carrying out their primary mission of education, state owned and operated schools may not disregard the constitutional rights of students. Meyer v. Nebraska, 262 U.S. 390; West Virginia State Board of Education v. Barnette, 319 U.S. 624; People of State of Ill. ex rel. McCollum v. Board of Education, 333 U.S. 203.

It is conceded that the Board of Trustees and administrative officials of state supported universities have the right to enforce rules and regulations governing the appearance of guest speakers. No one has the absolute, unlimited right to speak on a university campus; however, when the university opens its doors to visiting speakers, it must follow constitutional principles if it seeks to regulate those whom recognized groups may invite. The fundamental question in this lawsuit is whether the applicable constitutional principles require that the university's regulations on student-invited speakers not be vague or broad. If such a duty rests upon the defendants, then the Court must go further and determine whether existing regulations are too vague to meet the constitutional requirements.

In three recent decisions federal district courts have held that when state officials and legislatures undertake to restrict speaker invitations, they may not do so by rules which are too vague or too broad. Snyder v. Board of Trustees of Univ. of Ill., 286 F. Supp. 927 (three judges, N.D.Ill., 1968), arose from the university enforcement of a state statute which prohibited student invitations to speakers who were representatives of any "subversive, seditious, and un-American organizations." The Court held that the students' First Amendment rights were violated and that the statute was unconstitutional for vagueness and because it was in effect a prior restraint on speech which did not have procedural safeguards which might make prior restraint permissible.

A similar North Carolina statute limited university officials in allowing compus facilities to be used by speakers. A three-judge

District Court held, Dickson v. Sitterson, 280 F.Supp. 486 (M.D.
N.C., 1968), that the statute and university regulations pursuant
thereto were unconstitutional for vagueness.

The decision in Brooks v. Auburn Univ., 296 F.Supp. 188 (E.D.
Ala., February 5, 1969), differed from the two previous cases in
that no state statute was involved. Auburn's administrative officials denied approval of an invitation to and use of facilities to
a student-invited speaker and issued rules for inviting outside
speakers. After deciding that the rules were impermissibly broad
and vague if considered rules of conduct, the Court held that the
rules were regulations of pure speech and amounted to political
censorship.

Although appellate federal courts have not ruled on the specific issue, the decisions in the *Snyder, Dickson* and *Brooks* cases
appear to be in accord with related holdings of the Supreme
Court. In the recent decision of Tinker v. Des Moines Independent School Dist., 393 U.S. 503, February 24, 1969, the Supreme
Court held unconstitutional school rules against the wearing of
armbands in protest of the Vietnam War. The opinion states:

> "It (wearing armbands) was closely akin to 'pure speech'
> which, we have repeatedly held, is entitled to comprehensive
> protection under the First Amendment. (Citing cases)

> "First Amendment rights, applied in light of the special
> characteristics of the school environment, are available to
> teachers and students. It can hardly be argued that either
> students or teachers shed their constitutional rights to free-
> dom of speech or expression at the schoolhouse gate."

The Court indicated that the area in which school officials may
limit free speech is confined to speech that "would materially
and substantially disrupt the work and discipline of the school."

In another line of cases the Supreme Court has recognized the
right of states to protect their schools from subversion, but has
held that states may not use teacher oaths or disclosures of associations which are so vague or broad that they discourage
teachers from exercising freedom of speech and association.
Wieman v. Updegraff, 344 U.S. 183; Shelton v. Tucker, 364 U.S.
479; Keyishian v. Board of Regents, 385 U.S. 589.

Regulations which may limit the exercise of free speech and
assembly have often been subjected to the tests of vagueness and
broadness. A California statute making unlawful display of a
red flag as a symbol of opposition to organized government was
held to be so broad that it could prohibit constitutionally pro-

tected speech as well as unprotected speech. The Court held it unconstitutional for vagueness. Stromberg v. People of State of California, 283 U.S. 359.

The Supreme Court in one of its most recent cases, in dealing with a Birmingham, Alabama ordinance that vested power in the city commission to grant permits for parades and demonstration, said in part:

" . . . This ordinance as it was written, therefore, fell squarely within the ambit of the many decisions of this Court over the last 30 years, holding that a law subjecting the exercise of First Amendment freedoms to the prior restraint of a license, without narrow, objective, and definite standards to guide the licensing authority, is unconstitutional. 'It is settled by a long line of recent decisions of this Court that an ordinance which, like this one, makes the peaceful enjoyment of freedoms which the Constitution guarantees contingent upon the uncontrolled will of an official—as by requiring a permit or license which may be granted or withheld in the discretion of such official—is an unconstitutional censorship or prior restraint upon the enjoyment of those freedoms.' . . . " Shuttlesworth v. City of Birmingham, March 10, 1969, 394 U.S. 147.

See also, Cox v. Louisiana, 379 U.S. 536.

Unlike laws which penalize speech after it is uttered, as in the case with slander, the university's regulations on speakers have the effect of preventing speech before it is spoken. Prior restraints on speech come to the courts with a heavy presumption against their constitutional validity. Carroll v. President and Commissioners of Princess Anne, 393 U.S. 175.

The foregoing authorities establish that the defendant's regulations on student-invited speakers may not constitutionally be vague or broad beyond certain limits, when a statute or regulation either forbids or requires the doing of an act in terms so vague that men of common intelligence must necessarily guess at its meaning and differ as to its application, it violates the due process clause of the Fourteenth Amendment because of vagueness. Dickson v. Sitterson, supra. Stricter standards of vagueness apply where the statute potentially inhibits speech. Cramp v. Board of Public Instruction, 368 U.S. 278. Regulations may not withstand constitutional scrutiny which are so broad that they threaten speech which is protected by the First Amendment. Shelton v. Tucker, 364 U.S. 479.

Guideline No. 1 in the student handbook requires the guest speaker's competence and topic to be relevant to the approved constitutional purpose of the organization. Who is to judge the competence and the topic? What standards are to be used in so judging? Isn't competence, like real estate values, a relative term? Do people always agree as to whether a person is competent or incompetent? The term is so broad and vague that an administrator could, if he chose to do so, act as an unrestrained censor of the expression of ideas with which he does not agree.

Guidelines Nos. 2 and 3 provide in effect that there shall be no reason to believe that the speaker intends to present a personal defense against alleged misconduct or crime which is being adjudicated in the courts and no reason to believe that he will speak in a libelous, scurrilous or defamatory manner or in violation of public laws which prohibit incitement to riot and conspiracy to overthrow the government by force. Who is to judge these matters and what standards shall be used in finding the answers?

The final and Fourth Guideline provides that the University Faculty Committee in addition to the criteria to be considered in Guidelines 1, 2 and 3 must consider the general question of whether the invitation and its timing are in the best interests of the University. Any speaker could be debarred from the campus if it were determined that he was invited at the wrong time under this guideline. This vests in the administrative officials discretion to grant or withhold a permit upon criteria unrelated to proper regulation of school facilities and is impermissible. Kunz v. New York, 340 U.S. 290, 293; N. A. A. C. P. v. Button, 371 U.S. 415, 432; see Tinker v. Des Moines Independent School District, supra.

In holding unconstitutional New York's regulations on subversive activities and speech of teachers, the Supreme Court said in part:

"There can be no doubt of the legitimacy of New York's interest in protecting its education system from subversion. But 'even though the governmental purpose be legitimate and substantial, that purpose cannot be pursued by means that broadly stifle fundamental personal liberties when the end can be more narrowly achieved.' Shelton v. Tucker, 364 U.S. 479, 488.

"We emphasize once again that '[p]recision of regulation must be the touchstone in an area so closely touching our most precious freedoms,' N. A. A. C. P. v. Button, 371 U.S. 415, 438; '[f]or standards of permissible statutory vagueness are strict in the area of free expression. . . . Because First Amendment freedoms need breathing space to survive, government may regulate in the area only with narrow specificity.' Id., at 432–433." Keyishian v. Board of Regents, supra, 385 U.S. pp. 602–604.

It was the belief of our forefathers that censorship is the enemy of freedom and progress. We have lived by this principle since it was written by them in our Federal Constitution, and it has proved beneficial to the nation and its citizens. The interchange of ideas and beliefs is a constitutionally protected necessity for the advancement of society. See the comments of Mr. Justice Black, in the cases of Smith v. California, 361 U.S. 147, 160 and Feldman v. United States, 322 U.S. 487, 501.

The Court is constrained to hold that the plaintiffs are entitled to declaratory relief. The University has made it its policy to allow recognized student groups to invite speakers and to make university facilities available to both speaker and audience. The regulations by which the University denies permission for the appearance of speakers which students have selected are required by the Constitution to be clearly and narrowly worded. The existing regulations which appear in the Student Handbook do not satisfy those requirements.

The defendants are responsible citizens who occupy high positions in state government. We believe that they will abide by the declaration of this Court that the current policy of the University of Tennessee is not in accord with plaintiffs' First Amendment rights because the standards fixed for the selection of outside speakers are too broad and vague. For that reason injunctive relief is not granted at this time but plaintiffs may renew their application at an appropriate time if it becomes necessary.

Chapter 6

CONSTITUTIONAL GUIDELINES FOR
FREE EXPRESSION

At the root of all liberty is the liberty to learn
(Lord Acton)

As we have observed, lurking behind the question of where each college and university should draw the line between protected and unprotected expression, between which a viable standard of conduct must be formulated, lies not only the judiciary but a value judgment as well. The dilemma confronting public institutions of higher education in such a judgment is well-illustrated by noting two extremes, both unacceptable. On the one hand is the chaos of unlimited and unrestricted expression, but in this milieu no institution which properly may be called a college or university can exist. At the other end of the scale is the intolerable situation, also in no true sense an institution of higher learning, where any non-sanctioned expression is proscribed. Faced with this fundamental conflict and its implications for the vast system of American public education, the *Tinker* Court admitted the need for some degree of restriction on expression but then went on to define the edge of the conflict precisely: "Our problem lies in the area where students in the exercise of First Amendment rights collide with the rules of school authorities." [1]

It is at this tension point that the courts have a duty to determine which of the two conflicting interests demands the greater protection. "We must recognize," however, "that regulation of 'conduct' has all too frequently been employed by public authority as a cloak to hide censorship of unpopular ideas." [2] Thus First Amendment theory must deal not only with the powers of the state to restrict the right of expression but also with the obligations of the state to protect it and, in some instances, to encourage it. But to use the government itself—the traditional enemy of freedom of expression—as an instrument for promoting freedom of expression raises some intriguing questions and, in fact, calls for some unprecedented imagination and discipline.

1. Tinker v. Des Moines Independent Community School District, 393 U. S. 503, 507 (1965).

2. Justice Jackson concurring in Thomas v. Collins, 323 U.S. 516, 547 (1945).

The essential point is that the forces inherent in any system of administration tend to drive to excess, and the mere existence of a "conduct" enforcement apparatus can, if not carefully circumscribed, be in itself restrictive. Moreover, every organization is goal-directed. The official goals are expressed in the formal normative structure which defines the positions making up the organization. However, where officials occupying such positions are presumed to look objectively at the events around them, they tend to look selectively and subjectively at the events through the lenses of their organizational and bureaucratic perspectives.

Perhaps the most important characteristic which service organizations, such as public colleges and universities, share with one another is that they do not produce their own resources. They depend instead upon someone else to procure the resources for them. This dependence leads to the organizations' developing a very special relationship with those responsible for the allocation of resources. The organizations must, therefore, take into account the latter's wishes.

Another important characteristic of service organizations which is shared by public institutions of higher education is the powerlessness of the client. This powerlessness is both a cause and a consequence of organizational procedures. If the client is unable to muster sufficient support from individuals outside the organization who could cause "trouble" or "strain," then the decision of how to handle him will likely be determined, not according to the official goals of the organization, but solely on the grounds of what is organizationally efficient and (therefore) "right." Furthermore, much of the day-to-day contact with clients is usually relatively concentrated in the lower echelons of the bureaucracy. Often the lower level official's efficiency and possibility of advancement is measured in terms of being more organization—than client—minded. Success then tends to mean suppression of unpopular expression. On the other hand, "to be overly client-oriented and to transmit clients' demands upward is a relatively unrewarding experience in [these] organizations." [3]

Clearly, all of this has implications for students' First Amendment rights in public higher education. Thus in the remainder of this chapter an attempt is made to survey some of the chief

3. See Amitai Etzioni, *Modern Organization* (Englewood Cliffs, N.J.: Prentice-Hall, 1964), p. 100.

problems facing free expression in higher education and to suggest the legal doctrine by which they should be resolved. Such a hurried survey will, of course, leave many unanswered questions, doubts and possibly some disagreements. But the hope is that it will demonstrate at least how the issues ought to be framed if we are to achieve a meaningful and effective application of the First Amendment.

FIRST AMENDMENT PRINCIPLES

The Body Politic

The First Amendment simply states: "Congress shall make no law .   .   .   abridging the freedom of speech, or of the press; or the right of the people peaceably to assemble   .   .   ."—and the judiciary is the one institution (especially the Supreme Court of the United States) expressly assigned the role of protecting these guarantees. The character and significance of these rights, the kinds of forces loosed in prescribing limitations, the necessity for support by law, especially under conditions of public anxiety, all demand that the courts play a positive, indeed almost an aggressive role in this area.

Neither from a jurisprudential nor from any other point of view should there ever be any serious doubt that speech bears a special significance in a republican system. Republican government in fact begins with the understanding that the exercise of political power over others must be justified. Hence, a true republic sets about to ensure that people in positions of authority are compelled to offer justifications for their actions. The root purpose of the First Amendment, therefore, is to assure an effective system of free and open discussion.

The idea is that suppression of discussion makes a rational judgment impossible. In effect it substitutes force for logic. Moreover, suppression of expression conceals the real problems confronting a society. It is likely to result in neglect of the grievances which are the actual basis for unrest, and thus prevent their correction. Since it both hides the extent of opposition and hardens the position of all sides, it makes a rational compromise difficult or impossible. And finally, it weakens and debilitates the majority whose support for common decisions is necessary; for it hinders an intelligent understanding of the reasons for adopting such decisions and, John Stuart Mill observed, "beliefs not grounded on conviction are likely to give way before the slightest semblance of an argument." [4] In short (and what higher education officials in the sixties might have profitably considered), suppression of opposition may well mean that when change is finally forced on the community, it will come in more violent and radical form.

Thus the American theory of free expression means, as Justice Jackson said, "freedom to differ on things that go to the heart of the matter." But freedom of expression is not merely the personal right of individuals to have his or her say; it also means the right of the rest of us to hear them. In other words, the First Amendment protects the communication itself, and thus affords protection to both the source of the communication and its recipient. Justice Brennan, concurring in Lamont v. Postmaster General (1965), made the same point by stating that the "dissemination of ideas can accomplish nothing if otherwise willing addressees are not free to receive and consider them. It would be a barren marketplace of ideas that had only sellers and no buyers." [5] And John Stuart Mill again, whose "Essay on Liberty" is considered the classic defense of free expression, put it this way:

> The peculiar evil of silencing the expression of opinion is that it is robbing the human race. . . . If the opinion is right, they are deprived of the opportunity of exchanging error for truth; if wrong, they lose, what is almost as great a benefit, the clearer perception and livelier impression of truth, produced by its collision with error. [6]

Academic Freedom

The crucial point for higher education, however, is not that freedom of expression is politically useful, but that it is indispensable to the purpose of the higher learning—advancing knowledge and discovering truth. Once one accepts this premise it follows that members of the academic community must, in order to exercise their truth-seeking function, have great freedom both in forming individual judgment and in forming the common judgment.

Considered in this aspect, the theory of academic freedom coincides with that of democratic free expression in that both theories are based upon the premise that the soundest and most

4. John Stuart Mill, *On Liberty and Other Essays*, Vol. 20 (New York: The Book League of America, 1929), p. 42.

5. 381 U.S. 301, 308 (1965).

6. Mill, op. cit., p. 41.

rational judgment is arrived at by considering all facts and arguments which can be put forth in behalf of or against any proposition. Truth is most often a slippery and elusive object. Human judgment is a frail thing. People often err in being subject to emotion, prejudice or personal interest. Judgment frequently suffers from lack of information and insight, or inadequate thinking. In fact human judgment can seldom rest at the point any person carries it, but should always remain incomplete and subject to further extension, refinement, rejection or modification. Hence, an individual who seeks knowledge and truth must hear all sides of the question, especially as presented by those who feel strongly and argue for a different view. He should consider all alternatives, test his judgment by exposing it to opposition, make use of different minds to sift the true from the false. Conversely, the suppression of information, discussion, or the clash of opinions prevents one from reaching the most rational judgment, blocks the generation of new ideas, and tends to perpetuate error.

Furthermore, any judgment of a particular curriculum in higher education should be more than what a student's specialized intellectual experience ought to be. Yet, in an age increasingly reliant upon specialization it is altogether too easy to believe that training in the skills that lie at the core of a specialty is all there is to the matter. The central problem here, of course, is that specialized competence may be equivalent to social incompetence; it may either ignore the moral and political consequences of what the specialist does or may permit him to make decisions on behalf of society for which he is in fact unequipped.

Certainly this admonition must be taken to heart since that which distinguishes both intellectual and moral maturity is the development of critical responsibility. And critical responsibility is the obligation to make tacit values explicit. Hence it means more not less self-consciousness. It means that one should not recoil from the sometimes crushing burden of insight. It means that all the pronouncements of "conventional wisdom" should be met with "healthy skepticism," that it is all right—indeed, even preferable—to be shocked by social inequities and be prepared to admit that these inequities are maybe not accidental but rather the consequences of certain beliefs held by certain people with certain power.

To many people, however, the truth-seeking process suggests some kind of subsidized revolution. In fact, the process of truth seeking tends to make the institution of higher learning extremely vulnerable because the dynamics of that search means revising the view of the world as new evidence comes in, and these revisions inevitably come into conflict with many beliefs held dear to people. Nevertheless, no society, much less a free one, can long succeed without new ideas for its procedures and goals. Clearly, Mr. Justice Frankfurter expressed the same thoughts while concurring in Sweezy v. New Hampshire (1957):

> Insights into the mysteries of nature are born of hypothesis and speculation. The more so is this true in the pursuit of understanding in the groping endeavors of what are called the social sciences, the concern of which is man and society. . . . For society's good—if understanding be an essential need of society—inquiries into these problems, speculations about them, stimulation in others of reflections upon them, must be left as unfettered as possible. Political power must abstain from intrusion into the activity of freedom, pursued in the interest of wise government and the people's well-being, except for reasons that are exigent and obviously compelling.[7]

Nonetheless, the operation of a system of free expression must also involve a weighing of considerations in terms of the realities of maintaining such a system in the everyday world. As we have seen, often there are forces that distort and overextend the principles of free expression. Taking this into account, the *Tinker* Court held that constitutionally protected expression could be curtailed if, in its exercise, it clearly threatened to "materially and substantially disrupt" a legitimate activity of the school.[8]

The facts of the actual *Tinker* case, however, presented a fairly open-and-shut case with regard to freedom of speech. The factual index of what constitutes a "material and substantial disruption" varies, of course, with the circumstances. For example, it would normally take less to cause one in a library than on a campus lawn. And apparently courts have recognized that a continued distraction is more likely to "disrupt" than an isolated one. Nevertheless, it is difficult to imagine a quality education taking place in an institution simmering just below the level of "material and substantial disruption" as the result of free expression. Unlike the community at large, the campus is relatively confined (depending on its size), and lacks the numerous outlets to dissipate irritants.

7. 354 U.S. 234, 261–262 (1957).   8. *Tinker*, 393 U.S. at 509.

STUDENT PUBLICATIONS

As already noted, one of the fundamental purposes of higher education is the pursuit of truth. Not coincidentally, however, the concept of "truth" is a cornerstone of journalistic endeavor. In fact, the motto of the Society of Professional Journalists, Sigma Delta Chi, is "Truth, Talent and Energy," a credo of which any professional academician would approve. Nevertheless, administrators, staff, faculty and students often have different notions concerning the role and purpose of the campus press. But even more important, it seems that many newspaper advisers and administrators are either unaware of students' constitutionally protected rights, or simply choose to ignore them, hoping that the legal pendulum will swing the other way.

The Public Forum Principle

The direction in which that pendulum will swing remains to be seen. What is clear today is that students attending public colleges and universities do not "shed their constitutional rights to freedom of speech at the schoolhouse gate." [9] Moreover, the landmark aspect of the *Tinker* case is its holding that schools are appropriate places for First Amendment expression. Describing the nature of schools, the Court in *Tinker* said:

> It is a public place, and its dedication to specific uses does not imply that the constitutional rights of persons entitled to be there are to be gauged as if the premises were purely private property. [10]

Thus courts have rejected claims that college "ownership" or "sponsorship" of student publications *per se* justifies suppression of student expression. This means, in effect, that the issue of who is publisher is irrelevant in determining the First Amendment rights of students. For example, the district court in Antonelli v. Hammond (1970) reached the same conclusion. In this case, students producing a school-sponsored newspaper at a community college brought suit challenging the school's power to control the content of the publication. Upholding the student claims, the *Antonelli* court said:

> We are well beyond the belief that any manner of state regulation is permissible simply because it involves an ac-

9. *Tinker*, 393 U.S. at 506.

10. Id., at 512, fn.6; See also Antonelli v. Hammond, 308 F.Supp.

1329, 1336 (D.C.Mass.1970), where the court held that colleges and universities are proper forums for the dissemination of ideas.

tivity which is part of the university structure and is financed with funds controlled by the administration. *The state is not necessarily the unrestrained master of what it creates and fosters.* Thus in cases concerning school-supported publications or the use of school facilities, the courts have refused to recognize as permissible any regulations infringing free speech when not shown to be necessarily related to the maintenance of order and discipline within the educational process. . . .

Because of the potentially great social value of a free student voice . . ., it would be inconsistent with basic assumption of First Amendment freedoms to permit a campus newspaper to be simply a vehicle for ideas the state or the college administration deems appropriate. Power to prescribe classroom curricula in state universities may not be transferred to areas not designed to be part of the curriculum.[11]

All of this points up the fact that student journalists enjoy First Amendment protections to an even greater degree than do their counterparts employed by commercial publishers. Commercial publishers, after all, may dismiss employees who do not follow policies established by the publishers. Additionally, unlike school officials, commercial publishers may increase, decrease or reallocate funds without justification.

The ultimate control of a commercial publisher is financial, but it is without legal significance that a student publication is partially state-funded since the college administration does not stand in the shoes of a private publisher. Thus, in Joyner v. Whiting (1973), the Fourth Circuit Court of Appeals stated: "Censorship of constitutionally protected expression cannot be imposed . . . based on the institution's power of the purse." [12] In *Joyner*, a university president withdrew financial support for the school's newspaper because he objected to the paper's editorial content. The university's argument that with financial support came some degree of editorial control was rejected on the basis of a familiar legal principle:

It may well be that a college need not establish a campus newspaper, or, if a paper has been established, the college may permanently discontinue publication for reasons wholly unrelated to the First Amendment. But if a college has a

11.   308 F.Supp. 1329, 1337 (D.C.Mass.   12.   477 F.2d 456, 460 (4th Cir. 1973).
1970) (emphasis added).

student newspaper, its publication cannot be suppressed because college officials dislike its editorial comment. This rule is but a simple extension of the precept that freedom of expression may not be infringed by denying a privilege.[13]

In this respect, the decision to establish a student publication as a conduit for student expression is educational and political, and since there is no First Amendment obligation to create such a forum, the decision is one committed to the discretion of college officials. Once that decision is made, however, and a publication is created as a means for student communication and expression, constitutional protections attach and the publication must be operated in accord with First Amendment principles.[14] More specifically, the recurring theme of case law in this area is the judicial rejection of the notion that with financial support comes editorial control. Hence, once a forum for student expression is established, be it termed a college-sponsored forum, a college-funded forum, a curriculum-connected forum, an extracurricular forum, the creator of the forum, i. e., college authorities, may only restrict and censor, or punish students for past content, in a manner consistent with First Amendment guarantees.

The Publication as Instructional Tool or House Organ

In the law "labels" are irrelevant. A campus newspaper *is* what the facts indicate that it is, labels notwithstanding. Thus, the fact that a student publication is produced as an adjunct of journalism or a creative writing class or otherwise related to the college curriculum does not, in itself, give college authorities any greater control than they have over other publications. If a campus newspaper, however, is established principally, if not exclusively, as an instructional tool to develop the journalistic skills of enrolled students, then most likely, students cannot legitimate-

---

13. Id.

14. See, e. g. American Civil Liberties Union v. Radford, 315 F.Supp. 893, 896 (D.C.Va.1970), "[O]nce a public school makes an activity available to its students, faculty, or even the general public it must operate the activity in accord with first amendment principles."; Trujillo v. Love, 322 F.Supp. 1266, 1270 (D.C.Colo.1971), "Having established a particular forum for expression, officials may not then place limitations upon the use of that forum which interfere with protected speech and are not justified by an overriding state interest."; Pliscou v. Holtville Unified School District, 411 F.Supp. 842, 847 (D.C.Cal.1976), "It should be noted that a school district is not required to establish a newspaper . . . Once a newspaper is established, its publication cannot be suppressed because of its editorial content."

ly complain that their views are not allowed free expression since the purpose of the newspaper from the beginning was not to provide free expression, but to serve as an educational medium. Nevertheless where a college intends to use its newspaper principally as a teaching tool, it should not allow it to assume the characteristics of free expression; it should not allow students to dictate its form and content; it should provide journalism instruction for all student participants; it should supervise and criticize all work; submitted materials should meet established criteria and censorship allowed only when necessary to achieve a "quality" standard; and, inferentially at least, academic credit should be given for work performed.

A similar situation would prevail for what is commonly called the "house organ." The dictionary definition of a house organ is "a periodical issued by a business or other establishment primarily for its employees, presenting news of the activities of the firm, its executives and employees." Here again, the purpose of the house organ is other than providing a free mode of expression. Unlike the "laboratory" newspaper, the principal function of which is to develop journalism skills, the house organ is used to disseminate information. In fact, it may well be that in these days of increasing student press independence it would be advisable (and perhaps even necessary) for an institution to establish its own publication in order to communicate accurately and punctually certain essential information.

Clearly, the house organ, if it does not intermingle free expression with the "party line," retains independence from First Amendment proscriptions. The house organ actually presents few problems since it seldom, if ever, is under the control of students. On the other hand, it seems to be extremely difficult to categorize a student publication solely as a teaching vehicle. For example, in Bazaar v. Fortune (1973), a publication was produced by students with the advice of the University English Department for course credit as part of the Department's established curriculum. The magazine was created with the intention that student material from the course would make up the core of the publication with the possible addition of other student material which might be voluntarily submitted. The school sought content control on the grounds that (1) the publication was curricular in nature; (2) the publication would be identified as speaking for the institution; and (3) the position of the university was that of a private publisher possessing control over the publication's content. In response to these claims, the Fifth Circuit Court of Appeals stated:

> The University here is clearly an arm of the state and this single fact will always distinguish it from the purely private publisher as far as censorship is concerned. It seems a well-established rule that once a University recognizes a student activity which has elements of free expression, it can act to censor that expression only if it acts consistent with First Amendment constitutional guarantees.[15]

A somewhat analogous argument was also rejected in Bayer v. Kinzler (1974). In this case, students producing an official high school newspaper prepared a sex information supplement as a part of a regular issue of the school newspaper. The supplement was "primarily composed of articles dealing with contraception and abortion" but was "serious in tone and obviously intended to convey information rather than appeal to prurient interests."[16] The principal seized copies of the newspaper and ordered that no copies containing the supplement be distributed. However, when the school officials argued that their prior censorship was "reasonable" because publication of the supplement constituted an unauthorized intrusion into an area of secondary curriculum, the court disagreed:

> In this court's opinion, it is extremely unlikely that distribution of the supplement will cause material and substantial interference with schoolwork and discipline. Accordingly, the court finds that seizure of the supplement and refusal to allow the distribution were not reasonably necessary to avoid material and substantial interference with schoolwork or discipline. . . . Responsible presentation of information about birth control to high school students is not to be dreaded.[17]

In another leading case, Trujillo v. Love (1971), officials at Southern Colorado State College attempted to control and censor

---

15. 476 F.2d 570, 574 (5th Cir. 1973), modified en banc 489 F.2d 225 (per curium), cert. denied 416 U.S. 985 (1974).

16. 383 F.Supp. 1164, 1165 (D.C.N.Y. 1974), aff'd without opinion 515 F. 2d 504 (2d Cir. 1975); more specifically; some of the students' sex-survey questions were as follows: "Do you approve of pre-marital sexual relations? Do you consider yourself a heterosexual, homosexual or bisexual? Would you object to a homosexual or bisexual in a position of school authority?" Id. at 1166. Chances are, and for good reason, such a story on Page One might make a high school administrator a tad nervous.

17. Id., at 1166.

the content of a student newspaper, contending that it was intended as an instructional tool. The court rejected the school's
argument because the school in fact had not used the newspaper
as intended. The court found that the school officials had failed
to provide adequate journalistic instruction, failed to exercise
supervision over the newspaper and its staff, and had arbitrarily
reviewed the plaintiff's writing while leaving other students'
writing unreviewed. In the words of the court:

> [The] policy of the administration and faculty was not .   .
> put into effect with sufficient clarity and consistency to
> alter the function of the newspaper. As a result the news-
> paper continued to serve as a student forum and [therefore]
> the restraints placed on the student's writing did abridge
> her right of free expression.[18]

A similar conclusion was reached in the case of Zucker v.
Panitz (1969). In this case, a high school editor sought to run an
advertisement criticizing the American involvement in Vietnam.
In censoring the advertisement, school officials advanced the
argument "that the war is not a school related activity, and therefore not qualified for news, editorial and advertising treatment." [19] The court rejected this argument finding that the
paper was "more than a mere activity time and place sheet." The
school officials also alleged that the newspaper was only intended
as a teaching tool. However, after a "perusal" of past issues, the
court determined that the paper was largely an unsupervised student activity of general circulation.[20]

In short, the invalidity of most instructional arguments is highlighted by the problem of sufficiently eliminating the paper from
consideration as a free medium of expression. Yet, seeing this
from a different perspective, until recently such an issue was
moot. Most student publications were little more than house
organs—papers that published only what the board of trustees
and college administration wanted students to write and read.
Thus, whether instructional vehicles or not, these publications
tended to be school-approved pablum, fed to students in small,
bland doses.

Non-College Sponsored and "Underground" Publications

As noted above, *Tinker* established that schools are proper
forums for the expression of ideas. Therefore, the nature of the

18.   322 F.Supp. 1266, 1267 (D.C.Colo.   19.   299 F.Supp. 102, 103 (D.C.N.Y.
     1971).   1969).

20.   Id.

publication in question (publications produced by students on their own time, off campus and not funded by college sources) must be viewed in that light. Thus, a flat ban preventing the distribution of such alternate publications on campus is unconstitutional.[21] In other words, college officials cannot prohibit non-sponsored publications nor penalize students responsible for preparing or distributing them unless these publications violate First Amendment standards applicable to other published materials.

In this latter regard, however, the permissible limitations on First Amendment freedom of press guarantees are greater for college-sponsored than for non-college sponsored publications. Since the public college is an instrumentality of the state, it has an obligation to uphold the law, not merely to break the law and suffer the consequences therefrom. For example, the potential exposure to college liability for libel in school-sponsored publications might justify a limited degree of prepublication or predistribution regulation. On the other hand, colleges are not responsible for libel occurring in non-sponsored publications and thus can exercise prior publication or distribution control only in exceptional cases where such expression seriously threatens substantial disruption and material interference with the operation of the college.

The words "material" and "substantial" are crucial here, but this protection does not entirely rule out regulatory measures; that is, college officials may make reasonable rules regarding the time and place of distribution. However, a rule restricting the distribution of off-campus publications to a time and place that would prevent most students from getting the literature would be not reasonable. As you will recall, the First Amendment includes the right to receive as well as to disseminate information. Additionally, the general principle of constitutional law that is at the bottom of many "free expression" cases is the always present requirement of uniformity. Hence, policy designated by college administrators must be uniform as stated and as applied. Any attempt to discriminate between on-campus and off-campus literature, even though carefully framed and well-intentioned, may be susceptible to constitutional attack.

21. See, e. g., Eisner v. Stamford Bd. of Educ., 314 F.Supp. 832 (D.C. Conn.1970), aff'd 440 F.2d 803 (2d Cir. 1971); and Vail v. Board of Educ., 354 F.Supp. 592 (D.C.N.H. 1973).

In this regard, Brubaker v. Moelchert [22] is an excellent case in point since it deals with the on-campus distribution of printed materials by non-college groups. The plaintiffs, who were members of the United States Labor Party and the National Caucus of Labor Committees, filed suit in a federal district court alleging that University of North Carolina at Charlotte officials deprived them of their rights to freedom of speech, press, peaceable association and the equal protection of the laws by preventing them from assembling, approaching people and distributing their newspaper and political leaflets at places and times of their choice on campus.

These publications were critical of the Rockefellers and the CIA but were within the permissible limits of political comment since they were not calculated to disrupt the operations of the university. Nevertheless, in the distribution of their pamphlets and sale of their newspapers, the plaintiffs were restricted by the Assistant Dean of Students to the use of a table inside the Student Center. The Assistant Dean informed the plaintiffs that if they did not have a student organization sponsoring them, they "could distribute and congregate only (a) with prior permission at a table inside the Student Center; (b) in the Student Book Store; or (c) through a selling cage such as that used by local daily newspapers." [23] The Dean also warned them that they would be arrested if they failed to observe the regulations.

The district court took issue with the distinction drawn by the University regulations between sponsored and unsponsored organizations and expressly found that such a distinction could not "legally diminish the First Amendment rights of plaintiffs, since a partial dedication to First Amendment uses is effectively a dedication to the exercise of First Amendment rights by everyone." [24] Notably, the court declared the distinction arbitrary and pointed out that there was no evidence advanced to show that the outsiders were more likely to cause disruption or refuse to obey reasonable restrictions on the time, place and manner of distribution than were the insiders.

The district court likewise rejected the regulations as impermissibly vague on the ground that they gave the administrative officials an unchecked discretion to decide which uses of a campus space were to be allowed. In addition, the court found that the time lapse of several months between the plaintiffs' appeal to the

22. 405 F.Supp. 837 (D.C.N.C.1975).   24. Id.

23. Id., at 840.

Vice Chancellor for a modification of the Dean of Student's restrictions and the determination of that request violated the procedural safeguard of a brief, specified time in which the requested
decision should have been made.

Thus, the University's regulatory scheme of prior restraint on
the distribution of off-campus publications failed to pass even
minimum constitutional muster. But the court did note that the
University could "of course, make reasonable charges for the use
of its classrooms and auditoriums, and . . . prevent disruption of its classes. It may not, however, treat plaintiffs differently from others with respect to the exercise of First Amendment rights." [25] Finally, since the plaintiffs presented a serious
case of First Amendment injury to the court, the University officials drafted a proposed revision of the regulations and requested the comments of the court. This revision made several
significant changes and, in the court's opinion,

> eliminate[d] the chief constitutional problems with the ex-
> isting statement. The revised policy statement: (a) Estab-
> lishes uniform procedures and standards for those desiring
> to solicit funds and uniform locations for such solicitations;
> (b) Allows the distribution of non-commercial written ma-
> terials to be done in the open areas by anyone without per-
> mission or advance approval; (c) Permits assemblies of
> groups, whether or not university affiliated, to be conducted
> without sound amplification in Cove University Center Plaza
> and the Residence Hall Cafeteria Plaza; (d) Allows as-
> semblies in other areas upon written request at least forty-
> eight hours in advance to a designated office and telephone
> number, with approval assumed if no answer is received
> within thirty-six hours; (e) Provides a right of appeal to
> the Chancellor with a forthcoming decision required at least
> six hours before the scheduled event.[26]

Similarly, the Supreme Court of Arizona held that a University of Arizona regulation restricting the distribution of off-
campus newspapers to certain areas and imposing a fee for such
distribution violated the lawful free exercise of First Amendment
rights. The number of locations where papers could be placed
was ruled arbitrary, and, in reference to the fee, the Court concluded that it "constituted a license on the right to distribute
printed material" which was precluded by the First Amendment.[27]

25. Id., at 842.

26. Id., at 842–43.

27. New Times, Inc. v. Arizona Bd.
of Regents, 110 Ariz. 367, 373, 519
P.2d 169, 175 (1974).

The Court also ruled that "[t]he commercial nature of the activity is no justification for narrowing the protection of expression secured by the First Amendment."[28]

This line of reasoning was also followed by the Ninth Circuit Court of Appeals in Jones v. Board of Regents,[29] a case involving another regulation promulgated by the University of Arizona which this time prohibited the distribution of handbills on campus. The Court of Appeals held that

> . . . the challenged regulation completely prohibits the distribution of any handbills, at any time, in places open to the public generally. Such blanket prohibition is clearly unrelated to any valid regulatory purpose when applied to public property generally open to the public at large.[30]

On the other hand, the United States Court of Appeals for the Fifth Circuit ruled that a student editor of a university newspaper could constitutionally refuse a paid advertisement from an off-campus homosexual group (Mississippi Gay Alliance v. Goudelock).[31]

The case involved Bill Goudelock, editor of the Mississippi State student newspaper, *The Reflector,* who refused to accept both a paid ad and a subsequent unpaid public service announcement for the Mississippi Gay Alliance, an off-campus group offering counseling to gay students. *The Reflector* regularly published both types of ads, for both on-campus and off-campus groups.

As a result of the refusal, the MGA filed suit against the editor, charging that he had violated the group's First Amendment rights by refusing advertising on the basis of content. The federal district court, however, upheld the editor's action, saying that First Amendment protection required a showing of direct involvement by the state itself. Subsequently, the MGA appealed the district court's decision, declaring that *The Reflector* constituted a forum for the communication of ideas and was therefore an arm of the state and subject to the same restrictions. But, once again, the MGA was unsuccessful; that is, in upholding the district court's decision, the Court of Appeals pointed out

28. Id., at 176.

29. 436 F.2d 618 (9th Cir. 1970).

30. Id., at 620. See also Martin v. City of Struthers, 319 U.S. 141 (1943), which held that the right to distribute literature may not be withdrawn even if it creates a minor nuisance for the community which had the burden of cleaning up the litter from the streets.

31. 536 F.2d 1073 (5th Cir. 1976).

that since Goudelock had been selected as editor by the student body, there was no evidence that he was acting as a representative of the state. Thus,

> since there is not the slightest whisper that the University authorities had anything to do with the rejection of this material, offered by this off-campus cell of homosexuals, since such officials could not lawfully have done so, and since the record really suggests nothing but discretion exercised by an editor chosen by the student body, we think the First Amendment interdicts any judicial interference with the editorial decision.[32]

The Court further noted that the Mississippi statute which condemned "any intercourse which is unnatural, detestable and abominable" was not unconstitutional.[33]

Prior Restraint—Substantial Disruption and Material Interference Test

There is a heavy constitutional presumption in favor of a student's freedom of press. Moreover, given the Supreme Court's premise that a free press is a condition of a free society, "[a]ny prior restraint on expression comes to this Court with a 'heavy presumption' against its constitutional validity." [34] As such, the heavy burden of justifying prior restraint (any censorship before distribution, including seizure of publications) rests with college officials. Accordingly, it is the wise college official who exercises the utmost discretion prior to exercising any interference with free expression.

Excluding for a moment the issues of obscenity and libel, in order to constitute a valid interference with a student's right to prepare and distribute a publication on campus, there must be a strong showing of a present intention to incite violence or disrupt college activities. In fact, in view of *Tinker's* forecast rule, it should be obvious that school officials may not censor or withhold approval of literature without clear evidence that it is di-

---

32. Id., at 1075.

33. Id.

34. Nebraska Press Ass'n v. Stuart, 427 U.S. 539, 558 (1976). See also Smith v. University of Tennessee, 300 F.Supp. 777, 779 (D.C.Tenn. 1969), "Prior restraints on expression come to the courts with a heavy presumption against their constitutional validity"; and Poxon v. Board of Educ., 341 F.Supp. 256 (D.C.Cal.1971) where a school policy permitting prepublication review of student publications ruled *per se* unconstitutional.

rected to inciting imminent lawless action and is likely to incite
or produce such action:

"[S]chool officials cannot ignore expressions of feelings with
which they do not wish to contend. They cannot infringe on
their students' right to free and unrestricted expression as
guaranteed to them under the First Amendment to the Constitution, where the exercise of such rights in the school
buildings and schoolrooms do not materially and substantially interfere with the requirements of appropriate discipline
in the operation of the school." [35]

But whatever the strength of the state interest in maintaining
appropriate discipline in educational institutions, prior restraint
of expression may only be employed pursuant to precisely written
regulations which spell out what kinds of expression are prohibited in easily understood and exact terms. For example, in
striking down a challenged regulation, the court in Baugham v.
Freienmuth emphasized that criteria supporting prior restraint
must spell out "what is forbidden so that a reasonably intelligent
student will know what he may write and what he may not." [36]
Also, when school officials ordered two nonschool sponsored newspapers to cease publication, the court in Nitzberg v. Parks struck
down the supporting regulation "since it gives no guidance whatsoever as to what amounts to a 'substantial disruption of or material interference with' school activities   .   .   ." [37]

On the other hand, there is another line of case law that rejects any *routine* use of prior review of student expression. In
Fujishima v. Board of Educ., for instance, the court held:

Tinker in no ways suggests that students may be required
to announce their intentions of engaging in certain conduct
beforehand so school authorities may decide whether to prohibit the conduct. Such a concept of prior restraint is even
more offensive when applied to the long protected area of
publication. [38]

35. *Tinker*, 393 U.S. at 509, quoting
with approval Burnside v. Byars,
363 F.2d at 749 (5th Cir. 1966).

36. 478 F.2d 1345, 1351 (4th Cir.
1977); the Court also noted that
key terms must be defined by the
regulations and specifically indicat-

ed its disapproval of "vague labels."

37. 525 F.2d 378, 383 (4th Cir. 1975).

38. 460 F.2d 1355, 1358 (7th Cir.
1972).

In other words, the *Fujishima* Court held that *Tinker's* forecast rule is one that only applies in the context of a subsequent punishment and precludes a prior restraint system:

> The *Tinker* forecast rule is properly a formula for determining when the requirements of school discipline justify punishment of students for exercise of their First-Amendment rights. It is not a basis for establishing a system of censorship and licensing designed to prevent the exercise of First Amendment rights.[39]

Case law supporting the *Fujishima* position, however, seems to aim more at the rejection of any routine system of prior review than at nonroutine action taken on a reasonable forecast of substantial disruption of school activity. Moreover, it should be noted that the *Fujishima* position runs counter to a substantial portion of case law on this point. For example, the Second Circuit, in Eisner v. Stanford Board of Educ.,[40] indicated that prior submission of publications is constitutionally permissible if accompanied by carefully drawn regulations and elaborate procedural safeguards; and the Fourth Circuit, in Quarterman v. Byrd [41] and Baugham v. Freienmuth (above) ruled in like fashion.

But nonetheless, even assuming such a system of prior censorship would be constitutional, and there are some constitutional doubts, it is clear that precise regulations and adequate procedural safeguards must be part of that system. And in this regard the *Baugham* holding was that:

> A prior restraint system, even though precisely defining what may or may not be written is nevertheless invalid unless it provides for:
>
> (1) A definition of "Distribution" and its application to different kinds of material;
>
> (2) Prompt approval or
>
> (3) Specification of the effect to act promptly; and
>
> (4) An adequate and prompt appeal procedure.[42]

Under this latter system, therefore, it would seem that colleges need not *forsake* all forms of prior review over student publications. For instance, open exhortation to students to engage in disorderly and destructive activities, together with the demon-

---

39. Id., at 1359.

40. 440 F.2d 803 (2d Cir. 1971).

41. 453 F.2d 54 (4th Cir. 1971).

42. 478 F.2d at 1351.

strated probability of a riot, allowed college officials to enjoin pamphleteering in Norton v. Discipline Committee of East Tenn. State Univ.:

> It is not required that the college authorities delay action against the inciters until after the riot has started and buildings have been taken over and damaged. The college authorities had the right to nip such action in the bud and prevent it in its inception.[43]

Moreover, in Siegal v. Regents of the Univ. of Cal., a federal district court declared:

> Illegal conduct is not protected merely because it is in part initiated, evidenced, or carried out by language. [Expression] in a context of violence, involving a clear and present danger, can lose its significance as an appeal to reason and become part of an instrument of force and as such is unprotected by the Constitution.[44]

Prior Restraint—Obscenity

Today it seems almost traditional for student publications to be somewhat hostile and antagonistic toward school officials, sponsored or not. Adding considerable fuel to this antagonism, of course, is the practice of many young people (or would-be young) to use sexual display or "four-lettered words" quite deliberately as shock weapons against the "Establishment."

Quite understandably, the "new freedom" in moral expression has not been accepted easily by all educators, by all of the public, nor by all of the readers of campus publications. Yet, more and more, it seems that the knowable differences between "decent" and "indecent" expression can only be "dimly perceived." In effect, that which appeared "indecent" yesterday seems commonplace today: *Lady Chatterly's Lover, Fanny Hill, Tropic of Cancer, Portnoy's Complaint, Fear of Flying, Playboy, Playgirl, Penthouse,* and *Hustler,* for example, now circulate freely and legally. Then, too, such phenomena as sex therapy, sex surrogates and gay liberation movements abound today. It's all sort of a moral application of Fred Allen's sly insight: "Hush little bright line, don't you cry/you'll be a cliche by and by."

43. 419 F.2d 195 (6th Cir. 1969); however, one dissenting judge took issue with the court's factual finding of "sufficient evidence of probable eruption." Id. at 204. In fact the judge in his dissent claimed that there was not "even the slightest hint of probable or actual disruption." Id. at 205.

44. 308 F.Supp. 832, 838 (D.C.Cal. 1970).

Returning to campus, in the spring of 1977 two pert co-eds, both juniors at M.I.T., published a "consumer guide" in a student newspaper rating the sexual performances of thirty-six M.I.T. men. The ratings—from four stars to none—were purportedly based on the personal experience of the two women authors who, to the discredit of some of the more inept, named the men and described their sexual techniques; for example: "Lazy S.O.B.; couldn't maintain an erection except while lying on his back. I also got chronic vaginitis afterwards." The M.I.T. officials groaned, then referred the unfortunate mess to a disciplinary committee that later slapped the ladies with "formal probation." [45]

But in case one might think that this is the only such news from the nation's campuses, look again. In Scoville v. Board of Educ.,[46] two high school students were suspended for distributing an unofficial newspaper containing language deemed "inappropriate and indecent" by school officials. The court, however, ruled that the words at issue—"Oral sex may prevent tooth decay"—were not legally obscene and thus ordered the students to be reinstated. Interestingly, the court was also presented with a statement in the paper characterizing some remarks made by the school principal as the "product of a sick mind." Absent a showing that such criticism caused disruption, the court said, there was no basis to punish the students.[47]

Likewise, in Thonen v. Jenkins two East Carolina University students were expelled on the basis of a letter published in the school newspaper which was "critical of parietal regulations and ended with a 'four-letter' vulgarity referring to the president of the university." [48] In ruling that the expulsions were unconstitutional, the Fourth Circuit Court of Appeals held that "one [vulgar] word in an otherwise unexceptional letter does not constitute obscenity." [49] Similarly, in Bazaar v. Fortune, University of Mississippi students were upheld in their suit to prevent school officials from censoring a school-sponsored literary magazine. University authorities had attempted to suppress the magazine because, among other reasons, it had used "four-letter words, often colloquially referred to as 'obscenities' . . . [including]

45. "Want to Know What College Men are Like Today? Dial (617) 253-7977 and Ask for Roxanne," *Esquire*, September, 1977, p. 67.

46. 425 F.2d 10 (7th Cir. 1970).

47. Id., at 12–14.

48. 491 F.2d 722, 723 (4th Cir. 1973).

49. Id., at 723–724.

use of that four-letter word generally felt to be most offensive in
polite conversation." [50]

The *Bazaar* Court pointed out that

> . . . evidence establishes that . . . *Playboy* is sold
> on campus . . . [and] works in its library and . . .
> works that are assigned to students as required reading for
> courses contain the same words, used in much the same way,
> as are found in these stories to which the University now
> objects. . . . Similar language is also abundant in many
> recent best-sellers, including *Love Story, The Godfather,*
> *Portnoy's Complaint* . . . and *Valley of the Dolls.* Even
> the works of William Faulkner, an author indelibly associat-
> ed with Oxford and the University of Mississippi, contains a
> high number of "obscenities" much like the words under at-
> tack here. Thus, here the University is seeking to restrain
> the use of certain words which it acknowledges are often used
> in literary compositions and words which are found in the
> books it offers for student reading . . . .[51]

This, indeed, was a peculiar double standard, but, as in *Bazaar*,
such inconsistency on the part of a public institution is typically
regarded as fatal.

Then, in Papish v. Board of Curators of the Univ. of Missouri,[52]
the Supreme Court of the United States ruled that a thirty-two
year-old graduate student, Barbara Susan Papish, had been
wrongfully expelled for distributing on campus a paper containing the word "M_____-f_____" and featuring a cartoon showing a helmetted, clubwielding policeman raping the Statue of
Liberty and the Goddess of Justice. The Court ruled that neither
the language nor the cartoon could be ruled as "constitutionally
obscene or otherwise unprotected." Further, "The mere dissemination of ideas—no matter how offensive to good taste—on
a state university campus may not be shut off in the name alone
of 'conventions of decency.'" And notably, "the First Amendment leaves no room for the operation of a dual standard in the
academic community with respect to the content of speech."[53]

Thus, while the overall response might be "So what?", the
courts have specifically ruled that the use of vulgar language, profanity, or four-letter words does not alone constitute obscenity
(which is illegal). "One man's vulgarity," said Justice Harlan,

---

50. 476 F.2d at 573.

51. Id., at 577–578.

52. 410 U.S. 667 (1973).

53. Id., at 670–671.

"is another's lyric," and it was precisely "because governmental officials cannot make principled distinctions in this area" that the First Amendment left these "matters of taste and style so largely to the individual."[54]

Justice Harlan's remarkable opinion in Cohen v. California argued that if speech contained a residue of political significance, it was presumptively protected. The case involved a young man who walked through the corridors of the County Courthouse in Los Angeles wearing a jacket that bore the inscription "Fuck the Draft." According to Harlan, what Cohen was doing with his jacket was "asserting [a] position on the inutility or immorality of the draft" and thus presenting a statement—no less—on a matter of public policy. Thus, what Harlan denied was the existence of any standards for identifying expression that was truly offensive, because the offensiveness of the words depended entirely on the subjective feelings of the people who saw them.

The upshot of *Cohen,* then, would seem to indicate that neither the Supreme Court nor anyone else can any longer define obscenity (let alone propriety) within the context of political expression. In 1973, however, in Paris Adult Theatre I v. Slaton,[55] Chief Justice Burger pressed the point that obscenity proscriptions could not so simply be displaced from the law when he observed that the " 'live' performance of a man and woman locked in a sexual embrace at high noon in Times Square [would not be] protected by the Constitution because they simultaneously engaged in a valid political dialogue." Clearly, the Chief Justice made a most persuasive point; that is, the government could restrain the couple from their embrace without interfering in any important degree with their freedom to discuss political ideas. Hence, because their sexual demonstration is not strictly necessary to the protected discussion, the government might well be justified in acting out of concern for the sensibilities of other people in the public place.

Yet, though the Court considers a couple "locked in a sexual embrace at high noon in Times Square" as obscene and thus *not* entitled to constitutional protection, Supreme Court justices, like everyone else, have great difficulty in determining precisely what is obscene and what is not. As Justice Harlan pointed out: "The subject of obscenity has produced a variety of views among the members of the Court unmatched in any course of constitution-

54. Cohen v. California, 403 U.S. 15,   55. 413 U.S. 49 (1973).
    25 (1971).

al adjudication."[56] And as Justice Brennan wrote: "No other aspect of the First Amendment has, in recent years, commanded so substantial a commitment of our time, generated such disharmony of views, and remained so resistant to the formulation of stable and manageable standards."[57] Noting that "the number of obscenity cases on our docket gives ample testimony to the burden that has been placed upon this Court," quite rightfully remarked that "[t]he problem is . . . that one cannot say with certainty that material is obscene until at least five members of the Court, applying inevitably obscure standards, have pronounced it so."[58]

And therein lies the basic legal difficulty. Even though the First Amendment, despite permissive trends of recent years, does not protect expression which is legally obscene, "profanity" is protected. Simply stated, profanity is the use of what is commonly called a "four-letter word" or "swear word." Thus, the obvious problem for college administrators and students, as well as for impartial investigators of the problem, is that only courts of law can decide what is legally obscene, and guidelines for decision-making are far from precise. For example, according to current standards established in Miller v. California,[59] expression is obscene *only* when the following three questions can be answered affirmatively:

> (1) whether the *average* person, applying *contemporary community standards,* would find that the work, taken as a whole, appeals to *prurient interest* and (2) whether the work depicts or describes, in a patently offensive way, sexual conduct specifically defined by applicable state laws; and (3) whether the work, taken as a whole, *lacks* serious literary, artistic, political or scientific value.[60]

The Court also gave the following examples of what state obscenity laws could define for potential prohibition under part 2 of the 3-part above-mentioned test:

> (a) Patently offensive representations or descriptions of ultimate sexual acts, normal or perverted actual or simulated.

56. Interstate Circuit, Inc. v. City of Dallas, 390 U.S. 676, 704–705 (1968).

57. Paris Adult Theatre I v. Slaton, 413 U.S. at 73 (Brennan dissenting).

58. Id.

59. 413 U.S. 15 (1973).

60. Id., at 24 (emphasis added).

(b) Patently offensive representations or descriptions of masturbation, excretory functions, and lewd exhibition of the genitals.[61]

Each of the foregoing elements—prurient appeal, patent offensiveness, and social value—must be viewed in light of the contemporary moral standards of the *community*. In fact *Miller* expressly rejects the claim that obscenity be determined according to a national standard. But the difficulty attached to establishing a model representing an "average person" and to recognize with precision "contemporary community standards," "prurient appeal," and lack of social value is obvious. That four of the Supreme Court justices dissented from the *Miller* standard emphasizes further the potential for widespread disagreement even among highly qualified arbiters of obscenity disputes. How much greater, then, must be the potential for disagreement among lay educators and students concerned with obscenity problems in student publications.

Moreover, the basic difficulty is magnified by lack of consensus throughout society as to the need for obscenity legislation and control. For example, the 1970 *Report of the Commission on Obscenity and Pornography* reported that

A national survey of American public opinion sponsored by the Commission shows that a majority of American adults believe that adults should be allowed to read or see any sexual materials they wish. On the other hand, a substantial consensus of American adults favors prohibiting young persons access to some sexual materials. Almost half the population believes that laws against sexual materials are impossible to enforce. Americans also seem to have an inaccurate view of the opinions of others in their communities; the tendency is to believe that others in the community are more restrictive than they actually are.

(The *Report*, p. 43)

As a result, the Commission recommended the abolition of all of the obscenity laws as they apply to consenting adults. However, in rejecting the *Report*, President Nixon declared:

So long as I am in the White House, there will be no relaxation of the national effort to control and eliminate smut from our national life. . . . [T]he Commission contends that the proliferation of filthy books and plays has no lasting,

61.   Id., at 25.

harmful threat on man's character. . . . Centuries of civilization and ten minutes of common sense tell us otherwise. . . . American morality is not to be trifled with. [From the perspective of Watergate, an obvious double standard] The Commission on Pornography and Obscenity has performed a disservice, and I totally reject its report.[62]

However, whether or not a majority of the people oppose "smut," the First Amendment stands between the personal preference of those who do and the desired governmental action. Nevertheless, when substantial numbers of the public believe with Nixon that obscenity is a social evil that must be banned, while others—equally sincere and equally numerous—agree with the views of the Commission majority, finding a common meeting ground on which the opposing points of view may be reconciled becomes important. This is true especially in the campus setting where conflict of interests is always present, and because the lack of precision characteristic of obscenity—a lack which, when confronted with strong differences in philosophical and moral outlook—can lead only to bitter quarrel and legally incorrect decisions.

Thus, apart from moral and philosophical differences, the number of legal angles which might be made to dance on the point of a constitutional pin can sometimes endow even the reddest-eyed insomniac with a good fat dose of narcolepsy. Nonetheless, the problem of determining just how far the law can go in curtailing such anti-social behavior without endangering protected expression is important and complex. It should go without saying that First Amendment freedoms are delicate and vulnerable, as well as extremely precious in our society.

People, of course, are offended by many kinds of sexually oriented expression. They are also offended by certain political pronouncements and sociological themes which are contrary to moral standards and religious precepts. In other words, the list of activities, publications and pronouncements that offends someone is endless. Some of it goes on in private; some of it is inescapably public, as, for instance, when a student becomes a blatant offender of the moral sensibilities of his college community. And perhaps right here it is not entirely lunatic to imagine that, while outside in the streets the old Victorian world continues to fall about our ears, in the sanctum sanctorum of old Siwash's

---

62. Quoted in Stanley Fleishman. *The Supreme Court Obscenity Decisions* (San Diego, California: Greenleaf Classics, Inc., 1973), p. 19.

administrative chambers are some dedicated doctrinaires, locked away from reality, haggling over moral abstractions and fiddling with bits of paper. "I tell you, my friends, (waggling index finger at the ceiling) the Reds are not only under our beds; some of them are down at the journalism lab conniving at what Professor Higgins described as the cold-blooded murder of the English tongue."

The stodgy ineffectuality of this (hopefully) imaginary scene misconceives what it is that the First and Fourteenth Amendments protect. In fact, the Supreme Court in Kingsley Int'l. Pictures Corp. v. Regents cut through this kind of nonsense with the following classical statement:

> Its guarantee is not confined to the expression of the ideas that are conventional or shared by a majority. It protects advocacy of the opinion that adultery may sometimes be proper, no less than advocacy of socialism or the single tax. And in the realm of ideas it protects expression which is eloquent no less than that which is unconvincing.[63]

Still, even a confirmed optimist could find little realistic comfort in any suggestion that this statement marks the road to clarity in the determination of what is an obscene utterance and thus suppressible within constitutional standards. However, clarification can be enhanced by recognition of the fact that there are certain basic propositions of constitutional law upon which the courts are disposed to rely, faced with given factual situations.

First, as already noted, sex, "swear-words" and obscenity are not synonymous. In fact, there is nothing intrinsically obscene, for example, about sexual relations. Indeed, in Christian doctrine the sacrament of marriage is incomplete without this act of love. However, if we take the "pig in the parlor" [64] metaphor and apply it, say, to a situation where a dozen couples request permission to announce in the student newspaper that they plan to copulate on the campus green at high noon on Easter Sunday, their extrinsic exploitation of sex would constitute obscene behavior and it would be constitutionally permissible to censor such an announcement. Thus, when college authorities find that a pig is about to enter the parlor, the exercise of their regulatory power depends less on proof the pig is obscene than upon the context in which the pig is found.

---

63. 360 U.S. 684, 688–689 (1959).

64. Village of Euclid v. Ambler Realty Co., 272 U.S. 365, 388 (1926). "A nuisance," the Court held, "may be merely a right thing in the wrong place—like a pig in the parlor instead of the barnyard."

In other words, the offense of obscenity, or the use of obscenity under circumstances where it may be restrained or punished by a public institution, is largely confined to a "time, place and manner" common sense standard. The real nature, therefore, is essentially aesthetic. It is the use of certain behavior or kinds of expository styles under circumstances that will be repugnant to other people who are unwilling auditors. The *Goldberg* court in this respect is correct (see pages 84 and 85). The deliberate use of certain language, consequently, before a "captive audience" may appropriately be made the subject of restraint or discipline without violating First Amendment standards. However, in all likelihood it would be constitutionally impermissible to restrain or discipline the same language planned for or printed in, say, a student underground paper. The point is that it would be constitutionally awkward to claim that college authorities should be able to forbid the use of certain expressions in such publications since the consuming audience probably knowns in advance the nature of the publication and, in any event, must volunteer to read it.

It should be obvious that the "pig in the parlor" explanation does not mean that the next step could bring about a total ban on sexual intercourse anywhere, any time. This would simply miss the point that an act legal in itself can in different circumstances become a violation of public liberty. Yet, as we have seen, the contextual test of *Miller* (supra) must resort to such indefinite concepts as "contemporary community standards," "prurient interests," "patent offensiveness," "serious social value," and the like. Clearly, then, the uncertainty that surrounds such an approach can substantially erode protected speech and, hence, the next constitutional proposition.

Recognizing the inherent vagueness of any definition of obscenity, this proposition holds that the definition of obscenity must be drawn as narrowly as possible so as to minimize interference with protected expression. Therefore, even in exceptional cases where the power to restrain expression is recognized, there must first be regulations precisely defining prohibited expressions. For example, in Mississippi Gay Alliance v. Goudelock it was held that

> When no rules guide the decision to exclude a controversial message from what otherwise appears to be a public forum, the courts are properly very skeptical of any proffered justification for the exclusion.[65]

65. 536 F.2d 1073, 1089 (5th Cir. 1976).

And in Quarterman v. Byrd:

> What is lacking in the present regulation, and what renders
> its attempts at prior restraint invalid, is the absence of . .
> any criteria to be followed by school authorities in determin-
> ing whether to grant or deny permission . . .[66]

In short, where the state interest in the regulation of morality is
vague and ill-defined, interference with the guarantees of the
First Amendment is difficult to justify:

> This Court . . . has emphasized that the "vice of vague-
> ness" is especially pernicious where legislative power over
> an area involving speech, press, petition and assembly is in-
> volved. . . . For a statute broad enough to support in-
> fringement of speech, writings, thoughts, and public as-
> semblies, against the unequivocal command of the First
> Amendment necessarily leaves all persons to guess just what
> the law really means to cover, and fear of a wrong guess in-
> evitably leads people to forego the very rights the Constitu-
> tion sought to protect above all others. Vagueness becomes
> even more intolerable in this area if one accepts, as the
> Court today does, a balancing test to decide if First Amend-
> ment rights shall be protected. It is difficult at best to make
> a man guess—at the penalty of imprisonment—whether a
> court will consider the State's need . . . superior to
> society's interest in unfettered freedom. It is unconscion-
> able to make him choose . . . when the state supposedly
> establishing the "state interest" is too vague to give him
> guidance.[67]

Finally, the third basic constitutional proposition is that to
justify prior restraint in this area, procedural safeguards are required; that is, an adversary hearing, after adequate notice to all
interested parties, is normally essential to any procedure by which
freedom of expression is burdened by proper restraint. The
purpose of such procedural requirements, of course, is to protect
expression which might turn out to be constitutionally protected.

The Supreme Court, for example, has held that "a State is not
free to adopt whatever procedures it pleases for dealing with
obscenity. . . ."[68] "Rather, the First Amendment requires
that procedures be incorporated that 'ensure against the curtail-

---

66. 453 F.2d 54, 59 (4th Cir. 1971).

67. Barenblatt v. United States, 360
U.S. 109, 137–138 (1959).

68. Marcus v. Search Warrant, 367
U.S. 717, 731 (1961).

ment of constitutionally protected expression . . .' " [69] Thus, in Quarterman v. Byrd it was held that "restraints must be accompanied by procedural safeguards designed to minimize the impact of the restraints." [70]

Prior Restraint—Libel

Simply stated, libel is a common law action for a written statement which falsely defames the character of another. However, prior restraint (as well as the threat of libel prosecution after the expression) has often been a favorite weapon of those who would suppress criticism and prevent discussion of important issues. The realities pointing up this fact have been enumerated again and again. Thus, in examining the history of the Sedition Act of 1798, "which first crystallized a national awareness of the central meaning of the First Amendment," Justice Brennan found that "libel can claim no talismanic immunity from constitutional limitations. It must be measured by standards that satisfy the First Amendment." [71] Therefore, court interpretations of First Amendment freedom of press guarantees indicate that only very limited and reasonable measures can be adopted to preclude the distribution of unlawful, injurious and defamatory material.

Just as with obscenity, in other words, prior review of student publications to restrain libelous expression must be based upon adequate and specific regulations.[72] Nevertheless, the very concept of prior restraint is considered repulsive to the First Amendment. Hence, rather than employing a routine system of prior review, the more appropriate method would be for the college to have rules against libelous expression and be on record as strongly opposing such expression. Accordingly, students, not the college or its officials, would be personally liable to the individual defamed.

A nagging fear, nonetheless, is the possibility that failure to take appropriate and reasonable action to prevent the libelous expression of students may, under vicarious liability, make the col-

---

69. Blount v. Rizzi, 400 U.S. 410, 416 (1971), quoting from Bantam Books, Inc. v. Sullivan, 372 U.S. 58, 66 (1963).

70. 453 F.2d at 59.

71. New York Times Co. v. Sullivan, 376 U.S. 254, 297 (1964).

72. See, e. g., Quarterman v. Byrd, 453 F.2d at 59, regarding procedural

safeguards; and Nitzberg v. Parks, 525 F.2d at 383, where the court noted "that the definition of 'libelous' material contained in the regulation fails to apply the standard of New York Times v. Sullivan, and its progeny. On its face, therefore, the Board's regulations are void for vagueness and overbreadth."

lege or its officials legally responsible for damages. That is to say, institutions do not act by themselves but act through people. Hence, when institutions are held legally liable for acts of their employees (e. g., journalism teacher) the concept of vicarious liability is present.[73] Also present in this concept, moreover, is that a person can be held to respond in damages when another person, acting in his behalf, acts in a tortious way.[74]

Thus, by applying the doctrine of vicarious liability, some fear, for instance, that a college and its student newspaper adviser could be held legally responsible for the libelous publication of a student editor. Such a possibility, however, is extremely remote, particularly if reasonable care is exercised by providing appropriate regulations and instruction. But this cautionary recommendation in no way suggests a need for any system of prior censorship. In fact, to hold colleges and their officials legally responsible for libel published in such forums would seem rather inconsistent with the "forum theory" itself; that is, college officials, unlike commercial publishers, do not have absolute control over the content, staff and finances of these publications. In fact an analogy could well be drawn to Farmers Educational Cooperative Union v. WDAY, Inc.,[75] which suggests immunity from libel damages in a similar context. WDAY, a radio station, was sued for libel for broadcasting a political candidates' speech, but the Supreme Court held that since WDAY was prevented by the Communications Act from censoring a candidate's speech made pursuant to equal-time provisions, it would be "unconscionable" to permit civil liability to be imposed. Although in *Farmers* the station was denied censorship by statute, it would seem that a First Amendment restriction on such action in the college setting would apply with at least equal force.

The state of course has complete control to promulgate neutral regulations forbidding tortious conduct, but as already noted, con-

---

73. Also present is the concept of *respondeat superior*, which is the doctrine by which the principal is responsible for the act of his agent, and liability, therefore, is imputed to the principal.

74. In brief, a tortious act can be defined as the commission or omission of an act by one, without right, whereby another received some injury directly or indirectly to his person, property or reputation.

75. 360 U.S. 525 (1959). Also, such liability would seem inconsistent with the judicial holdings that only a court of law (not college officials) is empowered to determine when libel has occurred. As Justice Brennan pointed out in Freedman v. Maryland, 380 U.S. 51, 57 (1965): "Because the censor's business is to censor, there inheres the danger that he may be less responsive than a court . . . to the constitutionally protected interests in free expression."

tent control collides with First Amendment rights unless a compelling state interest can be demonstrated. Hence, in light of the recognition that a public institution subjects itself and its officials to civil rights liability when it acts unconstitutionally to restrain content, it would seem more "unconscionable" to hold that college authorities have a duty to prevent libel.[76]

Another factor which greatly reduces the possibility of obtaining libel judgments against either students or college officials is the New York Times Co. v. Sullivan ruling. Here the Supreme Court held that before any person may be subject either to civil damages or criminal conviction because of comments made about a matter of public policy or general interest, there must be proof that the comments were made with "actual malice . . . that is, with knowledge that it was false or with reckless disregard of whether it was false or not." [77] Also, the "*Sullivan* Rule" has broadened to include not only public officials, but other persons who can properly be called public figures by reason of being in the limelight and being widely known for one reason or the other.[78] The point is that by far the greatest amount of defamatory comment found in student newspapers is centered around public figures.

Prior Restraint vs. Post-Publication Regulation

On the basis of the principles discussed, therefore, it should be clear that only in the most exceptional circumstances—e. g., solid evidence of an imminent danger of substantial disruption and material interference with the operation of the institution— should college officials employ prior restraint. Clearly, college officials can best regulate inflammatory, obscene and libelous expression through instruction on what constitutes constitutionally unprotected expression (in terms of college-sponsored publications) and the explicit warning of carefully drawn regulations which precisely define such prohibited expression.

However, as noted earlier in this chapter, there are limits to post-publication regulation. To be specific, the usual test in this area is that the manifestation of expression, in terms of the style and manner of the communication, must rise above the level of

76. See chapter 3, pp. 96–102 for an explanation of liability under Section 1983 of the Civil Rights Act of 1871.

77. 376 U.S. 254, 280 (1964).

78. See, e. g., Curtis Pub. Co. v. Butts, 388 U.S. 130 (1965); Pauling v. Globe-Democrat Pub. Co., 362 F. 2d 188 (8th Cir. 1965); and Arnold Rose v. Gerda Koch, 278 Minn. 235, 154 N.W.2d 409 (1967).

mere inconvenience or annoyance to be constitutionally subject to regulation and disciplinary action.

The problems involved in the constitutional limitations on expression, of course, become larger when one looks at the painful issue of what happens when students print and distribute materials on campus which offend large numbers of a college's most generous benefactors, the public, and the public's mirror images— i. e., legislative bodies. The political pressure for censorship and discipline under such circumstances can be enormous, but any suggestion regarding the unconstitutional regulation of the editorial position of student publications should offend college officials profoundly. In fact the basic significance of academic freedom lies in the protection of intellectual freedoms: "the rights of professors to teach, of scholars to engage in the advancement of knowledge, of students to learn and to express their views, free from external pressures or interferences."[79] Moreover, college officials cannot, even by Boards of Trustees, be required to violate the Constitution of the United States—an obvious principle but frequently forgotten when explaining one's particular action or inaction to irate alumni, board members or legislators.

STUDENT ORGANIZATIONS

"It is beyond debate, that freedom to engage in association for the advancement of beliefs and ideas is an inseparable aspect of the 'liberty' assured by the Due Process Clause of the Fourteenth Amendment," Justice Harlan asserted in NAACP v. Alabama, and "abridgment of such rights, even though unintended, may inevitably follow from varied forms of governmental actions."[80]

Obviously, the heart of such protection lies in the fact that if substantial burdens were allowed to be imposed on associational efforts, freedom of speech and press and all the other rights listed in the First Amendment would be jeopardized. In other words, if government possessed an unrestrained power to determine when people could legally band together in associations, few people would dare to assemble without the imprimatur of government approval, and it would take rare courage for an individual, standing alone, to exercise his freedom to speak, write or petition on behalf of dissenting views.

79. "Rules and Regulations for the Maintenance of Public Order Pursuant to Article 129A of the Education Law," The Board of Higher Education of the City of New York in compliance with Chapter 191 of the Laws of 1969.

80. 357 U.S. 449, 450 (1958).

From another perspective, however, when one looks back at the determined and often unreasonable assaults on educational institutions by student groups during the 1960s, it becomes plain that freedom of association cannot be considered in absolute terms. Thus, as with other First Amendment rights, freedom of association must be applied "in the light of the special circumstances . . ." [81] Accordingly, in dealing with issues involving associational rights of college students, courts will predictably reinforce the idea that there always must be a balance between freedom of association and the need for restriction—but the need must be established clearly.

Recognition

On the institutional side of that balance sheet, college and university authorities may make rules and regulations necessary for the orderly management of the institution, which includes supervision of student organizations. Moreover, courts have acknowledged that student organizations do not have an unqualified right to be recognized by school officials. In fact, case law indicates that it is constitutionally permissible for colleges to require a student organization to apply for "official recognition," including the requirements that the institution be provided with a statement of the purpose of the student organization, the names of its officers,[82] and assurance that the organization will abide by reasonable college regulations." [83]

According to Healy v. James, the "primary impediment to freedom of association flowing from nonrecognition is the denial of use of campus facilities for meetings and other appropriate purposes." [84] At Virginia Commonwealth University, for example, registered student organizations enjoy the following perks:

(a) Inclusion in a directory, furnished to each student, setting forth the names and activities of student organizations which a student may join;

81. *Tinker*, 393 U.S. at 506.

82. See, e. g. Eisen v. Regents of the Univ. of Cal., 269 Cal.App.2d 696, 75 Cal.Rptr. 45 (1969); here the court held that the compelling interest of the public in being able to ascertain the names of the officers and the stated purposes of a registered student organization far outweighed any minimal infringement of First Amendment rights.

83. See, e. g. American Civil Liberties Union v. Radford College, 315 F.Supp. 893, 896 (D.C.Va.1970).

84. 408 U.S. 169, 187–188 (1972); in *Healy* the Students for a Democratic Society (SDS) sought official recognition as a campus organization at a state college. The Supreme Court sustained the group's right to be so registered subject to showing that SDS would "comply

    (b) the furnishing of VCU consultation services on financial management, budget preparation and financial records;

    (c) the use of VCU buildings for meetings and activities;

    (d) the use of the campus newspaper, the campus radio station, and the VCU bulletin boards to advertise the time and place of meetings and activities; and

    (e) eligibility to seek and obtain VCU funding for carrying on activities.[85]

But whatever the advantages, it is a basic principle of constitutional law that if a college, acting as an instrumentality of the state, refuses "official recognition," it must bear the heavy burden of demonstrating that the action taken was reasonably related to the protection of the state's interest and that "the incidental restriction on First Amendment freedoms was no greater than was essential to the furtherance of that interest." [86] Moreover, a college has no right to restrict peaceful advocacy of expression "simply because it finds the views expressed by any group abhorrent," [87] nor can the restriction be merely based on an "undifferentiated fear or apprehension" that the organization's activities will "materially and substantially disrupt the work and discipline of the school." [88]

Thus, when state colleges and universities once open up their facilities to some organizations, they must be made available to other groups unless there exists a clear and definite danger that unlawful means will be used to accomplish the organization's goals.[89] For that matter, if an organization simply refuses to affirm its willingness to adhere to reasonable campus rules, it is constitutionally permissible for the college to deny recognition. Presumably, the refusal is sufficient evidence to satisfy the *Tinker* forecast standard.[90]

It seems quite explicit, moreover, that insofar as termination of recognition is concerned—i. e., withdrawal of recognition from an established organization—that "[a]ssociational activities need not be tolerated where they infringe reasonable campus rules, in-

with reasonable campus regulations."

85. Gay Alliance of Students v. Matthews, 544 F.2d 162, 163 (4th Cir. 1976).

86. Id.

87. Healy v. James, 408 U.S. at 188, fn.20, quoting from United States v. O'Brien, 391 U.S. 367, 377 (1968).

88. Id., at 189, quoting from *Tinker*, 393 U.S. at 508.

89. ACLU v. Radford College, 315 F. Supp. at 896.

90. Healy v. James, 408 U.S. at 193.

terrupt classes, or substantially interfere with the opportunity of other students to obtain an education." [91] However, the First Amendment "does authorize advocacy . . . and espousal of change." Therefore, if an institution's restriction is directed at an organization's advocacy rather than its actual activities, there must be clear and substantial evidence that such advocacy was "directed to inciting or producing imminent lawless action and was likely to incite or produce such action." [92] In other words, "the critical line for First Amendment purposes must be drawn between advocacy, which is entitled to full protection, and action, which is not." [93] For example, student members of a campus organization, "may, if they so choose, preach the propriety of amending or even doing away with any or all campus regulations. They may not, however, undertake to flout these rules." [94]

Gay Student Organizations

Obviously, the establishment of a particular organization may be thought inconsistent with the purposes of a college—even an embarrassment—as is frequently the case when a homosexual organization applies for recognition. In this sense, "out of the closet" homosexuality is apparently at odds with the low-profile status our society would like to accord the homosexual. However, as previously noted, recognizable warning flags have been hoisted by the courts for some time in regards to any action taken by a college to impede the aims or ideas advocated by student groups. In fact, said one judge, as others on the bench nodded their agreement:

> . . . associations advocating any idea, any change in the law or policy of the general society, are as fully entitled to registration as is the plaintiff [the Gay Alliance of Students]. Thus, associations devoted to peaceful advocacy of decriminalization or social acceptance of sadism, euthanasia, masochism, murder, genocide, segregation, master-race theories, gambling, voodoo, and the abolishment of all higher education, to list a few, must be granted registration, upon

91. Id., at 189.

92. Id., quoting from Brandenburg v. Ohio, 395 U.S. 444, 447 (1969). See also Pickings v. Bruce, 430 F.2d 595 (8th Cir. 1970), where it was held that a college administration could not sanction a student organization, its officers and faculty advisors for failing to accede to an administration request to cancel a speaking invitation extended by the organization where there was no substantial evidence that material disruption would occur.

93. Id., at 192.

94. Id. at 192–193.

proper application and indicated compliance with reasonable regulations, if [the public college] continues to "register" associations.[95]

In this case, Gay Alliance of Students v. Matthews, Virginia Commonwealth University attempted to justify its non-recognition action on the general grounds that "the existence of GAS as a recognized campus organization would increase the opportunity for homosexual contacts, . . . would tend to encourage some students to join who otherwise might not join . . . [and] would tend to attract other homosexuals to VCU." [96] VCU stipulated further that "the record (depositions, affidavits and admissions in pleadings) contained evidence to support these conclusions and that the . . . court should not substitute its appraisal of the evidence for that of VCU." [97]

On the other side of the issue, the Gay Alliance of Students asserted that its purposes were "to develop a supportive community among individuals who believe in the right of self-determination with regard to sexual orientation, to convene educational situations for members of GAS and for members of the university community regarding homosexual life, and to advocate 'gay' rights in concert with the civil liberties of all people." [98]

The holding at the district court level was "that there was no cognizable constitutional deprivation imposed by the withholding of recognition *per se.*" [99] However, the district did order the VCU provide GAS with the use of its "physical facilities for organizational meetings and activities; access to the campus newspaper . . . and campus radio broadcast time [and] use of official VCU bulletin boards . . . " Moreover, it was ordered that VCU provide GAS with "sufficient space for the operation of an orientation booth during semester registration; and a listing of the name and description of GAS in the student directory." Nevertheless, the court did not require VCU to officially recognize GAS, and "refused to require VCU to provide . . . two other concomitants of formal recognition—the right to consultation services on financial management, budget preparation, etc., and the right to make application for funds through the Appropriations Board." [1] Because of these omissions GAS appealed the

95. Gay Alliance of Students v. Matthews, 544 F.2d at 167.

96. Id., at 164.

97. Id.

98. Id., at 163.

99. Id., at 164.

1. Id., at 164.

lower court's decision to the Circuit Court of Appeals claiming First Amendment and equal protection violations.

While relying heavily on *Healy,* the Court declared that GAS had correctly posited its claim to official recognition upon the First Amendment associational rights of its members:

> The very essence of the first amendment is that each individual makes his own decision as to whether joining an organization would be harmful to him, and whether any countervailing benefits outweigh the potential harm. We are aware that in recent years colleges and universities increasingly are voluntarily surrendering the role of *parens patriae* of their students which they formerly occupied. But even if not surrendering voluntarily, the state and its agents are forbidden from usurping the students' right to choose. In this respect, the governing bodies of schools have no greater authority than do other state officials. . . . VCU may not hinder the exercise of first amendment rights simply because it feels that exposure to a given group's ideas may be somehow harmful to certain students. . . . Individuals of whatever sexual persuasion have the fundamental right to meet, discuss current problems, and to advocate change in the *status quo,* so long as there is no "incitement of imminent lawless action." [2]

As to equal protection guarantees the Court concluded that

> . . . the withholding of recognition from GAS denies that organization the equal protection of the laws guaranteed by the fourteenth amendment. All of the justifications put forth by VCU for the denial of recognition are based upon the nature of the issues which GAS intended to confront. Where the exercise of first amendment rights is made dependent upon the content of the message to be conveyed, the discrimination "must be tailored to serve a substantial governmental interest." . . . Here, as discussed above in connection with the violations of the first amendment, VCU's asserted justifications do not meet that standard.[3]

Interestingly, the Court also noted that there was "no evidence that GAS [was] an organization devoted to carrying out illegal, specifically proscribed sexual practices." It pointed out that "Virginia law proscribes the practice of certain forms of homosexuality," but that "Virginia law does not make it a crime to be

---

2. Id., at 165–166.   3. Id., at 167.

a homosexual. Indeed, a statute criminalizing such status and prescribing punishment therefor would be invalid." [4] However, apparently in direct contradistinction, a federal district court in Gay Lib v. University of Missouri upheld a university's refusal to recognize a homosexual group on the grounds that

> . . . the First Amendment does not require that the university sanction and permit the free association of individuals as a student campus organization where, as the court now finds from the evidence, that association is likely to incite, promote, and result in acts contrary to and in violation of the sodomy statute of the state of Missouri. The members of Gay Lib, or for that matter any of those on the school campus who desire to do so, are free to express within the law their beliefs and views of homosexuality and of the Missouri Criminal Statutes on that subject. But it is a far different thing to show a right under the First Amendment to receive official school recognition of Gay Lib with all of the associational conditions that are likely to result therefrom. The legitimate interest of the university as a state institution includes the right to refuse the requested recognition and its concomitants where the result predictably is to bring on the commission of crimes against the sodomy statutes of the State of Missouri. [5]

Upon appeal, however, the Eighth Circuit reversed the district court's ruling, holding that

> . . . none of the purposes or aims of Gay Lib . . . evidences advocacy of present violations of state law (in a footnote here the court declared: "Surely, it is no longer a valid argument to suggest that an organization cannot be formed to peaceably advocate repeal of certain criminal laws.") or of university rules and regulations, and the district court made no finding that Gay Lib would infringe reasonable campus rules, interrupt classes, or substantially interfere with the opportunity of other students to obtain an education." Healy v. James, . . . Furthermore, . . . such an approach smacks of penalizing persons for their

---

4. Id., at 166. The Appeals Court referred to Robinson v. California, 370 U.S. 660 (1962), where the U.S. Supreme Court declared a state law making it a crime to be a drug addict unconstitutional. Since drug addiction was considered more an illness than a crime, the Court declared the law in violation of the Eighth Amendment's "cruel and unusual punishment" proscription.

5. 416 F.Supp. 1350, 1370 (D.C.Mo. 1976).

status rather than their conduct, which is constitutionally impermissible.[6]

Religious Organizations

The First Amendment states that government "shall make no law respecting an establishment of religion, or preventing the free exercise thereof . . ." but the United States Supreme Court "has struggled to find a neutral ground between the two Religion Clauses, both of which are cast in absolute terms, and either of which, if expanded to a logical extreme, would tend to clash with the other."[7] To illustrate, if a state university refuses to recognize a student religious organization, it might be violating the free exercise clause, but if it recognizes the group, it might be violating the establishment clause. Similarly, if organized religious activities are permitted on the university premises, it would appear to be in conflict with the establishment proscription; yet, if such activities are rejected, the policy would seem to run counter to the freedom of expression and association rights accorded to students in public educational institutions.

The problems presented by these apparent conflicts are indeed complex, especially so when one attempts to balance and reconcile the various constitutional provisions discussed above in the context of a public school campus. However, confusion is often accentuated here because public school authorities frequently place an oversweeping interpretation on religious decisions rendered by the Supreme Court. For instance, school officials generally adhere to the absolute "wall of separation" doctrine given by Justice Black in Everson v. Board of Educ. (1947):

> The "establishment of religion" clause . . . means at least this: Neither a state nor the Federal Government can set up a church. Neither can pass laws which aid one religion, aid all religions, or prefer one religion over another. Neither can force nor influence a person to go or to remain away from church against his will or force him to profess a belief or disbelief in any religion. No person can be pun-

6. 558 F.2d 848, 856 (8th Cir. 1977), review denied 435 U.S. 981 (1977). See also Gay Students Organization v. Univ. of New Hampshire, 509 F. 2d 652 (1st Cir. 1974), where the court held that in the absence of any illegal activity or conduct which would foreseeably lead to the physical disruption of university work or discipline, an officially recog- nized student organization may not be prohibited from holding social activities (in this case a dance) on campus similar to those engaged in by other organizations even though those activities may offend the community's sense of propriety.

7. Walz v. Tax Commission, 397 U.S. 664, 668 (1970).

ished for entertaining or professing religious beliefs or dis-
beliefs, for church attendance or non-attendance. No tax
in any amount . . . can be levied to support any religious activities or institutions, whatever they may be called,
or whatever form they may adopt to teach or practice religion. Neither a state nor the Federal Government can,
openly or secretly, participate in the affairs of any religious
organization or groups and vice versa. In the words of Jefferson, the clause against establishment of religion by law
was intended to erect "a wall of separation between Church
and State." [8]

Of course, some have argued that the establishment clause does
not forbid governmental support for religion but merely governmental favoritism toward a particular religion (the "no-preference" doctrine). However, the Supreme Court has unequivocally rejected this narrow construction.[9] All levels of government
must be strictly neutral, neither aiding a particular religion nor
all religions. "A given law might not *establish* a state religion
but nevertheless be one 'respecting' that end in the sense of being
a step that could lead to such establishment and hence offend
the First Amendment." [10] Thus, the establishment clause has
been used to forbid devotional exercises of any variety in the public schools, including denominationally neutral prayers, devotional reading of the Bible, or recitation of the Lord's Prayer; [11]
further, it has been used to prevent a state from proscribing from
its public school curriculum the teaching of Darwin's theory of
evolution because of "its supposed conflict with the Biblical account, literally read." [12]

On the other hand, laws requiring business establishments to
close on Sunday have passed constitutional muster; the Court
majority has reasoned that whatever the original purpose of these
Sunday closing laws, today they have taken on a secular cast
as a measure to promote family living by providing a common day
of rest and recreation.[13] Also it has been ruled constitutionally

8.   330 U.S. 1, 15 (1947).

9.   See, e. g., Abington School Dist. v.
     Schempp, 374 U.S. 203 (1963), and
     Engel v. Vitale, 370 U.S. 421 (1962).

10. Lemon v. Kurtzman, 403 U.S. 602,
     612 (1971).

11. *Abington School Dist.* and *Engel*
     cases, supra, fn. 9.

12. Epperson v. Arkansas, 393 U.S.
     97 (1968).

13. See, e. g., McGowan v. Mary-
     land, 366 U.S. 420 (1961). This
     interpretation would probably ap-
     ply with equal force to state-desig-
     nated school holidays such as
     Christmas and Easter vacations,
     but in order to maintain the re-
     quired secular cast many public ed-

permissible to use tax monies to furnish textbooks, lunches, and transportation to students in private religious schools.[14] These aids have been viewed as promoting the education, health, and safety of students rather than used to promote religious instruction. Further, the Court has ruled that the exemption of church property from taxation neither advances nor inhibits religion, represents neither sponsorship nor hostility, and unlike a direct subsidy does not involve excessive entanglement, and in fact involves less entanglement from religion than there would be if churches were subject to taxation.[15] Then, too, the Court has held that tax funds can be used as grants to church-operated colleges and universities to build facilities to be used for secular purposes.[16]

The point to be made from this rapid gallop across the landscape of Supreme Court decisions regarding government-connected religious relationships is that the Court has *not* required a strict "wall of separation" approach. Neither has it required governmental hostility toward religion. Instead, the approach that has been adopted by the Court has been one of "accommodating neutrality." In fact, óne commentator has specifically noted that this approach to the establishment clause has permitted "accommodation to and preferment of religion in order to safeguard free exercise values." [17]

The Court's *accommodating neutrality* approach in essence holds that the First Amendment was intended to maintain a proper relationship between government and religion, and though the "wall of separation" is present it is not an impregnable wall. Therefore, not all relationships between government and religion are unconstitutional. Instead, government can accommodate

---

ucational institutions now use the terms "Winter" and "Spring" recess in place of the traditional "Christmas" and "Easter" terms.

14. See, e. g., Cochran v. State Bd., 281 U.S. 370 (1930), Everson v. Board of Educ., 330 U.S. 1 (1947), and Board of Educ. v. Allen, 392 U.S. 236 (1968).

15. See, e. g., Walz v. Tax Commission, supra, fn. 7, and Diffendorfer v. Central Baptist Church, 404 U.S. 412 (1972). However, Justice Douglas stated that he could not see any constitutional difference between a direct money grant to a church and a tax exemption and thus believed that both were unconstitutional subsidies to religion. Some authorities in addition have questioned the constitutionality of providing tax exemption to church property not directly used for religious activities; e. g., apartment house buildings.

16. Tilton v. Richardson, 403 U.S. 672 (1971).

17. "The Constitutionality of the 1972 Amendment to Title VII's Exemption for Religious Organizations," 73 *Michigan Law Review*, p. 551.

(or oblige) religion in certain ways. Accordingly, the principle of accommodating neutrality was well stated by Justice William O. Douglas in Zorach v. Clauson (1952):

> When the state encourages religious instruction or cooperates with religious authorities by adjusting the schedule of public events to sectarian needs, it follows the best of our traditions. For it then respects the religious nature of our people and *accommodates* the public service to their spiritual needs.[18]

In fact, the Engel v. Vitale (1962) and Abington School Dist. v. Schempp (1963) decisions did not abandon accommodating neutrality but simply defined some of the limits of accommodation. It should be noted that Justice Douglas sensed the peril of a strict "wall of separation" approach in *Zorach* as he commented on the probable result if a state were not to accommodate religion:

> To hold that it may not would be to find in the Constitution a requirement that the government show a callous indifference to religious groups.   That would be preferring those who believe in no religion over those who do believe   .   .   .
> But we find no constitutional requirement which makes it necessary for government to be hostile to religion and to throw its weight against efforts to widen the effective scope of religious influence.[19]

Moreover, in the *Abington School Dist.* case Justice Goldberg indicated that a strict neutrality approach would lead to open hostility, and in taking the position of accommodation himself, he remarked:

> Untutored devotion to the concept of neutrality can lead to invocation or approval of results which partake not simply of that noninterference and noninvolvement with the religious which the Constitution commands, but a broadening and pervasive devotion to the secular and a passive or even active, hostility to the religious. Such results are not only not compelled by the Constitution, but, it seems to me, are prohibited by it.[20]

Later, in Walz v. Tax Comm. (1970), Chief Justice Burger pointed out that adherence "to the policy of neutrality that derives from an *accommodation* of the Establishment and Free

18.   343 U.S. 306, 313 (1952), (emphasis added).

19.   Id.

20.   374 U.S. at 306 (Goldberg concurring).

Exercise Clauses has prevented the kind of involvement that would tip the balance toward government control of churches or government restraint with religious practice." [21] He was also careful to point out that no "perfect or absolute separation is really possible" and that the First Amendment "seeks to mark boundaries to avoid excessive entanglement" between government and religion.[22] In this sense Chief Justice Burger noted that the central purpose of the establishment clause is directed primarily at three main evils: "sponsorship, financial support, and active involvement of the sovereign in religious activity." [23] But then he proclaimed: "Short of those expressly proscribed governmental acts there is room for play in the joints productive of a *benevolent neutrality* which will permit religious exercise to exist without sponsorship and without interference." [24]

More recently, in Roemer v. Board of Public Works of Maryland (1976), the doctrine of accommodating neutrality was further enhanced by the Court. Four Maryland citizens and taxpayers brought suit challenging the constitutionality (under the establishment clause) of a statute providing public aid in the form of noncategorical grants (given in the form of an annual fiscal year subsidy) to eligible colleges and universities. In upholding the Maryland statute, the Supreme Court, speaking through Justice Blackmun, said:

> A system of government that makes itself felt as pervasively as ours could hardly be expected never to cross paths with the church. In fact, our State and Federal governments impose burdens upon, and impart certain benefits to, virtually all our activities, and religious activity is not an exception. The Court has enforced a scrupulous neutrality by the State, as among religious and other activities, *but a hermetic separation of the two is an impossibility it has never required.*[25]

In terms of our present discussion, however, perhaps the Supreme Court of Delaware's decision in Keegan v. University of Delaware (1975) provides public higher education with its best case in point. Here, the Supreme Court of Delaware ruled that the establishment clause would not be violated by a state univer-

---

21. 397 U.S. at 670 (emphasis added).

22. Id.

23. Id., at 668.

24. Id., at 669 (emphasis added).

25. 426 U.S. 736, 745–746 (1976), (emphasis added).

sity allowing regular students worship services in the commons rooms of its dormitories:

> . . . we hold that the University cannot support its absolute ban of all religious worship on the theory that, without such a ban, University policy allowing all student groups, including religious groups, free access to dormitory common areas would necessarily violate the Establishment Clause. The Establishment cases decided by the United States Supreme Court indicate that neutrality is the safe harbor in which to avoid First Amendment violations: neutral "accommodation" of religion is permitted [citing Everson v. Board of Educ. and Zorach v. Clauson, supra] while "promotion" and "advancement" of religion are not [citing McCollum v. Board of Educ., 333 U.S. 203 (1948), and Abington School Dist. v. Schempp, supra]. University policy without the worship ban could be neutral towards religion and could have the primary effect of advancing education by allowing students to meet together in the commons room of their dormitory to exchange ideas and share mutual interests. If any religious groups or religion is accommodated or benefited thereby, such accommodation or benefit is purely incidental, and would not, in our judgment, violate the Establishment Clause [citing Tilton v. Richardson, supra].[26]

The State Supreme Court next indicated that "even an 'incidental burden' on the free exercise of religion must be justified by a 'compelling state interest' " and that under the factual situation at hand,

> . . . One must conclude it rises to a legally recognizable interest on the part of the students. The only activity proscribed by the regulation is worship regardless of whether one considers the proscription a direct or indirect burden on student activity. The commons area is already provided for student use and there is no request here that separate religious facilities be established. The area in question is a residence hall where students naturally assemble with their friends for many purposes. Religion, at least in part, is historically a communal setting.[27]

The Court continued with the statement that it found particular support for its views in two United States Supreme Court cases:

> In Tucker v. Texas, 326 U.S. 517 (1946), a freedom of press and religious case, the Supreme Court upheld the right of

26. 349 A.2d 14, 16 (Del.1975).   27. Id., at 17.

an ordained minister of Jehovah's Witnesses to distribute religious literature in a village owned by the United States, notwithstanding a request to leave by the manager of the village pursuant to his purported authority by federal regulation and Texas criminal law. The Court noted that the village "had the characteristics of a typical American town." The case thus has similarities to the University owned dormitory situation here. Similarly, in Healy v. James, 408 U.S. 169 (1972), it was held that a state supported college could not deny official recognition to student groups without justification, for such a denial would abridge the First Amendment rights of individuals to free expression and free association.[28]

The Court then concluded that "[s]ince the state policy here impedes the observance of religion and acts as a prior restraint upon all religious worship . . . it requires a showing of a compelling state interest for justification." [29]

Indeed, in light of the United States Supreme Court's principle of accommodating religious belief and practice, a strong case was made in *Keegan* that it is constitutionally permissible under the establishment clause for a state university to allow religious worship services to be conducted in the commons room of a dormitory; and that a state university regulation prohibiting such worship services could constitute an impermissible burden on students' constitutional right to freely exercise their religion. To say that the courts support a doctrine of accommodating neutrality, nevertheless, still brings us face to face with the vexing question of just what is the limit of that accommodation. For instance, would an officially recognized student religious organization show sufficient indicia of public sponsorship (e. g., assignment of faculty adviser and use of school facilities) so as to fall afoul of the establishment clause? If outside speakers from various religions were provided expense-free facilities and allowed to discuss their beliefs on a public campus, would this constitute an "excessive entanglement"?

Of course a particular situation may turn on its distinctive facts, but neither *Healy* nor *Keegan* specifically address these questions. Nonetheless, there are numerous precedents established in the public school sector indicating that sponsorship of a religious organization would constitute an establishment of religion violation. In fact, the use of tax-supported property for

28. Id., at 18.   29. Id., at 19.

religious activities, as a general rule, would be considered a prohibited aid to religion, and thus if the *Keegan* Court had relied
on the precedents established in the public school system, it would
have undoubtedly reached a different conclusion. Once again,
however, one must look at the situation "applied in light of the
special characteristics of the [particular] environment." [30]
Hence, it can be said that the public school cases dealt with a
captive audience rather than a voluntary one. Significantly, the
Supreme Court pointed out in a number of these cases that compulsory attendance in the public school system afforded sectarian
groups an invaluable aid.[31] Of course, attendance at a public
college is voluntary; moreover, college students are much less
susceptible to indoctrination than younger pupils.

With this added rationale, therefore, the *Keegan* holding might
well reflect a lawful accommodation of certain religious activities
on campus. Be leery, however, since precise precedents have not
yet been supplied. On the other hand, the following principles
appear to be well established:

(1) Official recognition of a student religious organization,
with it attendant indicia of sponsorship, would most likely run
afoul of the prescribed establishment tests; i. e., it would have an
effect that primarily advances religion, would reflect a sectarian
legislative purpose, and would foster excessive governmental entanglement with religion.

(2) Students may express religious views on campus in accordance with their free exercise of religion and expression guarantees if the college neither sponsors such views, nor actively
aids in the expression of such views, nor provides financial support to the expression of such views.

(3) Students may distribute religious literature on campus including handouts or leaflets advertising religious programs in
the community in accordance with established free expression
boundaries. Likewise, the use of bulletin boards by students to
post or advertise religious activities or programs in the community is permitted if the bulletin boards are placed on campus
pursuant to a policy of free expression and are not limited to religious announcements alone.

(4) Outside speakers representing various religions may be
invited to discuss their beliefs in an appropriate college setting

30. *Tinker*, 393 U.S. at 506.

31. See, e. g., Everson v. Board of
Educ., 330 U.S. 1 (1947), and McCol-

lum v. Board of Educ., 333 U.S.
203 (1948).

if the purpose is not the propagation of a religious faith or doctrine. As stated in Justice Goldberg's concurring opinion in Abington School Dist. v. Schempp: " . . . it seems clear to
me . . . that the Court would recognize the propriety
. . . of teaching *about* religion, as distinct from the teaching *of* religion, in the public schools." [32]

Fraternities and Sororities

Another form of student organization is the fraternity or sorority which for more than a century has raised legal questions.
The more current issues in this regard, however, have focused on
racial and religious discrimination practiced by some of these
organizations,[33] whereas earlier cases were concerned with the
larger question of whether fraternities and sororities had a legal
right to exist on campus. Of course today it would appear that
these organizations could not be banned or prohibited summarily
by either state law or institutional action, especially in view of the
Supreme Court's ruling in Healy v. James. Nonetheless, today's
constitutional principles on this subject, though seeming to be
totally unacceptable in terms of contemporary reasoning, were
spoken by Mr. Justice McKenna of the Supreme Court in Waugh
v. Mississippi Univ. (1915).[34]

The case involved a Mississippi law which barred students from
joining Greek letter fraternities and sororities and provided that
students who did so could be expelled from school. Naturally,
the law was attacked as violative of the Fourteenth Amendment.
It was argued that such organizations made their members
more moral, taught discipline, and inspired their members to
study harder and to obey the rules of discipline and order. The
Supreme Court, however, unanimously rejected these Fourteenth
Amendment arguments. The Court in the next to last paragraph
in its decision made this statement which, as it relates to fraternities and sororities, has not yet been overturned:

> It is said that the fraternity to which complainant belongs
> is a moral and of itself a disciplinary force. This need not
> be denied. But whether such membership makes against dis-
> cipline was for the State of Mississippi to determine. It is to

---

32. 374 U.S. at 306 (emphasis added).

33. See, e. g., Sigma Chi Fraternity
v. Regents of the Univ. of Colorado,
258 F.Supp. 515 (D.C.Colo.1966),
where the district court held that
the Board of Regents could place
any "fraternity, social organization,
or any other student group" on
probation for denying membership
to any person because of race, color,
or religion.

34. 237 U.S. 589 (1915).

be remembered that the University was established by the State and is under the control of the State, and the enactment may have been induced by the opinion that membership in the prohibited societies divided the attention of the students and distracted from that singleness of purpose which the State desired to exist in its public educational institutions. It is not for us to entertain conjectures in opposition to the views of the State and annul its regulations upon disputable considerations of their wisdom or necessity.[35]

Thus, it is on the foregoing argument that the courts will sustain a state's power to prohibit fraternities and sororities on its campuses. Even though the decision appears questionable in the modern context—and would be completely unacceptable, as we have observed, in regards to most other campus organizations— it remains as precedent in this particular regard.[36] But this in no way implies that the Greek letter organization is *per se* illegal on campus. In fact, before the 1960s Greek houses were still in their heyday. Their members were typically idealized as America's golden youth—the very epitome of all that was bright, engagingly aggressive and wholesome. They were considered part of a unique fellowship that would endure long after their last hurrah as undergraduates. Still, many Greek organizations practiced blatant racial and religious discrimination, even though in the late 1950s the national Greek offices began to declare such practices "un-American." Moreover, hazing continued to thrive in often brutal and senseless forms. However, as former members of Greek Row took on positions of responsibility in later life— especially as state legislators and trustees of prestigious universities—the holdover from their old shared enthusiasm was generally strong enough to influence their policy determinations. Thus, it was the rare state legislature or university board of trustees that opposed either the formation or continuation of Greek chapters.

Their comeuppance, therefore, did not essentially come from the law; instead it occurred during the Student Movement of the 1960s when Greek dominance was shattered at many campuses and students deserted them in droves. The Row, faced with the sullen new anti-establishment mood of students, became one of the

---

35. Id., at 596–597.

36. See, e. g., Webb v. State Univ. of New York, 125 F.Supp. 910 (D.C. N.Y.1954), and Beta Sigma Rho, Inc.

v. Moore, 46 Misc.2d 1030, 261 N.Y.S.2d 658 (1965), where both courts upheld the banning of fraternal organizations.

most visible and choicest targets for derision. However, during their wanderings many Greek groups turned to community service and even jettisoned much of their sadistic hazing and racial and social snobbery. But today—whether resulting from the new reformist spirit or new life styles—campus membership in nationally affiliated fraternity and sorority chapters has made a spectacular comeback. In fact, the Greek resurgence has now become such a nationwide phenomenon that even its severest critics can no longer ignore its popularity.

CONCLUDING OBSERVATION

Of course, the remainder of the book could be taken up citing another whole series of justifications in support of free expression on campuses. Indeed, higher education's vitality—its special purpose and extraordinary texture—comes from the richness of its peripheral cultural vision, from all the things going on that no one person will ever see. An ocean is very different from a swimming pool, even if the amount of swimming a person does is about the same. But at this point there would be something arrogant about attempting to cross that metaphorical ocean. Hence, four First Amendment cases follow which should reinforce and set the fundamental principles embodied in that amendment's relationship to public higher education.

PAPISH v. BOARD OF CURATORS OF UNIVERSITY OF MISSOURI

Supreme Court of the United States, 1973.
410 U.S. 667.

PER CURIAM.

Petitioner, a graduate student in the University of Missouri School of Journalism, was expelled for distributing on campus a newspaper "containing forms of indecent speech" in violation of a by-law of the Board of Curators. The newspaper, the Free Press Underground, had been sold on this state university campus for more than four years pursuant to an authorization obtained from the University Business Office. The particular newspaper issue in question was found to be unacceptable for two reasons. First, on the front cover the publishers had reproduced a political cartoon previously printed in another newspaper depicting policemen raping the Statue of Liberty and the Goddess of Justice. The caption under the cartoon read: " . . . With Liberty and Justice for All." Secondly, the issue contained an article entitled "M_____f_____ Acquitted," which discussed the trial and acquittal on an assault charge of a New York City youth who was a member of an organization known as "Up Against the Wall, M_____f_____."

Following a hearing, the Student Conduct Committee found that petitioner had violated Par. B of Art. V of the General Standards of Student Conduct which requires students "to observe generally accepted standards of conduct" and specifically prohibits "indecent conduct or speech." [37] Her expulsion, after affirmance first by the Chancellor of the University and then by its Board of Curators, was made effective in the middle of the spring semester. Although she was then permitted to remain on campus until the end of the semester, she was not given credit for the one course in which she made a passing grade.

. . . . She claimed that her expulsion was improperly premised on activities protected by the First Amendment. The District Court denied relief, 331 F.Supp. 1321, and the Court of Appeals affirmed, one judge dissenting. 464 F.2d 136. . . .

The District Court's opinion rests, in part, on the conclusion that the banned issue of the newspaper was obscene. The Court of Appeals found it unnecessary to decide that question. Instead, assuming that the newspaper was not obscene and that its distribution in the community at large would be protected by the First Amendment, the court held that on a university campus "freedom of expression" could properly be "subordinated to other interests such as, for example, the conventions of decency in the use and display of language and pictures." The court concluded that "[t]he Constitution does not compel the University . . . [to allow] such publications as the one in litigation to be publicly sold or distributed on its open campus."

This case was decided several days before we handed down Healy v. James, 408 U.S. 169 (1972), in which, while recognizing a state university's undoubted prerogative to enforce reasonable rules governing student conduct, we reaffirmed that "state colleges and universities are not enclaves immune from the sweep

---

37. In pertinent part, the bylaw states: "Students enrolling in the University assume an obligation and are expected by the University to conduct themselves in a manner compatible with the University's functions and missions as an educational institution. For that purpose students are required to observe generally accepted standards of conduct. . . . [I]ndecent conduct or speech . . . are examples of conduct which would contravene this standard. . . ." 464 F.2d, at 138.

of the First Amendment." See Tinker v. Des Moines Independent School District, 393 U.S. 503 (1969). We think *Healy* makes it clear that the mere dissemination of ideas—no matter how offensive to good taste—on a state university campus may not be shut off in the name alone of "conventions of decency." Other recent precedents of this Court make it equally clear that neither the political cartoon nor the headline story involved in this case can be labeled as constitutionally obscene or otherwise unprotected. There is language in the opinions below which suggests that the University's action here could be viewed as an exercise of its legitimate authority to enforce reasonable regulations as to the time, place, and manner of speech and its dissemination. While we have repeatedly approved such regulatory authority, the facts set forth in the opinions below show clearly that petitioner was expelled because of the disapproved *content* of the newspaper rather than the time, place, or manner of its distribution.

Since the First Amendment leaves no room for the operation of a dual standard in the academic community with respect to the content of speech, and because the state University's action here cannot be justified as a nondiscriminatory application of reasonable rules governing conduct, the judgments of the courts below must be reversed. Accordingly the petition for a writ of certiorari is granted, the case is remanded to the District Court, and that court is instructed to order the University to restore to petitioner any course credits she earned for the semester in question and, unless she is barred from reinstatement for valid academic reasons, to reinstate her as a student in the graduate program.

Reversed and remanded.

Mr. Chief Justice BURGER, dissenting.

I join the dissent of Justice REHNQUIST which follows and add a few additional observations.

. . .

In theory, at least, a university is not merely an arena for the discussion of ideas by students and faculty; it is also an institution where individuals learn to express themselves in acceptable, civil terms. We provide that environment to the end that students may learn the self-restraint necessary to the functioning of a civilized society and understand the need for those external restraints to which we must all submit if group existence is to be tolerable.

. . . Students are, of course, free to criticize the university, its faculty, or the Government in vigorous, or even harsh, terms. But it is not unreasonable or violative of the Constitution to subject to disciplinary action those individuals who distribute publications which are at the same time obscene and infantile. To preclude a state university or college from regulating the distribution of such obscene materials does not protect the values inherent in the First Amendment; rather, it demeans those values. The anomaly of the Court's holding today is suggested by its use of the now familiar "code" abbreviation for the petitioner's foul language.

The judgment of the Court of Appeals was eminently correct. It should be affirmed.

Mr. Justice REHNQUIST, with whom THE CHIEF JUSTICE and Mr. Justice BLACKMUN join, dissenting.

. . .

II

I continue to adhere to the dissenting views expressed in Rosenfeld v. New Jersey, 408 U.S. 901 (1972), that the public use of the word "M_____f_____" is "lewd and obscene" . . . .

. . . A state university is an establishment for the purpose of educating the State's young people, supported by the tax revenues of the State's citizens. The notion that the officials lawfully charged with the governance of the university have so little control over the environment for which they are responsible that they may not prevent the public distribution of a newspaper on campus which contained the language described in the Court's opinion is quite unacceptable to me and I would suspect would have been equally unacceptable to the Framers of the First Amendment. This is indeed a case where the observation of a unanimous Court in *Chaplinsky* that "such utterances are no essential part of any exposition of ideas and are of such slight social value as a step to truth that any benefit that may be derived from them is clearly outweighed by the social interest in order and morality" applies with compelling force.

III

The Court cautions that "disenchantment with Miss Papish's performance, understandable as it may have been, is no justification for denial of constitutional rights." Quite so. But a wooden insistence on equating, for constitutional purposes, the authority of the State to criminally punish with its authority to exercise even a modicum of control over the university which it operates, serves neither the Constitution nor public education well. There is reason to think that the "disenchantment" of which the Court speaks may, after this decision, become widespread among taxpayers and legislators. The system of tax-supported public universities which has grown up in this country is one of its truly great accomplishments; if they are to continue to grow and thrive to serve an expanding population, they must have something more than the grudging support of taxpayers and legislators. But one can scarcely blame the latter if, told by the Court that their only function is to supply tax money for the operation of the university, the "disenchantment" may reach such a point that they doubt the game is worth the candle.

SCHIFF v. WILLIAMS

United States Court of Appeals, Fifth Circuit, 1975.
519 F.2d 257.

CLARK, Circuit Judge:

Three students brought suit against the president of Florida Atlantic University alleging that he had dismissed them from their positions as editors of the school newspaper in violation of their First Amendment rights. The district court found in favor of the students, ordered them reinstated, and awarded them back pay, compensatory damages, and attorneys' fees. We affirm the decision insofar as it grants back pay and compensatory damages, but reverse the award of attorneys' fees.

The plaintiffs, Schiff, Littman and Vickers, were editors of the *Atlantic Sun,* the student newspaper of Florida Atlantic University. On April 27, 1973, the President of the University, Kenneth Williams, dismissed all three from their positions and began publishing the student newspaper using administrative personnel. He published his reasons for this action in a statement which read in pertinent part:

"I am today dismissing Mr. Ed Schiff as Editor of the Atlantic Sun and Mr. Tom Vickers and Ms. Carin Litman as Associate Editors. I take this action because I have become convinced that the level of editorial responsibility and competence has deteriorated to the extent that it reflects discredit and embarrassment upon the university. I am also convinced that the decreasing quality of the Atlantic Sun is irreversible under the present senior staff leadership.

"It is clear to me that the Editor does not respect, or is not able to interpret correctly, the guidelines [1] of the Board of Regents and the President. The Atlantic Sun currently reflects a standard of grammar, of spelling and of language expression unacceptable in any publication, certainly unacceptable and deplorable in a publication of an upper-level graduate university.

"The editorial policy of the Sun has increasingly emphasized villification and rumor mongering, instead of accurately reporting items likely to be of interest to the university community. Even articles on non-controversial issues such as enrollment trends recently have been incorrect and misleading. The editorials themselves have degenerated into immature and unsophisticated diatribes which reflect most negatively on the overall quality of our student body."

Under 42 U.S.C.A. §§ 1981, 1983, and 1985, the student editors sought injunctive and declaratory relief against Williams and his successor in office, Glenwood Creech, and requested general, special, and punitive damages and attorneys' fees for alleged violations of their rights. The court found that the protection of the First Amendment barred defendants' action, ordered plaintiffs reinstated, and enjoined the defendants from further control of the editorial content of the *Atlantic Sun*. The court also ordered that the students be awarded back pay; that nominal compensatory damages of one dollar be paid by Williams in his personal capacity to each plaintiff; and that the defendants in their official capacities pay the attorneys' fees incurred by plaintiffs in prosecuting the action.

Awaiting Supreme Court action on pending cases which could resolve controlling issues, we remanded the case for clarification,

---

1. The guidelines attached to the statement provide in part:

   a. . . . [W]e want only a newspaper which serves its public—the University family—in the tradition of all great newspapers. So long as it does this it will have our support and it will have earned the freedom it must have.

   b. What is it not?—
   —It is not a gripe sheet;
   —It is not a smear sheet;
   —It is not representative of shoddy, 'yellow journalism'; or of pornography; or of innuendo; or of invective;

   —It is not a platform to serve special interests of the administration, or of the faculty, or of any student clique.

   c. Primarily 'of, for and by' the students, it must serve the entire University family.

   d. It must accept responsibility for writing the truth and for presenting all sides of issues.

   e. It must reflect the best interests of the University community it serves.

   f. Low and vulgar language or art is prohibited.

since neither the source of the back pay award nor the source and rationale for the award of attorneys' fees appeared clear here. The supplemental record now filed discloses that back pay awards are to come from an activity fund contributed by students which the trial judge ordered placed in an account to be held by an appropriate state agency. The attorneys' fees award against the defendants in their official capacities was made as an integral part of the equitable remedy of injunctive reinstatement. The court made no finding of bad faith or obstinate conduct by the defendants.

The defendants' basic assertion of error relates to the court's finding that the dismissal of the editors was an actionable violation of their constitutional rights. They contend the question is not whether Williams restricted the editors' First Amendment freedom by regulation of the content of the newspaper, but whether the restriction was legally justified. The defendants maintain that since the editors were state employees, their free speech could be restricted by their employers if this right was outweighed by a more significant governmental interest—in this case, the university's interest in a publication which maintained high standards of grammar and literary value so as to project a proper view of the university and its student body. Defendants argue that the judge did not hear testimony on the significance of these nonconstitutional reasons for the students' dismissal (control of technical quality); wherefore he could not and did not balance them against the constitutional aspect of the dismissal (control of content).

The defendants' argument fails on two grounds. First, no evidence was presented on the university's nonconstitutional reasons except for the unsubstantiated reference to poor technical quality of the newspaper in the president's statement. In the absence of any evidence as to specific publications, it was not possible for the court to make a balancing type of evaluation.

Second, the right of free speech embodied in the publication of a college student newspaper cannot be controlled except under special circumstances. The cases relied on by the defendant all involve university employees performing tasks unrelated to the First Amendment, who, incidental to their employment, exercised their First Amendment freedoms to the displeasure of the university. By firing the student editors in this case, the administration was exercising direct control over the student newspaper. See generally Healy v. James, 408 U.S. 169, 183 (1972). The dispositive case in this circuit in the area of control of content of student publications is Bazaar v. Fortune, 476 F.2d 570, rehearing en banc 489 F.2d 225 (5th Cir. 1973). The rule of *Bazaar* is that special circumstances must be present to give a university the right to control student publications, for "once a University recognizes a student activity which has elements of free expression, it can act to censor that expression only if it acts consistent with First Amendment constitutional guarantees. . . . [T]he courts have refused to recognize as permissible any regulations infringing free speech when not shown to be necessarily related to the maintenance of order and discipline within the educational process." 476 F.2d at 574–75. See Antonelli v. Hammond, 308 F.Supp. 1329 (Mass.1970). In the case at bar the "special circumstances" relied on by the university—poor grammar, spelling and language expression—could embarrass, and perhaps bring some element of disrepute to the school; but, assuming the president's assessment was correct, these faults are clearly not the sort which could lead to significant disruption on the university campus or within its educational processes. See Bazaar v. Fortune, supra at 576. See also Papish v. Board of Curators of the University of Missouri, 410 U.S. 667 (1973).

The defendants also contest the award of compensatory damages by asserting that these public officials are immune from liability because they were performing discretionary duties and acted in good faith. The district court acknowledged that the president was not "motivated by malice . . . perhaps he thought he had a right to do what he did; he probably did think so." Nevertheless he found that President Williams did not seek legal advice prior to his actions and that the sort of motivation for his actions which the proof established did not constitute a defense to a charge that his acts had abridged First Amendment rights.

Recent precedent has broadened the qualified immunity available to public officials who are accused of constitutional wrongs while exercising discretionary duties within the scope of their authority. "These considerations suggest that, in varying scope, a qualified immunity is available to officers of the executive branch of Government, the variation [is] dependent upon the scope of discretion and responsibilities of the office and all the circumstances as they reasonably appeared at the time of the action on which liability is sought to be based. It is the existence of reasonable grounds for the belief formed at the time and in light of all the circumstances, coupled with good faith belief, that affords basis for qualified immunity . . . ." Scheuer v. Rhodes, 416 U.S. 232 (1974). "To be entitled to a special exemption from the categorical remedial language of § 1983 in a case in which his action violated a student's constitutional rights, a school [official], who has voluntarily undertaken the task of supervising the operation of the school and the activities of the students, must be held to a standard of conduct based not only on permissible intentions, *but also on knowledge of the basic unquestioned constitutional rights of his charges.* Such a standard neither imposes an unfair burden upon a person assuming a responsible public office requiring a high degree of intelligence and judgment for the proper fulfillment of its duties, nor an unwarranted burden in light of the value which civil rights have in our legal system." [Emphasis added.] Wood v. Strickland, 420 U.S. 308 (1975). The district court's finding that good faith immunity was not available was based on a proper concept of the character and scope of this defense. President Williams cannot avoid responsibility for his abridgment of First Amendment rights because his motives were to serve the best interest of the school.

The defendants urge that the back pay and attorneys' fees award expend themselves upon the treasury of Florida, and that under Edelman v. Jordan, 415 U.S. 651 (1974), the Eleventh Amendment bars federal jurisdiction over an action to recover a compensatory award which must inevitably come from general revenues of a state.

Insofar as the instant decree required past earnings be repaid to plaintiffs, *Edelman's* teaching applies full force. If this facet of the judgment had expended itself upon the state treasury, it could not stand.

Attorneys' fees, however, present a different question. *Edelman* recognizes that a very dim line divides prospective relief incident to a federal court's equitable power under Ex parte Young, 209 U.S. 123 (1908), which may be costly to the state but is permissible under the Amendment, from a compensatory or retroactive money judgment to which the judicial power of the United States does not extend. Cases testing awards of attorneys' fees in such situations are now pending on the Supreme Court's docket. We initially thought that the pendency of these cases required the withholding of our decision. After the district court's clarification, it now appears that both the back pay and attorneys' fees questions in the present litigation can be answered without raising the Eleventh Amendment issues which are awaiting resolution.

The supplemental record discloses that the back pay award was to come from a fund composed of payments by students of the university as part of their activity fee. The private monies in this fund were intended to be used for operating expenses of the paper, which included the salaries of *Atlantic Sun* personnel. The fund was not the property of the State of Florida. It had been entrusted to a state agency only to hold and invest pending the outcome of this appeal. Under these circumstances the judgment term requiring that monies from this fund be used to repay lost wages had no true impact on the state treasury; the effect of paying over such trust funds for their intended purpose would be an ancillary one at best. Such payments are not prohibited by the Eleventh Amendment. Hander v. San Jacinto Junior College, 519 F.2d 273 (5th Cir. 1975).

An intervening decision of the Supreme Court on a completely different ground has now effectively foreclosed the award of attorneys' fees to plaintiffs in this action. In Alyeska Pipeline Service Co. v. The Wilderness Society, 421 U.S. 240 (1975), the Court explicated the legal history of the "American rule" on awards of attorneys' fees—each party must bear the cost of its own attorneys' fees—and the traditional exceptions to that rule— 1) a contract between the parties; 2) a specific statute; 3) the common fund theory; or 4) cases involving willful disobedience of a court order or instances of bad faith, vexatious, wanton, or oppressive conduct. 95 S.Ct. at 1621–23. *Alyeska* has now made it plain that it was improper for the district court to make an award of attorneys' fees because the first three exceptions were not present and the award made was not based upon any conduct by the defendants which could qualify under the "bad faith" exception. The trial court stated that the award was bottomed upon the exercise of its chancery powers in the particular circumstances of the case. This statement does not constitute a basis which can bring the court's action within any traditional exception permitted by *Alyeska*. It therefore must be vacated. See Pupa v. Thompson, 517 F.2d 693 (5th Cir. 1975). The awards of nominal compensatory damages and back pay are affirmed. The award of attorneys' fees is reversed.

Affirmed in part and reversed in part.

HEALY v. JAMES

Supreme Court of the United States, 1972.
408 U.S. 169.

Mr. Justice POWELL, delivered the opinion of the Court.

. . .

Petitioners are students attending Central Connecticut State College (CCSC), a state-supported institution of higher learning. In September 1969 they undertook to organize what they then referred to as a "local chapter" of SDS. Pursuant to procedures established by the College, petitioners filed a request for official recognition as a campus organization with the Student Affairs Committee, a committee composed of four students, three faculty members, and the Dean of Student Affairs. The request specified three purposes for the proposed organization's existence. It would provide "a forum of discussion and self-education for students developing an analysis of American society"; it would serve as "an agency for integrating thought with action so as to bring about constructive changes"; and it would endeavor to provide "a coordinating body for relating the problems of leftist students" with other interested groups on campus and in the community. The Committee, while satisfied that the statement of purposes was clear and unobjectionable on its face, exhibited concern over the relationship between the proposed local group and the National SDS organization. In response to inquiries, representatives of the proposed organization stated that they would not affiliate with any national organization and that their group would remain "completely independent."

In response to other questions asked by Committee members concerning SDS' reputation for campus disruption, the applicants made the following statements which proved significant during the later stages of these proceedings:

"Q. How would you respond to issues of violence as other S. D. S. chapters have?

"A. Our action would have to be dependent upon each issue.

"Q. Would you use any means possible?

"A. No I can't say that; would not know until we know what the issues are.

. . .

"Q. Could you envision the S. D. S. interrupting a class?

"A. Impossible for me to say."

With this information before it, the Committee requested an additional filing by the applicants, including a formal statement regarding affiliations. The amended application filed in response stated flatly that "CCSC Students for a Democratic Society are not under the dictates of any National organization." . . .

By a vote of six to two the Committee ultimately approved the application and recommended to the President of the College, Dr. James, that the organization be accorded official recognition. . . .

Several days later, the President rejected the Committee's recommendation, and issued a statement indicating that petitioners' organization was not to be accorded the benefits of official campus recognition. His accompanying remarks, which are set out in full in the margin, indicate several reasons for his action. He found that the organization's philosophy was antithetical to the school's policies, and that the group's independence was doubtful. He concluded that approval should not be granted to any group that "openly repudiates" the College's dedication to academic freedom.

Their efforts to gain recognition having proved ultimately unsuccessful, and having been made to feel the burden of nonrecognition, petitioners resorted to the courts. . . .
. . .

At the outset we note that state colleges and universities are not enclaves immune from the sweep of the First Amendment. "It can hardly be argued that either students or teachers shed their constitutional rights to freedom of speech or expression at the schoolhouse gate." Tinker v. Des Moines Independent Community School District. Of course, as Mr. Justice Fortas made clear in *Tinker*, First Amendment rights must always be applied "in light of the special characteristics of the . . . environment" in the particular case. And, where state-operated educational institutions are involved, this Court has long recognized "the need for affirming the comprehensive authority of the States and of school officials, consistent with fundamental constitutional safeguards, to prescribe and control conduct in the schools." Yet, the precedents of this Court leave no room for the view that, because of the acknowledged need for order, First Amendment protections should apply with less force on college campuses than in the community at large. Quite to the contrary, "[t]he vigilant protection of constitutional freedoms is nowhere more vital than in the community of American schools." Shelton v. Tucker. The college classroom with its surrounding environs is peculiarly the " 'marketplace of ideas,' " and we break no new constitutional ground in reaffirming this Nation's dedication to safeguarding academic freedom. Keyishian v. Board of Regents . . . .

Among the rights protected by the First Amendment is the right of individuals to associate to further their personal beliefs. While the freedom of association is not explicitly set out in the Amendment, it has long been held to be implicit in the freedoms of speech, assembly, and petition. . . . There can be no doubt that denial of official recognition, without justification, to college organizations burdens or abridges that associational right. The primary impediment to free association flowing from nonrecognition is the denial of use of campus facilities for meetings and other appropriate purposes. The practical effect of nonrecognition was demonstrated in this case when, several days after the President's decision was announced, petitioners were not allowed to hold a meeting in the campus coffee shop because they were not an approved group.

Petitioners' associational interests also were circumscribed by the denial of the use of campus bulletin boards and the school newspaper. If an organization is to remain a viable entity in a campus community in which new students enter on a regular basis, it must possess the means of communicating with these students. Moreover, the organization's ability to participate in the intellectual give and take of campus debate, and to pursue its stated purposes, is limited by denial of access to the customary media for communicating with the administration, faculty members, and other students. Such impediments cannot be viewed as insubstantial.

Respondents and the courts below appear to have taken the view that denial of official recognition in this case abridged no constitutional rights. The District Court concluded that

> "President James' discretionary action in denying this application cannot be legitimately magnified and distorted into a constitutionally cognizable interference with the personal ideas or beliefs of any segment of the college students; neither does his action deter in any material way the individual advocacy of their personal beliefs; nor can his action be reasonably construed to be an invasion of, or having a chilling effect on academic freedom."

In that court's view all that was denied petitioners was the "administrative seal of official college respectability."

A majority of the Court of Appeals agreed that petitioners had been denied only the "college's stamp of approval."   .   .   .

We do not agree with the characterization by the courts below of the consequences of nonrecognition.   We may concede, as did Mr. Justice Harlan in his opinion for a unanimous Court in NA ACP v. Alabama ex rel. Patterson, 357 U.S., at 461, that the administration "has taken no direct action   .   .   .   to restrict the rights of [petitioners] to associate freely.   .   .   ."   But the Constitution's protection is not limited to direct interference with fundamental rights.   The requirement in *Patterson* that the NAACP disclose its membership lists was found to be an impermissible, though indirect, infringement of the members' associational rights.   Likewise, in this case, the group's possible ability to exist outside the campus community does not ameliorate significantly the disabilities imposed by the President's action.   We are not free to disregard the practical realities.   Mr. Justice Stewart has made the salient point: "Freedoms such as these are protected not only against heavy-handed frontal attack, but also from being stifled by more subtle governmental interference."
.   .   .

The opinions below also assumed that petitioners had the burden of showing entitlement to recognition by the College.   While petitioners have not challenged the procedural requirement that they file an application in conformity with the rules of the College, they do question the view of the courts below that final rejection could rest on their failure to convince the administration that their organization was unaffiliated with the National SDS.   For reasons to be stated later in this opinion, we do not consider the issue of affiliation to be a controlling one.   But, apart from any particular issue, once petitioners had filed an application in conformity with the requirements, the burden was upon the College administration to justify its decision of rejection.   .   .   .   It is to be remembered that the effect of the College's denial of   recognition was a form of prior restraint, denying to petitioners' organization the range of associational activities described above.   While a college has a legitimate interest in preventing disruption on the campus, which under circumstances requiring the safeguarding of that interest may justify such restraint, a "heavy burden" rests on the college to demonstrate the appropriateness of that action.   .   .   .

These fundamental errors—discounting the existence of a cognizable First Amendment interest and misplacing the burden of proof—require that the judgments below be reversed.   But we are unable to conclude that no basis exists upon which nonrecognition might be appropriate. Indeed, based on a reasonable reading of the ambiguous facts of this case, there appears to be at least one potentially acceptable ground for a denial of recognition. Because of this ambiguous state of the record we conclude that the case should be remanded and, in an effort to provide guidance to the lower courts upon reconsideration, it is appropriate to discuss the several bases of President James' decision. Four possible justifications for nonrecognition, all closely related, might be derived from the record and his statements. Three of those grounds are inadequate to substantiate his decision: a fourth, however, has merit.

A

From the outset the controversy in this case has centered in large measure around the relationship, if any, between petitioners' group and the National SDS. The Student Affairs Committee meetings, as reflected in its minutes, focused considerable attention on this issue; the court-ordered hearing also was directed primarily to this question. Despite assurances from petitioners and their counsel that the local group was in fact independent of the National organization, it is evident that President James was significantly influenced by his apprehension that there was a connection. Aware of the fact that some SDS chapters had been associated with disruptive and violent campus activity, he apparently considered that affiliation itself was sufficient justification for denying recognition.

Although this precise issue has not come before the Court heretofore, the Court has consistently disapproved governmental action imposing criminal sanctions or denying rights and privileges solely because of a citizen's association with an unpopular organization. . . . In these cases it has been established that "guilt by association alone, without [establishing] that an individual's association poses the threat feared by the Government," is an impermissible basis upon which to deny First Amendment rights. United States v. Robel, 389 U.S., at 265. The government has the burden of establishing a knowing affiliation with an organization possessing unlawful aims and goals, and a specific intent to further those illegal aims.

Students for a Democratic Society, as conceded by the College and the lower courts, is loosely organized, having various factions and promoting a number of diverse social and political views only some of which call for unlawful action. Not only did petitioners proclaim their complete independence from this organization, but they also indicated that they shared only some of the beliefs its leaders have expressed. On this record it is clear that the relationship was not an adequate ground for the denial of recognition.

B

Having concluded that petitioners were affiliated with, or at least retained an affinity for, National SDS, President James attributed what he believed to be the philosophy of that organization to the local group. He characterized the petitioning group as adhering to "some of the major tenets of the national organization," including a philosophy of violence and disruption. Understandably, he found that philosophy abhorrent. In an article signed by President James in an alumni periodical, and made a part of the record below, he announced his unwillingness to "sanction an organization that openly advocates the destruction of the very ideals and freedoms upon which the academic life is founded." He further emphasized that the petitioners' "philosophies" were "counter to the official policy of the college."

The mere disagreement of the President with the group's philosophy affords no reason to deny it recognition. As repugnant as these views may have been, especially to one with President James' responsibility, the mere expression of them would not justify the denial of First Amendment rights. Whether petitioners did in fact advocate a philosophy of "destruction" thus becomes immaterial. The College, acting here as the instrumentality of the State, may not restrict speech or association simply because it finds the views expressed by any group to be abhorrent. As Mr. Justice Black put it most simply and clearly:

> "I do not believe that it can be too often repeated that the freedoms of speech, press, petition and assembly guaranteed by the First Amendment must be accorded to the ideas we hate or sooner or later they will be denied to the ideas we cherish." Communist Party v. Subversive Activities Control Board, 367 U.S. 1, 137 (1961).

C

As the litigation progressed in the District Court, a third rationale for President James' decision—beyond the questions of affiliation and philosophy—began to emerge. His second statement, issued after the court-ordered hearing, indicates that he based rejection on a conclusion that this particular group would be a "disruptive influence at CCSC." This language was underscored in the second District Court opinion. In fact, the court concluded that the President had determined that CCSC–SDS' "prospective campus activities were likely to cause a disruptive influence at CCSC."

If this reason, directed at the organization's activities rather than its philosophy, were factually supported by the record, this Court's prior decisions would provide a basis for considering the propriety of nonrecognition. The critical line heretofore drawn for determining the permissibility of regulation is the line between mere advocacy and advocacy "directed to inciting or producing imminent lawless action and . . . likely to incite or produce such action." Brandenburg v. Ohio, 395 U.S. 444, 447 . . . . In the context of the "special characteristics of the school environment," the power of the government to prohibit "lawless action" is not limited to acts of a criminal nature. Also prohibitable are actions which "materially and substantially disrupt the work and discipline of the school." Tinker v. Des Moines Independent Community School District. Associational activities need not be tolerated where they infringe reasonable campus rules, interrupt classes, or substantially interfere with the opportunity of other students to obtain an education.

The "Student Bill of Rights" at CCSC, upon which great emphasis was placed by the President, draws precisely this distinction between advocacy and action. It purports to impose no limitations on the right of college student organizations "to examine and discuss *all* questions of interest to them." (Emphasis supplied.) But it also states that students have no right (1) "to deprive others of the opportunity to speak or be heard," (2) "to invade the privacy of others," (3) "to damage the property of others," (4) "to disrupt the regular and essential operation of the college," or (5) "to interfere with the rights of others." The line between permissible speech and impermissible conduct tracks the constitutional requirement, and if there were an evidential basis to support the conclusion that CCSC–SDS posed a substantial threat of material disruption in violation of that command the President's decision should be affirmed.

The record, however, offers no substantial basis for that conclusion. . . .

. . .

D

These same references in the record to the group's equivocation regarding how it might respond to "issues of violence" and whether it could ever "envision . . . interrupting a class," suggest a fourth possible reason why recognition might have been denied to these petitioners. These remarks might well have been read as announcing petitioners' unwillingness to be bound by reasonable school rules governing conduct. The College's Statement of Rights, Freedoms, and Responsibilities of Students contains, as we have seen, an explicit statement with respect to campus disruption. The regulation, carefully differentiating between advocacy and action, is a reasonable one, and petitioners have not questioned it directly. Yet their statements raise considerable question whether they intend to abide by the prohibitions contained therein.

As we have already stated in Parts B and C, the critical line for First Amendment purposes must be drawn between advocacy, which is entitled to full protection, and action, which is not. Petitioners may, if they so choose, preach the propriety of amending or even doing away with any or all campus regulations. They may not, however, undertake to flout these rules. Mr. Justice Blackmun, at the time he was a circuit judge on the Eighth Circuit, stated:

> "We . . . hold that a college has the inherent power to promulgate rules and regulations; that it has the inherent power properly to discipline; that it has power appropriately to protect itself and its property; that it may expect that its students adhere to generally accepted standards of conduct."
>
> . . .

Just as in the community at large, reasonable regulations with respect to the time, the place, and the manner in which student groups conduct their speech-related activities must be respected. A college administration may impose a requirement, such as may have been imposed in this case, that a group seeking official recognition affirm in advance its willingness to adhere to reasonable campus law. Such a requirement does not impose an impermissible condition on the students' associational rights. Their freedom to speak out, to assemble, or to petition for changes in school rules is in no sense infringed. It merely constitutes an agreement to conform with reasonable standards respecting conduct. This is a minimal requirement, in the interest of the entire academic community of any group seeking the privilege of official recognition.

HUDSON v. HARRIS

United States Court of Appeals, Tenth Circuit, 1973.
478 F.2d 244.

PER CURIAM.

This appeal is from the Western District of Oklahoma for summarily dismissing appellants' civil rights action. Appellants bring this class action as representatives of a class of students at Southwestern State College in Oklahoma who undertook the formation of two organizations entitled "Viet Nam Veterans Against the War" and "Students Against the War." Appellees are the college president and the dean of students who rejected appellants' applications for the antiwar organizations.

Southwestern State College is a public, tax-supported institution of higher learning maintained by the State of Oklahoma at Weatherford, Oklahoma. The appellants were students at Southwestern State who opposed the United States' policies in Southeast Asia. On two separate occasions appellants submitted applications to appellees requesting permission to establish an antiwar organization on campus. The applications were submitted pursuant to Southwestern State College regulations requiring any new organization on campus first to secure permission from the dean of students. On both occasions they received a letter from the dean denying their request. The reason behind the denials was "that we do not see a specific need for an organization of this type. We feel that the organization and functions of the Student Association permits all students to express their concerns in a constructive manner."

Appellants thereafter brought suit in federal court claiming jurisdiction under the First, Ninth and Fourteenth Amendments to the United States Constitution and 28 U.S.C.A. §§ 1331, 1343 and 42 U.S.C.A. § 1983. They also requested a temporary and permanent injunction prohibiting appellees from refusing to approve their proposed organizations as formal student groups. They also demanded a declaration that Southwestern State College as operated by appellees is violative of the Fourteenth Amendment's due process and equal protection clauses because guidelines for approval of campus organizations are vague and overbroad.

Appellants support their contentions by the following argument. Forty-seven honorary and professional organizations operate on the Southwestern State campus. Many of these organizations, such as the Oklahoma Young Republicans and Oklahoma Young Democrats, are at least in part political organizations. Many other organizations, such as Southwestern State Collegiate Farmers Union, take positions on political issues. Discrimination is also prevalent in the privileged status given certain off-campus organizations. For example, the Armed Forces are permitted to recruit on campus while antiwar organizations are denied use of the campus to solicit memberships and opposition to the Viet Nam war.

Appellees moved to dismiss the complaint on the ground no constitutional right of appellants had been denied, only the privilege of recognition. The motion was granted. It was the trial court's position that college regulations are matters for the legislature rather than the judiciary and only when school administrators act fraudulently, capriciously or arbitrarily may the judiciary interfere with administration of school affairs; that no constitutional right had been denied because neither freedom of expression nor advocacy of individual beliefs had been impeded; and that appellants had not been deprived of any federally protected right under color of state law, therefore are not entitled to proceed in federal court.

We cannot agree with the trial court's position in light of the recent Supreme Court decision in Healy v. James, 408 U.S. 169 (1972).[39] .   .   .   The Supreme Court, in holding for the SDS group, stated that First Amendment rights are available to students while on school premises.   .   .   .   The Court there also determined that governmental action denying rights and privileges of a citizen's association merely because it is an unpopular organization cannot be sanctioned.   .   .   .

We realize schools operate under unique circumstances and thus denial of approval should not be limited to acts of a criminal nature. "Associational activities need not be tolerated where they infringe reasonable campus rules, interrupt classes or substantially interfere with the opportunity of other students to obtain an education." Healy v. James, supra at 189. The test to be applied is whether such an organization would substantially and materially interfere with the discipline necessary to operate the college. Burnside v. Byars, 363 F.2d 744 (5th Cir. 1966).

At this stage of the proceedings we cannot determine whether appellants' organizations will substantially and materially inter-

---

39. The trial judge did not have the benefit of this case because the judgment appealed from was enter- ed on March 29, 1972, and the Healy case was not decided until June 26, 1972.

fere wtih the operation of Southwestern State College. There were no allegations of such fact in appellees' motion to dismiss. We must therefore follow the rule that a claim for relief should not be dismissed unless it appears beyond a reasonable doubt that appellants can prove no set of facts supporting their claim for relief. Conley v. Gibson, 355 U.S. 41 (1957); Williams v. Eaton, 443 F.2d 422 (10th Cir. 1971). On the face of appellants' complaint it appears their constitutional rights have been violated and thus it was error to grant a motion to dismiss.

The order granting the motion to dismiss is set aside, and the case is remanded to the trial court for further proceedings consistent herewith.

Part IV

EQUAL PROTECTION OF THE LAWS' GUARANTEES

Chapter 7

DeFUNIS AND BAKKE GO TO COURT: VICTIMS OF MAKING UP FOR PAST INJUSTICES?

No State shall make or enforce any law which shall
.   .   .   deny to any person within its jurisdiction the
equal protection of the laws.   .   .   .   The Congress
shall have power to enforce, by appropriate legislation,
the provisions of this article.

> (Amendment XIV, adopted in 1868, U.S. Constitution)

The object of the [Fourteenth] Amendment was undoubtedly to enforce the absolute equality of the two races before the law, but in the nature of things it could not have been intended to abolish distinctions based upon color, or to enforce social, as distinguished from political, equality, or a commingling of the two races upon terms unsatisfactory to either.

> (Justice Brown announcing the "separate but equal" doctrine in *Plessy v. Ferguson*, 1896)

Our Constitution is color-blind, and neither knows nor tolerates classes among citizens.   In respect of civil rights, all citizens are equal before the law.   The humblest is the peer of the most powerful.   The law regards man as man, and takes no account of his surroundings or of his color when his civil rights as guaranteed by the supreme law of the land are involved.   It is, therefore, to be regretted that this high tribunal, the final expositor of the fundamental law of the land, has reached the conclusion that it is competent for a State to regulate the enjoyment by citizens of their civil rights solely upon the basis of race.

> (Justice Harlan, the lone dissenting opinion in *Plessy v. Ferguson*, 1896)

297

The doctrine of "separate but equal" did not make its appearance in this Court until 1896 in the case of *Plessy v. Ferguson* involving not education but transportation. . . . Whatever may have been the extent of psychological knowledge at the time of Plessy . . . [its] finding is rejected . . . We conclude that in the field of public education the doctrine of "separate but equal" has no place. Separate educational facilities are inherently unequal.

> (Chief Justice Warren announcing Court's unanimous decision in *Brown v. Board of Educ.*, 1954)

Discriminatory preference for any group, minority or majority, is precisely and only what Congress has proscribed . . . Congress has not commanded that the less qualified be preferred over the better qualified simply because of minority origins. Far from disparaging job qualifications, Congress has made such qualifications the controlling factor, so that race, religion, nationality, and sex become irrelevant.

> (Chief Justice Burger for the majority in *Griggs v. Duke Power*, 1971)

Just as the use of race must be considered in determining whether a constitutional violation has occurred, so also race must be considered in formulating a remedy.

> (U. S. Supreme Court in *North Carolina State Bd. of Educ. v. Swann*, 1971)

Thus, the Constitution is color conscious to prevent the perpetuation of discrimination and to undo the effects of past segregation.

> (Justice Marshall A. Neill for the majority, Washington State Supreme Court, *DeFunis v. Odegaard*, 1973)

Regardless of its historical origin, the equal protection clause by its literal terms applies to "any person," and it's incompatible with the premise that some races may be afforded a higher degree of protection against unequal treatment than others.

> (Justice Stanley Mosk for the majority, California Supreme Court, *Bakke v. Regents of the Univ. of California*, 1976)

And so the battle goes.   Clearly, there is enormous competition for the shrinking number of jobs considered "desirable"— high paying, high prestige, meaningful.   Perhaps John Gardner, however, pointed out this dilemma more accurately:

> The sorting out of individuals according to ability is very nearly the most delicate and difficult process our society has to face.
>
> Those who receive the most education are going to move into virtually all the key jobs.   Thus the question "who should go to college?" translates itself into the more compelling question "Who is going to manage the society?"   That is not the kind of question one can treat lightly or cavalierly.   It is the kind of question that wars have been fought over.
>
> (John W. Gardner in *Excellence—Can We Be Equal and Excellent Too?* 1961.

Student activism wasn't the only problem in those turbulent sixties.   Gradually coming to a crossroads, higher education faced yet another classical dilemma.   Somewhere in the beginning of the sixties the leading edge of societal concern began to shift its social priorities away from attention to affluence and meritocratic principles toward increased preoccupation with justice for the minorities and the poor.   The movement of the fifties and early sixties to effect the civil rights of blacks in the South, of course, provided much of the stimulus, but soon the movement broadened in many directions.   Chicanos, Puerto Ricans and Native Americans, stimulated more or less by the black example, also began to assert their identity and to press for equality in education, housing, employment and income. There were many reactive results, including a resurgence of women's demands for rights and equal treatment, but perhaps the most significant result of this trend was that the federal government and then the states began to transform higher education into a public utility, a facility open to all.

Historically, much institutional action in dealing with minorities and women in colleges and universities had been not simply discriminatory, but massively and harshly so.   Right here, however, is not the place to analyze a complex national experience. What needs to be noted is that during this period the goal of equality for minorities and women began to be taken much more seriously, however contentious it was and however ineffective the results.

The crucial problem was that many of our colleges and universities were singularly ill-prepared for this transformation. These institutions tended to be ideologically egalitarian, but ecologically elitist. Their aims were largely dependent on principles of rigorous selection: the best students and the most qualified and distinguished professors. As a matter of fact, much of the nature of higher education was supposed to be selective with respect to degrees of ability, of effort, of performance, of difficulty, of importance. Thus, much of the higher learning was a classifying activity. But in an increasingly egalitarian democracy, selectarian institutions were ready-made objects of symbolic attack.

With the increasing social sophistication of the nation, it was realized that most barriers to further education were highly interrelated, operating quite consistently to exclude certain groups of people. With that realization, the national picture changed abruptly, and higher education found itself the target of one governmental action after another abolishing one barrier after another in rapid succession. But the notion of offering education to everyone who came had a profound effect upon the design of higher education. For instance, mounting pressures for college attendance pushed many reluctant and/or inadequately prepared learners into involuntary attendance at college. The business of picking those who would succeed in the type of higher education that we happened to offer was a very different task from educating those who came.

Under these new circumstances, the big educational questions became not so much how we could predict motivation, but how we could create it; not how well admissions criteria predicted grades, but how effectively they diagnosed learning strengths and weaknesses. In other words, the emphasis shifted from recruiting those who would be successful to the much more difficult task of determining how to make successful those who came. Needless to say, these demands placed great strains on the already attenuated resources and energy level of colleges and universities. We learned that the fashioning of pluralistic institutions was hardly a painless process. Everyone had to give up something; everyone had to do something more.

Whether our colleges and universities essentially mirror or determine society's goals is problematic. What seems certain is that at least since the 1950s there has been a steadily growing and generalized expectation that the nation's educational system provide a pace-setting example of equal opportunity. The focus has been on racial disparities vis-a-vis equal opportunity and this relationship has generally been understood in terms of both access to and quality of the schools.

In the spring of 1970, Vice President Spiro Agnew reacted to a University of Michigan announcement that it was increasing its black student enrollment to ten percent and, in setting such a goal, implying a clear preference in admissions. Agnew declared that such a policy was "some sort of madness" and added that "it just doesn't make sense to atone by discriminating against someone else." It was soon evident that this sentiment was shared by many others. Indeed, the impression one might have gleaned from anecdotal and popular sources was that of a horde of unqualified, marginally qualified, or certainly less-qualified individuals, especially blacks but not excluding other minorities, crowding out truly-deserving candidates for university enrollment and faculty positions.

Given this growing perception, the time appeared right and proper for a major case to test the legality, if not the morality, of what a short time ago had seemed one of the most promising innovations of the Great Society—a plan to break the residual effects of minority discrimination by shifting the emphasis of national policy from "equality of treatment" to "equality of results." The launching of this positive or "affirmative action" plan came about in 1965 when President Lyndon Johnson signed into effect Executive Order 11246. In a Howard University speech, President Johnson provided a critical and telling rationale for the program:

> You do not take a person who, for years, has been hobbled by chains and liberate him, bring him up to the starting line of a race and then say, "You are free to compete with all the others," and still justly believe that you have been fair.[1]

Accordingly, though the more blatant forms of discrimination had been curbed in the twelve years since the *Brown* ruling,[2] the fact of discrimination or the residual effect of discrimination remained a reality. In other words, even if overt discrimination

---

1. Quoted in "The Furor Over 'Reverse Discrimination,'" *Newsweek*, September 26, 1977, p. 5. Later, in a national address to the nation on June 27, 1967, President Johnson also recognized the link between discrimination and civil disorders: "The only genuine, long range solution for what has happened lies in an attack—mounted at every level—upon the conditions that breed despair and violence. All of us know what these conditions are: ignorance, discrimination, slums, poverty, disease, not enough jobs."

2. Brown v. Board of Educ., 347 U.S. 483 (1954).

had been completely eliminated, it could not have offset alto-gether such critical variables (chains) as low socioeconomic back-ground; marginal schooling and educational achievement; or the lack of social and familial networks or bridges that ease a person's pathway to competing in this society.

This analysis, if correct, shows that what we are really talk-ing about when we talk about civil rights is not only the ques-tion of whether black Americans or Mexican Americans or Native Americans or women, for instance, are to be given constitutional rights, but (and this is important) whether they will be extended the educational and social opportunities to take full part in the political system created by the American Constitution. Thus, the theory undergirding affirmative action was that prohibition against discrimination was not enough to break the grip of dis-advantage that locked certain groups into a lifetime of inequality. The best way to break that grip, therefore, was to break the vi-cious circle of unequal employment opportunity that led to un-equal housing opportunity, unequal educational opportunity, and back to continued unequal employment opportunity. Hence the drive for preferential treatment.

As the administrative guidelines were formulated to imple-ment affirmative action, it became clear that its major control mechanism would be contract compliance; that is, as a condition of obtaining or retaining federal contracts, contractors such as colleges and universities (both public and private) would have to do more than remain neutral with regard to race, color, sex, or national origin. "Affirmative action" therefore required these contractors to make additional efforts to recruit, employ, and promote qualified members of groups previously underrepresent-ed or excluded from employment, even in the absence of a de-termination that the employer had previously engaged in racial discrimination.

Additionally, it was soon recognized that a conscientious ef-fort to seek out and train minorities would be a significant ele-ment in the eventual success of affirmative action. "Preferen-tial admissions" certainly made sense, it seemed, because one of the goals of affirmative action was to lower barriers to higher level employment, and to accomplish this, trained people had to be around to take advantage of such opportunities. Besides, if this could be accomplished, special treatment would not be need-ed at a later stage.

Nevertheless, there was little doubt that preferential treat-ment in favor of certain groups over others would provide an imposing target for critics. To those unhappy with affirmative action, it seemed that the "chains" of disadvantage of one group were being removed and transferred to another group. Furthermore, it was one thing to prohibit, as the 1964 Civil Rights Act did, discrimination on the grounds of race, color, religion, national origin, or sex. That merely reaffirmed and extended the 1954 *Brown* doctrine. It was quite another to transmute anti-discrimination (equal opportunity) to affirmative action—a national policy where the majority would choose to discriminate against itself—justifiable though the shift might have been. Between the two, there was not merely a semantic gap, but a difference in stress. In fact, a new dimension was added. No longer was the situation simply a clash of civil rights and wrongs. That, of course, continued. There was also the matter of competing civil rights. Thus, preferential treatment may have been a remedy for one problem, but it also created another. For many, this was to become one of the most vexing, intractable issues of the age.

The resulting conflict, economically pervasive and politically explosive, was legally complex. More and more, it led to an emotional backlash from threatened white males. At the same time, the white backlash increasingly angered minorities who believed that they were still being denied their fair share of the American dream. And it was at the outer edge of this debacle that Marco DeFunis, a rejected law school applicant, stepped forward and filed a lawsuit that soon galvanized opinion—both public and professional—on "reverse discrimination." [3] He charged that the University of Washington Law School had discriminated against him, in violation of the "equal protection of the laws" clause of the Fourteenth Amendment, because he was white. In other words, DeFunis challenged the constitutional right of the University to reject him, a qualified white applicant, in order to accept less-qualified minority applicants.

Clearly, more was at stake in the court decision than which of the two immediately contending parties would win. A court must give reasons for its verdict, which can then help determine the outcome of future cases. Furthermore, the outcome of the case involved implications not only for university admissions but for similar affirmative action programs ranging from efforts

3. DeFunis v. Odegaard, 507 P.2d 1178 (1973), vacated as moot 416 U.S. 312 (1974).

to place more women on university faculties to hiring more blacks in the construction industry.

Thus as *DeFunis* slowly made its way to the U. S. Supreme Court, it became increasingly obvious that a major case was in the making. Interestingly, not least of all the forces propelling this case forward, past a thicket of procedural obstacles, was the fact that DeFunis had a patron: the law firm which skillfully argued the *DeFunis* case through the courts waived all professional fees. The extent of this largesse is best seen against the fact that out-of-pocket expenses, such as filing fees and duplicating costs, which DeFunis himself financed, had climbed to $10,000 by the time it reached the Supreme Court.[4] That the Goddess of Justice wore such an expensive price tag may seem a bit ironical, but the *DeFunis* case was filled with ironies. For instance, it involved charges of racial discrimination, but Marco DeFunis, the central figure, was white. For another, DeFunis was Jewish, but the issue he exposed in his lawsuit was so controversial and politically charged that it divided the Jewish community, one of the traditional allies of the civil rights movement.[5] Also, as the issue of reverse discrimination seemed to be reaching denouement in the U. S. Supreme Court, the Court suddenly declared the case moot; DeFunis was about to graduate from the same law school he was suing. Thus *DeFunis* came to have the dubious distinction of being perhaps the most celebrated noncase in the Court's history. Nonetheless, some four years later, DeFunis, now a Seattle lawyer, reappeared as the author of an *amicus* brief in support of Allen Bakke, filed on behalf of the Young Americans for Freedom.

4. Robert M. O'Neil, *Discriminating Against Discrimination* (Bloomington: Indiana University Press, 1975).

5. The use of quotas to exclude qualified American Jews from colleges and universities had a long history in American higher education. For example: "Many decades ago, as the late Professor Bickel reminds us in his brief for B'nai B'rith [supporting DeFunis], President Lowell of Harvard University argued in favor of a quota limiting the number of Jews who might be accepted by his university. He said that if Jews were accepted in numbers larger than their proportion of the population, as they certainly would have been if intelligence were the only test, then Harvard would no longer be able to provide to the world men of the qualities and temperament it aimed to produce, men, that is, who were more well rounded and less exclusively intellectual than Jews tended to be, and who, therefore, were better and more likely leaders of other men, both in and out of government." Ronald Dworkin, "The DeFunis Case: The Right to Go to Law School," *The New York Review*, February 5, 1976, pp. 30–31.

The Court majority in *DeFunis* evidently hoped that, given time, ways would be found to bring minorities into the professions without blatant reverse discrimination.   Yet the constitutional and ethical arguments changed little between *DeFunis* and *Bakke*.   In fact, both cases were strikingly similar with perhaps the most notable exception being that *Bakke* involved a medical school rather than a law school and that, unlike *DeFunis,* the U. S. Supreme Court did not declare the *Bakke* case moot.   Otherwise, both DeFunis and Bakke were white males who had failed to gain admission to a professional school, although their test scores and college grades were such that they would have been admitted if, for example, they had been black, Chicano, or Native American.   After commencing lawsuits in their respective state courts, both of them eventually had their cases heard by the U. S. Supreme Court, and in substance, they both asked the Court to declare the admissions procedures, which provided less exacting standards for minorities, in violation of their rights to equal protection of the laws under the Fourteenth Amendment.

Neither DeFunis nor Bakke claimed an absolute right to a law or medical school education nor a right that only "intelligence" be used as a standard for admission.   They did claim, however, that they had a right that race *not* be used as a standard for admission no matter how well a "benign" racial classification might work to overcome past discrimination.   Yet, one of the peculiar dilemmas of these cases was that perfectly rational arguments could be made on either side.   In essence, the cases caused two of America's most cherished values to collide head-on.   Arrayed on one side was the principle of governmental "color blindness," which purports that the color of a person's skin should have nothing to do with the distribution of benefits by the state.   Set against it was the goal of a truly integrated society, and the recognition that this objective could not be achieved unless race and color were taken into account by employers, educators, and other key decision makers, both public and private. Thus the cases raised intriguing moral and legal questions.   But central to their answer was the scope of permissible activity under the Fourteenth Amendment.

EQUAL PROTECTION UNDER THE LAWS— WHAT DOES IT MEAN?

The Fourteenth Amendment simply states: "No State [including any subdivision thereof] shall make or enforce any law

which shall   .   .   .   deny to any person under its jurisdiction
the equal protection of the laws." But the clause, while guaranteeing the equal protection of the laws, is set forth in language
that is at once specific and vague. For instance, it is specific
as to the guarantees but vague as to the substance of the guarantee; it specifically makes the guarantee a test of legislation, but
then is vague as to the application of that concept. In fact,
neither the text of the clause nor the decisions of the Supreme
Court decisively settle the question whether, as a matter of law,
the equal protection clause makes all racial classifications unconstitutional. Moreover, the equal protection guarantee does
not appear to be a distinct and independent right protected by
the Constitution specifically, like the freedom of religion and
speech; nor does it condemn racial classification directly as the
Constitution clearly condemns the establishment of a religion or
the censorship of expression.

Understandably, ambiguity such as this has caused a swell of
confusion. Constitutional scholars are still asking: Equality for
whom? Where? When? To what degree? Is the protection
absolute or qualified? And most germane to our discussion:
Is the Constitution "color-blind" or "color-sensitive"? Does
the Fourteenth Amendment allow discriminatory preference for
any group, minority or majority? Is there such a thing as
"good" discrimination and "bad" discrimination? Is racial preference in admissions and hiring a necessary step in promoting
equality, given the compelling interest of the state to overcome
the effects of past discrimination? Is a strategy that uses preferential treatment based on race a rational means of implementing
that interest? If race can legitimately be a factor in selecting
professional applicants (or in hiring), then *when* can race be
propertly decisive? Are traditional academic or intellectual qualifications to be temporarily suspended (how long is temporary)?
Does preferential admissions (or employment) imply some sort
of formula (goals or quotas) for proportional representation of
races (or sexes)? Does preferential treatment mean that a university is expected to freeze or set aside a certain number of professional school places for minorities even if this results in accepting less qualified candidates? And so it goes.

Certainly there is little doubt that the equal protection clause
has had great impact on state power, especially during the past
generation. Originally intended for the benefit of the Negro
freedmen, it was soon extended to orientals, particularly Chinese

living and working in California,[6] and in the same year to corporations which were declared to be "persons" within the meaning of the Amendment.[7] The official Supreme Court interpretation of the equal protection clause as of that period was that it required "merely that all persons subject to a law shall be treated alike, and under like circumstances and conditions, both in the privileges conferred and in the liabilities imposed." [8] Yet, whatever the judicial application, it is clear that the equal protection clause does not deprive a state of power to *classify,* provided such classification is not arbitrary or unreasonable.

It is also explicit that the legal status of "equal protection of the laws" is a line-drawing problem and that the line-drawing effort has never been static. In the course of history, the apparently simple words of that clause have been interpreted and reinterpreted, defined and redefined, idealized and compromised— each time in light of contemporary social experience. Until recent times, however, though cases which were successfully prosecuted under the equal protection clause were many and varied, one of their commonalities was that they involved discrimination *against* a particular group and not in *favor* of anyone.

Thus, as we attempt to understand the present condition and status of the equal protection clause, we find that the question broadens in many directions. As Pascal believed, everything counts. "If Cleopatra's nose had been an inch longer all history would have changed." Obviously, we cannot here examine the many guarantees suggested by that clause; instead we shall direct ourselves to a more detailed account of perhaps the key equal protection problem of our time—race. And the reader should bear in mind that some of its aspects—such as sex discrimination, campus housing, appearance, and out-of-state tuition issues—will be treated later in Chapter 8. Our present purpose is to deal with the evolution and meaning of the concept of equal protection in the racial sphere in general and with the racial classification aspect in particular.

It should also be noted that space does not permit extended discussion of all events relevant to past and contemporary racial

---

6. See Yick Wo v. Hopkins, 118 U.S. 356 (1886); issuing laundry permits to white San Franciscans but not to Chinese was an unconstitutional classification.

7. Santa Clara County v. Southern Pacific Railroad Co., 118 U.S. 394 (1886).

8. Hayes v. Missouri, 120 U.S. 68 (1887).

classification. In fact, brief notice of some of the more important must suffice. Moreover, it should be understood that discrete notice does not imply independent existence. On the contrary, a complex pattern of overlapping and interaction—which would be beyond tracing even in a multi-book treatment—obtains. And finally, it is essential to understand two indubitable truths. First, *tabula rasa* at any point in time is mere bizzare pretense in that the past lives in the present and largely conditions the future; thus, there is little that can be said about racial equality today without understanding the past. Second, the depth and validity of America's commitment to the principles it espouses has been, and always will be, judged by its actions and not simply by words.

The "Separate But Equal" Doctrine

In Roberts v. The City of Boston (1849),[9] nearly twenty years before the adoption of the Fourteenth Amendment, the plight of a five-year old black girl, Sarah Roberts, set in motion the precedent for what became one of the most historically significant doctrines in constitutional law, namely the doctrine of "Separate but Equal." The doctrine from this case reigned over educational jurisprudence thereafter for more than 100 years. The case also represented the beginning of the end of the "neighborhood school" concept for minority race children, as Sarah was excluded by the highest court in Massachusetts from the all-white school nearest her home.[10]

The precedent set by Chief Justice Shaw in the *Roberts* case may have been avoided if the Court had addressed itself not to the question of unlawful exclusion from a public school but rather to the one of whether or not Sarah Roberts had been denied equal protection of the laws. Justice Shaw, however, avoided the difficulty of defining precisely the term "equal protection" by interpreting his state's constitutional provision that all persons regardless of color, etc. are "equal before the law" as but a statement of broad principle, inapplicable in practice. Moreover, the Court decided, the state has no duty to provide a public education, and thus the right of a person to receive an education was ex-

---

9. 59 Mass. (5 Cushing) 198 (1849).

10. "SCHOLARS TO GO TO SCHOOL NEAREST THEIR RESIDENCE. Applicants for admission to the school (with the exception and provision referred to in the preceding rule) are especially entitled to enter the schools nearest their places of residence." *Regulation of the Primary School Committee,* quoted in Roberts, at 199. The exception was, of course, Negroes: " . . . those for whom special provisions have been made." Id.

pressly repudiated.[11]   In sum, the *Roberts* case reinforced the belief that education is a matter for the state which may leave the
responsibility for education solely to private means.   Furthermore, the decision approved of a classification drawn on the
basis of race for educational purposes.   That minority group
children had no inherent right to attend neighborhood schools
and that racial segregation for the purposes of education was both
acceptable and permissible under law, of course, was in keeping
with the thinking of the time.   Since then the courts generally held (but not after the 1954 *Brown* decision) that constitutional requirements of equality were met so long as there was
a reasonable basis for the classification adopted by the law.
Thus, not only the classification—blacks and whites educated in
separate schools—but the psychological burden which that classification placed on the black child was deemed reasonable and
not illegal:

> The increased distance, to which the plaintiff was obligated
> to go to school from her father's house, is not such, in our
> opinion, as to render the regulation in question unreason-
> able, still less illegal.[12]

The Fourteenth Amendment, of course, was nonexistent in
1849, and thus Shaw decided the case on the basis of his state's
law.   Nonetheless, the *Roberts* case, either overtly or implicitly,
set the course for judicial thinking about race and education for
many years to follow.   Laws requiring black children to attend
segregated schools and prohibiting their attendance in white
schools were passed by many state legislatures, as well as by
Congress under its general power of legislation over the District
of Columbia, and were generally, "if not uniformly, sustained by
the courts." [13]

In practice, the Fourteenth Amendment, adopted in 1868, has
never forbidden state governments from making distinctions
among people, for substantially all legislation involves classification of some sort.   Yet however necessary such classification
seems, the practice of such grouping, as we have seen, is a function which lends itself to abuse.   It is this abuse which the Fourteenth Amendment seeks to prevent, and it is to a consideration of
that prevention and its implications that we should now turn.

---

11. Id., at 207.

12. Id., at 210.

13. Plessy v. Ferguson, 163 U.S. 537
(1896); the *Roberts* case was cited
as "[o]ne of the earliest of these
cases . . ."

The Fourteenth Amendment and the "Separate But Equal" Doctrine

At the time the Fourteenth Amendment was being considered, it was obvious that the Southern States, left to their own devices, would subject the newly-freed blacks to numerous discriminatory laws and regulations designed to prevent them from achieving anything like a status of legal equality with the white citizens of the South. However, the equal protection clause does not mention blacks, but when it first came before the U. S. Supreme Court for interpretation in the *Slaughterhouse Cases* [14] in 1873, Mr. Justice Miller, with contemporary history and conditions in mind, observed: "We doubt very much whether any action of a state not directed by way of discrimination against the negroes as a class, or on account of their race, will ever be held to come within the purview of this provision." Mr. Justice Miller's appraisal of current history may have been correct, but his prophecy as to the limited use of the equal protection clause was way off mark. Actually, equal protection of the law over the years has come to afford broad and general relief against all forms of arbitrary classification and discrimination, regardless of the persons affected or the character of the rights involved. In fact, blacks could well constitute a minority of those who have invoked the equal protection clause against discriminatory treatment.

Even after the adoption of the Fourteenth Amendment, the efforts of the black community to secure the equal protection of the laws seemed doomed to failure. With the passing of the Reconstruction era and the return of the "white man's government" to the Southern States in 1877, state laws were again adopted reiminiscent of the "Black Codes" which had been passed during the Civil War to "Keep the Negro in his place." These

14. 83 U.S. (16 Wallace) 36 (1873). The *Slaughterhouse Cases* were the first cases brought under the Fourteenth Amendment, but they had nothing whatever to do with the rights of blacks. Actually the case arose as follows: The Reconstruction or "carpetbag" government in Louisiana, unquestionably under corrupt influence, had granted a monopoly of the slaughterhouse business to a single concern, thus preventing over 1,000 other persons and firms from continuing in that business. The validity of the law was challenged under the Fourteenth Amendment, but the majority of the Court (5–4) disposed of the challenge rather summarily by holding in substance that the due process clause was not a limitation on a state's police power and that the equal protection of the laws clause, equally inapplicable, was for the protection of the Negro. Of course, if the *Slaughterhouse Cases* were decided today, the Louisiana statute would be invalidated as a deprivation of liberty and property without due process and a denial of the equal protection of the laws.

laws established, and enforced by criminal penalties, a system of racial segregation under which members of the black and white races were required to be separated in the use of public and semi-public facilities. Thus, separate schools, colleges, parks, waiting rooms, and bus and railroad accommodations were required by law.

Where segregation was required by law, however, the question arose whether it violated the rights guaranteed to the newly freed blacks by the Fourteenth Amendment. This problem came to the Supreme Court for the first time in Plessy v. Ferguson (1896),[15] twenty-eight years after the Amendment had been adopted. At issue was a law passed by the legislature of Louisiana in 1890 requiring segregation of all intra-state railway carriers, but requiring them to provide "equal but separate accommodations for the white and colored races." A fine of twenty-five dollars or twenty days in jail was the penalty for sitting in the wrong compartment. Homer Plessy—who, incidently, was seven-eighths white and one-eighth Negro—had refused to vacate a seat in the white compartment of a railway car and was arrested for violating the statute. Subsequently, Mr. Plessy challenged the law on the basis that it violated his equal protection of the laws guarantee under the Fourteenth Amendment, and eventually, when the case reached the U. S. Supreme Court, the statute was upheld as a reasonable exercise of the state's police power; that is, as long as the facilities were equal, the separation of the races could be required by state law. Moreover, after citing Roberts v. The City of Boston (1849, supra), the Court stated that ". . . if the enforced separation of the two races stamps the colored race with the badge of inferiority . . . [it is] solely because the colored race chooses to put that construction upon [the separate-but-equal statute of the state].[16]

Thus the *Plessy* case established in American constitutional law for nearly six decades (until 1954) the doctrine that a black was not denied equal protection of the laws by compelling him to accept "equal but separate" accommodations. This decision, of course, became the constitutional pillar upon which the South based its system of racial segregation. Even so, there was some irony in the *Plessy* decision in that the majority opinion was written by Mr. Justice Brown, a Yale alumnus from the state of Michigan, while the eloquent protest against racial discrimination is found in the lone dissenting opinion of Mr. Justice Harlan, a Southerner from Kentucky and a former slave owner. In fact,

15. 163 U.S. 537 (1896).   16. Id., at 557.

the lone dissent by Mr. Justice John Marshall Harlan was not only eloquent but also equally angry: "The Constitution is color-blind," he wrote, "and neither knows nor tolerates classes among citizens."[17] Next, Harlan's dissent was remarkably prescient: "In my opinion, the judgment this day rendered will, in time, prove to be quite as pernicious as the decision made by this tribunal in the *Dred Scott Case*." [18]

Indeed, Harlan's dissent was an accurate prediction of the future course of events under the *Plessy* ruling.   (But his dissent also added some more irony in that Justice Harlan's observation that "The Constitution is color-blind" became one of the rallying cries of the civil rights movement in the 1950s, and, in a sense, became the law of the land with the Brown v. Board of Educ. decision in 1954; yet, on the other hand, in the 1970s the same "color-blind" claim became the "reverse discrimination" centerpiece of unsuccessful white professional school applicants who turned plaintiffs in preferential admissions litigation.)

Although Plessy v. Ferguson involved segregation only in the use of railroad facilities, there was not much reason to doubt that the Supreme Court would uphold state-imposed segregation in other areas, especially education.   This became clear when the Court, in Berea College v. Kentucky [19] (1908), held that the state could validly forbid a college, even though a private institution, to teach whites and blacks at the same time and place.   Of course, this removed whatever doubt there might have been at the time about the validity of the Southern laws requiring the education of white and black children in separate tax-supported schools.

By 1914, however, the Supreme Court began to show signs of requiring a much closer approach to equality under segregation.[20]

---

17. Id., at 559.

18.   Id., at 560. In the *Dred Scott Case* (1857), Chief Justice Taney ruled that "[Negroes] were not intended to be included, under the word 'citizen' in the Constitution, and can therefore claim none of the rights and privileges which that instrument provides for and secures for citizens of the United States. On the contrary, they were at that time considered as a subordinate and inferior class of beings, who had been subjugated by the dominant race, and, whether emancipated or not, yet remain subject to their authority .   .   ."   Of course the opening sentence of the Fourteenth Amendment reversed this decision: "All persons born or naturalized in the United States, and subject to the jurisdiction thereof, are citizens of the United States and of the State wherein they reside."

19.   211 U.S. 45 (1908); a fine had been imposed on Berea College (and upheld on appeal by the U.S. Supreme Court) for *not* maintaining separate education for the races.

20.   See, e. g., McCabe v. Atchison, T. and S. F. Ry. Co., 235 U.S. 151 (1914).

On a number of occasions, the Court struck down segregated facilities provided by the states as not being "equal"—never going so far, however, as to hold the separate-but-equal doctrine itself unconstitutional.   In fact, the tougher attitude of the Court toward what equality under segregation meant was made abundantly clear in 1938 in the case of Missouri ex rel. Gaines v. Canada.[21] Here, Gaines, a Negro graduate of Lincoln University and a citizen of Missouri, was refused admission to the University of Missouri Law School solely upon the ground that he was a Negro. The state, however, agreed to pay his tuition in the law school of any adjacent state which would accept him, pending such time as Missouri should itself establish a Negro law school. The Supreme Court held that this was a violation of the separate-but-equal doctrine, and ruled that ".   .   .   petitioner was entitled to be admitted to the law school of the State University in the absence of other and proper provision for his legal training within the State." [22]   The Court further said:

> The basic consideration is not as to what sort of opportunities other States provide, or whether they are as good as those in Missouri, but as to what opportunities Missouri itself furnishes to white students and denies to negroes solely upon the ground of color.   .   .   .   Manifestly, the obligation of the State to give the protection of equal laws can be performed only where its laws operate, that is, within its own jurisdiction.[23]

The paramount significance of this decision is that it brought the segregation states, most of them poor economically, to the critical question of whether to try to duplicate their professional training institutions (law, medicine, education, business administration, dentistry, and so on) for their black students or to abolish them for whites. This was obviously a no-win type of choice since they could not abolish, and they could not, without great sacrifice, duplicate the institutional arrangements.

A similar case to that of *Gaines* occurred when a young black woman was refused admission to the law school of the University of Oklahoma, and when the refusal was appealed to the Supreme Court in 1948, Sipuel v. University of Oklahoma, the Court in a one-page opinion reaffirmed the ruling in the *Gaines* case. It said:

> The petitioner is entitled to secure legal education afforded by a state institution. To this time it has been denied her

21. 305 U.S. 337 (1938).

22. Id., at 352.

23. Id., at 350.

although during the same period many white applicants have been afforded legal education by the State. The State must provide it for her in conformity with the equal protection clause of the Fourteenth Amendment and provide it as soon as it does for applicants of any other group.[24]

Hence, once again a segregated state was given three choices: (1) admit the black student to the professional school; (2) provide a black professional school of comparable quality; or (3) close its professional school.

The next logical step was for blacks to demand admission to white schools regardless of the state having educational alternatives for blacks, and in Sweatt v. Painter (1950),[25] such a challenge was made. The issue here, therefore, was not whether the segregation of whites and blacks was valid. Instead, the question was based on the theory that separate facilities were valid only if they were equal. Of course, in common usage there are no degrees of equality; things or conditions are either equal or they are not equal. But the Supreme Court had not yet taken this view. Rather, at this point it had held that equality in accommodations meant not exact or mathematical equality but only "substantial" equality. In earlier cases, the Court had been extremely lenient in construing what "equality" required in the segregated educational systems of the South.[26] But in Sweatt v. Painter, in spite of the fact that the state of Texas had created a separate law school for blacks, the Court held that the black school was by no means the equal of the white school:

> Whether the University of Texas Law School is compared with the original or the new law school for Negroes, we cannot find substantial equality in the educational opportunities offered white and Negro law students by the State. In terms of number of the faculty, variety of courses and opportunity for specialization, size of the student body, scope of the library, availability of law review and similar activities, the University of Texas Law School is superior. What is more important, the University of Texas Law School possesses to a far greater degree those qualities which are incapable of ob-

24. 332 U.S. 631, 632–633 (1948).

25. 339 U.S. 629 (1950).

26. See, e. g., Cumming v. County Bd. of Educ., 175 U.S. 528 (1899); here the Supreme Court found no denial of equal protection of the laws in the failure of a Southern county to provide a high school for sixty black children, although it maintained a high school for white children. The Court seemed satisfied with the county's defense that it could not afford to build a high school for the blacks.

jective measurement but which make for greatness in a law school. Such qualities, to name but a few, include reputation of the faculty, experience of the administration, position and influence of the alumni, standing in the community, traditions and prestige. It is difficult to believe that one who had a free choice between these law schools would consider the question close.[27]

Thus the Court ruled that blacks had been denied equal protection of the laws.

At the same time, in McLaurin v. Oklahoma State Regents [28] the Supreme Court invalidated segregation of races within a single institution. This case involved a black graduate student who had been admitted to the College of Education of the University of Oklahoma, but was required to sit in a row in the classroom specified for black students, at a designated table in the library, and at a special table in the cafeteria. This, the Court held, hindered the black student's effective intellectual exchange with other students, and therefore, under the equal protection clause, the black student must be given the same treatment by the state as students of the white race.

In retrospect, perhaps the *Plessy* decision was forward-looking for its time, but the separate but equal formula and the passage of time did little to lessen the effects of discrimination. In 1950, in all the segregated states, there were fourteen medical schools for whites, none for blacks; sixteen law schools for whites, five for blacks; fifteen engineering schools for whites, none for blacks; five dentistry schools for whites, none for blacks. Following the *Sweatt*, and *McLaurin* decisions, however, most southern states quietly opened their colleges and universities to blacks. By 1952, only five states—Alabama, Florida, Georgia, Mississippi and South Carolina—still barred black students from their publicly supported institutions of higher education.[29] Normally, and in less controversial cases, a rule of constitutional law proclaimed by the high court in a particular case will be accepted and complied with by all those throughout the country to whom the rule clearly applies. But this compliance is technically voluntary, since only the parties to the case are immediately bound by the Court's ruling. It followed, therefore, that the more obstinate states could be compelled to comply with these Supreme Court rulings only as

27. 339 U.S. 629, 633–634 (1950).

28. 339 U.S. 637 (1950).

29. John Brubacher and Willis Rudy, *Higher Education in Transition* (New York: Harper and Row, Publishers, 1976), p. 78.

cases were brought against them in the courts and those courts applied to them such rules. Moreover, in the cases dealing with segregation that reached the Supreme Court after Plessy v. Ferguson, the "separate but equal" doctrine of that case was followed and never reexamined; and so the Court, following the rule that it will not decide constitutional issues if it can avoid doing so, granted relief to blacks, not because they were segregated, but because they were unequally treated under segregation.

Brown v. Board of Education—The End of "Separate But Equal"

Thus, the door had been opened a crack, but still the Court had not overruled Plessy v. Ferguson. Rather, by admitting that separate could sometimes be unequal, the Court had applied the equal protection clause to improve black opportunities in higher education. In the fall of 1952, however, the Supreme Court had on its docket cases from four states (Kansas, South Carolina, Virginia and Delaware) and from the District of Columbia, challenging the constitutionality of racial segregation in public elementary and secondary schools. In all of these cases the facts showed that ". . . the Negro and white schools involved have been equalized, or are being equalized, with respect to buildings, curricula, qualifications and salaries of teachers, and other 'tangible' factors." [30] Nonetheless, the black parents who filed these suits could easily have proved that the "tangible factors" of their children's education were not equal in most respects to that of white children in the same school districts. But they were through with that approach. Instead, they applied the "intangible factors" of inequality resulting from de jure segregation and thus attacked the constitutionality of segregation per se. So, after nearly sixty years, the Court had squarely before it the question of whether the "separate but equal" doctrine of Plessy v. Ferguson should be affirmed or reversed.

The five cases were argued together in December, 1952, and the nation waited in tense anticipation for the Court's decision. The Court, however, moved with careful deliberation, and on June 8, 1953, instead of handing down a decision, it ordered the cases restored to the docket to be reargued the next December. Apparently, there was some apprehension among the justices that any disagreement in the Court on the decision, or disagreement on the reasons for the decision, would aid those who would

30. The situation as restated in Brown v. Board of Educ. of Topeka, 347 U.S. 483 (1954).

resent and seek to thwart its ruling. So after three days of re-argument in December, 1953, the Court handed down its decision on May 17, 1954. But, as an indication of the high sense of responsibility felt by the justices in deciding a case of such vital national significance, the decision was given the Court's maximum weight: first, by issuing a unanimous decision; second, by writing only one opinion, not half a dozen; third, by having the Chief Justice write the opinion; and fourth, by setting for argument at a later time the problem of the nature of the decree by which its decision might best be given effect.

The decision, of course, dealt a death blow to the "separate but equal" doctrine in elementary and secondary education. "We conclude," wrote Chief Justice Earl Warren, "that in the field of public education the doctrine of 'separate but equal' has no place. Separate educational facilities are inherently unequal." Therefore, the black plaintiffs had been, ". . . by reason of the segregation complained of, deprived of the equal protection of the laws guaranteed by the Fourteenth Amendment." [31] The belief that segregated schooling could not be equal to desegregated schooling was explained as follows:

> We come then to the question presented: Does segregation of children in public schools solely on the basis of race, even though the physical facilities and other 'tangible' factors may be equal, deprive the children of the minority group of equal educational opportunities? We believe that it does.
> . . . . The effect of this separation on their educational opportunities was well stated by a finding in the Kansas case by a court which nevertheless felt compelled to rule against the Negro plaintiffs:
>
> "Segregation of white and colored children in public schools has a detrimental effect upon the colored children. The impact is greater when it has the sanction of law; for the policy of separating the races is usually interpreted as denoting the inferiority of the Negro group. A sense of inferiority affects the motivation of a child to learn. Segregation with the sanction of law, therefore, has a tendency to retard the educational and mental development of Negro children and to deprive them of some of the benefits they would receive in a racially integrated school system." Whatever may have been the extent of psychological knowledge at the time of Plessy v. Ferguson, this finding is amply

31. Id., at 495.

supported by modern authority. Any language in Plessy v. Ferguson contrary to this finding is rejected.[32]

In May, 1955—almost exactly one year after the first *Brown* decision—the Court announced the procedures to be followed for the orderly conversion of segregated public school systems to completely integrated ones. Reasonable time for alteration was given to local school officials with the appropriate United States district court judges expected to adjudicate fairly any petitions asking for immediate desegregation; [33] but in 1968, fourteen years after its first ruling against school segregation, the Court specifically withdrew its earlier grant of time to school authorities to work out the problems in bringing about desegration. The Court stated, "The time for mere 'deliberate speed' has run out. . . . Delays in desegregating school systems are no longer tolerable. . . . The burden of a school board today is to come forward with a plan that promises realistically to work and promises realistically to work now." [34]

Extension of the Brown Doctrine

In the wake of the *Brown* decision, the Board of Trustees of the University of North Carolina resolved to deny admissions to members of the Negro race. But, in Frasier v. Board of Trustees of the Univ. of North Carolina,[35] a suit was brought against the Board and the United States District Court held that Negroes as a class could not be excluded from the University solely because of their race. The court suggested that the *Brown* position of separate educational facilities as inherently unequal applied with greater force to students at the college-university level with its observation that "Indeed it is fair to say that [this prohibition] applies with greater force to students . . . in the concluding years of their formal education as they are about to engage in

32. Id., at 494. Technically there were four cases involving state schools and a fifth case involving the District of Columbia, which is under the legislative control of Congress. The four state-school cases were decided simultaneously and a single opinion written for all, while the fifth, Bolling v. Sharpe, 347 U.S. 497 (1954), was decided separately. Since the Constitution places no equal protection obligation on the federal government, the Court applied the due process clause in the Fifth Amend-ment in *Bolling* saying that ". . . discrimination may be so unjustifiable as to be violative of due process."

33. Brown v. Board of Educ., 349 U.S. 294 (1955).

34. Green v. County School Bd. of New Kent County, 391 U.S. 430, 438–439 (1968).

35. 134 F.Supp. 589 (D.C.N.C.1955); aff'd 350 U.S. 979 (1956).

the serious business of adult life." [36]   At the same time, the court carefully pointed out that the Board of Trustees retained the power to establish qualifications other than race for admission.

Subsequently, the applicability of the *Brown* doctrine to public higher education was specifically sanctioned by the U. S. Supreme Court through its affirming the *Frasier* decision.[37]   As in this case, during the last half of the fifties, the extension of the *Brown* decision's validation of black constitutional claims to equality was largely done by the Court through the technique of affirming lower court decisions without opinion.   It was clear that selective admission policies based on race were defunct, and, in fact, that the basic doctrine of the *Brown* case was broad enough to reach and strike down segregation in all of the remaining areas in which it still existed under state or federal law.

As observed earlier, however, more difficult equal protection issues were soon presented by the various affirmative action programs that deliberately weighted the scales in favor of blacks and other minority groups.   These programs reflected an increasing awareness that the mere elimination of formal barriers against minorities could not actually produce equality of opportunity. Therefore, proponents of such preferential treatment generally acknowledged an obligation to justify these programs as an exception to the "strict scrutiny" rule, often arguing that strict scrutiny applied only in cases of "invidious" discrimination and not majority discrimination.

Nonetheless, a growing number of affirmative-action opponents began to insist that the use of racial criteria violated the equal protection clause by discriminating against whites and thus that any such program be subjected to the "strict scrutiny" test—a standard which almost universally meant the "kiss of death" to governmental action when so reviewed.

Standards of Review Under Equal Protection

The Constitution does not forbid government from making distinctions among people, for it could hardly legislate without doing so.   What the Constitution forbids is an *unreasonable* classification.[38]   In general, a classification is unreasonable when there is

36. Id., at 592.

37. Frasier v. Board of Trustees of the Univ. of North Carolina, 134 F. Supp. 589 (D.C.N.C.1955); aff'd 350 U.S. 979 (1956).

38. Although there is no equal protection clause limiting the national government, the Fifth Amendment's due process clause has been construed to impose the same restraints on the national govern-

no "rational relationship" between the classification it creates and a permissible governmental purpose. For example, in 1971 a unanimous Supreme Court in Reed v. Reed stated that the preference Idaho gave to fathers over mothers in the administration of their children's estates "cannot stand in the face of the Fourteenth Amendment's command that no State deny the equal protection to any person within its jurisdiction. A criterion based on sex for the purpose of administering estates," said the Court, "is arbitrary and wholly unrelated to the objective of the statute." [39] Similarly, the Supreme Court has held that a state may not make ownership of property a requirement to serve on a school board,[40] nor may a state make it a crime for a doctor to prescribe a contraceptive device to an unmarried person.[41]

Nevertheless, under the traditional "limited scrutiny" or "rational basis" test, the judiciary tends to defer almost completely to the legislature. Briefly, the limited scrutiny test assumes the constitutional validity of the law and thus places the burden of proof upon those challenging the law. In effect, to pass this test a classification must be "reasonable, not arbitrary, and must rest upon some ground of difference having a fair and substantial relation to the object of the legislation, so that all persons similarly circumstanced shall be treated alike." [42] Therefore, if any facts can be pointed out that would justify a classification, it will be sustained. "It's enough that the State action be rationally based and free from invidious discrimination. . . . It does not offend the Constitution because the classification is not made with mathematical nicety or because in practice it results in some inequality." [43] To illustrate, the courts have upheld state university regulations requiring freshmen and sophomores to live in university housing [44] and regulations denying married students the privilege of having their children live with them in campus housing.[45] In sum, the extent of judicial deference under limited scrutiny is evidenced by an early statement of Chief Justice Earl Warren:

> [T]he States [are permitted] a wide scope of discretion in enacting laws which affect some groups of citizens differ-

ment. See, e. g., Bolling v. Sharpe, 347 U.S. 497 (1954).

39. 404 U.S. 71 (1971).

40. Turner v. Fouche, 396 U.S. 346 (1970).

41. Eisenstadt v. Baird, 405 U.S. 438 (1972).

42. F. S. Royster Guano Co. v. Virginia, 253 U.S. 412, 415 (1920).

43. Dandridge v. Williams, 397 U.S. 471, 483–485 (1970).

44. Prostrollo v. University of South Dakota, 507 F.2d 775 (8th Cir. 1974).

45. Bynes v. Toll, 512 F.2d 252 (2d Cir. 1975).

ently than others. The constitutional safeguard is offended only if the classification rests on grounds wholly irrelevant to the achievement of the State's objective. State legislatures are presumed to have acted within their constitutional power despite the fact that, in practice, their laws result in some inequality. A statutory discrimination will not be set aside if any state of facts reasonably may be conceived to justify it.[46]

Indeed, the limited scrutiny formulation proved so permissive that the equal protection clause was largely powerless to constrain legislative classifications. However, in the wake of the *Brown* decision it was soon recognized that certain "suspect" classifications affecting "fundamental interests" [47] required much more exacting justification. Thus today the judicial deference to the judgment of the legislature and its use of the less exacting "limited scrutiny" or "rational basis" test does not hold when a suspect classification or a fundamental right is involved. At this point the normal presumption of constitutionality is reversed and a more rigorous "strict scrutiny" test applies which requires the state to show that the classification serves a "compelling public interest" and that no less-restrictive alternative methods are available to achieve the same end.[48] Moreover, when applying strict scrutiny, courts refuse to speculate in order to discover a rationale for the classification,[49] and the courts will not uphold a classifying statute unless it provides the necessary means for im-

---

46. McGowan v. Maryland, 366 U.S. 420, 425–426 (1961).

47. The fundamental interests recognized by the Supreme Court have not been confined to those expressly guaranteed by the Constitution such as religion, speech, press and assembly. Others that have been included are the right to interstate travel, Shapiro v. Thompson, 394 U.S. 618 (1969), the right to vote, Harper v. Virginia Bd. of Elections, 383 U.S. 663 (1966), and the right to criminal appeals, Griffin v. Illinois, 351 U.S. 12 (1956). The Burger Court has generally refused to continue expanding the list. For example, where welfare benefits, Dandridge v. Williams, 397 U.S. 471 (1970) housing, Lindsey v. Normet, 405 U.S. 56 (1972) and education, San Antonio Independent School Dist. v. Rodriguez, 411 U.S. 1 (1973) were asserted to be fundamental rights, the Court did not require "strict scrutiny." On the other hand, Burger Court decisions in Stanley v. Illinois, 405 U.S. 645 (1972), Vlandis v. Kline, 412 U.S. 441 (1973), and Board of Educ. v. LaFleur, 414 U.S. 632 (1974), indicate that where important interests like parenthood, education and employment are adversely affected, a state may not make classifications without allowing an opportunity to show that they are appropriate.

48. See, e. g., Shapiro v. Thompson, 394 U.S. 618, 634 (1969).

49. See, e. g., McDonald v. Board of Election Commissioners, 394 U.S. 802, 809 (1969).

plementing and achieving its purpose under the "compelling state interest" and "least means" aspect of the strict scrutiny test.[50]

In this regard, the Supreme Court has declared that there are certain classifications that are "odious to our system," "constitutionally suspect," "subject to the most rigid scrutiny" and "in most circumstances irrelevant" to "any constitutionally acceptable legislative purpose." [51] Constitutionally suspect classifications, explained the Court, are those involving persons "saddled with such disabilities, or subject to such a history of purposeful unequal treatment, or relegated to such positions of powerlessness as to command extraordinary protection from the majoritarian political process." [52]

For some time, however, it appeared that the sharpest bite of the *Brown* decision was that *all* racial classifications involving the distribution of preferences and benefits were *per se* unconstitutional; that is, the Supreme Court seemed to agree with the first Justice Harlan, who, while dissenting in Plessy v. Ferguson, stated, "The Constitution is color-blind." Yet, Justice White's statement for the Court in Hunter v. Erikson (1969)— "The majority needs no protection against discrimination" [53] signaled an exception ("benign" discrimination). And in 1971, in North Carolina State Bd. v. Swann, the Supreme Court recognized that exclusive resort to a "color-blind" formalism "against the background of segregation, would render illusory the promise of Brown v. Board of Educ." The Court then noted:

> Just as the race of students must be considered in determining whether a constitutional violation has occurred, so must race be considered in formulating a remedy. To forbid, at this stage, all assignments made on the basis of race, would deprive school authorities of the one tool absolutely essential to fulfillment of their constitutional obligation to eliminate existing dual school systems.[54]

Subsequently, a federal district court held in Geier v. Dunn (1972) [55] that if good faith recruiting efforts to attract a more mixed student body failed to produce significant results, "the court may exact more" and that there is an affirmative duty im-

---

50. See, e. g., Loving v. Virginia, 388 U.S. 1, 11 (1967).

51. See, e. g., San Antonio Independent School Dist. v. Rodriguez, 411 U.S. 1 (1973), and Frontiero v. Richardson, 411 U.S. 677 (1973) and cases cited therein.

52. San Antonio Independent School Dist. v. Rodriguez, 411 U.S. at 28.

53. 393 U.S. 385, 391 (1969).

54. 402 U.S. 43, 45–46 (1971).

55. 337 F.Supp. 573 (D.C.Tenn.1972).

posed upon the state by the Fourteenth Amendment to dismantle the dual system of higher education. Also, in the same year another federal district judge in Adams v. Richardson [56] rebuked officials of the Department of Health, Education and Welfare (HEW) for what he regarded as their lack of aggressiveness in enforcing civil rights laws in secondary and higher education.

Of course the above examples are not intended as exhaustive; rather, they are merely illustrative of the fact that some years prior to *DeFunis* and *Bakke* racial classifications for remedial purposes had been approved by the courts. Obviously, therefore, a white complainant would not be successful by espousing the now overly simplistic position that a special admissions program was constitutionally invalid merely because it was based on racial and ethnic criteria. Still, a major issue was not yet settled; that is, none of these court decisions resulted in the denial of benefits or opportunities to the white majority class.

THE PREFERENTIAL ADMISSIONS CASES

DeFunis v. Odegaard

The *DeFunis* case, which reached the Supreme Court in 1974, marks the beginning of reverse discrimination lawsuits in higher education. It is a case which has become famous and one which offers a good view of the twists and turns often found in the history of a major case and a look as well into the admissions procedures which figure rather prominently in the lawsuit. It has been said that judges do not understand the nuances and subtleties involved in the professional school admission process, and many in higher education seem to share this view, but judges interpret and apply the law and, as we will see, show a disinclination to accept "nuances and subtleties" in admissions practices when viewed as whimsical and even unprofessional.

DeFunis v. Odegaard commenced in a Washington superior court in the fall of 1971 and eventually made its way to the United States Supreme Court where it was disposed of in the spring of 1974. In its three-year judicial history, *DeFunis* produced a flood of public comment (twenty six *amici curiae* at the U. S. Supreme Court level), placed a noticeable strain on the traditional friendly alliance between Jews and nonwhite minorities, and generated considerable anxiety and frustration in a nation with a palpable need for closure.

56. 351 F.Supp. 636 (D.C.D.C.1972).

Marco DeFunis, Jr., resident of the state of Washington, applied to the University of Washington School of Law for the class beginning September, 1971. Having been denied admission the previous year, DeFunis was understandably sensitive to the strength of the credentials supporting his application and the vulnerability of the competition for the limited number of places in the first year class. While not overwhelming, DeFunis' academic record was solid—an overall GPA of 3.7 (University of Washington) and a Law School Aptitude Test Score average of 582. He had taken the test three times; the last time, 1970, he had obtained a score of 668 placing him in the top seven percent of all law school applicants nationwide during the previous three year period. DeFunis also presented evidence of having financed much of his college education by working.

DeFunis' application was duly reviewed by the admissions committee along with 1601 others. A total of 275 applicants were notified of acceptance, and an additional 55 were placed on a waiting list. DeFunis was placed in the bottom quartile of the latter group and a short time later was informed that his application had been denied. Suspecting that he did not belong at the bottom of the scholastic heap, DeFunis promptly sued the University of Washington, its president, Charles Odegaard, and other University officials. The suit took particular aim at the University's affirmative action policy which gave preferential treatment to certain minority groups, namely, blacks, Chicanos, American Indians, and Philippine Americans.

In the complaint filed in superior court, DeFunis alleged that he had been wrongfully denied admission to the University of Washington School of Law, and, more to the point, that (1) persons with lesser qualifications than his had been admitted, and (2) no preference had been given him as a resident of the state of Washington. The main basis of the suit was an alleged violation of the Equal Protection Clause of the Fourteenth Amendment. The suit asked that the court order the defendants to admit and enroll DeFunis in the law school in the fall of 1971 and that upon failure to do so that the court award damages in the sum of $50,000. The court also was asked to restrain the law school from selecting students during the pendency of the action.

As shall be seen, the heart of DeFunis' contention was that he was the victim of reverse discrimination. How clear and compelling a case could he make? During the course of the nonjury trial the following facts were developed: (1) The University of Washington was indeed operating under an affirmative action policy which gave favored treatment in admissions to the four racial minorities mentioned. The University in court documents asserted its right to "constitutionally take into account, as one element in selecting from among qualified applicants for the study of law, the races of applicants in pursuit of a state policy to *mitigate* gross under-representation of certain minorities in the law school and in the membership of the bar." (2) Of the 330 applicants either admitted or placed on the waiting list, 224 had lower junior-senior GPA's than DeFunis and 106 had higher ones. For each applicant, the law school calculated a predicted first year average (PFYA). Included in this average were the junior-senior GPA and the average Law School Aptitude Test score. DeFunis obtained a PFYA of 76.23. Of the 155 students enrolled in the first year class in 1971, 29 had higher PFYA's and 74, including 38 minorities, lower PFYA's. There were 6 minorities admitted with higher PFYA's and 16 non-minorities admitted with lower PFYA's. (3) There was a significant subjective element in the admissions process which throughout the course of the litigation some judicial opinion found reasonable in amount and effect and, as shall be shown, other judicial opinion found arbitrary and capricious.

In October, 1971, the trial court entered its judgment in favor of DeFunis. The court ruled that in denying DeFunis admission to the law school and accepting less-qualified persons in his stead, the University of Washington had violated his rights under the Equal Protection Clause of the Fourteenth Amendment. The court said:

> In 1954, the United States Supreme Court decided that public education must be equally available to all regardless of race. After that decision the Fourteenth Amendment could no longer accommodate the needs of any race. .   .   . In my opinion the only safe rule is to treat all races alike
> .   .   . [57]

The court ordered the University to cease admitting to the law school "in a number which would preclude the admission of plaintiff, Marco DeFunis, Jr., to the 1971–72 first year class, should his admission eventually be ordered by this court." Not waiting to be so ordered, the University promptly admitted DeFunis to the law school and appealed to the Washington State Supreme Court.

---

57. As quoted in the Washington Supreme Court decision, DeFunis v. Odegaard, 82 Wash. 11, 507 P.2d 1169, 1178 (1973).

It was not until March, 1973, that the Washington State Supreme Court handed down its lengthy decision. The Court split 4:2 with the chief points of the majority opinion as follows:

> The law school sought to carry forward this University policy in its admission program, not only to obtain a reasonable representation from minorities within its classes, but to increase participation within the legal profession by persons from racial and ethnic groups which have been historically denied access to the profession and which, consequently, are grossly underrepresented within the legal system. In doing so, the Admissions Committee followed certain procedures which are the crux of plaintiff's claimed denial of equal protection of the laws.[58]

> The dean of the law school testified that the law school has no fixed admissions quota for minority students, but that the committee sought a reasonable representation of such groups in the law school. He added that the law school has accepted no unqualified minority applicants, but only those whose records indicated that they were capable of successfully completing the law school program.[59]

> *Brown* did not hold that all racial classifications are *per se* unconstitutional; rather, it held that invidious racial classifications—i. e., those that stigmatize a racial group with the stamp of inferiority—are unconstitutional. Even viewed in a light most favorable to plaintiff, the "preferential" minority admissions policy administered by the law school is clearly not a form of invidious discrimination. The goal of this policy is not to separate the races, but to bring them together. And, as has been observed, preferential admissions do not represent a covert attempt to stigmatize the majority race as inferior. . . . Subsequent decisions of the United States Supreme Court have made it clear that in some circumstances a racial criterion *may* be used—and indeed in some circumstances *must* be used—by public educational institutions in bringing about racial balance.[60]

And in answering the oft-quoted opinion of Justice John Harlan in the famous 1896 case of Plessy v. Ferguson that "Our Constitution is color-blind" the Washington Supreme Court added:

> Thus, the Constitution is color conscious to prevent the perpetuation of discrimination and to undo the effects of past segregation.[61]

58. Id., at 1175.

59. Id., at 1176.

60. Id., at 1179.

61. Id., at 1180.

However, the Court did select the "strict scrutiny" test:

> The burden is upon the law school to show that its consideration of race in admitting students is necessary to the accomplishment of a compelling state interest.[62]

And then indicated that the preferential admissions program passed the "compelling state interest" and "least means" muster:

> In light of the serious underrepresentation of minority groups in the law schools, and considering that minority groups participate on an equal basis in the tax support of the law school, we find the state interest in eliminating racial imbalance within public legal education to be compelling.[63]

> No less restrictive means would serve the governmental interest here; we believe the minority admissions policy of the law school to be the only feasible plan "that promises realistically to work, and promises realistically to work *now*." [64]

Finally, and of considerable significance, the Court pointed out:

> We particularly note that while race was a major factor, it was not the only factor considered by the committee in reviewing minority applications. No minority quota was established; rather, a reasonable representation of such groups in the law school was sought. Also, the dean of the law school testified (and the trial court did not find otherwise) that only "qualified" minority applicants were admitted . . . [65]

The Court's Chief Justice and an associate justice, however, saw the facts and issues quite differently. In a lengthy dissenting opinion the Chief Justice wrote:

> Racial bigotry, prejudice and intolerance will never be ended by exalting the political rights of one group or class over that of another. The circle of inequality cannot be broken by shifting the inequities from one man to his neighbor. To aggrandize the first will, to the extent of the aggrandizement, diminish the latter. There is no remedy at law except to abolish all class distinctions heretofore existing in law. For that reason, the constitutions are, and ever ought to be, color blind. Now the court says it would hold

62. Id., at 1182.

63. Id.

64. Id., at 1184 and quoting from Green v. County School Bd., 391 U.S. 430, 439 (1968).

65. Id., at 1185.

the constitutions color conscious and they may stay color blind. I do not see how they can be both color blind and color conscious at the same time toward the same persons and on the same issues, so I dissent.[66]

In view of the findings of at least one subsequent case, the dissenting justices' opinion regarding an arbitrary and capricious admissions process deserves more than passing notice. Evidently the dissent was based upon the fact that a number of minorities were admitted with far lesser qualifications (one example cited: GPA of 2.37 and LSAT of 475), but also upon the discovery of some rather odd admissions files. One file of an apparently successful minority applicant with a GPA of 2.63 bore the notation: "Excellent recommendations, sound record. Divorced with five kids. Could make it if her personal situations could be worked out, lightened load possibility? Admit." [67] Another admitted applicant's file (from a student with a 2.89 GPA) carried the lament: "We seem to have bungled this one pretty conclusively. He's got us." [68] The dissent objected, sometimes vigorously, to the casualness with which, in its view, applications were processed. Student members of the admissions committee, in particular, came in for harsh criticism.

Insofar as legal precedents were concerned, the Chief-Justice cited a 1972 district court ruling which held that it is unconstitutional to give preference in employment and promotions to members of ethnic minorities in administrative and supervisory positions. The case was Anderson v. San Francisco Unified School Dist. wherein the court said:

No one race or ethnic group should ever be accorded preferential treatment over another. . . . There is no place for race or ethnic groupings in America. Only in individual accomplishment can equality be achieved. [citation omitted] [69]

An interesting situation now existed. The Washington State Supreme Court had reversed the trial court's judgment. The Court had generously refrained from ordering DeFunis to turn in his horn books, but second year law student DeFunis apparently did not feel securely ensconced in school. He quickly appealed to U. S. Supreme Court Judge William Douglas, the justice responsible for stays in the nine western states, for an order stay-

---

66. Id., at 1189.

67. Id., at 1195.

68. Id.

69. Id., at 1197.

ing the State Supreme Court ruling until the case could be heard
by the U. S. Supreme Court. Justice Douglas issued such a stay
order thus setting the stage for a full-dress review of this powerful issue.

When all the *DeFunis* briefs, both pro and con, were assembled
at the U. S. Supreme Court, it became clear that many of the
greatest forces in America had an interest in the case. Supporting DeFunis' position were groups such as the Anti-Defamation
League of B'nai B'rith, the American Jewish Committee and the
AFL–CIO. Among the organizations on the other side were
the National Association for the Advancement of Colored People,
the American Bar Association, and the National Urban League.
The famous Harvard Law professor, Archibald Cox, presented a
brief supporting the University's position. Cox's brief made the
point that a university should have the freedom to establish criteria that will achieve the institution's objectives, and this included giving added weight to the applications of disadvantaged minorities. He said:

> In recent years, many institutions of higher education have
> determined that their objectives should include removing
> the special obstacles facing disadvantaged minority groups
> in access to higher education, business and professional op-
> portunities, and professional services—obstacles which are
> deeply-ingrained consequences of the hostile public and pri-
> vate discrimination pervading the social structure. Giving
> favorable weight to minority status in selecting qualified
> students for admission is an important method of reducing
> these disadvantages.

On the other side, Alexander Bickel and Philip Kurland argued
that race may be used as a factor for preference only where there
is a specific finding of past discrimination and even then it may
only be used to provide a remedy for such discrimination. They
said:

> A racial quota creates a status on the basis of factors that
> have to be irrelevant to any objectives of a democratic so-
> ciety, the factors of skin color or parental origin. A racial
> quote derogates the human dignity and individuality of all
> to whom it is applied. A racial quota is invidious in prin-
> ciple as well as in practice. . . . The evil of the racial
> quota lies not in its name but in its effect. A quota by any
> other name is still a divider of society, a creator of castes,
> and it is all the worse for its racial base, especially in a so-

ciety desperately striving for an equality that will make race
irrelevant, politically, economically and socially.

Oral arguments were heard by the Supreme Court on February 26, 1974 and with the many interested parties and a host of
onlookers poised to receive from the nine venerated justices
the law of the land, the Court announced its decision April 23,
1974. Splitting in its strikingly characteristic way, 5:4, the Court
declared DeFunis v. Odegaard moot.[70] In a brief six-page opinion, the Court explained why it should not rule on the case. The
Court observed that DeFunis was at that moment enrolled in his
final quarter at the University of Washington School of Law
and that therefore his rights would not be affected by the Court's
ruling—no matter which way it went. The Court recalled North
Carolina v. Rice (1971) where it had ruled that "federal courts
are without power to decide questions that cannot affect the
rights of litigants in the case before them." The Court continued:

> The inability of the federal judiciary to review moot cases
> derives from the requirement of Art. III of the Constitution
> under which the exercise of judicial power depends upon the
> existence of a case or controversy.[71]

The Court pointed out that DeFunis had not cast his case as
a class action; some have inferred from the Court's opinion that,
had DeFunis done so, the Court would have felt more obliged to
render a decision.

Not surprisingly, the Supreme Court's refusal to rule on the
case hardly served to quiet the national debate. Indeed, there
was a torrent of criticism of the Court for its failure to face
squarely the important issues raised by DeFunis. Yet, as if to
underscore the case's mootness, DeFunis quickly graduated from
law school.

Not the least odd of the episodes in the lengthy adjudicatory
history of *DeFunis* is the fact that the Court opinion—before too
much time had passed—was eclipsed by a dissenting opinion.
Justice William Douglas, often regarded as one of the most liberal
justices ever to sit on the Supreme Court, had written a spirited
and lengthy dissent to *DeFunis*. The Douglas dissent has since
been analyzed in dozens of articles and quoted by courts deciding
similar cases. The Douglas opinion might strike the reader as a

---

70. 82 Wash. 11, 507 P.2d 1169 (1973),
    vacated as moot 416 U.S. 312 (1974).   71. 416 U.S. at 312.

curious piece; in fact, extracts from it have appeared in briefs and articles prepared by diametrically-opposed interests.

First, Douglas asserted that the case was not moot: "Because of the significance of the issues raised I think it is important to reach the merits." [72] Yet, Douglas seems to have seen merits distributed fairly widely. Those who believe that Douglas rejected the idea of preferential treatment must contend with the following statement from his opinion:

> I cannot conclude that the admissions procedure of the Law School of the University of Washington that excluded DeFunis is violative of the Equal Protection clause of the Fourteenth Amendment. [73]

Yet, Douglas was clearly troubled over the type of admission policy which gave rise to the *DeFunis* case.

> What places this case in a special category is the fact that the school did not choose one set of criteria but two, and then determined which to apply to a given applicant on the basis of his race. The Committee adopted this policy in order to achieve "a reasonable representation" of minority groups in the Law School. Although it may be speculated that the cultural or racial biases in the LSAT or in the candidates' undergraduate records, the record in this case is devoid of any evidence of such bias .   .   . [74]

Perhaps the best remembered quote from Douglas is the following:

> The Equal Protection Clause commands the elimination of racial barriers, not their creation in order to satisfy our theory as to how society ought to be organized. [75]

Douglas implied that even if the law might be properly employed to advance the progress of certain minority groups, somebody should take note of the poor Appalachian white and the second generation Chinese in San Francisco.

72. Id., at 320.

73. Id., at 344.

74. Id., at 325–326.

75. Id., at 331. Douglas also claimed that under the Fourteenth Amendment professional school applications must be considered in a "racially neutral way." Id., at 340.

Moreover: "So far as race is concerned, any state-sponsored preference [of] one race over another .   .   . is in my view 'invidious' and violative of the Equal Protection Clause" but then weakened this point by concluding that he could not say whether DeFunis was discriminated against because of his race. Id., at 343–344.

While the legal equation yielded a law degree for Marco DeFunis, it left everyone else—spectators and interested parties alike—empty-handed and frankly in something of a muddle. Three courts had looked at the case and had seen it quite differently. It is worth noting that the case essentially was handled by state courts—somewhat surprising in view of the trend toward more federal involvement in cases affecting individual rights in the constitutional law area.

At the time *DeFunis* reached the Supreme Court it was hailed as a test case—a timely case capable of establishing an important precedent. In retrospect, such a claim is hard to support. Reading a signal from such a decision—a decision not to decide—led to speculation regarding the Court's "real" thinking on the case. Was it simply maintaining the tradition of minimal judicial involvement in university affairs? Or, was it that the Court was exercising prudence in deferring to time and the wisdom of administrators in education, industry, and government to refine affirmative action and thereby gain broader acceptance of the principle? A host of other rationales might be mentioned in addition to the one the Court used, i. e., the case technically was moot.

Whatever the Court's motive—if a collective motive can be assumed—a question about the value of *DeFunis* as a test case remains. As a general rule, the law requires that the plaintiff show that a significant *injury* has occurred. Often, the more dramatic and irreversible the injury, the more likely the settlement or judgment favorable to the plaintiff. Though there is little doubt that it would be possible to argue convincingly that denied admission to law school resulted in an injury, it is suggested that a clearer, more conventional example of injury could be found in a noneducational preferential treatment case. And if the test case must come from education, it certainly could be argued that it come not from denied admission to law school but to medical school.

In the first place, accessibility to law school is far greater than to medical school. There has been developing in recent years a substantial network of alternative law schools for those unable to attend mainline law schools. In the case of DeFunis, denied admission to the University of Washington School of Law did not foreclose a legal education. In fact, DeFunis was accepted at no less than four major law schools.

There are not only far fewer major medical schools than major law schools, there are essentially no minor or alternative medical schools. In addition, it could be argued that a clearer example of injury could be shown in denied medical school admission inasmuch as the premedical curriculum is typically narrower and as such, more deterministic than the prelaw curriculum.

If measured by the amount of coverage and comment in both popular and professional publications, *DeFunis* certainly ranks as an extremely important case. More recently, however, a California case, Bakke v. Regents of the Univ. of California, presented *DeFunis* with a serious challenge for pre-eminence in the reverse discrimination field. It involved an unsuccessful medical school applicant and was heard in the October, 1977 term of the United States Supreme Court.

Bakke v. Regents of the Univ. of California

Allen Bakke was a blond, blue-eyed honor student in engineering at the University of Minnesota and served with the Marines in Vietnam, rising to the rank of Captain. He later married, settled in the San Francisco suburbs and began a promising career as a space-agency engineer. Then, Bakke decided that he really wanted to be a doctor. His enthusiasm was so strong that in off hours he took pre-med courses and worked as a hospital volunteer. In 1973, at the age of 32, he applied to the University of California at Davis School of Medicine. Rejected for two consecutive years (1973 and 1974) Bakke learned that his college grades and aptitude-test scores ranked well above many of the students who had been accepted. The only explanation, as far as he could determine, was that they were black or Mexican-American or Asian-Americans, and he was white.

Thus, like Marco DeFunis, Jr., Allan Bakke was white and a rejected professional-school applicant; and, in a similar fashion, Bakke filed a "reverse discrimination" lawsuit against the Regents of the University, seeking an order compelling the University to admit him to the medical school. Moreover, when the case reached the U. S. Supreme Court in 1977, many of the groups which had submitted friends-of-the-court briefs in the *DeFunis* case, submitted briefs in *Bakke*. In fact, nearly 60 separate legal briefs, many on behalf of several organizations, were filed in the *Bakke* case, the greatest number of *amicus* briefs in Supreme Court history.

In the 1973 and 1974 entering classes to which Bakke applied, the Davis medical school was faced with 2,644 and 3,737 applicants respectively, but the school, which had not been founded until 1968, could only admit 100 students to its freshman classes. The policy of the medical school admissions authorities was to determine a numerical rating for each applicant based upon an assessment of the applicant derived from grade point average (GPA), scores on the national Medical College Admission Test (MCAT), letters of recommendation, the application and interview summary, as well as consideration of the applicant's motivation, character, imagination, and the type and locale of the practice he/she anticipated entering in the future. The composite numerical score was then calculated to establish a "benchmark" criterion for selection, although exceptions to strict numerical ranking could be made in special circumstances. However, the evidence at trial in the state superior court indicated that the medical school maintained two separate admissions programs— a special program for "disadvantaged students" with 16 places to fill, which could have included white students but never did, and a regular admissions program for the other students with 84 places to fill.

Students identified on their application forms as disadvantaged members of minorities (black, Chicano, American Indian, among others) were placed under the special committee as a separate admissions pool to compete only against each other. In making its selection, however, the special committee, unlike the regular committee, did not summarily reject an applicant with a GPA of less than 2.5 (out of a possible 4.0). Moreover, the trial court found that white students were barred from the special admissions program. Nonetheless, in both years that Bakke applied for admission he presented impressive credentials. His GPA was 3.51, his MCAT average was at the 90th percentile. When all admissions factors were considered, Bakke had a composite score of 468 out of a possible 500 (1973) and 549 out of a possible 600 (1974). On the other hand, admitted minority students from the disadvantaged pool for the two years in question had a mean MCAT slightly below the 50th percentile. In 1973, the lowest GPA of a successful minority applicant was 2.11, in 1974, 2.21.

At the heart of Bakke's complaint before the superior court, therefore, was his contention that he was qualified for admission but that he was denied admission solely because he was a member of the caucasian race. Bakke thus alleged that he had been denied "equal protection of the laws" under the Fourteenth Amendment, as the special admissions programs for minorities had applied separate preferential admissions standards resulting in less qualified persons being admitted.

The trial court agreed—to a point. It found that Bakke was entitled to have his application evaluated without regard to his race or the race of any other applicant but refused to order the University to admit him since the court determined that he would not have been selected even if there had been no special program for minorities.

The result was plainly unsatisfactory to both plaintiff and defendant. Bakke was left with a hollow victory, and the University's special admission program was in serious jeopardy. Both sides in the dispute therefore appealed—the University appealed the first part of the trial court's order, Bakke appealed the second part.

Customarily, the case would have been heard on appeal in a state court of appeal, but as California Supreme Court Justice Stanley Mosk explained in the California Supreme Court decision: "We transferred the cause directly here, prior to a decision in the Court of Appeal, because of the importance of the issues involved." [76]

The subsequent California Supreme Court decision, although the Court treated the case as applicable only to education, seemed to be a sweeping and stunning setback for affirmative action in general and preferential admissions procedures in professional schools in particular. In a near unanimous decision, splitting only 6:1, perhaps the most prestigious state court in the country rejected the Davis Medical School procedure by affirming the lower court's finding that its special admissions program was invalid. In striking down the special admissions program the Court stated:

> To uphold the University would call for the sacrifice of principle for the sake of dubious expediency and would represent a retreat in the struggle to assure that each man and woman shall be judged on the basis of individual merit alone, a struggle which has only lately achieved success in removing legal barriers to racial equality. The safest course, the one most consistent with the fundamental interests of all races and with the design of the constitution is to hold, as we do, that the special admission program is unconstitutional because it violates the rights guaranteed to the majority by the equal

---

76. Bakke v. Regents of the Univ. of California, 132 Cal.Rptr. 680, 684, 553 P.2d 1152, 1156 (1976). Declaring that the University could not take race into account in making admissions decisions, the trial court held the challenged program in violation of the Fourteenth Amendment (equal protection), the State Constitution, and Title VI of the Civil Rights Act of 1964.

protection clause of the Fourteenth Amendment of the United States Constitution.[77]

The Court also reversed the trial court's ruling that the burden of proof was upon the plaintiff to demonstrate that he would have been admitted to the 1973 or 1974 entering class in the absence of the invalid preferences. The Court's reasoning was that since Bakke had successfully demonstrated the University's unconstitutional discrimination against him that the burden of proof had then shifted to the University. However, the Court remanded this part of the case to the trial court to determine under the proper burden of proof whether Bakke would have been admitted absent the special admissions program.[78] So, as far as Bakke was concerned, all that expensive, protracted and complicated litigation was almost for naught—he was two years older and still not in med school. And worse, the University of California promptly appealed the decision to the United States Supreme Court. Thus, along side a nagging feeling of *deja vu*, Bakke must have felt that such triumphs were indeed costly, perhaps best illuminated by a flashback to Pyrrhus' remark—"Another such victory and we are undone."

But before checking out Bakke's final win-loss record, we should examine the legal rationale upon which the California Supreme Court based its decision; it will be an essential step towards an understanding of the subsequent United States Supreme Court hearing where Bakke, now 37 years old and still wanting to be a doctor, awaited some kind of determinative judgment. At the very least, the California Ruling seemed to auger well for the opponents of affirmative action.

The California Supreme Court first noted that although the special admissions program classified applicants by race, that fact did not render the procedure *per se* unconstitutional. Rather, the Court indicated that classification by race had been upheld in a number of federal court cases where the purpose of the classification was to benefit rather than to disable minority groups; for example, such classification had been approved to achieve integra-

---

77. Id., at 1171.

78. However, when the University later conceded that it could not meet the burden of proving that Bakke would have been rejected, regardless of the special admissions program, the trial court entered an order directing his admission to the school. At this point, the U.S. Supreme Court, on application of the university, intervened by staying the order until a petition for *certiorari* could be filed.

tion in the public schools. On the other hand, the Court observed:

> These cases differ from the special admission program in at
> least one critical respect, however. In none of them did the
> extension of a right or benefit to a minority have the effect
> of depriving persons who were not members of a minority
> group of benefits which they would otherwise have en-
> joyed. . . . The disadvantages suffered by a child who
> must attend school some distance from his home or is trans-
> ferred to a school not of his qualitative choice cannot be
> equated with the absolute denial of a professional education,
> as occurred in the present case.[79]

The Court next rejected the University claim that it was not
choosing between "qualified" and "unqualified" applicants, but
simply exercising discretion among qualified students who differed only by degree. The Court instead noted that Bakke was
also qualified for admission and that his allegation that he was
better qualified for admission than the minority students accepted
under the special admissions program at least had not been dis-
proved by the University. The Court therefore concluded that the
question it had to decide was whether the rejection of a better-
qualified applicant on racial grounds was constitutional:

> The issue to be determined thus narrows to whether a racial
> classification which is intended to assist minorities, which
> also has the effect of depriving those who are not so classified
> of benefits they would enjoy but for their race, violates the
> constitutional rights of the majority. . . . Two dis-
> tinct inquiries emerge at this point; first, what test is to be
> used in determining whether the program violates the equal
> protection clause; and second, does the program meet the
> requirements of the applicable test.[80]

The Court indicated that as a general rule a classification could
be made by government regulations, without violating the equal
protection clause, "if any stated facts reasonably may be conceived" for its justification (the "rational basis" test). The
Court, however, stated that where such classification was made on
the basis of race and worked to the detriment of the complaining

79. Id., at 1160–1161.

80. Id., at 1162. Without passing
on the state constitutional or federal statutory (Title VI) grounds
cited in the trial court's judgment,
the California Supreme Court instead focused exclusively upon the
validity of the special admissions
program under the equal protection clause of the Fourteenth
Amendment.

party, it became a "suspect classification" and thus subject to "strict scrutiny." Under these circumstances the Court noted that (1) the purpose of the classification must serve a "compelling state interest," and (2) it must also be shown by rigid scrutiny that the state could not have accomplished its compelling interests by means which would have imposed lesser limitations on the rights of the parties disadvantaged by the classification.[81] A key related point was that the burden of proof in both respects shifted to the government.

The University contended, however, that the "strict scrutiny" test was only applicable to a racial classification that discriminated against a minority, not majority discrimination. The Court also rejected this argument saying that the "lofty purpose" of the equal protection clause of the Fourteenth Amendment, "to secure equality of treatment to all, is incompatible with the premises that some races may be afforded a higher degree of protection against unequal treatment than others." [82] Thus, the Court ruled that the "strict scrutiny" test was applicable.

As a result, the University sought to justify its special admissions program by arguing that the use of race as one of its criteria constituted a compelling interest of the people of California. The point was that by increasing the number of minority students, many of whom could be expected to practice in ghetto areas, it would not only improve health care to the poor and minorities, but minority doctors would also serve as models for minority youngsters considering medicine. Moreover, it was argued, minority physicians would have a better relationship with patients of their own race and a greater desire to treat diseases which were especially prevalent among their groups.

The Court strongly rejected most of these assertions in terms of meeting the "strict scrutiny" test inasmuch as the University failed to meet its burden of demonstrating that reasonable alternatives were not available to meet such goals. The Court therefore turned to the question of appropriate alternatives:

> We observe and emphasize in this connection that the University is not required to choose between a racially neutral admission standard applied strictly according to grade point averages and test scores, and a standard which accords preference to minorities because of their race. . . . The University is entitled to consider, as it does with respect to applicants in the special program, that low grades and test

81. Id.   82. Id., at 1163.

scores may not accurately reflect the abilities of some disadvantaged students; and it may reasonably conclude that although their academic scores are lower, their potential for
success in the school and the profession is equal to or greater
than that of an applicant with higher grades who has not
been similarly handicapped. . . . In addition, the University may properly as it in fact does, consider other factors
in evaluating an applicant, such as the personal interview,
recommendations, character, and matters relating to the
needs of the profession and society, such as an applicant's
professional goals. In short, the standards for admission employed by the University are not constitutionally infirm except to the extent that they are utilized in a racially discriminatory manner. Disadvantaged applicants of all races
must be eligible for sympathetic consideration, and no applicant may be rejected because of his race, in favor of
another who is less qualified, as measured by standards applied without regard to race. We reiterate, in view of the
dissent's misrepresentation, that we do not compel the University to utilize only the "highest objective academic credentials" as the criterion for admission.[83]

The Court continued:

In addition to flexible admission standards, the University
might increase minority enrollment by instituting aggressive programs to identify, recruit, and provide remedial
schooling for disadvantaged students of all races who are
interested in pursuing a medical career and have an evident
talent for doing so.[84]

The Court then suggested that the state might consider increasing
the number of places available in the medical schools, either by
allowing additional students to enroll in existing schools or by
expanding the schools. Finally, the Court concluded:

None of the foregoing measures can be related to race, but
they will provide for consideration and assistance to individual applicants who have suffered previous disabilities,
regardless of their surname or color. So far as the record
discloses, the University has not considered the adoption of
these or other nonracial alternatives to the special admission
program.[85]

83. Id., at 1165.   85. Id.

84. Id., at 1166.

Thus, though the majority opinion clearly sympathized with the University's desire to enroll more minority group members, it still felt compelled to strike down the program:

> While a program can be damned by semantics, it is difficult to avoid considering the University scheme as a form of an education *quota*, benevolent in concept perhaps, but a revival of quotas nevertheless. *No college admission policy in history has been so thoroughly discredited in contemporary times as the use of racial percentages.* Originated as a means of exclusion of racial and religious minorities from higher education, *a quota becomes no less offensive when it serves to exclude a racial majority.*[86]

The lone dissenting opinion of Justice Tobriner vigorously disagreed with the majority on two levels, both on the choice of "strict scrutiny" as the controlling standard and on the practicalities of its application to the situation presented. That is, he first asserted that the majority used the wrong standard of review by erroneously equating the University's classifications with traditional racial classifications. In so doing, the majority failed "to distinguish between *invidious racial classifications* and remedial or *'benign' racial classifications.*"[87] Secondly, he faulted the majority for its determination that the minority students were less qualified than the rejected nonminority students; he believed that the majority had overemphasized the importance of the standardized criteria. Because school officials have discretion to determine admissions criteria, Justice Tobriner reasoned that the departure from strictly objective criteria was a permissible policy choice.[88]

Regardless, the California Supreme Court had spoken and ruled that the University's admissions policy, which included a quota for nonwhites, was a violation of the Fourteenth Amendment. A nagging question about the sweep of the California decision, however, remained. In a rare interview, Justice Mosk hinted that the result might have been different had the University established a history of discrimination against nonwhite applicants.

---

86. Id., at 1171 (emphasis added).

87. Id., at 1173 (emphasis in original).

88. Justice Tobriner compared the Davis program with the preference granted by many universities to athletes and relatives of alumni. Id., at 1174. It should be kept in mind that the admission program in question, though purportedly allowing all who were considered to be economically or educationally disadvantaged to be reviewed under the special program, had never accepted a nonminority during the five years since its inception in 1969. Id., at 1156–1157.

Mosk stated that such evidence would have had "some significance legally." He also stated his opinion that under Title VII of the Civil Rights Act of 1964, " . . . minorities are entitled to a preference if they have been previously discriminated against in employment" and then indicated that it was possible to analogize employment to school admissions.[89]

Whether a finding of past discrimination would have overcome other objections expressed by the Court is problematical. But the Court left little doubt that it would not accept the argument that the small number of minorities enrolled in professional schools constituted such evidence. Neither did the Court seem inclined to relax traditional admissions standards because of the University's argument that standardized tests had a drastic impact on minority enrollments:

> In the recent case of Washington v. Davis [426 U.S. 229, 1976] the United States Supreme Court has made it clear that the standard for adjudicating claims of racial discrimination on constitutional grounds is not the same as the standard applicable to cases decided under Title VII, and that absent a racially discriminatory purpose, *a test is not invalid solely because it may have a racially disproportionate impact.*[90]

Other Pertinent Preferential Treatment Cases

It is interesting to note that the majority opinion in *Bakke* pointed out that there were not yet any United States Supreme Court decisions directly in point. The majority, however, did appear to rely on one recent high court ruling, McDonald v. Santa Fe Trail Transportation Co. (1976),[91] to demonstrate the Supreme Court's present tendency to evaluate discrimination in the same manner for both blacks and whites.[92] But Justice Trobriner

---

89. Arval A. Morris, "Mosk Defends U.C. Handling of 'Reverse Bias Case,'" *Los Angeles Times*, August 24, 1977, p. 24.

90. 553 P.2d at 1169 (emphasis added). In Griggs v. Duke Power Co., 401 U.S. 424 (1971), for example, the Supreme Court held invalid a private employer's rule forbidding future employment or promotion of persons who did not have the educational equivalent of a high school diploma. The rule was invalidated on the basis of Title VII because it eliminated proportionally more blacks than whites and the compa-

ny could not show that a diploma or an equivalency test demonstrated job-related skills. These factors interacted to create preferential treatment for white applicants. The decision striking down the criterion did not create preferential treatment for uneducated blacks; it merely eliminated a nonfunctional device which had the effect of giving whites preferred treatment.

91. 427 U.S. 273 (1976).

92. 553 P.2d at 1164.

responded that in *McDonald* the Court pointedly refrained from ruling on the permissibility of affirmative action programs, "whether judicially required or otherwise prompted." [93]

McDonald is noteworthy for several reasons. Very briefly, the facts are that McDonald and another white employee of Santa Fe were discharged after being accused of misappropriating company property. Another employee who was black was similarly charged but not dismissed. The whites sought, unsuccessfully, to obtain relief from the Equal Employment Opportunity Commission (EEOC) and then sued in federal court, alleging impermissible racial discrimination under Title VII of the Civil Rights Act of 1964. Their case was dismissed and the United States Court of Appeals affirmed.

To the surprise of many, the Supreme Court granted certiorari and in June, 1976, handed down its decision. The opinion was written by Justice Marshall, the Court's only black, and there were but two limited dissents. The Court found for the plaintiffs and in the process reversed the lower courts' decisions on two critical points.

On the question of Title VII, which specifically prohibits discharge from employment on the basis of race, Marshall wrote that EEOC has

> . . . consistently interpreted Title VII to proscribe racial discrimination in private employment against whites on the same terms as racial discrimination against nonwhites, holding that to proceed otherwise would constitute a dereliction of Congressional mandate to eliminate all practices which operate to disadvantage the employment opportunities of any group protected by Title VII, including Caucasians.[94]

Justice Marshall, however, directed most of his attention to Section 1981 of the Civil Rights Act of 1866. The position of Santa Fe was that 1981, providing that "all persons . . . shall have the same right . . . to make and enforce contracts . . . as is enjoyed by white citizens . . ." was

---

93. Id., at 1176 fn. 3 and quoting *McDonald*, 427 U.S. at 281 fn. 8.

94. 427 U.S. at 279–280. Still, eight federal circuit courts had either upheld or spoken approvingly of preferential hiring quotas under Title VI which disadvantaged whites. In two of these cases the Supreme Court denied certiorari. See, e. g., Carter v. Gallagher, 452 F.2d 315, 328 (8th Cir.), cert. denied 406 U.S. 950 (1972); and United States v. Lathers Local 46, 471 F.2d 408, 414 (2d Cir.), cert. denied 412 U.S. 939 (1973).

inapplicable to whites. Santa Fe maintained that the implication of the wording was that nonwhites were the intended beneficiaries of the protection, the position that had been upheld by the lower federal courts. Marshall, for the Court, took vigorous exception:

> The bill ultimately enacted as the Civil Rights Act of 1866 was introduced by Senator Trumbill of Illinois as a "Bill to protect all persons in the United States in their civil rights" and was initially described by him as applying to "every race and color." [95]

McDonald, therefore, reflected a strong Supreme Court reluctance to apply different standards when determining the rights of minority and majority group members. It also suggested that the protection of the Fourteenth Amendment applies to "any person" regardless of race. Surely the Davis Medical School quota system, though promoted as benign, was not benign to a more qualified white applicant when denied admission because of his non-preferred racial status. Nevertheless, *McDonald* did not, nor had any other Supreme Court holding at that time, require a "strict scrutiny" standard of review for both benign and invidious classifications.

In fact in Alevy v. Downstate Medical Center of New York (1976),[96] a New York Court of Appeals affirmed a lower court's refusal to use a strict scrutiny approach since the discrimination alleged was "benign" in purpose. The plaintiff, a white male and *magna cum laude* graduate of Brooklyn College, applied for admission to the Medical Center but was eventually turned down. Subsequently he alleged that the Medical Center had "arbitrarily granted preferential treatment" to minority applicants.[97]

Alevy's quantitative credentials were as impressive as Bakke's. He had an undergraduate GPA of 3.47 and an MCAT average at the 94th percentile. His science MCAT score was at the 99th percentile. The Medical Center maintained that due to the large number of applicants, factors readily discerned through the interviewing process were given more weight than actual quantitative factors, but then admitted that applicants from minority groups were screened separately and further conceded that "had the petitioner been a minority group member he probably would have been accepted." [98]

95. Id., at 287.

96. 39 N.Y.2d 326, 384 N.Y.S.2d 82, 348 N.E.2d 537 (1976).

97. Id., at 85.

98. Id., at 86.

Although the Court of Appeals unanimously upheld the Medical Center and its special admissions program, the Court sounded a note of caution:

> Our recognition that benign discrimination is permissible should not be taken as tacit approval of such practices. We reiterate that preferential policies, laudable in origin and goal, may be laden with substantial detrimental side effects which make their use undesirable.[99]

After reviewing the rigidity of the two-tiered equal protection approach and noting that the United States Supreme Court more recently seemed to be striking a middle ground in terms of result, the Court of Appeals indicated how it would have decided had it been necessary to apply the equal protection clause to instances of "reverse discrimination":

> The Fourteenth Amendment was adopted to guarantee equality for Blacks, and by logical extension has come to include all minority groups. . . . It would indeed be ironic and, of course, would cut against the very grain of the amendment, were the equal protection clause used to strike down measures designed to achieve real equality for persons whom it was intended to aid. We reject, therefore, the strict scrutiny test for benign discrimination as, in our view, such an application would be contrary to the salutary purposes for which the Fourteenth Amendment was intended.[1]

Thus, the Court indicated that the standard should be one of rationality, and the question to ask is whether the preferential treatment satisfies a substantial state interest.

> However the interest need not be urgent, paramount or compelling since it need ony be found that, on balance, the gain to be derived from the preferential policy outweighs possible detrimental effects.[2]

Under this middle-ground test, therefore, the "compelling state interest" component of the strict scrutiny test would be replaced by the less compelling "substantial state interest."

> In sum, in proper circumstances, reverse discrimination is constitutional. However, to be so, it must be shown that a substantial interest underlies the policy and practice and, further, that no nonracial, or less objectionable racial, classifications will serve the same purpose.[3]

---

99. Id., at 91.

1. Id., at 90.

2. Id.

3. Id.

On the other hand, a few weeks before the California Supreme Court ruled that Allan Bakke had been unconstitutionally discriminated against by the University of California at Davis, a United States District Court in Hupart v. Board of Higher Educ.[4] ruled that 25 Caucasian and Asian students had been the victims of "intentional racial discrimination" by the City College of New York in its six-year biomedical program.[5]

In the admissions procedure which resulted in the rejection of Hupart and the other plaintiffs, the court found no formal quotas but "rather ill-defined standards." [6] Nevertheless, it was determined that the manner in which the special admissions program was administered "the pervasive and overriding criterion" was race which in effect amounted to a 50 percent quota for blacks and Hispanics.[7]

At first it was thought, like the University of California, the New York Board had deliberately adopted a policy of minority preference to fulfill the goals of integration and improved medical service in minority communities. As the case developed, however, it became clear that the committee's use of race as the sole basis for making many of the selections was guided by an unwritten and unapproved 50 percent quota for blacks and Latins, leaving Caucasians, Asians, and others in the remaining 50 percent. Actually, the College and the Board's own policy forbade the use of race as an admissions standard under any circumstances.

The facts of *Hupart*, therefore, only demonstrated unauthorized racial discrimination by an agent of the state.[8] However, even though the need for the court to be specific about its equal protection standard was thus eliminated, the decision is noteworthy in a number of respects. First, the court stressed its conviction that the state or its agencies (such as City College) must have arrived at its racial preference through a deliberate and conscious choice, or it will fail to meet even a rational basis test.

> Whatever standard of scrutiny is ultimately fashioned in "reverse discrimination" cases, it is clear that the State cannot justify making distinctions on the basis of race without having first made a deliberate choice to do so . . . .

---

4. 420 F.Supp. 1087 (D.C.N.Y.1976).

5. Id., at 1105.

6. Id., at 1091.

7. Id., at 1107.

8. The court noted that the NAACP Legal Defense and Educational Fund, which had intended to participate as *amicus* in the case, withdrew when these facts became apparent. Id., at 1105 fn. 40.

While perhaps not every classification by race is "odious," every distinction made on a racial basis is at least suspect and must be justified . . . . It is not for the court to supply a rational or compelling basis (or something in between) to sustain the questioned state action.[9]

The clear message of the court was that racial classifications must always be justified and that the state must supply that justification. It is also interesting to note that the court refused to speculate as to the possible justifications for the classification but nevertheless implied a middle ground.

Second, the court found that not only had the committee's admissions process violated equal protection but due process as well:

It is by now familiar law that an agency's violation of its own regulations may in and of itself constitute a violation of the process. . . . Defendants cannot sustain their burden of justification by coming to court with an array of hypothetical and "post facto" justifications for discrimination that has occurred either with their approval or without their conscious and formal choice to discriminate as a matter of official policy.[10]

In the next case, Flanagan v. President and Directors of Georgetown College,[11] scholarship aid came under fire under the claim of "reverse discrimination." Flanagan, a white law student who had been denied financial aid, sued the College under Title VI of the Civil Rights Act of 1964.[12] He claimed that he was the victim of race discrimination because sixty percent of the available scholarship funds were allocated to eleven percent of the students who were members of minority groups.

The College claimed that "minority" status was accorded to whites suffering from social, educational, cultural or economic disadvantages, as well as to decernible ethnic and racial groups. The court found this insufficient, however, since blacks, Hispanics, American Indians, and Asian Americans qualified automatically, whereas whites had to make a special showing to

9. Id., at 1106.

10. Id., at 1107.

11. 417 F.Supp. 377 (D.C.D.C.1976).

12. Title VI provides that: "No person in the United States shall, on the ground of race, color, or national origin, be excluded from participation in, be denied the benefits of, or be subjected to discrimination under any program or activity receiving Federal financial assistance."

receive consideration.[13]   Next, the College claimed that it had adopted a bona fide affirmative action plan in 1972 to increase minority representation in the law school.   The court also rejected this approach:

> Defendants would have this court conclude that affirmative action is any action which gives a preference to "minorities" regardless of its impact on "non-minorities." While there is authority for the proposition that any affirmative action granting preferences to one race or sex is constitutionally infirm, Cramer v. Virginia Commonwealth Univ., 415 F.Supp. 673 (1976), this court need not rely on such an extreme position.   Affirmative action may be justified provided it does not violate the non-discrimination provisions of Title VI and is administered on a racially *neutral* basis.[14]

Furthermore, said the court, financial need cuts across racial, cultural and social lines:

> There is no justification for saying that a "minority" student with a demonstrated financial need of $2,000 requires more scholarship aid than a "non-minority" student with a demonstrated financial need of $3,000.   To take such a position, which the defendants have, is *reverse discrimination* on the basis of race which cannot be justified by a claim of affirmative action.[15]

Title VI, of course, applies to most private as well as public schools, and it is generally assumed that the equal-protection issue will control the interpretation of Title VI.[16]   Also of particular interest in interpreting the meaning of Title VI with respect to minority preference programs are two implementing regulations issued by HEW.   The first provides that recipients of federal assistance (both public and private institutions) "may properly give special consideration to race, color or national origin to make the benefits of its program more widely available." [17]   And the other provides that:

> In administering a program regarding which the recipient has previously discriminated against persons on the ground

---

13.   417 F.Supp. at 382.

14.   Id., at 384 (emphasis in original).

15.   Id. (emphasis added).

16.   It was this assumption that formed part of the basis for many

of the *amici curiae* briefs submitted in *DeFunis* and *Bakke*.

17.   38 Fed.Reg. 17979, July 9, 1973:- 45 CFR 80.5(j).

of race, color or national origin, the recipient *must* take affirmative action to overcome the effects of prior discrimination. *Even in the absence of such prior discrimination a recipient in administering a program may take affirmative action to overcome the effects and conditions which resulted in limiting participation by persons of a particular race, color or national origin.*[18] (emphasis added)

In *Flanagan,* however, it was held that unless an institution could show a history of prior discrimination, the strict scrutiny approach would apply to a racially-preferred classification [19] —a test which usually leads to an automatic conclusion that the classsification at issue is unconstitutional. Moreover, the court rejected the college's affirmative action program and insisted that any benefits distributed under Title VI provisions must be "racially *neutral.*" The *DeFunis* and *Bakke* decisions also took under consideration past discrimination, but in *DeFunis* it was not considered a controlling factor since it was decided that the state interest in integrating the legal profession did not become less compelling because the admission procedures were not implemented to remedy a prior constitutional violation.[20] In fact, while purporting to use the same strict scrutiny approach *DeFunis* reached a different result.

On the other hand, the strict scrutiny approach was flatly rejected in *Alevy* since the reverse discrimination alleged was "benign" in purpose. Instead, and similar to the implication in *Hupart,* the court suggested a compromise between strict scrutiny and rational basis—a middle-ground "substantial interest" approach. Significantly, none of the aforementioned cases employed the rational basis standard of review, even though they all involved benign classifications. Yet, the United States Supreme Court on one occasion had approved "benign" discrimination by using the rational basis standard. That is, in Morton v. Mancari (1974)[21] the Court unanimously upheld a statutory and administrative policy giving preference to qualified Indians

---

18. 38 Fed.Reg. 17979, July 9, 1973:- 45 CFR 80.3(b)(vii)(6); made applicable to admissions at 45 CFR 80.4(d)(1) and (2) and at 45 CFR 80.5(e).

19. 417 F.Supp. at 384. See, e. g., Rosenstock v. Board of Governors of the Univ. of North Carolina, 423 F.Supp. 1321, 1325 (D.C.N.C.1976), where the court held that since the university was guilty of prior discrimination and because its special admissions program sought "to include, rather than isolate, students of different races" the program was "not subject to strict scrutiny."

20. 507 P.2d at 1183.

21. 417 U.S. 535 (1974).

in the Bureau of Indian Affairs (BIA). The Court explained the practice as one not involving race at all, but "reasonably designed to further the cause of Indian self-government and to make the BIA more responsive to the needs of its constituent groups." [22] Of course this reason is strikingly similar to one of the arguments advanced in support of preferential admissions: the need for more minority professionals to serve minority communities.

It is also interesting to note that the United States Supreme Court in Lau v. Nichols [23] upheld the same Title VI regulations as condemned in *Flanagan* and required the San Francisco school system to provide special bilingual education to students of Chinese ancestry. In other words, the Supreme Court held that the school system *must* classify children on the basis of race and then provide members of that class special instructional programs in their native language. However, in comparing *Flanagan* and *Lau* it must be noted that while both cases dealt with the issue of bestowing a benefit on one class and not another, *Lau* did not deny an opportunity to one class in order to grant a benefit to the other. As with Marco DeFunis, Allan Bakke, Martin Alevy and Hupart, it was the loss of opportunity that Flanagan was fighting.

Of course, much of the concern about preferential treatment has focused on its practical consequences for non-preferred individuals. But the *Morton* and *Lau* distinction is important because it shifts the focus from the rights of individuals to the appropriateness of the remedy in overcoming the effects of continuing discrimination. Thus, even though the Supreme Court deliberately ducked the issue in *DeFunis, Bakke* presented the Court with the opportunity once again to clarify what was presently a very confused area of the law. The issue was the same as addressed by the California Supreme Court: "whether a racial classification which is intended to assist minorities, but which also has the effect of depriving those who are not so

---

22. Id., at 554. A federal district court apparently took this logic one step further in Grove v. Ohio State Univ. College of Veterinary Medicine, 424 F.Supp. 377 (D.C.Ohio 1976). In this case a thrice-rejected white applicant alleged that school officials denied him due process and equal protection by admitting less qualified students.

The court, however, dodged the underlying preferential treatment issue with: "Strict scrutiny was not necessary since there was no indication that race, alienage, national origin, or sex had been a factor in the unequal treatment."

23. 414 U.S. 563 (1974).

classified of benefits they would enjoy but for their race, violates the constitutional rights of the majority." [24]

There is no question about the need to bring minority group members into the mainstream of society. Still, the problem is one of means, not of ends. And added to the problem of means is the fact that the entire history of American jurisprudence has been one of expanding legal rights for everyone. Indeed, the position of the California Supreme Court was that Allan Bakke should receive the same protection as a member of any other race.[25] But the United States Supreme Court is the final arbiter of what that protection is, and thus it was hoped that the Court would clarify this point in a well-reasoned and deliberate decision.

Indisputably, some hoped that the Court would differentiate between invidious and benign classifications and therefore subject the latter to a more lenient middle-tier analysis. At the very least it was believed that preferential treatment could be justified as an emergency measure—much like the Court upheld Japanese exclusion orders in *Korematsu*.[26] Yet others believed just as strongly that any government-sponsored preference of one race over another was in violation of the equal protection clause.

Bakke and the United States Supreme Court

The variety and intensity of the social, political and emotional arguments involved in the discussion of affirmative action in general, and Regents of the Univ. of California v. Bakke [27] in particular, presented the Supreme Court with a very real dilemma. Apocalyptics on both sides were predicting an explosion if their views failed to exit victorious. However, with the dexterous performance of Justice Powell the Court responded with a low-key formulation and perhaps defused a bomb.

First, Justice Powell joined four brethren—Chief Justice Burger and Justices Stevens, Stewart and Rehnquist—to declare the Davis Medical School's admissions program in violation of Title VI and the Fourteenth Amendment and to require Bakke's

24. 553 P.2d at 1162.

25. Id., at 1163.

26. The Court is on record as having upheld invidious discrimination twice, both times within the context of World War II as a "compelling" measure necessary to national survival in time of war, Korematsu v. United States, 323 U.S. 214 (1944); Hirabayashi v. United States, 320 U.S. 81 (1943).

27. 98 S.Ct. 2733 (1978).

admission to the School. Then, Powell joined the other four Justices—Brennan, White, Marshall and Blackman—to concede that race could be a proper factor to consider in admissions policies.[28]

Thus, it appeared that Powell would speak for the Court, but, as we shall see, that is questionable.

Justice Powell began by pointing out that the interpretation of Title VI would be controlled as a constitutional issue:

> Examination of the voluminous legislative history of Title VI reveals a congressional intent to halt federal funding of entities that violate a prohibition of racial discrimination similar to that of the Constitution. . . . [Thus], Title VI must be held to proscribe only those racial classifications that would violate the Equal Protection Clause . . . .[29]

Next, Justice Powell provided a revealing clue as to the final outcome:

> The guarantees of the Fourteenth Amendment extend to persons. Its language is explicit: "No state shall . . . deny to any person within its jurisdiction the equal protection of the laws". . . . The guarantee of equal protection cannot mean one thing when applied to one individual and something else when applied to a person of another color. If both are not accorded the same protection, then it is not equal. . . . It is far too late to argue that the guarantee of equal protection to *all* persons permits the recognition of special wards entitled to a degree of protection greater than that accorded others.[30]

The University of California, however, claimed that Bakke's exclusion from medical school subjected him to no stamp of inferiority; that is, the classification was "benign" rather than "invidious" and therefore asserted that the program was constitutional. Nonetheless, Powell was disinclined to accept either

---

28. More precisely, the Court split into three groups: Stevens, Stewart, Rehnquist and Burger, who argued that the Davis special admissions program violated Title VI; Brennan, White, Marshall and Blackman, who contended that the special admissions program was legitimate because race is a proper factor to consider; and, finally, Powell, who agreed with the first group that the admissions program was invalid and agreed with the second group on the point that race is a permissible factor under both Title VI and the Fourteenth Amendment.

29. 98 S.Ct. at 2745, 2748.

30. Id., at 2748, 2751 (emphasis in original).

the toothless rational basis test or a middle-standard of review simply because the classification lacked "invidiousness." Instead, he found the University rationale unsupportable and thus turned towards the fatal "strict scrutiny" approach:

> Petitioner [the University of California] urges us to adopt for the first time a more [lenient] view of the Equal Protection Clause and hold that discrimination against members of the white "majority" cannot be suspect if its purpose can be characterized as "benign." . . . [31] These individuals are likely to find little comfort in the notion that the deprivation they are asked to endure is merely the price of membership in the dominent majority and that its imposition is inspired by the supposedly benign purpose of aiding others.[32]

> Moreover, there are serious problems of justice connected with the idea of preference itself. First, it may not always be clear that a so-called preference is in fact benign. . . . Second, preferential programs may only reinforce common stereotypes holding that certain groups are unable to achieve success without special protection based on a factor having no relationship to individual worth. . . . Third, there is a measure of inequity in forcing innocent persons in respondent's [Bakke's] position to bear the burdens of redressing grievances not of their making.[33]

Another defect in the special program was its similarity to historically suspect quota systems in "that white applicants could not compete for the 16 places reserved solely" for minorities.[34] "Whether this limitation is described as a quota or a goal, it is a line drawn on the basis of race and ethnic status." [35] Hence, Powell recognized serious, in fact fatal, constitutional questions in plans that used quota systems irrespective of qualifications.

Nevertheless, [the University] argues that the [California Supreme Court] erred in applying strict scrutiny to the special admissions programs because white males, such as [Bakke], are not a "discrete and insular minority" requiring extraordinary protection from the majoritarian political process. . . . This rationale, however, has never

---

31. Id., at 2750–2751.

32. Id., at 2751, fn. 34.

33. Id., at 2752–2753.

34. Id., at 2748, fn. 26.

35. Id., at 2748.

been invoked as a prerequisite to subjecting racial or ethnic distinctions to strict scrutiny. Nor has this Court held that discreteness and insularity constitute necessary preconditions to a holding that a particular classification is invidious.[36]

Justice Powell in fact flatly refuted the position that only discrimination against minorities was suspect and therefore invidious, since any "denial to innocent persons of equal rights and opportunities may outrage those so deprived and therefore may be perceived as invidious." [37] Even though the motives behind a policy using racial criteria might be socially worthy, "[r]acial and ethnic distinctions of any sort are inherently suspect and thus call for the most exacting judicial examination." [38] Therefore, Powell rejected the University's assertion that "benign" classifications should be distinguished because no absolute deprivation is imposed on the majority class, or because racial classifications might be used remedially.

Disparate constitutional tolerance of such classifications well may serve to exacerbate racial and ethnic antagonisms rather than alleviate them. . . . Also, the mutability of a constitutional principle, based upon shifting political and social judgments, undermines the chances for consistent application of the Constitution from one generation to the next, a critical factor of its coherent interpretation. . . . Political judgments regarding the necessity for the particular classification may be weighed in the con-

36. Id. Reference is made to Justice Stone's famous *Carolene Products* footnote which called for "more searching judicial inquiry" where "prejudice against discrete and insular minorities may be a special condition." United States v. Carolene Products Co., 304 U.S. 144, 152 fn. 4 (1938). Thus, the University's position was that strict scrutiny should be applied only to those classifications designed to exclude, disadvantage, or stigmatize "discrete and insular minorities." Also, according to the dissent—Justices Brennan, White, Marshall and Blackman—the notion of "stigma" is the crucial element in analyzing racial classifications. Id., at 2785.

37. Id., at 2751, fn. 34.

38. Id., at 2749. Powell pointed out that the Court "declared as much in the first cases explicitly to recognize racial distinctions as suspect: 'Distinctions between citizens solely because of their ancestry are by their very nature odious to a free people whose institutions are founded upon the doctrine of equality.'" *Hirabayashi*, 320 U.S. 81, 100 (1943); and: "'. . . [A]ll legal restrictions which curtail the rights of a single racial group are immediately suspect. That is not to say that all such restrictions are unconstitutional. It is to say that courts must subject them to the most rigid scrutiny.'" *Korematsu*, 323 U.S. 214, 216 (1944).

stitutional balance . . . but the standard of justification [strict scrutiny] will remain the same.[39]

Though not necessarily explicit, certain implications in Powell's remarks seem clear. If the Supreme Court permitted the use of reverse discrimination as a temporary corrective measure to reach the ultimate goal of a color-blind society, it would eventually encounter the difficulty of recognizing when the need for correction no longer existed, and in eliminating a preference which certain minorities would have come to expect. Moreover, once a minority preference was rooted in the law, courts would then be faced with deciding which ethnic groups qualified as minority classes and, in extreme cases, would have to decide whether a particular individual was or was not a member of a preferred race. Thus, the courts would be faced with the classic "Gordian Knot" in unraveling the limits of racial preference—even if such preference is acknowledged as temporarily desirable.

Next, in response to the University's claim "that on several occasions this Court has approved preferential classifications without applying the most exacting scrutiny," Justice Powell declared any such analogy faulty. First, these cases involved clearly determined prior discrimination—"not just by society at large"—whereas in *Bakke* there was no prior intentional discrimination by the University. Another distinguishing factor he noted was that no complete deprivation of benefits had occurred in these cases, whereas a person such as Bakke suffered an absolute deprivation of a benefit when denied a place in a professional school.[40]

Thus, "[w]hen a classification denies an individual opportunities or benefits enjoyed by others solely because of his race or ethnic background, it must be regarded as suspect," and strict scrutiny applies. Of course the most difficult inquiry mandated by the strict scrutiny standard is that regarding a "compelling state interest." At this point, however, Powell seemed to suggest a reduced or middle-tiered approach: "a State must show

39. Id., at 2753.

40. Id., at 2753–2756. E. g., the school desegregation decisions, which seemed to approve racial classifications employed to desegregate educational institutions, were discounted because in that context the classifications resulted in no clear detriment to the majority. Employment decisions were also inapplicable as precedent because the preferences in those cases were approved only after a Court or administrative unit found a pattern of previous invidious discrimination.

that its purpose of interest is *substantial,* and that its use of the classification is 'necessary . . . to the accomplishment' of its purpose or the safeguarding of its interests." [41] He also indicated that the two-track admissions program is impermissible in the absence of appropriate "judicial, legislative, or administrative bindings of constitutional or statutory violations," [42] which, despite the problem of "shifting political and social judgments," opens the possibility for schools to turn to the political process (e. g., state legislatures or civil rights commissions) for the necessary findings and tailoring of remedies.

Nevertheless, the University failed to answer the "substantial interest" inquiry to Powell's satisfaction. He then suggested some alternatives (e. g., Harvard's and Princeton's admissions policies) which did not call for racial classifications and concluded that the Davis Medical School's special admissions program was not necessary:

> If petitioner's purpose is to assure within its student body some specified percentage of a particular group merely because of its race or ethnic origin, such a preferential purpose must be rejected not as insubstantial but as facially invalid. Preferring members of any one group for no reason other than race or ethnic origin is discrimination for its own sake. This the Constitution forbids.[43]

> [One] . . . goal asserted by petitioner is the attainment of a diverse student body. This clearly is a constitutionally permissible goal for an institution of higher education. . . . It may be assumed that the reservation of a specified number of seats in each class for individuals from the preferred ethnic groups would contribute to the attainment of considerable ethnic diversity in the student body. *But petitioner's argument that this is the only effective means of serving the interest of diversity is seriously flawed. . . . The diversity that furthers a compelling state interest encompasses a far broader array of qualifications and characteristics of which racial or ethnic origin is but a single important element.*[44]

In summary, it is evident that the Davis special admission[s] program involves the use of an explicit racial clas-

---

41. Id., at 2756–2757 (emphasis added). The state's ability to choose "substantial interests" would be far less limited than "compelling interest."

42. Id., at 2758.

43. Id., at 2757.

44. Id., at 2761 (emphasis added).

sification never before countenanced by this Court. It tells applicants who are not Negro, Asian, or "Chicano" that they are totally excluded from a specific percentage of the seats in an entering class. No matter how strong their qualifications, quantitative and extracurricular, including their own potential for contribution to educational diversity, they are never afforded the opportunity to compete with applicants from the preferred groups for the special admission seats. At the same time, the preferred applicants have the opportunity to compete for every seat in the class.

The fatal flaw in petitioner's preferential program is its disregard of individual rights as guaranteed by the Fourteenth Amendment. . . . Such rights are not absolute. But when a State's distribution of benefits or imposition of burdens hinges on the color of a person's skin or ancestry, that individual is entitled to a demonstration that the challenged classification is necessary to promote a substantial state interest. Petitioner has failed to carry this burden. For this reason, that portion of the California court's judgment holding petitioner's special admissions program invalid under the Fourteenth Amendment must be affirmed.[45]

Justice Powell, however, next suggested constitutional support for carefully tailored flexible affirmative action plans:

In enjoining [the University] from ever considering the race of any applicant, however, the courts below failed to recognize that the State has a substantial interest that legitimately may be served by a properly devised admissions program involving the competitive consideration of race and ethnic origin. For this reason, so much of the California court's judgment as enjoins petitioner from any consideration of the race of any applicant must be reversed.[46]

In fact at this point the Court's decision becomes difficult to comprehend because of a multitude of elements. That is, there is some doubt whether Justice Powell spoke for the Court on a number of the issues discussed so far. Not one of the other eight Justices concurred with Powell in his discussion of an appropriate standard of review or permissible and impermissible purposes for considering race in admissions decisions. The

---

45. Id., at 2764.   46. Id.

concurring Justices agreed with Justice Powell on two narrow points:

> . . . that Title VI . . . prohibits [quota-type] programs such as that at the Davis Medical School . . . [and,] [a]ccordingly, these Members of the Court form a majority of five affirming the judgment of the Supreme Court of California insofar as it holds that respondent Bakke "is entitled to an order that he be admitted to the University." [47]

Moreover, the four dissenting Justices believed that the special admissions program was valid and laudable since it was voluntarily designed to overcome the effects of past discrimination in this country.

Under the circumstances, it is not at all clear what educators might do to make race-conscious admissions programs pass judicial muster, but future cases will almost certainly shed some more light on what constitutes permissible affirmative action.

CONCLUDING OBSERVATIONS

The reverse discrimination cases discussed in this chapter, particularly *DeFunis* and *Bakke*, seem to reveal the following:

1.   If possible, courts will avoid definitive statements on the constitutionality and legality of preferential admissions, presumably because they lack unambiguous guidance from the United States Supreme Court.

2.   Private institutions are no longer well insulated against challenges involving preferential treatment.

3.   A student litigant's chances of successfully pressing a reverse discrimination allegation depend largely upon the strength of his credentials and upon the magnitude of disparity between his credentials and that of preferred minority applicants.

4.   Courts generally view quite skeptically any special admissions practices resembling a quota.

5.   Courts are more sympathetic to preferential treatment in the presence of hard evidence of past discrimination by the institution.

6.   Courts will look at the care with which an institution has designed its special admissions program; a high standard of

47. Id., at 2766.

professionalism in implementing such programs should be maintained.

It is in this latter area—"the lack of demonstrable, systematic, clearly documented guidelines for making judgments about applicants"—where institutions of higher education appear most vulnerable to "the stultifying consequences of litigation." According to Winton H. Manning, Senior Vice President for Research and Development, Educational Testing Service, "educational due process requires that institutions adhere to 'Principles of Good Practice in Admissions.'" In summarizing this chapter, it would be difficult to improve on Manning's ten basic principles:

(1) Educational institutions should clearly describe their admissions policies and explicitly state how these policies are related to the goals and objectives of the institution.

(2) Institutions should publicly describe their admissions criteria and provide information to applicants that is complete enough to permit students to make a reasonable estimate of the likelihood of their meeting these standards.

(3) Whatever criteria are used, the educational institution should routinely allow applicants the procedural opportunity to demonstrate that those particular criteria or standards are inappropriate for assessing their qualifications.

(4) Institutions should use the same admissions process for all candidates considered for the same program.

(5) Where exceptions to uniformity of process, criteria and standards are made for particular *classes* of applicants, this policy should be publicly articulated with particular attention to the legal restraints on such actions.

(6) The criteria employed in the admissions process must be validated—that is, demonstrably shown to measure qualities relevant to the legitimate educational objectives of the educational program. Additionally, criteria should not be used that cannot be shown to be *reliably* assessed.

(7) Upon request, a rejected applicant should be given a statement of the reason(s) for his or her rejection and a

means of appeal if he or she challenges the institution's explanation.

(8) Selection criteria used by institutions should represent a reasonably abroad array of those qualities shown to be relevant, rather than relying solely upon a single index of competence derived from ability tests and grades.

(9) Institutions should ensure that all those who participate in the process of implementing admissions decisions are trained and competent in performing the complex task of evaluating candidates for admission.

(10) Institutions should periodically invite external audit of their admissions policies and practices in order to assure the public and other constituencies that the process that actually goes on conforms with publicly stated policies, principles and procedures.[48]

---

48. Carnegie Council on Policy Studies in Higher Education, *Public Policy and Academic Policy.* (In a Report of the Carnegie Policy Council on Studies in Higher Education, entitled *Selective Admissions in Higher Education.*) San Francisco: Jossey-Bass, 1977, pp. 1–17.

Chapter 8

EQUAL PROTECTION: SEX, HOUSING, HANDICAPPED, OUT–OF–STATE TUITION, APPEARANCE

I thank thee, O Lord, that thou has not created me a
woman.

> (Daily Orothodox Jewish Prayer for males;
> also Sophie Portnoy's complaint)

But two hundred years ago Judith Murray wrote:

> Is it upon mature consideration we adopt the idea
> that nature is partial in her distributions? Is it indeed
> a fact that she hath yielded to one half the human spe-
> cies so unquestionable a mental superiority? May we
> not trace the source [of this judgment that men are in-
> tellectually superior to women] in the difference in edu-
> cation and continued advantages? . . . [Is] it rea-
> sonable, that a candidate for immortality, for joys of
> heaven, an intelligent being, . . . should at present
> be so degraded, as to be allowed no other ideas, than
> those which are suggested by the mechanism of a pud-
> ding, or the sowing of the seams of a garment?

> (quoted in Eleanor Flexner, *Century of Struggle*)

SEX DISCRIMINATION

As a majority of humankind, women clearly comprise the larg-
est "group" in the world and share every racial, class, ethnic,
religious, and regional alignment that one might imagine. But
women also constitute the only group which is both treated unequally as a whole and whose members live in greater intimacy
with their "oppressors" than with each other.

In America, the assertion that equal opportunity exists for all is
generally defended on the grounds that there is equal access to the
opportunity structure. Nevertheless, prior to 1861 and the Civil
War, there were only ten institutions of higher education where
women, like men, could pursue a full four-year course of studies
leading to an A.B. The normative definition of "woman's place"
as set forth by the dominant culture was that a woman's first goal

360

in life was to marry and have children and that such a role largely excluded other possibilities. Thus, in 1837, two hundred and one years after Harvard opened its doors to men, when Oberlin College granted admission to four women, it was still something more than premature to say that conditions had really changed in higher education.

And to make the equal-access problem even worse for women, as late as 1913 the eminent educational psychologist, Edward L. Thorndike, could make the statement that women could not possibly learn as well as men because their brains were smaller (and have the theory generally accepted as true). Hence, even in the 1950s and eary 1960s, it seldom occurred to most female students to question why male students outnumbered them three to one; perhaps it simply meant more Saturday night dates. Nor did they seem troubled because they were required to live in campus dorms while many of their male classmates lived off campus. If their dorm roommates opted for home economics while their boyfriends took premed and prelaw, that seemed to be merely a matter of choice. If all their professors happened to be male, and their advisors too, that was simply the way of the world. After all they were fortunate just to be there.

By the early 1960s, however, behavior and attitudes toward and among women were changing sharply. Undoubtedly, much of this change came about as a result of the black civil rights movement and the growing recognition that blacks had equal rights under the law, and thereby equal access to the opportunity structure. In fact a constellation of social and economic factors had come together, each reinforcing the others, to create a total pattern that ensured a quickening transformation of "woman's place." Simply put, a new awareness was beginning to jog women out of their complacency.

Higher education today, therefore, faces the challenge of meeting the needs of female students who are entering college in increasing numbers and diversity. The federal government, not only in official reports, but in legislation has increasingly shown extensive interest in providing women educational opportunities.

One of the first of these reports was the result of work accomplished by the President's Commission on the Status of Women. Entitled *American Women* (1963), it recommended that the "structure of adult education . . . be drastically revised" in order to "provide practicable and accessible opportunities, developed with regard for the needs of women . . . to continue education beyond high school." [1]

Title VII of the Civil Rights Act of 1964, Executive Order 11375, and Public Law 92–318 (Title IX) followed. Yet before concluding our brief story that everyone lived happily ever after, it is necessary to face up to the fact that tradition dies hard and that women have not found these changes as emancipating as they expected them to be.

In 1964, for instance, the Chairman of the House Rules Committee, Howard W. Smith, who opposed the Civil Rights Bill then being debated in the House of Representatives, inadvertently rather than purposefully helped the cause of women's rights. Assuming he could get the whole bill laughed off the floor by injecting a foolish note, Smith suggested adding the word "sex" wherever the phrase "race, color, or national origin" appeared in Title VII, the section of the bill spelling out equal employment opportunities. Of course much laughing and joking followed his proposal, and in fact the occasion became known as "ladies day." Nonetheless, the Civil Rights Act passed with its "foolish" addition, and Title VII has since become the legal basis for thousands of cases concerning employer discrimination against a worker because of sex. And to add to the irony of that bit of "foolishness," Title VII is recognized as formulating the basis and the development for the enactment of Title IX of the Education Amendments of 1972 (PL92–318), a law that would attempt to strike at the heart of society's sex-biased "hidden curriculum."

The point to be made is that most of us think that if injustice exists, it can be remedied by ensuring the aggrieved equal protection under the law. But Thomas Jefferson perhaps pinpointed the irony of this notion best when he described the "natural aristocracy" which would evolve in the new nation as being based upon each person (black?) having the same opportunity to maximize his (her?) talents. No mention was made of sharing resources or, even more important, of somehow changing culture-induced race or sex stereotypes.

Title IX of the Education Amendments of 1972

When Congress passed Title IX, Education Amendments Act of 1972, on June 23, 1972, it was attempting to end all sex discrimination in federally assisted educational programs. On June 20,

1. President's Commission on the Status of Women, *American Wom-en*, (Washington, D.C.: Government Printing Office, 1963), p. 113.

1974, the Department of Health, Education and Welfare issued proposed regulations to implement Title IX and solicited public comments in reference to the regulations through October 15, 1974. As a result, Congress acted to exempt social fraternities and sororities and certain youth organizations from coverage under the Title. A few other substantive changes to the regulations were made, but, although forcefully presented with the issue of athletics, Congress was unable to reach a consensus. Nonetheless, on May 27, 1975, a former University of Michigan Football center, Gerald Ford, as President of the United States, signed into law the Title IX guidelines and on July 21, 1975, the regulations governing Title IX's implementation became effective. Interestingly, 1975 had been designated International Women's Year.

The implementing regulations essentially cover the following aspects of sex discrimination in education: admissions, access to courses and programs, counseling, financial assistance, athletics, employment, and general treatment of students. The Office of Civil Rights of HEW is responsible for ensuring compliance, and enforcement is through a cutoff of federal funds; Title IX does not authorize private suits for damages. Moreover, virtually every educational institution in the country from elementary school to college and university, public and private, is covered by some portion of the law, so long as it receives federal financial assistance.

Overall, Public Law 92–318, Education Amendments of 1972, provides the following:

TITLE IX—PROHIBITION OF SEX DISCRIMINATION

Sex Discrimination Prohibited

Sec. 901. (a) No person in the United States shall, on the basis of sex, be excluded from participation in, be denied the benefits of, or be subjected to discrimination under any education program or activity receiving Federal financial assistance, except that:

(1) in regard to admissions to educational institutions, this section shall apply only to institutions of vocational education, professional education, and graduate higher education, and to public institutions of undergraduate higher education;

(2) in regard to admissions to educational institutions, this section shall not apply (A) for one year from the date of enactment of this Act, nor for six years after such date in the case of an educational institution which has begun the process of changing from being an institution which admits

only students of one sex to being an institution which admits students of both sexes but only if it is carrying out a plan for such a change which is approved by the Commissioner of Education or (B) for seven years from the date an educational institution begins the process of changing from being an institution which admits only students of only one sex to being an institution which admits students of both sexes, but only if it is carrying out a plan for such a change which is approved by the Commissioner of Education, whichever is the later;

(3) this section shall not apply to an educational institution which is controlled by a religious organization if the application of this subsection would not be consistent with the religious tenets of such organization;

(4) this section shall not apply to an educational institution whose primary purpose is the training of individuals for the military services of the United States, or the merchant marine; and

(5) in regard to admissions this section shall not apply to any public institution of undergraduate higher education which is an institution that traditionally and continually from its establishment has had a policy of admitting only students of one sex.

(b) Nothing contained in subsection (a) of this section shall be interpreted to require any educational institution to grant preferential or disparate treatment to the members of one sex on account of an imbalance which may exist with respect to the total number or percentage of persons of that sex participating in or receiving the benefits of any federally supported program or activity, in comparison with the total number or percentage of persons of that sex in any community, State, section, or other area: *Provided*, That this subsection shall not be construed to prevent the consideration in any hearing or proceeding under this title of statistical evidence tending to show that such an imbalance exists with respect to the participation in, or receipt of the benefits of, any such program or activity by the members of one sex.

(c) For purposes of this title an educational institution means any public or private preschool, elementary, or secondary school, or any institution of vocational, professional, or higher education, except that in the case of an educational institution composed of more than one school, college, or department which are administratively separate units, such term means each such school, college, or department.

With the broad overview in mind, the following discussion will focus on some of the more pertinent regulations with respect to colleges and universities.

Admissions:

The final regulation covers recruitment as well as all admissions policies and practices of those recipients not exempt as to admissions. It includes specific prohibitions of sex discrimination through separate ranking of applicants, application of sex-based quotas, administration of sex-biased tests or selection criteria, and granting of preference to applicants based on their attendance at particular institutions if the preference results in sex discrimination. The final regulation also forbids application in a discriminatory manner of rules concerning marital or parental status, and prohibits discrimination on the basis of pregnancy and related conditions, providing that recipients shall treat pregnancy and disabilities related to pregnancy in the same way as any other temporary disability or physical condition.

Generally, comparable efforts must be made by recipients to recruit members of each sex. Where discrimination previously existed, additional recruitment efforts directed primarily toward members of one sex must be undertaken to remedy the effects of the past discrimination. (Not included with regard to admissions requirements are private undergraduate colleges and those public undergraduate colleges which have been traditionally and continuously single-sex since their establishments).

Section § 86.21 provides the following:

(a) *General.* No person shall, on the basis of sex, be denied admission, or be subject to discrimination in admission, by any recipient to which this Subpart applies . . .

(b) *Specific prohibitions.* (1) In determining whether a person satisfies any policy or criterion for admission, or in making any offer of admission, a recipient to which this Subpart applies shall not:

(i) give preference to one person over another on the basis of sex, by ranking applicants separately on such basis, or otherwise:

(ii) apply numerical limitations upon the number or proportion of persons of either sex who may be admitted; or

(iii) otherwise treat one individual differently from another on the basis of sex.

(2) A recipient shall not administer or operate any test or other criterion for admission which has a disproportionately adverse effect on persons on the basis of sex unless the use of such test or criterion is shown to predict validly success in the education program or activity in question and alternative tests or criteria which do not have such a disproportionately adverse effect are shown to be unavailable.

Access to Courses and Programs:

The basic principle underlying consideration of equality in access to course offerings is the avoidance of stereotypic patterns by providing all students full encouragement and support in selecting courses and programs on the basis of their interests, values and abilities. Thus, § 86.34 provides that an institution or agency may not:

> Provide any course or otherwise carry out any of its education program or activity separately on the basis of sex, or require or refuse participation therein by any of its students on such basis, including health, physical education, industrial, business, vocational, technical, home economics, music and adult education courses.

Counseling:

Male and female students must not be discriminated against on the basis of sex in counseling. Generally, a counselor may not use different materials in testing or guidance based on the student's sex unless this is essential in eliminating bias and then, provided the materials cover the same occupations and interest areas. Also, if a school finds that a class or program contains a disproportionate number of students of one sex, it must be sure that this disproportion is not the result of sex-biased counseling or materials.

> (a) *Counseling.* A recipient shall not discriminate against any person on the basis of sex in the counseling or guidance of students or applicants for admissions.

> (b) *Use of appraisal and counseling materials.* A recipient which uses testing or other materials for appraising or counseling students shall not use different materials for students on the basis of their sex or use materials which permit or require different treatment of students on such basis unless such different materials cover the same occupations

and interest areas and the use of such different materials is shown to be essential to eliminate sex bias. Recipients shall develop and use internal procedures for ensuring that such materials do not discriminate on the basis of sex. Where the use of a counseling test or other instrument results in a substantially disproportionate number of members of one sex in any particular course of study or classification, the recipient shall take such action as is necessary to assure itself that such disproportion is not the result of discrimination in the instrument or its application.

(c) *Disproportion in classes.* Where a recipient finds that a particular class contains a substantially disproportionate number of individuals of one sex, the recipient shall take such action as is necessary to assure itself that such disproportion is not the result of discrimination on the basis of sex in counseling or appraisal materials or by counselors.

Financial Assistance:

The issue of sex equality in financial assistance as addressed by § 86.37 prohibits institutions from discriminating in making available any benefits, services, scholarships, loans, grants-in-aid, assistance in obtaining employment, work-study programs, or insurance policies in connection with its educational program or activities.

A key concept in the requirements for nondiscriminatory financial assistance is referred to as "pooling" as outlined in § 86.-37(c). With the pooling provision, a college may administer a sex-restricted scholarship (e. g., Rhodes) created by a will, trust, or similar legal instrument under a two-step procedure.

Step One requires an institution to select students to be awarded financial aid on the basis of criteria other than a student's sex. Once students have been thus identified, a school's financial aid office would award the aid from both sex-restrictive and non sex-restrictive sources. If not enough aid is then available through non-restrictive sources for members of one sex, the school would then be required to obtain funds from other sources or award less funds from sex-restricted sources.

Athletics:

The basic intent of Title IX, of course, is to eliminate discrimination based on stereotyped sex-characterizations. As already noted, internalized notions of appropriate roles for females and males have served as significant obstacles in this task, but the challenge has been nowhere more difficult than in the area of athletics. As in other areas, the fundamental dilemma is that traditional feminine fulfillment seems to depend upon one set of psychological attitudes—attitudes of submissiveness and passivity—while masculine fulfillment seems to depend upon an opposite set—attitudes of competiveness and self-assertion. But in athletics, the long-term home of the "masculine mystique," the conflict between traditional and emerging male-female roles is more immediate and less subtle.

These stereotypes are being weakened, nevertheless, and a woman running track or playing basketball, for instance, is decreasingly seen as devient. Once these stereotypes are eliminated, furthermore, it should be possible for boys and girls, men and women, to choose freely activities formerly associated with the stereotypes, but this time without suffering any of the limitations or inhibitions that once accompanied those activities.

Accordingly, § 86.34 of Title IX provides that schools may not schedule separate male or female physical education classes. However, the section contains the following qualifications:

> (b) This section does not prohibit grouping of students in physical education classes and activities by ability as assessed by objective standards of individual performance developed and applied without regard to sex.
>
> (c) This section does not prohibit separation of students by sex within physical education classes or activities during participation in wrestling, boxing, rugby, ice hockey, football, basketball and other sports the purpose or major activity of which involves bodily contact.
>
> (d) Where use of a single standard of measuring skill or progress in a physical education class has an adverse effect on members of one sex, the recipient shall use appropriate standards which do not have such effect.

§ 86.41, the most controversial section in Title IX, provides the following:

> (a) *General.* No person shall, on the basis of sex, be excluded from participation in, be denied the benefits of, be treated differently from another person or otherwise be discriminated against in any interscholastic, intercollegiate, club or intramural athletics offered by a recipient, and no recipient shall provide any such athletics separately on such basis.

(b) *Separate Teams.* Notwithstanding the requirements of paragraph (a) of this section, a recipient may operate or sponsor separate teams for members of each sex where selection for such teams is based upon competitive skill or the activity involved is a contact sport. However, where a recipient operates or sponsors a team in a particular sport for members of one sex but operates or sponsors no such team for members of the other sex, and athletic opportunities for members of that sex have been previously limited, members of the excluded sex must be allowed to try out for the team offered unless the sport involved is a contact sport. For the purposes of this Part, contact sports include boxing, wrestling, rugby, ice hockey, football, basketball and other sports the purpose or major activity of which involves bodily contact.

(c) *Equal Opportunity.* A recipient which operates or sponsors interscholastic, intercollegiate, club or intramural athletics shall provide equal athletic opportunity for members of both sexes. In determining whether equal opportunities are available, the Director will consider, among other factors:

  (i)   whether the selection of sports and levels of competition effectively accommodate the interests and abilities of members of both sexes

  (ii) the provision of equipment and supplies

  (iii) scheduling of games and practice time

  (iv) travel and per diem allowance

  (v)   opportunity to receive coaching and academic tutoring

  (vi) assignment and compensation of coaches and tutors

  (vii) provision of locker rooms, practice and competitive facilities

  (viii) provision of medical and training facilities and services

  (ix) provision of housing and dining facilities and services

  (x)   publicity

Unequal aggregate expenditures for members of each sex or unequal expenditures for male and female teams

if a recipient operates or sponsors separate teams will
not constitute compliance with this section, but the Director may consider the failure to provide necessary
funds for teams for one sex in assessing equality of opportunity for members of each sex.

This section has been particularly controversial because many
educators believe (d) that the regulation mandated a dollar-for-
dollar matching expenditure for each sex; however, the last sentence in the above regulation is crucial in determining funding
requirements.   That is, unequal expenditures for members of
each sex or unequal expenditures for male and female teams, if
separate teams are operated or sponsored, is not necessarily considered as non-complying.   In other words, funding differentials
alone cannot be considered as non-compliance with the regulation.   Rather, the thrust of compliance is based on whether the
intercollegiate athletic teams are being adequately equipped,
coached and supported as are other teams in the institution.
"[F]ailure to provide necessary funds for teams for one sex,"
therefore, is the qualifier "in assessing equality of opportunity
. . ."

Nevertheless, the amount of money now spent on athletic
programs for male students far exceeds that typically allocated
women's athletics.   While the regulations do not require equal
expenditures for males and females, the cost of upgrading those
areas for women (e. g., facilities, supplies, travel allowances)
examined to determine whether equal opportunities are available
is bound to run high.

Employment:

Obviously, institutionalized sex preference in employment comprises another aspect of the "hidden curriculum" in that it can
substantially influence students' academic, career and personal
options and choices.   Title IX, therefore, provides comprehensive
prohibitions of discrimination in the employment policies and
practices of educational institutions.

General Treatment of Students:

Overall, the basic intent of those portions of Title IX which
prohibit sex discrimination in the treatment of students is to ensure that both females and males are provided equal benefits,
opportunities and responsibilities throughout their educational
experience.   Some examples: locker rooms, showers, and other
facilities provided for women must be comparable to those pro-

vided for men. An institution listing off-campus housing for its students must ensure that comparable off-campus housing is available in equal proportion to those members of each sex expressing an interest in such. An institution hiring its own students for part-time work cannot discriminate. Rules and regulations governing student conduct must be essentially the same for both sexes.

In sum, there are obviously too many Title IX regulations to be either reproduced or discussed here (see either Code of Federal Regulations—CFR, Title 45, Part 86 or the Federal Register, Vol. 40, No. 108 at P. 24128). Nevertheless, these regulations should be carefully studied. Compliance and affirmative remedial action is required by the law; moreover, institutions must "adopt and publish grievance procedures providing for prompt and equitable resolution of student and employee complaints alleging any action . . . prohibited by [the regulations]."

When all is said and done, Title IX provides the professional educator—male or female—with an opportunity and a challenge. People who want academia or any other sphere of life to be characterized by cooperative, egalitarian social relations need to actively concern themselves with questions regarding the true meaning of "equal educational opportunity" and its potential influence on every aspect of human life and social relations within our society.

The Fourteenth Amendment and Sex Discrimination

The constitutional issues with regard to sex discrimination sometimes seem less settled than even those connected with race. In fact, in determining whether sex-based legislation violates the equal protection clause, the Supreme Court has been divided as to whether or not "strict scrutiny" would be the appropriate standard of review. A majority of the Court, however, does consider the minimum "rational basis" test as generally no longer appropriate, but while sex classifications have been frequently elevated to a higher level of constitutional protection than most other classifications, a Court majority has never treated sex as race—that is, as a suspect class triggering the "strict scrutiny" standard of review.

In the fall of 1971, for example, a unanimous Court in Reed v. Reed [2] found unconstitutional a portion of an Idaho probate code which granted males a mandatory preference over females in

---

2.   404 U.S. 71 (1971).

competing for the right to administer an estate without regard for the individual qualifications of the female applicant. One of the reasons which the Idaho Supreme Court gave for upholding the statute was that the "legislature when it enacted the statute evidently concluded that in general men are better qualified to act as an administrator than are women." [3] Because of this, in the Idaho Supreme Court opinion, eliminating females from consideration "is neither an illogical nor an arbitrary method devised by the legislature to resolve an issue that would otherwise require a hearing as to the relative merits . . . of the two petitioning relatives." [4]

The United States Supreme Court concluded that the preference for men was arbitrary:

> To give a mandatory preference to members of either sex over members of the other, merely to accomplish the elimination of hearings on the merits, is to make the very kind of arbitrary legislative choice forbidden by the Equal Protection Clause of the Fourteenth Amendment; . . . By providing dissimilar treatment for men and women who are . . . similarly situated, the challenged section violates the Equal Protection Clause.[5]

The United States Supreme Court did admit, however, that "[c]learly the objective of reducing the workload on probate courts . . . is not without legitimacy" [6] and thus agreed that the law had at least a conceivable justification (a rational connection is all that is required under minimum scrutiny) so it is not difficult to discern that the Court was doing something differently.[7] Moreover, after the *Reed* decision some argued that the Equal Rights Amendment would be superfluous since *Reed* seemed to make classifications based on sex, like those based on race, presumptively unconstitutional.[8]

---

3. 93 Idaho 511, 514, 465 P.2d 635, 638 (1970).

4. Id.

5. 404 U.S. at 76–77.

6. Id., at 76.

7. For example, in McDonald v. Board of Election Commissioners, 394 U.S. 802, 809 (1969), the Court explained the rational basis test as follows: "Legislatures are pre-sumed to have acted constitutionally even if source materials normally resorted to for ascertaining their grounds for action are otherwise silent, and their statutory classifications will be set aside only if *no* grounds can be conceived to justify them." (emphasis added.)

8. However, the proposed 27th Amendment (ERA) if passed, will make such classifications totally unacceptable.

Two years later, in Frontiero v. Richardson,[9] the Court struck down a federal law which allowed male Air Force officers dependency benefits for their wives but only for husbands of female officers who were dependent on their wives for over one half of their support. Justice Brennan, speaking for a plurality, ruled that sex, like race, was a suspect classification and applied the strict scrutiny standard. "Indeed," he wrote, "there can be no doubt that our Nation has had a long and unfortunate history of sex discrimination. Traditionally, such discrimination was rationalized by an attitude of 'romantic paternalism' which, in practical effect put women, not on a pedestal, but in a cage." [10]

It is significant to note that Brennan, while conceding that this had not always been the construction of the Constitution, explicitly stated that the Reed decision fully justified a "departure from 'traditional' rational-basis analysis." [11]   Three Justices agreed with Brennan; however, the other four Justices concurred in the judgment but refrained from holding that sex is a suspect classification. Thus, four Justices specifically stated that sex was a suspect classification, four refrained from doing so, and one dissented. Nevertheless, Frontiero can be read as bolstering the Reed position that something more than "rational basis" is required as a standard to review sex discrimination cases.[12]

Interestingly, in Craig v. Boren,[13] the Court used the same type of analysis in striking down a statute allowing females to drink beer at age eighteen, while males could not drink until age twenty-one. In doing so the Court again reaffirmed Reed's more strict analysis.[14] That is, even though the state presented statistics correlating a lower drinking age for males with increased automobile accidents, the Court rejected the justification because of the "weak congruence between gender and the characteristic or trait that gender purported to represent." [15] The standard announced by the Court was that "classifications by gender must serve some important governmental objectives and must be substantially related to achievement of these objectives." [16]

9. 411 U.S. 677 (1973).

10. Id., at 684.

11. Id.

12. A number of lower federal courts, however, have treated sex-based classifications as suspect. See, e. g., Held v. Missouri Pacific R. R., 373 F.Supp. 996 (D.C.Tex. 1974); Daugherty v. Daley, 370 F. Supp. 338 (D.C.Ill.1974); Wiesenfeld v. Secretary of HEW, 367 F. Supp. 981 (D.C.N.J.1973), aff'd 420 U.S. 636 (1974).

13. 429 U.S. 190 (1976).

14. Id., at 204.

15. Id., at 199.

16. Id., at 204.

However, despite the fact that the Supreme Court has applied the *Reed* language in rather consistent fashion, the result was remarkably different in Kahn v. Shevin.[17] Here the Court sustained a Florida statute granting widows, but not widowers, an annual $500 tax exemption. In upholding the statute, the Court, speaking through Justice Douglas, quoted the *Reed* test as controlling in that gender—classifications must have some "fair and substantial relation to the object of the legislation."[18] The object of the legislation was to reduce the economic disparity between men and women, apparently a more substantial justification than the mere administrative convenience in *Reed* and *Frontiero*. However, on the surface the *Kahn* justification does not appear more substantial than that attempted in *Craig*. But the justification in *Kahn,* and this is important, was that of compensating for the effects of past discrimination that had deprived women of equal economic opportunity.

Thus, despite the fact that the Court ostensibly applied the *Reed* language in *Kahn,* it is evident that not all sex-based classifications will be invalidated. Apparently gender-based classifications designed to compensate for past discrimination find it rather easy to pass constitutional muster while classifications stereotyping men and women into old masculine-feminine roles must survive a more rigorous judicial analysis. Today the courts have obviously become sensitive to the problems of sex discrimination so that no longer can such classifications be justified by reliance on "outdated images . . . of women as peculiarly delicate and impressionable creatures in need of protection from the rough and tumble of unvarnished humanity."[19]

Yet a number of public colleges and universities today continue to discriminate on the basis of sex—by total exclusion of students of one sex—and the courts have generally upheld the practice on the grounds of what might be termed the "separate but equal" doctrine. For example, in Williams v. McNair[20] a federal district court upheld a challenged South Carolina statute which limited regular admissions in one of the state's eight public colleges and universities to females. While applying the rational basis analysis, the court pointed out that there were "still a substantial number of private and public institutions, which limit

17. 416 U.S. 351 (1974).

18. Id., at 355.

19. Seidenberg v. McSorleys' Old Ale House, Inc., 317 F.Supp. 593, 606 (D.C.N.Y.1970).

20. 316 F.Supp. 134 (D.C.S.C.1970).

their enrollment to one sex and do so because they feel it offers better educational advantages." [21]   The court then explained that the single-sex college "is merely a part of an entire system of State-supported higher education.   .   .   .   If the State operated only one [such] college   .   .   .   there can be no question that to deny males admission thereto would be impermissible under the Equal Protection Clause." [22]

On the other hand, in Kirstein v. Rector and Visitors of the Univ. of Virginia,[23] another federal district court appeared to reach a different conclusion.   It found that denial of admission based on sex constituted a violation of the equal protection clause. However, the court then explicitly qualified its decision: "We are urged to go further and to hold that Virginia may not operate *any* educational institution separated according to the sexes. We decline to do so." [24]   But the real key to this remark is that the women-plaintiffs were seeking admission to the University of Virginia (at that time reserved for men only) and it was conceded that the University occupied a position of preeminence among the State-supported institutions of Virginia and offered a far wider range of curriculum.   No such situation existed in *Williams*.   There South Carolina offered the male students essentially the same quality education as the female students but in a different location, whereas in *Kirstein* the women-plaintiffs had been *deprived* of comparable benefits rather than being offered them on the same basis as the opposite sex.

Actually, even if Title IX had been in existence at the time of *Williams,* it would not have been of any greater help than the Constitution to the plaintiffs in obtaining admission to the allfemale college, as long as there was another college with com-

21. Id., at 137. This view would find considerable support in Alexander Astin's recent findings. After culling data from more than 200,000 students in a national sample of more than 300 institutions of higher education and then conducting follow-up surveys ranging from 1–10 years after the students' college entry, Astin found that "Single-sex colleges show a pattern of effects on both sexes that is almost universally positive. Students of both sexes become more academically involved, interact with faculty more frequently, show larger increases in intellectual self-esteem, and are more satisfied with practically all aspects of the college experience . . . compared with their counterparts in coeducational institutions." Astin, "On the Failures of Educational Policy," *Change* (Sept., 1977), p. 41.

22. Id. See also Heaton v. Bristol, 317 S.W.2d 86 (Tex.Civ.App.1958), where the Texas Court of Civil Appeals also ruled affirmatively on the constitutionality of public supported single-sex colleges.

23. 309 F.Supp. 184 (D.C.Va.1970).

24. Id., at 187 (emphasis added).

parable courses, services and facilities available to them. Yet, whereas challenges to separate (but equal) facilities with identical admissions standards are likely to be unsuccessful under either the Constitution or Title IX, both are more likely to support challenges by female plaintiffs where academically elite or specialized schools require higher admissions standards for female applicants than for males. For example, the Ninth Circuit, using a "strict rationality" standard, held the differential standards of an elite academic high school in San Francisco to be an unconstitutional violation of the equal protection clause.[25]

HOUSING

As is by now abundantly clear from the preceding pages, Title IX regulations all but blanket the area of sex discrimination in the schools. In the area of housing, for instance, § 86.32(c) states that a federally assisted institution "shall not, on the basis of sex, administer different policies or practices concerning occupancy by its students of housing other than that provided by the recipient." Of course colleges which are not in compliance can have their federal aid revoked and/or be barred from eligibility for future awards, but it should be recalled that Title IX does not authorize a private right of action against an institution.[26] Thus, rather than invoking Title IX, in Texas Woman's Univ. v. Chayklintaste, female students brought action against the institution challenging the constitutionality of a regulation allowing "male students, but not female students, to live in off-campus housing." [27]

The regulation in the instant case, however, seemed not to be an issue for the recent admission of men; that is, the University had adequate on-campus housing facilities for women but, because of the previous composition of the student body, did not anticipate any need for male housing. Under these circumstances the University made an exception to its policy and allowed male students to live off-campus. And yes, the exception received a sound

25. Berkelman v. San Francisco Unified School Dist., 501 F.2d 1264 (9th Cir. 1974). See also Bray v. Lee, 337 F.Supp. 934 (D.C.Mass.1972). Title IX regulations also prohibit the use of sex-differential admissions criteria; see pp. 456–457, supra.

26. See, e. g., Cannon v. University of Chicago, 406 F.Supp. 1257 (D.C.

Ill.1976), aff'd 559 F.2d 1063 (7th Cir. 1977). The Seventh Circuit held that while Title IX provides for an administrative hearing, Congress did not envision "the rather drastic remedy of individual lawsuits." Id., at 1077.

27. 521 S.W.2d 949 (Tex.Civ.App. 1975).

thumping when challenged in the Texas trial court. Subsequently, the University appealed to the Court of Civil Appeals where,
in a sort of "let's treat everybody equally from here on in" remark, the Court began with the observation "that our courts
are about to embark upon tasks like unto that made necessary by
the litigation over racial discrimination. Hopefully it will be neither as extended, nor as bitter." [28] The Court then quickly affirmed the lower court's ruling by concluding that the regulation "is hereby declared invalid, void, and unenforceable as
. . . prohibited by the Equal Protection Clause of the 14th
Amendment and by Article I, Section 3 of the Texas Constitution." [29] And, in an interesting corollary, the Court also asserted that, "[h]aving provided housing facilities for women, [the
University] is unconstitutionally discriminating against its male
students when it does not provide substantially equivalent and
equal housing facilities for men." [30]

The University responded by changing its housing regulation
to apply equally to men and women and appealed the decision to
the State Supreme Court.[31] Obviously, the Supreme Court determined that the modification eliminated the constitutionally objectionable sex classification and thus declared the issue moot and
hypothetical. Nonetheless, it also determined that since the
amended regulation applied only to men and women under the
age of twenty-three, the issue now rested upon the constitutionality of an age classification. Hence, in this determination, the
standard of review articulated by the Court was that "[w]hen
no suspect categories are involved, any rational basis may justify
the classification." [32] Not surprisingly, under this criterion the
Court found the age-based classification reasonable, not arbitrary,
and constitutionally permissible because the University established the classification for a legitimate educational purpose. But
lack of evidence certainly was not a problem. The University
presented affidavits from numerous educators and professional
literature (e. g., *Educational Record,* Summer 1973 and *Educational Research* 8, April 1970) demonstrating that on-campus
living benefited the intellectual and social development of students. Moreover, two witnesses from the University testified
that they believed the age bracket within the regulation repre-

28. Id., at 950.

29. Id., at 951 and quoting verbatim
   the lower court's conclusion.

30. Id.

31. 530 S.W.2d 927 (Tex.1975).

32. Id., at 928.

sented "that group of students that would benefit most from the living-learning concept . . . " [33]

Interestingly, the Texas Supreme Court acted unhesitatingly to fill in one apparent gap in the University's rationale: occupancy of the dormitories was now essential for the University to meet its bonded indebtedness incurred in the construction of new dormitories for men. But in Mollere v. Southeastern Louisiana College,[34] a somewhat similar regulation was struck down because the *only* reason given for requiring unmarried women students and freshman men to live on campus was that the particular group approximated the number needed to fill dormitory vacancies. "This," the federal district court concluded, "is the type of irrational discrimination impermissible under the Fourteenth Amendment." In other words, "[t]o select a group less-than-all to fulfill [a financial] obligation which should fall equally on all, is a violation of equal protection no matter how the group is selected." [35]

The court in *Mollere*, nevertheless, did imply that the disputed classification would have been permissible had it been connected to a legitimate social-educational purpose. Moreover, the rationale used to support the classification in *Chayklintaste* emphasized the "living-learning concept." In fact, though a precise blueprint cannot be provided, case law strongly suggests that something more than a fiscal-solvency rationale is needed to justify mandatory residency classifications of this sort.[36] In any case, the need for a regulation treating different students in different ways will always be substantially more rational and convincing to a judge if it can be connected to academic and social benefits. For example, in Robinson v. Board of Regents of Eastern Kentucky Univ., the University justified sex-differential curfew regulations by asserting "that women are more likely to be criminally attacked at night, and are less capable of defending themselves than men." [37] The Sixth Circuit, in affirming the district court's dismissal of the challenge, concluded that the "[g]oal of safety was legitimate concern . . . of state university, and its regulations imposing dormitory curfew restrictions upon women but

33. Id., at 921.

34. 304 F.Supp. 826 (D.C.La.1969).

35. Id., at 828.

36. See, e. g., Pratz v. Louisiana Polytechnic Institute, 316 F.Supp.

872 (D.C.La.1970); Poynter v. Drevdahl, 359 F.Supp. 1137 (D.C.Mich. 1972); and Prostrollo v. University of South Dakota, 507 F.2d 775 (8th Cir. 1974).

37. 475 F.2d 707, 711 (6th Cir. 1973), cert. denied 416 U.S. 982 (1974).

not upon men were rationally related to effectuation of such goal and were not violative of equal protection." [38]

Thus, despite the powerful trend to change traditional patterns of university housing—especially reflected in the effects of Title IX and the lowering of the age of majority in most states from 21 to 18—the courts seem to be reaffirming a position held for years; that is, while some universities may wish to liberalize housing regulations, there is nothing in the Constitution requiring all universities to do so, as long as traditional restrictions are rationally connected to the benefit of students.

THE HANDICAPPED

Yet whatever one's feelings about the reasonableness of university classifications, the inequitable classification of the physically and mentally handicapped is, without doubt, the most insensitive and debasing form of discrimination existing in our society, and the implications of this fact are worthy of the most serious consideration by higher education. But more than that, this consideration is now mandated as a result of the Rehabilitation Act of 1973.[39]

Rehabilitation Act of 1973

In language closely mirroring provisions in Title VI of the Civil Rights Act of 1974, and Title IX of the Education Amendments of 1972, the Rehabilitation Act (§ 504) states:

No otherwise qualified handicapped individual in the United States, as defined in 7(6) of this title shall, solely by reason of his handicap, be excluded from participation in, be denied the benefits of, or be subjected to discrimination under any program or activity receiving Federal financial assistance.

According to § 84.3(j), the definition of "handicapped individuals" for the purposes of the law are ". . . any person who (i) has a physical or mental impairment [40] which substantially limits one or more of such person's major life activities,[41] (ii) has a rec-

---

38. Id., at 708.

39. Public Law 93–112, 87 Stat. 355; now codified as amended at 29 U.S. C.A. §§ 701–794 [hereinafter referred to as "Section 504"].

40. ". . . mental impairment means . . . any mental or psychological disorder, such as mental retardation, organic brain syn-

drome, emotional or mental illness, and specific learning disabilities." 84.3(j)(i). The regulations are codified in 45 CFR §§ 80.1–84.

41. "'Major life activities' means functions such as caring for one's self, performing manual tasks, walking, seeing, hearing, speaking, breathing, learning, and working." § 84.3(j)(ii).

ord of such impairment, or (iii) is regarded as having such an impairment."

The regulations clearly prohibit any federally assisted institution, public or private, from barring admission or employment to handicapped persons solely because of their disabilities, or from imposing quotas or giving admissions tests that have "a disproportionate, adverse effect on handicapped persons." This means that colleges must give tests to those who cannot speak, hear or write which "accurately reflect the applicant's aptitude or achievement level or whatever other factor the test purports to measure, rather than reflecting the applicant's impair[ment]." Moreover, the regulations bar colleges from asking, prior to admission, whether an applicant has a handicap, unless they plan remedial or voluntary action "to overcome the limited participation of handicapped persons" in their institutions. In that case, colleges must make it clear to applicants that they are not required to supply such information. However, the regulations do allow inquiries after admission and before actual enrollments.[42]

Although all college facilities need not be changed, they must "as a whole" be made accessible to the handicapped,[43] but all buildings constructed after the law went into effect must be "designed and constructed in such manner that the facility . . . is readily accessible to and usable by handicapped persons."[44] Handicapped students are also entitled to "convenient and accessible" campus housing at the same cost as provided to other students, and handicapped students, such as deaf or blind persons, who are capable of living in campus housing, must be offered the same variety and "scope" of rooms offered to nonhandicapped persons.[45]

Handicapped bias in counseling, placement, social activities, educational programs, physical education and athletics is also prohibited. Colleges must "adopt grievance procedures that incorporate appropriate due process standards and that provide for the prompt and equitable resolution of complaints. . . ."[46] Further, the regulations broadly prohibit discrimination in financial aid, student employment[47] and regular employment.[48]

42. § 84.42 et seq.

43. § 84.22(a).

44. § 84.23(a).

45. § 84.44(a).

46. 84.43 et seq.

47. § 84.46 et seq.

48. §§ 84.11–84.14

In addition to the provisions listed above, the regulations impose obligations upon colleges to provide auxiliary aids to handicapped students:

A recipient to which this subject applies shall take such steps as are necessary to ensure that no handicapped student is denied the benefits of, excluded from participation in, or otherwise subjected to discrimination under the education program or activity operated by the recipient because of the absence of educational auxiliary aids for students with impaired sensory, manual, or speaking skills.

Auxiliary aids may include taped texts, interpreters or other effective method of making orally delivered materials available to students with hearing impairments, readers in libraries for students with visual impairments, classroom equipment adapted for use by students wtih manual impairments, and other similar services and actions. Recipients need not provide attendants, individually prescribed devices, readers for personal use or study, or other devices or services of a personal nature.[49]

The position of HEW is that colleges must accommodate disabilities by providing appropriate auxiliary aids. The rationale is perhaps obvious:

In drafting a regulation to prohibit exclusion and discrimination, it became clear that different or special treatment of handicapped persons, because of their handicaps, may be necessary in a number of contexts, in order to ensure equal opportunity. Thus, for example, it is meaningless to "admit" a handicapped person in a wheelchair to a program if the program is offered only on the third floor of a walk-up building. Nor is one providing equal educational opportunity to a deaf child by admitting him or her to a classroom but providing no means for the child to understand the teacher or receive instruction.[50]

However, higher education officials have estimated that it will cost at least $1.5 billion to bring the nation's colleges and universities into compliance with the law, and apparently little if any financial help will be forthcoming from the federal govern-

---

49. § 84.44(d).

50. 42 Fed.Reg. 22676 (1977). This also means that colleges may not bar aids such as tape recorders or brailler's from the classroom. In regard to concerns that recording lectures may infringe upon a professor's copyright protection, it is suggested having students agree in writing not to release tapes.

ment. Thus, though no one can argue with the goal of full access and participation by handicapped persons in higher education, questions are legitimately raised as to who can and should bear the costs inherent in serving that goal.

In this respect, Dr. Gary Brooks, an attorney and an Assistant Dean at Dartmouth College, pointed out the following:

It is submitted, however, that failure to pay for auxiliary aids does not constitute discrimination within the meaning of § 504. It is not "solely by reason of his handicap" that the handicapped individual may be denied full participation in the classroom. Rather, it is by reason of the absence of some necessary person or thing constituting an auxiliary aid. The affirmative obligation of the institution is arguably satisfied by admission of the student and the provision of barrier-free access to the facilities.[51] Therefore, providing additional services to the student should be voluntary on the part of the private institution, or at least any such obligation should be limited to assisting the student in finding such services or funds to pay for such services from existing federal-state programs or other external sources.

The requirement of additional services exceeds Congressional intent and ignores relevant differences in ability to pay.[52] Moreover, it subjects private institutions to a "catch-22" situation in which they are forbidden to deny admission to an otherwise qualified handicapped individual, but once that individual is admitted, are required to pay for auxiliary aids. Presumably the regulations would prohibit an institution from denying admission on the grounds that it had insufficient funds to pay for the auxiliary aid which would be required.[53]

51. Brooks, "Section 504 of the Rehabilitation Act of 1973 and the Private College: Barnes v. Converse," 29 *Mercer Law Review* (1978) p. 750. At fn. 84: Snowden v. Birmingham-Jefferson City Transit Auth., 407 F.Supp. 394 (N.D.Ala.1975), aff'd 551 F.2d 862 (5th Cir. 1977); United Handicapped Federation v. Andre, 409 F. Supp. 1297 (D.Minn.1976). In *Snowden*, the court stressed the "solely by reason of his handicap" language in holding that § 504 did not require the provision of auxiliary mechanical aids to lift persons in wheelchairs from the street to the bus. The court found that the provision of access, by permitting persons in wheelchairs to ride the bus, was all that § 504 required.

52. Id., at fn. 85: In Mourning v. Family Service Publications, Inc., 411 U.S. 356 (1973) and Thorpe v. Housing Authority, 393 U.S. 268 (1969), there is an implicit recognition that the impact of the burden imposed on a regulated entity is a relevant factor in determining the reasonableness of regulations.

53. Id.

Court Cases

Indeed, the Rehabilitation Act (and its regulations) represents some laudable goals, but it has also created problems associated with the implementation of those goals. As shall be seen, a number of court cases provide some interesting insight into the nature of these problems.

In the first case, Davis v. Southeastern Community College,[54] a young lady afflicted with a hearing disability brought an action against a community college. She claimed that the college's refusal to admit her to a program for the training of registered nurses constituted a violation of the Rehabilitation Act of 1973, as well as her equal protection and due process rights under the Fourteenth Amendment.

The federal district court sustained the decision of the college, holding that no Fourteenth Amendment violation had occurred since the refusal to admit her was neither "arbitrary" nor "unreasonable" and that the college was required to admit Ms. Davis as an "otherwise qualified" person only if in spite of her handicap she would be able to succeed in the training program and profession.[55] But even though the district court ruled against Ms. Davis, it at least implied that a Section 504 complainant could by-pass HEW and go directly to court. Moreover, upon appeal, the Fourth Circuit held that the district court applied the wrong interpretation of the term "otherwise qualified":

> . . . [T]he district court erred by considering the nature of Davis's handicap in order to determine whether or not she was "otherwise qualified" for admittance to the nursing program, . . . rather than by focusing upon her academic and technical qualifications as required by the newly promulgated regulations.[56]

Thus, read literally, "otherwise qualified" handicapped persons would seem to include persons who are qualified *except* for their handicap, rather than *in spite* of their handicap. Under such a literal reading, however, a blind person possessing all the qualifications for flying an airplane except sight could be said to be "otherwise qualified" for the job of an airline pilot. It would be difficult to believe that Congress intended such a possibility, and, at this writing, Southeastern Community College has appealed the *Davis* appellate decision to the U.S. Supreme Court.

---

54. 424 F.Supp. 1341 (D.C.N.C.1976).

55. Id., at 1345.

56. 574 F.2d 1158, 1161 (4th Cir. 1978).

In fact, the American Council of Education has filed a brief on behalf of the College, arguing that "sound logic" and "common sense" require a college to "take into consideration the nature of a person's handicap to see if he or she is qualified for *admission into a particular program of* study *in spite* of that handicap." [57] Also, with respect to a handicapped student's right to by-pass HEW in a "private right of action," the Cannon v. University of Chicago decision due from the U.S. Supreme Court in the spring of 1979 should resolve this issue.[58]

In Crawford v. University of North Carolina,[59] where a deaf graduate student invoked the Rehabilitation Act against his university because it had denied his request for interpreter services, the court made it clear that: "It is at least a serious question as to whether the plaintiff has a private cause of action insofar as he seeks benefits." [60] But, while determining that HEW had primary jurisdiction in enforcing the provisions of the Act, the court observed that this alone does not render "moot the question of whether preliminary relief should issue to safeguard plaintiff's rights from irreparable injury pending administrative determination." [61] The court then permitted an independent cause of action to be asserted and explained that "the public interest lies on the side of the plaintiff. Congress has enacted the Rehabilitation Act . . . and H.E.W. has formulated regulations which indicate that plaintiff has the right (at some time) to receive that which he seeks in the complaint." [62] Thus, the court ordered the university to provide the interpretive services, but in doing so the court noted its reluctance—particularly be-

57. Quoted in Thomas J. Flygare, "Schools and the Law," 60 *Phi Delta Kappan* (February 1979), p. 456.

58. 559 F.2d 1063 (7th Cir. 1976), cert. granted 98 S.Ct. 3142 (1978). At this writing, Geraldine Cannon (a surgical nurse), on appeal from the Seventh Circuit's holding that Title IX does not provide a private cause of action, is pressing her charges that the University of Chicago and Northwestern both unlawfully denied her admission to their medical schools because she was a woman. If Cannon wins, all sides agree that it will also open the way for individual lawsuits under Section 504 of the 1973 Rehabilita-

tion Act. The many civil rights advocate groups supporting Cannon insist that HEW enforcement just isn't enough; that is, HEW doesn't have the resources to investigate every case of alleged discrimination, and even when it does find illegal bias, it is loath to stop federal payments for fear of hurting some of the very students the programs were set up to help.

59. 440 F.Supp. 1047 (D.C.N.C.1977).

60. Id., at 1056.

61. Id., at 1058.

62. Id., at 1059.

cause of the tremendous burden that might be placed on institutions in fully implementing the Act. Also, as a condition of such relief, the court ordered the student to initiate an action against the university with HEW and to post a $3,000 security bond pending its outcome.[63]

Though apparently following a similar approach, a different outcome resulted in the case of Doe v. New York Univ.[64] The circumstances here centered around a student (named in the suit as Jane Doe) who had completed the first term of medical school at New York University and then took a leave of absence to obtain psychiatric treatment. She alleged that she had regained sufficient emotional stability to return to medical school, but the University refused to readmit her. As a result, she sought a preliminary injunction against the University claiming that it had discriminated against her on the basis of her handicap—a mental disability—in violation of the Rehabilitation Act.

The court found that the Act provided an enforcement mechanism, but that the plaintiff had made no attempt to utilize it.

> It is clear .   .   .   that administrative remedies exist to handle this plaintiff's complaint, and that the most authoritative court to analyze the issue whether a private right exists under Section 504 concluded that when such administrative machinery did come into being, any private right under the statute would be subject to the requirement that such administrative remedies must be exhausted before plaintiff can obtain judicial review of his complaint. Although the Court is not overly optimistic as to the expeditiousness or efficiency of such a scheme of administrative enforcement, particularly when it appears that H.E.W.'s enforcement machinery in other areas of civil rights complaints is inefficacious, at best, it is simply too early to find this specific administrative remedy inadequate.[65]

63. Id., at 1059–1060.

64. 442 F.Supp. 522 (D.C.N.Y.1978).

65. Id., at 523. See 45 CFR 80.6–80.10 which includes provisions for compliance reports, investigations, procedures for effecting compliance including termination of federal financial assistance, opportunity for hearing, and post-administrative judicial review. See also Lloyd v. Regional Transportation Auth., 548 F.2d 1277, 1286 fn. 29 (7th Cir., 1977); where, in permitting an independent cause of action in the absence of administrative remedial machinery, the Seventh Circuit explained: "We expressly leave open as premature the question of whether, after consolidated procedural enforcement regulations are issued to implement section 504, the judicial remedy available must be limited to post-administrative remedy judicial review. .   .   .   But

However, the court cautioned that "if H.E.W. does not or cannot provide an effective remedy, a decision to bypass the administrative machinery would rest on substantial ground." [66]   Further, in contrasting this case with Crawford v. University of North Carolina (supra), the court observed that it did "not agree that such would be a proper manner to proceed in this case." That is, in *Crawford* the "balance of hardship tipped decidedly in favor of the plaintiff," while in this case University officials "have made a strong showing that compelling them to readmit a student who might suffer from a substantial emotional disability could pose a danger not only to the plaintiff and her fellow students, but also to patients with whom first-year medical students come into regular contact." [67]   Hence, the court deemed it inadvisable to issue an injunction.

Clearly, it is in the application of these principles that the tough issues of handicap discrimination arise, for Section 504 of the Rehabilitation Act grants affirmative relief.   But fashioning such relief in these situations necessitates not only the development of an effective enforcement mechanism to ensure that the Act's express purpose is being met (stated positively to bring about equal educational and employment opportunity for the handicapped), but in balancing that purpose with the ability of federal or state assistance to realize the mandate as well.   Absent the latter corollary, the negative financial impact on already hard-pressed educational institutions will only serve to freeze the process at the level of apology and quarrel.

OUT–OF–STATE TUITION

It has been estimated that approximately three-fourths of educational costs at state colleges and universities are met by taxes. Of course herein lies the crux of a major conflict between states and mobile students because, in attempting to partially equalize the cost of public higher education between in-state and out-of-state citizens, state institutions "almost universally" charge nonresident students higher tuition fees than residents.[68]   Naturally,

assuming a meaningful administrative enforcement mechanism, the private cause of action under section 504 should be limited to *a posteriori* judicial review."

66. Id., at 524.

67. Id.

68. Carnegie Commission on Higher Education, *Tuition* (Berkely, California: CCHE, 1974), pp. 13, 25. See also Robert F. Carbone, *Students and State Borders* (Iowa City: ACT Publications, 1973), at pp. 14–19, where it is claimed that perhaps half the nation's public institutions also have higher admissions stan-

the constitutionality of such discrimination has been challenged in the courts.

In Starns v. Malkerson,[69] for instance, two woman moved from Illinois to Minnesota when their husbands obtained employment there; shortly after the move they attempted to register at the University of Minnesota as residents but were classified as non-residents and charged higher tuition fees. The reason given for the differential tuition status was that under Minnesota's durational residency requirement, any person who had not continuously resided in the state one year immediately prior to registration could only qualify for the lower in-state rates by living within the state for another year in student status. Subsequently, the two women challenged the regulation on the grounds that classifying citizens by the length of time they lived in a state embodied an unconstitutional interference with the right of interstate travel and violated equal protection of the laws guarantees. Moreover, they buttressed their argument by the fact that such grounds had already been recognized by the Supreme Court in Shapiro v. Thompson,[70] in which the Court struck down a one-year waiting period provided for in a state's welfare laws.

Thus, it appeared to the *Starns* plaintiffs that even if one accepted the University's argument that the regulation operated to apportion tuition rates on the basis of past tax contributions by students—personally or through their families—that justification under *Shapiro* would still give rise to grave constitutional problems. In other words, in *Shapiro* the Court rejected the contention that a challenged classification could be sustained as an attempt to distinguish betwen contributions people had made to the state through past payment of taxes. That rationale, the Court pointed out, "would logically permit the State to bar new residents from schools, parks, and libraries or deprive them of police and fire protection   .   .   .   The Equal Protection Clause prohibits such an apportionment of state services."[72] In addition, the Court ruled that the classification violated the constitutional right to travel, a right which derives from "our constitutional concepts of personal liberty."[73]

dards and/or quotas for nonresident students.

69.   326 F.Supp. 234 (D.C.Minn.1970), aff'd 401 U.S. 985 (1971).

70.   394 U.S. 618 (1969).

71.   326 F.Supp. at 236–237.

72.   394 U.S. at 632–633.

73.   Id., at 645–655.

But the *Starns* three-judge panel refused to accept the analogy between state expenditures for welfare and state expenditures for higher education, holding that *Shapiro* dealt with an admitted attempt to "fence-out" indigents by denying them life's basic necessities, whereas attendance at a public institution of higher education did not present such an immediate and pressing need. Thus, the *Starns* decision expressly rejected the argument that a right to interstate movement is involved in any dispute over whom a state may legitimately classify as a nonresident student and upheld states' rights to discriminate against nonresidents as rationally connected to a valid interest in equalizing contributions toward the support of their higher education programs.[74] It should be noted, however, that in *Starns* the court was dealing with a provision that permitted out-of-state students to establish in-state status after one year's residence.

The constitutionality of a one-year waiting period for receipt of in-state tuition benefits, therefore, was upheld and then summarily affirmed by the United States Supreme Court. Obviously, other courts have followed suit.[75] Nevertheless, courts have refused to accept a provision that would force retention of out-of-state status throughout a student's attendance at a state college or university.[76] In fact, any doubt that existed on this point was dispelled when the United States Supreme Court, in Vlandis v. Kline, struck down a Connecticut statute interpreted as denying persons who applied from another state the opportunity ever to qualify for resident tuition rates.[77] More specifically, the Connecticut statute at issue in *Vlandis* created an "irreversible and irrebuttable . . . presumption that because a student's legal address was outside the State at the time of his application for admission or at some point during the preceding year, he remains a nonresident for as long as he is a student there." [78]

---

74.   326 F.Supp. at 240–241. See also Johns v. Redecker, 406 F.2d 878, 883 (8th Cir. 1969) for an explanation that reasonable tuition charges to nonresident students tend to make the tuition charged more nearly approximate the cost per student.

75.   See, e. g., Weaver v. Kelton, 357 F.Supp. 1106 (D.C.Tex.1973); Hooban v. Boling, 503 F.2d 648 (6th Cir. 1974); and Sturgis v. Washington, 368 F.Supp. 38 (D.C.Wash. 1973), aff'd 414 U.S. 1057 (1973).

76.   See, e. g., Clarke v. Redecker, 259 F.Supp. 117 (D.C.Iowa 1966).

77.   412 U.S. 441, 453 (1973). In light of the *Vlandis* holding, for example, the decision in Glusman v. Trustees of Univ. of North Carolina, 284 N.C. 225, 200 S.E.2d 9 (1973), was vacated and remanded, 412 U.S. 947 (1973).

78.   412 U.S. at 445.

It was "this conclusive presumption" that two women graduate students challenged as invalid in that it allowed "the State to classify as 'out-of-state students' those who are, in fact, bona fide residents of the State." The students claimed that they had "a constitutional right to controvert that presumption of nonresidence by presenting evidence that they [were] bona fide residents." The district court agreed and in affirming that judgment the Supreme Court quoted from the district court's holding: " 'Assuming that it is permissible for the state to impose a heavier burden of tuition and fees on non-resident than on resident students, the state may not classify as "out-of-state students" those who do not belong in that class.' " [79]

At the same time, however, the Supreme Court assured states "the right to impose on a student, as one element in demonstrating bona fide residence, a reasonable durational residency requirement, which can be met while in student status." Thus, the one year durational residency requirement, which has been affirmed summarily two years before in *Starns* (supra, fn. 70) was this time explicitly approved.

Still, the *Vlandis* restriction left unsettled a number of troublesome questions. For instance, before the ratification of the Twenty-Sixth Amendment (1971), it was extremely difficult for out-of-state students to prove legal emancipation from their nonresident parents prior to their twenty-first birthday and thus qualify for lower resident rates before their twenty-second. In effect, this gave states an almost *de facto* four-year period in which they could collect higher tuition rates from each incoming group of out-of-state undergraduates. But with 18-year-old majority could states deny resident status to legal adults solely on the ground that they received financial assistance from out-of-state parents? If so, the economic impact of *Vlandis* might be softened, but even though in Pelletreau v. Savage [80] a federal district court held that resident status could be so conditioned—it was a wise sage who said that "one robin a spring does not make."

Also, *Vlandis* did not establish precise guidelines for the determination of bona fide residence. Thus, the Sixth Circuit held that proof of state residency for voting purposes did not by itself

79. Id., at 445–446.

80. 381 F.Supp. 582 (D.C.N.H.1974). Perhaps the saying should be changed to "two robins a spring does not make" since in Florida Bd. of Regents v. Harris, 338 So.2d 215, 219 (Fla.App.1976), the Florida District Court of Appeals held that "an unemancipated minor cannot, of his own accord, select or change his domicile."

constitute proof for purposes of reduced university tuition,[81] for *Vlandis* noted approval of the Connecticut Attorney General's revised scheme in which voter registration was treated as but one of many criteria relevant to an individual determination of domicile. The Attorney General's criteria were quoted as follows:

"In reviewing a claim of in-state status, the issue becomes essentially one of domicile. In general, the domicile of an individual is his true, fixed and permanent home and place of habitation. It is the place to which, whenever he is absent, he has the intention of returning. This general statement, however, is difficult of application. Each individual case must be decided on its own particular facts. In reviewing a claim, relevant criteria include year-round residence, voter registration, place of filing tax returns, property ownership, driver's license, car registration, marital status, vacation employment, etc." [82]

On the other hand, the Sixth Circuit held that a state may *not* require proof of a postgraduation employment contract as a requisite element in such criteria, for this is a condition which may be "completely beyond the control of the applicant . . . , an impassable barrier to good faith residents." [83]

Although *Vlandis* did not speak directly to the question of financial aid (e. g., scholarships, loans) for nonresidents, it appears that "residents only" assistance is no more objectionable than the policy of providing lower tuition rates for residents. Most state scholarships, in fact, are reserved for in-state high school graduates, a practice which obviously places a permanent and irrebuttable stamp of ineligibility on out-of-state newcomers. Of course for tuition purposes this practice would not pass the *Vlandis* muster, but at least for the awarding of state scholarships its constitutionality is now well settled.[84] However, a fed-

---

81. Hayes v. Board of Regents of Kentucky State Univ., 495 F.2d 1326 (6th Cir. 1974).

82. 412 U.S. at 454.

83. Kelm v. Carlson, 473 F.2d 1267, 1272 (6th Cir. 1973). However, such evidence would undoubtedly carry considerable weight since states recognize that they are likely to realize less benefit from education invested in nonnatives; that is, these persons, having fewer roots in a state are more likely than na-tives to leave, carrying with them their socially valuable skills and taxable earning power. This point is discussed in Kirk v. Board of Regents of the University of California, 273 Cal.App.2d 430, 444, 78 Cal. Rptr. 260, 265 (1969) appeal dismissed, 396 U.S. 554 (1970).

84. See, e. g., Spatt v. State of New York, 361 F.Supp. 1048 (D.C.N.Y. 1973), aff'd 414 U.S. 1058 (1973), where New York's practice of restricting its Regents Scholarship to in-state high school graduates

eral district court in Connecticut struck down a permanent and irrebuttable presumption of nonresidency for purposes of Federally Insured Student Loan eligibility. Nevertheless, in applying the logic of *Vlandis*, at the same time it upheld a one-year waiting period.[85]

There is also the question of whether states may constitutionally classify resident aliens as nonresidents for purposes of charging them higher tuition fees or denying them financial assistance. The answer is obviously no, and even though *Vlandis* and its program are not directly articulated as such, the courts have consistently disapproved of such practices. In reaching this conclusion, courts have held that classifications based on alienage are "inherently suspect," and subject to "strict judicial scrutiny." As observed in chapter 7, such heightened judicial solicitude typically applies the "kiss of death" to these forms of classification. For example, in Jagnandan v. Giles,[86] resident student aliens attending Mississippi State University were successful in having declared unconstitutional this kind of discriminatory classification:

> Hence, although defendants may be concerned with the strain of educational financing and budget balancing—concededly such considerations do bear a rational relationship between the classification and a legitimate state purpose—they nevertheless fall short of constituting compelling need for the State to justify the classification . . . Most assuredly, this is not to say that aliens may not be subjected to any residency requirement whatever for tuition purposes, but only that Mississippi cannot permissibly draw a distinction between residency requirements imposed on the student who is a United States citizen and one who is a lawfully admitted alien.[87]

APPEARANCE

A Hairy Issue

Like UFO's it seems that the younger generation will always puzzle older people. But the sixties was somehow different.

and for use within the state was upheld. More specifically, it was determined that New York had no obligation to assist a Regents Scholarship winner who decided to attend an out-of-state institution.

85. Clark v. Hammer, 360 F.Supp. 476 (D.C.Conn.1973).

86. 379 F.Supp. 1178 (D.C.Miss.1974).

87. Id., at 1186. See also Moreno v. University of Maryland, 420 F. Supp. 541 (D.C.Md.1976); and Mauclet v. Nyguist, 406 F.Supp. 1233 (D.C.N.Y.1976).

Hair styles and bizarre costumes adopted by youth certainly aggravated the mystery. Young people also appeared a little more restless than usual, but then any parent knows that children are often a little like Miniver Cheevy, who "wept that he was ever born, and he had his reasons."

Later, however, the new physical trappings of youth began to enrage most adults. That is, once the association between long hair, beards and "ghastly" clothes on the one hand, and radicalism and dope on the other, was established, adult America declared war. In fact, the mania against long hair on one occasion was fatal. United Press International ran a story in April 1970 which reported a father had shot his son to death in a row over long hair and "a negative attitude toward society." That body hair could be of such significance in structuring an interpersonal response would have made even Dr. Freud's hair curl, but fortunately cases such as this were rare. Nevertheless, cases of body-hair discrimination in housing, school attendance, jobs, and commercial establishments, to mention a few, were numerous. John Kerns, for instance, placement officer at Stanford University stated that long-haired young men graduating from college in 1971 would likely find themselves lacking in job opportunities: "The length of a male's hair is directly proportionate to the job opportunities he can find . . . . In other words, the longer the hair, the fewer the jobs." [88]

Thus, in many places long hair (and beards) represented a hostile act which invited reprisal. Moreover, in the sixties school systems and colleges everywhere began to wage a relentless struggle against long hair. Often the long-haired male student was accused, tried and convicted in the blink of an eye as being one of "them." But the more they were persecuted, the more they seemed to cling to their hair styles. In fact, the progress of the generational struggle during the sixties and early seventies can be almost measured by the spread of these fashions.

Court Cases

Naturally, the authority of school administrators to impose hair-length prescriptions was tested in the courts, and at the college level, Zachry v. Brown [89] represents one of the earlier challenges. In this case, two students were administratively withdrawn from Jefferson State Junior College for failing to

---

88. Executive's Research Council, *Personnel Management Week* (January 25, 1971).

89. 299 F.Supp. 1360 (D.C.Ala.1967).

comply with a campus hair-length regulation (both students were members of a student band which had adopted the page-boy haircuts at issue). At the trial the college admitted that neither plaintiff had been a disciplinary problem, that both had passed their college entrance examinations placing them in the upper ten percent of the nation, and that their withdrawal had been motivated solely by dislike for what the college considered exotic hair styling. In fact, plaintiff Zachry had been a candidate for his class presidency and "would have been elected had he not been forced to withdraw." And, as if things did not look bad enough for the college, it made no allegation that the "plaintiffs' hair styling had any effect upon the health, discipline or decorum of the institution.[90]

The court had little difficulty in finding for the plaintiffs:

> The wide latitude permitted legislatures of the states and therefore the administrators of public colleges to classify students with respect to dress, appearance and behavior must be respected and preserved by the courts. However, the equal protection clause of the fourteenth amendment prohibits classification upon an unreasonable basis. This court is of the firm opinion that the classification of male students attending Jefferson State Junior College by their hair style is unreasonable and fails to pass constitutional muster.

> It needs to be emphasized that the defendants have not sought to justify such classification for moral and social reasons. The only reason stated upon the hearing of this case was their understandable personal dislike to long hair on men students. The requirement that these plaintiffs cut their hair to conform to normal or conventional styles is just as unreasonable as would palpably be a requirement that all male students of the college wore their hair down over their ears and collars.[91]

The court then indicated that "[o]n its facts, this case is clearly distinguishable from Ferrell v. Dallas Independent School Dist. . . . ."[92] Of course the *Ferrell*[93] case had also taken place in Texas and in the same United States Circuit, the Fifth. In fact, the issue in *Ferrell* was strikingly similar to that in *Zachry*; it involved Beatle-style haircuts which ran afoul of school hair regulations. Thus, aside from the fact that it in-

90. Id., at 1361.

91. Id., at 1362.

92. Id.

93. 261 F.Supp. 545 (D.C.Tex.1966).

volved a high school rather than a college, it might seem that *Ferrell's* ruling upholding the right of schools to impose such restrictions would have served as precedent for the ruling in *Zachry*. However, in *Ferrell* the hair-length regulation was upheld because the school was able to demonstrate a need for such a restriction in order to control disruptions attributable to controversies over student hair length.

Interestingly, the district court's rationale in *Ferrell* was affirmed by the Fifth Circuit; [94] that is, it accepted the principal's testimony that problems had been caused by boys wearing Beatle-type haircuts in school—for example, other boys deciding that a haircut was too long and threatening to take matters into their own hands by trimming it themselves, obscene remarks made by short-haired boys to long-haired ones, the long-haired boys being challenged to fights by the boys who did not like long hair. Thus, the test of compelling reason in this case—the interest of the state in maintaining an effective and efficient school system—was obvious, the Court said, as it affirmed the expulsion of the "long hairs." However, while recognizing the reasonableness and necessity of the regulation, both the district court and the Fifth Circuit recognized the general right of students to govern their personal appearance.

Later, in Stevenson v. Board of Educ. of Wheeler County, Georgia, the Fifth Circuit made clear that "[t]he touchstone for sustaining such regulations is the demonstration that they are necessary to alleviate interference with the educational process." [95] But the problem with such logic is that the legality of these regulations are not tested by any constitutional right to be different but by the reactions of others to that difference. Constitutionality by majority rule is a rather unique approach indeed. In fact, Judge Tuttle's dissenting opinion in *Ferrell* suggests that the short-haired boys were the ones causing the disturbance: "It seems to me it cannot be said too often that the constitutional rights of an individual cannot be denied him because his exercise of them produces violent reaction by those who would deprive him of the very right he seeks to assert." [96]

In later cases, including Breen v. Kahl [97] and Richards v. Thurston,[98] the Seventh and First Circuits recognized the impli-

---

94. 392 F.2d 697 (5th Cir. 1968).

95. 426 F.2d 1154, 1158 (5th Cir. 1970).

96. 392 F.2d at 705.

97. 419 F.2d 1034 (7th Cir. 1969).

98. 424 F.2d 1281 (1st Cir. 1970).

cations in Judge Tuttle's language and thus refused to recognize any inherent authority for a school administrator to suspend a student whose hair style seemed unconventional. Both opinions emphasized the position that a person cannot be restrained from performing a lawful act merely because hostile individuals or groups might cause a disturbance. In *Breen,* for instance, the Court pointed out that "[t]o uphold arbitrary school rules which 'sharply implicate basic constitutional values' for the sake of some nebulous concept of school discipline is contrary to the principle that we are a government of laws which are passed pursuant to the United States Constitution." [99]

Today, fortunately, few colleges and universities attempt to regulate the dress and hair styles of their students. Indeed, "[m]ankind's experience has demonstrated that in this area of fashion, fads constantly come and go as the pendulum unceasingly swings from extreme to extreme." [1] Of course, the problem still arises at the elementary and high level where decisions may be found both upholding and striking down such regulations, but the Supreme Court has so far ducked the issue.[2] Also, both the Ninth and Tenth Circuits believe that either such problems should be left to local authorities [3] or that this issue does not involve a question of substantial constitutional dimension.[4] Nevertheless, a state's invasion into the personal rights and liberty of an individual of whatever age or description should present a justiciable issue worthy of judicial review.

In general, then, colleges and universities should recognize personal appearance as a constitutionally protected right. However, if it can be shown that some aspect of a student's appearance will adversely affect his safety, the safety of others, or his ability to perform, then the institution should and may require change.

99. 419 F.2d at 1037.

1. Sims v. Colfax Community School Dist., 307 F.Supp. 485, 489 (D.C. Iowa 1970).

2. Some attempts have been made to equate appearance with symbolic expression and thus apply the *Tinker* holding. However, the Court in that case said: "The problem posed by the present case [black armbands] does not relate to regulation of the length of skirts or the type of clothing, to hair style or deportment." 393 U.S. 507–508 (1969).

3. King v. Saddleback Jr. College Dist., 445 F.2d 932 (9th Cir. 1971). Students in the 9th Circuit should be wary of this decision since it upheld grooming regulations on unbelievably flimsy grounds and recognized neither 1st nor 14th Amendment rights in this area.

4. Freeman v. Flake, 448 F.2d 258 (10th Cir. 1971).

VLANDIS v. KLINE

Supreme Court of the United States, 1973.
412 U.S. 441.

Mr. Justice STEWART delivered the opinion of the Court.

Like many other States, Connecticut requires nonresidents of the State who are enrolled in the state university system to pay tuition and other fees at higher rates than residents of the State who are so enrolled.   .   .   .   The constitutional validity of that requirement is not at issue in the case before us. What is at issue here is Connecticut's statutory definition of residents and nonresidents for purposes of the above provision.

[The statute] provides that an unmarried student shall be classified as a nonresident, or "out of state," student if his "legal address for any part of the one-year period immediately prior to his application for admission at a constituent unit of the state system of higher education was outside of Connecticut." With respect to married students,   .   .   .   the Act provides that such a student, if living with his spouse, shall be classified as "out of state" if his "legal address at the time of his application for admission to such a unit was outside of Connecticut." These classifications are permanent and irrebuttable for the whole time that the student remains at the university since   .   .   .   the Act commands that: "The status of a student, as established at the time of his application for admission at a constituent unit of the state system of higher education under the provisions of this section, shall be his status for the entire period of his attendance at such constituent unit." The present case concerns the constitutional validity of this conclusive and unchangeable presumption of nonresident status from the fact that, at the time of application for admission, the student, if married, was then living outside of Connecticut, or, if single, had lived outside the State at some point during the preceding year.

One appellee, Margaret Marsh Kline, is an undergraduate student at the University of Connecticut. In May of 1971, while attending college in California, she became engaged to Peter Kline, a lifelong Connecticut resident. Because the Klines wished to reside in Connecticut after their marriage, Mrs. Kline applied to the University of Connecticut from California. In late May, she was accepted and informed by the University that she would be considered an in-state student. On June 26, 1971, the appellee and Peter Kline were married in California, and soon thereafter took up residence in Storrs, Connecticut, where they have established a permanent home. Mrs. Kline has a Connecticut driver's license, her car is registered in Connecticut, and she is registered as a Connecticut voter. In July 1971, Public Act No. 5 went into effect. Accordingly, the appellant, Director of Admissions at the University of Connecticut, irreversibly classified Mrs. Kline as an out-of-state student, pursuant to   .   .   .   that Act. As a consequence, she was required to pay $150 tuition and a $200 nonresident fee for the first semester, whereas a student classified as a Connecticut resident paid no tuition; and upon registration for the second semester, she was required to pay $425 tuition plus another $200 nonresident fee, while a student classified as a Connecticut resident paid only $175 tuition.

The other appellee, Patricia Catapano, is an unmarried graduate student at the same University. She applied for admission from Ohio in January 1971, and was accepted in February of that year. In August 1971, she moved her residence from Ohio to Connecticut and registered as a full-time student at the University. Like Mrs. Kline, she has a Connecticut driver's license, her car is registered in Connecticut, and she is registered as a Connecticut voter. Pursuant to   .   .   .   the 1971 Act, the appellant classified her permanently as an out-of-state student. Consequently, she, too, was required to pay $150 tuition and a $200 nonresident fee for her first semester, and $425 tuition plus a $200 nonresident fee for her second semester.

Appellees then brought suit in the District Court pursuant to the Civil Rights Act of 1871, 42 U.S.C.A. § 1983, contending that they were bona fide residents of Connecticut, and that § 126 of Public Act No. 5, under which they were classified as nonresidents for purposes of their tuition and fees, infringed their rights to due process of law and equal protection of the laws, guaranteed by the Fourteenth Amendment to the Constitution. After the convening of a three-judge District Court, that court unanimously held §§ 126 (a) (2), (a) (3), and (a) (5) unconstitutional, as violative of the Fourteenth Amendment, and enjoined the appellant from enforcing those sections. The court also found that before the commencement of the spring semester in 1972, each appellee was a bona fide resident of Connecticut; and it accordingly ordered that the appellant refund to each of them the amount of tuition and fees paid in excess of the amount paid by resident students for that semester. On December 4, 1972, we noted probable jurisdiction of this appeal.

.   .   .

Statutes creating permanent irrebutable presumptions have long been disfavored under the Due Process Clauses of the Fifth and Fourteenth Amendments. In Heiner v. Donnan, 285 U.S. 312 (1932), the Court was faced with a constitutional challenge to a federal statute that created a conclusive presumption that gifts made within two years prior to the donor's death were made in contemplation of death, thus requiring payment by his estate of a higher tax. In holding that this irrefutable assumption was so arbitrary and unreasonable as to deprive the taxpayer of his property without due process of law, the Court stated that it had "held more than once that a statute creating a presumption which operates to deny a fair opportunity to rebut it violates the due process clause of the Fourteenth Amendment." Id., at 329.

The more recent case of Bell v. Burson, 402 U.S. 535, involved a Georgia statute which provided that if an uninsured motorist was involved in an accident and could not post security for the amount of damages claimed, his driver's license must be suspended without any hearing on the question of fault or responsibility. The Court held that since the State purported to be concerned with fault in suspending a driver's license, it could not, consistent with procedural due process, conclusively presume fault from the fact that the uninsured motorist was involved in an accident, and could not, therefore, suspend his driver's license without a hearing on that crucial factor.

Likewise, in Stanley v. Illinois, 405 U.S. 645, the Court struck down, as violative of the Due Process Clause of the Fourteenth Amendment, Illinois' irrebuttable statutory presumption that all unmarried fathers are unqualified to raise their children. Because of that presumption, the statute required the State, upon the death of the mother, to take custody of all such illegitimate children, without providing any hearing on the father's parental fitness. It may be, the Court said, "that most unmarried fathers are unsuitable and neglectful parents. . . . But all unmarried fathers are not in this category; some are wholly suited to have custody of their children." Id., at 654. Hence, the Court held that the State could not conclusively presume that any individual unmarried father was unfit to raise his children; rather, it was required by the Due Process Clause to provide a hearing on that issue. According to the Court, Illinois "insists on presuming rather than proving Stanley's unfitness solely because it is more convenient to presume than to prove. Under the Due Process Clause that advantage is insufficient to justify refusing a father a hearing . . . . " Id., at 658.

The same considerations obtain here. It may be that most applicants to Connecticut's university system who apply from outside the State or within a year of living out of State have no real intention of becoming Connecticut residents and will never do so. But it is clear that not all of the applicants from out of State inevitably fall in this category. Indeed, in the present case, both appellees possess many of the indicia of Connecticut residency, such as year-round Connecticut homes, Connecticut drivers' licenses, car registrations, voter registrations, etc.; and both were found by the District Court to have become bona fide residents of Connecticut before the 1972 spring semester. Yet, under the State's statutory scheme, neither was permitted any opportunity to demonstrate the bona fides of her Connecticut residency for tuition purposes, and neither will ever have such an opportunity in the future so long as she remains a student.

The State proffers three reasons to justify that permanent irrebuttable presumption. The first is that the State has a valid interest in equalizing the cost of public higher education between Connecticut residents and nonresidents, and that by freezing a student's residential status as of the time he applies, the State ensures that its bona fide in-state students will receive their full subsidy. The State's objective of cost equalization between bona fide residents and nonresidents may well be legitimate, but basing the bona fides of residency solely on where a student lived when he applied for admission to the University is using a criterion wholly unrelated to that objective. As is evident from the situation of the appellees, a student may be a bona fide resident of Connecticut even though he applied to the University from out of State. Thus, Connecticut's conclusive presumption of nonresidence, instead of ensuring that only its bona fide residents receive their full subsidy, ensures that certain of its bona fide residents, such as the appellees, do *not* receive their full subsidy, and can never do so while they remain students.

Second, the State argues that even if a student who applied to the University from out of State may at some point become a bona fide resident of Connecticut, the State can nonetheless reasonably decide to favor with the lower rates only its established residents, whose past tax contributions to the State have been higher. According to the State, the fact that established residents or their parents have supported the State in the past justifies the conclusion that applicants from out of State—who are presumed not to be such established residents—may be denied the lower rates, even if they have become bona fide residents.

Connecticut's statutory scheme, however, makes no distinction on its face between established residents and new residents. Rather, . . . the State purports to distinguish, for tuition purposes, between residents and nonresidents by granting the lower rates to the former and denying them to the latter. In these circumstances, the State cannot now seek to justify its classification of certain bona fide residents as nonresidents, on the basis that their Connecticut residency is "new."

. . .

The third ground advanced to justify § 126 is that it provides a degree of administrative certainty. The State points to its interest in preventing out-of-state students from coming to Connecticut solely to obtain an education and then claiming Connecticut residence in order to secure the lower tuition and fees. The irrebuttable presumption, the State contends, makes it easier to separate out students who come to the State solely for its educational facilities from true Connecticut residents, by eliminating the need for an individual determination of the bona fides of a person who lived out of State at the time of his application. Such an individual determination, it is said, would not only be an expensive administrative burden, but would also be very difficult to make, since it is hard to evaluate when bona fide residency exists. Without the conclusive presumption, the State argues, it would be almost impossible to prevent out-of-state students from claiming a Connecticut residence merely to obtain the lower rates.

In Stanley v. Illinois, supra, however, the Court stated that "the Constitution recognizes higher values than speed and efficiency." 405 U.S., at 656. The State's interest in administrative ease and certainty cannot, in and of itself, save the conclusive presumption from invalidity under the Due Process Clause where there are other reasonable and practicable means of establishing the pertinent facts on which the State's objective is premised. In the situation before us, reasonable alternative means for determining bona fide residence are available. Indeed, one such method has already been adopted by Connecticut; after § 126 was invalidated by the District Court, the State established reasonable criteria for evaluating bona fide residence for purposes of tuition and fees at its university system. These criteria, while perhaps more burdensome to apply than an irrebuttable presumption, are certainly sufficient to prevent abuse of the lower, in-state rates by students who come to Connecticut solely to obtain an education.

In sum, since Connecticut purports to be concerned with residency in allocating the rates for tuition and fees in its university system, it is forbidden by the Due Process Clause to deny an individual the resident rates on the basis of a permanent and irrebuttable presumption of nonresidence, when that presumption is not necessarily or universally true in fact, and when the State has reasonable alternative means of making the crucial determination. Rather, standards of due process require that the State allow such an individual the opportunity to present evidence showing that he is a bona fide resident entitled to the in-state rates. Since § 126 precluded the appellees from ever rebutting the presumption that they were nonresidents of Connecticut, that statute operated to deprive them of a significant amount of their money without due process of law.

We are aware, of course, of the special problems involved in determining the bona fide residence of college students who come from out of State to attend that State's public university. Our holding today should in no wise be taken to mean that Connecticut must classify the students in its university system as residents, for purposes of tuition and fees, just because they go to school there. Nor should our decision be construed to deny a State the right to impose on a student, as one element in demonstrating bona fide residence, a reasonable durational residency requirement, which can be met while in student status. We fully recognize that a State has a legitimate interest in protecting and preserving the quality of its colleges and universities and the right of its own bona fide residents to attend such institutions on a preferential tuition basis.

We hold only that a permanent irrebuttable presumption of nonresidence—the means adopted by Connecticut to preserve that legitimate interest—is violative of the Due Process Clause, because it provides no opportunity for students who applied from out of State to demonstrate that they have become bona fide Connecticut residents. The State can establish such reasonable criteria for in-state status as to make virtually certain that students who are not, in fact, bona fide residents of the State, but who have come there solely for educational purposes, cannot take advantage of the in-state rates. .   .   .

.   .   .   .

Because we hold that the permanent irrebuttable presumption of nonresidence . . . violates the Due Process Clause of the Fourteenth Amendment, the judgment of the District Court is affirmed. It is so ordered.

. . .

Mr. Justice MARSHALL, with whom Mr. Justice BRENNAN joins, concurring.

I join the opinion of the Court except insofar as it suggests that a State may impose a one-year residency requirement as a prerequisite to qualifying for in-state tuition benefits. . . . That question is not presented by this case since here we deal with a permanent, irrebuttable presumption of nonresidency based on the fact that a student was a nonresident at the time he applied for admission to the state university system. I recognize that in Starns v. Malkerson, 401 U.S. 985, we summarily affirmed a district court decision sustaining a one-year residency requirement for receipt of in-state tuition benefits. But I now have serious question as to the validity of that summary decision in light of well-established principles, under the Equal Protection Clause of the Fourteenth Amendment, which limit the States' ability to set residency requirements for the receipt of rights and benefits bestowed on bona fide state residents. See Dunn v. Blumstein, 405 U.S. 330; Shapiro v. Thompson, 394 U.S. 618. Because the Court finds sufficient basis in the Due Process Clause of the Fourteenth Amendment to dispose of the constitutionality of the Connecticut statute here at issue, it has no occasion to address the serious equal protection questions raised by this and other tuition residency laws. In the absence of full consideration of those equal protection questions, I would leave the validity of a one-year residence requirement for a future case in which the issue is squarely presented.

. . .

Mr. Justice WHITE, concurring in the judgment.

. . .

I concur in the judgment, . . . because Connecticut, although it may legally discriminate between its residents and nonresidents for purposes of tuition, here invidiously discriminates among at least three classes of bona fide Connecticut residents. First, there are those unmarried students who have resided in Connecticut one year prior to application or who later reside in Connecticut for a year without going to school. They pay the substantially lower in-state tuition. Second, there are the married students who have a legal address in Connecticut at the time of application. They also pay the lower tuition, whether or not they have resided in Connecticut for a year prior to application. Third, there are the unmarried students whose legal address has been outside Connecticut at some time during the year prior to application but who later become legal residents of Connecticut, before or after application or before or after matriculation, and remain such for at least one year. These students, although yearlong residents, must continue to pay out-of-state tuition for as long as they are in school.

This discrimination between classes of bona fide residents of the State is sought to be justified, as I understand it, on the sole ground that too few students from out of State actually become Connecticut residents to require the State to sort out this small number by investigating the inevitably larger number of residency claims which would be submitted if the rule were otherwise but which for the most part would be bogus.

. . .

Here, it is enough for me that the interest involved is that of obtaining a higher education, that the difference between in-state and out-of-state tuition is substantial, and that the State, without sufficient justification, imposes a one-year residency requirement on some students but not on others, and also refuses, no matter what the circumstances, to permit the requirement to be satisfied through bona fide residence while in school. It is plain enough that the State has only the most attenuated interest in terms of administrative convenience in maintaining this bizarre pattern of discrimination among those who must or must not pay a substantial tuition to the University. The discrimination imposed by the State is invidious and violates the Equal Protection Clause.

Mr. Chief Justice BURGER, with whom Mr. Justice REHNQUIST joins, dissenting.

I find myself unable to join the action taken today because the Court in this case strays from what seem to me sound and established constitutional principles in order to reach what it considers a just result in a particular case; this gives meaning to the ancient warning that "hard cases make bad law." The Court permits this "hard" case to make some very dubious law.

A state university today is an establishment with capital costs of many millions of dollars of investment. Its annual operating costs likewise may run into the millions. Parents and other taxpayers willingly carry this heavy burden because they believe in the values of higher education. It is not narrow provincialism for the State to think that each State should carry its own educational burdens. Until we redefine our system of government—as we are free to do by constitutionally prescribed means—the States may restrict subsidized education to their own residents. This much the Court recognizes and it likewise recognizes that the statutory scheme under review reasonably tends to support that end.

. . .

Distressingly, the Court applies "strict scrutiny" and invalidates Connecticut's statutory scheme without explaining why the statute impairs a genuine constitutional interest truly worthy of the standard of close judicial scrutiny. The real issue here is not whether holes can be picked in the Connecticut scheme; of course, that is readily done with this "bad" statute. Whether we deal with statutes of Connecticut or of Congress, we can find flaws, gaps, and hard and unseemly results at times. But our function in constitutional adjudication is not to see whether there is some conceivably "less restrictive" alternative to the statutory classifications under review. The Court's task is to explain why the "strict scrutiny" test, previously confined to other areas, should now in practical effect be read into the Due Process Clause. . . .

There will be, I fear, some ground for a belief that the Court now engrafts the "close judicial scrutiny" test onto the Due Process Clause whenever we deal with something like "permanent irrebuttable presumptions." But literally thousands of state statutes create classifications permanent in duration, which are less than perfect, as all legislative classifications are, and might be improved on by individualized determinations so as to avoid the untoward results produced here due to the very unusual facts of this case. Both the anomaly present here and the arguable alternatives to it do not differ from those present when, for example, a State provides that a person may not be licensed to practice medicine or law unless he or she is a graduate of an accredited professional graduate school; a perfectly capable practitioner may as a consequence be barred "permanently and irrebuttably" from pursuing his calling, without ever having an opportunity to prove his personal skills. The doctrinal difficulties of the Equal Protection Clause are indeed trying, but today the Court makes an uncharted drift toward complications for the Due Process Clause comparable in scope and seriousness with those we are encountering in the equal protection area. Can this be what we are headed for?

The pressure of today's holding may well push the States to enact reciprocal statutes to the end that Connecticut will undertake to admit as "resident" students only those students from other States that give the same status to Connecticut residents. When a State allocates a large share of its resources to create and maintain a university whose quality is found attractive to many students from other States, its very success and stature may well operate to cripple it because then, not unnaturally, it will be flooded with applications from students from afar. Perhaps on less "high ground" students who favor winter sports will flock to the Northeast and Northwest and the sun worshipers will head South. Is the Court willing to say that Connecticut may not grant partial scholarships to persons who have attended a Connecticut secondary school for—let us say— at least one full school year and then set nonresident tuition as it does now? We should not be surprised at the natural response of States which, having placed high value on universities, having developed great institutions at large cost, believe that other States should do the same and therefore seek ways to keep the institution in being for its own citizens. . . .

The urge to cure every disadvantage human beings can experience exerts an inexorable pressure to expand judicial doctrine. But that urge should not move the Court to erect standards that are unrealistic and indeed unexplained for evaluating the constitutionality of state statutes.

Mr. Justice REHNQUIST, with whom THE CHIEF JUSTICE and Mr. Justice DOUGLAS join, dissenting.

The Court's opinion relegates to the limbo of unconstitutionality a Connecticut law that requires higher tuition from those who come from out of State to attend its state universities than from those who come from within the State. The opinion accomplishes this result by a highly theoretical analysis that relies heavily on notions of substantive due process that have been authoritatively repudiated by subsequent decisions of the Court. Believing as I do that the Connecticut statutory scheme is a constitutionally permissible means of dealing with an increasingly acute problem facing state systems of higher education, I dissent.

This country's system of higher education presently faces a serious crisis, produced in part by escalating costs of furnishing educational services and in part by sharply increased demands for those services. Because state systems have available to them state financial resources that are not available to private institutions, they may find it relatively easier to grapple with the financial aspect of this crisis. But for this very reason, States have generally felt that state resources should be devoted, at least in large part, to the education of children of the State's own residents, and that those who come from elsewhere to attend a state university should have to make a more substantial contribution toward the full costs of the education they would receive than the all but nominal tuition required of those who come from within the State.

One way to accomplish such a differentiation would be to make the tuition differential turn on whether or not the student was a "resident" or "nonresident" of the State at the time tuition is paid. The Court, at least by implication, concedes that such a differentiation would violate no command of the Constitution, but even a capsule examination of how such a plan would operate indicates why it did not commend itself to the Connecticut Legislature. The very act of enrolling in a Connecticut university with the intention of completing a program of studies leading to a degree necessitates the physical presence of the student in the State of Connecticut. Additional indicia of residency, by which the Court apparently sets great store—obtaining a Connecticut motor vehicle registration or driver's license, registering to vote in Connecticut—impose no significant burden on the out-of-state student in comparison with the thousands of dollars he will save in tuition and fees during the pursuit of a four-year course in undergraduate studies. Thus, what the Court concedes to the States in the way of distinguishing between resident and nonresident students, while perhaps a valuable bit of authority in issuing fishing and hunting licenses, is all but useless in making students who come from out of State pay even a portion of their fair share of the cost of the education that they seek to receive in Connecticut state universities.

. . .

. . . The Court's opinion deals with the situation of the particular litigants here involved, doubtless chosen with an eye to illustrating the Connecticut system at its worst, and with still other hypothetical examples upon which it expatiates during the course of its opinion. But the fact that a generally valid rule may have rough edges around its perimeter does not make it unconstitutional under the Due Process Clause of the Fourteenth Amendment:

> "[T]he law need not be in every respect logically consistent with its aims to be constitutional. It is enough that there is an evil at hand for correction, and that it might be thought that the particular legislative measure was a rational way to correct it." Williamson v. Lee Optical Co., 348 U.S. 483, 487–488.

Throughout the Court's opinion are found references to the "irrebuttable" presumption as to residency created by the Connecticut statutes. But a fair reading of these laws indicates that Connecticut has not chosen to define eligibility for a state-subsidized education in terms of "residency" at the moment that the applicant seeks admission to the university system, but instead has insisted that the applicant have some prior connection with the State of Connecticut independent of the desire to attend a state-supported university. Thus, it would not satisfy Connecticut's goals in seeking to subsidize the education of Connecticut's young people in Connecticut state universities to impose a classic residency test as of the moment of entry into the system of higher education. All students, and not only those with substantial Connecticut connections, will be present in Connecticut on this date, and those who have been astute enough to consult counsel will have obtained Connecticut drivers' licenses, registered their cars in Connecticut, and registered to vote in Connecticut.

Meaningful differentiation between children of families who have supported the state educational system by payment of taxes to the State of Connecticut, and children from families who have not done this, would be impossible if the test were residency as of the date of admission, or the date on which tuition is due, at least as the Court enunciates such a test. But this is not what Connecticut tried to do, and, as I read the Court's opinion Connecticut is not limited to the imposition of such an easily circumvented test. For the Court reaffirms Starns v. Malkerson, 326 F.Supp. 234 (Minn.1970), aff'd, 401 U.S. 985, in which the State of Minnesota had by regulation provided that no student could qualify as a resident for tuition purposes unless he had been a bona fide domiciliary of the State for at least a year immediately prior thereto. A regulation such as Minnesota's enables the State partially to maintain the distinction that Connecticut has sought to protect here. The Court indicates that the critical distinction between the Minnesota regulation and the Connecticut statute is that the Minnesota regulation operated to fix nonresidency only for the first year of attendance at the university. But this supposed distinction merely highlights the error in the Court's approach to this entire problem. Minnesota was no more concerned during the first year than is Connecticut with "residency" as that term is used in other legal contexts. One who had his vehicle licensed in Minnesota, obtained a Minnesota driver's license, and registered to vote in Minnesota could make the same attack on the "irrebuttable" presumption of residency involved in *Starns* as these appellees do on the Connecticut statute. The Court's response is that while Minnesota's fixing of residency as of a date prior to application endured for only one year, Connecticut's endures for four years. This is admittedly a factual difference, but one may read the Court's opinion in vain to ascertain why it is a difference of constitutional significance.

.   .   .

Part V

MISCELLANY

Chapter 9

WHO CARES?

I became an academic administrator in 1923. For more than 51 years, I have seen educational institutions from the kindergarden up settle their programs by log-rolling, by public relations, by political pressure and most of all by asking where the money is. I have met with committees of great universities to discuss education and research, and I have found them talking about those mystic initials ADA and FTE, average daily attendance and full-time equivalents. This is what they wanted to talk about because manipulating these letters produces the revenue, through a kind of mystical algebra, derived from the state. What this led to was public relations as determinant of policy. They tried to think of courses that would attract students. It mattered not whether these courses had any intellectual content. Things have not changed.

(Robert M. Hutchins, 1974)

There are serious drawbacks to an imagery based on students as consumers or receivers of an educational product or service. In large measure, consumerist rhetoric conjures up an image of unwitting victims pitted against unscrupulous villains bent on gaining a quick profit. The reality of post-secondary study is much different: Students are active participants in the learning process, not passive recipients of a service. A specific product cannot be expected; although the institution can provide opportunities for learning, the result for any particular student depends heavily on individual interest and effort. And most institutions conscientiously seek to provide good instructional and other services, even if actual performance falls short of that mark.

(E. H. El-khawas in "Putting the Student Consumer in Perspective," *Educational Record,* Spring, 1977)

409

TORT LIABILITY

Is there a doctor (Ph.D.) in the house? With that the better question for the good doctor (professor) might be which way to run. In legal parlance, that is, the question is really whether there is a "reasonable person" in the house, "a fictitious person who never has existed on land or sea."[1] But in a court of law such cynical doubt is never entertained; in the words of no less than H. P. Herbert, reasonable-person models abound in courtrooms across the land: "this excellent but odious character [who] stands like a monument in our courts of justice, vainly appealing to his fellow-citizens to order their lives after his own excellent example."[2]

Indeed, at the moment there is nothing on the horizon that would lead one to believe that the interaction between lawyers and educators, colleges and courts, will decline. Widespread feelings of distrust of educators seem likely to continue for, among other things, these feelings are rooted in growing expectations about colleges and universities and their role in promoting the good life. As in a theater, it is the actors who are at fault if they do not give satisfaction; it is never the audience that is obtuse, insensitive or unreasonable.

Still, the very nature of the academic enterprise involves the question of what role educators should play. As shall be seen, the courts repeatedly underscore the principle that the function of teaching-learning imposes the duty to exercise reasonable care in its discharge; and the standard of care is that of a reasonably prudent educator, not that of a reasonably prudent layman. Moreover, there is also the implication that since institutions of higher education do exist to serve students, as consumers they should have a voice to indicate, and with some force, whether their needs are being well or poorly served.

The picture then is one of increasing litigation with the court of justice as the culprit or hero. In fact, though the issues of due process and equal protection are laden with legal significance, one of the most fertile sources of litigation continues to be in the area of tortious conduct. Here, once again, is that reasonable standard of care which higher education personnel must adhere to with respect to students; and faculty members and administra-

1. William L. Prosser, *Law of Torts*, 4th ed. (St. Paul, Minn.: West Publishing Co., 1971), p. 24.

2. As quoted in Prosser, Id., p. 125.

tors are seldom immune from such a standard irrespective of whether they are employed in public or private institutions. Nonetheless, any definition of a "tort" is likely to encounter disagreement and lack of uniformity in its application, but sufficient for our purpose one legal authority defines a tort as

> . . . a term applied to a miscellaneous and more or less unconnected group of civil wrongs, *other than a breach of contract,* for which a court of law will afford a remedy in the form of an action for damages. The law of torts is concerned with the compensation of losses suffered by private individuals in their legally protected interests, through conduct of others which is regarded as socially unreasonable.[3]

Tort liability, therefore, covers an expansive and varied category of civil law actions exclusive of contract. Generally the courts are asked to right a wrong suffered by one party during a social interaction with one or more parties, by obligating the defendant to compensate the plaintiff for damages suffered. The disputed action most commonly falls into one of two causal categories:

1. An *intentional* tort which assumes the injurious action to have been intentional or planned, but not necessarily intended as hostile (e. g., a practical joke not meant to cause harm or injury). The most frequent intentional torts occurring in campus interaction are assault, battery and defamation (see chapter 6, pp. 256–258 for discussion of defamation liability).

2. A *negligence* tort which assumes that unintentional injurious action could have been prevented with reasonable care and proper foresight.

Tort cases are generally decided on the basis of common law precedent, but without attempting to exhaust all possible torts, the discussion that follows will be centered around negligence torts which seem to occur with reasonable frequency in the everyday operation of colleges and universities.

Elements of Negligence Torts

Negligence liability stems from a social relationship wherein a person establishing a relationship with another must assume the risk of that association, and, as noted above, it implies unintentional conduct which causes an injury or damages to another person. Hence, negligence may be defined as conduct falling be-

---

3. Prosser, *Law of Torts,* 3rd ed.
(1964), p. 1 (emphasis added).

low that of a reasonable person who, if in the position of the actor, would have anticipated the harmful results. Moreover, according to the familiar judicial formula, the requisite elements to a cause of action are (1) facts showing a duty on the part of the defendant to protect the plaintiff against unreasonable risks; (2) negligence on the part of the defendant constituting a breach of that duty; and (3) injury to the plaintiff as a proximate result of the defendant's conduct.[4]

Obviously, in the educational setting there exists a special relationship between professors and others in the teaching profession and students. And as the foreseeable risk involved in this relationship increases, the standard of care required likewise increases. For instance, the standard of care of a chemistry teacher for the protection of students is generally greater than that of the college librarian. This is true, of course, because the risk of injury involved in handling chemicals is much greater than the risk of being injured while reading a book.

Defenses to Negligence Suits

There are three basic defenses to a negligence suit, any one of which may either reduce liability or bar altogether a plaintiff's effort to recover damages from a defendant. These are "contributory negligence," "assumption of risk," and "immunity."

Contributory negligence is negligent conduct on the part of the plaintiff which, combined with the negligence of the defendant, is the proximate cause of the injury suffered by the plaintiff.

4. Since it is a community ideal, the model for the "reasonable person" varies. However, a California court in Lehmuth v. Long Beach Unified School Dist., 53 Cal.2d 544, 2 Cal.Rptr. 279, 348 P.2d 887 (1960) provided a generally accepted framework: (1) the physical attributes of the defendant himself; (2) normal intelligence; (3) normal perception and memory with a minimum level of information and experience common to the community; and (4) such superior skill and knowledge as the actor has or holds himself out as having. However, "duty [to care] is not sacrosanct in itself, but only an expression of the sum total of those considerations of policy which lead the law to say that the particular plaintiff is entitled to protection." Prosser, 3rd ed. (1971), pp. 332–333. Also, Rowland v. Christian, 69 Cal.2d 108, 70 Cal.Rptr. 97, 100, 443 P.2d 561, 564 (1968), lists the principal considerations: "the foreseeability of harm to the plaintiff, the degree of certainty that the plaintiff suffered injury, the closeness of the connection between the defendant's conduct and the injury suffered, the moral blame attached to the defendant's conduct and the injury suffered, the future harm, the extent of the burden to the defendant and consequences to the community of imposing a duty to exercise care with resulting liability for breach, and the availability, cost, and prevalence of insurance for the risk involved.

To illustrate, contributory negligence by the plaintiff student in Kiser v. Snyder [5] was apparent enough to the presiding judge to hold the tort action alleging instructor negligence invalid.

The injury under consideration in this case involved a 19-year-old male student who had two fingertips mashed while learning to operate a metal shearer at a tax-supported technical institute. The student, along with others in the class, received instruction in the use and operation of the machine and, while demonstrating how to operate the machine when working with a short piece of metal, the instructor warned the class not to place their fingers under the guardrail. The student, however, forgot to recheck his finger position after looking away to check the position of his foot and, with the resulting injury, instructor negligence was claimed on the basis of lack of specific instruction to recheck the hand position.

The court found that the instructor had provided adequate instruction and then went on to point out that regardless of any instructor negligence, the student was contributorily negligent since he was old enough and had the capacity to exercise reasonable care for his own safety; that is, the law also imposes a duty on the individual to protect himself. Therefore, the negligence, if any, on the part of the defendant instructor was not the "substantial" cause of the harm to the plaintiff. Clearly, in reaching this determination the age of the student was of paramount importance to the court.

In most negligence cases, however, the courts will not emphasize proximate cause but will instead rely almost solely on the duty or obligation of the defendant and the standard of conduct required to avoid liability. Proximate cause as a criterion of negligence liability is most often used when some doubt is present as to whether the injured party was within a zone of obvious danger.[6] For example, in the college or university setting there are often risks involved in the teaching-learning function, as in the above *Kiser* case, but unlike *Kiser,* the courts here will generally place more emphasis on the required standard of conduct than the proximate cause. This is evident in the next case, Butler v. Louisiana State Bd. of Educ.,[7] wherein this time the court ruled for the student as it focused its attention on a standard of care in relation to an unambiguous hazard.

---

5. 21 N.C.App. 708, 205 S.E.2d 619 (1974).

6. Prosser, 4th ed. (1971), 252.

7. 331 So.2d 192 (La.App.1976).

The hazardous condition in this case centered around the action of a University of Southwestern Louisiana biology professor who allowed a student to conduct an experiment which required the extraction of blood from student volunteers. After blood had been taken from the plaintiff, a freshman coed, she fainted while being walked to a table (no wheelchair or bed was available) and fell forward on the floor whereupon six of her teeth were broken or badly damaged. Her suit, therefore, alleged that the professor had been negligent for not having properly instructed the student who performed the blood extraction as to the procedure which should be followed and that the professor had not provided ready access to a bed or a means of carrying a patient to such a facility had one been needed.

The defendant contended that the plaintiff was barred from collecting damages since her own negligence was a substantial factor in bringing about the injury that befell her. More specifically, it was alleged that she had insisted upon returning to her dormitory and thus misled the student who extracted the blood by telling him that she felt fine after the extraction, when she in fact was feeling faint. Testimony contrary to that claim, however, was heard and accepted by the trial court, and upon appeal, the Court of Appeal of Louisiana affirmed the lower court's holding that the defendant failed to establish contributory negligence.

In regard to the professor's duty and required standard of conduct, the Court of Appeal pointed out that where risks are greater to students, the teacher has an increased level of obligation or duty to protect the students. And in reinforcing the special nature of this duty, the Court declared that "the law is well settled that nurses and medical technicians who undertake to perform medical services are subject to the same . . . duty of care and to liability as are physicians in the performance of professional services." [8] The Court then held that the same duty of care applied to a university professor "who approves and undertakes to supervise a project which includes the performance of a medical function such as the withdrawal of blood from volunteer students." [9] As to the proximate cause of the injury, the Court held that because of the nature of such relationships, a professor can be liable for an omission to act as well as for an affirmative act; thus, since the professor failed to properly instruct the student conducting the experiment and failed to pro-

8. Id., at 196.   9. Id.

vide for the necessary facilities, such omissions constituted negligence and were the "proximate cause of the accident." [10]

In another tort case on appeal to the Supreme Judicial Court of Maine, Isaacson v. Husson College,[11] a judgment against a college was likewise sustained as both courts concentrated on the required standard of conduct as it related to a distinct and manifest danger. Isaacson, the plaintiffs and a student at Husson College, one evening slipped and fell on a patch of ice on his way from the dining hall along an unlighted direct walkway to his dormitory. As a result he sustained a "permanent impairment" to his right knee and was awarded damages in the amount of $12,000 by the jury in the trial court.

The judgment was based on evidence indicating that the College failed to exercise reasonable care under the foreseeably hazardous conditions of severely cold weather "which exposed [the plaintiff] to an unreasonable risk of harm [that] was present for a time of sufficient duration prior to the accident to enable the reasonably prudent person to discover and remedy it." [12] In respect to the defendant's allegation that the plaintiff was contributorily negligent, the higher court succinctly pointed out that "despite his [the plaintiff's] precautions of wearing rippled-soled shoes and walking in a 'shuffling' manner, he fell forward injuring his right knee. When he fell plaintiff felt and saw that he had slipped on a patch of ice not previously visible to him because of the absence of illumination in the area." [13]

State law differs as to whether pleas of contributory or comparative negligence will be available to a defendant. In some states a showing of contributory negligence will result in a judgment for the defendant and has the effect of barring any kind of recovery. Other states have adopted comparative negligence statutes. Where this concept is practiced, both the plaintiff and the defendant may be found negligent and a proration of the damages will therefore be decided on a light, ordinary, or gross basis with the jury determining the degree of carelessness on the part of both parties. On a finding of slight negligence on the part of the defendant the plaintiff may have to bear the major loss.

Of course the best defense for an educator in these kinds of situations would be proof that he had acted without negligence or that his professional performance measured up to that expected of a reasonably prudent professional in the same or similar

10. Id. at 197.

11. 332 A.2d 757 (Me.1975).

12. Id., at 760.

13. Id., at 769.

circumstances. If, for instance, a professor gave adequate instruction as to the hazards involved in an activity and at the same time provided proper supervision, he later would have a compelling and convincing response to any charge of negligence. A simple denial of negligence is not enough to satisfy a jury.

Occasionally, a plea of an "act of God" may be available in this kind of situation. Such a circumstance might include a situation where a student is hit by a bolt of lightning while playing golf as a member of a college team. The point is that this occurrence would be a direct, immediate, and exclusive operation of the forces of nature and thus no amount of care or foresight could prevent such an injury. Moreover, the legal doctrine of "assumed risk" often gets lively play in such cases. For example, in Mintz v. State,[14] the Appellate Division of the State Supreme Court of New York affirmed a lower court's dismissal of a negligence action filed by the parents of two university students who had drowned during an overnight canoe outing. The drownings occurred during a fierce storm, but the lower court, even though accepting the fact that the university had encouraged the outing and then subsequently failed to supervise it properly, expressed great doubt as to whether the students had been encouraged to enter a zone of obvious danger. Not negligence, but the unforeseen weather storm was the proximate cause according to the court. In affirming the lower court, the higher court pointed out that a 20-year-old student is capable of understanding the risk in such an activity and furthermore does not need the supervision of a 10-year-old.

Assumption of risk, though a minor element in the *Mintz* decision, is a commonly used defense in the area of contact sports. A college-age student who voluntarily participates in football or ice hockey, for instance, knows before he joins the team that occasional injuries occur. Hence, when he participates with this knowledge he also assumes those inherent and obvious risks of the sport. Such a defense is often asserted against a spectator watching a sporting event of this kind; however, as pointed out by the State Supreme Court of Iowa in Dudley v. William Penn College,[15] the assumption of risk for athletes participating in a sport is far greater.

Dudley, a pitcher and an outstanding ball player for the William Penn team, was struck in the eye by a fly ball while seated

14. 47 A.D.2d 570, 362 N.Y.S.2d 619   15. 219 N.W.2d 484 (Iowa 1974).
(1975).

on a bench during a game in which he was one of the players. The bench did not have a protective screen, and thus the issue before the court was whether the college had taken reasonable care in protecting its players. The lower court answered in the affirmative and found no negligence on the part of the college as alleged by the plaintiff. On appeal, the State Supreme Court affirmed the trial court's findings, pointing out that Dudley was not a spectator but a member of the team. Risks are inherent in "the rough and tumble" action of athletic events, the Court declared, and therefore the plaintiff had not been exposed to any "unreasonable risk of harm." [16]

The Supreme Court, however, cited two examples of what it would consider to be an unreasonable risk in a sporting event and therefore negligence on the part of a defendant. In Scott v. State (158 N.Y.S.2d 617 (1956)), the defendant college had erected a flag pole within the confines of the playing field itself, and an "outfielder, in his excitement and concentration, forgot about the pole and ran into it while chasing a fly." Obviously, "the pole subjected players to unreasonable risk of harm." In Frieze v. Rosenthal (269 N.Y.S. 1010 (1934)), "in which [a] player prevailed, a proprietor permitted a large rock to remain between third base and home plate, protruding three or four inches above ground and concealed by grass. A player fell over it." [17]

A different result might have been reached, therefore, if the injury had been foreseeable and could have been prevented by reasonable care on the part of the defendant. Thus, even though the critical question in an assumption of risk determination is whether the plaintiff had been, or should have been, aware of the risk assumed when he voluntarily participated in that risk, such a conclusion alone does not necessarily overcome the defendant's "duty to care," as we shall see in the following example.

In Wells v. Colorado College,[18] a female student at a private institution, while enrolled in a self-defense course, suffered a severe back injury resulting from a hip throw performed by her instructor in a class demonstration. Though considered an excellent athlete prior to the accident, after two operations to correct her spinal problem, she could not engage in anything more strenuous than walking. Hence, the student and her father filed a negligence suit against the college in a federal dis-

16. Id., at 486.

17. Id.

18. 478 F.2d 158 (10th Cir. 1973).

trict court in Colorado which resulted in a jury award of $150,-000 in damages.

In an appeal to the Tenth Circuit, the Court of Appeals affirmed the judgment of the District Court while pointing out that (1) the self-defense class was not a "sporting" activity in the usually perceived sense, (2) though it might be held that the plaintiff was aware of the normal risks associated with such an activity, there was no basis to hold that the plaintiff was or should have been aware of the possibility of her being thrown on the hardwood floor instead of the mat, and (3) the college duty to exercise care intensifies as the risks increase.

Immunity, the third and final defense mentioned, is based upon the common law principle of "sovereign immunity," a legal doctrine insulating, to the extent of its applicability, public institutions and, in certain situations, their officers and employees, from liability in tort. However, this doctrine has been modified or abolished by either judicial or legislative action in most states. In 1959, for instance, in a precedent-establishing case, the Supreme Court of Illinois repudiated common-law immunity, indicating that it was a carryover of the medieval doctrine of the "King can do no wrong" and was no longer consonant with modern concepts of right and justice.[19]

Of course some states retain all or part of the immunity principle, while others have modified the effects of tort litigation against public educators by passing "save harmless" statutes.[20] Nonetheless, immunity does not apply to private institutions and their employees, unless specifically provided for by a statute. Moreover, under modern trends a dependency upon the immunity protection brings to mind that classic "weak reed." On the other hand, the rule of privileged communication offers support for limiting the extent of tort liability for both public and private institutions and their employees. However, only a legislature can grant an absolute privilege, and the relationship covered can vary from state to state as well as upon the nature of the institution, the communication, or its officers. For example, the protective privilege in special relationships

---

19. Molitor v. Kaneland Community Unit District No. 302, 18 Ill.2d 11, 163 N.E.2d 89 (1959). See also Holytz v. City of Milwaukee, 17 Wis.2d 26, 115 N.W.2d 618 (1962); Spanel v. Mounds View School Dist. No. 621, 264 Minn. 279, 118 N. W.2d 795 (1962); and Hicks v. State, 88 N.M. 588, 544 P.2d 1153 (1975).

20. These acts relieve public educators from paying damages adjudged against them in activities within the professional's scope of employment.

versus public peril was the basic issue addressed in Tarasoff v. Regents of the Univ. of California.[21]

Briefly, the issue in *Tarasoff* centered around a murder committed by a person who had informed a University of California-employed psychologist that he was going to do so and in fact had named the person. The psychologist did not warn the victim, her parents, or others who might have informed her of the danger. The victim's parents, therefore, filed a negligence suit on the grounds that the University psychologist and others failed to detain a dangerous person and failed to warn plaintiffs of the murderer's intention to kill their daughter. The California Supreme Court ruled in favor of the plaintiffs.

> The revelation of a communication under the above circumstances is not a breach of trust or a violation of professional ethics; as stated in the Principles of Medical Ethics of the American Medical Association (1957) section 9: "A physician may not reveal the confidences entrusted to him in the course of medical attendance . . . *unless he is required to do so by law or unless it becomes necessary in order to protect the welfare of the individual or of the community.*" We conclude that the public policy favoring protection of the confidential character of patient-psychotherapist communications must yield in instances in which disclosure is essential to avert danger to others. The protective privilege ends where the public peril begins.[22]

THE ACADEMIC CONTRACT

While constitutional principles of due process and equal protection apply to disciplinary action taken by a public institution of higher education, this does not mean that enrollment in the institution precludes any contractual relationship between the student and his college. Rather, excluding the area of student conduct, the legal relationships is primarily contractual.[23] Also, "[t]he basic legal relation between a student

---

21. 13 Cal.3d 177, 118 Cal.Rptr. 129, 529 P.2d 553 (1974).

22. Id., at 561 (Court's emphasis).

23. See, e. g. Healy v. Larson, 67 Misc.2d 374, 323 N.Y.S.2d 625 (1971); Andersen v. Regents of the Univ. of California, 22 Cal.App.3d 763, 99 Cal.Rptr. 531 (1972); and Cal.Jur.2d, Universities and Colleges at p. 505: "By the act of matriculation, together with payment of required fees, a contract between the student and institution is created containing two implied conditions: (1) that the student will not be arbitrarily expelled, and (2) that

and a private university or college is contractual in nature. The catalogues, bulletins, circulars, and regulations of the institution become a part of the contract." [24]

In view of the acceptance of this theory, one might naturally assume that judges would apply standard principles of contract law to legal disputes arising between the student and the institution as parties to the contract. However, three basic problems are involved in most student contract actions: (1) the demonstrated judicial reluctance to interfere with the internal conduct of college life, (2) the typically college-oriented contract terms contained in college catalogues and other publications, and (3) the unreceptive judicial attitude toward student challenges in the academic area. (See chapter 3, pp. 91–95). Nonetheless, several important suits have been brought against both public and private colleges for breach of the student-institution contract.

Published "Promises" and Regulations

The first case, Trustees of Columbia Univ. v. Jacobsen,[25] reads almost like a college prank and represents one of the most frivolous attempts to hold a university liable for failing to deliver what it "promised." The issue here centered on a promissory note from a student for payment of his college tuition and arose as a counterclaim to the Columbia University action to collect his unpaid back tuition. In other words, the student refused payment because, he alleged, the university had promised in catalogues, brochures and in language inscribed on college buildings to provide him with "wisdom, truth, character, enlightenment, understanding, justice, liberty, honesty, courage, beauty and similar virtues and qualities" and had obviously not done so since it refused to graduate him because of low scholastic standing.

Ultimately the student reduced his counterclaim to the charge that Columbia had not taught wisdom as it had claimed. Thus, the student placed squarely before the court an interesting ques-

---

the student will submit himself to reasonable rules and regulations for the breach of which, in a proper case, he may be expelled, . . ."

24. Zumbrun v. University of Southern California, 25 Cal.App.3d 1, 101 Cal.Rptr. 499, 504 (1972); see also DeMarco v. University of Health Sciences, The Chicago Medical School, 40 Ill.App.3d 474, 352 N.E. 2d 356 (1976): "A contract between a private institution and a student confers duties on both parties which cannot be arbitrarily disregarded and may be judicially enforced."

25. 53 N.J.Super. 574, 148 A.2d 63 (1959).

tion: what distinction, if any, is there between teaching knowledge and wisdom? Fortunately, the court saved the day by granting a summary judgment to the university while, at the same time, pointing out that no college in its right mind would ever confuse knowledge with wisdom:

> [W]isdom is not a subject which can be taught and . . . no rational person would accept such a claim made by any man or institution. We find nothing in the record to establish that Columbia represented, expressly or even by way of impression, that it could or would teach wisdom or the several qualities which defendant insists are "synonyms for or aspects of the same quality." The matter is perhaps best summed up in the supporting affidavit of the dean of Columbia College, where he said that "All that any college can do through its teachers, libraries, laboratories, and other facilities is to endeavor to teach the student the known facts, acquaint him with the nature of those matters which are unknown, and thereby assist him in developing mentally, morally, and physically. Wisdom is a hoped-for end product of education, experience, and ability which many seek and many fail to attain." [26]

In another case, Depperman v. University of Kentucky,[27] a medical student was placed on probation pursuant to a university regulation purporting " . . . to insure conduct becoming potential physicians." In a letter from the chairman of the Promotions Committee the student was told that he had demonstrated an inability " . . . to function effectively with other people." After withdrawing from school and undergoing psychiatric counseling in order to be considered for readmission, he was denied readmission by the school admissions committee. As a result, the student brought suit claiming that he had been treated arbitrarily and capriciously and that, above all, the regulation under which he had been suspended was unconstitutionally vague.

The court, however, was unsympathetic to the charges; in regard to the vagueness claim it pointed out that academic regulations "are not judged by the degree of specificity as is required for penal status" and that such regulations "are not used in a vacuum" but rather must be interpreted in the context of their intended import.[28]

26. Id., at 66.

27. 371 F.Supp. 73 (D.C.Ky.1974).

28. Id., at 78.

In a similar context there is the problem of additional requirements that a college might add after a student enrolls in a program of studies. But recognizing the possibility of breach-of-
contract suits, most colleges insert disclaimers in their catalogs,
such as "courses, programs and degree requirements are subject
to change without notice." An example of the legal implications
involved in the area of disclaimers is provided in Mahavongsanan
v. Hall.[29]

In this case a graduate student at Georgia State University,
working on a master's degree in the School of Education, Department of Curriculum and Instruction, completed the required
courses for the degree but failed on two occasions a comprehensive examination which had become a requirement after she
had enrolled in the program. Understandably, the student, a
citizen of Thailand, filed suit claiming, among other things, that
the University bulletins and catalogues in effect at the time she
enrolled constituted a contract, that the new examination requirement should not have applied to her, and that the University should therefore be required to grant her the degree. In her
support the catalog stated: "A student will normally satisfy the
degree requirements in effect at the time of entrance." Moreover, the catalog also provided that " . . . academic regulations, other than degree requirements, are subject to change at
the end of any quarter."

University officials, however, claimed that the comprehensive
examination was an academic regulation rather than a degree
requirement: "The examination [was] simply a standard of performance, a method of evaluating the student's mastery of the
subject matter of the program instructed and that the catalogue
reserves within the faculty the right to change or add to the
standard of performance required at any time." But a federal
district court disagreed with this interpretation and ruled in the
student's favor, by ordering the University to grant the student
a degree. Subsequently, the University appealed to the Fifth Circuit Court of Appeals which reversed the lower court.

The Court of Appeals noted that even though the University
had granted the degree to the plaintiff, the case was not moot
because the University's academic integrity had been jeopardized.
As to the student's charge that the University had breached its
contract wtih her, the Court concluded:

> Implicit in the student's contract with the university upon
> matriculation is the student's agreement to comply with the

29. 529 F.2d 448 (5th Cir. 1976).

university's rules and regulations, which the university clearly is entitled to modify so as to properly exercise its educational responsibility.[30]

A similar conclusion was reached in Balogun v. Cornell Univ.,[31] a case involving a student who was refused a Doctor of Veterinary Medicine degree when the faculty voted 39 to 1 not to allow him to graduate due to unsatisfactory academic performance. In the legal action that followed the refusal, professors submitted affidavits and officials attested to the fact that the student's performance was unsatisfactory and that he was therefore dismissed in accordance with the school's published "Scholastic Requirements":

> "Although a weighted average of 70% is passing, the determination of whether a student has done satisfactory or unsatisfactory work is not based on any set percentile grade but rather upon the appraisal of the student's record and potential. The New York State Veterinary College has a responsibility to maintain a standard of excellence determined by the faculty." [32]

Balogun's problem, the defendants pointed out, was that even though he had passing grades in the academic and basic fields, he was seriously deficient in the clinical areas; as a result, Balogun ranked 54th in a class of 54 as his total grade point average slipped to 1.516 in his senior year.

In response, the student claimed that the grading standards as applied to him in the clinical areas were "malicious, arbitrary and capricious" and constituted an additional requirement for graduation to those set out in the College bulletin. Moreover, the student also claimed that since he was a native of Nigeria and black that he had been discriminated against. The court, however, ruled that there was no showing that the "denial of the degree was arbitrary, malicious, capricious or in any way discriminatory." [33] It pointed out that the same procedures of grading were applied equally to all members of the class and that the published "Scholastic Requirements" clearly reserved the right of the faculty to review the total record and potential of a student. "This is not a case where the court may further review the discretionary acts of the College's academic committee or substitute its judgment for theirs." [34]

---

30. Id., at 450.

31. 70 Misc.2d 474, 333 N.Y.S.2d 838 (1971).

32. Id., at 841.

33. Id., at 842.

34. Id.

Cancellation of Classes

Campus turmoil requiring the cancellation of classes also raised some interesting questions bearing upon the nature of the academic contract. In Paynter v. New York Univ.,[35] for instance, a father of a student at N.Y.U. sought a refund of tuition for nineteen days of classes when instruction was suspended during student disorders over the invasion of Cambodia. The suit was filed in the Small Claims Court of New York City with the allegation that the defendant university breached its contract by cancelling classes. The Court ruled in favor of the plaintiff, awarding him a $277.40 refund. Yet on appeal, the lower court's decision was reversed.[36]

In overturning the lower court's decision, the Appellate Court turned to a New York Education Law which gave private colleges and universities broad powers of academic self-regulation and ruled that self-regulation, if not arbitrary and capricious, permitted the institution to make "minor" and "unsubstantial" changes in scheduling:

> In the light of the events on the defendant's campus and in college communities throughout the country on May 4th to 5th, 1970, the Court [Small Claims] erred in substituting its judgment for that of the University Administrators and in concluding that the University was unjustified in suspending classes for the time remaining in the school year prior to the examination period. Moreover, while in a strict sense, a student contracts with a college or university for a number of courses to be given during the academic year, the services rendered by the university cannot be measured by the time spent in the classroom. The circumstances of the relationship permit the implication that the professor or the college may make minor changes in this regard. The insubstantial change made in the schedule of classes does not permit a recovery of tuition.[37]

In contrast, a California court presented with an analogous situation i. e., the cancellation of a class because of the 1970 Cambodian crisis—remanded the case to a lower court to determine whether the plaintiff's damages were minimal. In this case, Zumbrun v. University of Southern California (supra, p. 420 fn.

35. 64 Misc.2d 226, 314 N.Y.S.2d 676 (1970).

36. 66 Misc.2d 92, 319 N.Y.S.2d 893 (1971).

37. Id., at 894.

24), a sixty-three-year-old woman student sought a tuition refund because of a professor's cancellation of a sociology class
and arbitrarily assigning a grade of B during the 1970 turmoil.
Basically, the court accepted the woman's contention that when
she enrolled in the class the university had accepted her tuition
in exchange for a set number of lectures and a final examination:
"It is obvious that plaintiff did not receive all she bargained for
when she enrolled in 'Sociology 200.' " [38]

Though the *Paynter* and *Zumbrun* decisions were different in
result, their significance is that both courts recognized the validity of suits by students against their universities for breach of
contract. In comparing the two cases, moreover, a well-respected
teacher and attorney provided a probable rationale for the different conclusions:

> The fact that [the *Paynter* and *Zumbrun* cases] reached
> different conclusions might be at least attributable to the
> different factual situations involved as to any critical dif-
> ferences in theory applied. That is, in *Paynter* it was the
> university administration (not a teacher acting independ-
> ently) which cancelled classes, and the reason was a fear of
> violent disruption on campus (not one individual's personal
> ideology).[39]

Advising as Contract

In any event, it is apparent that institutions have wide discretion to refuse course credit, to dismiss students for academic
deficiency, and to deny degrees. However, the prerogatives of
colleges and universities in the academic area are not without
limits. For example, in Blank v. Board of Educ. of New York
City,[40] the Supreme Court of that state granted relief to a student
who had relied on his faculty advisor's incorrect interpretation
of some academic regulations. The Court held that " . . .
the dean of faculty may not escape the binding effect of the acts
of his agents performed within the scope of their apparent authority, and the consequences that must equitably follow therefrom." [41] Similarly, in Healy v. Larsson [42] a New York court
ruled in favor of a student who had been denied a degree but had

38. 101 Cal.Rptr. at 504–505.

39. John H. Mancuso, "Legal Rights
to Reasonable Rules, Fair Grades,
and Quality Courses," *New Directions for Higher Education,*
(Spring, 1976), p. 85.

40. 51 Misc.2d 724, 273 N.Y.S.2d 796
(1966).

41. Id., at 730.

42. 67 Misc.2d 374, 323 N.Y.S.2d 625
(1971).

successfully completed all requirements outlined for him by proper officials prior to his enrollment.

Grading

Despite the technically sound legal arguments that can be made in support of student breach-of-contract suits against colleges and universities, the wary plaintiff's attorney will have to enter the courtroom with sound and compelling arguments to reinforce the legal tap dance he must perform in convincing a skeptical judge to abandon the traditional hands-off policy in all academic matters. As noted in Chapter 3, the courts have stated again and again that they are reluctant to intervene in scholastic affairs. In fact a Minnesota court, while holding that requirements imposed by common law on private universities parallel those imposed by the due process clause on public universities, not surprisingly followed the traditional "abstention rule" as it distinguished the protections between disciplinary and academic dismissals:

> But when a student is expelled for academic deficiencies, these protections are less appropriate. An adjudicative hearing will not determine whether a student's educational performance was unsatisfactory. That issue would be resolved only by regarding the student's examinations which is a professor's and not a judge's function.[43]

In Morpurgo v. United States,[44] a federal district court held that plaintiff's unsupported and reiterated assertions that she had passed examinations that had been recorded as "F," did not entitle her to have the court, as opposed to her professors, review her academic performance. Likewise, in Horne v. Cox,[45] a state court held that there was no legal basis for granting students the rights or privileges with respect to grades for academic performance. Again, in Jansen v. Emory Univ.[46] a federal district court ruled that academic matters were issues "wholly between the student and school," and thus the court refused to get involved in determining whether the plaintiff was qualified to be graduated from dental school: "Respect for the discretion of those best qualified to make such judgments dictates that the university not

43. Abbariao v. Hamline Univ. School of Law, 258 N.W.2d 108, 112 (Minn.1977).

44. 437 F.Supp. 1135 (D.C.N.Y.1977).

45. 551 S.W.2d 690 (Tenn.1977).

46. 440 F.Supp. 1060 (D.C.Ga.1977).

the federal courts should determine the qualifications of students to continue their postgraduate education." [47]

At Salve Regina College, a three-member grade appeals committee recommended to the dean that a student's petition to change an "F" to an "Incomplete" be honored. When the dean refused to change the grade on the basis that the committee was simply a recommending body, the student sought relief in the courts by requesting an order requiring the college to change the grade, to reinstate her for the purpose of completing the courses required for a nursing degree, and to pay money damages. The court refused to provide such relief, however, holding that nothing in the catalog implied that the committee decision was mandatory.[48]

Once again, what all of this means is that courts will typically refrain from imposing their judgment in the area involving the heart of higher education—its academic programs and standards —unless justice clearly requires intervention. Such determinations are usually considered within the competence of the faculty and administration. Thus, in questioning the judgment of professors and officials in academic matters, the burden of proof is always upon the student to show arbitrary, capricious or discriminatory action. And at least as far as professors are concerned, the negative effects of academic second-guessing by the judiciary would far outweigh the positive results for students.

Nevertheless, when one looks at this situation from the student's side, the application of the judicial "abstention rule" appears to create a kind of *Catch-22*. In effect, the courts require the student to demonstrate arbitrariness, for instance, but will not review the primary proof of that arbitrariness—the student's graded examinations or papers. The difficulty of performing this task is further highlighted by the fact that, unlike students who have been disciplined by public colleges for misconduct, those who have been dismissed for academic reasons need not be given a hearing before any tribunal—judicial, collegiate or otherwise. The glaring weakness in the constitutional distinction between academic and disciplinary dismissals is that under both circumstances a student stands to lose an important interest (to remain in college).

It seems that where a dismissal hinges on a particular grade, at least some minimal procedural safeguard for the student should

47. Id., at 1064.   48. Lyons v. Salve Regina College, 565 F.2d 200 (1st Cir. 1977).

be required if requested. In this sense, and quite appropriately, a student author of a law review article has suggested,

> where a failing grade leads to expulsion, the student's strong interest [should] require more than the opinion of a single faculty member. Although it may be too difficult for a court to set down the specific requirements of fair academic proceeding, it could remand with the instruction that the school fashion a more appropriate means of reaching such an important decision—for example by honoring student requests that failing papers be re-read by another member of the department.[49]

ACADEMIC MALPRACTICE

The unreceptive judicial attitude toward student challenges in the academic area has been discussd above, but now that 18-year-olds are constitutionally recognized as adults, with the right to enter into contractual agreements, students are beginning to realize that they also have a legal right to complain about the product they buy. For instance, one student sued the University of Bridgeport because she had not received anything of value from a course. Another student at George Washington University claimed a course she took was "pure junk" and the University settled out of court for the balance of her tuition.[50] Clearly, these will not be the last such complaints.

Despite examples such as these, however, most suits have thus far been resolved in favor of the institution, in part because the legal definition of academic malpractice has yet to be agreed upon. When this condition is coupled with the general reluctance of the judiciary to interfere in the educational process, the growing concern over the future outlook of malpractice suits might bring to mind the anxiety of Tristam Shandy's mother, who was worried that her husband might one day forget to wind all the clocks and therefore neglect his conjugal obligations. Perhaps apropos is the fact that the first educational malpractice suit attracting national attention, Peter W. v. San Francisco Unified School Dist. (1976),[51] flunked in court. Nonetheless, in the

---

49. "Developments in the Law-Academic Freedom," 81 *Harvard Law Review* (1968), p. 1139 as quoted in *Mancuso*, op. cit., p. 86.

50. "Academics—The New Legal Battleground," *The School Law Newsletter*, Vol. 6, No. 2, p. 208.

51. 60 Cal.App.3d 814, 131 Cal.Rptr. 854 (1976); at trial court level the case was entitled Doe v. San Francisco Unified School Dist.

"court of public opinion," the case proved to be a great embarrassment to professional educators everywhere. What left the educational establishment red-faced was the pathetic irony of Peter having graduated from high school while being functionally illiterate.

The plaintiff, Peter's mother, thus understandably alleged that her son "suffered a loss of earning capacity by his limited ability to read and write" because of the negligence and carelessness of the school district and its agents. She therefore sued for general damages "by reason of such 'negligence, acts and omissions of defendants.' " [52] However, both the trial court and the Court of Appeal refused to offer relief. In making that judgment, the California Court of Appeal explained its position:

> substantial professional authority attests that the achievement of literacy in the schools, or its failure, are influenced by a host of factors which affect the pupil subjectively, from outside the formal teaching process, and beyond the control of its ministers. They may be physical, neurological, emotional, cultural, environmental; they may be present but not perceived, recognized but not identified.[53]

Thus, the Court held that, "[u]nlike the activity of the highway or the marketplace, classroom methodology affords no readily acceptable standards of care, or cause, or injury." Interestingly, the Court also pointed out a well-understood truism, at least among professional educators: "The science of pedagogy itself is fraught with different and conflicting theories of how or what a [student] should be taught, and any layman might—and commonly does—have his own emphatic views on the subject." [54] But more significant, the Court stated that "the failure of educational achievement may not be characterized as an injury within the meaning of tort law." [55]

The Court also stated its worries about the financial problems that educational malpractice suits could create for the taxpayer. That is, any money won from a school district by a defendant would be paid from taxes, and the Court feared that school systems would collapse under the weight of damages if every student who failed to learn sued and won.[56] Nevertheless, disenchant-

52. Id., at 856.

53. Id., at 861.

54. Id., at 860–861.

55. Id., at 862.

56. Id., at 861. "The ultimate consequences, in terms of public time and money, would burden them—and society—beyond calculation."

ment with education abounds in our society today, and one should recall that the United States is a country that settles many, if not most, of its disagreements in the courts.

In the meantime, law journals are attempting to clarify the issue by defining academic malpractice more precisely. *The School Law Newsletter,* for example, recently characterized it as "improper, injurious, or negligent and/or action which has a negative effect on the student's academic standing." [57] As noted earlier, college registration has been considered by the courts as an implied contractual agreement between buyer and seller. Perhaps it will not be long before they recognize college publications as a form of advertising—thereby introducing the issue of false advertising into academic litigation. Indeed, with declining enrollments, many colleges and universities are already setting the stage for such challenges by taking a cue from Madison Avenue and turning to the "sales pitch." It represents what Harvard Sociologist David Riesman has described as "the war of all, against all, for student body count." [58]

Names matter, as advertisers have long known. At Southern Oregon State College, for example, astronomy was re-titled "Outer Space," and the University of Montana christianed a course on Mexican history, "Cow Chips and Revolution." Astronomy is too "heavy" for this generation, one is given to mutter. Instead, the current temptation is to ape "with-it" words that reflect much of the adolescent view of the world, to cater to these new sentiments like some politician entreating his skeptical constituents. Maybe this is why most students are enough impressed by posturing politicians to elect them to high office. However, since colleges and universities are increasingly finding themselves in a "buyer's market," the temptation among these institutions to commercialize and even to oversell their products is correspondingly increased. Naturally, such temptations become difficult to resist when the alternative is empty classrooms, and this is unquestionably why more and more professors are ingratiating themselves with students by offering "snap" courses—with a reputation for easy grades—and/or resorting to informal rap sessions. One might wonder about how many "Peter W's" are currently being awarded the long-cherished college diploma.

It all sounds preposterous, of course, but it signals a serious trend. "The free market works very badly in higher education,"

57. "Academics—The New Legal Battleground," op. cit., p. 213.

58. "Hard Sell for Higher Learning," *Time* (October 2, 1978), p. 80.

sighed Riesman.[59] Yet the new selling of higher education not only bodes ill for academic integrity, it involves some rather ominous legal implications as well. As college-goers increasingly see themselves as buyers of education rather than passive receivers, they will concomitantly begin to demand that they receive a proper return for their educational dollar. Thus, though the basis for the inevitable suits will primarily be breach of contract, the complaints being made will not only be that the college evaluated the student unfairly, but also that the "service" provided by the institution failed to measure up to what was promised in college publications and recruiting activities.

If this unhappy situation actually develops in fact, college teaching will become an even more beleaguered profession. There has always been a strongly held conviction, at least among professors, that what happens within the individual classroom should be kept free from outside interference. Any significant incursion by the courts into the educational process could well lead to the imposition of a pall of orthodoxy over the classroom and eventually even the disestablishment of our Nineteenth Century adoption of German *Lehrfreiheit*—which allows the university professor "freedom of inquiry and freedom of teaching, the right to study and to report on his findings in an atmosphere of consent."

On the other hand, there might be some advantages; if the economic and legalistic crunch on higher education results in something like "teach or perish" instead of "publish or perish," such adversity might prove sweet indeed for the college student. But such possibilities notwithstanding, the student consumer movement continues to grow. A 1977 editorial in *Change* explains this development with the observation that today's students are older, more experienced, and have a greater sense of a right "to be informed of the facts of what they are buying for their educational dollars, a right they hold as unassailable as that of breathing reasonably unpolluted air." [60]

Equally important is the fact that information supplied to prospective students by colleges and universities is beginning to receive considerable attention from the federal government. This attention, now incorporated into law through the student consumer information sections of the Education Amendments of

---

59. Id.

60. G. W. Bonham, "Consumer Information and Student Choice," *Change* (May, 1977), pp. 10–11.

1976, requires accurate disclosure by educational institutions on such items as financial assistance, instructional programs, refund policies, tuition and related costs, facilities, faculty, student retention, and employment prospects.[61] Also, the new federal guardianship is lodged in eligibility requirements for participation in various student aid programs, and thus the college may become a prisoner of its own rhetoric.

FAMILY EDUCATION RIGHTS AND PRIVACY ACT OF 1974

Legislative Background

During the 1960s, the decision-making process for counselors, teachers and administrators was enhanced by more readily available and sophisticated information. For example, in 1968 the Phoenix, Arizona High School District established a cumulative record system that allowed a staff member to pick up any school phone, push a button, dial a code number, and dictate comments about a student into a remote recorder. One could also play back comments made by other staff members.[62] However, a number of problems resulted from such personal information systems. Errors in computerized information, for instance, were sometimes magnified, and compounded before corrections could be made, but information received through this system still seemed to carry a special validity because of its source. And apart from the computer, dossiers were often casually compiled with anecdotal comments made therein frequently becoming the student's mysterious adversary. With some justification, therefore, the Privacy Protection Study Commission lamented:

> Never before have records substituted for face-to-face contact in so many relationships between individuals and organizations and thus never before have records been able to affect an individual as easily, as broadly, and potentially as unfairly as they can today.[63]

But just as disturbing was the fact that the average student had no way to find out what information about him was in a record or how it was used. In the parlance of most schools, a "confiden-

---

61. Public Law 94–482. See Appendix F, pp. 583–588, for the Final Regulations, Student Consumer Information.

62. D. Divoky, "Cumulative Records Assault on Privacy," *National Edu-*

cation Association Journal, Vol. 47 (1973), pp. 16–18.

63. *Personal Privacy in an Information Society* (Washington, D.C. Government Printing Office, 1977), p. 413.

tial" record was not revealed to a student; however, it seemed to be accessible to virtually anyone else. Thus, as damaging as the record might be, there was generally no way for the student to challenge, correct or amend that record.

By the late 1960s, electronic data processing had become the prevailing mode for managing student data files. Indeed, the computer's efficient storage, retrieval and manipulative capabilities made it possible not only to accommodate larger quantities of data but also to more thoroughly and imaginatively correlate that data to reveal patterns of belief and behavior that might previously have escaped notice. Under such conditions, the student's lack of privacy and personal disclosure rights were clearly magnified, but a corollary problem to the increasing use of the computer was even less recognized. Later, John Lautsch, chairperson of the American Bar Association's sub-committee on the regulation of computers, warned of the possibilities for tampering with information stored in college computers, especially since many institutions' students had access to the school computers. "Computer fraud is rapidly becoming a kind of 'white collar crime wave.'" [64]

In a 1973 report entitled *Records, Computers and the Rights of Citizens* written by the HEW Advisory Committee on Automated Personal Data Systems, the fundamental principles of fair information practices were outlined:

1. There must be no personal-data recordkeeping systems whose very existence is secret.

2. There must be a way for an individual to find out what information about him is in a record and how it is used.

3. There must be a way for an individual to prevent information about him obtained for one purpose from being used or made available for other purposes without his consent.

4. There must be a way for an individual to correct or amend a record of identifiable information about him.

5. Any organization creating, maintaining, using, or disseminating records of identifiable personal data must assure the reliability of the data for their intended use

---

64. E. Cougilan, "Colleges, Computers and the Law," *Chronicle of*   *Higher Education* (July 18, 1977), p. 4.

and must take reasonable precautions to prevent misuse of the data.[65]

The report had a major impact on the drafting of two federal privacy laws: The Privacy Act of 1974 and the Family Education Rights and Privacy Act of 1974.

On May 9, 1974, when Senator James Buckley (Republican, New York) announced his intention to add a rider to pending legislation that ultimately became the Education Amendments of 1974, he deplored what he characterized as the

. . . systematic violation . . . of the right of privacy of millions of children in the schools across the nation whose school records are routinely made available to governmental and other busy-bodies, and the rights of their parents, who are too often denied access to such information.[66]

Senator Buckley's rider became a part of Public Law 93–380; however, the original Buckley Amendment was a hastily designed piece of legislation that was quickly passed and signed against the background of the Watergate hearings. Although it was primarily designed to remedy problems in elementary and secondary schools, it was made applicable to higher education on perhaps the too simple basis that the problems in both areas were similar and consequently that the same principles would apply equally well in both areas. Yet, to practically every one of the higher education associations, it was just another example of Congress not doing its homework. Thus, these organizations urged delay of implementation citing problems with "confidentiality of letters of recommendation" and certain "ambiguities in the Act and consequences that . . . Congress may not have intended."[67] Among other things, the ambiguities and unintended consequences involved the implication that students could view the confidential financial statements submitted by parents and the possibility of student access to their psychiatric records. Also, most of these groups predicted wide-spread demands by students to inspect their records.

65. Report published by the United States Government Printing Office in 1973. The information quoted can be found on pp. xx–xxi of the Report.

66. Congressional Record, 1974, p. 7536.

67. C. M. Mattessich, "The Buckley Amendment—Opening School Files for Student and Parental Review," Catholic University Law Review 24 (1975), p. 597.

On the other hand, student groups supported the new law. The president of the United States Student Association, for instance, noted that the amendment "provides a long overdue mechanism for correcting misinformation and errors in students' records which may be vital to their careers," and claimed that it would "curb the arbitrary power that has so often been misused by school administrators and agencies allowed easy access to students' records." [68] And the National Committee for Citizens in Education also supported the Buckley Amendment and branded the appeals for delay and modification by the various professional education groups as "incomprehensible and frightening." [69]

Yielding to the criticism of the professional educators, however, the corrective measure, which became Public Law 93–568, was introduced shortly before the end of the 93rd Congress, attached to a House Resolution authorizing a 1977 White House Conference on libraries and information services. On December 31, 1974, President Ford signed this new amendment co-authored by Senators Buckley and Pell. In terms of its applicability to higher education, the new legislation set forth the following major changes: (1) denied students access to confidential letters and statements of recommendation placed in the education records prior to January 1, 1975; (2) denied students access to financial information submitted by parents; (3) allowed students only limited or conditional access to their medical records; and (4) allowed students to voluntarily waive rights to see confidential letters of recommendation.

The Law

The discussion that follows draws mainly from what is commonly referred to as the Buckley Amendment [70] (the Family Education Rights and Privacy Act of 1974, Public Law 93–380, as amended by Public Law 93–568) but with the law's relevancy to postsecondary institutions specifically in mind. Because of this focus, the rights of parents and students under the age of 18 and the responsibilities of elementary and secondary institutions will not be included.

The Buckley Amendment deals with one subject only: educational records. On the one hand, the law grants students

---

68. Id., at 596.

69. E. Wentworth, "Unlocking School Files: The Buckley Amendment," *Washington Post*, Nov. 17, 1974, p. 5.

70. On June 17, 1976, final regulations were published in the *Federal Register* at 41 FR 24662 wherein much of the following information was taken.

guaranteed access to their educational records; such access includes the right to challenge or supplement information on file in order to prevent flawed interpretation. On the other hand, it takes from postsecondary institutions the privilege of indiscriminate disclosures; prior consent is required before educational records can be released to nonexempt agencies or persons. That, essentially, is what the Amendment does.

It is important to know, therefore, how the term "educational record" is defined by the law. Accordingly, whether handwriting, print, tape, film, or some other medium, a record is considered an educational record if it is directly related to a student and if it is "maintained by" an educational agency, institution or party (e. g., a computer bank system acting for the agency or institution). More specifically, the educational record includes:

> all official records, files, and data directly related to [students], including all material that is incorporated into each student's cumulative record folder, and intended for school use or to be available to parties outside the school or school system, and specifically including, but not necessarily limited to, identifying data, academic work completed, level of achievement (grades, standardized achievement test scores), attendance data, scores on standardized intelligence, aptitude, and psychological tests, interest inventory results, health data, family background information, teacher or counselor ratings and observations, and various reports of serious or recurrent behavior patterns.[71] [At the college level, medical or law enforcement records are not included].

The phrases "maintained by" and "official records," however, have confused many educators. How "official," for instance, must a record be before it is considered "maintained"?

According to a clarification provided by the Fair Information Practice Staff, the HEW office responsible for enforcing the Buckley Amendment, any record which remains in the possession of a school employee and which has been shared with or is accessible to another individual is considered an educational record. However, if a teacher, counselor, administrator or school psychologist has sole possession of some notes on one or more students (e. g., memory joggers) and shows them to no one else, they are not considered an educational record and hence are exempt from student access. But once these notes are shared with others, they are part of a student's educational record. The fact that

71. 20 U.S.C.A. 821 § 438(a)(1).

such shared notes may be kept in various places all over the college does not affect their official status.

Other types of records exempt from the regulations are law enforcement and employment records as long as they are kept separate. Financial information on parents is also excluded. Medical records kept for treatment purposes may be accessed by a doctor of the student's choice. Confidential letters written prior to January 1, 1975 are exempt, and students may voluntarily waive rights to see confidential letters of recommendation. Those other than students having access to their records include employees of the educational system having "legitimate educational interests" and accrediting organizations. A reasonable attempt must be made to notify a student of subpoena before complying. In the case of an emergency, information may be released if it is necessary to protect the health and safety of the student and other persons, but the person given the information must be in a position to act.[72]

Colleges and universities must develop policies in accordance with the Act and its regulations and "inform . . . students of the rights accorded them . . . " Each institution must specify in its policy what constitutes "directory information" and may be released publicly as such. However, students have the right to restrain institutions from releasing this kind of information. Directory information may include: "student's name, address, telephone listing, date and place of birth, major field of study, participation in officially recognized activities and sports, weight and height of members of athletic teams, dates of attendance, degrees and awards received, . . . the most recent previous educational agency or institution attended by the student" and other similar information.[73]

The regulations provide that a "student who believes that information contained in the education records . . . is inac-

---

72. Federal Register, Vol. 41, No. 42, §§ 99.11–99.35. See also Mattie T. v. Johnston, 74 F.R.D. 498, 499 (1976): "Family Education Rights and Privacy Act [does] not bar the disclosure of subpoenaed documents . . . . Act places burden on . . . institution, and not party who subpoenaed the documents, of notifying . . . students prior to compliance; . . . ."; and Arizona v. Birdsall, 116 Ariz. 196, 568 P.2d 1094, 1097 (1977), where the court held that the Buckley Amendment "prohibits a practice or policy of disclosure of educational records except in designated instances and expressly recognizes that disclosure may be made in response to a subpoena duces tecum or other judicial order."

73. Id., at § 99.3(a).

curate or misleading or violates [his] privacy or other rights
. . . may request that the . . . institution . . .
amend them." If a change is made as a result of the challenge,
the institution must inform the student in writing. However, if
the institution decides not to amend the record then it must inform the student of its refusal in writing and also advise the
student of his right to a hearing before a neutral observer and/or
panel designated by the institution. Most significantly, the regulations permit the student to be represented at the hearing by an
attorney or other person of his choice but at his own expense.
Moreover, the hearing officer must be someone who has no direct
interest in the outcome, and if it is determined at the hearing
that the record is not inaccurate and thus will not be changed,
then the student must be informed of his right to insert explanatory comments into his record. The institution must treat the
explanatory comments as a permanent and integral part of the
record. This includes the obligation to disclose such comments
whenever disclosing the related record.[74]

Even though the Buckley Amendment specifies the circumstances and data elements that can be released, a violation of any
of its provisions carries no tort liability *per se.* An alleged violation is reported to HEW which investigates complaints and
seeks to bring about compliance through voluntary means, but
failure to achieve compliance will result in a hearing before an
HEW review board which may recommend to the Secretary the
withdrawal of Office of Education funds from the institution.[75]

In Student Bar Ass'n Bd. of Governors v. Byrd, for example,
students sought to enjoin the faculty of the University of North
Carolina School of Law from allowing its official meetings to be
closed. The student action was based on North Carolina's Open
Meetings Law, but the University claimed that under the provisions of the Buckley Amendment it legally could not hold open
faculty meetings since individual students might be discussed
without their consent, "and since the Buckley Amendment is part
of the Supreme Law of the Land, pursuant to Article VI, section
2, of the Constitution of the United States, it controls the Open
Meetings Law." [76] However, the Supreme Court of North Carolina held that an educational agency is not compelled to observe

---

74. Id., at §§ 99.10–99.22. Students
may not contest a grade *per se,*
but they may contest the recording
of a grade which they believe was
inaccurately entered in their record.

75. Id., at §§ 99.66–99.69.

76. 239 S.E.2d 415, 419 (N.C.1977).

any given individual's rights under the published provisions of the Family Education Rights and Privacy Act:

> The Buckley Amendment does not forbid such disclosure of information concerning a student and, therefore, does not forbid opening to the public a faculty meeting at which such matters are discussed. The Buckley Amendment simply cuts off Federal funds, otherwise available to an educational institution which has a policy or practice of permitting the release of such information. Thus, if the Open Meetings Law applies to a meeting of the faculty of the School of Law at which such matters are discussed, the right of the public to attend such meeting would continue. Only the availability of Federal funds in aid of the institution would be affected. Of course, a violation of the Buckley Amendment could well result, not only in termination of any otherwise available Federal financial aid to the School of Law but also in the termination of any such aid to the entire University.[77]

This case is interesting because it also points out that privacy issues and disclosure issues are two sides of the same coin— i. e., a person's freedom from intrusive practices or "the right to be let alone by other people" as opposed to an institution's duty of disclosure or the "public's right to be informed." Thus, privacy is often in conflict with other valued social interests such as effective government, law enforcement, and the public's right to know, but in this case the interest in privacy prevailed. Of course, the Court was obviously concerned about "the possibility that all further Federal financial aid to the entire University of North Carolina, including all its component institutions, may be jeopardized by an [overbroad] interpretation of the Open Meetings Law." Moreover, the Court feared that a broad interpretation of the statute would then "afford no basis for distinguishing between enrolled students in the School of Law, rejected applicants for admission, prospective applicants for admission, . . . or other members of the public seeking only a warm shelter on a cold winter's day."[78] Under such a construction the statute would provide "no basis for distinction between the faculty of the School of Law, the faculty of the English Department, the Athletic Department or the football coaching staff, the faculty of a public elementary school or of a

77. Id.   78. Id., at 417.

public kindergarten." Under these circumstances, the Court ominously presaged:

> It would, in all probability, create substantial consternation in the headquarters of the Athletic Department . . . if a rival school's coach appeared and demanded admission to a conference of the University's football coaching staff called to consider strategy to be pursued in a forthcoming contest with the team of such other institutions, or a meeting of a subcommittee called to discuss the qualifications of prospects for recruitment for next year's team.[79]

With these concerns in mind, the Court construed the Open Meetings Law narrowly, finding that the "faculty of the School of Law is not a 'subsidiary or component part' of the [University] Board of Governors, but is simply a group of employees of the Board. Furthermore, the faculty does not act as a 'body politic.' "[80] Therefore, it was held that the North Carolina "sunshine" statute did not apply to a meeting of the law school faculty because it was not a governing body.

A similar result was reached in Marston v. Gainesville Pub. Co.[81] This case involved an appeal from a lower court's determination that student disciplinary hearings of the University of Florida Honor Court were subject to the open-meetings requirement of Florida law. The lower court had thus enjoined the Honor Court from conducting further closed hearings and declared void all Honor Court actions resulting from deliberations, discussions or rulings in closed hearings. The Appeals Court indicated that the Buckley Amendment did not provide a private remedy but nevertheless reversed the lower court's ruling, holding that the decision was a violation of privacy based on a 1973 Florida law protecting the confidentiality of school records. Hence, the Appeals Court held that students who appeared before the Honor Court were entitled to privacy protection and that such hearings and their pursuant reports could not be made public without the consent of the students.

Even before the Buckley Amendment, the concern for individual privacy had many implications for institutional policy. In Dixon v. Alabama State Bd. of Educ., for instance, the collateral implications of expelling a student from college were recognized:

> It is most unlikely that a public college would accept a student expelled from another public college from the same

---

79. Id., at 417–418.
80. Id., at 421.

81. 341 So.2d 783 (Fla.App.1976).

state. Indeed, expulsion may well prejudice the student in completing his education at any other institution.[82]

In Javits v. Stevens it was held "that reinstatement does not moot the controversy because the 'collateral consequences' of the suspension may prejudice the students." [83] In other words, the fact that a suspension remained on a student's record might prevent him from obtaining future employment or admission to college or graduate school. Moreover, because of these collateral implications there must be due process:

> Neither the property interest in educational benefits temporarily denied nor the liberty interest in reputation, which is also implicated, is so insubstantial that suspension may constitutionally be imposed by any procedure the school chooses, no matter how arbitrary.[84]

However, the due process clause does not shield a student from a suspension properly imposed: "The student's interest is to avoid unfair or mistaken exclusion from the educational process, with all of its unfortunate consequences." [85]

Thus, the Buckley Amendment and its explicit requirement for written institutional policy regarding disclosure practices and privacy protections should be seen as a part of a continuing issue in public policy. The Fair Credit Reporting Act of 1970, the Freedom of Information Act, the Consumer Protection Act, the Buckley Amendment, and the Privacy Act of 1974, as well as state open-meetings and freedom of information laws, to name a few examples, exemplify the law's unprecedented state of flux with respect to the twin problems of privacy and disclosure. These laws attempt to mitigate threats to privacy believed to be inherent in the records-keeping function of institutions and the extensive information needs of both government and society. But aside from federal and state statutes, perhaps the larger dimensions of the issue involve privacy protections under constitutional and tort law.

Court Cases—Privacy Rights

In Public Utilities Comm. v. Pollack, Justice Douglas wrote: "Liberty in the constitutional sense must mean more than freedom from unlawful governmental restraint; it must include privacy as well, . . . The right to be let alone is indeed the

---

82. 294 F.2d 150, 157 (5th Cir. 1961).

83. 382 F.Supp. 131, 135 (D.C.N.Y. 1974).

84. Goss v. Lopez, 419 U.S. 565, 576 (1975).

85. Id., at 579.

beginning of all freedom." [86]   Thus, though privacy is not mentioned explicitly in the United States Constitution, courts have recognized that rights of personal privacy or guarantees of certain zones of privacy exist under the Constitution.   For example, in Griswold v. Connecticut the Supreme Court held that inherent in the Bill of Rights is the right to privacy:

> Various guarantees create zones of privacy.   The right of association contained in the penumbra of the First Amendment is one, as we have seen.   The Third Amendment in its prohibition against the quartering of soldiers "in any house" in time of peace without the consent of the owner is another facet of that privacy.   The Fourth Amendment explicitly affirms the "right of the people to be secure in their person, houses, papers, effects, against unreasonable searches and seizures."   The Fifth Amendment in its self-incrimination clause enables the citizen to create a zone of privacy which government may not force him to surrender to his detriment.   The Ninth Amendment provides: "The enumeration in the Constitution, of certain rights, shall not be construed to deny or disparage others retained by the people." The Fourth and Fifth Amendments were described in Boyd v. United States as protection against all government invasions "of the sanctity of a man's home and the privacies of life."   We recently referred in Mapp v. Ohio to the Fourth Amendment as creating a "right to privacy, no less important than any other right carefully and particularly reserved to the people." [87]

In Katz v. United States, the Supreme Court articulated a standard definition for zones of privacy as places where people have "a reasonable expectation of privacy," [88] and in Roe v. Wade, Justice Blackmun described the right to privacy as being among a set of "personal rights that can be deemed 'fundamental' or 'implicit in the concept of ordered liberty.' " [89]   Accordingly, privacy is a personal liberty or fundamental right against which states are constrained from acting or intruding except where

86.   343 U.S. 451, 467 (1952).

87.   381 U.S. 479, 484–485 (1965). This position on privacy was reaffirmed in Roe v. Wade, 410 U.S. 113 (1973), as the Court held that the right of privacy, founded in the Fourteenth Amendment's conception of personal liberty and in the Ninth Amendment's reservation of rights to the people, was broad enough to cover a wide array of subjects and situations.

88.   389 U.S. 347, 352–353 (1967).

89.   410 U.S. at 153 (1973).

some "compelling state interest of overriding significance" is established. The courts, moreover, have been rapidly expanding the privacy zone.

In Stanley v. Georgia,[90] the Supreme Court struck down a law that forbade the showing of obscene films in the privacy of one's home. Thus, "a man's home is his castle" insofar as obscenity laws are concerned; a person may engage in conduct or possess materials in the privacy of his home which would be punishable as obscenity elsewhere. The right of privacy also encompasses and protects "the personal intimacies of the home, the family, marriage, motherhood, procreation and child-rearing."[91] In Griswold v. Connecticut, supra, the Court invalidated a state law which made it a crime for any person to use contraceptives, or aid or abet another using them. The Court held that the statute infringed upon a constitutionally protected "zone of marital privacy." Later, in Eisenstadt v. Baird,[92] the Court held that the decision whether to use contraceptives was one of individual privacy and hence that the right belonged to single as well as married persons.

A woman's decision as to whether to terminate her pregnancy was declared by the Court to be within her constitutionally protected right of privacy and could not be made subject to parental or spousal consent.[93] In fact there have been several lower court decisions ruling that minors are eligible for an abortion without parental consent.[94] But in Roe v. Wade, supra, the Supreme Court declared that at some point during pregnancy, the state's interest in protecting the woman's life and in protecting prenatal life becomes sufficiently "compelling" to justify reasonable state regulation of the abortion decision.

Thus, constitutional rights to privacy involve some subtle contours and are frequently in conflict with other interests and rights. As one commentator pointed out, "we will know which rights are and which are not within the zone only case by case, with lines drawn and redrawn, in response to individual and societal initiatives and the imaginativeness of lawyers."[95] In this

90. 394 U.S. 557 (1969).

91. Paris Adult Theater v. Slaton, 413 U.S. 49 (1973).

92. 405 U.S. 438 (1972).

93. Planned Parenthood of Central Missouri v. Danforth, 428 U.S. 52 (1976).

94. See e. g., Foe v. Vanderhoof, 389 F.Supp. 947 (1975); and State v. Koome, 84 Wash.2d 901, 530 P.2d 260 (1975).

95. L. Henkin, "Privacy and Autonomy," 74 *Columbia Law Review* (1974), p. 1426.

sense the Supreme Court in Whalen v. Roe seems to have implicitly acknowledged at least three facets of the constitutional privacy right carrying potential constitutional dimensions in higher education. In a footnote the Court quoted Professor Kurland as follows:

"The concept of a constitutional right of privacy still remains largely undefined. There are at least three facets that have been partially revealed, but their form and shape remain to be fully ascertained. The first is the right of the individual to be free in his private affairs from governmental surveillance and intrusion. The second is the right of an individual not to have his private affairs made public by the government. The third is the right of an individual to be free in action, thought, experience, and belief from governmental compulsion." [96]

The first of those interests dealing with unwanted "governmental surveillance and intrusion" was primarily implicated in the Moore v. Student Affairs Committee of Troy State Univ. (1968) and Smyth and Smith v. Lubbers (1975) cases discussed in Chapter 4. In *Moore* the court said that a "reasonable right of inspection is necessary to the institution's performance . . . even though it may infringe on the outer boundaries of a dormitory student's Fourth Amendment rights." [97] In contrast, seven years later the *Smyth* court said that a student's "interest in the privacy of his room is not at the 'outer limits' as the College argues, but on the contrary is at the very core of the Fourth Amendment's protections." [98] Of course, to determine in any given case what procedures due process requires, a court must carefully determine and balance the nature of private interests affected with the government interests involved, taking account of history and the precise circumstances surrounding the case at hand. Obviously, circumstances had changed considerably between *Moore* and *Smyth*. Aside from the Supreme Court rulings in *Tinker* (1969) and *Healy* (1972) and the ratification of the Twenty-Sixth Amendment (1971), the *Smyth* court mentioned the Buckley Amendment wherein "Congress ha[d] recently recognized the extreme importance of a student's 'record' by close-

96. 429 U.S. 589, 599 fn. 24 (1977), quoting from Kurland, "The Private I," *The University of Chicago Magazine* 7, 8 (Autumn, 1976).

97. 284 F.Supp. 725, 729 (D.C.Ala. 1968).

98. 398 F.Supp. 777, 786 (D.C.Mich. 1975). See also the discussion of *Moore*, *Smyth* and other Fourth Amendment cases in Chapter 4, pp. 132–140.

ly regulating the circumstances under which student records may be released by school authorities." [99] According to the court, this in itself presupposed careful attention to students' privacy rights. In other words, the court believed that the seriousness of recording suspensions on student records required it to seriously and sympathetically consider the students' privacy claim:

> [I]n our credentialed society, an individual wishing to transfer to another school, to attend graduate school, or to find a job with responsibility and possibility for advancement has no choice but to provide any information which prospective schools or employers request . . . . In the interest of order and discipline, the College is claiming the power to shatter career goals, and to make advancement in our highly competitive society much more difficult for an individual than it already is.[1]

As will be recalled, the court determined inter alia that for Fourth Amendment purposes, adult college students have the same interest in the privacy of their rooms as any adult has in the privacy of his home; that a blanket authorization for inspection in contracts for dormitory rooms does not waive Fourth Amendment rights; that colleges cannot search dormitory rooms for contraband without probable cause and, absent exigent circumstances, without a warrant; and that evidence seized in illegal searches cannot be used in college disciplinary proceedings.[2] Thus, even though a specific student is suspected of criminal activity, college officials should be wary of breeching that student's privacy rights. In fact, if the matter is a criminal one, it is entirely outside the control of the college, and the search and seizure in question should be placed in the hands of proper law enforcement authorities.

The second of those interests mentioned in Whalen v. Roe—that is, "the right of an individual not to have his private affairs made public by the government"—was the central issue in Merriken v. Cressman (1973) [3] and Lora v. Bd. of Educ. of City of New York (1977).[4] These cases were at the secondary and elementary school levels, but nevertheless provide some indication of what the bounds of "unwanted publicity" can be in higher education, especially in behavioral research, as well as some in-

99. Id., at 795.

1. Id., at 797.

2. Id., at 786–795.

3. 364 F.Supp. 913 (D.C.Pa.1973).

4. 74 F.R.D. 565 (D.C.N.Y.1977).

sight into the judicial process of balancing the right of an individual to privacy with the right of government to invade that privacy for the sake of public interest.

The *Merriken* case arose when a junior high school student and his mother filed suit to enjoin a school district from continuing a newly-instituted program entitled Critical Period of Intervention (CPI) administered to eighth grade students. The program was described "as a drug prevention approach . . . designed to aid the local school district in identifying potential abusers, prepare the necessary interventions, identify resources to train and aid district personnel to remediate the problems and, finally, to evaluate the results." [5] The questionnaire used to identify potential drug users in the school consisted of questions about a student's family life, "including the reason for the absence of one or both parents, and . . . whether the student's family life is 'very close, somewhat close, not too close, . . . not close at all' " and if a student's parents "hugged and kissed him good-night when he was small" . . . ; whether they told him how 'much they loved him or her' and other such intimate inquiries.[6]

The federal district court observed that such questions went directly to the heart of family relationships and child rearing and thus looked upon the intrusion as a potential "violation of one's Constitutional right to privacy." Significantly, the court added "that the right to privacy is on an equal or possibly more elevated pedestal than some other individual Constitutional rights and should be treated with as much deference as free speech." [7] Thus, since a fundamental right was involved, the court shifted the burden to the state (school district) to show some compelling state interest and to authenticate its means—e. g., least intrusive alternative—for reaching that interest.

Of course drug prevention is a legitimate state objective, but the method used by the school to reach that objective failed to pass constitutional muster. "The reasons for this are that the test itself and the surrounding results of that test are not sufficiently presented to both the child and the parent . . . as to its authenticity and credibility in fighting the drug problem . . . " Moreover, in balancing the competing interest of individual "privacy against the public need for a program to learn

5. 364 F.Supp. at 914.

6. Id., at 916, 918.

7. Id., at 918.

and possibly prevent drug abuse in a society which has become highly aware of the dangers and effects of drug abuse," the court held that "[a]s the Program now stands the individual loses more than society can gain in its fight against drugs." Hence, the court held that the CPI Program constituted an involuntary invasion of the constitutionally protected privacy rights of the plaintiffs under "the First, Fourth, Fifth, Ninth and Fourteenth Amendments of the United States Constitution," and thus "permanently enjoined and restrained" the school district and its agents "from implementing or in any other way proceeding with the CPI Program . . ." [8]

The *Merriken* case, therefore, clarifies the constitutional protections required in terms of the confidentiality of personal information gathered in various forms of social and behavioral research, and the proper bounds of information that might be requested and used in decisions and judgments concerning an individual's educational or social progression. The case has numerous implications for college record systems and behavioral research, and hence those involved in these activities should take special note of some specifics that lay behind the court's reasoning. That is, the problems involved in the implementation of the CPI Program pointed out by the court amounted to more than the intrusiveness of the Program's questionnaire. For instance, the court noted that the letter sent to parents was "a 'selling device,' 'an attempt to convince the parent to allow the child to participate'" which contained nothing "'critical or negative about the CPI Program.'" The court determined that this was misleading since the letter mentioned none of the dangers involved in the Program:

> Two child psychiatrists testified without contradiction as to several negative, and indeed dangerous aspects of the CPI Program, none of which are mentioned or referred to in any of the materials to be made available to parents. These dangers include the risk that the CPI Program will operate as a self fulfilling prophecy in which a child labelled as a potential drug abuser will by virtue of the label decide to be that which people already think he or she is anyway . . . In fact, the CPI Program manual itself, not available to parents, acknowledges this risk . . . Another danger mentioned is that of scapegoating in which a child might be marked out by his peers for unpleasant treatment either

8. Id., at 920–922.

because of refusal to take the CPI test or because of the results of the test . . . That this is not a mere hypothetical risk was illustrated by an incident involving Plaintiff, Michael Merriken, in which fellow students accused him of being a drug user because his mother does not want him to participate in the CPI Program . . . Drs. Gordon and Hanford also described the severe loyalty conflict that might result by asking children the types of personal questions about their relationship with parents and siblings which are included in the CPI questionnaire . . . A final example has to do with the qualifications of the personnel who will administer the so-called interventions once the results of the CPI questionnaire have been evaluated. As both psychiatrists pointed out, the types of psychotherapy that are suggested as interventions in the CPI Program are quite sophisticated and require the skills of trained psychotherapists, psychiatrists, psychologists, etc. who have undergone many years of training. However, the CPI Program contemplates that these sophisticated psychotherapy techniques will be administered by school personnel, including teachers without any particular qualifications who have undergone only a short crash course.[9]

Later, the court admitted its lack of expertise in the area of "personality testing and confidentiality, and the problems of informed consent." Hence, the court turned to a recent law journal article for some guidance:

"The average American parent has a great and naive faith in 'scientifically' constructed tests. This faith is reinforced by the unconscious desire of the more insecure parents to avoid involvement and to depend on 'professionals' to make the difficult decisions in the education and maturation of their children . . . ..

"In all probability, he is not clear regarding the qualifications of the school 'psychologist' who is likely to hold a master's degree in school psychology, not from the psychology department of a college or university, but from an education school or department. Chances are great he has not had significant supervision in a hospital, or outpatient clinic, or from a clinical psychologist or psychiatrist. He is likely to be considered 'untrained' by the persons that parents have in mind when they 'picture' a psychologist . . . Informed

9. Id., at 915.

consent for personality testing should be comparable to the
informed consent ideally obtained by a physician prior to
the performance of surgery . . . " [10]

With this in mind, the court held that "[t]he attempt to make
the letter requesting consent similar to a promotional inducement
buy, lacks the necessary substance to give a parent the opportunity to give knowing, intelligent and aware consent," but then
stated that its ultimate concern was the Program's remediation
stage because of "the use of teachers, guidance counsellors and
others, who have had little training in the area of psychological
therapy in either individual or group therapy sessions . . .
How many children would be labeled as potential drug abusers
who in actuality are not, and would be subjected to the problem
of group therapy sessions conducted by inexperienced individuals? " [11]

The purported confidentiality of the CPI Program also received
some harsh criticism:

> Although the CPI Program constantly refers to confidential-
> ity, no specifics are given in the Program itself as to how
> confidentiality is to be maintained after evaluation. Mr.
> Streit did testify on this subject but that testimony is far
> different from what appears in the printed CPI materials.
> The Program, by its own terms, contemplates the develop-
> ment of a 'massive data bank' and also dissemination of data
> relating to specific students to various school personnel, in-
> cluding superintendents, principals, guidance counsellors,
> athletic coaches, social workers, PTA officers, and school
> board members . . . In fact, at a meeting of the Nor-
> ristown School Board on Monday, October 23, 1972, parents
> were advised that teams of faculty members had already
> been selected to receive data back from the CPI Program
> in order to implement the intervention stage of the Program
> in the various schools in Norristown . . .

> Even if those who are to be working with the CPI Program
> were to try and be as confidential as possible, in accordance
> with Mr. Streit's testimony, there is absolutely no assurance
> that the materials which have been gathered would be free
> from access by outside authorities in the community who

10.　Id., at 919–920, quoting from
Charles W. Sheerer and Ronald A.
Roston, "Some Legal and Psycho-
logical Concerns About Personality
Testing in the Public Schools,"

Federal Bar Journal III (1971), pp.
114–115.

11.　Id. at 920.

have subpoena power. Thus, there is no assurance that should an enterprising district attorney convene a special grand jury to investigate the drug problem in Montgomery County, the records of the CPI Program would remain inviolate from subpoenas and that he could not determine the identity of children who have been labled by the CPI Program as potential drug abusers.[12]

Interestingly, the privacy boundaries charter in *Merriken* are essentially identical with those to be found in an HEW regulation published a few years thereafter. To illustrate, 45 CFR 46 protects research subjects by requiring two fundamental assurances: (1) risks to subjects will not outweigh the value of the knowledge to be gained, and (2) subjects have given informed consent to participate. Informed consent is defined as having the following crucial elements:

1.   Notification that participation is voluntary and that one is free to withdraw from participation at any time without prejudice.

2.   An adequate explanation of procedures to be used, their purposes, and disclosure of any alternative procedures that might be to the subject's advantage.

3.   Offering to answer any inquiries about the procedure.

4.   A fair description of risks, discomforts, and benefits to be expected.

Educators, therefore, are well-advised to monitor any behavioral research accordingly. In the judicial search for the proper balance between protected privacy and acceptable intrusion, both the risks and benefits involved in a contested program will be weighed carefully; and since the right to privacy is rooted in the Constitution, "informed consent" will be the critical element in clearing the Brady v. United States barrior:

> Waivers of constitutional rights not only must be voluntary but must be knowing, intelligent and done with sufficient awareness of the relevant circumstances and likely consequences.[13]

There are exceptional circumstances, however, wherein informed consent may not be required in order to justify disclosure. Such was the case in Lora v. Board of Educ. of City of New York; here, in contrast to *Merriken,* the court reached a different conclusion in the "right to privacy"—"right to know" boundary dis-

12. Id., at 916.

13.   397 U.S. 742, 748 (1969), and quoted in *Merriken* at 919.

pute. As Justice Powell noted in his concurring opinion in Branzburg v. Hayes:

> The balance of . . . vital constitutional and societal interests on a case-by-case basis accords with the tried and traditional way of adjudicating such questions.[14]

The plaintiffs in the *Lora* case were all Black and Hispanic children assigned to "Special Day Schools for Socially Maladjusted and Emotionally Disturbed Children (SMED)." With the assistance of the Legal Aid Society and the NAACP, they had charged that the New York City school system's standards for the identification, evaluation and educational placement of emotional handicapped children were "vague, ambiguous and overbroad, and . . . applied in a capricious, arbitrary and racially discriminatory manner that [was] violative of their federal constitutional and statutory rights to due process of law and equal educational opportunity." [15] To provide evidentiary support for these charges, the plaintiffs sought a pretrial discovery order to compel the production of 50 randomly selected, anonymous diagnostic and referral files. They thus raised important issues concerning the rights of non-party students to privacy as well as protections under the psychiatrist-patient privilege.

The court set the stage for its decision with a familiar and fundamental formula for adjudicating such matters: "Only strong countervailing public policies should be permitted to prevent disclosure when, as here, a suit is brought to redress a claim for violation of civil rights under the Constitution." [16] Of course the "strong countervailing public policies" included both the constitutional protection against the disclosure of embarrassing or intimate biographical information by the government and the privilege of therapist-patient interchanges. Nonetheless, the court explained that "[b]y its very nature the need for privacy must inevitably conflict with society's compelling need for information in a myriad of circumstances." When such circumstances arise, a balancing of competing interests is required to determine whether privacy protections should be extended to particular communications:

> Whether claims to privacy and privilege of the sort made here are ultimately rooted in the Constitution, or in non-

---

14. 408 U.S. 665, 710 (1972), and quoted in *Lora*, 74 F.R.D. at 576.

15. Lora v. Board of Educ., 74 F.R. D. 565, 568 (D.C.N.Y.1977); consti-

tutional and statutory rights invoked were the Fourteenth Amendment and 42 U.S.C.A. §§ 1981, 1983.

16. Id., at 579.

constitutional considerations of public policy, they are not absolute. Like rights and interests generally, they are qualified and must be balanced against legitimate and weighty competing private and state interests . . . "It should also be recognized that not every threat to private personality is a matter of sufficient concern to warrent social protection. Similarly, not every technical trespass is serious enough to warrent social redress. The test is always this: Is the threat or the invasion unreasonable, or intolerable?" [17]

Thus, under the special circumstances here presented, the court began its process of weighing relevant factors.

Obviously, the best source for evidence to prove the alleged pattern of racial discrimination in the SMED evaluation and placement process rested in the referral and diagnostic files sought by the plaintiffs. Equally as obvious was the value of a just determination of such charges. After pointing out that "for more than two decades this nation has charted a course to eradicate racial discrimination in our schools," the court said:

Remedial education of the emotionally disturbed and handicapped, if tainted by capricious or discriminatory administration, may have devastating consequences not only for the victimized students, but for society generally. The possibility that SMED schools are, as plaintiffs allege, responsible for a tragic waste of human resources and the concomitant threat to physical well-being and social order posed by a class of ill-educated, emotionally disturbed outcasts, make accurate fact finding in this case imperative.[18]

Since it was primarily methodology that concerned the plaintiffs, moreover, they requested neither the names nor other identifying data with the files. In fact, it was agreed that any such information would be redacted:

In addition to requiring that all identifying data be redacted and the files coded, the court may order that the information they contain be used solely for the purpose of the pending litigation; strict confidentiality may be enforced under penalty of contempt; the number of copies to be made of the documents may be rigidly regulated; files submitted to the court may be ordered sealed; and all material may be required to be returned to the defendants immediately

---

17. Id., at 576–577, and quoting in part from O. Ruebhausen and O. G. Brim, "Privacy and Behavioral Re-

search," 65 *Columbia Law Review* (1965) p. 1190.

18. Id., at 579.

upon conclusion of this suit. Under such a protective scheme the invasion of the children's privacy will be minimal.[19]

Under these conditions, any invasion of privacy attendant upon dissemination of the files would be *de minimus*. In this connection the court stated that in deciding "a suit under the Freedom of Information Act, the Supreme Court held that disclosure contained in personnel and medical files that would otherwise 'constitute a clearly unwarranted invasion of privacy,' would be permissible where the names and identifying characteristics of the subjects were deleted." [20]

In sum, as a result of the special circumstances surrounding the case—issues affecting significant public interests, unavailability of alternate sources to settle such issues, limited subjective expectations of secrecy on the part of affected students and parents, and protective orders ensuring confidentiality of disclosed information—the value of compelled disclosure outweighed any speculative costs to privacy and to the psychotherapist-patient privilege:

> The minimal invasion of privacy the students might suffer, weighed against their interest, even as non-parties, in an accurate determination of these charges, convinces us that they would reject this assertion of confidentiality on their behalf.

> Given this view of the facts, it might appear desirable to limit examination of files to those students whose consent could actually be obtained. That path is foreclosed, however, since such a procedure would eliminate the necessary randomness of the sample.[21]

Similarly, in Rios v. Read,[22] a case in which Spanish-speaking plaintiffs sought records of individual students in connection with a class action based on a school district's alleged failure to remedy students' English language deficiencies, it was held that the weight fell clearly on the side of compelled disclosure. The court did point out that the Buckley Amendment "places a significantly heavier burden on a party seeking access to student records to justify disclosure than exists with respect to discovery of other kinds of information such as business records." [23] Nonetheless, it held that "in view of the significant role of private lawsuits

---

19. Id., at 582–583.

20. Id., 581, and citing Department of the Air Force v. Rose, 425 U.S. 352, 375 (1976).

21. Id., at 586.

22. 73 F.R.D. 589 (D.C.N.Y.1977).

23. Id., at 498.

in ending various forms of discrimination in school systems, 'the Family Education Rights and Privacy Act' should not serve as a cloak for alleged discriminatory practices . . . " [24] As already noted, moreover, it was made clear that the Act does not prohibit the release of information, but sets up guidelines for such release and specifically provides for release pursuant to judicial order.

Indeed, only recently the Supreme Court emphasized a strong policy in favor of full development of the facts in federal litigations to the end that justice be served. The Court observed in United States v. Nixon:

> We have elected to employ an adversary system of . . . justice in which the parties contest all issues before a court of law. The need to develop all relevant facts in the adversary system is both fundamental and comprehensive . . . . The very integrity of the judicial system and public confidence in the system depend on full disclosure of all the facts, within the framework of the rules of evidence.[25]

Viewed from this perspective, then, "privacy" and "disclosure" are simply alternative ways of referring to the same problem. But the line-drawing problem can be difficult for educational institutions since the privacy collision with someone else's need to know is classic and continuous. In fact, the third concept of the constitutional right to privacy mentioned in Professor Kurland's article and quoted in Whalen v. Roe—i. e., "the right of an individual to be free in action, thought, experience, and belief from governmental compulsion" is directly implicated in such "privacy"—"disclosure" collisions. For instance, in Carter v. Fench [26] a student government association's budget was held to be disclosable under Louisiana's Public Records Act and thus right-to-know interests prevailed. In another lawsuit, Associated Students, Univ. of Cal. at Riverside v. Attorney General,[27] the students obtained a ruling that a California statute banning the publication and mailing of birth control information—a sort of "right-*not*-to-know" protection—was unconstitutional. Then, too, in Papadopoulos v. State Bd. of Higher Educ.,[28] the Oregon State University administration was placed in the awkward position of disclosing a confidential report when the state's highest

24. Id., at 600.

25. 418 U.S. 683, 709 (1974).

26. 322 So.2d 305 (La.App.1975).

27. 368 F.Supp. 11 (D.C.Cal.1973).

28. 8 Or.App. 445, 494 P.2d 260 (1972).

court ruled that the report had been paid for by public funds and therefore came under the disclosure provisions of Oregon's "right-to-know" statute.

On the other hand, in a case which arose from the exclusion of a student for failure to comply with grooming regulations, Black v. Cothren,[29] a federal district court in Nebraska held that one had the right to privacy in the development of one's personality even though it was not specifically mentioned in the Constitution. That is, its existence as a fundamental right was no longer open to question. (See discussion of the constitutionality of grooming regulations in Chapter 8, pp. 391–395). Similarly, in Richards v. Thurston [30] a federal district court in Massachusetts held the suspension of a student for refusing to cut his hair to a length satisfactory to the school administration to be in violation of the Constitution. The only basis for the suspension, the court contended, appeared to be the administration's personal prejudices, conventions in this period of history, and the views of some who may or may not be a majority in the community. The court asserted that the educational institution should not be a bastion of governmentally imposed conformity, but should allow for nonconformity as well. Likewise, in Breen v. Kahl [31] a federal district court in Wisconsin was also disturbed by a school's seeming attempt to promote an unwarranted conformity among students by its imposition of grooming regulations.

The opinions of the judges in these grooming cases reveal a belief that students have a wide zone of constitutionally protected privacy in which they are free from governmentally compelled conformity. Although not always stated precisely so, this view implies the idea that education should foster diversity and personal choice; at a minimum, this view supports the idea that educational institutions should not be operated as quasi-military or penal institutions; yet, in Brooks v. Wainwright, where a prison inmate protested that the rule that he "shave twice a week and receive periodic haircuts," the Fifth Circuit revealingly cited a high school grooming case to support its holding that the prison regulation did not violate the inmate's "freedom of expression." [32] It should be noted, moreover, that the majority of decisions re-

---

29. 316 F.Supp. 468 (D.C.Neb.1970).

30. 304 F.Supp. 449 (D.C.Mass.1969), aff'd 424 F.2d 1281 (1st Cir. 1970).

31. 296 F.Supp. 702 (D.C.Wis.1969), aff'd 419 F.2d 1034 (7th Cir. 1969), cert. denied 398 U.S. 937 (1970).

32. 428 F.2d 655, 664 (5th Cir. 1970), citing Ferrell v. Dallas Independent School Dist., 261 F.Supp. 545 (D.C. Tex.1966), aff'd 392 F.2d 697 (5th Cir. 1968), cert. denied 393 U.S. 856 (1968).

garding school grooming regulations have upheld the prison warden's viewpoint.

One final case worthy of considerable attention here is that of White v. Davis [33] in which the Supreme Court of California ruled that it is unconstitutional under the Federal and California Constitutions for policemen to pose as students in a university classroom. The holding in this case arose from a taxpayer's suit filed by Hayden White, a professor of history at UCLA and taxpaying resident of Los Angeles, charging that Edward Davis, Chief of Police of the City of Los Angeles, authorized an illegal expenditure of public funds in connection with the police department's conduct of covert intelligence gathering activities at UCLA.

Justice Tobriner, in response to this charge and speaking for the majority, declared that "the presence in a university classroom of undercover officers taking notes to be preserved in police dossiers must inevitably inhibit the exercise of free speech both by professors and students." The First Amendment protection of private expression under like circumstances, he contended, has been affirmed by the United States Supreme Court:

> Thus, for example, in NAACP v. Alabama, . . . 357 U.S. 449, 462 . . . [1958], the Supreme Court struck down a court order requiring the NAACP to disclose its membership lists, declaring: "It is hardly a novel perception that compelled disclosure of affiliation with groups engaged in advocacy may constitute [an] effective . . . restraint on freedom of association . . . . *Inviolability of privacy in group association* may in many circumstances be indispensible to preservation of freedom of association, particularly where a group espouses dissident beliefs" . . .
>
> In like manner, covert police surveillance and intelligence gathering may potentially impose a significant inhibiting effect on the free expression of ideas. As the United States Supreme Court . . . observed: "Official surveillance, whether its purpose be criminal investigation or ongoing intelligence gathering, risks infringement of *constitutionally protected privacy of speech*." (United States v. United States District Court, . . . 407 U.S. 297, 320 [1972] . . . .) [34]

33. 13 Cal.3d 757, 120 Cal.Rptr. 94, 533 P.2d 222 (1975).

34. Id., at 229 (emphasis added). In respect to the NAACP v. Alabama holding on the "inviolability of privacy in group association," however, it should be noted that the courts have allowed the college to require that a student organization

In a footnote, Tobriner noted that "if either a teacher or student speaks in class he takes the 'risk' that a class member will take note of the statement and perhaps recall it in the future." Nonetheless, he claimed "such a risk is qualitatively different than that posed by a governmental surveillance system involving the filing of reports in permanent police records." [35] In fact, when "police surveillance activities focus upon university classrooms and their environs," he observed "[t]he threat to First Amendment freedoms . . . is considerably exacerbated" inasmuch as there now exists one significant factual difference: "academic freedom." [36] He then pointed with approbation to the Sweezy v. New Hampshire case "in which governmental inquiry sought to reach inside the classroom itself; the Supreme Court's stinging condemnation of that intrusive investigative effort illuminates the constitutional [exacerbation] presented by the instant case":

> Chief Justice Warren, . . . declared: "The essentiality of freedom in the community of American universities is almost self-evident . . . . Scholarship cannot flourish in an atmosphere of suspicion and distrust." (354 U.S. at p. 250, [1957] . . .) Justice Frankfurter, in a concurrence joined by Justice Harlan, was even more emphatic: "These pages need not be burdened with proof . . of the dependence of a free society on free universities. *This means the exclusion of governmental intervention in the intellectual life of a university. It matters little whether such intrusion occurs avowedly or through action that inevitably tends to check the ardor and fearlessness of scholars, qualities at once so fragile and so indispensible for fruitful academic labor* . . . [I]n these matters of the spirit inroads on legitimacy must be resisted at their incipiency." [37]

Thus, having established that the facts in the instant case demonstrated a First Amendment violation of free speech and association, Tobriner turned to the second part of the complaint: that the police surveillance activities violated "students' and teachers' constitutional right of privacy." Rather than applying the privacy protections of the First (which had been implied in answering the first allegation), Fourth, Fifth, Ninth, and Four-

provide the institution with the names of its officers. (See Chapter 6, p. 260.)

35. Id., at fn. 4.

36. Id., at 229–230.

37. Id., at 230 (emphasis added by Tobriner).

teenth Amendments, however, the Justice turned to the 1972 California Constitutional provision guaranteeing the right of privacy. Based upon the statement drafted by the proponents of the provision included in the state's election brochure, Trobriner observed:

> First, the statement identifies the principal "mischiefs" at which the amendment is directed: (1) government snooping and the secret gathering of personal information; (2) the overbroad collection and retention of unnecessary personal information by government and business interests; (3) the improper use of information properly obtained for a specific purpose, for example, the use of it for other purpose or disclosure of it to some third party; and (4) the lack of a reasonable check on the accuracy of existing record. Second, the statement makes clear that the amendment does not purport to prohibit all incursion into individual privacy but rather that any such intervention must be justified by a compelling interest. Third, the statement indicates that the amendment is intended to be self-executing, i. e., that the constitutional provision, in itself, "creates a legal and enforceable right of privacy for every Californian." [38]

The Justice, in response to this observation, held:

> In several respects, the police surveillance operation challenged in the instant complaint epitomizes the kind of government conduct which the new constitutional amendment condemns. In the first place, the routine stationing of covert, undercover police agents in university classrooms and association meetings, both public and private, constitutes "government snooping" in the extreme. Second, as noted above, the instant complaint alleges that the information gathered by the undercover agents, from class discussion and organization meetings "pertains to no illegal activity or acts"; if this allegation is true, and we must assume it is at this stage of the proceedings, a strong suspicion is raised that the gathered material, preserved in "police dossiers," may be largely unnecessary for any legitimate, let alone "compelling" governmental interest.
>
> In view of these considerations, we believe that the allegations of the present complaint state a prima facie violation of the state constitutional right of privacy. At trial, of course, defendant will be free to contest any of the allega-

---

38. Id., at 234.

tions of the complaint as well as to designate the compelling governmental interests upon which they rely for their intrusive conduct . . . .

As far as we are concerned, the extensive routine, covert police surveillance of university classes and organization meetings alleged by the instant complaint are unprecedented in our nation's history.[39]

Still, a note of caution must be sounded for school authorities who would study any of the constitutional privacy decisions with a view to implementing their stated holdings. First, constitutional rights to privacy protect individuals only against acts of federal or state governments. The key to a successful constitutional claim is "state action." Where none can be shown, no constitutional violation exists. Private colleges in only rare exceptions have been held to be in the position of public parties vis-a-vis their students. As noted throughout the book, however, public colleges clearly do act as state instrumentalities and therefore must respect their students' constitutional rights.

Second, fundamental rights can be abridged if a public institution can demonstrate a "compelling" state interest which justifies the resulting abridgement and which cannot be served by alternative means less intrusive on fundamental rights.[40] Moreover, the constitutional right of privacy has the limitation that it must not only be balanced with "right-to-know" interests, but with the concomitant freedoms of speech and press as well. In Cox Broadcasting Corp. v. Cohn, for instance, the United States Supreme Court recognized that the sphere in which claims of privacy most directly confront the constitutional freedoms of speech and press is the publication of information which is embarrassing or painful to an individual. In this sphere of collision the Court spelled out press liability protection when reporting the contents of public records:

> At the very least, the First and Fourteenth Amendments will not allow exposing the press to liability for truthfully publishing information related to the public in official records; if there are privacy interests to be protected in judicial proceedings, the states must respond by means which avoid public documentation or other exposure of private information, but once true information is disclosed in public court documents open to public inspection, the press cannot be sanc-

---

39. Id., at 234–235.

40. See, e. g., Shelton v. Tucker, 364 U.S. 479, 488 (1960).

tioned for publishing it, and reliance must rest on those who decide what to publish or broadcast.[41]

With this reasoning the Court struck down a Georgia statute which expressly forbade the publication of a rape victim's identity. But a more significant qualification of privacy rights occurs when legitimate public interest in published information is substantial, especially when an individual willingly enters the public sphere.

For example, based upon the "public interest in having free and unhindered debate on matters of public importance," the Supreme Court in New York Times Co. v. Sullivan established the principle that "public officials" cannot recover damages for false or misleading publication of their official activities unless they can show "that the statement was made with 'actual malice'— that is, with knowledge that it was false or with reckless disregard of whether it was false or not." [42] Then, in Curtis Pub. Co. v. Butts, the Court expanded the "public officials" ruling to cover "public figures" which it defined as individuals "intimately involved in the resolution of important public questions, or by reason of their fame, shape events in areas of concern to society at large." [43] Finally, in Gertz v. Robert Welch, Inc., the Court provided a further distinction between public officials or public figures and private individuals by identifying the latter as persons not in a position to seek redress via "selfhelp"—"the first remedy of any victim of defamation." [44] However, while appreciating this distinction, the Court also recognized that the threat of costly punitive damages would present an inhibiting constraint on First Amendment rights to speech and press. Thus, though the Court held that private individuals would not have to allege and prove actual malice to sustain a cause of action, as public officials and public figures must do, it held that in the absence of a showing of actual malice, private individuals would be limited to compensation for "actual injury." What is "actual injury"? The Court partially answered the question by stating:

> We need not define "actual injury," as trial courts have wide experience in framing appropriate jury instructions in tort actions. Suffice it to say that actual injury is not limited to out-of-pocket loss. Indeed, the more customary types of actual harm inflicted by defamatory falsehood include im-

41. 420 U.S. 469, 473 (1975).

42. 376 U.S. 254, 279–280 (1964).

43. 388 U.S. 130, 164 (1967).

44. 418 U.S. 323, 344–345 (1974).

pairment of reputation and standing in the community, personal humiliation, and mental anguish and suffering. Of course, juries must be limited by appropriate instructions, and all awards must be supported by competent evidence concerning the injury, although there need be no evidence which assigns an actual dollar value to the injury.[45]

All of this rather obviously points out that constitutional protections of privacy, speech and press are interwoven with interests in privacy protected by common-law tort or by statute. As Justice Fortas wrote in a dissenting opinion:

A distinct right of privacy is now recognized either as a "common law" right or by statute, in at least 35 states. Its exact scope varies in the respective jurisdictions. It is, simply stated, the right to be let alone; to live one's life as one chooses, free from assault, intrusion or invasion except as they can be justified by the clear needs of community living under a government of law.[46]

As explained earlier in this chapter, tort law is that branch of common law which deals with legal wrongs committed by one person against the person or property of another. Moreover, interests in privacy are protected by tort law, but, as Fortas observed above: "Its exact scope varies in the respective" states. With this caution noted, then, Prosser categorizes the tort of "invasion of privacy" as:

1. Appropriation of a person's name or likeness for another person's benefit or advantage.

2. Unreasonable intrusion upon a person's physical solitude or seclusion.

3. Public disclosure of another's private life.

4. Publicity that places another in a false light before the public.

Thus, Prosser's analysis of privacy describes its violation almost exclusively in terms of being a tort or a complex of four torts. Just as with other torts, he implies, the common thread woven into these invasions of privacy is the idea of unreasonable interference with others. Also, it is not simply that a particular wrong has been committed; closely attendant to either a judgment or an assessment of resulting damages are the defendant's

---

45. Id., at 349–350.

46. Times, Inc. v. Hill, 385 U.S. 374, 399 (1965).

motives and conduct in committing the wrong.[47] That such refinements are critical can perhaps be explained in a brief accounting of two cases.

In the first case, Porten v. Univ. of San Francisco,[48] a University of San Francisco student filed a complaint for damages against the University for disclosing to the California State Scholarship and Loan Commission grades he had earned while attending Columbia University. Porten's claim for damages was essentially based upon Prosser's above "public-disclosure-of-another's-private-life" category of the invasion of privacy. He had specifically asked that his grades not be released to a third party; moreover, the Scholarship and Loan Commission had not asked the University to send Porten's Columbia University transcript. Nonetheless, the court held that the University's disclosure of the Columbia transcript to the Commission was not a communication to the public in general or to a large number of persons; rather, it was a communication to an individual or a few persons. Hence, the court held that the University's communication at issue could not be interpreted as a cause of action based upon public disclosure of private facts.

The other case, Wallace v. Weiss,[49] involved Prosser's first category—the appropriation of another's likeness. It was on this basis that the plaintiff in the case sued the University of Rochester and one of its student organizations for the unauthorized use of her photograph on the front cover of a magazine published and distributed by the named student organization. However, the outcome in the defendants' favor turned in part on the plaintiff's failure to show commercial exploitation of the photograph: "The defendant organization was not a commercial venture and was not engaged in trade." Further, the court applied *Gertz* and found "that she suffered no personal humiliation, mental anguish and suffering" and "incurred no out of pocket loss, except for attorney's fees for the commencement of this action. These attorney fees do not [here] constitute an item of damage . . . ."[50]

In sum, the individual is concerned about information that is distributed about him, and constitutional, statutory and tort law

47. W. L. Prosser, *Handbook of the Law of Torts*, 4th ed. (St. Paul, Minn.: West Publishing Co., 1971), et seq.

48. 64 Cal.App.3d 825, 134 Cal.Rptr. 839 (1976).

49. 82 Misc.2d 1053, 372 N.Y.S.2d 416 (1975).

50. Id., at 420–421.

are powerful guardians of that interest. As we have observed, these protections have numerous implications for the student-college relationship. Clearly, the liberty interest of the student is strongly implicated and in this respect perhaps one brief statement from Goss v. Lopez provides the best summary:

> The Due Process Clause . . . forbids arbitrary deprivations of liberty. "Where a person's good name, reputation, honor, or integrity is at stake because of what the government is doing to him," the minimal requirements of the clause must be satisfied.[51]

---

51. 419 U.S. 565, 579 (1975), and quoting in part from Wisconsin v. Constantineau, 400 U.S. 433, 437 (1971).

Chapter 10

EPILOGUE

The vigilant protection of constitutional freedoms is nowhere more vital than in the community of American
schools.

(*Shelton v. Tucker*, 364 U.S. 479, 487 (1960))

We are not free to disregard the practical realities. Mr.
Justice Stewart has made the salient point: "Freedoms
such as these are protected not only against heavy-
handed frontal attack, but also from being stifled by
more subtle governmental interference."

(*Healy v. James*, 408 U.S. 169, 183 (1972),
quoting from *Bates v. City of Little Rock*,
361 U.S. 516, 523 (1960))

No person who follows the march of national news, however
casually, can be unmindful of the fact that the college campus
is a decidedly more tranquil place today than it was in the sixties.
Time passes, metabolisms change, and many of the younger generation who passionately believed that anyone over thirty was
not to be trusted are now losing their hair. But college students
in all decades have had at least one thing in common—a certain
number of them inevitably get into trouble.

Before those turbulent sixties, however, most colleges and universities claimed authority to make disciplinary rules and to
adopt procedures, if any, for expulsion or suspension at their
discretion. Moreover, such procedural devices were typically
truncated at best. In fact, as early as 1887 one court warned
against giving school officials a completely free hand in setting
up hearing procedures. The case in which this warning was
made involved a student who had been expelled from college
wherein the court apparently learned that although administrators and faculty may be learned in other fields, "their conceptions of what would be competent evidence of guilt may be at
variance with all established legal principles." [1] As an example
of this possibility, the court quoted the testimony of one of the
faculty members to the effect that the student turned pale when

1. Hill v. McCauley, 3 Pa.County
Ct. 77, 88 (1887).

464

he was brought before the college hearing committee was evidence that he understood, without being told, that he was being called upon to explain his participation in riotous conduct. The court also pointed out that evidence received against the student at the college hearing from a janitor of known incredibility and from a student who was never identified "ought not to be and would not be received as competent testimony in the determination of the most trivial rights in the most petty tribunal in the land." [2]

For these reasons, the court ordered the reinstatement of the student, but, as by now well known, a reading of the record of those times clearly reveals that such decisions were rare indeed. Thus, today, the classic starting point for an inquiry into the rights of students at state educational institutions of higher education is Dixon v. Alabama State Bd. of Educ. where, while recognizing that some type of orderly proceeding is the cornerstone of justice, the Fifth Circuit Court of Appeals opened the constitutional door for students. And *no* court since *Dixon* has denied that a student must be given prior notice of the grounds on which a charge is based and the opportunity to respond and the knowledge of and the right to demand a hearing before a final action is taken.

What subsequently passed through that constitutional door, moreover, can be generally reviewed in five Supreme Court decisions: Goss v. Lopez (1975), Horowitz v. Board of Curators (1978), Tinker v. Des Moines School Dist. (1969), Healy v. James (1972), and Papish v. Board of Curators (1973).

Goss recognized that there may be situations in which prior notice and hearing need not be given. Specific illustration of this exception was made as to students who present a "continuing danger to persons or property or an ongoing threat of disrupting the academic process." [3] Under these conditions a student may be removed temporarily, but he is entitled to a prompt, subsequent hearing before final action is taken. Additionally, *Goss* made it clear that even in short-term suspensions, the due process clause applied with its holding that "in connection with a suspension of 10 days or less, . . . the student be given oral or written notice of the charges against him and, if he denies them, an explanation of the evidence the authorities have and an opportunity to present his side of the story." [4] The require-

2. Id., at 83.

3. 419 U.S. 565, 582 (1975).

4. Id., at 581.

ment here, however, was no more than a brief conversation between the school official and the student charged with the infraction of school rules before this type of sanction could be meted out:

> There need be no delay between the time "notice" is given and the time of the hearing. In the great majority of cases the disciplinarian may informally discuss the alleged misconduct with the student minutes after it has occurred. We hold only that, in being given an opportunity to explain his version at this discussion, the student first be told what he is accused of doing and what the basis of the accusation is.[5]

Goss did not discuss removal resulting from a student's failure to maintain required academic standards, but in *Horowitz* the Court held that academic punishment did not require due process procedures since such matters are not amenable to the legal process:

> Such a judgment is by its nature more subjective and evaluative than the typical factual questions presented in the average disciplinary decision. Like the decision of an individual professor as to the proper grade for a student in his course, the determination whether to dismiss a student for academic reasons requires an expert evaluation of cumulative information and is not readily adapted to the procedural tools of judicial or administrative decisionmaking.
>
> Under such circumstances, we decline to ignore the historic judgment of educators and thereby formalize the academic dismissal process by requiring a hearing.[6]

Thus, absent arbitrariness or capriciousness, academic dismissals are not subject to judicial scrutiny.

Then, in *Tinker*, *Healy* and *Papish*, the Court staked out the substantive due process zones of protection for students. The clear implication of elaborating language in *Tinker* is to the effect that mere anticipation of disruption is not enough to justify a restriction of freedom of expression: "In order for the State in the person of school officials to justify prohibition of a particular expression of opinion, it must be able to show that its action was caused by something more than a mere desire to avoid the discomfort and unpleasantness that always accompany

5. Id., at 582.   6. 98 S.Ct. 948, 955 (1978).

an unpopular viewpoint." [7] In response to this observation, the Court held: "Clearly, the prohibition of expression of one particular opinion, at least without evidence that it is necessary to avoid material and substantial interference with school work or discipline, is not constitutionally permissible." [8]

Of course, *Tinker* made it clear that First Amendment rights must always be applied "in light of the special characteristics of the environment," and, where state-operated educational institutions are involved, it recognized "the need for affirming the comprehensive authority of the States and of school officials, consistent with fundamental constitutional safeguards, to prescribe and control conduct in the schools." [9] Still, *Healy* pointed out that "the precedents of this Court leave no room for the view that, because of the acknowledged need for order, First Amendment protections should apply with less force on college campuses than in the community at large. Quite to the contrary," the Court observed, "[t]he college classroom with its surrounding environs is peculiarly the 'marketplace of ideas,' and we break no new constitutional ground in reaffirming this Nation's dedication to academic freedom."

Healy then set forth another protected province of students— "freedom of association . . . long . . . held to be implicit in the freedoms of speech, assembly, and petition." [10] The Court concluded that "the College's denial of recognition" to a student organization on the basis that its philosophy was counter to the official policy of the college, "was a form of prior restraint denying to petitioner organization the range of associational activities" protected by the First and Fourteenth Amendments. "While a college has a legitimate interest in preventing disruption on the campus, which under circumstances requiring the safeguarding of that interest may justify such restraint, a 'heavy burden' rests on the college to demonstrate the appropriateness of that action." [11]

Finally, *Papish* held that "[t]he mere dissemination of ideas —no matter how offensive to good taste—on a state university campus may not be shut off in the name alone of 'conventions of decency.' " [12] Although not a factor in these cases, other courts

---

7.   393 U.S. 503, 509 (1969).

8.   Id., at 511.

9.   Id., at 506–507.

10.   408 U.S. 169, 180–181 (1972).

11.   Id., at 184.

12.   410 U.S. 667, 670–671 (1973).

have pointed out that a conduct regulation may be held invalid if it is so vague and standardless that it leaves the student uncertain as to the conduct prohibited. Board of Regents v. Bakke might also be mentioned here but would require some careful legal navigation transcending this brief synopsis. Nonetheless, the general constitutional principle at the bottom of the equal-protection logic is that college policy be uniformly applied.

All of the above and more is now (or should be) inside a rather large tent called public higher education. But it is with mixed feelings that some educators view this special province that has been staked out for students. The problem in this area is a familiar one: colleges and universities must have the power to establish and enforce rules, both disciplinary and academic, in order to further important educational interests, while students charged with violating these rules have the opposing interest of protecting themselves from being arbitrarily deprived of equally important educational opportunities.

Of course, the granting or withholding of any privilege requires the balancing of competing interests, but a growing number of educators today are spinning endless tales about courtroom horror stories and do so with a bright-eyed intensity once witnessed mostly at revival meetings. Somehow, it seems, we have transformed academe into a giant courtroom, and the jury, as luck would have it, is always on the other side. No matter how strong or logical or certain your case may be, the argument goes, you are cooked. But this aggrieved antijudicial mood is probably best typified in the words of Grant Gilmore: "The better the society, the less law there will be. In Heaven there will be no law, and the lion will lie down with the lamb . . . . The worse the society, the more law there will be. In Hell there will be nothing but law, and due process will be meticulously observed." [13]

And today it is the student who is the lion, and so on.

In the words of Dicken's Coachman (in *The Pickwick Papers*): "That remark's political, or what is much the same, it ain't true." Yet there is a kernel of truth to it. Still, I'd like to argue, as a member in more or less good standing in the vast congregation of university professors, that this sort of windy hyperbole is just plain dumb. And maybe slightly dangerous, too, especially if one considers that the alternative might well be "to shoot it out in the streets."

13. Quoted in Mark G. Yudof, "Educational Policy and the Law— Who Runs the Schools?" *American Educator* (Fall, 1978), p. 9.

For one thing, it might be hoped that the experience of the sixties would at least now be instructive. But even without this illuminating experience, as early as 1907 the Supreme Court put its finger on what I mean to say:

> The right to sue and defend in the courts is the alternative of force. In an organized society it is the right conservative of all other rights, and lies at the foundation of orderly government.[14]

Even so, admittedly college officials are, or should be, in a better position than the courts to administer discipline; but then should an attitude of judicial self-restraint in such matters allow an injustice to be countenanced?

Beyond that lies the traditional argument against courts interfering in cases of college disciplinary action premised on the historical independence of universities from outside intervention in their internal affairs—admittedly again, an interest that should be guarded jealously. However, there is also the fact that once you claim something, you are likely to be held responsible for acting on it; but let me quickly add that I am not headed for that intellectually fraudulent we-are-all-guilty terrain. What the college officials did, for example, at Alabama State College, including not resisting the intervention of state officials, is not what "someone" or "everyone" else did or did not do. My observation is simply that specific college officials at a specific institution got caught, *flagrante delecti*, and, with all the high stakes involved, it came down to the precedent-setting Dixon v. Alabama State Bd. of Educ. (1961) case and a good decision made by a good man, Judge Rives—a decider who was not afraid of facing the implications of what he saw, whose instincts and empathies were good, and thus had the guts to turn around this really unfair and dangerous brand of second-class citizenship.

Dixon, moreover, has been woven into the fabric of the law, and, as discussed throughout the book, later cases have added to prevailing judicial expectations regarding the governance of student conduct. Thus, as I see it, rather than squabbling about judicial intervention, we should do something about reducing the need for it; and the quintessence of this argument is that specific individuals stop deluding themselves with greeting-card-like sentiments of fairness and justice. That is not to say that we should

14. Chambers v. Baltimore and Ohio Railroad Co., 207 U.S. 142, 148 (1907).

recast our decisional processes in the mold of the courtroom hearing; that is neither required nor would it be wise. Rather, the important factor in this equation is the need for a full recognition of student rights—that a student may not be dismissed or otherwise deprived of educational advantages because of the exercise of those rights, and that a student has the right to a full and disinterested development of the facts surrounding a dispute over whether he will lose any such educational advantages.

Appendix A

UNITED STATES CONSTITUTION

THE CONSTITUTION OF THE UNITED STATES

PREAMBLE

We the People of the United States, in Order to form a more perfect Union, establish Justice, insure domestic Tranquility, provide for the common defence, promote the general Welfare, and secure the Blessings of Liberty to ourselves and our Posterity, do ordain and establish this Constitution for the United States of America.

ARTICLE I

Section 1. All legislative Powers herein granted shall be vested in a Congress of the United States, which shall consist of a Senate and House of Representatives.

Section 2. [1] The House of Representatives shall be composed of Members chosen every second Year by the People of the several States, and the Electors in each State shall have the Qualifications requisite for Electors of the most numerous Branch of the State Legislature.

[2] No Person shall be a Representative who shall not have attained to the Age of twenty five Years, and been seven Years a Citizen of the United States, and who shall not, when elected, be an Inhabitant of that State in which he shall be chosen.

[3] Representatives and direct Taxes shall be apportioned among the several States which may be included within this Union, according to their respective Numbers, which shall be determined by adding to the whole Number of free Persons, including those bound to Service for a Term of Years, and excluding Indians not taxed, three fifths of all other Persons. The actual Enumeration shall be made within three Years after the first Meeting of the Congress of the United States, and within every subsequent Term of ten Years, in such Manner as they shall by Law direct. The Number of Representatives shall not exceed one for every thirty Thousand, but each State shall have at Least one Representative; and until such enumeration shall be made, the State of New Hampshire shall be entitled to chuse three, Massachusetts eight, Rhode Island and Providence Plantations one, Connecticut five, New York six, New Jersey four, Pennsylvania eight, Delaware one, Maryland six, Virginia ten, North Carolina five, South Carolina five, and Georgia three.

[4] When vacancies happen in the Representation from any State, the Executive Authority thereof shall issue Writs of Election to fill such Vacancies.

[5] The House of Representatives shall chuse their Speaker and other Officers; and shall have the sole Power of Impeachment.

Section 3. [1] The Senate of the United States shall be composed of two Senators from each State, chosen by the Legislature thereof, for six Years; and each Senator shall have one Vote.

[2] Immediately after they shall be assembled in Consequence of the first Election, they shall be divided as equally as may be into three Classes. The Seats of the Senators of the first Class shall be vacated at the Expiration of the Second Year, of the second Class at the Expiration of the fourth Year, and of the third Class at the Expiration of the sixth Year, so that one third may be chosen every second Year; and if Vacancies happen by Resignation, or otherwise, during the Recess of the Legislature of any State, the

Executive thereof may make temporary Appointments until the next Meeting of the Legislature, which shall then fill such Vacancies.

[3] No Person shall be a Senator who shall not have attained to the Age of thirty Years, and been nine Years a Citizen of the United States, and who shall not, when elected, be an Inhabitant of that State for which he shall be chosen.

[4] The Vice President of the United States shall be President of the Senate, but shall have no Vote, unless they be equally divided.

[5] The Senate shall chuse their other Officers, and also a President pro tempore, in the Absence of the Vice President, or when he shall exercise the Office of President of the United States.

[6] The Senate shall have the sole Power to try all Impeachments. When sitting for that Purpose, they shall be on Oath or Affirmation. When the President of the United States is tried, the Chief Justice shall preside: And no Person shall be convicted without the Concurrence of two thirds of the Members present.

[7] Judgment in Cases of Impeachment shall not extend further than to removal from Office, and disqualification to hold and enjoy any Office of honor, Trust, or Profit under the United States: but the Party convicted shall nevertheless be liable and subject to Indictment, Trial, Judgment, and Punishment, according to Law.

Section 4. [1] The Times, Places and Manner of holding Elections for Senators and Representatives, shall be prescribed in each State by the Legislature thereof; but the Congress may at any time by Law make or alter such Regulations, except as to the Places of chusing Senators.

[2] The Congress shall assemble at least once in every Year, and such Meeting shall be on the first Monday in December, unless they shall by Law appoint a different Day.

Section 5. [1] Each House shall be the Judge of the Elections, Returns, and Qualifications of its own Members, and a Majority of each shall constitute a Quorum to do Business; but a smaller Number may adjourn from day to day, and may be authorized to compel the Attendance of absent Members, in such Manner, and under such Penalties as each House may provide.

[2] Each House may determine the Rules of its Proceedings, punish its Members for disorderly Behavior, and, with the Concurrence of two thirds, expel a Member.

[3] Each House shall keep a Journal of its Proceedings, and from time to time publish the same, excepting such Parts as may in their Judgment require Secrecy; and the Yeas and Nays of the Members of either House on any question shall, at the Desire of one fifth of those Present, be entered on the Journal.

[4] Neither House, during the Session of Congress, shall, without the Consent of the other, adjourn for more than three days, nor to any other Place than that in which the two Houses shall be sitting.

Section 6. [1] The Senators and Representatives shall receive a Compensation for their Services, to be ascertained by Law, and paid out of the Treasury of the United States. They shall in all Cases, except Treason, Felony and Breach of the Peace, be privileged from Arrest during their Attendance at the Session of their respective Houses, and in going to and returning from the same; and for any Speech or Debate in either House, they shall not be questioned in any other Place.

[2] No Senator or Representative shall, during the Time for which he was elected, be appointed to any civil Office under the Authority of the United States, which shall have been created, or the Emoluments whereof shall have been increased during such time; and no Person holding any Office under the United States, shall be a Member of either House during his Continuance in Office.

Section 7. [1] All Bills for raising Revenue shall originate in the House of Representatives; but the Senate may propose or concur with Amendments as on other Bills.

[2] Every Bill which shall have passed the House of Representatives and the Senate, shall, before it become a Law, be presented to the President of the United States; If he approve he shall sign it, but if not he shall return it, with his Objections to the House in which it shall have originated, who shall enter the Objections at large on their Journal, and proceed to reconsider it. If after such Reconsideration two thirds of that House shall agree to pass the Bill, it shall be sent together with the Objections, to the other House, by which it shall likewise be reconsidered, and if approved by two thirds of that House, it shall become a Law. But in all such Cases the Votes of both Houses shall be determined by yeas and Nays, and the Names of the Persons voting for and against the Bill shall be entered on the Journal of each House respectively. If any Bill shall not be returned by the President within ten Days (Sundays excepted) after it shall have been presented to him, the Same shall be a Law, in like Manner as if he had signed it, unless the Congress by their Adjournment prevent its Return in which Case it shall not be a Law.

[3] Every Order, Resolution, or Vote, to Which the Concurrence of the Senate and House of Representatives may be necessary (except on a question of Adjournment) shall be presented to the President of the United States; and before the Same shall take Effect, shall be approved by him, or being disapproved by him, shall be repassed by two thirds of the Senate and House of Representatives, according to the Rules and Limitations prescribed in the Case of a Bill.

Section 8. [1] The Congress shall have Power To lay and collect Taxes, Duties, Imposts and Excises, to pay the Debts and provide for the common Defence and general Welfare of the United States; but all Duties, Imposts and Excises shall be uniform throughout the United States;

[2] To borrow money on the credit of the United States;

[3] To regulate Commerce with foreign Nations, and among the several States, and with the Indian Tribes;

[4] To establish an uniform Rule of Naturalization, and uniform Laws on the subject of Bankruptcies throughout the United States;

[5] To coin Money, regulate the Value thereof, and of foreign Coin, and fix the Standard of Weights and Measures;

[6] To provide for the Punishment of counterfeiting the Securities and current Coin of the United States;

[7] To Establish Post Offices and Post Roads;

[8] To promote the Progress of Science and useful Arts, by securing for limited Times to Authors and Inventors the exclusive Right to their respective Writings and Discoveries;

[9] To constitute Tribunals inferior to the supreme Court;

[10] To define and punish Piracies and Felonies committed on the high Seas, and Offenses against the Law of Nations;

[11] To declare War, grant Letters of Marque and Reprisal, and make Rules concerning Captures on Land and Water;

[12] To raise and support Armies, but no Appropriation of Money to that Use shall be for a longer Term than two Years;

[13] To provide and maintain a Navy;

[14] To make Rules for the Government and Regulation of the land and naval Forces;

[15] To provide for calling forth the Militia to execute the Laws of the Union, suppress Insurrections and repel Invasions;

[16] To provide for organizing, arming, and disciplining, the Militia, and for governing such Part of them as may be employed in the Service of the United States, reserving to the States respectively, the Appointment of the Officers, and the Authority of training the Militia according to the discipline prescribed by Congress;

[17] To exercise exclusive Legislation in all Cases whatsoever, over such District (not exceeding ten Miles square) as may, by Cession of particular States, and the Acceptance of Congress, become the Seat of the Government of the United States, and to exercise like Authority over all Places purchased by the Consent of the Legislature of the State in which the Same shall be, for the Erection of Forts, Magazines, Arsenals, dock-Yards, and other needful Buildings;—And

[18] To make all Laws which shall be necessary and proper for carrying into Execution the foregoing Powers, and all other Powers vested by

this Constitution in the Government of the United States, or in any Department or Officer thereof.

Section 9. [1] The Migration or Importation of Such Persons as any of the States now existing shall think proper to admit, shall not be prohibited by the Congress prior to the Year one thousand eight hundred and eight, but a Tax or duty may be imposed on such Importation, not exceeding ten dollars for each Person.

[2] The privilege of the Writ of Habeas Corpus shall not be suspended, unless when in Cases of Rebellion or Invasion the public Safety may require it.

[3] No Bill of Attainder or ex post facto Law shall be passed.

[4] No Capitation, or other direct, Tax shall be laid, unless in Proportion to the Census or Enumeration herein before directed to be taken.

[5] No Tax or Duty shall be laid on Articles exported from any State.

[6] No Preference shall be given by any Regulation of Commerce or Revenue to the Ports of one State over those of another: nor shall Vessels bound to, or from, one State be obliged to enter, clear, or pay Duties in another.

[7] No money shall be drawn from the Treasury, but in Consequence of Appropriations made by Law; and a regular Statement and Account of the Receipts and Expenditures of all public Money shall be published from time to time.

[8] No Title of Nobility shall be granted by the United States: And no Person holding any Office of Profit or Trust under them, shall, without the Consent of the Congress, accept of any present, Emolument, Office, or Title, of any kind whatever, from any King, Prince, or foreign State.

Section 10. [1] No State shall enter into any Treaty, Alliance, or Confederation; grant Letters of Marque and Reprisal; coin Money; emit Bills of Credit; make any Thing but gold and silver Coin a Tender in Payment of Debts; pass any Bill of Attainder, ex post facto Law, or Law impairing the Obligation of Contracts, or grant any Title of Nobility.

[2] No State shall, without the Consent of the Congress, lay any Imposts or Duties on Imports or Exports, except what may be absolutely necessary for executing it's inspection Laws: and the net Produce of all Duties and Imposts, laid by any State on Imports or Exports, shall be for the Use of the Treasury of the United States; and all such Laws shall be subject to the Revision and Controul of the Congress.

[3] No State shall, without the Consent of Congress, lay any Duty of Tonnage, keep Troops, or Ships of War in time of Peace, enter into any Agreement or Compact with another State, or with a foreign Power, or engage in War, unless actually invaded, or in such imminent Danger as will not admit of delay.

ARTICLE II

Section 1. [1] The executive Power shall be vested in a President of the United States of America. He shall hold his Office during the Term of four Years, and, together with the Vice President, chosen for the same Term, be elected, as follows:

[2] Each State shall appoint, in such Manner as the Legislature thereof may direct, a Number of Electors, equal to the whole Number of Senators and Representatives to which the State may be entitled in the Congress; but no Senator or Representative, or Person holding an Office of Trust or Profit under the United States, shall be appointed an Elector.

[3] The Electors shall meet in their respective States, and vote by Ballot for two Persons, of whom one at least shall not be an Inhabitant of the same State with themselves. And they shall make a List of all the Persons voted for, and of the Number of Votes for each; which List they shall sign and certify, and transmit sealed to the Seat of the Government of the United States, directed to the President of the Senate. The President of the Senate shall, in the Presence of the Senate and House of Representatives, open all the Certificates, and the Votes shall then be counted. The Person having the greatest Number of Votes shall be the President, if such Number be a Majority of the whole Number of Electors appointed; and if there be more than one who have such Majority, and have an equal Number of Votes, then the House of Representatives shall immediately chuse by Ballot one of them for President; and if no Person have a Majority, then from the five highest on the List the said House shall in like Manner chuse the President. But in chusing the President, the Votes shall be taken by States the Representation from each State having one Vote; A quorum for this Purpose shall consist of a Member or Members from two thirds of the States, and a Majority of all the States shall be necessary to a Choice. In every Case, after the Choice of the President, the Person having the greater Number of Votes of the Electors shall be the Vice President. But if there should remain two or more who have equal Votes, the Senate shall chuse from them by Ballot the Vice President.

[4] The Congress may determine the Time of chusing the Electors, and the Day on which they shall give their Votes; which Day shall be the same throughout the United States.

[5] No person except a natural born Citizen, or a Citizen of the United States, at the time of the Adoption of this Constitution, shall be eligible to the Office of President; neither shall any Person be eligible to that Office who shall not have attained to the Age of thirty five Years, and been fourteen Years a Resident within the United States.

[6] In case of the removal of the President from Office, or of his Death, Resignation or Inability to discharge the Powers and Duties of the

said Office, the Same shall devolve on the Vice President, and the Congress may by Law provide for the Case of Removal, Death, Resignation or Inability, both of the President and Vice President, declaring what Officer shall then act as President, and such Officer shall act accordingly, until the Disability be removed, or a President shall be elected.

[7] The President shall, at stated Times, receive for his Services, a Compensation, which shall neither be increased nor diminished during the Period for which he shall have been elected, and he shall not receive within that Period any other Emolument from the United States, or any of them.

[8] Before he enter on the Execution of his Office, he shall take the following Oath or Affirmation: "I do solemnly swear (or affirm) that I will faithfully execute the Office of President of the United States, and will to the best of my Ability, preserve, protect and defend the Constitution of the United States."

Section 2. [1] The President shall be Commander in Chief of the Army and Navy of the United States, and of the militia of the several States, when called into the actual Service of the United States; he may require the Opinion, in writing, of the principal Officer in each of the Executive Departments, upon any Subject relating to the Duties of their respective Offices, and he shall have Power to grant Reprieves and Pardons for Offenses against the United States, except in Cases of Impeachment.

[2] He shall have Power, by and with the Advice and Consent of the Senate to make Treaties, provided two thirds of the Senators present concur; and he shall nominate, and by and with the Advice and Consent of the Senate, shall appoint Ambassadors, other public Ministers and Consuls, Judges of the supreme Court, and all other Officers of the United States, whose Appointments are not herein otherwise provided for, and which shall be established by Law; but the Congress may by Law vest the Appointment of such inferior Officers, as they think proper, in the President alone, in the Courts of Law, or in the Heads of Departments.

[3] The President shall have Power to fill up all Vacancies that may happen during the Recess of the Senate, by granting Commissions which shall expire at the End of their next Session.

Section 3. He shall from time to time give to the Congress Information of the State of the Union, and recommend to their Consideration such Measures as he shall judge necessary and expedient; he may, on extraordinary Occasions, convene both Houses, or either of them, and in Case of Disagreement between them, with Respect to the Time of Adjournment, he may adjourn them to such Time as he shall think proper; he shall receive Ambassadors and other public Ministers; he shall take Care that the Laws be faithfully executed, and shall Commission all the Officers of the United States.

Section 4. The President, Vice President and all civil Officers of the United States, shall be removed from Office on Impeachment for, and Conviction of, Treason, Bribery, or other high Crimes and Misdemeanors.

ARTICLE III

Section 1.   The judicial Power of the United States, shall be vested in one supreme Court, and in such inferior Courts as the Congress may from time to time ordain and establish.   The Judges, both of the supreme and inferior Courts, shall hold their Offices during good Behaviour, and shall, at stated Times, receive for their Services a Compensation, which shall not be diminished during their Continuance in Office.

Section 2.   [1]   The judicial Power shall extend to all Cases, in Law and Equity, arising under this Constitution, the Laws of the United States, and Treaties made, or which shall be made, under their Authority;—to all Cases affecting Ambassadors, other public Ministers and Consuls;—to all Cases of admiralty and maritime Jurisdiction;—to Controversies to which the United States shall be a Party;—to Controversies between two or more States;—between a State and Citizens of another State;—between Citizens of different States;—between Citizens of the same State claiming Lands under the Grants of different States, and between a State, or the Citizens thereof, and foreign States, Citizens or Subjects.

[2]   In all Cases affecting Ambassadors, other public Ministers and Consuls, and those in which a State shall be a Party, the supreme Court shall have original Jurisdiction.   In all the other Cases before mentioned, the supreme Court shall have appellate Jurisdiction, both as to Law and Fact, with such Exceptions, and under such Regulations as the Congress shall make.

[3]   The trial of all Crimes, except in Cases of Impeachment, shall be by Jury; and such Trial shall be held in the State where the said Crimes shall have been committed; but when not committed within any State, the Trial shall be at such Place or Places as the Congress may by Law have directed.

Section 3.   [1]   Treason against the United States, shall consist only in levying War against them, or, in adhering to their Enemies, giving them Aid and Comfort.   No Person shall be convicted of Treason unless on the Testimony of two Witnesses to the same overt Act, or on Confession in open Court.

[2]   The Congress shall have Power to declare the Punishment of Treason, but no Attainder of Treason shall work Corruption of Blood, or Forfeiture except during the Life of the Person attainted.

ARTICLE IV

Section 1.   Full Faith and Credit shall be given in each State to the public Acts, Records, and judicial Proceedings of every other State.   And the Congress may by general Laws prescribe the Manner in which such Acts, Records and Proceedings shall be proved, and the Effect thereof.

Section 2. [1] The Citizens of each State shall be entitled to all Privileges and Immunities of Citizens in the several States.

[2] A Person charged in any State with Treason, Felony, or other Crime, who shall flee from Justice, and be found in another State, shall on demand of the executive Authority of the State from which he fled, be delivered up, to be removed to the State having Jurisdiction of the Crime.

[3] No Person held to Service or Labour in one State, under the Laws thereof, escaping into another, shall, in Consequence of any Law or Regulation therein, be discharged from such Service or Labour, but shall be delivered up on Claim of the Party to whom such Service or Labour may be due.

Section 3. [1] New States may be admitted by the Congress into this Union; but no new State shall be formed or erected within the Jurisdiction of any other State; nor any State be formed by the Junction of two or more States, or Parts of States, without the Consent of the Legislatures of the States concerned as well as of the Congress.

[2] The Congress shall have Power to dispose of and make all needful Rules and Regulations respecting the Territory or other Property belonging to the United States; and nothing in this Constitution shall be so construed as to Prejudice any Claims of the United States, or of any particular State.

Section 4. The United States shall guarantee to every State in this Union a Republican Form of Government, and shall protect each of them against Invasion; and on Application of the Legislature, or of the Executive (when the Legislature cannot be convened) against domestic Violence.

Article V

The Congress, whenever two thirds of both Houses shall deem it necessary, shall propose Amendments to this Constitution, or, on the Application of the Legislatures of two thirds of the several States, shall call a Convention for proposing Amendments, which, in either Case, shall be valid to all Intents and Purposes, as part of this Constitution, when ratified by the Legislatures of three fourths of the several States, or by Conventions in three fourths thereof, as the one or the other Mode of Ratification may be proposed by the Congress; Provided that no Amendment which may be made prior to the Year One thousand eight hundred and eight shall in any Manner affect the first and fourth Clauses in the Ninth Section of the first Article; and that no State, without its Consent, shall be deprived of its equal Suffrage in the Senate.

Article VI

[1] All Debts contracted and Engagements entered into, before the Adoption of this Constitution shall be as valid against the United States under this Constitution, as under the Confederation.

[2]   This Constitution, and the Laws of the United States which shall be made in Pursuance thereof; and all Treaties made, or which shall be made, under the Authority of the United States, shall be the supreme Law of the Land; and the Judges in every State shall be bound thereby, any Thing in the Constitution or Laws of any State to the Contrary notwithstanding.

[3]   The Senators and Representatives before mentioned, and the Members of the several State Legislatures, and all executive and judicial Officers, both of the United States and of the several States, shall be bound by Oath or Affirmation, to support this Constitution; but no religious Test shall ever be required as a Qualification to any Office or public Trust under the United States.

Article VII

The Ratification of the Conventions of nine States shall be sufficient for the Establishment of this Constitution between the States so ratifying the Same.

ARTICLES IN ADDITION TO, AND AMENDMENT OF, THE CONSTITUTION OF THE UNITED STATES OF AMERICA, PROPOSED BY CONGRESS, AND RATIFIED BY THE LEGISLATURES OF THE SEVERAL STATES PURSUANT TO THE FIFTH ARTICLE OF THE ORIGINAL CONSTITUTION.

Amendment I [1791]

Congress shall make no law respecting an establishment of religion, or prohibiting the free exercise thereof; or abridging the freedom of speech, or of the press; or the right of the people peaceably to assemble, and to petition the Government for a redress of grievances.

Amendment II [1791]

A well regulated Militia, being necessary to the security of a free State, the right of the people to keep and bear Arms, shall not be infringed.

Amendment III [1791]

No Soldier shall, in time of peace be quartered in any house, without the consent of the Owner, nor in time of war, but in a manner to be prescribed by law.

Amendment IV [1791]

The right of the people to be secure in their persons, houses, papers, and effects, against unreasonable searches and seizures, shall not be violated, and no Warrants shall issue, but upon probable cause, supported by Oath or affirmation, and particularly describing the place to be searched, and the persons or things to be seized.

AMENDMENT V [1791]

No person shall be held to answer for a capital, or otherwise infamous crime, unless on a presentment or indictment of a Grand Jury, except in cases arising in the land or naval forces, or in the Militia, when in actual service in time of War or public danger; nor shall any person be subject for the same offence to be twice put in jeopardy of life or limb; nor shall be compelled in any criminal case to be a witness against himself, nor be deprived of life, liberty, or property, without due process of law; nor shall private property be taken for public use, without just compensation.

AMENDMENT VI [1791]

In all criminal prosecutions, the accused shall enjoy the right to a speedy and public trial, by an impartial jury of the State and district wherein the crime shall have been committed, which district shall have been previously ascertained by law, and to be informed of the nature and cause of the accusation; to be confronted with the witnesses against him; to have compulsory process for obtaining witnesses in his favor, and to have the Assistance of Counsel for his defence.

AMENDMENT VII [1791]

In Suits at common law, where the value in controversy shall exceed twenty dollars, the right of trial by jury shall be preserved, and no fact tried by jury, shall be otherwise re-examined in any Court of the United States, than according to the rules of the common law.

AMENDMENT VIII [1791]

Excessive bail shall not be required, nor excessive fines imposed, nor cruel and unusual punishments inflicted.

AMENDMENT IX [1791]

The enumeration in the Constitution, of certain rights, shall not be construed to deny or disparage others retained by the people.

AMENDMENT X [1791]

The powers not delegated to the United States by the Constitution, nor prohibited by it to the States, are reserved to the States respectively, or to the people.

Amendment XI [1798]

The Judicial power of the United States shall not be construed to extend to any suit in law or equity, commenced or prosecuted against one of the United States by Citizens of another State, or by Citizens or Subjects of any Foreign State.

Amendment XII [1804]

The Electors shall meet in their respective states and vote by ballot for President and Vice-President, one of whom, at least, shall not be an inhabitant of the same state with themselves; they shall name in their ballots the person voted for as President, and in distinct ballots the person voted for as Vice-President, and they shall make distinct lists of all persons voted for as President, and of all persons voted for as Vice-President, and of the number of votes for each, which lists they shall sign and certify, and transmit sealed to the seat of the government of the United States, directed to the President of the Senate;—The President of the Senate shall, in the presence of the Senate and House of Representatives, open all the certificates and the votes shall then be counted;—The person having the greatest number of votes for President, shall be the President, if such number be a majority of the whole number of Electors appointed; and if no person have such majority, then from the persons having the highest numbers not exceeding three on the list of those voted for as President, the House of Representatives shall choose immediately, by ballot, the President. But in choosing the President, the votes shall be taken by states, the representation from each state having one vote; a quorum for this purpose shall consist of a member or members from two-thirds of the states, and a majority of all the states shall be necessary to a choice. And if the House of Representatives shall not choose a President whenever the right of choice shall devolve upon them before the fourth day of March next following, then the Vice-President shall act as President, as in the case of the death or other constitutional disability of the President.— The person having the greatest number of votes as Vice-President, shall be the Vice-President, if such number be a majority of the whole number of Electors appointed, and if no person have a majority, then from the two highest numbers on the list, the Senate shall choose the Vice-President; a quorum for the purpose shall consist of two-thirds of the whole number of Senators, and a majority of the whole number shall be necessary to a choice. But no person constitutionally ineligible to the office of President shall be eligible to that of Vice-President of the United States.

Amendment XIII [1865]

Section 1. Neither slavery nor involuntary servitude, except as a punishment for crime whereof the party shall have been duly convicted, shall exist within the United States, or any place subject to their jurisdiction.

Section 2.   Congress shall have power to enforce this article by appropriate legislation.

AMENDMENT XIV [1868]

Section 1.   All persons born or naturalized in the United States, and subject to the jurisdiction thereof, are citizens of the United States and of the State wherein they reside.   No State shall make or enforce any law which shall abridge the privileges or immunities of citizens of the United States; nor shall any State deprive any person of life, liberty, or property, without due process of law; nor deny to any person within its jurisdiction the equal protection of the laws.

Section 2.   Representatives shall be apportioned among the several States according to their respective numbers, counting the whole number of persons in each State, excluding Indians not taxed.   But when the right to vote at any election for the choice of electors for President and Vice President of the United States, Representatives in Congress, the Executive and Judicial officers of a State, or the members of the Legislature thereof, is denied to any of the male inhabitants of such State, being twenty-one years of age, and citizens of the United States, or in any way abridged, except for participation in rebellion, or other crime, the basis of representation therein shall be reduced in the proportion which the number of such male citizens shall bear to the whole number of male citizens twenty-one years of age in such State.

Section 3.   No person shall be a Senator or Representative in Congress, or elector of President and Vice President, or hold any office, civil or military, under the United States, or under any State, who having previously taken an oath, as a member of Congress, or as an officer of the United States, or as a member of any State legislature, or as an executive or judicial officer of any State, to support the Constitution of the United States, shall have engaged in insurrection or rebellion against the same, or given aid or comfort to the enemies thereof.   But Congress may by a vote of two-thirds of each House, remove such disability.

Section 4.   The validity of the public debt of the United States, authorized by law, including debts incurred for payment of pensions and bounties for services in suppressing insurrection or rebellion, shall not be questioned. But neither the United States nor any State shall assume or pay any debt or obligation incurred in aid of insurrection or rebellion against the United States, or any claim for the loss or emancipation of any slave; but all such debts, obligations and claims shall be held illegal and void.

Section 5.   The Congress shall have power to enforce, by appropriate legislation, the provisions of this article.

AMENDMENT XV [1870]

Section 1.   The right of citizens of the United States to vote shall not be denied or abridged by the United States or by any State on account of race, color, or previous condition of servitude.

Section 2.   The Congress shall have power to enforce this article by appropriate legislation.

AMENDMENT XVI [1913]

The Congress shall have power to lay and collect taxes on incomes, from whatever source derived, without apportionment among the several States, and without regard to any census or enumeration.

AMENDMENT XVII [1913]

[1]   The Senate of the United States shall be composed of two Senators from each State, elected by the people thereof, for six years; and each Senator shall have one vote.   The electors in each State shall have the qualifications requisite for electors of the most numerous branch of the State legislatures.

[2]   When vacancies happen in the representation of any State in the Senate, the executive authority of such State shall issue writs of election to fill such vacancies: *Provided*, That the legislature of any State may empower the executive thereof to make temporary appointments until the people fill the vacancies by election as the legislature may direct.

[3]   This amendment shall not be so construed as to affect the election or term of any Senator chosen before it becomes valid as part of the Constitution.

AMENDMENT XVIII [1919]

Section 1.   After one year from the ratification of this article the manufacture, sale, or transportation of intoxicating liquors within, the importation thereof into, or the exportation thereof from the United States and all territory subject to the jurisdiction thereof for beverage purposes is hereby prohibited.

Section 2.   The Congress and the several States shall have concurrent power to enforce this article by appropriate legislation.

Section 3.   This article shall be inoperative unless it shall have been ratified as an amendment to the Constitution by the legislatures of the several States, as provided in the Constitution, within seven years from the date of the submission hereof to the States by the Congress.

AMENDMENT XIX [1920]

[1]   The right of citizens of the United States to vote shall not be denied or abridged by the United States or by any State on account of sex.

[2]   Congress shall have power to enforce this article by appropriate legislation.

Amendment XX [1933]

Section 1. The terms of the President and Vice President shall end at noon on the 20th day of January, and the terms of Senators and Representatives at noon on the 3d day of January, of the years in which such terms would have ended if this article had not been ratified; and the terms of their successors shall then begin.

Section 2. The Congress shall assemble at least once in every year, and such meeting shall begin at noon on the 3d day of January, unless they shall by law appoint a different day.

Section 3. If, at the time fixed for the beginning of the term of the President, the President elect shall have died, the Vice President elect shall become President. If the President shall not have been chosen before the time fixed for the beginning of his term, or if the President elect shall have failed to qualify, then the Vice President elect shall act as President until a President shall have qualified; and the Congress may by law provide for the case wherein neither a President elect nor a Vice President elect shall have qualified, declaring who shall then act as President, or the manner in which one who is to act shall be selected, and such person shall act accordingly until a President or Vice President shall have qualified.

Section 4. The Congress may by law provide for the case of the death of any of the persons from whom the House of Representatives may choose a President whenever the right of choice shall have devolved upon them, and for the case of the death of any of the persons from whom the Senate may choose a Vice President whenever the right of choice shall have devolved upon them.

Section 5. Sections 1 and 2 shall take effect on the 15th day of October following the ratification of this article.

Section 6. This article shall be inoperative unless it shall have been ratified as an amendment to the Constitution by the legislatures of three-fourths of the several States within seven years from the date of its submission.

Amendment XXI [1933]

Section 1. The eighteenth article of amendment to the Constitution of the United States is hereby repealed.

Section 2. The transportation or importation into any State, Territory, or possession of the United States for delivery or use therein of intoxicating liquors, in violation of the laws thereof, is hereby prohibited.

Section 3. This article shall be inoperative unless it shall have been ratified as an amendment to the Constitution by conventions in the several States, as provided in the Constitution, within seven years from the date of the submission hereof to the States by the Congress.

Amendment XXII [1951]

Section 1. No person shall be elected to the office of the President more than twice, and no person who has held the office of President, or acted as President, for more than two years of a term to which some other person was elected President shall be elected to the office of President more than once. But this Article shall not apply to any person holding the office of President when this Article was proposed by the Congress, and shall not prevent any person who may be holding the office of President, or acting as President, during the term within which this Article becomes operative from holding the office of President or acting as President during the remainder of such term.

Section 2. This article shall be inoperative unless it shall have been ratified as an amendment to the Constitution by the legislatures of three-fourths of the several States within seven years from the date of its submission to the States by the Congress.

Amendment XXIII [1961]

Section 1. The District constituting the seat of Government of the United States shall appoint in such manner as the Congress may direct:

A number of electors of President and Vice President equal to the whole number of Senators and Representatives in Congress to which the District would be entitled if it were a State, but in no event more than the least populous state; they shall be in addition to those appointed by the states, but they shall be considered, for the purposes of the election of President and Vice President, to be electors appointed by a state; and they shall meet in the District and perform such duties as provided by the twelfth article of amendment.

Section 2. The Congress shall have power to enforce this article by appropriate legislation.

Amendment XXIV [1964]

Section 1. The right of citizens of the United States to vote in any primary or other election for President or Vice President, for electors for President or Vice President, or for Senator or Representative in Congress, shall not be denied or abridged by the United States or any State by reason of failure to pay any poll tax or other tax.

Section 2. The Congress shall have power to enforce this article by appropriate legislation.

Amendment XXV [1967]

Section 1. In case of the removal of the President from office or of his death or resignation, the Vice President shall become President.

Section 2. Whenever there is a vacancy in the office of the Vice President, the President shall nominate a Vice President who shall take office upon confirmation by a majority vote of both Houses of Congress.

Section 3. Whenever the President transmits to the President pro tempore of the Senate and the Speaker of the House of Representatives his written declaration that he is unable to discharge the powers and duties of his office, and until he transmits to them a written declaration to the contrary, such powers and duties shall be discharged by the Vice President as Acting President.

Section 4. Whenever the Vice President and a majority of either the principal officers of the executive departments or of such other body as Congress may by law provide, transmit to the President pro tempore of the Senate and the Speaker of the House of Representatives their written declaration that the President is unable to discharge the powers and duties of his office, the Vice President shall immediately assume the powers and duties of the office as Acting President.

Thereafter, when the President transmits to the President pro tempore of the Senate and the Speaker of the House of Representatives his written declaration that no inability exists, he shall resume the powers and duties of his office unless the Vice President and a majority of either the principal officers of the executive department or of such other body as Congress may by law provide, transmit within four days to the President pro tempore of the Senate and the Speaker of the House of Representatives their written declaration and the President is unable to discharge the powers and duties of his office. Thereupon Congress shall decide the issue, assembling within forty-eight hours for that purpose if not in session. If the Congress, within twenty-one days after receipt of the latter written declaration, or, if Congress is not in session, within twenty-one days after Congress is required to assemble, determines by two-thirds vote of both Houses that the President is unable to discharge the powers and duties of his office, the Vice President shall continue to discharge the same as Acting President; otherwise, the President shall resume the powers and duties of his office.

AMENDMENT XXVI [1971]

Section 1. The right of citizens of the United States, who are eighteen years of age or older, to vote shall not be denied or abridged by the United States or by any State on account of age.

Section 2. The Congress shall have power to enforce this article by appropriate legislation.

AMENDMENT XXVII [Proposed]

Section 1. Equality of rights under the law shall not be denied or abridged by the United States or by any State on account of sex.

Section 2. The Congress shall have the power to enforce, by appropriate legislation, the provisions of this article.

Section 3. This amendment shall take effect two years after the date of ratification.

Appendix B

JOINT STATEMENT ON RIGHTS AND FREEDOMS OF STUDENTS

AMERICAN ASSOCIATION OF UNIVERSITY PROFESSORS

Policy Documents and Reports 67–69 (1973).

In June, 1967, a joint committee, comprised of representatives from the American Association of University Professors, U.S. National Student Association, Association of American Colleges, National Association of Student Personnel Administrators, and National Association of Women Deans and Counselors, met in Washington, D.C., and drafted the Joint Statement on Rights and Freedoms of Students published below.

Since its formulation, the Joint Statement has been endorsed by each of its five national sponsors, as well as by a number of other professional bodies.

PREAMBLE

Academic institutions exist for the transmission of knowledge, the pursuit of truth, the development of students, and the general well-being of society. Free inquiry and free expression are indispensable to the attainment of these goals. As members of the academic community, students should be encouraged to develop the capacity for critical judgment and to engage in a sustained and independent search for truth. Institutional procedures for achieving these purposes may vary from campus to campus, but the minimal standards of academic freedom of students outlined below are essential to any community of scholars.

Freedom to teach and freedom to learn are inseparable facets of academic freedom. The freedom to learn depends upon appropriate opportunities and conditions in the classroom, on the campus, and in the larger community. Students should exercise their freedom with responsibility.

The responsibility to secure and to respect general conditions conducive to the freedom to learn is shared by all members of the academic community. Each college and university has a

489

duty to develop policies and procedures which provide and safeguard this freedom. Such policies and procedures should be developed at each institution within the framework of general standards and with the broadest possible participation of the members of the academic community. The purpose of this statement is to enumerate the essential provisions for student freedom to learn.

I. FREEDOM OF ACCESS TO HIGHER EDUCATION

The admissions policies of each college and university are a matter of institutional choice provided that each college and university makes clear the characteristics and expectations of students which it considers relevant to success in the institution's program. While church-related institutions may give admission preference to students of their own persuasion, such a preference should be clearly and publicly stated. Under no circumstances should a student be barred from admission to a particular institution on the basis of race. Thus, within the limits of its facilities, each college and university should be open to all students who are qualified according to its admission standards. The facilities and services of a college should be open to all of its enrolled students, and institutions should use their influence to secure equal access for all students to public facilities in the local community.

II. IN THE CLASSROOM

The professor in the classroom and in conference should encourage free discussion, inquiry, and expression. Student performance should be evaluated solely on an academic basis, not on opinions or conduct in matters unrelated to academic standards.

A. Protection of Freedom of Expression

Students should be free to take reasoned exception to the data or views offered in any course of study and to reserve judgment about matters of opinion, but they are responsible for learning the content of any course of study for which they are enrolled.

B. Protection against Improper Academic Evaluation

Students should have protection through orderly procedures against prejudiced or capricious academic evaluation. At the same time, they are responsible for maintaining standards of academic performance established for each course in which they are enrolled.

C. Protection against Improper Disclosure

Information about student views, beliefs, and political associations which professors acquire in the course of their work as instructors, advisers, and counselors should be considered confidential. Protection against improper disclosure is a serious professional obligation. Judgments of ability and character may be provided under appropriate circumstances, normally with the knowledge or consent of the student.

III. STUDENT RECORDS

Institutions should have a carefully considered policy as to the information which should be part of a student's permanent educational record and as to the conditions of its disclosure. To minimize the risk of improper disclosure, academic and disciplinary records should be separate, and the conditions of access should be set forth in an explicit policy statement. Transcripts of academic records should contain only information about academic status. Information from disciplinary or counseling files should not be available to unauthorized persons on campus, or to any person off campus without the express consent of the student involved except under legal compulsion or in cases where the safety of persons or property is involved. No records should be kept which reflect the political activities or beliefs of students. Provisions should also be made for periodic routine destruction of noncurrent disciplinary records. Administrative staff and faculty members should respect confidential information about students which they acquire in the course of their work.

IV. STUDENT AFFAIRS

In student affairs, certain standards must be maintained if the freedom of students is to be preserved.

A. Freedom of Association

Students bring to the campus a variety of interests previously acquired and develop many new interests as members of the academic community. They should be free to organize and join associations to promote their common interests.

1. The membership, policies, and actions of a student organization usually will be determined by vote of only those persons

who hold bona fide membership in the college or university community.

2. Affiliation with an extramural organization should not of itself disqualify a student organization from institutional recognition.

3. If campus advisers are required, each organization should be free to choose its own adviser, and institutional recognition should not be withheld or withdrawn solely because of the inability of a student organization to secure an adviser. Campus advisers may advise organizations in the exercise of responsibility, but they should not have the authority to control the policy of such organizations.

4. Student organizations may be required to submit a statement of purpose, criteria for membership, rules of procedures, and a current list of officers. They should not be required to submit a membership list as a condition of institutional recognition.

5. Campus organizations, including those affiliated with an extramural organization, should be open to all students without respect to race, creed, or national origin, except for religious qualifications which may be required by organizations whose aims are primarily sectarian.

B. Freedom of Inquiry and Expression

1. Students and student organizations should be free to examine and discuss all questions of interest to them, and to express opinions publicly and privately. They should always be free to support causes by orderly means which do not disrupt the regular and essential operation of the institution. At the same time, it should be made clear to the academic and the the larger community that in their public expressions or demonstrations students or student organizations speak only for themselves.

2. Students should be allowed to invite and to hear any person of their own choosing. Those routine procedures required by an institution before a guest speaker is invited to appear on campus should be designed only to insure that there is orderly scheduling of facilities and adequate preparation for the event, and that the occasion is conducted in a manner appropriate to an academic community. The institutional control of campus facilities should not be used as a device of censorship. It should be made clear to the academic and large community that sponsorship of guest

speakers does not necessarily imply approval or endorsement of the views expressed, either by the sponsoring or the institution.

C.   Student Participation in Institutional Government

As constituents of the academic community, students should be free, individually and collectively, to express their views on issues of institutional policy and on matters of general interest to the student body.   The student body should have clearly defined means to participate in the formulation and application of institutional policy affecting academic and student affairs.   The role of the student government and both its general and specific responsibilities should be made explicit, and the actions of the student government within the areas of its jurisdiction should be reviewed only through orderly and prescribed procedures.

D.   Student Publications

Student publications and the student press are a valuable aid in establishing and maintaining an atmosphere of free and responsible discussion and of intellectual exploration on the campus. They are a means of bringing student concerns to the attention of the faculty and the institutional authorities and of formulating student opinion on various issues on the campus and in the world at large.

Whenever possible the student newspaper should be an independent corporation financially and legally separate from the university.   Where financial and legal autonomy is not possible, the institution, as the publisher of student publications, may have to bear the legal responsibility for the contents of the publications.   In the delegation of editorial responsibility to students the institution must provide sufficient editorial freedom and financial autonomy for the student publications to maintain their integrity of purpose as vehicles for free inquiry and free expression in an academic community.

Institutional authorities, in consultation with students and faculty, have a responsibility to provide written clarification of the role of the student publications, the standards to be used in their evaluation, and the limitations on external control of their operation.   At the same time, the editorial freedom of student editors and managers entails corollary responsibilities to be governed by the canons of responsible journalism, such as the avoidance of libel, indecency, undocumented allegations, attacks on personal integrity, and the techniques of harassment and innuendo.   As safeguards for the editorial freedom of student publications the following provisions are necessary.

1. The student press should be free of censorship and advance approval of copy, and its editors and managers should be free to develop their own editorial policies and news coverage.

2. Editors and managers of student publications should be protected from arbitrary suspension, or public disapproval of editorial policy or content. Only for proper and stated causes should editors and managers be subject to removal and then by orderly and prescribed procedures. The agency responsible for the appointment of editors and managers should be the agency responsible for their removal.

3. All university published and financed student publications should explicitly state on the editorial page that the opinions there expressed are not necessarily those of the college, university, or student body.

V. OFF–CAMPUS FREEDOM OF STUDENTS

A. Exercise of Rights of Citizenship

College and university students are both citizens and members of the academic community. As citizens, students should enjoy the same freedom of speech, peaceful assembly, and right of petition that other citizens enjoy and, as members of the academic community, they are subject to the obligations which accrue to them by virtue of this membership. Faculty members and administrative officials should insure that institutional powers are not employed to inhibit such intellectual and personal development of students as is often promoted by their exercise of the rights of citizenship both on and off campus.

B. Institutional Authority and Civil Penalties

Activities of students may upon occasion result in violation of law. In such cases, institutional officials should be prepared to apprise students of sources of legal counsel and may offer other assistance. Students who violate the law may incur penalties prescribed by civil authorities, but institutional authority should never be used merely to duplicate the function of general laws. Only where the institution's interests as an academic community are distinct and clearly involved should the special authority of the institution be asserted. The student who incidentally violates institutional regulations in the course of his off-campus activity, such as those relating to class attendance, should be subject to no greater penalty than would normally be imposed. Institutional action should be independent of community pressure.

Appendix C

TITLE IX—FINAL REGULATIONS

PART 86—NONDISCRIMINATION ON THE BASIS OF SEX UNDER FEDERALLY ASSISTED EDUCATION PROGRAMS AND ACTIVITIES

Subpart A—Introduction

Subpart D—Discrimination on the Basis of Sex in Education Programs and Activities Prohibited

Subpart E—Discrimination on the Basis of Sex in Employment in Education Programs and Activities Prohibited

Subpart F—Procedures

Subpart A—Introduction

§ 86.1 Purpose and effective date

The purpose of this part is to effectuate title IX of the Education Amendments of 1972, as amended by Pub.L. 93–568, 88 Stat. 1855 (except sections 904 and 906 of those Amendments) which is designed to eliminate (with certain exceptions) discrimination on the basis of sex in any education program or activity receiving Federal financial assistance, whether or not such program or activity is offered or sponsored by an educational institution as defined in this part. This part is also intended to effectuate section 844 of the Education Amendments of 1974, Pub.L. 93–380, 88 Stat. 484. The effective date of this part shall be July 21, 1975.

§ 86.2 Definitions

As used in this part, the term—

(a) *"Title IX"* means title IX of the Education Amendments of 1972, Pub.L. 92–318, as amended by section 3 of Pub.L. 93–568, 88 Stat. 1855, except §§ 904 and 906 thereof; 20 U.S.C. §§ 1681, 1682, 1683, 1685, 1686.

(b) *"Department"* means the Department of Health, Education, and Welfare.

(c) *"Secretary"* means the Secretary of Health, Education, and Welfare.

(d) *"Director"* means the Director of the Office for Civil Rights of the Department.

(e) *"Reviewing Authority"* means that component of the Department delegated authority by the Secretary to appoint, and to review the decisions of, administrative law judges in cases arising under this Part.

(f) *"Administrative law judge"* means a person appointed by the reviewing authority to preside over a hearing held under this Part.

(g) *"Federal financial assistance"* means any of the following, when authorized or extended under a law administered by the Department:

(1) A grant or loan of Federal financial assistance, including funds made available for:

(i) The acquisition, construction, renovation, restoration, or repair of a building or facility or any portion thereof; and

(ii) Scholarships, loans, grants, wages or other funds extended to any entity for payment to or on behalf of students admitted to that entity, or extended directly to such students for payment to that entity.

(2) A grant of Federal real or personal property or any interest therein, including surplus property, and the proceeds of the sale or transfer of such property, if the Federal share of the fair market value of the property is not, upon such sale or transfer, properly accounted for to the Federal Government.

(3) Provision of the services of Federal personnel.

(4) Sale or lease of Federal property or any interest therein at nominal consideration, or at consideration reduced for the purpose of assisting the recipient or in recognition of public interest to be served thereby, or permission to use Federal property or any interest therein without consideration.

(5) Any other contract, agreement, or arrangement which has as one of its purposes the provision of assistance to any education program or activity, except a contract of insurance or guaranty.

(h) *"Recipient"* means any State or political subdivision thereof, or any instrumentality of a State or political subdivision thereof, any public or private agency, institution, or organization, or other entity, or any person, to whom Federal financial assistance is extended directly or through another recipient and which operates an education program or activity which receives or benefits from such assistance, including any subunit, successor, assignee, or transferee thereof.

(i) *"Applicant"* means one who submits an application, request, or plan required to be approved by a Department official, or by a recipient, as a condition to becoming a recipient.

(j) *"Educational institution"* means a local educational agency (L.E.A.) as defined by section 801(f) of the Elementary and Secondary Education Act of 1965 (20 U.S.C. 881), a preschool, a private elementary or secondary school, or an applicant or recipient of the type defined by paragraph (k), (*l*), (m), or (n) of this section.

(k) *"Institution of graduate higher education"* means an institution which:

(1) Offers academic study beyond the bachelor of arts or bachelor of science degree, whether or not leading to a certificate of any higher degree in the liberal arts and sciences; or

(2) Awards any degree in a professional field beyond the first professional degree (regardless of whether the first professional degree in such field is awarded by an institution of undergraduate higher education or professional education); or

(3) Awards no degree and offers no further academic study, but operates ordinarily for the purpose of facilitating research by persons who have received the highest graduate degree in any field of study.

(*l*) *"Institution of undergraduate higher education"* means:

(1) An institution offering at least two but less than four years of college level study beyond the high school level, leading to a diploma or an associate degree, or wholly or principally creditable toward a baccalaureate degree; or

(2) An institution offering academic study leading to a baccalaureate degree; or

(3) An agency or body which certifies credentials or offers degrees, but which may or may not offer academic study.

(m) *"Institution of professional education"* means an institution (except any institution of undergraduate higher education) which offers a program of academic study that leads to a first professional degree in a field for which there is a national specialized accrediting agency recognized by the United States Commissioner of Education.

(n) *"Institution of vocational education"* means a school or institution (except an institution of professional or graduate or undergraduate higher education) which has as its primary purpose preparation of students to pursue a technical, skilled, or semiskilled occupation or trade, or to pursue study in a technical field, whether or not the school or institution offers certificates, diplomas, or degrees and whether or not it offers fulltime study.

(*o*) *"Administratively separate unit"* means a school, department or college of an educational institution (other than a local educational agency) admission to which is independent of admission to any other component of such institution.

(p) *"Admission"* means selection for part-time, full-time, special, associate, transfer, exchange, or any other enrollment, membership, or matriculation in or at an education program or activity operated by a recipient.

(q) *"Student"* means a person who has gained admission.

(r) *"Transition plan"* means a plan subject to the approval of the United States Commissioner of Education pursuant to section 901(a)(2) of the Education Amendments of 1972, under which an educational institution operates in making the transition from being an educational institution which admits only students of one sex to being one which admits students of both sexes without discrimination.

§ 86.3   Remedial and affirmative action and self-evaluation

(a) *Remedial action.* If the Director finds that a recipient has discriminated against persons on the basis of sex in an education program or activity, such recipient shall take such remedial action as the Director deems necessary to overcome the effects of such discrimination.

(b) *Affirmative action.* In the absence of a finding of discrimination on the basis of sex in an education program or activity, a recipient may take affirmative action to overcome the effects of conditions which resulted in limited participation therein by persons of a particular sex. Nothing herein shall be interpreted to alter any affirmative action obligations which a recipient may have under Executive Order 11246.

(c) *Self-evaluation.* Each recipient education institution shall, within one year of the effective date of this part:

(i) Evaluate, in terms of the requirements of this part, its current policies and practices and the effects thereof concerning admission of students, treatment of students, and employment of both academic and non-academic personnel working in connection with the recipient's education program or activity;

(ii) Modify any of these policies and practices which do not or may not meet the requirements of this part; and

(iii) Take appropriate remedial steps to eliminate the effects of any discrimination which resulted or may have resulted from adherence to these policies and practices.

(d) *Availability of self-evaluation and related materials.* Recipients shall maintain on file for at least three years following competition of the evaluation required under paragraph (c) of this section, and shall provide to the Director upon request, a description of any modifications made pursuant to subparagraph (c)(ii) and of any remedial steps taken pursuant to subparagraph (c)(iii).

§ 86.4   Assurance required

(a) *General.* Every application for Federal financial assistance for any education program or activity shall as condition of its approval contain or be accompanied by an assurance from the applicant or recipient, satisfactory to the Director, that each education program or activity operated by the applicant or recipient and to which this part applies will be operated in compliance with this part. An assurance of compliance with this part shall not be satisfactory to the Director if the applicant or recipient to whom such assurance applies fails to commit itself to take whatever remedial action is necessary in accordance with § 86.3(a) to eliminate existing discrimination on the basis of sex or to eliminate the effects of past discrimination whether occurring prior or subsequent to the submission to the Director of such assurance.

(b) *Duration of obligation.* (1) In the case of Federal financial assistance extended to provide real property or structures thereon, such assurance shall obligate the recipient or, in the case of a subsequent transfer, the transferee, for the period during which the real property or structures are used to provide an education program or activity.

(2) In the case of Federal financial assistance extended to provide personal property, such assurance shall obligate the recipient for the period during which it retains ownership or possession of the property.

(3) In all other cases such assurance shall obligate the recipient for the period during which Federal financial assistance is extended.

(c) *Form.* The Director will specify the form of the assurances required by paragraph (a) of this section and the extent to which such assurances will be required of the applicant's or recipient's subgrantees, contractors, subcontractors, transferees, or successors in interest.

§ 86.5 Transfers of property

If a recipient sells or otherwise transfers property financed in whole or in part with Federal financial assistance to a transferee which operates any education program or activity, and the Federal share of the fair market value of the property is not upon such sale or transfer properly accounted for to the Federal Government both the transferor and the transferee shall be deemed to be recipients, subject to the provisions of Subpart B.

§ 86.6 Effect of other requirements

(a) *Effect of other Federal provisions.* The obligations imposed by this part are independent of, and do not alter, obligations not to discriminate on the basis of sex imposed by Executive Order 11246, as amended; sections 799A and 845 of the Public Health Service Act (42 U.S.C. 295h–9 and 298b–2); Title VII of the Civil Rights Act of 1964 (42 U.S.C. 2000e et seq.); the Equal Pay Act (29 U.S.C. 206 and 206(d)); and any other Act of Congress or Federal regulation.

(b) *Effect of State or local law or other requirements.* The obligation to comply with this part is not obviated or alleviated by any State or local law or other requirement which would render any applicant or student ineligible, or limit the eligibility of any applicant or student, on the basis of sex, to practice any occupation or profession.

(c) *Effect of rules or regulations of private organizations.* The obligation to comply with this part is not obviated or alleviated by any rule or regulation of any organization, club, athletic or other league, or association which would render any applicant or student ineligible to participate or limit the eligibility or participation of any applicant or student, on the basis of sex, in any education program or activity operated by a recipient and which receives or benefits from Federal financial assistance.

§ 86.7   Effect of employment opportunities

The obligation to comply with this Part is not obviated or alleviated because employment opportunities in any occupation or profession are or may be more limited for members of one sex than for members of the other sex.

§ 86.8   Designation of responsible employee and adoption of grievance procedures

(a) *Designation of responsible employee.* Each recipient shall designate at least one employee to coordinate its efforts to comply with and carry out its responsibilities under this part, including any investigation of any complaint communicated to such recipient alleging its noncompliance with this part or alleging any actions which would be prohibited by this part. The recipient shall notify all its students and employees of the name, office address and telephone number of the employee or employees appointed pursuant to this paragraph.

(b) *Complaint procedure of recipient.* A recipient shall adopt and publish grievance procedures providing for prompt and equitable resolution of student and employee complaints alleging any action which would be prohibited by this part.

§ 86.9 Dissemination of policy

(a) *Notification of policy.* (1) Each recipient shall implement specific and continuing steps to notify applicants for admission and employment, students and parents of elementary and secondary school students, employees, sources of referral of applicants for admission and employment, and all unions or professional organizations holding collective bargaining or professional agreements with the recipient, that it does not discriminate on the basis of sex in the educational programs or activities which it operates, and that is required by title IX and this part not to discriminate in such a manner. Such notification shall contain such information, and be made in such manner, as the Director finds necessary to apprise such persons of the protections against discrimination assured them by title IX and this part, but shall state at least that the requirement not to discriminate in education programs and activities extends to employment therein, and to admission thereto unless Subpart C does not apply to the recipient, and that inquiries concerning the application of title IX and this part to such recipient may be referred to the employee designated pursuant to § 86.8, or to the Director.

(2) Each recipient shall make the initial notification required by paragraph (a) (1) of this section within 90 days of the effective date of this part or of the date this part first applies to such recipient, whichever comes later, which notification shall include publication in: (i) Local newspapers; (ii) newspapers and magazines operated by such recipient or by student, alumnae, or alumni groups for or in connection with such recipient; and (iii) memoranda or other written communications distributed to every student and employee of such recipient.

(b) *Publications.* (1) Each recipient shall prominently include a statement of the policy described in paragraph (a) of this section in each announcement, bulletin, catalog, or application form which it makes available to any person of a type described in paragraph (a) of this section, or which is otherwise used in connection with the recruitment of students or employees.

(2) A recipient shall not use or distribute a publication of the type described in this paragraph which suggests, by text or illustration, that such recipient treats applicants, students, or employees differently on the basis of sex except as such treatment is permitted by this part.

(c) *Distribution.* Each recipient shall distribute without discrimination on the basis of sex each publication described in paragraph (b) of this section, and shall apprise each of its admission and employment recruitment representatives of the policy of non-discrimination described in paragraph (a) of this section, and require such representatives to adhere to such policy.

Subpart B—Coverage

§ 86.11 Application

Except as provided in this subpart, this Part 86 applies to every recipient and to each education program or activity operated by such recipient which receives or benefits from Federal financial assistance.

§ 86.12 Educational institutions controlled by religious organizations

(a) *Application.* This part does not apply to an educational institution which is controlled by a religious organization to the extent application of this part would not be consistent with the religious tenets of such organization.

(b) *Exemption.* An educational institution which wishes to claim the exemption set forth in paragraph (a) of this section, shall do so by submitting in writing to the Director a statement by the highest ranking official of the institution, identifying the provisions of this part which conflict with a specific tenet of the religious organization.

§ 86.13 Military and merchant marine educational institutions

This part does not apply to an educational institution whose primary purpose is the training of individuals for a military service of the United States or for the merchant marine.

§ 86.14 Membership practices of certain organizations

(a) *Social fraternities and sororities.* This part does not apply to the membership practices of social fraternities and sororities which are exempt from taxation under Section 501(a) of the Internal Revenue Code of 1954, the active membership of which consists primarily of students in attendance at institutions of higher education.

(b) *YMCA, YWCA, Girl Scouts, Boy Scouts and Camp Fire Girls.* This part does not apply to the membership practices of the Young Men's Christian Association, the Young Women's

Christian Association, the Girl Scouts, the Boy Scouts and Camp Fire Girls.

(c) *Voluntary youth service organizations.* This part does not apply to the membership practices of voluntary youth service organizations which are exempt from taxation under Section 501(a) of the Internal Revenue Code of 1954 and the membership of which has been traditionally limited to members of one sex and principally to persons of less than nineteen years of age.

§ 86.15   Admissions

(a) Admissions to educational institutions prior to June 24, 1973, are not covered by this part.

(b) *Administratively separate units.* For the purposes only of this section, §§ 86.15 and 86.16, and Subpart C, each administratively separate unit shall be deemed to be an educational institution.

(c) *Application of Subpart C.* Except as provided in paragraphs (c) and (d) of this section, Subpart C applies to each recipient. A recipient to which Subpart C applies shall not discriminate on the basis of sex in admission or recruitment in violation of that subpart.

(d) *Educational institutions.* Except as provided in paragraph (e) of this section as to recipients which are educational institutions, Subpart C applies only to institutions of vocational education, professional education, graduate higher education, and public institutions of undergraduate higher education.

(e) *Public institutions of undergraduate higher education.* Subpart C does not apply to any public institution of undergraduate higher education which traditionally and continually from its establishment has had a policy of admitting only students of one sex.

§ 86.16   Educational institutions eligible to submit transition plans

(a) *Application.* This section applies to each educational institution to which Subpart C applies which:

(1) Admitted only students of one sex as regular students as of June 23, 1972; or

(2) Admitted only students of one sex as regular students as of June 23, 1965, but thereafter admitted as regular students, students of the sex not admitted prior to June 23, 1965.

(b) *Provision for transition plans.* An educational institution to which this section applies shall not discriminate on the basis of sex in admission or recruitment in violation of Subpart C unless it is carrying out a transition plan approved by the United States Commissioner of Education as described in § 86.17, which plan provides for the elimination of such discrimination by the earliest practicable date but in no event later than June 23, 1979.

§ 86.17   Transition plans

(a) *Submission of plans.* An institution to which § 86.15 applies and which is composed of more than one administratively separate unit may submit either a single transition plan applicable to all such units, or a separate transition plan applicable to each such unit.

(b) *Content of plans.* In order to be approved by the United States Commissioner of Education, a transition plan shall:

(1) State the name, address, and Federal Interagency Committee on Education (FICE) Code of the educational institution submitting such plan, the administratively separate units to which the plan is applicable, and the name, address, and telephone number of the person to whom questions concerning the plan may be addressed. The person who submits the plan shall be the chief administrator or president of the institution, or another individual legally authorized to bind the institution to all actions set forth in the plan.

(2) State whether the educational institution or administratively separate unit admits students of both sexes, as regular students and, if so, when it began to do so.

(3) Identify and describe with respect to the educational institution or administratively separate unit any obstacles to admitting sudents without discrimination on the basis of sex.

(4) Describe in detail the steps necessary to eliminate as soon as practicable each obstacle so identified and indicate the schedule for taking these steps and the individual directly responsible for their implementation.

(5) Include estimates of the number of students, by sex, expected to apply for, be admitted to, and enter each class during the period covered by the plan.

(c) *Nondiscrimination.* No policy or practice of a recipient to which § 86.16 applies shall result in treatment of applicants to or students of such recipient in violation of Subpart C unless such treatment is necessitated by an obstacle identified in paragraph

(b) (3) of this section and a schedule for eliminating that obstacle has been provided as required by paragraph (b) (4) of this section.

(d) *Effects of past exclusion.* To overcome the effects of past exclusion of students on the basis of sex, each educational institution to which § 86.16 applies shall include in its transition plan, and shall implement, specific steps designed to encourage individuals of the previously excluded sex to apply for admission to such institution. Such steps shall include instituting recruitment programs which emphasize the institution's commitment to enrolling students of the sex previously excluded.

§§ 86.18–86.20 [Reserved]

Subpart C—Discrimination on the Basis of Sex in Admission and Recruitment Prohibited

§ 86.21 Admission

(a) *General.* No person shall, on the basis of sex, be denied admission, or be subjected to discrimination in admission, by any recipient to which this subpart applies, except as provided in §§ 86.16 and 86.17.

(b) *Specific prohibitions.* (1) In determining whether a person satisfies any policy or criterion for admission, or in making any offer of admission, a recipient to which this Subpart applies shall not:

(i) Give preference to one person over another on the basis of sex, by ranking applicants separately on such basis, or otherwise;

(ii) Apply numerical limitations upon the number or proportion of persons of either sex who may be admitted; or

(iii) Otherwise treat one individual differently from another on the basis of sex.

(2) A recipient shall not administer or operate any test or other criterion for admission which has a disproportionately adverse effect on persons on the basis of sex unless the use of such test or criterion is shown to predict validly success in the education program or activity in question and alternative tests or criteria which do not have such a disproportionately adverse effect are shown to be unavailable.

(c) *Prohibitions relating to marital or parental status.* In determining whether a person satisfies any policy or criterion for admission, or in making any offer of admission, a recipient to which this subpart applies:

(1) Shall not apply any rule concerning the actual or potential parental, family, or marital status of a student or applicant which treats persons differently on the basis of sex;

(2) Shall not discriminate against or exclude any person on the basis of pregnancy, childbirth, termination of pregnancy, or recovery therefrom, or establish or follow any rule or practice which so discriminates or excludes;

(3) Shall treat disabilities related to pregnancy, childbirth, termination of pregnancy, or recovery therefrom in the same manner and under the same policies as any other temporary disability or physical condition; and

(4) Shall not make pre-admission inquiry as to the marital status of an applicant for admission, including whether such applicant is "Miss" or "Mrs." A recipient may make pre-admission inquiry as to the sex of an applicant for admission, but only if such inquiry is made equally of such applicants of both sexes and if the results of such inquiry are not used in connection with discrimination prohibited by this part.

§ 86.22   Preference in admission

A recipient to which this subpart applies shall not give preference to applicants for admission, on the basis of attendance at any educational institution or other school or entity which admits as students or predominantly members of one sex, if the giving of such preference has the effect of discriminating on the basis of sex in violation of this subpart.

§ 86.23   Recruitment

(a) *Nondiscriminatory recruitment.* A recipient to which this subpart applies shall not discriminate on the basis of sex in the recruitment and admission of students. A recipient may be required to undertake additional recruitment efforts for one sex as remedial action pursuant to § 86.3(a), and may choose to undertake such efforts as affirmative action pursuant to § 86.3(b).

(b) *Recruitment at certain institutions.* A recipient to which this subpart applies shall not recruit primarily or exclusively at educational institutions, schools or entities which admit as students only or predominantly members of one sex, if such actions have the effect of discriminating on the basis of sex in violation of this subpart.

§§ 86.24–86.30 [Reserved]

Subpart D—Discrimination on the Basis of Sex in Education Programs and Activities Prohibited

§ 86.31 Education programs and activities

(a) *General.* Except as provided elsewhere in this part, no person shall, on the basis of sex, be excluded from participation in, be denied the benefits of, or be subjected to discrimination under any academic, extracurricular, research, occupational training, or other education program or activity operated by a recipient which receives or benefits from Federal financial assistance. This subpart does not apply to actions of a recipient in connection with admission of its students to an education program or activity of (1) a recipient to which Subpart C does not apply, or (2) an entity, not a recipient, to which Subpart C would not apply if the entity were a recipient.

(b) *Specific prohibitions.* Except as provided in this subpart, in providing any aid, benefit, or service to a student, a recipient shall not, on the basis of sex:

(1) Treat one person differently from another in determining whether such person satisfies any requirement or condition for the provision of such aid, benefit, or service;

(2) Provide different aid, benefits, or services or provide aid, benefits, or services in a different manner;

(3) Deny any person any such aid, benefit, or service;

(4) Subject any person to separate or different rules of behavior, sanctions, or other treatment;

(5) Discriminate against any person in the application of any rules of appearance;

(6) Apply any rule concerning the domicile or residence of a student or applicant, including eligibility for in-state fees and tuition;

(7) Aid or perpetuate discrimination against any person by providing significant assistance to any agency, organization, or person which discriminates on the basis of sex in providing any aid, benefit or service to students or employees;

(8) Otherwise limit any person in the enjoyment of any right, privilege, advantage, or opportunity.

(c) *Assistance administered by a recipient educational institution to study at a foreign institution.* A recipient educational institution may administer or assist in the administration of scholarships, fellowships, or other awards established by foreign or domestic wills, trusts, or similar legal instruments, or by acts of foreign governments and restricted members of one sex, which are designed to provide opportunities to study abroad, and which are awarded to students who are already matriculating at or who are graduates of the recipient institution; *Provided,* a recipient educational institution which administers or assists in the administration of such scholarships, fellowship, or other awards which are restricted to members of one sex provides, or otherwise makes available reasonable opportunities for similar studies for members of the other sex. Such opportunities may be derived from either domestic or foreign sources.

(d) *Programs not operated by recipient.* (1) This paragraph applies to any recipient which requires participation by any applicant, student, or employee in any education program or activity not operated wholly by such recipient, or which facilitates, permits, or considers such participation as part of or equivalent to an education program or activity operated by such recipient, including participation in educational consortia and cooperative employment and student-teaching assignments.

(2) Such recipient:

(i) Shall develop and implement a procedure designed to assure itself that the operator or sponsor of such other education program or activity takes no action affecting any applicant, student, or employee of such recipient which this part would prohibit such recipient from taking; and

(ii) Shall not facilitate, require, permit, or consider such participation if such action occurs.

§ 86.32 Housing

(a) *Generally.* A recipient shall not, on the basis of sex, apply different rules or regulations, impose different fees or requirements, or offer different services or benefits related to housing, except as provided in this section (including housing provided only to married students).

(b) *Housing provided by recipient.* (1) A recipient may provide separate housing on the basis of sex.

(2) Housing provided by a recipient to students of one sex, when compared to that provided to students of the other sex, shall be as a whole:

(i) Proportionate in quantity to the number of students of that sex applying for such housing; and

(ii) Comparable in quality and cost to the student.

(c) *Other housing.* (1) A recipient shall not, on the basis of sex, administer different policies or practices concerning occupancy by its students of housing other than provided by such recipient.

(2) A recipient which, through solicitation, listing, approval of housing, or otherwise, assists any agency, organization, or person in making housing available to any of its students, shall take such reasonable action as may be necessary to assure itself that such housing as is provided to students of one sex, when compared to that provided to students of the other sex, is as a whole:

(i) Proportionate in quantity and

(ii) comparable in quality and cost to the student. A recipient may render such assistance to any agency, organization, or person which provides all or part of such housing to students only of one sex.

§ 86.33   Comparable facilities

A recipient may provide separate toilet, locker room, and shower facilities on the basis of sex, but such facilities provided for students of one sex shall be comparable to such facilities provided for students of the other sex.

§ 86.34   Access to course offerings

A recipient shall not provide any course or otherwise carry out any of its education program or activity separately on the basis of sex, or require or refuse participation therein by any of its students on such basis, including health, physical education, industrial, business, vocational, technical, home economics, music, and adult education courses.

(a) With respect to classes and activities in physical education at the elementary school level, the recipient shall comply fully with this section as expeditiously as possible but in no event later than one year from the effective date of this regulation. With respect to physical education classes and activities at the secondary and post-secondary levels, the recipient shall comply fully with this section as expeditiously as possible but in no event later than three years from the effective date of this regulation.

(b) This section does not prohibit grouping of students in physical education classes and activities by ability as assessed by objective standards of individual performance developed and applied without regard to sex.

(c) This section does not prohibit separation of students by sex within physical education classes or activities during participation in wrestling, boxing, rugby, ice hockey, football, basketball and other sports the purpose or major activity of which involves bodily contact.

(d) Where use of a single standard of measuring skill or progress in a physical education class has an adverse effect on members of one sex, the recipient shall use appropriate standards which do not have such effect.

(e) Portions of classes in elementary and secondary schools which deal exclusively with human sexuality may be conducted in separate sessions for boys and girls.

(f) Recipients may make requirements based on vocal range or quality which may result in a chorus or choruses of one or predominantly one sex.

§ 86.35   Access to schools operated by L.E.A.s

A recipient which is a local educational agency shall not, on the basis of sex, exclude any person from admission to:

(a) Any institution of vocational education operated by such recipient; or

(b) Any other school or educational unit operated by such recipient, unless such recipient otherwise makes available to such person, pursuant to the same policies and criteria of admission, courses, services, and facilities comparable to each course, service, and facility offered in or through such schools.

§ 86.36   Counseling and use of appraisal and counseling materials

(a) *Counseling.* A recipient shall not discriminate against any person on the basis of sex in the counseling or guidance of students or applicants for admission.

(b) *Use of appraisal and counseling materials.* A recipient which uses testing or other materials for appraising or counseling students shall not use different materials for students on the basis of their sex or use materials which permit or require different treatment of students on such basis unless such different materials cover the same occupations and interest areas and the use of such different materials is shown to be essential to eliminate sex bias. Recipients shall develop and use internal procedures for ensuring that such materials do not discriminate on the basis of sex. Where the use of a counseling test or other instrument results in a substantially disproportionate number of members of one sex in any particular course of study or classification, the recipient shall take such action as is necessary to assure itself that such disproportion is not the result of discrimination in the instrument or its application.

(c) *Disproportion in classes.* Where a recipient finds that a particular class contains a substantially disproportionate number of individuals of one sex, the recipient shall take such action as is necessary to assure itself that such disproportion is not the result of discrimination on the basis of sex in counseling or appraisal materials or by counselors.

§ 86.37   Financial assistance

(a) *General.* Except as provided in paragraphs (b), (c) and (d) of this section, in providing financial assistance to any of its students, a recipient shall not: (1) On the basis of sex, provide different amount or types of such assistance, limit eligibility for such assistance which is of any particular type or source, apply different criteria, or otherwise discriminate;   (2) through solicitation, listing, approval, provision of facilities or other services, assist any foundation, trust, agency, organization, or person which provides assistance to any of such recipient's students in a manner which discriminates on the basis of sex;   or (3) apply any rule or assist in application of any rule concerning eligibility for such assistance which treats persons of one sex differently from persons of the other sex with regard to marital or parental status.

(b) *Financial aid established by certain legal instruments.*   (1) A recipient may administer or assist in the administration of scholarships, followships, or other forms of financial assistance established pursuant to domestic or foreign wills, trusts, bequests, or similar legal instruments or by acts of a foreign government which requires that awards be made to members of a particular sex specified therein;   *Provided,* that the overall effect of the award of such sex-restricted scholarships, fellowships, and other forms of financial assistance does not discriminate on the basis of sex.

(2) To ensure nondiscriminatory awards of assistance as required in subparagraph (b)(1) of this paragraph, recipients shall develop and use procedures under which:

(i) Students are selected for award of financial assistance on the basis of nondiscriminatory criteria and not on the basis of availability of funds restricted to members of a particular sex;

(ii) An appropriate sex-restricted scholarship, fellowship, or other form of financial assistance is allocated to each student selected under subparagraph (b)(2)(i) of this paragraph; and

(iii) No student is denied the award for which he or she was selected under subparagraph (b)(2)(i) of this paragraph because of the absence of a scholarship, fellowship, or other form of financial assistance designated for a member of that student's sex.

(c) *Athletic scholarships.* (1) To the extent that a recipient awards, athletic scholarships or grants-in-aid, it must provide reasonable opportunities for such awards for members of each sex in proportion to the number of students of each sex participating in interscholastic or intercollegiate athletics.

(2) Separate athletic scholarships or grants-in-aid for members of each sex may be provided as part of separate athletic teams for members of each sex to the extent consistent with this paragraph and § 86.41 of this part.

§ 86.38 Employment assistance to students

(a) *Assistance by recipient in making available outside employment.* A recipient which assists any agency, organization or person in making employment available to any of its students:

(1) Shall assure itself that such employment is made available without discrimination on the basis of sex; and

(2) Shall not render such services to any agency, organization, or person which discriminates on the basis of sex in its employment practices.

(b) *Employment of students by recipients.* A recipient which employs any of its students shall not do so in a manner which violates Subpart E.

§ 86.39 Health and insurance benefits and services

In providing a medical, hospital, accident, or life insurance benefit, service, policy, or plan to any of its students, a recipient shall not discriminate on the basis of sex, or provide such benefit, service, policy, or plan in a manner which would violate Subpart

E if it were provided to employees of the recipient. This section shall not prohibit a recipient from providing any benefit or service which may be used by a different proportion of students of one sex than of the other, including family planning services. However, any recipient which provides full coverage health service shall provide gynecological care.

§ 86.40 Marital or parental status

(a) *Status generally.* A recipient shall not apply any rule concerning a student's actual or potential parental, family, or marital status which treats students differently on the basis of sex.

(b) *Pregnancy and related conditions.* (1) A recipient shall not discriminate against any student, or exclude any student from its education program or activity, including any class or extracurricular activity, on the basis of such student's pregnancy, childbirth, false pregnancy, termination of pregnancy or recovery therefrom, unless the student requests voluntarily to participate in a separate portion of the program or activity of the recipient.

(2) A recipient may require such a student to obtain the certification of a physician that the student is physically and emotionally able to continue participation in the normal education program or activity so long as such a certification is required of all students for other physical or emotional conditions requiring the attention of a physician.

(3) A recipient which operates a portion of its education program or activity separately for pregnant students, admittance to which is completely voluntary on the part of the student as provided in paragraph (b)(1) of this section shall ensure that the instructional program in the separate program is comparable to that offered to non-pregnant students.

(4) A recipient shall treat pregnancy, childbirth, false pregnancy, termination of pregnancy and recovery therefrom in the same manner and under the same policies as any other temporary disability with respect to any medical or hospital benefit, service, plan or policy which such recipient administers, operates, offers, or participates in with respect to students admitted to the recipient's educational program or activity.

(5) In the case of a recipient which does not maintain a leave policy for its students, or in the case of a student who does not otherwise qualify for leave under such a policy, a recipient shall

treat pregnancy, childbirth, false pregnancy, termination of pregnancy and recovery therefrom as a justification for a leave of absence for so long a period of time as is deemed medically necessary by the student's physician, at the conclusion of which the student shall be reinstated to the status which she held when the leave began.

§ 86.41 Athletics

(a) *General.* No person shall, on the basis of sex, be excluded from participation in, be denied the benefits of, be treated differently from another person or otherwise be discriminated against in any interscholastic, intercollegiate, club or intramural athletics offered by recipient, and no recipient shall provide any such athletics separately on such basis.

(b) *Separate teams.* Notwithstanding the requirements of paragraph (a) of this section, a recipient may operate or sponsor separate teams for members of each sex where selection for such teams is based upon competitive skill or the activity involved is a contact sport. However, where a recipient operates or sponsors a team in a particular sport for members of one sex but operates or sponsors no such team for members of the other sex, and athletic opportunities for members of that sex have previously been limited, members of the excluded sex must be allowed to try-out for the team offered unless the sport involved is a contact sport. For the purposes of this part, contact sports include boxing, wrestling, rugby, ice hockey, football, basketball and other sports the purpose of major activity of which involves bodily contact.

(c) *Equal opportunity.* A recipient which operates or sponsors interscholastic, intercollegiate, club or intramural athletics shall provide equal athletic opportunity for members of both sexes. In determining whether equal opportunities are available the Director will consider, among other factors:

(i) Whether the selection of sports and levels of competition effectively accommodate the interests and abilities of members of both sexes;

(ii) The provision of equipment and supplies;

(iii) Scheduling of games and practice time;

(iv) Travel and per diem allowance;

(v) Opportunity to receive coaching and academic tutoring;

(vi) Assignment and compensation of coaches and tutors;

(vii) Provision of locker rooms, practice and competitive facilities;

(viii) Provision of medical and training facilities and services;

(ix) Provision of housing and dining facilities and services;

(x) Publicity.

Unequal aggregate expenditures for members of each sex or unequal expenditures for male and female teams if a recipient operates or sponsors separate teams will not constitute noncompliance with this section, but the Director may consider the failure to provide necessary funds for teams for one sex in assessing equality of opportunity for members of each sex.

(d) *Adjustment period.* A recipient which operates or sponsors interscholastic, intercollegiate, club or intramural athletics at the elementary school level shall comply fully with this section as expeditiously as possible but in no event later than one year from the effective date of this regulation. A recipient which operates or sponsors interscholastic, intercollegiate, club or intramural athletics at the secondary or post-secondary school level shall comply fully with this section as expeditiously as possible but in no event later than three years from the effective date of this regulation.

§ 86.42 Textbooks and curricular material

Nothing in this regulation shall be interpreted as requiring or prohibiting or abridging in any way the use of particular textbooks or curricular materials.

§§ 86.43–86.50 [Reserved]

Subpart E—Discrimination on the Basis of Sex in Employment in Education Programs and Activities Prohibited

§ 86.51 Employment

(a) *General.* (1) No person shall, on the basis of sex, be excluded from participation in, be denied the benefits of, or be subjected to discrimination in employment, or recruitment, consideration, or selection therefor, whether full-time or part-time, under any education program or activity operated by a recipient which receives or benefits from Federal financial assistance.

(2) A recipient shall make all employment decisions in any education program or activity operated by such recipient in a

nondiscriminatory manner and shall not limit, segregate, or classify applicants or employees in any way which could adversely affect any applicant's or employee's employment opportunities or status because of sex.

(3) A recipient shall not enter into any contractual or other relationship which directly or indirectly has the effect of subjecting employees or students to discrimination prohibited by this Subpart, including relationships with employment and referral agencies, with labor unions, and with organizations providing or administering fringe benefits to employees of the recipient.

(4) A recipient shall not grant preferences to applicants for employment on the basis of attendance at any educational institution or entity which admits as students only or predominantly members of one sex, if the giving of such preferences has the effect of discriminating on the basis of sex in violation of this part.

(b) *Application.* The provisions of this subpart apply to:

(1) Recruitment, advertising, and the process of application for employment;

(2) Hiring, upgrading, promotion, consideration for and award of tenure, demotion, transfer, layoff, termination, application of nepotism policies, right of return from layoff, and rehiring;

(3) Rates of pay or any other form of compensation, and changes in compensation;

(4) Job assignments, classifications and structure, including position descriptions, lines of progression, and seniority lists;

(5) The terms of any collective bargaining agreement;

(6) Granting and return from leaves of absence, leave for pregnancy, childbirth, false pregnancy, termination of pregnancy, leave for persons of either sex to care for children or dependents, or any other leave;

(7) Fringe benefits available by virtue of employment, whether or not administered by the recipient;

(8) Selection and financial support for training, including apprenticeship, professional meetings, conferences, and other related activities, selection for tuition assistance, selection for sabbaticals and leaves of absence to pursue training;

(9) Employer-sponsored activities, including social or recreational programs; and

(10) Any other term, condition, or privilege of employment.

§ 86.52 Employment criteria

A recipient shall not administer or operate any test or other criterion for any employment opportunity which has a disproportionately adverse effect on persons on the basis of sex unless:

(a) Use of such test or other criterion is shown to predict validly successful performance in the position in question; and

(b) Alternative tests or criteria for such purpose, which do not have such disproportionately adverse effect, are shown to be unavailable.

§ 86.53 Recruitment

(a) *Nondiscriminatory recruitment and hiring.* A recipient shall not discriminate on the basis of sex in the recruitment and hiring of employees. Where a recipient has been found to be presently discriminating on the basis of sex in the recruitment or hiring of employees, or has been found to have in the past so discriminated, the recipient shall recruit members of the sex so discriminated against so as to overcome the effects of such past or present discrimination.

(b) *Recruitment patterns.* A recipient shall not recruit primarily or exclusively at entities which furnish as applicants only or predominantly members of one sex if such actions have the effect of discriminating on the basis of sex in violation of this subpart.

§ 86.54 Compensation

A recipient shall not make or enforce any policy or practice which, on the basis of sex:

(a) Makes distinctions in rates of pay or other compensation;

(b) Results in the payment of wages to employees of one sex at a rate less than that paid to employees of the opposite sex for equal work on jobs the performance of which requires equal skill, effort, and responsibility, and which are performed under similar working conditions.

§ 86.55 Job classification and structure

A recipient shall not:

(a) Classify a job as being for males or for females;

(b) Maintain or establish separate lines of progression, seniority lists, career ladders, or tenure systems based on sex; or

(c) Maintain or establish separate lines of progression, seniority systems, career ladders, or tenure systems for similar jobs, position descriptions, or job requirements which classify persons on the basis of sex, unless sex is a bona-fide occupational qualification for the positions in question as set forth in § 86.51.

§ 86.56 Fringe benefits

(a) *"Fringe benefits" defined.* For purposes of this part, "fringe benefits" means: any medical, hospital, accident, life insurance or retirement benefit, service, policy or plan, any profit-sharing or bonus plan, leave, and any other benefit or service of employment not subject to the provision of § 86.54.

(b) *Prohibitions.* A recipient shall not:

(1) Discriminate on the basis of sex with regard to making fringe benefits available to employees or make fringe benefits available to spouses, families, or dependents of employees differently upon the basis of the employee's sex;

(2) Administer, operate, offer, or participate in a fringe benefit plan which does not provide either for equal periodic benefits for members of each sex, or for equal contributions to the plan by such recipient for members of each sex; or

(3) Administer, operate, offer, or participate in a pension or retirement plan which establishes different optional or compulsory retirement ages based on sex or which otherwise discriminates in benefits on the basis of sex.

§ 86.57 Marital or parental status

(a) *General.* A recipient shall not apply any policy or take any employment action:

(1) Concerning the potential marital, parental, or family status of an employee or applicant for employment which treats persons differently on the basis of sex; or

(2) Which is based upon whether an employee or applicant for employment is the head of household or principal wage earner in such employee's or applicant's family unit.

(b) *Pregnancy.* A recipient shall not discriminate against or exclude from employment any employee or applicant for employment on the basis of pregnancy, childbirth, false pregnancy, termination of pregnancy, or recovery therefrom.

(c) *Pregnancy as a temporary disability.* A recipient shall treat pregnancy, childbirth, false pregnancy, termination of pregnancy, and recovery therefrom and any temporary disability resulting therefrom as any other temporary disability for all job related purposes, including commencement, duration and extensions of leave, payment of disability income, accrual of seniority and any other benefit or service, and reinstatement, and under any fringe benefit offered to employees by virtue of employment.

(d) *Pregnancy leave.* In the case of a recipient which does not maintain a leave policy for its employees, or in the case of an employee with insufficient leave or accrued employment time to qualify for leave under such a policy, a recipient shall treat pregnancy, childbirth, false pregnancy, termination of pregnancy and recovery therefrom as a justification for a leave of absence without pay for a reasonable period of time, at the conclusion of which the employee shall be reinstated to the status which she held when the leave began or to a comparable position, without decrease in rate of compensation or loss of promotional opportunities, or any other right or privilege of employment.

§ 86.58   Effect of State or local law or other requirements

(a) *Prohibitory requirements.* The obligation to comply with this subpart is not obviated or alleviated by the existence of any State or local law or other requirement which imposes prohibitions or limits upon employment of members of one sex which are not imposed upon members of the other sex.

(b) *Benefits.* A recipient which provides any compensation, service, or benefit to members of one sex pursuant to a State or local law or other requirement shall provide the same compensation, service, or benefit to members of the other sex.

§ 86.59   Advertising

A recipient shall not in any advertising related to employment indicate preference, limitation, specification, or discrimination based on sex unless sex is a *bona-fide* occupational qualification for the particular job in question.

§ 86.60   Pre-employment inquiries

(a) *Marital status.* A recipient shall not make pre-employment inquiry as to the marital status of an applicant for employment, including whether such applicant is "Miss or Mrs."

(b) *Sex.* A recipient may make pre-employment inquiry as to the sex of an applicant for employment, but only if such inquiry is made equally of such applicants of both sexes and if the results of such inquiry are not used in connection with discrimination prohibited by this part.

§ 86.61 Sex as a bona-fide occupational qualification

A recipient may take action otherwise prohibited by this subpart provided it is shown that sex is a bona-fide occupational qualification for that action, such that consideration of sex with regard to such action is essential to successful operation of the employment function concerned. A recipient shall not take action pursuant to this section which is based upon alleged comparative employment characteristics or stereotyped characterizations of one or the other sex, or upon preference based on sex of the recipient, employees, students, or other persons, but nothing contained in this section shall prevent a recipient from considering an employee's sex in relation to employment in a locker room or toilet facility used only by members of one sex.

§§ 86.62–86.70 [Reserved]

Subpart F—Procedures [Interim]

§ 86.71 Interim procedures

For the purposes of implementing this part during the period between its effective date and the final issuance by the Department of a consolidated procedural regulation applicable to title IX and other civil rights authorities administered by the Department, the procedural provisions applicable to title VI of the Civil Rights Act of 1964 are hereby adopted and incorporated herein by reference. These procedures may be found at 45 CFR §§ 80–6–80–11 and 45 CFR Part 81.

Appendix D

REHABILITATION ACT OF 1973—
FINAL REGULATIONS

Subpart A—General Provisions

Subpart B—Employment Practices

Subpart C—Program Accessibility

Subpart D—Preschool, Elementary, and Secondary Education

APPENDIX A—ANALYSIS OF FINAL REGULATION

AUTHORITY: Sec. 504, Rehabilitation Act of 1973, Pub.L. 93–112, 87 Stat. 394 (29 U.S.C. 794); sec. 111(a), Rehabilitation Act Amendments of 1974, Pub.L. 93–516, 88 Stat. 1619 (29 U.S.C. 706); sec. 606, Education of the Handicapped Act (20 U.S.C. 1405), as amended by Pub.L. 94–142, 89 Stat. 795; sec. 321, Comprehensive Alcohol Abuse and Alcoholism Prevention, Treatment, and Rehabilitation Act of 1970, 84 Stat. 182 (42 U.S.C. 4581), as amended; sec. 407, Drug Abuse Office and Treatment Act of 1972, 86 Stat. 78 (21 U.S.C. 1174), as amended.

Subpart A—General Provisions

§ 84.1 Purpose

The purpose of this part is to effectuate section 504 of the Rehabilitation Act of 1973, which is designed to eliminate discrimination on the basis of handicap in any program or activity receiving Federal financial assistance.

§ 84.2 Application

This part applies to each recipient of Federal financial assistance from the Department of Health, Education, and Welfare and to each program or activity that receives or benefits from such assistance.

§ 84.3 Definitions

As used in this part, the term:

(a) "The Act" means the Rehabilitation Act of 1973, Pub.L. 93–112, as amended by the Rehabilitation Act Amendments of 1974, Public Law 93–516, 29 U.S.C. 794.

(b) "Section 504" means section 504 of the Act.

(c) "Education of the Handicapped Act" means that statute as amended by the Education for all Handicapped Children Act of 1975, Pub.L. 94–142, 20 U.S.C. 1401 et seq.

(d) "Department" means the Department of Health, Education, and Welfare.

(e) "Director" means the Director of the Office for Civil Rights of the Department.

(f) "Recipient" means any state or its political subdivision, any instrumentality of a state or its political subdivision, any public or private agency, institution, organization, or other entity, or any person to which Federal financial assistance is extended directly or through another recipient, including any successor, assignee, or transferee of a recipient, but excluding the ultimate beneficiary of the assistance.

(g) "Applicant for assistance" means one who submits an application, request, or plan required to be approved by a Department official or by a recipient as a condition to becoming a recipient.

(h) "Federal financial assistance" means any grant, loan, contract (other than a procurement contract or a contract of insurance or guaranty), or any other arrangement by which the Department provides or otherwise makes available assistance in the form of:

(1) Funds;

(2) Services of Federal personnel; or

(3) Real and personal property or any interest in or use of such property, including:

(i) Transfers or leases of such property for less than fair market value or for reduced consideration; and

(ii) Proceeds from a subsequent transfer or lease of such property if the Federal share of its fair market value is not returned to the Federal Government.

(i) "Facility" means all or any portion of buildings, structures, equipment, roads, walks, parking lots, or other real or personal property or interest in such property.

(j) "Handicapped person." (1) "Handicapped persons" means any person who (i) has a physical or mental impairment which substantially limits one or more major life activities, (ii) has a record of such an impairment, or (iii) is regarded as having such an impairment.

(2) As used in paragraph (j) (1) of this section, the phrase:

(i) "Physical or mental impairment" means (A) any physiological disorder or condition, cosmetic disfigurement, or anatomical loss affecting one or more of the following body systems: neurological; musculoskeletal; special sense organs; respiratory, including speech organs; cardiovascular; reproductive, digestive; genito-urinary; hemic and lymphatic; skin; and endocrine; or (B) any mental or psychological disorder, such as mental retardation, organic brain syndrome, emotional or mental illness, and specific learning disabilities.

(ii) "Major life activities" means functions such as caring for one's self, performing manual tasks, walking, seeing, hearing, speaking, breathing, learning, and working.

(iii) "Has a record of such an impairment" means has a history of, or has been misclassified as having, a mental or physical impairment that substantially limits one or more major life activities.

(iv) "Is regarded as having an impairment" means (A) has a physical or mental impairment that does not substantially limit major life activities but that is treated by a recipient as constituting such a limitation; (B) has a physical or mental impairment that substantially limits major life activities only as a result of the attitudes of others toward such impairment; or (C) has none of the impairments defined in paragraph (j) (2) (i) of this section but is treated by a recipient as having such an impairment.

(k) "Qualified handicapped person" means:

(1) With respect to employment, a handicapped person who, with reasonable accommodation, can perform the essential functions of the job in question;

(2) With respect to public preschool elementary, secondary, or adult educational services, a handicapped person (i) of an age during which nonhandicapped persons are provided such services, (ii) of any age during which it is mandatory under state law to provide such services to handicapped persons, or (iii) to whom a state is required to provide a free appropriate public education under § 612 of the Education of the Handicapped Act; and

(3) With respect to postsecondary and vocational education services, a handicapped person who meets the academic and technical standards requisite to admission or participation in the recipient's education program or activity;

(4) With respect to other services, a handicapped person who meets the essential eligibility requirements for the receipt of such services.

(l) "Handicap" means any condition or characteristic that renders a person a handicapped person as defined in paragraph (j) of this section.

§ 84.4 Discrimination Prohibited

(a) *General.* No qualified handicapped person shall, on the basis of handicap, be excluded from participation in, be denied the benefits of, or otherwise be subjected to discrimination under any program or activity which receives or benefits from Federal financial assistance.

(b) *Discriminatory actions prohibited.* (1) A recipient, in providing any aid, benefit, or service, may not, directly or through contractual, licensing, or other arrangements, on the basis of handicap:

(i) Deny a qualified handicapped person the opportunity to participate in or benefit from the aid, benefit, or service;

(ii) Afford a qualified handicapped person an opportunity to participate in or benefit from the aid, benefit, or service that is not equal to that afforded others;

(iii) Provide a qualified handicapped person with an aid, benefit, or service that is not as effective as that provided to others;

(iv) Provide different or separate aid, benefits, or services to handicapped persons or to any class of handicapped persons unless such action is necessary to provide qualified handicapped persons with aid, benefits, or services that are as effective as those provided to others;

(v) Aid or perpetuate discrimination against a qualified handicapped person by providing significant assistance to an agency, organization, or person that discriminates on the basis of handicap in providing any aid, benefit, or service to beneficiaries of the recipients program;

(vi) Deny a qualified handicapped person the opportunity to participate as a member of planning or advisory boards; or

(vii) Otherwise limit a qualified handicapped person in the enjoyment of any right, privilege, advantage, or opportunity enjoyed by others receiving an aid, benefit, or service.

(2) For purposes of this part, aids, benefits, and services, to be equally effective, are not required to produce the identical result or level of achievement for handicapped and nonhandicapped persons, but must afford handicapped persons equal opportunity to obtain the same result, to gain the same benefit, or to reach the same level of achievement, in the most integrated setting appropriate to the person's needs.

(3) Despite the existence of separate or different programs or activities provided in accordance with this part, a recipient may not deny a qualified handicapped person the opportunity to participate in such programs or activities that are not separate or different.

(4) A recipient may not, directly or through contractual or other arrangements, utilize criteria or methods of administration (i) that have the effect of subjecting qualified handicapped persons to discrimination on the basis of handicap, (ii) that have the purpose or effect of defeating or substantially impairing accomplishment of the objectives of the recipient's program with respect to handicapped persons, or (iii) that perpetuate the discrimination of another recipient if both recipi-

ents are subject to common administrative control or are agencies of the same State.

(5) In determining the site or location of a facility, an applicant for assistance or a recipient may not make selections (i) that have the effect of excluding handicapped persons from, denying them the benefits of, or otherwise subjecting them to discrimination under any program or activity that receives or benefits from Federal financial assistance or (ii) that have the purpose or effect of defeating or substantially impairing the accomplishment of the objectives of the program or activity with respect to handicapped persons.

(6) As used in this section, the aid, benefit, or service provided under a program or activity receiving or benefiting from Federal financial assistance includes any aid, benefit, or service provided in or through a facility that has been constructed, expanded, altered, leased or rented, or otherwise acquired, in whole or in part, with Federal financial assistance.

(c) *Programs limited by Federal law.* The exclusion of non-handicapped persons from the benefits of a program limited by Federal statute or executive order to handicapped persons or the exclusion of a specific class of handicapped persons from a program limited by Federal statute or executive order to a different class of handicapped persons is not prohibited by this part.

§ 84.5 Assurances Required

(a) *Assurances.* An applicant for Federal financial assistance for a program or activity to which this part applies shall submit an assurance, on a form specified by the Director, that the program will be operated in compliance with this part. An applicant may incorporate these assurances by reference in subsequent applications to the Department.

(b) *Duration of obligation.* (1) In the case of Federal financial assistance extended in the form of real property or to provide real property or structures on the property, the assurance will obligate the recipient or, in the case of a subsequent transfer, the transferee, for the period during which the real property or structures are used for the purpose for which the Federal financial assistance is extended or for another purpose involving the provision of similar services or benefits.

(2) In the case of Federal financial assistance extended to provide personal property, the assurance will obligate the re-

cipient for the period during which it retains ownership or possession of the property.

(3) In all other cases the assurance will obligate the recipient for the period during which Federal financial assistance is extended.

(c) *Covenants.*   (1) Where Federal financial assistance is provided in the form of real property or interest in the property from the Department, the instrument effecting or recording this transfer shall contain a covenant running with the land to assure nondiscrimination for the period during which the real property is used for a purpose for which the Federal financial assistance is extended or for another purpose involving the provision of similar services or benefits.

(2) Where no transfer of property is involved but property is purchased or improved with Federal financial assistance, the recipient shall agree to include the covenant described in paragraph (b)(2) of this section in the instrument effecting or recording any subsequent transfer of the property.

(3) Where Federal financial assistance is provided in the form of real property or interest in the property from the Department, the covenant shall also include a condition coupled with a right to be reserved by the Department to revert title to the property in the event of a breach of the covenant. If a transferee of real property proposes to mortgage or otherwise encumber the real property as security for financing construction of new, or improvement of existing, facilities on the property for the purposes for which the property was transferred, the Director may, upon request of the transferee and if necessary to accomplish such financing and upon such conditions as he or she deems appropriate, agree to forbear the exercise of such right to revert title for so long as the lien of such mortgage or other encumbrance remains effective.

§ 84.6   Remedial Action, Voluntary Action, and Self-evaluation

(a) *Remedial action.*   (1) If the Director finds that a recipient has discriminated against persons on the basis of handicap in violation of section 504 or this part, the recipient shall take such remedial action as the Director deems necessary to overcome the effects of the discrimination.

(2) Where a recipient is found to have discriminated against persons on the basis of handicap in violation of section 504 or this part and where another recipient exercises control over

the recipient that has discriminated, the Director, where appropriate, may require either or both recipients to take remedial action.

(3) The Director may, where necessary to overcome the effects of discrimination in violation of section 504 or this part, require a recipient to take remedial action (i) with respect to handicapped persons who are no longer participants in the recipient's program but who were participants in the program when such discrimination occurred or (ii) with respect to handicapped persons who would have been participants in the program had the discrimination not occurred.

(b) *Voluntary action.* A recipient may take steps, in addition to any action that is required by this part, to overcome the effects of conditions that resulted in limited participation in the recipient's program or activity by qualified handicapped persons.

(c) *Self-evaluation.* (1) A recipient shall, within one year of the effective date of this part:

(i) Evaluate, with the assistance of interested persons, including handicapped persons or organizations representing handicapped persons, its current policies and practices and the effects thereof that do not or may not meet the requirements of this part;

(ii) Modify, after consultation with interested persons, including handicapped persons or organizations representing handicapped persons, any policies and practices that do not meet the requirements of this part; and

(iii) Take, after consultation with interested persons, including handicapped persons or organizations representing handicapped persons, appropriate remedial steps to eliminate the effects of any discrimination that resulted from adherence to these policies and practices.

(2) A recipient that employs fifteen or more persons shall, for at least three years following completion of the evaluation required under paragraph (c)(1) of this section, maintain on file, make available for public inspection, and provide to the Director upon request: (i) a list of the interested persons consulted, (ii) a description of areas examined and any problems identified, and (iii) a description of any modifications made and of any remedial steps taken.

§ 84.7 Designation of Responsible Employee and Adoption of Grievance Procedures

(a) *Designation of responsible employee.* A recipient that employs fifteen or more persons shall designate at least one person to coordinate its efforts to comply with this part.

(b) *Adoption of grievance procedures.* A recipient that employs fifteen or more persons shall adopt grievance procedures that incorporate appropriate due process standards and that provide for the prompt and equitable resolution of complaints alleging any action prohibited by this part. Such procedures need not be established with respect to complaints from applicants for employment or from applicants for admission to post-secondary educational institutions.

§ 84.8 Notice

(a) A recipient that employs fifteen or more persons shall take appropriate initial and continuing steps to notify participants, beneficiaries, applicants, and employees, including those with impaired vision or hearing, and unions or professional organizations holding collective bargaining or professional agreements with the recipient that it does not discriminate on the basis of handicap in violation of section 504 and this part. The notification shall state, where appropriate, that the recipient does not discriminate in admission or access to, or treatment or employment in, its programs and activities. The notification shall also include an identification of the responsible employee designated pursuant to § 84.7(a). A recipient shall make the initial notification required by this paragraph within 90 days of the effective date of this part. Methods of initial and continuing notification may include the posting of notices, publication in newspapers and magazines, placement of notices in recipients' publication, and distribution of memoranda or other written communications.

(b) If a recipient publishes or uses recruitment materials or publications containing general information that it makes available to participants, beneficiaries, applicants, or employees, it shall include in those materials or publications a statement of the policy described in paragraph (a) of this section. A recipient may meet the requirement of this paragraph either by including appropriate inserts in existing materials and publications or by revising and reprinting the materials and publications.

§ 84.9   Administrative Requirements for Small Recipients

The Director may require any recipient with fewer than fifteen employees, or any class of such recipients, to comply with §§ 84.7 and 84.8, in whole or in part, when the Director finds a violation of this part or finds that such compliance will not significantly impair the ability of the recipient or class of recipients to provide benefits or services.

§ 84.10   Effect of State or Local Law or Other Requirements and Effect of Employment Opportunities

(a) The obligation to comply with this part is not obviated or alleviated by the existence of any state or local law or other requirement that, on the basis of handicap, imposes prohibitions or limits upon the eligibility of qualified handicapped persons to receive services or to practice any occupation or profession.

(b) The obligation to comply with this part is not obviated or alleviated because employment opportunities in any occupation or profession are or may be more limited for handicapped persons than for nonhandicapped persons.

Subpart B—Employment Practices

§ 84.11   Discrimination Prohibited

(a) *General.* (1) No qualified handicapped person shall, on the basis of handicap, be subjected to discrimination in employment under any program or activity to which this part applies.

(2) A recipient that receives assistance under the Education of the Handicapped Act shall take positive steps to employ and advance in employment qualified handicapped persons in programs assisted under that Act.

(3) A recipient shall make all decisions concerning employment under any program or activity to which this part applies in a manner which ensures that discrimination on the basis of handicap does not occur and may not limit, segregate, or classify applicants or employees in any way that adversely affects their opportunities or status because of handicap.

(4) A recipient may not participate in a contractual or other relationship that has the effect of subjecting qualified handicapped applicants or employees to discrimination prohibited by this subpart. The relationships referred to in this subpara-

graph include relationships with employment and referral agencies, with labor unions, with organizations providing or administering fringe benefits to employees of the recipient, and with organizations providing training and apprenticeship programs.

(b) *Specific activities.* The provisions of this subpart apply to:

(1) Recruitment, advertising, and the processing of applications for employment;

(2) Hiring, upgrading, promotion, award of tenure, demotion, transfer, lay-off, termination, right of return from lay-off, and rehiring;

(3) Rates of pay or any other form of compensation and changes in compensation;

(4) Job assignments, job classifications, organizational structures, position descriptions, lines of progression, and seniority lists;

(5) Leaves of absence, sick leave, or any other leave;

(6) Fringe benefits available by virtue of employment, whether or not administered by the recipient;

(7) Selection and financial support for training, including apprenticeship, professional meetings, conferences, and other related activities, and selection for leaves of absence to pursue training;

(8) Employer sponsored activities, including social or recreational programs; and

(9) Any other term, condition, or privilege of employment.

(c) A recipient's obligation to comply with this subpart is not affected by any inconsistent term of any collective bargaining agreement to which it is a party.

§ 84.12 Reasonable Accommodation

(a) A recipient shall make reasonable accommodation to the known physical or mental limitations of an otherwise qualified handicapped applicant or employee unless the recipient can demonstrate that the accommodation would impose an undue hardship on the operation of its program.

(b) Reasonable accommodation may include: (1) making facilities used by employees readily accessible to and usable by handicapped persons, and (2) job restructuring, part-time or modified work schedules, acquisition or modification of equipment or devices, the provision of readers or interpreters, and other similar actions.

(c) In determining pursuant to paragraph (a) of this section whether an accommodation would impose an undue hardship on the operation of a recipient's program, factors to be considered include:

(1) The overall size of the recipient's program with respect to number of employees, number and type of facilities, and size of budget;

(2) The type of the recipient's operation, including the composition and structure of the recipient's workforce; and

(3) The nature and cost of the accommodation needed.

(d) A recipient may not deny any employment opportunity to a qualified handicapped employee or applicant if the basis for the denial is the need to make reasonable accommodation to the physical or mental limitations of the employee or applicant.

§ 84.13   Employment Criteria

(a) A recipient may not make use of any employment test or other selection criterion that screens out or tends to screen out handicapped persons or any class of handicapped persons unless: (1) the test score or other selection criterion, as used by the recipient, is shown to be job-related for the position in question, and (2) alternative job-related tests or criteria that do not screen out or tend to screen out as many handicapped persons are not shown by the Director to be available.

(b) A recipient shall select and administer tests concerning employment so as best to ensure that, when administered to an applicant or employee who has a handicap that impairs sensory, manual, or speaking skills, the test results accurately reflect the applicant's or employee's job skills, aptitude, or whatever other factor the test purports to measure, rather than reflecting the applicant's or employee's impaired sensory, manual, or speaking skills (except where those skills are the factors that the test purports to measure).

§ 84.14   Preemployment Inquiries

(a) Except as provided in paragraphs (b) and (c) of this section, a recipient may not conduct a preemployment medical examination or may not make preemployment inquiry of an applicant as to whether the applicant is a handicapped person or as to the nature or severity of a handicap. A recipient may, however, make preemployment inquiry into an applicant's ability to perform job-related functions.

(b) When a recipient is taking remedial action to correct the effects of past discrimination pursuant to § 84.6(a), when a recipient is taking voluntary action to overcome the effects of conditions that resulted in limited participation in its federally assisted program or activity pursuant to § 84.6(b), or when a recipient is taking affirmative action pursuant to section 503 of the Act, the recipient may invite applicants for employment to indicate whether and to what extent they are handicapped, *Provided*, That:

(1) The recipient states clearly on any written questionnaire used for this purpose or makes clear orally if no written questionnaire is used that the information requested is intended for use solely in connection with its remedial action obligations or its voluntary or affirmative action efforts; and

(2) The recipient states clearly that the information is being requested on a voluntary basis, that it will be kept confidential as provided in paragraph (d) of this section, that refusal to provide it will not subject the applicant or employee to any adverse treatment, and that it will be used only in accordance with this part.

(c) Nothing in this section shall prohibit a recipient from conditioning an offer of employment on the results of a medical examination conducted prior to the employee's entrance on duty, *Provided*, That: (1) All entering employees are subjected to such an examination regardless of handicap, and (2) the results of such an examination are used only in accordance with the requirements of this part.

(d) Information obtained in accordance with this section as to the medical condition or history of the applicant shall be collected and maintained on separate forms that shall be accorded confidentiality as medical records, except that:

(1) Supervisors and managers may be informed regarding restrictions on the work or duties of handicapped persons and regarding necessary accommodations;

(2) First aid and safety personnel may be informed, where appropriate, if the condition might require emergency treatment; and

(3) Government officials investigating compliance with the Act shall be provided relevant information upon request.

§§ 84.15–84.20   [Reserved]

Subpart C—Program Accessibility

§ 84.21   Discrimination Prohibited

No qualified handicapped person shall, because a recipient's facilities are inaccessible to or unusable by handicapped persons, be denied the benefits of, be excluded from participation in, or otherwise be subjected to discrimination under any program or activity to which this part applies.

§ 84.22   Existing Facilities

(a) *Program accessibility.*   A recipient shall operate each program or activity to which this part applies so that the program or activity, when viewed in its entirety, is readily accessible to handicapped persons.   This paragraph does not require a recipient to make each of its existing facilities or every part of a facility accessible to and usable by handicapped persons.

(b) *Methods.*   A recipient may comply with the requirement of paragraph (a) of this section through such means as redesign of equipment, reassignment of classes or other services to accessible buildings, assignment of aides to beneficiaries, home visits, delivery of health, welfare, or other social services at alternate accessible sites, alteration of existing facilities and construction of new facilities in conformance with the requirements of § 84.23, or any other methods that result in making its program or activity accessible to handicapped persons.   A recipient is not required to make structural changes in existing facilities where other methods are effective in achieving compliance with paragraph (a) of this section.   In choosing among available methods for meeting the requirement of paragraph (a) of this section, a recipient shall give priority to those methods that offer programs and activities to handicapped persons in the most integrated setting appropriate.

(c) *Small health, welfare, or other social service providers.* If a recipient with fewer than fifteen employees that provides health, welfare, or other social services finds, after consultation with a handicapped person seeking its services, that there is no method of complying with paragraph (a) of this section other than making a significant alteration in its existing facilities, the recipient may, as an alternative, refer the handicapped person to other providers of those services that are accessible.

(d) *Time period.* A recipient shall comply with the requirement of paragraph (a) of this section within sixty days of the effective date of this part except that where structural changes in facilities are necessary, such changes shall be made within three years of the effective date of this part, but in any event as expeditiously as possible.

(e) *Transition plan.* In the event that structural changes to facilities are necessary to meet the requirement of paragraph (a) of this section, a recipient shall develop, within six months of the effective date of this part, a transition plan setting forth the steps necessary to complete such changes. The plan shall be developed with the assistance of interested persons, including handicapped persons or organizations representing handicapped persons. A copy of the transition plan shall be made available for public inspection. The plan shall, at a minimum:

(1) Identify physical obstacles in the recipient's facilities that limit the accessibility of its program or activity to handicapped persons;

(2) Describe in detail the methods that will be used to make the facilities accessible;

(3) Specify the schedule for taking the steps necessary to achieve full program accessibility and, if the time period of the transition plan is longer than one year, identify steps that will be taken during each year of the transition period; and

(4) Indicate the person responsible for implementation of the plan.

(f) *Notice.* The recipient shall adopt and implement procedures to ensure that interested persons, including persons with impaired vision or hearing, can obtain information as to the existence and location of services, activities, and facilities that are accessible to and usable by handicapped persons.

§ 84.23 New Construction

(a) *Design and construction.* Each facility or part of a facility constructed by, on behalf of, or for the use of a recipient shall be designed and constructed in such manner that the facility or part of the facility is readily accessible to and usable by handicapped persons. If the construction was commenced after the effective date of this part.

(b) *Alteration.* Each facility or part of a facility which is altered by, on behalf of, or for the use of a recipient after the effective date of this part in a manner that affects or could affect the usability of the facility or part of the facility shall, to the maximum extent feasible, be altered in such manner that the altered portion of the facility is readily accessible to and usable by handicapped persons.

(c) *American National Standards Institute accessibility standards.* Design, construction, or alteration of facilities in conformance with the "American National Standard Specifications for Making Buildings and Facilities Accessible to, and Usable by, the Physically Handicapped," published by the American National Standards Institute, Inc.   (ANSI A117.1–1961 (R1971)),[1] which is incorporated by reference in this part, shall constitute compliance with paragraphs (a) and (b) of this section.   Departures from particular requirements of those standards by the use of other methods shall be permitted when it is clearly evident that equivalent access to the facility or part of the facility is thereby provided.

§§ 84.24–84.30   [Reserved]

Subpart D—Preschool, Elementary, and Secondary Education

§ 84.31   Application of This Subpart

Subpart D applies to preschool, elementary, secondary, and adult education programs and activities that receive or benefit from federal financial assistance and to recipients that operate, or that receive or benefit from federal financial assistance for the operation of, such programs or activities.

§ 84.32   Location and Notification

A recipient that operates a public elementary or secondary education program shall annually:

(a) Undertake to identify and locate every qualified handicapped person residing in the recipient's jurisdiction who is not receiving a public education; and

(b) Take appropriate steps to notify handicapped persons and their parents or guardians of the recipient's duty under this subpart.

---

1. Copies obtainable from American National Standards Institute, Inc.,   1430 Broadway New York, N.Y. 10018.

§ 84.33 Free Appropriate Public Education

(a) *General.* A recipient that operates a public elementary or secondary education program shall provide a free appropriate public education to each qualified handicapped person who is in the recipient's jurisdiction, regardless of the nature or severity of the person's handicap.

(b) *Appropriate education.* (1) For the purpose of this subpart, the provision of an appropriate education is the provision of regular or special education and related aids and services that (i) are designed to meet individual educational needs of handicapped persons as adequately as the needs of nonhandicapped persons are met and (ii) are based upon adherence to procedures that satisfy the requirements of §§ 84.34, 84.35, and 84.36.

(2) Implementation of an individualized education program developed in accordance with the Education of the Handicapped Act is one means of meeting the standard established in paragraph (b)(1)(i) of this section.

(3) A recipient may place a handicapped person in or refer such person to a program other than the one that it operates as its means of carrying out the requirements of this subpart. If so, the recipient remains responsible for ensuring that the requirements of this subpart are met with respect to any handicapped person so placed or referred.

(c) *Free education*—(1) *General.* For the purpose of this section, the provision of a free education is the provision of educational and related services without cost to the handicapped person or to his or her parents or guardian, except for those fees that are imposed on nonhandicapped persons or their parents or guardian. It may consist either of the provision of free services or, if a recipient places a handicapped person in or refers such person to a program not operated by the recipient as its means of carrying out the requirements of this subpart, of payment for the costs of the program. Funds available from any public or private agency may be used to meet the requirements of this subpart. Nothing in this section shall be construed to relieve an insurer or similar third party from an otherwise valid obligation to provide or pay for services provided to a handicapped person.

(2) *Transportation.* If a recipient places a handicapped person in or refers such person to a program not operated by the recipient as its means of carrying out the requirements of this

subpart, the recipient shall ensure that adequate transportation to and from the program is provided at no greater cost than would be incurred by the person or his or her parents or guardian if the person were placed in the program operated by the recipient.

(3) *Residential placement.* If placement in a public or private residential program is necessary to provide a free appropriate public education to a handicapped person because of his or her handicap, the program, including nonmedical care and room and board, shall be provided at no cost to the person or his or her parents or guardian.

(4) *Placement of handicapped persons by parents.* If a recipient has made available, in conformance with the requirements of this section and § 84.34, a free appropriate public education to a handicapped person and the person's parents or guardian choose to place the person in a private school, the recipient is not required to pay for the person's education in the private school. Disagreements between a parent or guardian and a recipient regarding whether the recipient has made such a program available or otherwise regarding the question of financial responsibility are subject to the due process procedures of § 84.36.

(d) *Compliance.* A recipient may not exclude any qualified handicapped person from a public elementary or secondary education after the effective date of this part. A recipient that is not, on the effective date of this regulation, in full compliance with the other requirements of the preceding paragraphs of this section shall meet such requirements at the earliest practicable time and in no event later than September 1, 1978.

§ 84.34 Educational Setting

(a) *Academic setting.* A recipient to which this subpart applies shall educate, or shall provide for the education of, each qualified handicapped person in its jurisdiction with persons who are not handicapped to the maximum extent appropriate to the needs of the handicapped person. A recipient shall place a handicapped person in the regular educational environment operated by the recipient unless it is demonstrated by the recipient that the education of the person in the regular environment with the use of supplementary aids and services cannot be achieved satisfactorily. Whenever a recipient places a person in a setting other than the regular educational environment pursuant to this paragraph, it shall take into account the proximity of the alternate setting to the person's home.

(b) *Nonacademic settings.* In providing or arranging for the provision of nonacademic and extracurricular services and activities, including meals, recess periods, and the services and activities set forth in § 84.37(a)(2), a recipient shall ensure that handicapped persons participate with nonhandicapped persons in such activities and services to the maximum extent appropriate to the needs of the handicapped person in question.

(c) *Comparable facilities.* If a recipient, in compliance with paragraph (a) of this section, operates a facility that is identifiable as being for handicapped persons, the recipient shall ensure that the facility and the services and activities provided therein are comparable to the other facilities, services, and activities of the recipient.

§ 84.35 Evaluation and Placement

(a) *Preplacement evaluation.* A recipient that operates a public elementary or secondary education program shall conduct an evaluation in accordance with the requirements of paragraph (b) of this section of any person who, because of handicap, needs or is believed to need special education or related services before taking any action with respect to the initial placement of the person in a regular or special education program and any subsequent significant change in placement.

(b) *Evaluation procedures.* A recipient to which this subpart applies shall establish standards and procedures for the evaluation and placement of persons who, because of handicap, need or are believed to need special education or related services which ensure that:

(1) Tests and other evaluation materials have been validated for the specific purpose for which they are used and are administered by trained personnel in conformance with the instructions provided by their producer;

(2) Tests and other evaluation materials include those tailored to assess specific areas of educational need and not merely those which are designed to provide a single general intelligence quotient; and

(3) Tests are selected and administered so as best to ensure that, when a test is administered to a student with impaired sensory, manual, or speaking skills, the test results accurately reflect the student's aptitude or achievement level or whatever

other factor the test purports to measure, rather than reflecting the student's impaired sensory, manual, or speaking skills (except where those skills are the factors that the test purports to measure).

(c) *Placement procedures.* In interpreting evaluation data and in making placement decisions, a recipient shall (1) draw upon information from a variety of sources, including aptitude and achievement tests, teacher recommendations, physical condition, social or cultural background, and adaptive behavior, (2) establish procedures to ensure that information obtained from all such sources is documented and carefully considered, (3) ensure that the placement decision is made by a group of persons, including persons knowledgeable about the child, the meaning of the evaluation data, and the placement options, and (4) ensure that the placement decision is made in conformity with § 84.34.

(d) *Reevaluation.* A recipient to which this section applies shall establish procedures, in accordance with paragraph (b) of this section, for periodic reevaluation of students who have been provided special education and related services. A reevaluation procedure consistent with the Education for the Handicapped Act is one means of meeting this requirement.

§ 84.36   Procedural Safeguards

A recipient that operates a public elementary or secondary education program shall establish and implement, with respect to actions regarding the identification, evaluation, or educational placement of persons who, because of handicap, need or are believed to need special instruction or related services, a system of procedural safeguards that includes notice, an opportunity for the parents or guardian of the person to examine relevant records, an impartial hearing with opportunity for participation by the person's parents or guardian and representation by counsel, and a review procedure. Compliance with the procedural safeguards of section 615 of the Education of the Handicapped Act is one means of meeting this requirement.

§ 84.37   Nonacademic Services

(a) *General.* (1) A recipient to which this subpart applies shall provide nonacademic and extracurricular services and activities in such manner as is necessary to afford handicapped students an equal opportunity for participation in such services and activities.

(2) Nonacademic and extracurricular services and activities may include counseling services, physical recreational athletics, transportation, health services, recreational activities, special interest groups or clubs sponsored by the recipient, referrals to agencies which provide assistance to handicapped persons, and employment of students, including both employment by the recipient and assistance in making available outside employment.

(b) *Counseling services.* A recipient to which this subpart applies that provides personal, academic, or vocational counseling, guidance, or placement services to its students shall provide these services without discrimination on the basis of handicap. The recipient shall ensure that qualified handicapped students are not counseled toward more restrictive career objectives than are nonhandicapped students with similar interests and abilities.

(c) *Physical education and athletics.* (1) In providing physical education courses and athletics and similar programs and activities to any of its students,, a recipient to which this subpart applies may not discriminate on the basis of handicap. A recipient that offers physical education courses or that operates or sponsors interscholastic, club, or intramural athletics shall provide to qualified handicapped students an equal opportunity for participation in these activities.

(2) A recipient may offer to handicapped students physical education and athletic activities that are separate or different from those offered to nonhandicapped students only if separation or differentiation is consistent with the requirements of § 84.34 and only if no qualified handicapped student is denied the opportunity to compete for teams or to participate in courses that are not separate or different.

§ 84.38 Preschool and Adult Education Programs

A recipient to which this subpart applies that operates a preschool education or day care program or activity or an adult education program or activity may not, on the basis of handicap, exclude qualified handicapped persons from the program or activity and shall take into account the needs of such persons in determining the aid, benefits, or services to be provided under the program or activity.

§ 84.39 Private Education Programs

(a) A recipient that operates a private elementary or secondary education program may not, on the basis of handicap, exclude a qualified handicapped person from such program if the person can, with minor adjustments, be provided an appropriate education, as defined in § 84.33(b)(1), within the recipient's program.

(b) A recipient to which this section applies may not charge more for the provision of an appropriate education to handicapped persons than to nonhandicapped persons except to the extent that any additional charge is justified by a substantial increase in cost to the recipient.

(c) A recipient to which this section applies that operates special education programs shall operate such programs in accordance with the provisions of §§ 84.35 and 84.36. Each recipient to which this section applies is subject to the provisions of §§ 84.34, 84.37, and 84.38.

§ 84.40   [Reserved]

Subpart E—Postsecondary Education

§ 84.41   Application of This Subpart

Subpart E applies to postsecondary education programs and activities, including postsecondary vocational education programs and activities, that receive or benefit from federal financial assistance and to recipients that operate, or that receive or benefit from federal financial assistance for the operation of, such programs or activities.

§ 84.42   Admissions and Recruitment

(a) *General.* Qualified handicapped persons may not, on the basis of handicap, be denied admission or be subjected to discrimination in admission or recruitment by a recipient to which this subpart applies.

(b) *Admissions.* In administering its admission policies, a recipient to which this subpart applies:

(1) May not apply limitations upon the number or proportion of handicapped persons who may be admitted;

(2) May not make use of any test or criterion for admission that has a disproportionate, adverse effect on handicapped persons or any class of handicapped persons unless (i) the test or criterion, as used by the recipient, has been validated as a predictor of success in the education program or activity in question and (ii) alternate tests or criteria that have a less dispro-

portionate, adverse effect are not shown by the Director to be available;

(3) Shall assure itself that (i) admissions tests are selected and administered so as best to ensure that, when a test is administered to an applicant who has a handicap that impairs sensory, manual, or speaking skills, the test results accurately reflect the applicant's aptitude or achievement level or whatever other factor the test purports to measure, rather than reflecting the applicant's impaired sensory, manual, or speaking skills (except where those skills are the factors that the test purports to measure); (ii) admissions tests that are designed for persons with impaired sensory, manual, or speaking skills are offered as often and in as timely a manner as are other admissions tests; and (iii) admissions tests are administered in facilities that, on the whole, are accessible to handicapped persons; and

(4) Except as provided in paragraph (c) of this section, may not make preadmission inquiry as to whether an applicant for admission is a handicapped person but, after admission, may make inquiries on a confidential basis as to handicaps that may require accommodation.

(c) *Preadmission inquiry exception.* When a recipient is taking remedial action to correct the effects of past discrimination pursuant to § 84.6(a) or when a recipient is taking voluntary action to overcome the effects of conditions that resulted in limited participation in its federally assisted program or activity pursuant to § 84.6(b), the recipient may invite applicants for admission to indicate whether and to what extent they are handicapped, *Provided*, That:

(1) The recipient states clearly on any written questionnaire used for this purpose or makes clear orally if no written questionnaire is used that the information requested is intended for use solely in connection with its remedial action obligations or its voluntary action efforts; and

(2) The recipient states clearly that the information is being requested on a voluntary basis, that it will be kept confidential, that refusal to provide it will not subject the applicant to any adverse treatment, and that it will be used only in accordance with this part.

(d) *Validity studies.* For the purpose of paragraph (b)(2) of this section, a recipient may base prediction equations on first year grades, but shall conduct periodic validity studies against the criterion of overall success in the education program or activity in question in order to monitor the general validity of the test scores.

§ 84.43   Treatment of Students; General

(a) No qualified handicapped student shall, on the basis of handicap, be excluded from participation in, be denied the benefits of, or otherwise be subjected to discrimination under any academic, research, occupational training, housing, health, insurance, counseling, financial aid, physical education, athletics, recreation, transportation, other extracurricular, or other post-secondary education program or activity to which this subpart applies.

(b) A recipient to which this subpart applies that considers participation by students in education programs or activities not operated wholly by the recipient as part of, or equivalent to, an education program or activity operated by the recipient shall assure itself that the other education program or activity, as a whole, provides an equal opportunity for the participation of qualified handicapped persons.

(c) A recipient to which this subpart applies may not, on the basis of handicap, exclude any qualified handicapped student from any course, course of study, or other part of its education program or activity.

(d) A recipient to which this subpart applies shall operate its programs and activities in the most integrated setting appropriate.

§ 84.44   Academic Adjustments

(a) *Academic requirements.* A recipient to which this subpart applies shall make such modifications to its academic requirements as are necessary to ensure that such requirements do not discriminate or have the effect of discriminating, on the basis of handicap, against a qualified handicapped applicant or student. Academic requirements that the recipient can demonstrate are essential to the program of instruction being pursued by such student or to any directly related licensing requirement will not be regarded as discriminatory within the meaning of this section. Modifications may include changes in the length of time permitted for the completion of degree requirements, substitution of specific courses required for the completion of degree requirements, and adaptation of the manner in which specific courses are conducted.

(b) *Other rules.* A recipient to which this subpart applies may not impose upon handicapped students other rules, such as the prohibition of tape recorders in classrooms or of dog guides in campus buildings, that have the effect of limiting the participation of handicapped students in the recipient's education program or activity.

(c) *Course examinations.* In its course examinations or other procedures for evaluating students' academic achievement in its program, a recipient to which this subpart applies shall provide such methods for evaluating the achievement of students who have a handicap that impairs sensory, manual, or speaking skills as will best ensure that the results of the evaluation represents the student's achievement in the course, rather than reflecting the student's impaired sensory, manual, or speaking skills (except where such skills are the factors that the test purports to measure).

(d) *Auxiliary aids.* (1) A recipient to which this subpart applies shall take such steps as are necessary to ensure that no handicapped student is denied the benefits of, excluded from participation in, or otherwise subjected to discrimination under the education program or activity operated by the recipient because of the absence of educational auxiliary aids for students with impaired sensory, manual, or speaking skills.

(2) Auxiliary aids may include taped texts, interpreters or other effective methods of making orally delivered materials available to students with hearing impairments, readers in libraries for students with visual impairments, classroom equipment adapted for use by students with manual impairments, and other similar services and actions. Recipients need not provide attendants, individually prescribed devices, readers for personal use or study, or other devices or services of a personal nature.

§ 84.45 Housing

(a) *Housing provided by the recipient.* A recipient that provides housing to its nonhandicapped students shall provide comparable, convenient, and accessible housing to handicapped students at the same cost as to others. At the end of the transition period provided for in Subpart C, such housing shall be available in sufficient quantity and variety so that the scope of handicapped students' choice of living accommodations is, as a whole, comparable to that of nonhandicapped students.

(b) *Other housing.* A recipient that assists any agency, organization, or person in making housing available to any of its students shall take such action as may be necessary to assure itself that such housing is, as a whole, made available in a manner that does not result in discrimination on the basis of handicap.

§ 84.46 Financial and Employment Assistance to Students

(a) *Provision of financial assistance.* (1) In providing financial assistance to qualified handicapped persons, a recipient to which this subpart applies may not (i), on the basis of handicap, provide less assistance than is provided to nonhandicapped persons, limit eligibility for assistance, or otherwise discriminate or (ii) assist any entity or person that provides assistance to any of the recipient's students in a manner that discriminates against qualified handicapped persons on the basis of handicap.

(2) A recipient may administer or assist in the administration of scholarships, fellowships, or other forms of financial assistance established under wills, trusts, bequests, or similar legal instruments that require awards to be made on the basis of factors that discriminate or have the effect of discriminating on the basis of handicap only if the overall effect of the award of scholarships, fellowships, and other forms of financial assistance is not discriminatory on the basis of handicap.

(b) *Assistance in making available outside employment.* A recipient that assists any agency, organization, or person in providing employment opportunities to any of its students shall assure itself that such employment opportunities, as a whole, are made available in a manner that would not violate Subpart B if they were provided by the recipient.

(c) *Employment of students by recipients.* A recipient that employs any of its students may not do so in a manner that violates Subpart B.

§ 84.47 Nonacademic Services

(a) *Physical education and athletics.* (1) In providing physical education courses and athletics and similar programs and activities to any of its students, a recipient to which this subpart applies may not discriminate on the basis of handicap. A recipient that offers physical education courses or that operates or sponsors intercollegiate, club, or intramural athletics shall provide to qualified handicapped students an equal opportunity for participation in these activities.

(2) A recipient may offer to handicapped students physical education and athletic activities that are separate or different only if separation or differentiation is consistent with the re-

quirements of § 84.43(d) and only if no qualified handicapped student is denied the opportunity to compete for teams or to participate in courses that are not separate or different.

(b) *Counseling and placement services.* A recipient to which this subpart applies that provides personal, academic, or vocational counseling, guidance, or placement services to its students shall provide these services without discrimination on the basis of handicap. The recipient shall ensure that qualified handicapped students are not counseled toward more restrictive career objectives than are nonhandicapped students with similar interests and abilities. This requirement does not preclude a recipient from providing factual information about licensing and certification requirements that may present obstacles to handicapped persons in their pursuit of particular careers.

(c) *Social organizations.* A recipient that provides significant assistance to fraternities, sororities, or similar organizations shall assure itself that the membership practices of such organizations do not permit discrimination otherwise prohibited by this subpart.

§§ 84.48–84.50 [Reserved]

Subpart F—Health, Welfare, and Social Services

§ 84.51 Application of This Subpart

Subpart F applies to health, welfare, and other social service programs and activities that receive or benefit from federal financial assistance and to recipients that operate, or that receive or benefit from federal financial assistance for the operation of, such programs or activities.

§ 84.52 Health, Welfare, and Other Social Services

(a) *General.* In providing health, welfare, or other social services or benefits, a recipient may not, on the basis of handicap:

(1) Deny a qualified handicapped person these benefits or services;

(2) Afford a qualified handicapped person an opportunity to receive benefits or services that is not equal to that offered nonhandicapped persons;

(3) Provide a qualified handicapped person with benefits or services that are not as effective (as defined in § 84.4(b)) as the benefits or services provided to others;

(4) Provide benefits or services in a manner that limits or has the effect of limiting the participation of qualified handicapped persons; or

(5) Provide different or separate benefits or services to handicapped persons except where necessary to provide qualified handicapped persons with benefits and services that are as effective as those provided to others.

(b) *Notice.* A recipient that provides notice concerning benefits or services or written material concerning waivers of rights or consent to treatment shall take such steps as are necessary to ensure that qualified handicapped persons, including those with impaired sensory or speaking skills, are not denied effective notice because of their handicap.

(c) *Emergency treatment for the hearing impaired.* A recipient hospital that provides health services or benefits shall establish a procedure for effective communication with persons with impaired hearing for the purpose of providing emergency health care.

(d) *Auxiliary aids.* (1) A recipient to which this subpart applies that employs fifteen or more persons shall provide appropriate auxiliary aids to persons with impaired sensory, manual, or speaking skills, where necessary to afford such persons an equal opportunity to benefit from the service in question.

(2) The Director may require recipients with fewer than fifteen employees to provide auxiliary aids where the provision of aids would not significantly impair the ability of the recipient to provide its benefits or services.

(3) For the purpose of this paragraph, auxiliary aids may include brailled and taped material, interpreters, and other aids for persons with impaired hearing or vision.

§ 84.53   Drug and Alcohol Addicts

A recipient to which this subpart applies that operates a general hospital or outpatient facility may not discriminate in admission or treatment against a drug or alcohol abuser or alcoholic who is suffering from a medical condition, because of the person's drug or alcohol abuse or alcoholism.

§ 84.54   Education of Institutionalized Persons

A recipient to which this subpart applies and that operates or supervises a program or activity for persons who are institutionalized because of handicap shall ensure that each qualified handicapped person, as defined in § 84.3(k)(2), in its program or activity is provided an appropriate education, as defined in § 84.33 (b). Nothing in this section shall be interpreted as altering in any way the obligations of recipients under Subpart D.

§§ 84.55–84.60 [Reserved]

Subpart G—Procedures

§ 84.61 Procedures

Note: Incorporation by reference provisions approved by the Director of the Federal Register, May 27, 1975. Incorporated documents are on file at the Office of the Federal Register.

The procedural provisions applicable to title VI of the Civil Rights Act of 1964 apply to this part. These procedures are found in §§ 80.6–80.10 and Part 81 of this Title.

[§§ 80.6–80.10 are reprinted here for the convenience of the reader. Part 81 is not reprinted since it deals with practices and procedures for hearings prior to termination of Federal funding and would be of value only to attorneys.]

§§ 84.62–84.99 [Reserved]

§ 80.6 Compliance Information

(a) *Cooperation and assistance.* The responsible Department official shall to the fullest extent practicable seek the cooperation of recipients in obtaining compliance with this part and shall provide assistance and guidance to recipients to help them comply voluntarily with this part.

(b) *Compliance reports.* Each recipient shall keep such records and submit to the responsible Department official or his designee timely, complete and accurate compliance reports at such times, and in such form and containing such information, as the responsible Department official or his designee may determine to be necessary to enable him to ascertain whether the recipient has complied or is complying with this part. For example, recipients should have available for the Department racial and ethnic data showing the extent to which members of minority groups are beneficiaries of and participants in federally-assisted programs. In the case of any program under which a primary recipient extends Federal financial assistance to any other recipient, such other recipient shall also submit such compliance reports to the primary recipient as may be necessary to enable the primary recipient to carry out its obligations under this part.

(c) *Access to sources of information.* Each recipient shall permit access by the responsible Department official or his designee during normal business hours to such of its books, records, accounts, and other sources of information, and its facilities as may be pertinent to ascertain compliance with this part. Where any information required of a recipient is in the exclusive possession of any other agency, institution or person and this agency, institution or person shall fail or refuse to furnish this information the recipient shall so certify in its report and shall set forth what efforts it has made to obtain the information. Asserted considerations of privacy or confidentiality may not operate to bar the Department from evaluating or seeking to enforce compliance with this Part. Information of a confidential nature obtained in connection with compliance evaluation or enforcement shall not be disclosed except where necessary in formal enforcement proceedings or where otherwise required by law.

(d) *Information to beneficiaries and participants.* Each recipient shall make available to participants, beneficiaries, and other interested persons such information regarding the provisions of this regulation and its applicability to the program for which the recipient receives Federal financial assistance, and make such information available to them in such manner, as the responsible Department official finds necessary to apprise such persons of the protections against discrimination assured them by the Act and this regulation.

§ 80.7   Conduct of Investigations

(a) *Periodic compliance reviews.* The responsible Department official or his designee shall from time to time review the practices of recipients to determine whether they are complying with this part.

(b) *Complaints.* Any person who believes himself or any specific class of individuals to be subjected to discrimination prohibited by this part may by himself or by a representative file with the responsible Department official or his designee a written complaint. A complaint must be filed not later than 180 days from the date of the alleged discrimination, unless the time for filing is extended by the responsible Department official or his designee.

(c) *Investigations.* The responsible Department official or his designee will make a prompt investigation whenever a compliance review, report, complaint, or any other information indicates a possible failure to comply with this part. The investigation should include, where appropriate, a review of the pertinent practices and policies of the recipient, the circumstances under which the possible noncompliance with this part occurred, and other factors relevant to a determination as to whether the recipient has failed to comply with this part.

(d) *Resolution of matters.* (1) If an investigation pursuant to paragraph (c) of this section indicates a failure to comply with this part, the responsible Department official or his designee will so inform the recipient and the matter will be resolved by informal means whenever possible. If it has been determined that the matter cannot be resolved by informal means, action will be taken as provided for in § 80.8.

(2) If an investigation does not warrant action pursuant to subparagraph (1) of this paragraph the responsible Department official or his designee will so inform the recipient and the complainant, if any, in writing.

(e) *Intimidatory or retaliatory acts prohibited.* No recipient or other person shall intimidate, threaten, coerce, or discriminate against any individual for the purpose of interfering with any right or privilege secured by section 601 of the Act or this part, or because he has made a complaint, testified, assisted, or participated in any manner in an investigation, proceeding or hearing under this part. The identity of complainants shall be kept confidential except to the extent necessary to carry out the purposes of this part, including the conduct of any investigation, hearing, or judicial proceeding arising thereunder.

§ 80.8　Procedure for Effecting Compliance

(a) *General.* If there appears to be a failure or threatened failure to comply with this regulation, and if the noncompliance or threatened noncompliance cannot be corrected by informal means, compliance with this part may be effected by the suspension or termination of or refusal to grant or to continue Federal financial assistance or by any other means authorized by law. Such other means may include, but are not limited to, (1) a reference to the Department of Justice with a recommendation that appropriate proceedings be brought to enforce any rights of the United States under any law of the United States (including other titles of the Act), or any assurance or other contractual undertaking, and (2) any applicable proceeding under State or local law.

(b) *Noncompliance with § 80.4.* If an applicant fails or refuses to furnish an assurance required under § 80.4 or otherwise fails or refuses to comply with a requirement imposed by or pursuant to that section Federal financial assistance may be refused in accordance with the procedures of paragraph (c) of this section. The Department shall not be required to provide assistance in such a case during the pendency of the administrative proceedings under such paragraph except that the Department shall continue assistance during the pendency of such proceedings where such assistance is due and payable pursuant to an application therefor approved prior to the effective date of this part.

(c) *Termination of or refusal to grant or to continue Federal financial assistance.* No order suspending, terminating or refusing to grant or continue Federal financial assistance shall become effective until (1) the responsible Department official has advised the applicant or recipient of his failure to comply and has determined that compliance cannot be secured by voluntary means, (2) there has been an express finding on the record, after opportunity for hearing, of a failure by the applicant or recipient to comply with a requirement imposed by or pursuant to this part, (3) the expiration of 30 days after the Secretary has filed with the committee of the House and the committee of the Senate having legislative jurisdiction over the program involved, a full written report of the circumstances and the grounds for such action. Any action to suspend or terminate or to refuse to grant or to continue Federal financial assistance shall be limited to the particular political entity, or part thereof, or other applicant or recipient as to whom such a finding has been made and shall be limited in its effect to the particular program, or part thereof, in which such noncompliance has been so found.

(d) *Other means authorized by law.* No action to effect compliance by any other means authorized by law shall be taken until (1) the responsible Department official has determined that compliance cannot be secured by voluntary means, (2) the recipient or other person has been notified of its failure to comply and of the action to be taken to effect compliance, and (3) the expiration of at least 10 days from the mailing of such notice to the recipient or other person. During this period of at least 10 days additional efforts shall be made to persuade the recipient or other person to comply with the regulation and to take such corrective action as may be appropriate.

§ 80.9 Hearing

(a) *Opportunity for hearing.* Whenever an opportunity for a hearing is required by § 80.8(c), reasonable notice shall be given by registered or certified mail, return receipt requested, to the affected applicant or recipient. This notice shall advise the applicant or recipient of the action proposed to be taken, the specific provision under which the proposed action against it is to be taken, and the matters of fact or law asserted as the basis for this action, and either (1) fix a date not less than 20 days after the date of such notice within which the applicant or recipient may request of the responsible Department official that the matter be scheduled for hearing or (2) advise the applicant or recipient that the matter in question has been set down for hearing at a stated place and time. The time and place so fixed shall be reasonable and shall be subject to change for cause. The complainant, if any, shall be advised of the time and place of the hearing. An applicant or recipient may waive a hearing and submit written information and argument for the record. The failure of an applicant or recipient to request a hearing for which a date has been set shall be deemed to be a waiver of the right to a hearing under section 602 of the Act and § 80.8(c) of this regulation and consent to the making of a decision on the basis of such information as may be filed as the record.

(b) *Time and place of hearing.* Hearings shall be held at the offices of the Department in Washington, D. C., at a time fixed by the responsible Department official unless he determines that the convenience of the applicant or recipient or of the Department requires that another place be selected. Hearings shall be held before a hearing examiner designated in accordance with 5 U.S.C. 3105 and 3344 (section 11 of the Administrative Procedure Act).

(c) *Right to counsel.* In all proceedings under this section, the applicant or recipient and the Department shall have the right to be represented by counsel.

(d) *Procedures, evidence, and record.* (1) The hearing, decision, and any administrative review thereof shall be conducted in conformity with sections 5–8 of the Administrative Procedure Act, and in accordance with such rules of procedure as are proper (and not inconsistent with this section) relating to the conduct of the hearing, giving of notices subsequent to those provided for in paragraph (a) of this section, taking of testimony, exhibits, arguments and briefs, requests for findings, and other related matters. Both the Department and the applicant or recipient shall be entitled to introduce all relevant evidence on the issues as stated in the notice for hearing or as determined by the officer conducting the hearing at the outset of or during the hearing. Any person (other than a Government employee considered to be on official business) who, having been invited or requested to appear and testify as a witness on the Government's behalf, attends at a time and place scheduled for a hearing provided for by this part, may be reimbursed for his travel and actual expenses of attendance in an amount not to exceed the amount payable under the standardized travel regulations to a Government employee traveling on official business.

(2) Technical rules of evidence shall not apply to hearings conducted pursuant to this part, but rules or principles designed to assure production of the most credible evidence available and to subject testimony to test by cross-examination shall be applied where reasonably necessary by the officer conducting the hearing. The hearing officer may exclude irrelevant, immaterial, or unduly repetitious evidence. All documents and other evidence offered or taken for the record shall be open to examination by the parties and opportunity shall be given to refute facts and arguments advanced on either side of the issues. A transcript shall be made of the oral evidence except to the extent the substance thereof is stipulated for the record. All decisons shall be based upon the hearing record and written findings shall be made.

(e) *Consolidated or Joint Hearings.* In cases in which the same or related facts are asserted to constitute noncompliance with this regulation with respect to two or more programs to which this part applies, or noncompliance with this part and the regulations of one or more other Federal departments or agencies issued under Title VI of the Act, the responsible Department official may, by agreement with such other departments or agencies where applicable, provide for the conduct of consolidated or joint hearings, and for the application to such hearings of rules of procedures not inconsistent with this part. Final decisions in such cases, insofar as this regulation is concerned, shall be made in accordance with § 80.10.

§ 80.10   Decisions and Notices

(a) *Decisions by hearing examiners.* After a hearing is held by a hearing examiner such hearing examiner shall either make an initial decision, if so authorized, or certify the entire record including his recommended findings and proposed decision to the reviewing authority for a final decision, and a copy of such initial decision or certification shall be mailed to the applicant or recipient and to the complainant, if any. Where the initial decision referred to in this paragraph or in paragraph (c) of this section is made by the hearing examiner, the applicant or recipient or the counsel for the Department may, within the period provided for in the rules of procedure issued by the responsible Department official, file with the reviewing authority exceptions to the initial decision, with his reasons therefor. Upon the filing of such exceptions the reviewing authority shall review the initial decision and issue its own decision thereof including the reasons therefor. In the absence of exceptions the initial decision shall constitute the final decision, subject to the provisions of paragraph (c) of this section.

(b) *Decisions on record or review by the reviewing authority.* Whenever a record is certified to the reviewing authority for decision or it reviews the decision of a hearing examiner pursuant to paragraph (a) or (c) of this section, the applicant or recipient shall be given reasonable opportunity to file with it briefs or other written statements of its contentions, and a copy of the final decision of the reviewing authority shall be given in writing to the applicant or recipient and to the complainant, if any.

(c) *Decisions on record where a hearing is waived.* Whenever a hearing is waived pursuant to § 80.9(a) the reviewing authority shall make its final decision on the record or refer the matter to a hearing examiner for an initial decision to be made on the record. A copy of such decision shall be given in writing to the applicant or recipient, and to the complainant, if any.

(d) *Rulings required.* Each decision of a hearing examiner or reviewing authority shall set forth a ruling on each finding, conclusion, or exception presented, and shall identify the requirement or requirements imposed by or pursuant to this part with which it is found that the applicant or recipient has failed to comply.

(e) *Review in certain cases by the Secretary.* If the Secretary has not personally made the final decision referred to in paragraphs (a), (b), or (c) of this section, a recipient or applicant or the counsel for the Department may request the Secretary to review a decision of the Reviewing Authority in accordance with rules of procedure issued by the responsible Department official. Such review is not a matter of right and shall be granted only where the Secretary determines there are special and important reasons therefor. The Secretary may grant or deny such request, in whole or in part. He may also review such a decision upon his own motion in accordance with rules of procedure issued by the responsible Department official. In the absence of a review under this paragraph, a final decision referred to in paragraphs (a), (b), (c) of this section shall become the final decision of the Department when the Secretary transmits it as such to Congressional committees with the report required under section 602 of the Act. Failure of an applicant or recipient to file an exception with the Reviewing Authority or to request review under this paragraph shall not be deemed a failure to exhaust administrative remedies for the the purpose of obtaining judicial review.

(f) *Content of orders.* The final decision may provide for suspension or termination of, or refusal to grant or continue Federal financial assistance, in whole or in part, to which this regulation applies, and may contain such terms, conditions, and other provisions as are consistent with and will effectuate the purposes of the Act and this regulation, including provisions designed to assure that no Federal financial assistance to which this regulation applies will thereafter be extended under such law or laws to the applicant or recipient determined by such decision to be in default in its performance of an assurance given by it pursuant to this regulation, or to have otherwise failed to comply with this regulation unless and until it corrects its noncompliance and satisfies the responsible Department official that it will fully comply with this regulation.

(g) *Post-termination proceedings.* (1) An applicant or recipient adversely affected by an order issued under paragraph (f) of this section shall be restored to full eligibility to receive Federal financial assistance if it satisfies the terms and conditions of that order for such eligibility or if it brings itself into compliance with this part and provides reasonable assurance that it will fully comply with this part. An elementary or secondary school or school system which is unable to file an assurance of compliance with § 80.3 shall be restored to full eligibility to receive Federal financial assistance, if it files a court order or a plan for desegregation which meets the requirements of § 80.4(c), and provides reasonable assurance that it will comply with the court order or plan.

(2) Any applicant or recipient adversely affected by an order entered pursuant to paragraph (f) of this section may at any time request the responsible Department official to restore fully its eligibility to receive Federal financial assistance. Any such request shall be supported by information showing that the appli-

cant or recipient has met the requirements of subparagraph (1) of this paragraph. If the responsible Department official determines that those requirements have been satisfied, he shall restore such eligibility.

(3) If the responsible Department official denies any such request, the applicant or recipient may submit a request for a hearing in writing, specifying why it believes such official to have been in error. It shall thereupon be given an expeditious hearing, with a decision on the record, in accordance with rules of procedure issued by the responsible Department official. The applicant or recipient will be restored to such eligibility if it proves at such hearing that it satisfied the requirements of subparagraph (1) of this paragraph. While proceedings under this paragraph are pending, the sanctions imposed by the order issued under paragraph (f) of this section shall remain in effect.

Appendix E

FAMILY EDUCATION AND PRIVACY ACT (BUCKLEY AMENDMENT)—FINAL REGULATIONS

Subpart A—General

Subpart B—Inspection and Review of Education Records

Subpart C—Amendment of Education Records

Subpart D—Disclosure of Personally Identifiable Information From Education Records

561

AUTHORITY: Sec. 438, Pub.L. 90–247, Title IV, as amended, 88 Stat.
571–574 (20 U.S.C. 1232g) unless otherwise noted.

Subpart A—General

§ 99.1   Applicability of Part

(a) This part applies to all educational agencies or institutions
to which funds are made available under any Federal [program
for which the U. S. Commissioner of Education has administrative responsibility, as specified by law or by delegation of authority pursuant to law.]

(b) This part does not apply to an educational agency or institution solely because students attending that nonmonetary agency
or institution receive benefits under one or more of the Federal
programs referenced in paragraph (a) of this section, if no funds
under those programs are made available to the agency or institution itself.

(c) For the purposes of this part, funds will be considered to
have been made available to an agency or institution when funds
under one or more of the programs referenced in paragraph (a)
of this section: (1) Are provided to the agency or institution by
grant, contract, subgrant, or subcontract, or   (2) are provided

to students attending the agency or institution and the funds may be paid to the agency or institution by those students for educational purposes, such as under the Basic Educational Opportunity Grants Program and the Guaranteed Student Loan Program (Titles IV–A–1 and IV–B, respectively, of the Higher Education Act of 1965, as amended).

(d) Except as otherwise specifically provided, this part applies to education records of students who are or have been in attendance at the educational agency or institution which maintains the records.

§ 99.2 Purpose

The purpose of this part is to set forth requirements governing the protection of privacy of parents and students under section 438 of the General Education Provisions Act, as amended.

§ 99.3 Definitions

As used in this Part:

"Act" means the General Education Provisions Act, Title IV of Pub.L. 90–247, as amended.

"Attendance" at an agency or institution includes, but is not limited to: (a) attendance in person and by correspondence, and (b) the period during which a person is working under a work-study program.

"Commissioner" means the U. S. Commissioner of Education.

"Directory information" includes the following information relating to a student: the student's name, address, telephone number, date and place of birth, major field of study, participation in officially recognized activities and sports, weight and height of members of athletic teams, dates of attendance, degrees and awards received, the most recent previous educational agency or institution attended by the student, and other similar information.

"Disclosure" means permitting access or the release, transfer, or other communication of education records of the student or the personally identifiable information contained therein, orally or in writing, or by electronic means, or by any other means to any party.

"Educational institution" or "educational agency or institution" means any public or private agency or institution which is the recipient of funds under any Federal program referenced in § 99.1(a). The term refers to the agency or institution recipient as a whole, including all of its components (such as schools or departments in a university) and shall not be read to refer to one or more of these components separate from that agency or institution.

"Education records" (a) means those records which: (1) Are directly related to a student, and (2) are maintained by an educational agency or institution or by a party acting for the agency or institution.

(b) The term does not include:

(1) Records of instructional, supervisory, and administrative personnel and educational personnel ancillary thereto which:

(i) Are in the sole possession of the maker thereof, and

(ii) Are not accessible or revealed to any other individual except a substitute. For the purpose of this definition, a "substitute" means an individual who performs on a temporary basis the duties of the individual who made the record, and does not refer to an individual who permanently succeeds the maker of the record in his or her position.

(2) Records of a law enforcement unit of an educational agency or institution which are:

(i) Maintained apart from the records described in paragraph (a) of this definition;

(ii) Maintained solely for law enforcement purposes, and

(iii) Not disclosed to individuals other than law enforcement officials of the same jurisdiction; *Provided,* That education records maintained by the educational agency or institution are not disclosed to the personnel of the law enforcement unit.

(3) (i) Records relating to an individual who is employed by an educational agency or institution which:

(A) Are made and maintained in the normal course of business;

(B) Relate exclusively to the individual in that individual's capacity as an employee, and

(C) Are not available for use for any other purpose.

(ii) This paragraph does not apply to records relating to an individual in attendance at the agency or institution who is employed as a result of his or her status as a student.

(4) Records relating to an eligible student which are:

(i) Created or maintained by a physician, psychiatrist, psychologist, or other recognized professional or paraprofessional acting in his or her professional or paraprofessional capacity, or assisting in that capacity;

(ii) Created, maintained, or used only in connection with the provision of treatment to the student, and

(iii) Not disclosed to anyone other than individuals providing the treatment; *Provided,* That the records can be personally reviewed by a physician or other appropriate professional of the student's choice. For the purpose of this definition, "treatment" does not include remedial educational activities or activities which are part of the program of instruction at the educational agency or institution.

(5) Records of an educational agency or institution which contain only information relating to a person after that person was no longer a student at the educational agency or institution. An example would be information collected by an educational agency or institution pertaining to the accomplishments of its alumni.

"Eligible student" means a student who has attained eighteen years of age, or is attending an institution of postsecondary education.

"Financial Aid", as used in § 99.31(a)(4), means a payment of funds provided to an individual (or a payment in kind of tangible or intangible property to the individual) which is conditioned on the individual's attendance at an educational agency or institution.

"Institution of postsecondary education" means an institution which provides education to students beyond the secondary school level; "secondary school level" means the educational level (not beyond grade 12) at which secondary education is provided, as determined under State law.

"Panel" means the body which will adjudicate cases under procedures set forth in §§ 99.65–99.67.

"Parent" includes a parent, a guardian, or an individual acting as a parent of a student in the absence of a parent or guardian. An educational agency or institution may presume the parent has the authority to exercise the rights inherent in the Act unless the agency or institution has been provided with evidence that there is a State law or court order governing such matters as divorce, separation or custody, or a legally binding instrument which provides to the contrary.

"Party" means an individual, agency, institution or organization.

"Personally identifiable" means that the data or information includes (a) the name of a student, the student's parent, or other family member, (b) the address of the student, (c) a personal identifier, such as the student's social security number or student number, (d) a list of personal characteristics which would make the student's identity easily traceable, or (e) other information which would make the student's identity easily traceable.

"Record" means any information or data recorded in any medium, including, but not limited to: handwriting, print, tapes, film, microfilm, and microfiche.

"Secretary" means the Secretary of the U. S. Department of Health, Education, and Welfare.

"Student" (a) includes any individual with respect to whom an educational agency or institution maintains education records.

(b) The term does not include an individual who has not been in attendance at an educational agency or institution. A person who has applied for admission to, but has never been in attendance at a component unit of an institution of postsecondary education (such as the various colleges or schools which comprise a university), even if that individual is or has been in attendance at another component unit of that institution of postsecondary education, is not considered to be a student with respect to the component to which an application for admission has been made.

§ 99.4   Student Rights

(a) For the purposes of this part, whenever a student has attained eighteen years of age, or is attending an institution of postsecondary education, the rights accorded to and the consent required of the parent of the student shall thereafter only be accorded to and required of the eligible student.

(b) The status of an eligible student as a dependent of his or her parents for the purposes of § 99.31(a)(8) does not otherwise affect the rights accorded to and the consent required of the eligible student by paragraph (a) of this section.

(c) Section 438 of the Act and the regulations in this part shall not be construed to preclude educational agencies or institutions from according to students rights in addition to those accorded to parents of students.

§ 99.5   Formulation of Institutional Policy and Procedures

(a) Each educational agency or institution shall, consistent with the minimum requirements of section 438 of the Act and this part, formulate and adopt a policy of—

(1) Informing parents of students or eligible students of their rights under § 99.6;

(2) Permitting parents of students or eligible students to inspect and review the education records of the student in accordance with § 99.11, including at least:

(i) A statement of the procedure to be followed by a parent or an eligible student who requests to inspect and review the education records of the student;

(ii) With an understanding that it may not deny access to an education record, a description of the circumstances in which the agency or institution feels it has a legitimate cause to deny a request for a copy of such records;

(iii) A schedule of fees for copies, and

(iv) A listing of the types and locations of education records maintained by the educational agency or institution and the titles and addresses of the officials responsible for those records;

(3) Not disclosing personally identifiable information from the education records of a student without the prior written consent of the parent of the student or the eligible student, except as otherwise permitted by §§ 99.31 and 99.37; the policy shall include, at least: (i) A statement of whether the educational agency or institution will disclose personally identifiable information from the education records of a student under § 99.31(a)(1) and, if so, a specification of the criteria for determining which parties are "school officials" and what the educational agency or institution considers to be a "legitimate educational interest", and (ii) a specification of the personally identifiable information to be designated as directory information under § 99.37;

(4) Maintaining the record of disclosures of personally identifiable information from the education records of a student required to be maintained by § 99.32, and permitting a parent or an eligible student to inspect that record;

(5) Providing a parent of the student or an eligible student with an opportunity to seek the correction of education records of the student through a request to amend the records or a hearing under Subpart C, and permitting the parent of a student or

an eligible student to place a statement in the education records of the student as provided in § 99.21(c);

(b) The policy required to be adopted by paragraph (a) of this section shall be in writing and copies shall be made available upon request to parents of students and to eligible students.

§ 99.6   Annual Notification of Rights

(a) Each educational agency or institution shall give parents of students in attendance or eligible students in attendance at the agency or institution annual notice by such means as are reasonably likely to inform them of the following:

(1) Their rights under section 438 of the Act, the regulations in this part, and the policy adopted under § 99.5; the notice shall also inform parents of students or eligible students of the locations where copies of the policy may be obtained; and

(2) The right to file complaints under § 99.63 concerning alleged failures by the educational agency or institution to comply with the requirements of section 438 of the Act and this part.

(b) Agencies and institutions of elementary and secondary education shall provide for the need to effectively notify parents of students identified as having a primary or home language other than English.

§ 99.7   Limitations on Waivers

(a) Subject to the limitations in this section and § 99.12, a parent of a student or a student may waive any of his or her rights under section 438 of the Act or this part. A waiver shall not be valid unless in writing and signed by the parent or student, as appropriate.

(b) An educational agency or institution may not require that a parent of a student or student waive his or her rights under section 438 of the Act or this part. This paragraph does not preclude an educational agency or institution from requesting such a waiver.

(c) An individual who is an applicant for admission to an institution of postsecondary education or is a student in attendance at an institution of postsecondary education may waive his or her right to inspect and review confidential letters and confidential statements of recommendation described in § 99.12(a)(3) except that the waiver may apply to confidential letters and statements only if: (1) The applicant or student is, upon request, notified of the names of all individuals providing the letters or statements; (2) the letters or statements are used only for the purpose for which they were originally intended, and (3) such waiver is not required by the agency or institution as a condition of admission to or receipt of any other service or benefit from the agency or institution.

(d) All waivers under paragraph (c) of this section must be executed by the individual, regardless of age, rather than by the parent of the individual.

(e) A waiver under this section may be made with respect to specified classes of: (1) Education records, and (2) persons or institutions.

(f) (1) A waiver under this section may be revoked with respect to any actions occurring after the revocation.

(2) A revocation under this paragraph must be in writing.

(3) If a parent of a student executes a waiver under this section, that waiver may be revoked by the student at any time after he or she becomes an eligible student.

§ 99.8 Fees

(a) An educational agency or institution may charge a fee for copies of education records which are made for the parents of students, students, and eligible students under section 438 of the Act and this part; *Provided,* That the fee does not effectively prevent the parents and students from exercising their right to inspect and review those records.

(b) An educational agency or institution may not charge a fee to search for or to retrieve the education records of a student.

Subpart B—Inspection and Review of Education Records

§ 99.11 Right to Inspect and Review Education Records

(a) Each educational agency or institution, except as may be provided by § 99.12, shall permit the parent of a student or an eligible student who is or has been in attendance at the agency or institution, to inspect and review the education records of the student. The agency or institution shall comply with a request within a reasonable period of time, but in no case more than 45 days after the request has been made.

(b) The right to inspect and review education records under paragraph (a) of this section includes:

(1) The right to a response from the educational agency or institution to reasonable requests for explanations and interpretations of the records; and

(2) The right to obtain copies of the records from the educational agency or institution where failure of the agency or institution to provide the copies would effectively prevent a parent or eligible student from exercising the right to inspect and review the education records.

(c) An educational agency or institution may presume that either parent of the student has authority to inspect and review the education records of the student unless the agency or institution has been provided with evidence that there is a legally binding instrument, or a State law or court order governing such matters as divorce, separation or custody, which provides to the contrary.

§ 99.12 Limitations on Right to Inspect and Review Education Records at the Postsecondary Level

(a) An institution of postsecondary education is not required by section 438 of the Act or this part to permit a student to inspect and review the following records:

(1) Financial records and statements of their parents or any information contained therein;

(2) Confidential letters and confidential statements of recommendation which were placed in the education records of a student prior to January 1, 1975; *Provided*, That:

(i) The letters and statements were solicited with a written assurance of confidentiality, or sent and retained with a documented understanding of confidentiality, and

(ii) The letters and statements are used only for the purposes for which they were specifically intended;

(3) Confidential letters of recommendation and confidential statements of recommendation which were placed in the education records of the student after January 1, 1975:

(i) Respecting admission to an educational institution;

(ii) Respecting an application for employment, or

(iii) Respecting the receipt of an honor or honorary recognition; *Provided*, That the student has waived his or her right to inspect and review those letters and statements of recommendation under § 99.7(c).

(b) If the education records of a student contain information on more than one student, the parent of the student or the eligible student may inspect and review or be informed of only the specific information which pertains to that student.

§ 99.13   Limitation on Destruction of Education Records

An educational agency or institution is not precluded by section 438 of the Act or this part from destroying education records, subject to the following exceptions:

(a) The agency or institution may not destroy any education records if there is an outstanding request to inspect and review them under § 99.11;

(b) Explanations placed in the education record under § 99.21 shall be maintained as provided in § 99.21 (d), and

(c) The record of access required under § 99.32 shall be maintained for as long as the education record to which it pertains is maintained.

Subpart C—Amendment of Education Records

§ 99.20   Request to Amend Education Records

(a) The parent of a student or an eligible student who believes that information contained in the education records of the student is inaccurate or misleading or violates the privacy or other rights of the student may request that the educational agency or institution which maintains the records amend them.

(b) The educational agency or institution shall decide whether to amend the education records of the student in accordance with the request within a reasonable period of time of receipt of the request.

(c) If the educational agency or institution decides to refuse to amend the education records of the student in accordance with the request it shall so inform the parent of the student or the eligible student of the refusal, and advise the parent or the eligible student of the right to a hearing under § 99.21.

§ 99.21   Right to a Hearing

(a) An educational agency or institution shall, on request, provide an opportunity for a hearing in order to challenge the content of a student's education records to insure that information in the education records of the student is not inaccurate, misleading or otherwise in violation of the privacy or other rights of students. The hearing shall be conducted in accordance with § 99.22.

(b) If, as a result of the hearing, the educational agency or institution decides that the information is inaccurate, misleading or otherwise in violation of the privacy or other rights of students, it shall amend the education records of the student accordingly and so inform the parent of the student or the eligible student in writing.

(c) If, as a result of the hearing, the educational agency or institution decides that the information is not inaccurate, misleading or otherwise in violation of the privacy or other rights of students, it shall inform the parent or eligible student of the right to place in the education records of the student a statement commenting upon the information in the education records and/or setting forth any reasons for disagreeing with the decision of the agency or institution.

(d) Any explanation placed in the education records of the student under paragraph (c) of this section shall:

(1) Be maintained by the educational agency or institution as part of the education records of the student as long as the record or contested portion thereof is maintained by the agency or institution, and

(2) If the education records of the student or the contested portion thereof is disclosed by the educational agency or institution to any party, the explanation shall also be disclosed to that party.

§ 99.22   Conduct of the Hearing

The hearing required to be held by § 99.21 (a) shall be conducted according to procedures which shall include at least the following elements:

(a) The hearing shall be held within a reasonable period of time after the educational agency or institution has received the request, and the parent of the student or the eligible student shall be given notice of the date, place and time reasonably in advance of the hearing;

(b) The hearing may be conducted by any party, including an official of the educational agency or institution, who does not have a direct interest in the outcome of the hearing;

(c) The parent of the student or the eligible student shall be afforded a full and fair opportunity to present evidence relevant to the issues raised under § 99.21, and may be assisted or represented by individuals of his or her choice at his or her own expense, including an attorney;

(d) The educational agency or institution shall make its decision in writing within a reasonable period of time after the conclusion of the hearing; and

(e) The decision of the agency or institution shall be based solely upon the evidence presented at the hearing and shall include a summary of the evidence and the reasons for the decision.

Subpart D—Disclosure of Personally Identifiable Information From Education Records

§ 99.30   Prior Consent for Disclosure Required

(a) (1) An educational agency or institution shall obtain the written consent of the parent of a student or the eligible student before disclosing personally identifiable information from the education records of a student, other than directory information, except as provided in § 99.31.

(2) Consent is not required under this section where the disclosure is to (i) the parent of a student who is not an eligible student, or (ii) the student himself or herself.

(b) Whenever written consent is required, an educational agency or institution may presume that the parent of the student or the eligible student giving consent has the authority to do so unless the agency or institution has been provided with evidence that there is a legally binding instrument, or a State law or court order governing such matters as divorce, separation or custody, which provides to the contrary.

(c) The written consent required by paragraph (a) of this section must be signed and dated by the parent of the student or the eligible student giving the consent and shall include:

(1) A specification of the records to be disclosed,

(2) The purpose or purposes of the disclosure, and

(3) The party or class of parties to whom the disclosure may be made.

(d) When a disclosure is made pursuant to paragraph (a) of this section, the educational agency or institution shall, upon request, provide a copy of the record which is disclosed to the parent of the student or the eligible student, and to the student who is not an eligible student if so requested by the student's parents.

§ 99.31 Prior Consent for Disclosure Not Required

(a) An educational agency or institution may disclose personally identifiable information from the education records of a student without the written consent of the parent of the student or the eligible student if the disclosure is—

(1) To other school officials, including teachers, within the educational institution or local educational agency who have been determined by the agency or institution to have legitimate educational interests;

(2) To officials of another school or school system in which the student seeks or intends to enroll, subject to the requirements set forth in § 99.34;

(3) Subject to the conditions set forth in § 99.35, to authorized representatives of:

(i) The Comptroller General of the United States,

(ii) The Secretary,

(iii) The Commissioner, the Director of the National Institute of Education, or the Assistant Secretary for Education, or

(iv) State educational authorities;

(4) In connection with financial aid for which a student has applied or which a student has received; *Provided*, That personally identifiable information from the education records of the student may be disclosed only as may be necessary for such purposes as:

(i) To determine the eligibility of the student for financial aid,

(ii) To determine the amount of the financial aid,

(iii) To determine the conditions which will be imposed regarding the financial aid, or

(iv) To enforce the terms or conditions of the financial aid;

(5) To State and local officials or authorities to whom information is specifically required to be reported or disclosed pursuant to State statute adopted prior to November 19, 1974. This subparagraph applies only to statutes which require that specific information be disclosed to State or local officials and does not apply to statutes which permit but do not require disclosure. Nothing in this paragraph shall prevent a State from further limiting the number or type of State or local officials to whom disclosures are made under this subparagraph;

(6) To organizations conducting studies for, or on behalf of, educational agencies or institutions for the purpose of developing, validating, or administering predictive tests, administering student aid programs, and improving instruction; *Provided*, That the studies are conducted in a manner which will not permit the personal identification of students and their parents by individuals other than representatives of the organization and the information will be destroyed when no longer needed for the purposes for which the study was conducted; the term "organizations" includes, but is not limited to, Federal, State and local agencies, and independent organizations;

(7) To accrediting organizations in order to carry out their accrediting functions;

(8) To parents of a dependent student, as defined in section 152 of the Internal Revenue Code of 1954;

(9) To comply with a judicial order or lawfully issued subpoena; *Provided*, That the educational agency or institution makes a reasonable effort to notify the parent of the student or the eligible student of the order or subpoena in advance of compliance therewith; and

(10) To appropriate parties in a health or safety emergency subject to the conditions set forth in § 99.36.

(b) This section shall not be construed to require or preclude disclosure of any personally identifiable information from the education records of a student by an educational agency or institution to the parties set forth in paragraph (a) of this section.

§ 99.32   Record of Disclosures Required to be Maintained

(a) An educational agency or institution shall for each request for and each disclosure of personally identifiable information from the education records of a student, maintain a record kept with the education records of the student which indicates:

(1) The parties who have requested or obtained personally identifiable information from the education records of the student, and

(2) The legitimate interests these parties had in requesting or obtaining the information.

(b) Paragraph (a) of this section does not apply to disclosures to a parent of a student or an eligible student, disclosures pursuant to the written consent of a parent of a student or an eligible student when the consent is specific with respect to the party or parties to whom the disclosure is to be made, disclosures to school officials under § 99.31(a)(1), or to disclosures of directory information under § 99.37.

(c) The record of disclosures may be inspected;

(1) By the parent of the student or the eligible student,

(2) By the school official and his or her assistants who are responsible for the custody of the records, and

(3) For the purpose of auditing the recordkeeping procedures of the educational agency or institution by the parties authorized in, and under the conditions set forth in § 99.31(a)(1) and (3).

§ 99.33 Limitation on Redisclosure

(a) An educational agency or institution may disclose personally identifiable information from the education records of a student only on the condition that the party to whom the information is disclosed will not disclose the information to any other party without the prior written consent of the parent of the student or the eligible student, except that the personally identifiable information which is disclosed to an institution, agency or organization may be used by its officers, employees and agents, but only for the purposes for which the disclosure was made.

(b) Paragraph (a) of this section does not preclude an agency or institution from disclosing personally identifiable information under § 99.31 with the understanding that the information will be redisclosed to other parties under that section; *Provided,* That the recordkeeping requirements of § 99.32 are met with respect to each of those parties.

(c) An educational agency or institution shall, except for the disclosure of directory information under § 99.37, inform the party to whom a disclosure is made of the requirement set forth in paragraph (a) of this section.

§ 99.34 Conditions for Disclosure to Officials of Other Schools and School Systems

(a) An educational agency or institution transferring the education records of a student pursuant to § 99.31(a)(2) shall:

(1) Make a reasonable attempt to notify the parent of the student or the eligible student of the transfer of the records at the last known address of the parent or eligible student, except:

(i) When the transfer of the records is initiated by the parent or eligible student at the sending agency or institution, or

(ii) When the agency or institution includes a notice in its policies and procedures formulated under § 99.5 that it forwards education records on request to a school in which a student seeks or intends to enroll; the agency or institution does not have to provide any further notice of the transfer;

(2) Provide the parent of the student or the eligible student, upon request, with a copy of the education records which have been transferred; and

(3) Provide the parent of the student or the eligible student, upon request, with an opportunity for a hearing under Subpart C of this part.

(b) If a student is enrolled in more than one school, or receives services from more than one school, the schools may disclose information from the education records of the student to each other without obtaining the written consent of the parent of the student or the eligible student; *Provided*, That the disclosure meets the requirements of paragraph (a) of this section.

§ 99.35 Disclosure to Certain Federal and State Officials for Federal Program Purposes

(a) Nothing in section 438 of the Act or this part shall preclude authorized representatives of officials listed in § 99.31(a)(3) from having access to student and other records which may be necessary in connection with the audit and evaluation of Federally supported education programs, or in connection with the enforcement of or compliance with the Federal legal requirements which relate to these programs.

(b) Except when the consent of the parent of a student or an eligible student has been obtained under § 99.30, or when the collection of personally identifiable information is specifically authorized by Federal law, any data collected by officials listed in § 99.31(a)(3) shall be protected in a manner which will not permit the personal identification of students and their parents by other than those officials, and personally identifiable data shall be destroyed when no longer needed for such audit, evaluation, or enforcement of or compliance with Federal legal requirements.

§ 99.36 Conditions for Disclosure in Health and Safety Emergencies

(a) An educational agency or institution may disclose personally identifiable information from the education records of a student to appropriate parties in connection with an emergency if knowledge of the information is necessary to protect the health or safety of the student or other individuals.

(b) The factors to be taken into account in determining whether personally identifiable information from the education records of a student may be disclosed under this section shall include the following:

(1) The seriousness of the threat to the health or safety of the student or other individuals;

(2) The need for the information to meet the emergency;

(3) Whether the parties to whom the information is disclosed are in a position to deal with the emergency; and

(4) The extent to which time is of the essence in dealing with the emergency.

(c) Paragraph (a) of this section shall be strictly construed.

§ 99.37 Conditions for Disclosure of Directory Information

(a) An educational agency or institution may disclose personally identifiable information from the education records of a student who is in attendance at the institution or agency if that information has been designated as directory information (as defined in § 99.3) under paragraph (c) of this section.

(b) An educational agency or institution may disclose directory information from the education records of an individual who is no longer in attendance at the agency or institution without following the procedures under paragraph (c) of this section.

(c) An educational agency or institution which wishes to designate directory information shall give public notice of the following:

(1) The categories of personally identifiable information which the institution has designated as directory information;

(2) The right of the parent of the student or the eligible student to refuse to permit the designation of any or all of the categories of personally identifiable information with respect to that student as directory information; and

(3) The period of time within which the parent of the student or the eligible student must inform the agency or institution in writing that such personally identifiable information is not to be designated as directory information with respect to that student.

Subpart E—Enforcement

§ 99.60　Office and Review Board

(a) The Secretary is required to establish or designate an office and a review board under section 438(g) of the Act. The office will investigate, process, and review violations, and complaints which may be filed concerning alleged violations of the provisions of section 438 of the Act and the regulations in this part. The review board will adjudicate cases referred to it by the office under the procedures set forth in §§ 99.65–99.67.

(b) The following is the address of the office which has been designated under paragraph (a) of this section: The Family Educational Rights and Privacy Act Office (FERPA), Department of Health, Education, and Welfare, 330 Independence Ave. SW., Washington, D. C. 20201.

§ 99.61　Conflict with State or Local Law

An educational agency or institution which determines that it cannot comply with the requirements of section 438 of the Act or of this part because a State or local law conflicts with the provisions of section 438 of the Act or the regulations in this part shall so advise the office designated under § 99.60(b) within 45 days of any such determination, giving the text and legal citation of the conflicting law.

§ 99.62　Reports and Records

Each educational agency or institution shall (a) submit reports in the form and containing such information as the Office of the Review Board may require to carry out their functions under this part, and (b) keep the records and afford access thereto as the Office or the Review Board may find necessary to assure the correctness of those reports and compliance with the provisions of section 438 of the Act and this part.

§ 99.63　Complaint Procedure

(a) Complaints regarding violations of rights accorded parents and eligible students by section 438 of the Act or the regulations in this part shall be submitted to the Office in writing.

(b) (1) The Office will notify each complainant and the educational agency or institution against which the violation has been alleged, in writing, that the complaint has been received.

(2) The notification to the agency or institution under paragraph (b)(1) of this section shall include the substance of the alleged violation and the agency or institution shall be given an opportunity to submit a written response.

(c)(1) The Office will investigate all timely complaints received to determine whether there has been a failure to comply with the provisions of section 438 of the Act or the regulations in this part, and may permit further written or oral submissions by both parties.

(2) Following its investigation the Office will provide written notification of its findings and the basis for such findings, to the complainant and the agency or institution involved.

(3) If the Office finds that there has been a failure to comply, it will include in its notification under paragraph (c)(2) of this section, the specific steps which must be taken by the agency or educational institution to bring the agency or institution into compliance. The notification shall also set forth a reasonable period of time, given all of the circumstances of the case, for the agency or institution to voluntarily comply.

(d) If the educational agency or institution does not come into compliance within the period of time set under paragraph (c)(3) of this section, the matter will be referred to the Review Board for a hearing under §§ 99.64–99.67, inclusive.

§ 99.64   Termination of Funding

If the Secretary, after reasonable notice and opportunity for a hearing by the Review Board, (1) finds that an educational agency or institution has failed to comply with the provisions of section 438 of the Act, or the regulations in this part, and (2) determines that compliance cannot be secured by voluntary means, he shall issue a decision, in writing, that no funds under any of the Federal programs referenced in § 99.1(a) shall be made available to that educational agency or institution (or, at the Secretary's discretion, to the unit of the educational agency or institution affected by the failure to comply) until there is no longer any such failure to comply.

§ 99.65   Hearing Procedures

(a) *Panels.* The Chairman of the Review Board shall designate Hearing Panels to conduct one or more hearings under § 99.64. Each Panel shall consist of not less than three members of the Review Board. The Review Board may, at its discretion, sit for any hearing or class of hearings. The Chairman of the Review Board shall designate himself or any other member of a Panel to serve as Chairman.

(b) *Procedural rules.* (1) With respect to hearings involving, in the opinion of the Panel, no dispute as to a material fact the resolution of which would be materially assisted by oral testimony, the Panel shall take appropriate steps to afford to each party to the proceeding an opportunity for presenting his case at the option of the Panel (i) in whole or in part in writing or (ii) in an informal conference before the Panel which shall afford each party: (A) Sufficient notice of the issues to be considered (where such notice has not previously been afforded); and (B) an opportunity to be represented by counsel.

(2) With respect to hearings involving a dispute as to a material fact the resolution of which would be materially assisted by oral testimony, the Panel shall afford each party an opportunity, which shall include, in addition to provisions required by subparagraph (1)(ii) of this paragraph, provisions designed to assure to each party the following:

(i) An opportunity for a record of the proceedings;

(ii) An opportunity to present witnesses on the party's behalf; and

(iii) An opportunity to cross-examine other witnesses either orally or through written interrogatories.

§ 99.66 Hearing Before Panel or a Hearing Officer

A hearing pursuant to § 99.65(b)(2) shall be conducted, as determined by the Panel Chairman, either before the Panel or a hearing officer. The hearing officer may be (a) one of the members of the Panel or (b) a nonmember who is appointed as a hearing examiner under 5 U.S.C. 3105.

§ 99.67 Initial Decision; Final Decision

(a) The Panel shall prepare an initial written decision, which shall include findings of fact and conclusions based thereon. When a hearing is conducted before a hearing officer alone, the hearing officer shall separately find and state the facts and conclusions which shall be incorporated in the initial decision prepared by the Panel.

(b) Copies of the initial decision shall be mailed promptly by the Panel to each party (or to the party's counsel), and to the Secretary with a notice affording the party an opportunity to submit written comments thereon to the Secretary within a specified reasonable time.

(c) The initial decision of the Panel transmitted to the Secretary shall become the final decision of the Secretary, unless, within 25 days after the expiration of the time for receipt of written comments, the Secretary advises the Review Board in writing of his determination to review the decision.

(d) In any case in which the Secretary modifies or reverses the initial decision of the Panel, he shall accompany that action with a written statement of the grounds for the modification or reversal, which shall promptly be filed with the Review Board.

(e) Review of any initial decision by the Secretary shall be based upon the decision, the written record, if any, of the Panel's proceedings, and written comments or oral arguments by the parties, or by their counsel, to the proceedings.

(f) No decision under this section shall become final until it is served upon the educational agency or institution involved or its attorney.

Appendix F

EDUCATION AMENDMENTS OF 1976
PUBLIC LAW 94–482

FINAL REGULATIONS
STUDENT CONSUMER INFORMATION

(Federal Register, Vol. 42, No. 231)

AUTHORITY: Sec. 493A of Title IV of the Higher Education Act of 1965 as added by sec. 131 of Pub.L. 94–482, 90 Stat. 2148–2149 (20 U.S.C. 1088b–1), unless otherwise noted.

§ 178.1 Purpose and Scope

This part establishes rules for the dissemination of information required by section 493A of the Higher Education Act of 1965. It applies to any institution or school which receives a payment under section 411(d), 428(e), or 493 of that Act (20 U.S.C. 1070 a(d), 1078(e) and 1088b). Section 411(d) refers to payments made to an institution of higher education under the Basic Grant Program. Section 428(e) refers to payments to an eligible institution under the Guaranteed Student Loan Program. Section 493 refers to payments received by an institution of higher education because of its participation in the Supplemental Educational Opportunity Grant, College Work-Study, or National Direct Student Loan Programs and to payments received by an area vocational school because of its participation in the College Work-Study Program.

§ 178.2 Definitions

As used in this part: (a) "Act" means the Higher Education Act of 1965, as amended.

(b) "Administrative cost allowance" means the payment to any institution pursuant to section 411(d), 428(e), or 493 of the Act.

(c) "Award period" means the period of time between July 1 of one year and June 30 of the subsequent year.

(d) "Institution" means an institution of higher education as defined in section 1201(a) of the Act, a proprietary institution of higher education as defined in section 491(b) of the Act, an eligible institution as defined in section 435 of the Act, or an area vocational school as defined in section 195(2) of the Vocational Education Act of 1963.

(e) "Prospective student" means any individual who has contacted an institution requesting information for the purpose of enrolling at that institution.

§ 178.3 Information Dissemination Requirements

Each institution which receives an administrative cost allowance for any award period shall, for that award period, (a) prepare material, if necessary, on the topics set forth in § 178.4 and (b) disseminate that information, or any requested portions of that information, to enrolled or prospective students who request all or part of that material.

§ 178.4 Information Dissemination Topics

The information to be prepared and disseminated to students includes:

(a)(1) A description of all student financial aid programs available to students who enroll at that institution that provide assistance to students to meet the cost of attending that institution. These programs include the Guaranteed Student Loan type program and programs for which the primary criterion of student eligibility is demonstrated financial need for the assistance because of the financial condition of the student or the student's family.

(2) For purposes of compliance with this section, the institution must describe:

(i) Programs authorized under Title IV of the Act.

(ii) Programs administered by the State in which the institution is located, and

(iii) The institution's own programs of student financial aid. The institution may, at its option, describe its own programs by listing them by general categories.

(3) The institution must describe for these programs the procedures and forms for applying for such aid, the student eligibility requirements, the criteria for selecting recipients from the group of eligible applicants, and the criteria for determining the amount of a student's award;

(b) A statement of the rights and responsibilities of students receiving financial aid under the Basic Educational Opportunity Grant, Supplemental Educational Opportunity Grant, College Work-Study, National Direct Student Loan, or Guaranteed Student Loan Programs. This information includes:

(1) Criteria for continued eligibility for each program;

(2) Criteria for determining that a student is in good standing and maintaining satisfactory progress in his course of study, as required by Section 497(e)(1) of the Act for the purposes of receiving financial aid payments, and the criteria by which a student who has failed to maintain a satisfactory progress or good standing may reestablish his eligibility for payment;

(3) The means by which payment of awards will be made to students and the frequency of such payments;

(4) The terms of any loan received by a student as part of his student financial aid and sample loan repayment schedules for sample loans; and

(5) The general conditions and terms applicable to any employment provided to a student as part of his financial aid;

(c) The cost of attending the institution, including tuition and fees, books and supplies, estimates of typical room and board and transportation costs for students living on-campus, off-campus, or at home, and any additional cost of the program in which the student is enrolled or expresses a specific interest:

(d) The refund policy of the institution for the return of unearned tuition and fees or other refundable portion of cost paid to that institution as described in paragraph (c) of this section;

(e) The academic program of the institution, including the current degree programs and other educational and training programs; the instructional, laboratory, and other physical facilities which relate to the academic program; and the faculty and other instructional personnel;

(f) Data regarding student retention which takes into account the enrollment pattern of that institution, including a description of the types of students that were included and excluded in compiling the retention information;

(g) The number and percentage of students completing the program in which a student is enrolled or expresses interest, if such data are available at the institution; and

(h) The titles of persons designated under § 178.5 and information regarding how and where such persons may be contacted.

§ 178.5   Availability of Employees for Information Dissemination Purposes

(a) Except as provided in paragraph (b) of this section, each institution which receives an administrative cost allowance for any award period shall designate, for that award period, an employee or group of employees who shall be available on a full-time basis to assist students or prospective students in obtaining the information specified in § 178.4. If the institution designates one person, that person shall be available, upon reasonable notice, to any interested student or prospective student throughout the normal administrative working hours of that institution. If more than one person is designated, their combined schedules shall be arranged in such a manner that at least one of them is available, upon reasonable notice, throughout the normal administrative working hours of that institution.

(b) *Waiver.* (1) The Commissioner may waive the requirement set out in paragraph (a) of this section for an institution that submits a timely application for the waiver when the total enrollment, or the portion of the enrollment participating in student financial aid programs authorized under Title IV of the Act (the Basic Educational Opportunity Grant, Supplemental Educational Opportunity Grant, College Work-Study, National Direct Student Loan, Guaranteed Student Loan, and State Student Incentive Grant Programs), is too small to necessitate the availability of an employee or group of employees on a full-time basis. In determining whether an institution's total enrollment or the number of recipients of Title IV assistance is too small, the Commissioner will consider whether there will be an insufficient demand for information dissemination services among its students or prospective students to necessitate the full-time availability of an employee or group of employees.

(2) The granting of a waiver under subparagraph (1) of this paragraph does not exempt an institution from designating a

specific employee or group of employees to carry out the provisions of this section.

§ 178.6   Use of Funds

Any institution which receives an administrative cost allowance for any award period shall first use such funds to carry out the provisions of this part for that award period.   If any funds remain, the institution shall use those funds for other costs of administering the student financial aid programs authorized under Title IV of the Act for that award period.

§ 178.7   Compliance Procedures and Records

(a) *Retention of records.*   Each institution which receives an administrative cost allowance for any award period shall keep intact and accessible all records relating to the receipt and expenditure of Federal funds in accordance with Section 434(a), General Education Provisions Act (20 U.S.C. 1232c), including all accounting records and related original and supporting documents that substantiate costs, for a period of five years after the close of the award period for which the payments were received, except as provided in paragraph (b) of this section.

(b) *Audit questions.*   The records involved in any claim or expenditure which has been questioned by audit shall be further retained until resolution of any such audit questions: *Provided, however,* That records need not be retained if they relate to a payment with respect to which actions by the United States to recover for diversion of Federal funds are barred by the statute of limitations in 20 U.S.C. 2415(b).

(c) *Audit and examination.*   The Secretary of Health, Education, and Welfare and the Comptroller General of the United States, or any of their duly authorized representatives, shall have access, for the purpose of audit and examination, to the records specified in paragraph (a) of this section and to any other pertinent documents, paper, and records of the institution.

§ 178.8   Audits—Non-Federal

(a) A comprehensive audit of an institution's transactions relating to its use of administrative cost allowances received shall be performed by the institution or at the institution's direction to determine, at a minimum, the fiscal integrity of financial transactions and reports and whether such transactions are in compliance with applicable laws and regulations.   Such audits shall be performed in accordance with the Department of Health, Education, and Welfare "Audit Guide" for student financial aid programs. If the institution participates in the Supplemental Educational Opportunity Grant, College Work-Study, or National Direct Student Loan Programs, then the audit required by this part shall be included as part of an audit performed for any of those programs. If the institution does not participate in any of the above three programs, then the audit required by this part shall be performed at least once every two years.

(b) Audit report shall be submitted to the HEW Audit Agency at the regional office of the Department of Health, Education, and Welfare serving the region in which the institution is located for its review. The Audit Agency and the Commissioner shall also be given access to records or other documents as may be necessary to review the results of such audits.

Appendix G

GLOSSARY

The terms listed are defined in the senses in which they are used in this book. They may have additional meanings in other areas of the law or subject matters.

Ab Initio: from the beginning.

Accommodating Neutrality: a position which permits religion to exist without sponsorship and without interference.

Action: a legal proceeding (strictly speaking, at common law) to enforce one's rights against another.

Ad Hoc: for this special purpose.

Administrative Law: orders, regulations and individual decisions by the administrative agencies that are part of the executive branch of government, generally based on statutes (spelling out statutory requirements) and subject to court review.

Adversary System: characteristic of American judicial system in that courtroom is viewed as combat arena where contending parties attempt to convince the court of the righteousness of their respective claims; based on theory that truth is produced by the clash of contending views.

Advisory Opinion: an opinion rendered by a court as to the constitutional or legal effect of a bill, statute or regulation when no actual case is before it. However, the Supreme Court of the United States (and therefore lower Federal courts) refuses to render such opinions on the ground that it would be engaging in nonjudicial activity. When rendered by state courts, advisory opinions generally have no binding force. See declaratory judgment.

Affidavit: a written statement of facts that a person makes voluntarily and confirms by oath or affirmation before an officer having authority to administer the oath, such as a notary public.

Affirm: to declare that a judgment, decree or order by a lower court is valid and legally correct even if the reasoning behind the judgment is rejected.

589

Affirmative Action: a term that apparently originated in the 1930s and is contained in the National Labor Relations Act designed to protect union employees. At present, in hiring and promoting employees and admitting students, special efforts are suggested in regard to minorities and women. However, the precise meaning, requirements and implications are far from clear.

A Fortiori: for the more compelling reason; all the more.

Allegation: a statement by a party to a legal controversy the truth of which he proposes to prove in court.

Amicus Curiae: a friend of the court. When a case raises questions of concern to people other than the parties to the case, these individuals or organizations sometimes request permission from the court to file briefs and even to present oral arguments raising issues that might be different from those raised by the parties. These are called friend of the court briefs and appearances because they enable the court to reach its decision on broader grounds or with a wider perspective than that presented by the actual parties to the case. The plural is *"amici curiae."*

Appellant: the party who loses a case in a lower court and takes the case to the next level of courts for review. The opposing party is called the *"appellee"* or *"respondent."*

Appellate Court: a court of appeal (not a court of original jurisdiction, i. e., where the case is first heard). The appeals court—e. g., a United States Circuit Court of Appeal—consists of three or more judges sitting to review decisions of lower courts by studying the records of the litigation, trial, and previous appeals, reading briefs, and hearing oral arguments by the attorneys for the parties, but rarely hearing any live testimony themselves. The United States Supreme Court is the ultimate court of appeal; there is one level of intermediate appellate courts in the federal system, and there are one or more levels of intermediate appellate courts in each of the fifty state systems.

Arbitrary: autocratic; without adequate determining principle; nonrational; careless; capricious.

Assumption of Risk: plaintiff voluntarily exposes himself to an obvious and known risk; one of the primary defenses to a negligence action.

Balancing Doctrine: theory that no rights or freedoms are absolute, but must be weighed against competing interests.

Breach of the Peace: the misdemeanor of disturbing the public order and tranquillity by an act of violence, or by an act inciting to violence.

Brief: a statement written by an attorney for one side (or by an amicus curiae) setting forth the facts and arguments so as to convince the judge or judges to decide in the favor of his side. A brief may be short, but it often belies its name.

Case: any suit, action, or other proceeding in law or equity contested before a court.

Case Law: the body of law developed by case decisions, as opposed to statutory or administrative law. See also "common law."

Cause of Action: the door through which a party bringing a lawsuit passes to gain a full (judicial) review of his allegations; it must contain all the elements necessary to justify a court in passing judgment on the dispute.

Certiorari: a plea (based on a petition to an appellate court), and an order when granted, for a lower court to "certify" its record of a particular case and to send it up to the appellate court for review. The appellate court may grant or deny certiorari (agree or refuse to review the case) as it sees fit, without stating reasons.

Civil Rights: those rights guaranteed to the individual against encroachment by his government; in part found enumerated in the national and state constitutions and include substantive rights, such as freedom of religion, speech, press and assembly, and procedural rights, such as protection against punishment without a fair trial, as well as equal protection guarantees against discriminatory treatment by government. These rights also include positive legislation such as the Civil Rights Acts of 1866, 1870, 1871, 1875, 1957 and 1964 guaranteeing certain liberties to the individual against encroachment by other individuals or groups.

Civil Suit: a legal proceeding started by one party against another to enforce a right, to protect property, or to redress or prevent a wrong. Judgment for the plaintiff requires the defendant to do an act or pay money in damages rather than to be imprisoned or fined as in a criminal case.

Class Action Suit: a lawsuit filed by a plaintiff not only to right a wrong done by the defendant to him individually but also on behalf of everyone in the same situation or class as the plaintiff in regard to the defendant and his actions.

Clear and Present Danger: the modern criterion for determining the validity of laws or acts restricting freedom of expression; i. e., whether the danger of a particular expression to public interest outweighs the interest in free expression (*imminency* of danger is an essential requirement).

Common law: the continually developing law through court decisions as distinguished from statutes and regulations.

Complainant: a party who applies to a court or administrative agency for legal redress; one who instigates an action or accuses a person of some unlawful act.

Complaint: the filing of allegations in any civil lawsuit stating the cause of action and describing the facts requiring a judicial decision.

Concurring Opinion: an opinion filed by an appellate judge or justice that agrees with the conclusions of the majority decision but differs on the reasoning.

Concurrent Jurisdiction: authority shared by two or more courts to deal with the same subject matter. When federal and state courts have concurrent jurisdiction the parties to the dispute may usually decide where a case is brought.

Concurrent Powers: powers shared by the national and state governments.

Confession of Judgment: an accused party who does not plead guilty but, by failure to appear at the hearing upon proper notification, implies acceptance of the hearing body's judgment *in absentia.*

Contempt of Court: any intentional act likely to embarrass, hinder or obstruct a judge in the administration of justice or to lessen his authority or dignity. A contemptuous act may be committed in or out of the presence of a judge by a party, a witness, an attorney, a member of the audience, or some other person.

Contract: a legally enforceable agreement between two or more parties under the terms of which the parties agree to perform some act or refrain from performing some act.

Contributory Negligence: negligence of the plaintiff which, combined with the negligence of the defendant, was the proximate cause of the injury at issue; one of the primary defenses to a negligence action.

Constructive Knowledge: a legal concept charging a person with knowledge he did not have on the theory that he should have had it.

De Facto: a condition existing in fact but not in law; for example, racial segregation in public schools existing in fact (as in the North and West) although not required by law (as in parts of the South before 1954).

Declaratory Judgment: a judicial declaration, in an actual controversy, of the existing rights of parties under a statute, regulation, contract or other document, without executory process granting relief, but binding upon the parties. It is not necessary to show that any wrong has been done, as in an action for damages; or that any is immediately threatened as in an injunction proceeding. In most states, and in the federal courts since 1934, this remedy has been made available by statute as a means of ascertaining the rights of parties without expensive litigation.

Defamation: words written or spoken concerning another, tending to the injury of a person's reputation, for which an action for damages will lie. See also, "libel" and "slander."

De Jure: a condition existing according to law.

De Minimus: insufficient injury to support a cause of action.

Demurrer: allegation of a defendant admitting that matters of fact alleged in complaint are true, but that they are insufficient for plaintiff to proceed upon or to oblige defendant to answer.

Dicta: remarks made by a judge that are not technically part of a decision and/or court order; not binding on other judges but nevertheless often studied carefully. (The singular is "*dictum*.")

Dissenting Opinion: a judge's explicit disagreement with the majority decision.

Ejusdem Generis: of the same kind, class, or nature.

Enumerated Powers: powers specifically granted to the national government by the Constitution.

Equal Protection: requirement of the Fourteenth Amendment that classification of persons be reasonably adapted to the accomplishment of proper governmental purposes.

Equity: a branch of remedial justice following principles of fairness and reason in circumstances where the common law is unable to ensure justice. For example, under the common law, a person whose property rights are about to be injured has no choice but to wait until the injury has taken place and then to seek money damages. But the injury may do irreparable harm for which money damages cannot provide adequate compensation. Accordingly, under equity, a person may go to a judge, show why the common-law remedy is inadequate, and ask for equitable relief to prevent an act that threatens irreparable harm. In equity cases there are no juries, and violations of decrees—e. g., a specific performance order or an injunction—are punished as contempt of court.

Evidence: legally admissible information submitted to a court or investigating body orally, in writing, or as an exhibit, in order to determine the truth concerning any matter at issue.

Ex Cathedra: from the chair; by the authority of one's position.

Executive Order: a rule or regulation issued by the President or some administrative authority under his direction for the purpose of interpreting, implementing or giving administrative effect to a provision of the Constitution or of some law or treaty.

Ex Parte: pertaining to a proceeding where there is no adverse party or where the adverse party is absent or without opportunity to be heard.

Ex Post Facto: literally, "after the fact"; a retroactive criminal law which is unconstitutional when it declares an act a crime which was not a crime when it was done; or, with retrospective effect, increases a penalty; or alters the rules of evidence to the disadvantage of an accused person; or in other ways decreases the protection which the law previously provided.

Ex Rel: legal proceedings instituted in the name and behalf of the government, but on the information and at the instigation of an individual who has a private interest in the matter.

Felony: a serious crime so classified in law and thus distinguished from a misdemeanor; punishable by incarceration in a state or federal prison (usually for more than one year) and/or a fine.

Finding: a conclusion of fact certified after inquiry by a judicial or other body.

Fraud: an act characterized by deceit, cunning, or misrepresentation.

Full Faith and Credit: clause in Constitution (Art. IV) requiring that each state recognize civil judgments rendered by courts of other states.

Fundamental Right: any right explicitly or implicitly guaranteed by the Constitution. The "strict scrutiny" test applies whenever a classification burdens or affects a fundamental right.

Grant-In-Aid: national funds made available to states who meet certain conditions.

Hearsay: evidence not coming from the personal knowledge of the witness, but merely repeating what he has heard someone else say.

Holding: a determination of a question of law. See also "finding."

In Camera: in private.

Implied Powers: powers that by inference belong to the national government as a result of its enumerated powers; e. g., Congressional power to investigate is implied from its enumerated power to legislate.

Inherent Powers: undelegated powers belonging to government by virtue of its existence.

Injunction: an order issued by a court of equity commanding a person to do, or to refrain from doing, a particular act.

In Loco Parentis: literally, "in place of the parent," having full responsibility for a child in the parent's absence.

In Re: in the matter of; concerning. When used in the title of a case it merely designates that there are not adversary parties.

Inter Alia: among other things.

In Toto: entirely; in full.

Invidious Discrimination: a maligning or vilifying classification of a minority group; a classification that stamps the mark of inferiority upon a particular racial or ethnic group.

Judgment: an authoritative determination of the legal rights and duties of the parties to a controversy usually rendered by a court.

Judicial Review: the authority of any court to hold a specific enactment of a legislative body or a particular act of an administrative official to be unconstitutional and hence unenforceable.

Jurisdiction: the authority of a court to hear and decide cases within a defined geographic area and/or concerning particular subject matters or parties. See also "concurrent" and "original jurisdiction."

Jurisprudence: the science of philosophy of law; the principles of law and legal relations.

Justiciability: the nature of a question that makes it proper for a court to decide it.

Liable: responsible, accountable, answerable, chargeable, compellable to compensate or make restitution.

Libel: an untrue statement deliberately made in writing, picture or effigy that injures the reputation of another person.

Litigant: a party to a lawsuit.

Litigation: the formal contesting of legal issues; a lawsuit.

Majority Opinion: a statement of the reasons for a decision agreed to by a majority of the appellate court judges when the court is not unanimous. If the majority judges disagree on the reasons, they usually write separate concurring opinions.

Malfeasance: the performance of an illegal act, especially on the part of a public official.

Malice: the intentional performance of a wrongful act without just cause and with an intent to inflict injury or with reckless disregard of the harmful effect.

Malpractice: an offense against law which consists of ignorant or wrongful practice of a professional resulting in an injury to his client or patient.

Malum In Se: an act inherently wrong and essentially evil in itself; i. e., immoral in its nature.

Malum Prohibitum: an act which is wrong because prohibited; i. e., an act which is not inherently immoral but becomes so because its commission is prohibited by law.

Mandamus: a writ issued by a court against a public officer requiring him to perform a nondiscretionary public duty.

Minority Opinion: statement of the reasons given by a majority of appellate court judges who do not agree with the majority opinion. If the minority judges do not agree on the reasons for their disapproval, they usually write separate dissenting opinions.

Misdemeanor: a minor criminal offense not serious enough to constitute a felony.

Misfeasance: the performance of a lawful act in an improper or illegal manner, to the detriment of another person.

Mootness: a concept directly related to Article III of the Constitution which allows federal courts to decide only "cases" and "controversies"; i. e., for a plaintiff to have "standing" and an issue to have "justiciability," the case must present a "live" issue. Hence, if a party once had a real and live controversy but events have changed the situation so that there is no longer a sufficient injury at the time the case is before a federal court, the court will not decide any of the issues the case presents because it has become "moot." See also "justiciability" and "standing."

Nexus: a connection that must be found between an alleged wrongful act and an alleged resultant injury. See also "state action."

Nolens Volens: whether willing or unwilling; consenting or not.

Nonfeasance: an unreasonable failure to perform some lawful act.

Non Sequitur: it does not follow; a fallacious conclusion.

No-Preference: a contention that government may aid religion and religious activities as long as no preference is shown in its support to different religions and creeds; a theory that has been unequivocally rejected by the Supreme Court. See also accommodating neutrality and wall-of-separation.

Obscenity: constitutionally unprotected expression; each of the foregoing elements—prurient appeal, patent offensiveness and lack of social value—must be viewed in light of contemporary community standards. Obscenity is ultimately a question of law and since its determination has constitutional ramifications, the Supreme Court stands as the ultimate arbiter of the issue. Thus, when a public college regulates expression for lesser reasons than obscenity, it must be acting to prevent disruption. See also "substantial disruption and material interference."

Original Jurisdiction: jurisdiction of a court to entertain a case in its inception, as contrasted with appellate jurisdiction.

Overbreadth: laws or regulations legitimately affecting First Amendment freedoms may not be written or applied so broadly as to infringe protected behavior. See also "vagueness."

Pending: started but not yet decided or concluded.

Per Curiam: "by the court"; a phrase used in case reports to distinguish an unsigned opinion of the court from an opinion written by one judge and subscribed to by the other judges.

Peremptory: absolute, final, positive; not requiring any cause to be shown.

Per Se: in itself; taken alone; inherently; without explanation.

Plaintiff: the party who initiates the lawsuit; the one who alleges he has been wrongfully treated.

Plenary: entire; complete; unabridged.

Post Factum: by the fact itself.

Preferred Position: formula which gives a special or privileged position to First Amendment freedoms.

Prima Facie: at first sight; on the face of it; presumed to be true.

Prior Restraint: action taken to prevent someone from exercising a liberty guaranteed in the First Amendment, and comes to the courts with a heavy presumption against its constitutional validity.

Procedural Due Process: a major limitation on acts of public colleges and universities which affect the "liberty" or "property" rights of its students; procedural safeguards— e. g., "adequate notice" and a "fair hearing"—are insisted upon as prerequisite to governmental action which has more than "de minimus" impact on a student's rights.

Public Forum: an appropriate place for First Amendment expression; e. g., the landmark aspect of *Tinker* is its holding that educational institutions are proper places for the dissemination of ideas. It is only when expression actually threatens, or in fact causes, disruption of the school that restriction is permissible. However, the creation of a public forum, like most other state benefits, is the decision of the governing body responsible for such action. But once the benefit is granted, First Amendment protections apply. Of course the college may place *neutral* conditions upon the use of the forum (time, place, manner).

Quasi: as if; analogous to; e. g., quasi-judicial meaning the power held by some agencies to both execute and interpret regulations.

Rational Basis: limited or traditional equal protection test which, until recent years, was the sole test employed by the courts in determining the reasonableness of a statutory classification. Where *no* "fundamental right" or "suspect criteria" involved, classification generally presumed constitutionally valid if *any* rational state of facts can reasonably be conceived that would justify the classification. Burden of proof is on the complainant to show that the classification 1) is an irrational one, 2) furthers no proper governmental purpose, or 3) treats persons unequally within the classification.

Relief: the specific remedies a complainant seeks from the court.

Remand: the action of an appellate court, after reviewing and deciding a case, sending it back to the lower court it came from for a trial, retrial or other action on it.

Reserved Powers: powers not delegated to the national government nor prohibited to the states.

Residual Discrimination: a term suggesting the lingering effects of pervasive discrimination against certain minorities.

Res Judicata: a matter judicially acted upon or decided.

Respondeat Superior: the responsibility of an employer for the acts of his employees.

Reverse Discrimination: though a somewhat loaded term, it is commonly used to describe the allegation of disadvantage or disqualification simply on account of belonging to the majority race or male sex; less pejorative terms are "benign" or "inverse" discrimination.

Self-Incrimination: a proscription guaranteed by the Fifth Amendment: "no person shall be compelled in a criminal case to be a witness against himself." Generally not applicable in student disciplinary cases.

Slander: the oral utterance of a falsehood that is intended to defame a person or injure his reputation.

Slot Machine Theory: pictures judges as technicians merely matching cases and judicial precedent.

Sovereign Immunity: a rule of law that protects government agencies and officials from suits for damages for their wrongful acts on the theory that "the king can do no wrong." Many states have passed statutes limiting sovereign immunity.

Standing: the right to raise an issue in lawsuit. A person does not have standing to sue if he was not sufficiently damaged by the illegal or wrongful act of the defendant.

Stare Decisis: to stand by decided cases; a principle of Anglo-American jurisprudence that a precedent once established in a decision of a case should be followed in other like cases unless it is found to be in conflict with established principles of justice.

State Action: for the due process and equal protection of the laws guarantees of the Fourteenth Amendment to apply, there must be a substantial government involvement in the act alleged to be in violation of those guarantees. This is the "state action" principle and it constitutes the threshold of litigation in many civil rights cases involving private colleges and universities.

Statute of Limitations: a statute which fixes a limited period of time during which existing claims may be collected, judgments enforced, crimes punished or in which a lawsuit must be started or else the right to sue is lost. The statute of limitations is different for different civil and criminal wrongs, and varies from jurisdiction to jurisdiction.

Statutory Law: laws enacted by a legislative body as opposed to case law, handed down by the judicial branch, and administrative law, issued by the executive branch.

Stay: to stop or delay; to refrain from.

Strict Scrutiny: the stricter equal protection test which applies when a statutory classification affects some "fundamental right" or is based on "suspect criteria." Not only must the statutory classification meet the traditional "rational basis" test, but it must *also* be 1) necessary to promote some compelling state interest, and 2) the least burdensome alternative available. See "fundamental right," "suspect criteria" and "rational basis."

Subpoena: a command from a court ordering a witness to appear and give testimony and imposing a penalty for refusal to obey. It may also include an order to bring certain documents into court.

Substantial Disruption and Material Interference: student expression in a public educational institution may be regulated when "necessary to avoid material and substantial interference with schoolwork or discipline." However, before college authorities interfere with student expression, either by direct censorship or by subsequent punishment, there must be a valid showing that student expression will or has produced "substantial disruption of or material interference with school activities . . ." (Tinker v. Sch. Dist., 393 U.S. 503, 1969). See also "clear and present danger."

Substantial Evidence: the weight of evidence generally required for a determination in a student disciplinary hearing; i. e., just enough evidence (weight) on one side to tip the scales.

Substantive Due Process: the requirement that all legislation be reasonable; in general the following factors are used in determining the "reasonableness" of challenged legislation: (1) is the purpose of the legislation a proper subject matter of legislative power, and (2) do the means selected by the legislative body bear a real and substantial relation to the purpose sought to be accomplished?

Sui Generis: of its own kind; unique.

Supremacy Clause: constitutional provision (Art. VI) providing for the supremacy of the Constitution, laws and treaties of the United States over the constitutions and laws of the states.

Suspect Criteria: pertaining to the "traditional indicia of suspectness" such as race, religion, or national origin; though the Supreme Court has never defined precisely what "suspect criteria" are, it has noted the general characteristics as 1) a class determined by characteristics which are solely an accident of birth; or 2) a class subjected to such a history of purposefully unequal treatment, or relegated to a position of such political powerlessness, as to command extraordinary protection from the majority. When a suspect classification comes before a court, the normal presumption of constitutionality is reversed and the "strict scrutiny" test applies.

Symbolic Speech: representation of ideas through such symbols as a clenched fist, black armband, etc.; e. g., wearing of black armbands by public school students to protest American policies in Vietnam was held to be a "symbolic act . . . closely akin to pure speech" and hence protected under the First and Fourteenth Amendments (Tinker v. Sch. Dist., 393 U.S. 503, 1969).

Tailoring the Procedure: a judicially allowable scaling down from higher procedural safeguards required in student expulsion cases to lower requirements in proceedings involving lighter sanctions.

Test: a standard or criterion used by courts to determine specific issues.

Test Case: a suit designed to pose a general challenge to the enforcement of a statute, regulation or precedent, as well as to determine the rights of the particular parties to the suit.

Tort: a civil wrong or injury not involving a contract; a violation of a duty imposed by law.

Trial De Novo: a new trial of a case in a higher court, ordered after error is found in the original trial in the lower court; it is conducted as if no trial whatever had been held in the court below.

Vacate: to annul, set aside, cancel, rescind, or render void.

Vagueness: a standard assuming the invalidity of any law or regulation legitimately affecting First Amendment freedoms that is "so vague that men of common intelligence must necessarily guess at its meaning . . ." See also "overbreadth."

Vicarious Liability: a legal principle attributing responsibility to the master (e. g., employer) for the actions of his servants or agents. See also "respondeat superior."

Ultra Vires: acts done by a corporation or public agency which are void for want of legal power conferred in the corporation's charter or public agency's enabling statute(s).

Wall-of-Separation: doctrine holding that First and Fourteenth Amendments prohibit both national and state governments from aiding any and all religions and religious activities. See also "accommodating neutrality" and "no-preference."

Warrant: an order from a magistrate or other authority requiring a police officer or other official to arrest a particular person or search specified premises.

•

TABLE OF CASES

The principal cases are in italic type. Cases cited or discussed are in roman type. References are to Pages.

*

BIBLIOGRAPHY

General

American Digest System. General Digest. 3rd Series. St. Paul, Minn.: West Publishing Co., 1976.

American Jurisprudence. Vol. 15. New York: Lawyer's Publishing Co., 1976.

American Law Reports, Annotated. Vol. 26. New York: Lawyer's Publishing Co., 1976.

Black, C. The People and the Court. New York: Macmillan, 1960.

Black, C. Perspectives on Constitutional Law. Englewood Cliffs, New Jersey: Prentice-Hall, 1963.

Brubacher, J., and Rudy, W. Higher Education in Transition. 3rd Ed. New York: Harper and Row, 1976.

Cohen, M. L. Legal Research in a Nutshell. 2nd Ed. St. Paul, Minn.: West Publishing Co., 1971.

Corpus Juris Secundum. Vol. 14. New York: American Law Book Co., 1976.

Corwin, E. S. Constitutional Revolution. Claremont Associated Colleges, 1941.

DeTocqueville, A. Democracy in America. Ed. P. Bradley. New York: Vintage Books, 1945.

Greenberg, J. Cases and Materials on Judicial Process and Social Change: Constitutional Litigation. St. Paul, Minn.: West Publishing Co., 1977.

Halstead, K. Statewide Planning. Washington, D. C.: U. S. Government Printing Office, 1974.

Holmes, O. W. The Common Law. Boston: Little, Brown, 1881.

Isreal, B. Can Higher Education Recapture Public Support? New York: International Council for Educational Development, 1974.

General—Cont'd

Kaplan, K. "The Idealogies of Tough Times." Change, VIII, August, 1976.

Llewellyn, K. The Bramble Bush. New York: Oceana, 1951.

Llewellyn, K. "Law and the Social Sciences—Especially Sociology." American Sociological Review, 14, August, 1949.

Morris, A. The Constitution and American Education. St. Paul, Minn.: West Publishing Co., 1974.

Pound, R. Social Control Through Law. New Haven: Yale University Press, 1942.

Shepard's Federal Citations. Colorado Springs, Colorado: Shepard's Citations, 1977.

Sherrill, R. Why They Call It Politics. New York: Harcourt Brace Jovanovich, Inc., 1974.

Student Protest and the Law. Ed. G. Holmes. Ann Arbor: Institute of Continuing Legal Education, 1969.

Swindler, W. Court and Constitution in the 20th Century. Indianapolis: Bobbs-Merrill, 1974.

Swisher, C. The Supreme Court in Modern Role. New York: New York University Press, 1958.

Trumen, D. The Governmental Process: Political Interests and Public Opinion. New York: Alfred A. Knopf, 1951.

Van Alstyne, W. "Student Academic Freedom and the Rule-Making Power of Public Universities." Law in Transition Quarterly, I, Winter 1965.

Young, D. P., and Gehring, D. D. The College Student and the Courts. Asheville, North Carolina: College Administration Publications, Inc., 1978.

General—Cont'd

Zoglin, M. *Power and Politics in the Community College.* Palm Springs, Calif.: ETC Publications, 1976.

Part I

Buess, T. "A Step Towards Guaranteed Student Rights, The University as Agency." *Student Lawyer Journal,* May 1968.

Cowley, W. H. "The College Guarantees Satisfaction." *Educational Record,* Vol. 16, January 1935.

Hogan, J. C. *The Schools, the Courts and the Public Interest.* Lexington, Mass.: D. C. Heath and Co., 1974.

Legal Issues for Postsecondary Education. Vols. I and II. Ed. D. Blumer. Washington, D. C.: American Association of Community and Junior Colleges, 1975.

MacIntosh, A. *Behind the Academic Curtain.* New York: Harper and Row, 1948.

Mayhew, L. B. "American Higher Education Now and in the Future: Ed. M. Bressler. *The Annals.* Philadelphia: The American Academy of Political and Social Science, 1972.

O'Leary, R. E. "The College Student and Due Process in Disciplinary Proceedings." *University of Illinois Law Forum,* 1962.

O'Neil, R. M. "Private Universities and Public Law." *Buffalo Law Review,* 1970.

Pound, R. *The Spirit of the Common Law.* Boston: Marshall Jones, 1921.

Seavey, W. A. "Dismissal of Students: Due Process." *Harvard Law Review,* 1957.

Strang, R. "Democracy in the College." *Journal of Higher Education,* January, 1940.

Part II

Crandal, D. *The Personal Liability of Community College Officials.* Los Angeles: ERIC, UCLA, 1977.

Part II—Cont'd

Fischer, T. C. *Due Process in the Student-Institutional Relationship.* Washington, D. C.: American Association of State Colleges and Universities, 1970.

Goldman, A. L. "The University and the Liberty of Its Students—a Fiduciary Theory." *Kentucky Law Journal,* 1966.

Johnson, M. T. "Constitutional Rights of College Students." *Texas Law Review,* 1964.

Sherry, A. "Governance of the University: Rules, Rights, and Responsibilities." *California Law Review,* 1966.

Van Alstyne, W. "Procedural Due Process and State University Students." *UCLA Law Review,* 1963.

Wigmore, J. H. *Evidence in Trials at Common Law.* Boston: Little, Brown, 1940.

Wright, C. A. "The Constitution on the Campus." *Vanderbilt Law Review,* 1969.

Part III

Berkeley Student Revolt. Eds. S. M. Lipset and S. S. Wolin. Garden City, New York: Doubleday, 1965.

Bloustein, E. J. "The New Student and His Role in American Colleges," in Metzger, Kadish, DeBardeleben and Bloustein, *Dimensions of Academic Freedom.* Urbana: University of Illinois Press, 1969.

Fager, C. B. "Ownership and Control of the Student Press: A First Amendment Analysis," (mimeographed) Washington, D. C.: The Student Press Law Center, 1976.

Feuer, L. S. *The Conflict of Generations/The Character and Significance of Student Movements.* New York: Basic Books, 1969.

Fleishman, S. *The Supreme Court Obscenity Decisions.* San Diego, Calif.: Greenleaf Classics, 1973.

Part III—Cont'd

Frankel, C. "Reflections on a Worn-Out Model." *Daedalus*, Fall, 1974.

Glaser, N. *Remembering the Answers*. New York: Basic Books, 1970.

Heller, L. G. *The Death of the American University*. New Rochelle, New York: Arlington House, 1973.

Jacobs, P. and Landau, S. *The New Radicals: A Report with Documents*. New York: Vintage Books, 1966.

Newfield, J. *A Prophetic Minority*. New York: The New American Library, 1966.

O'Neill, W. L. *Coming Apart*. Chicago: Quadrangle Books, 1971.

Perkins, J. A. *The University in Transition*. Princeton University Press, 1967.

Schauer, F. F. *The Law of Obscenity*. Washington, D. C.: The Bureau of National Affairs, Inc., 1976.

Schwab, J. J. *College Curriculum and Student Protest*. Chicago: University of Chicago Press, 1969.

Part IV

Brooks, G. T. "Section 504 of the Rehabilitation Act and the Private College: Barnes v. Converse." *Mercer Law Review*, 1978.

Calkins, C. C. *The Story of America*. Pleasantville, New York: The Reader's Digest Association, Inc., 1975.

Carbone, R. F. *Students and State Borders*. Iowa City: ACT Publications, 1973.

Carnegie Commission on Higher Education. *Tuition*. CCHE, 1974.

Carnegie Council on Policy Studies in Higher Education. *Public Policy and Academic Policy*. (In a report of the Carnegie Policy Council on Studies in Higher Education, *Selective Admissions in Higher Education*.) San Francisco: Jossey-Bass, 1977.

Part IV—Cont'd

Ely, J. H. "The Constitutionality of Reverse Discrimination." *University of Chicago Law Review*, 1974.

Flexner, E. *Century of Struggle*. Cambridge, Mass.: Harvard University Press, 1959.

Flygare, T. "Appeals Court Says Individuals Cannot Sue Under Title IX." *Phi Delta Kappan*, 1977.

Glickstine, H. *Equal Educational Opportunity: The State of the Law*. New York: Columbia University Press, 1976.

Hogan, C. L. "Shedding Light on Title IX." *Woman Sports*, February 1976.

Morris, A. A. "Equal Protection, Affirmative Action and Racial Preference in Law Admissions." *Washington Law Review*, 1973.

O'Neil, R. M. *Discriminating Against Discrimination: Preferential Admissions and the DeFunis Case*. Bloomington: Indiana University Press, 1975.

Palley, D. B. "Resolving the Nonresident Student Problem." *Journal of Higher Education*, January/February 1976.

President's Commission on the Status of Women. *American Women*. Washington, D. C.: Government Printing Office, 1963.

Part V

"Academics—The New Legal Background." *The School Law Newsletter*, Vol. 6, No. 2.

Bonham, G. W. "Consumer Information and Student Choice." *Change*, May 1977.

Divoky, D. "Cumulative Records Assault on Privacy." *National Education Association Journal*, Vol. 47, 1973.

El-Khawas, E. H. "Putting the Student Consumer in Perspective." *Educational Record*, Spring 1977.

Mancuso, J. H. "Legal Rights to Reasonable Rules, Fair Grades, and

Part V—Cont'd

Quality Courses." *New Directions for Higher Education*, Spring 1976.

Mattessich, C. M. "The Buckley Amendment—Opening School Files for Student and Parental Review." *Catholic University Law Review*, 24, 1975.

Privacy Protection Study Commission. *Personal Privacy in an In-*

Part V—Cont'd

formation Society. Washington, D. C.: Government Printing Office, 1977.

Prosser, W. L. *Law of Torts.* 4th Ed. St. Paul, Minn.: West Publishing Co., 1971.

Yudof, M. G. "Educational Policy and the Law—Who Runs the Schools," *American Educator*, Fall, 1978.

INDEX

BUCKLEY AMENDMENT
See Family Education Rights and Privacy Act

BUREAU OF INDIAN AFFAIRS (BIA), 349

BURGER, JUSTICE WARREN E.
Dissenting opinions, 278–279, 403–405
Majority opinions, 249–251, 269–270, 298

CENSORSHIP
See Expression, Freedom of; Press, Freedom of

CENTRAL INTELLIGENCE AGENCY (CIA), 181, 187, 240

CERTIORARI, WRIT
See Appendix G, 591

CHICANOS
See also Hispanics; Mexican-Americans
Generally, 299

CIVIL LAW, EXPLANATION OF, XXI–XXII

CIVIL RIGHTS ACTS
(42 USCA § 1981), 51, 69, 342–343
Text of, 52
Application in private-school discrimination, 52
Application not restricted to minorities, 342–343
(42 USCA § 1983),
For public agencies, immunity from liability,
Eleventh Amendment and sovereign immunity, 97–98
For public officials, qualified immunity, 97, 98–102
Good-faith test, 100–101
In denial of First Amendment freedoms, 219, 281–282, 294–295
In denial of procedural due process, 98–102
Malice and constructive-knowledge test, 99–100
Inapplicability of exhaustion-of-administrative-remedies doctrine, 95–96

CIVIL RIGHTS ACTS—Cont'd
(42 USCA § 1983)—Cont'd
Increased use of, 96–97
Text of, 96
(42 USCA § 1985),
Conspiracy to deny students' constitutional rights by private university, 70
1964 Act, 51, 303, 341, 346, 362, 379
Title VI,
Text of, 346
Admissions, 351–357
Application to language difficulties, 349
Application to minority preference, 346–348
Financial aid, 346–348
Title VII,
See also Immunity; Negligence; Tort Liability
Application to employment discrimination, 342
In race discrimination, 341

CIVIL RIGHTS MOVEMENT, 15, 17, 36–39 *passim*, 165, 168, 174

CLEAR – AND – PRESENT – DANGER TEST, 176, 178, 192, 196, 197

COMMISSION ON OBSCENITY AND PORNOGRAPHY, 251–252

COMMON LAW, EXPLANATION OF, XXV

COMMONER, BARRY, 188

COMMUNISTS, 176, 190, 192, 193, 195

CONFRONTATION OF WITNESSES, RIGHT TO, 127–129

CONGRESS OF RACIAL EQUALITY (CORE), 37, 183

CONSPIRACY CHARGES, 70

CONSTITUTIONAL LAW, EXPLANATION OF, XXVII, XXIV

CONSUMER PROTECTION ACT, 441

CONTRACEPTION, 320, 443, 454

†